PETER BERRESFORD ELLIS is a foremost authority on the Celts and the author of many books in the field including *The Celtic Empire* (1990), *Celt and Saxon* (1993), *Celt and Greek* (1997), *Celt and Roman* (1998) and *The Ancient World of the Celts* (1998). Under the pseudonym Peter Tremayne he is the author of the bestselling Sister Fidelma murder mysteries set in Ireland in the seventh Century.

Praise for *Celtic Myths and Legends*

'For those interested in our Celtic past this selection will be a tremendous source of enjoyment and instruction.'
Contemporary Review

'The introduction is the most comprehensive and lucid explanation of Celtic lore.' Alan Lambert, *The New Humanity*

'Peter Berresford Ellis brings to bear not only his extensive knowledge of the source material but also his acclaimed skills of storytelling to produce an original and enthralling collection.' *Ipswich Evening News*

Other titles by the same author

A Brief History of the Druids
Celt and Saxon
The Celtic Empire
Celtic Women
Celt and Roman
The Ancient World of the Celts
A Dictionary of Irish Mythology
A Dictionary of Celtic Mythology

CELTIC MYTHS AND LEGENDS

Peter Berresford Ellis

CARROLL & GRAF PUBLISHERS
New York

Carroll & Graf Publishers
An imprint of Avalon Publishing Group, Inc.
161 William Street
New York
NY 10038 2607

ISBN 0-7394-3289-3

Printed in the United States of America

Contents

This volume is respectfully dedicated to the memory of my good friend, mentor and guide in matters Celtic – Pádraig Ó Conchúir (1928–1997).

I was a listener in the woods,
I was a gazer at the stars,
I was not blind where secrets were concerned,
I was silent in a wilderness,
I was talkative among many,
I was mild in the mead-hall,
I was stern in battle,
I was gentle towards allies,
I was a physician of the sick,
I was weak towards the feeble,
I was strong towards the powerful,
I was not parsimonious lest I should be burdensome,
I was not arrogant though I was wise,
I was not given to vain promises though I was strong,
I was not unsafe though I was swift,
I did not deride the old though I was young,
I was not boastful though I was a good fighter,
I would not speak about any one in their absence,
I would not reproach, but I would praise,
I would not ask, but I would give.

Cormac Mac Cuileannáin
King and Poet of Cashel, AD 836–908

Introduction

The mythology, legends and folklore of the Celtic peoples are among the oldest and most vibrant of Europe. The Celts were, in fact, the first European people north of the Alps to emerge into recorded history. They were delineated from their fellow Europeans by virtue of the languages which they spoke and which we now identify by the term "Celtic".

This linguistic group is a branch of the greater Indo-European family. The Indo-European family of languages encompasses most of the languages spoken in Europe, with a few notable exceptions such as Basque, Finnish, Estonian and Hungarian. The Indo-European group also covers Iran and northern India.

Since the old classical language of India, Sanskrit, was identified in the eighteenth century, the concept of linguistic evolution and language relationships has become a science. What this means is that we can see from the linguistic relationship of the Indo-European languages that, at some point in remote antiquity, there was a single parent language, which we call Indo-European, for want of a better designation. This parent language diversified into dialects, as its speakers began to migrate from the geographic location where it was originally spoken. These dialects then became the ancestors of the present major European and Northern Indian language groups – Italic or Latin (now called Romance), Germanic, Slavonic, Baltic, Celtic, Iranian, Indo-Aryan and so forth.

Even today, there remain relative forms of construction and vocabulary among the Indo-European languages which are not found in other languages: features which help us identify them as such. Features common to Indo-European include clear formal distinction of noun and verb, a basically inflective structure and decimal numeration. An experiment which demonstrates the relationship is to note the cardinal numbers – one to ten – in each Indo-European language and one will find the same sound values indicating the common parent.

Where was the Indo-European parent originally spoken and when did it begin to break up? It is probable, and only probable, that the speakers of the parent tongue originated somewhere between the Baltic and the Black Sea. It also seems probable that the parent tongue was already breaking into dialects before waves of migrants carried them westward into Europe and eastward into Asia.

The first Indo-European literature that we have records of is Hittite, a language spoken in what is now eastern Turkey. The Hittites formed an empire which eventually incorporated Babylonia and even briefly exerted authority over Egypt. Hittite writing emerged from 1900 BC and vanished around 1400 BC. Hittite literature survives on tablets written in cuneiform syllabics which were not deciphered until 1916.

Scholars argue that the Celtic dialect of Indo-European, which became the parent of all Celtic languages, emerged at about 2000 BC. The Celtic peoples began to appear as a distinctive culture in the area of the headwaters of the Danube, the Rhine and the Rhône. In other words, in what is now Switzerland and South-West Germany.

A study of early place names of this region show that rivers, mountains, woodland and even some of the towns, still retain the Celtic original. The three great rivers we have mentioned retain their Celtic names. The Danube, first recorded as the Danuvius, was named after the Celtic goddess Danu, whose name means "divine waters". The Rhône, first recorded as Rhodanus, also incorporates the name of the goddess prefixed by the Celtic *ro*, or "great". The Rhine, originally recorded as Rhenus, is a Celtic word for "sea way".

This is the area, then, where the Celts developed their distinctive culture. Archaeologists now date that identifiable culture through the medium of artifacts, called the Hallstatt Culture, from 1200 BC to 475 BC. This was so called because the first identifiable artifacts were found on the west bank of Lake Hallstatt in Upper Austria. Previously, archaeologists only dated the culture from 750 BC, but new finds have made them revise their dating. A later distinctive Celtic culture, developing out of Hallstatt, was called La Tène, from the finds found at La Tène on the northern edge of Lake Neuchatel.

The discovery of iron smelting by the Celts around the start of the first millennium BC gave them a superiority over their neighbours. Celtic smithies assumed a new role in society and artisans were considered among the nobility. With iron spears, swords, shield fittings, axes, saws, hammers and billhooks, the Celts started their expansion through the previously impenetrable forests of northern Europe. As an agricultural society, they had a new weapon to tame the earth in the iron ploughshare. The Celts were even able to develop threshing machines. Their iron axes and saws helped them to build roads throughout Europe. It is interesting that the Old Irish word for a road was *slighe*, from *sligim*, "I hew". Over-population and, perhaps, conflict between tribes seems a reasonable cause for the start of the Celtic expansion from their original homelands.

Some Celtic tribes had already crossed the Alps and settled in the Po Valley by the 7th century BC. They came into conflict with the Etruscan empire and pushed it back south of the Appenines. The Senones tribe crossed the Appenines, searching for land to settle on, around 390 BC. They encountered resistance from the Etruscans and then the new overlords of the Etruscans – Rome itself.

The Celtic Senones defeated the Roman legions at the battle of Allia and marched on Rome, occupying the city for seven months before the Roman Senate agreed to pay a ransom to free their city. The Senones settled on the eastern seaboard of Italy around Ancona. This turbulent period appears in Celtic mythological tales and was recorded by

Geoffrey of Monmouth in his *Historia Regum Britanniae* (History of the Kings of Britain) in the twelfth century; this work popularised the Arthurian sagas.

Practically a hundred years after the defeat of the Romans, Celtic tribes pushed into the Greek peninsula, defeating the armies that had once conquered the known world for Alexander. They defeated the combined armies of Greece at Thermopylae and then marched on to the holy shrine of Delphi, which they sacked.

The Celts (as *Keltoi*) had first emerged into recorded history, so far as surviving records show, in the writings of Greek travellers and historians in the sixth century BC. Herodotus of Halicarnassus says that a merchant from Samos, named Colaeus, landed at the mouth of the Tartessus, the modern river Guadalquivir, just north of Cadiz in Spain, about 630 BC. He found Celts were long settled throughout the Iberian peninsula and exploiting the silver mines of the region. This was the first known encounter between the Greeks and the Celts and Greek merchants began a thriving business with the Celtic mine-owners in the area. The first historical accounts of the Celts came from the pens of Herodotus of Halicarnassus and Hecataeus of Miletus.

By the third century BC, the Celtic peoples had reached their greatest expansion. They were domiciled from the west in Ireland to the east on the central plain of Turkey (the Celtic "commonwealth" of Galatia, which became the first non-Jewish peoples to accept Christianity and to whom Paul wrote a famous epistle), and north from Belgium, which is still named after the Celtic "Belgae", south through France (what was then Gaul) through the Iberian peninsula as far south as Cadiz, and also across the Alps into the Po Valley (Cisalpine Gaul) and along the Danube Valley. Switzerland is still designated by the name of the Celtic people who lived there – the Helvetii. Thrace had become a Celtic kingdom for a century or so, and isolated Celtic groups were to be found into Poland and Russia, as far as the Sea of Azov.

It should be pointed out that, by this time, there were several Celtic dialects – not all Celts spoke the same Celtic language which had further sub-divided.

The tide of the Celtic expansion began to turn in the first century BC with the rise of Rome's great military empire. Then the expansions of the Slavs and finally the Germanic peoples pushed the Celts back, so that today, the survivors of that once vast Celtic civilisation are now confined to the north-west periphery of Europe. They had survived into modern times as the Irish, the Manx and the Scottish (speaking Goidelic or Q-Celtic) and the Welsh, Cornish and Breton (speaking Brythonic or P-Celtic).

Linguists argue that the form of Celtic we term as Goidelic is the more archaic branch of Celtic. It is suggested that around the seventh century BC, the Celtic languages subdivided, when the form which we called Brythonic emerged. From a Goidelic parent, Brythonic modified and evolved in several ways.

The basic change was the famous substitution of "Q", the sound now represented by a hard "C", into "P". To give a simple example, the word for "son" in Irish is *mac*; in Welsh this became *map* and in modern Welsh is shortened to *ap*. "Everyone", or *cách*, in Old Irish, is *paup* in Old Welsh. The word for a "feather" in Old Irish, *clúmh*, became *pluf* in Old Welsh. Thus the "Q" is substituted for the "P" and hence the identification of "P" and "Q" Celtic and perhaps the origin of the phrase about "minding your 'p's' and 'q's' ".

Language repression and persecution has nearly destroyed the Celtic languages. Census returns and estimations show that, out of the sixteen millions now living in the Celtic areas, only some two-and-a-half million speak a Celtic language. In studying Celtic mythology, it is essential to study the Celtic languages in which that mythology is first recorded.

Although our first surviving inscription in a Continental Celtic language dates from the sixth century BC, and we have over two hundred inscriptions mainly from the fourth and third centuries BC, Celtic mythology was not recorded until the Christian era: and then only in the insular Celtic languages, mainly Irish and Welsh.

At one point, the Coligny calendar was regarded as the longest text in a Celtic language from pre-Christian times. In August 1983, a text of 160 words on a lead tablet was found in Larzac, which dates to the first century BC. More recently, two bronze tablets, one containing 200 words in Celtic and apparently a legal document, were found at Botoritta, the ancient site of Contrebia Belaisca near Saragossa, Spain. These are said to be dated back to the second and first centuries BC. The argument that the ancient Celts were illiterate, so often put forward, is patently a false one.

To put the surviving Celtic inscriptions into context, we should point out that, while our first surviving Latin inscription dates from the sixth century, as does the first surviving Celtic inscription, few Latin inscriptions are to be found before the third century BC. As a literary language, Latin did not develop until the second century BC.

There is an irony here, in that a young Celtic warrior of the Insubres from Mediolanum (Milan) in the Po Valley, taken prisoner when the Romans defeated the Celts at Telamon in 222 BC, became a slave in Rome and was given the name Caecilius Statius. He learnt Latin and then became the chief comic dramatist of his day. Some forty-two titles of his works are known but only fragments survive. He was one of the earliest literary "Roman" writers. Many other Celts helped to make Latin a major literary vehicle.

A problem in Celtic terms seems to be that there was some pre-Christian religious prohibition on the Celts writing extensively in their own language. This was due to the mystic significance which the pagan Celts placed on words. However, it did not appear to prevent individual Celts, such as Caecilius Statius, using Latin as a medium for literary expression. However, it is why we had to wait until the Christian period before we saw a flowering of Celtic literature.

Irish became the third literary language of Europe, after Greek and Latin. Professor Calvert Watkins of Harvard University pointed out that both Greek and Latin literatures were written by people using the language as a *lingua franca* and not as their mother tongue. It could be argued, he says, that "Irish has the oldest *vernacular* literature of Europe".

When the Celtic myths, as represented in Old Irish and Old Welsh, came to be written down, Christianity had taken a firm hold and those who were writing the stories tended to be Christian scribes working in religious houses. Therefore there was a tendency to bowdlerise the more ancient stories about the gods and goddesses. The priests of the former pagan religion were denigrated as wizards and sorcerers. A Christian veneer was given to the pagan vibrancy of the myths and tales. Even the gods and goddesses were demoted into Otherworld spirits and entities and even fairies.

Lugh Lámhfada, Lugh of the Long Hand, the senior of the gods and patron of all arts and crafts, was eventually demoted into *Lugh-chromain*, "stooping Lugh", and from there Anglicized into "leprechaun".

Because of this Christian bowdlerisation of the stories, some scholars have argued that our knowledge of Celtic mythology is highly fragmentary. In its strictest sense, mythology would refer to the sum total of religious narratives which are thought to interpret and affirm the cultural experience of a people, as well as religious and social institutions. Dr Bernhard Maier is inclined to believe that the medieval records are no true reflection of pre-Christian Celtic mythology. I would venture that, examining these stories from an Indo-European viewpoint, the pre-Christian motifs can be discerned.

It is from the Irish tradition that we have our oldest mythological tales and sagas. Dr Georges Dottin has argued that "it is probable that the most ancient pieces of epic literature of Ireland were written before the middle of the seventh century; but how long previously they had been preserved by oral tradition – this is a point difficult to estimate".

The fact that many of the surviving Irish tales show some remarkable resemblances to themes, stories and even names in the sagas of the Indian *Vedas*, written in Sanskrit at the start of the first millennium BC, shows just how ancient they may be. The being which emerges as the Mother Goddess of the Celts – whose name is given as Danu and sometimes Anu in Old Irish, and is cognate with Dôn in Old Welsh, as well as surviving in the epigraphy of the Continental Celts – also emerges in the literature of Vedas, Persia and in Hittite myth.

The name Danu means "divine waters". River names throughout Europe acknowledge her.

The story associated with the Danuvius – arguably, the first great Celtic sacred river – has similarities with myths about the Boyne (from the goddess Boann) and Shannon (from the goddess Sionan) in Ireland. More importantly, it bears a resemblance to the story of the Hindu goddess Ganga. Both Celts and Hindus worshipped in the sacred rivers and made votive offerings there. In the Vedic myth of Danu, the goddess appears in the famous Deluge story called *The Churning of the Ocean.*

The Irish texts are, in fact, probably the best demonstration of those seeking tangible evidence of Indo-European cultural origins. Time and again we see remarkable resemblances between Irish culture on the western fringe of Europe and Hindu culture in India. Even the language of the Old Irish law texts, the *Fenéchus* or Brehon Laws, and the Vedic Laws of Manu, show an original point of origin, both in concept and, even more amazingly, in vocabulary.

Professor Myles Dillon, in *Celts and Aryans: Survivals of Indo-European Speech and Society* (1975) has pointed out that "parallelism between the Irish and Hindu law-books, both of them the work of a privileged professional class, is often surprisingly close; it extends not merely to form and technique but even to diction". As Professor Calvert Watkins of Harvard has argued, of all the Celtic linguistic remains, Old Irish represents an extraordinarily archaic and conservative linguistic tradition within the Indo-European field. Its nominal and verbal systems, he says, are a far truer reflection of Indo-European than Classical Greek or Latin and the structure of Old Irish can be compared only with that of Vedic Sanskrit or Hittite of the Old Kingdom.

The *Vedas*, four books of learning composed in North India, in the period 1000–500 BC, are named from the Sanskrit root *vid*, meaning "knowledge". This same root occurs in Old Irish as *uid*, meaning "observation, perception and knowledge". Most people will immediately recognise it as one of the two roots of the compound Celtic word Druid – *dru-vid*, arguably meaning "thorough knowledge".

To demonstrate some of the similarities of vocabulary between Old Irish and Sanskrit, we may refer to the following: *arya* (freeman) in Sanskrit, from which that much maligned word Aryan comes from. In Old Irish, the cognate is *aire* meaning "a noble". *Naib* (good) in Sanskrit is cognate with *noeib* (holy) in Old Irish and from which the word *naomh* (saint) comes.

Minda (physical defect) in Sanskrit is cognate with *menda* ("one who stammers") in Old Irish. *Namas* (respect) in Sanskrit is cognate with *nemed* (respect or privilege) in Old Irish. *Badhura* (deaf) in Sanskrit is cognate with *bodhar* (deaf) in Old Irish. As a matter of interest, this word was borrowed from Irish into English in the 18th century to become the English word "bother".

Most easily recognisable is the word *raj* (king) which is cognate with the Irish *rí* and this word is demonstrated also in the Continental Celtic *rix* and the Latin *rex*. Most Indo-European languages, at one time, used this concept. However, the Germanic group developed another word, i.e. *cyning*, *koenig* and *king*. But English did not abandon it altogether, for that ancient word for king is still to be found in the etymology of *reach*. The Indo-European concept was of a king as one "who reaches or stretches out his hand to protect his people".

This concept of "reaching out to protect the tribe or people" is one found many in Indo-European myths. In the *Vedas*, the sky-god was called Dyaus and is recorded in the *Rig Veda* as one who stretches forth a long hand. This is cognate with *deus* in Latin, *dia* in Irish and *devos* in Slavonic. It means, significantly, "bright one". Presumably it has a sun-deity significance.

In the *Vedas*, we find Dyaus was called Dyaus-Pitir – Father Dyaus; in Greek this became Zeus – also a father god; in Latin Jovis-Pater – Father Jove. Julius Caesar observed that the Celts had a Dis-Pater – a father god and we certainly find an Irish reference to *Ollathair* – the All-Father. He is a sky god and Lugh is given this role. Lugh also appears in Welsh myth as Lleu. Significantly, the name means "bright one" and the Irish god is Lugh Lámhfada (Lugh of the Long

Hand) while his Welsh counterpart is Lleu Llaw Gyffes (Lleu of the Skilful Hand).

The goddess Boann, whose name means "cow white", gave her name to the River Boyne; she was mother to Aonghus Óg, the love god, and was called *guou-uinda*, or cow finder. Now this appears, almost exactly the same, in the Vedic name Govinda, which was an epithet for the god Krishna. Govinda is still used by Hindus as a name today.

The motifs of the sacred cow or bull are easily found in Celtic, particularly in Irish myths, as well as Vedic or Hindu myths. The Gaulish god Esus equates with Asura (the powerful) and, as Asvapati, it is an epithet for Indra. The Gaulish Ariomanus is also cognate with the Vedic Aryaman.

The horse rituals, once common to the Indo-Europeans, are found in Irish myth and ritual as well as in the Vedic sources. The kingship ritual of the symbolic union of horse and ruler survives in both. This must date back to the time when the Indo-Europeans domesticated horses, a development which allowed them not only to commence their initial expansions but to become more proficient in their agricultural and pastoral and warrior life. Horses meant power.

In Ireland, the ritual of the symbolic union of a mare with the king survived for a long time and was mentioned by Giraldus Cambrensis in his *Topographia Hibernica*, in the eleventh century. In India, a similar symbolic ritual of a union of a stallion and queen survived, as we see in the myth of Saranyu in the *Rig Veda*.

Another important aspect found in common is the "Act of Truth" which Professor Myles Dillon has discussed so well in "The Hindu Act of Truth in Celtic Tradition" (*Modern Philology*, February, 1947). The ancient Irish text *Auraicept Moraind* could well be mistaken as a passage from the *Upanishad*. The symbolism in Irish myth of Mochta's Axe, which, when heated in a fire of blackthorn, would burn a liar but not harm someone telling the truth; or Luchta's iron, which had the same quality; or Cormac Mac Art's cup – three lies would cause it to fall apart and three truths would make it whole again: all have their counterparts in the *Chandogya Upanishad*.

Even terms relating to cosmology may be seen to have comparisons in Celtic and Vedic culture. The similarities of the Hindu calendar and Celtic calender – the latter example being the Coligny calendar, found in 1897 – have been seen to be remarkably close. Dr Garrett Olmsted, who has made the most recent examination of the calendar, points out that the calendar's original computation and its astronomical observations and calculations put its origin to 1100 BC. There is also evidence from the early tracts that the Celts practised a form of astrology based on the twenty-seven lunar mansions, or *nakshatras*, as the modern Hindus still do, and not the Western form which was, of course, imported from Babylonia via Greece.

So the most exciting thing about the study of Celtic linguistics and mythology is that we are not just pursuing the cultural origins of the Celts, we are actually pushing back the boundaries of our knowledge of an all Indo-European culture. The comparisons of language, myths, cultural philosophies and social structure, mathematics and calendrical studies (for the ancient Celts were foremost in this field) with Hindu and Hittite, lead one irrevocably towards a developing picture of the common Indo-European roots whose progeny now spreads through Europe, Asia Minor to North India.

Celtic mythology, the legends and oral storytelling traditions, constitute one of the brightest gems of European culture. It is both unique and dynamic. It is a mythology and folklore which should be as well-known and valued as its sister Indo-European cultures of Greece and Rome. Perhaps it should be prized that much more because it gives us a direct path back to the dim origins of civilisation in this part of the world.

The oldest surviving complete manuscript books that provide the sources for Irish mythology date from the twelfth century. There are, of course, earlier fragmentary texts. The oldest complete sources are the *Leabhar na hUidre*, known as the Book of the Dun Cow, the *Leabhar Laignech*, or Book of Leinster, and an unnamed book known simply by its Bodleian Library reference, Rawlinson Manuscript B502. They represent the tip of an extraordinary rich literary mountain.

And the textural remains of Middle Irish literature have not even been exhausted.

Professor Kuno Meyer, in his introduction to the beautiful tale *Liadain and Curithir: A Love Story* (1900), listed four hundred sagas and tales in these manuscript books known to scholars. To this he added a further hundred texts which had been discovered since he had started to make his list. He then added a possible further fifty to a hundred tales which could be in repositories still undiscovered. In all, he believed that there were some five to six hundred tales of which only a hundred and fifty had been translated and annotated at the time when he was writing. Eleanor Hull, in her introduction to *The Cuchullin Saga in Irish Literature* (1898) made a similar estimation.

It is quite extraordinary that this figure has not changed much during the last century. This means that there are great libraries of Irish manuscripts still uncatalogued, let alone examined, in various libraries and archives, such as that of the Regensburg archive in Vienna.

Of course, Old Irish was the standard literary language throughout the Gaelic-speaking world, until the late medieval period. The spoken language of the Manx and the Scots had begun to diverge from the standard during the sixth and seventh centuries AD. Therefore the myths and legends of Ireland, the Isle of Man and Scotland are often the same, sometimes differentiated by local embellishments. The evidence shows that bards and storytellers wandered freely from one country to another plying their craft. We have an account of the chief bard of Ireland, Seanchán Torpeist (*ca* AD 570–647) arriving on the Isle of Man with his entourage and entering into a literary contest there. Yet an identifiable Manx written literature, as distinct from Irish, did not emerge until the seventeenth century.

It was not until the sixteenth century that a distinctive Scottish Gaelic literature began to emerge from that shared with Ireland. *The Book of the Dean of Lismore* (Lismore in Argyll) was a miscellany compiled in 1516 and included sagas of the Fianna of Fionn Mac Cumhaill and other stories. However, like the Isle of Man, the main wealth of mythological and legendary traditions lay in a continued oral tradition, which was only extensively committed to writing in the eighteenth and nineteenth centuries and then predominantly in English translations.

Welsh began to emerge from its common British Celtic parent, along with Cornish and Breton, in the fifth and sixth centuries AD. It is in Welsh that the main early Brythonic myths and legends have survived. The Welsh material is nowhere near as extensive nor as old as the Irish tales and sagas. While Welsh was certainly flourishing as a literary language by the eighth century AD, apart from fragmentary remains, the oldest book wholly in Welsh is *Llyfr Du Caerfyrddin*, the Black Book of Carmarthen, dated to the thirteenth century. Among the poems it contains are a few on the Myrddin (Merlin) legends. But the mythological texts are preserved in two sources: *Llyfr Gwyn Rhydderch*, the White Book of Rhydderch (1300–1325), and *Llyfr Coch Hergest*, the Red Book of Hergest (1375–1425). The stories in these two books constitute what is called in Welsh the *Mabinogi*, or in English "The Four Branches of the Mabinogion".

The *Mabinogi* consists of eleven tales and romances. There is evidence that at least three tales originated from a period far earlier than the surviving written texts. *Culhwch and Olwen*, for example, which is given in the current volume as *The Quest for Olwen*, reflects a period of style, vocabulary and custom of at least two centuries earlier.

Like the Irish, the Welsh produced a wealth of manuscript archive material during the later medieval period. The best introduction to this is Andrew Breeze's *Medieval Welsh Literature* (1997). This book presents the controversial thesis that several of the *Mabinogi* tales were actually written by a Welsh princess named Gwenllian who was killed in battle against the Anglo-Normans in 1136–37. I have discussed this in my preface to the Welsh tales.

Although the Cornish had produced written forms by the tenth century, nothing survives in Cornish that is reflective of the myths and legends of the *Mabinogi*. But, like the Goidelic Celtic *seanachaidhe* or wandering storytellers or bards, the Brythonic Celts had their *cyfarwydd*. These bards were constantly travelling between Wales, Cornwall and Brittany, even down to Tudor times. Common characteristics in tales are to be found in all three countries.

It is arguable that an Arthurian poem, translated by John of Cornwall into Latin hexameters during the twelfth century, is a genuine translation from an earlier Cornish manuscript. Glosses in Cornish on the manuscript date it to the tenth century. This is *The Prophecy of Merlin*, and the oldest surviving copy of this text is dated 8 October 1474. It is in the Vatican Library. It belongs to the Arthurian cycle of tales.

The oldest text in Breton dates from 1450 and is *Dialog etre Arzur Roe d'an Bretounet ha Guynglaff* (Dialogue of Arthur, King of the Bretons). The work is of Breton provenance and not merely a copy of the Welsh sagas or French or German extensions of the Arthurian tales.

By the end of the fifteenth century, it could be argued that Breton literature had started in earnest. Saints plays and other material were being written in Breton. *Buhez santaz Nonn hag he nap Deuy* (The Life of St Nonn, Son of Devy) is one of the first major works of this tradition. But the main communication of the legends and sagas remained an oral tradition until 1839 when Théodore Hersart de la Villemarqué published his ground-breaking *Barzaz Breiz: Chants Populaires de la Bretagne*, an anthology of poems, ballads and folklore which first introduced Breton folklore to a wider audience.

Whenever anyone mentions the Celtic myths and legends there are two subjects that always seem to spring to mind. The first is the Arthurian sagas and the second is the romance of Tristan and Iseult.

Arthur was a sixth-century historical Celtic personality fighting for the independence of his people against the ravages of the Anglo-Saxons. He is first mentioned in a sixth century poem, *Y Gododdin*, originally written in British Celtic in southern Scotland – then British Celtic speaking – but now claimed for Welsh literature. The Gododdin were a tribe whose capital was at Edinburgh.

The Welsh chronicler Nennius, writing in the early ninth

century, also refers to Arthur and his battles and significantly calls him a warlord but not a king, pointing out that the British Celtic kings appointed him leader in battle. The *Annales Cambriae*, compiled *c.* AD 955, also mention him and his great victory at Badon and his death at Camlann. It was from Geoffrey of Monmouth (*c.* 1100–1155) in his Latin *Historia Regum Britanniae* – which he said was a translation from "a very ancient book in the British tongue" – who began to develop Arthur as a mythical being. From here, Arthur headed off into European literature via the Norman poets, such as Wace and Chrétien de Troyes and Layamon, who introduced Arthur to continental literatures.

It became clear, as I have argued in *Celt and Saxon: The Struggle for Britain* AD 410–937, that after the defeat of the historical Arthur by the Anglo-Saxons, the British Celts would gather around their storytellers and these storytellers would tell sagas of the hero. Over the centuries, the historical deeds were lost in the mists of the storytelling. Searching for new themes to enliven their sagas, the bards borrowed freely from many of the Irish tales associated with the popular Fionn Mac Cumhaill and his legendary warriors, the Fianna. Even *Sir Gawain and the Green Knight* borrowed from the Cúchulainn saga. The story with the same motif appears in the *Feast of Bricriu* in which Cúchulainn plays the role later assigned to Gawain.

Arthur and his knights actually appear in one of the Irish myths in which he steals the hound of Fionn Mac Cumhaill. Arthurian tales had a vogue in medieval Irish literature, but he never replaced the popularity of Fionn Mac Cumhaill as the chief hero. However, at least twenty-five Arthurian tales in Irish have been identified from this period.

In Welsh mythology, *Culhwch and Olwen* is the earliest known fully-fledged Arthurian tale, which linguists claim dates several centuries before it was first written down, in the eleventh century. There are three other later Arthurian tales in the *Mabinogi*: *The Lady of the Fountain*, *Peredur, Son of Efrawg* and *Gereint, Son of Erbin*. Arthur also appears as a character in a tenth-century poem called *The Spoils of Annwn* which is a prototype for the Holy Grail legend.

It is fascinating that Arthur has now become part of a world folklore, but is no longer seen through Celtic eyes as a great champion fighting against the ancestors of the English. Indeed, Arthur has become an archetypal English king, with the additions of European medieval chivalry, courtly love and a whole host of appendages that did not appear in the original stories.

Similarly, the romance of Tristan and Iseult has also left its Celtic homeland to become part of a wider European cultural myth. Tristan was the nephew of King Mark of Cornwall, and Iseult the daughter of an Irish King of Munster. The origins now matter little, as the story has been recorded in hundreds of different versions in practically every European language – the earliest, outside of the Celtic orbit, being in French, German and English. Joseph Bédier (*Le Roman de Tristan par Thomas*, Paris, 1902) maintained that all the known Tristan stories could be traced back to one extant manuscript written by Beroul, about whom nothing is known, in the middle of the twelfth century. Bédier argues that Beroul, writing in French, was translating from a Breton source who probably derived it from a Cornish source.

The saga is, of course, one of the world's greatest love stories. The central motif is the traditional Celtic elopement tale, known in Irish as *aithedha*, of which there are many famous examples, such as the story of Deirdre and that of Gráinne. In the Tristan and Iseult case, the elopement is of the king's new wife with her lover, the king's nephew. Many of the essential characteristics of the tale are to be found in other Celtic elopement tales.

Interestingly, we find that there was a real King Mark and a real Tristan in Cornwall. Castle Dore, Mark's "castle", is two miles north of Fowey; it is an earthwork fortification dating back to the second century BC and was inhabited in the sixth century. A mile or so from Fowey, towards Par and near the disused entrance to Menabilly House, there is an engraved stone dated to the mid-sixth century. The accepted reading of the Latin inscription is *Drustaus* (or *Drustanus*) hic iacit Cunomori filius – here lies Drustanus, son of Cunomorus.

Philologically, the name Drustanus equates with Tristan.

King Mark's full name in the records is given as "Marcus Cunomorus". The name Mark does not come from the Roman *praenomen* "Marcus" but from the Celtic word for horse: in Cornish *Margh*, in Breton *Marc'h* and in Welsh *March*. Cunomorus means "hound of the sea". The *Life of St Pol de Léon*, written about AD 880 by Urmonek, a monk of Landévennec in Brittany, not only refers to the king as having "ears like a horse" but explains that Marc'h was also called "Cunomorus".

Returning to the important fact given in the inscription at Fowey – how much more poignant this elopement tale would be if Tristan, indeed, had eloped with his stepmother!

The first complete Celtic language version of the Tristan and Iseult story only survives from the sixteenth century. This is in Welsh.

In the current collection of retellings, I have chosen to introduce the tales with a recreation of the Celtic "creation myth" – *The Ever-Living Ones* – and attempted to delete the Christian glosses added to it when it was first written down. I have incorporated into this the elements from *Cath Maige Tuired* (The Battle of Mag Tuired), arguably the most important tale in the "Mythological Cycle", in which the gods and goddesses of Danu fight with evil Fomorii (Under-Sea Dwellers). There are two early versions of this, one surviving in a sixteenth century copy, while the second version survives in a manuscript *c.* 1650.

The stories given in the *Leabhar Gábhala* (The Book of Invasions, often given in the old form *Lebor Gabála Érenn*), which is found in the *Leabhar Laignech* of the twelfth century, is the nearest to the Celtic origin myth that we have. The *Leabhar Gábhala* tells of the mythical invasions of Ireland, including that of the "Ever-Living Ones", the Children of Danu or "The Tuatha Dé Danaan".

In the Irish creation myth, the Christian writers made Cesair the granddaughter of the biblical Noah. Her parents are Bith and Birren and they set out in three ships to find a place which would escape the Deluge. Only one ship survives and lands at Corca Dhuibhne, on the Dingle Peninsula in Co. Kerry. There are fifty women and three men. As well as Bith, there is Ladra the pilot and Fionntan. When Bith and Ladra die, Fionntan, left alone with the women, feels inadequate and flees. He and the women eventually perish. Among the variants of this tale is the story that one of the women had a magic cask which, when opened, flowed for so long that water covered the earth and drowned them.

The Welsh Christian creation myth is found in the medieval *Trioedd Ynys Prydain*, a collection of triads which served as a mnemonic device for cataloguing a variety of facts and precepts. It speaks of Llyon-Llion, the Lake of the Waves, which overflows due to Addanc, a monster who lives in the lake. He is finally disposed of by being hauled from his lair by the oxen of Hu Gadarn. In some versions, he is killed by Peredur. However, he creates the overflow and thereby the Deluge. Indeed, he seems to be cognate with Griva who has a similar role in Hindu Deluge myth. Nefyed Naf Nefion then builds a ship, in which Dwyvan and his wife Dwyvach escape. Nefyed is cognate to the Irish Nemed, who is said to have arrived in Ireland after the Deluge.

While there are hints of a pre-Christian origin, especially with the story of Addanc, other sources compare more with *The Churning of the Ocean* in which many comparative figures to Celt myth also appear, such as Dhanu; Surabhi, the divine cow; the Tree of Knowledge; Dhanvantari – the equivalent of the Irish Dian Cécht, the physician of the gods; and others.

In many ways, the *Leabhar Gábhala* is the equivalent of the Hindu *Mahabharata*. It was necessary, therefore, to check other references, make comparisons with similar origin myths in the *Vedas* and in other Indo-European myths, in order to clarify points which have been lost in the bowdlerisation by the Christian scribes. Thus, it was my intention to return the story to its original pre-Christian Celtic vibrancy.

The pre-Christian themes certainly are in evidence in the *Leabhar Gábhala* and also in the *Dindsenchas*, a collection of sagas which explain the meaning of place-names, the oldest version being found in the *Leabhar Laignech* from texts first recorded from the ninth to twelfth centuries. In fact, there are three versions of the *Dindsenchas*, surviving in over forty manuscripts.

Each one of the six surviving Celtic peoples is represented here by six stories. I have prefaced each section and given some essential sources for the tales of that country. Some of them will be familiar to some ardent followers of Celtic myth and legend but others, I hope, will not be so familiar. I have tried to seek out some new tales and new versions.

It should be noted that seven of the stories included in this collection were first published in *The Giant Book of Myths and Legends*, edited by Mike Ashley, Magpie Books, London, 1995. These stories appeared there under my fiction-writing pseudonym of Peter Tremayne and were: *The Ever-Living Ones*; *The Sons of Tuireann*; *Island of the Ocean God*; *The Shadowy One*; *Bran and Branwen*; *Tewdrig, Tyrant of Treheyl* and *The Destruction of Ker-Ys*. My thanks to Mike Ashley and Nick Robinson of Magpie Books, for allowing them to be reprinted in the current volume.

In Celtic mythology and legend, one enters a fascinating world of fantasy, which is remote from the world of Greek and Latin myths, but which holds a strange resonance with Hindu myths. Even though the insular Celts have spent at least three millennia in their north-west homelands, separated from their Indo-European parent, it is curious that there is a warmth and lightness rather than the brooding bleakness that permeates the sagas of the Germanic and Nordic cultures. It is hard to believe, at times, that we are considering a north-west European culture. A bright, happy spirit pervades even the tragedies. There is a spirit of eternal optimism. Even in the tragedy of *The Children of Lir* there is nothing *final* about the end.

Death is never the conqueror and we are reminded that the ancient Celts were one of the first cultures to evolve a sophisticated doctrine of the immortality of the soul, in a form of reincarnation. Their teaching was of such interest to the Classical world that scholars of the Greek Alexandrian school are divided as to whether Pythagoras, via his Thracian servant Zalmoxis, borrowed the concept or whether Zalmoxis had taught it to the Celts. However, on examination, the Celtic theory of immortality and reincarnation was unlike the theory expounded by Pythagoras.

The Celts taught that death is only a change of place and that life goes on, with all its forms and goods, in the Otherworld. When a soul dies in this world, it is reborn in the Otherworld and when a soul dies in the Otherworld, it is reborn in this one. Thus birth was greeted with mourning and death with exaltation and celebration. These customs were regarded with some surprise by the Greeks and Latins. And from such ancient customs there survived until modern times the Irish funereal celebrations of the wake.

It is important to remember that, for the ancient Celts, the soul reposed in the head. Thus the cult of "head collecting" was used by the Romans to denigrate the Celts. The ancient Celts would take and keep the heads of those people they respected, embalming them with cedar oil, and thus paying reverence to great souls. They were not, as some have claimed, head *hunters*. Only the heads of those already slain in battle, friend or foe, were taken as trophies: and always people worthy of respect. Sometimes the heads were placed in sanctuaries or, more often, were placed in the sacred Celtic rivers as votive offerings.

Even in London, signs of this Celtic practice have been found. Countless skulls from the Celtic period were found in the River Thames and in Walbrook, a brook running into the Thames. Scholars have argued whether Tacitus, who first records the Latin form of the name *Londinium* was recording this from the Celtic *Lugdunum* (fortress of Lug) or from another Celtic word, a word still surviving in the Irish root, *londo* – the wild place. London, as a Celtic trading town of the Trinovantes, stood on the north bank of the Thames, or *Tamesis*, as it was recorded. *Tamesis* means "the dark river", cognate with the Sanskrit *Tamesa*, meaning exactly the same. Now the River Tamesa is a tributary of the Ganges, a sacred river of the Hindus, in which votive offerings were placed.

Is it any surprise, therefore, that we find many rich votive offerings and skulls placed in the Thames by the ancient Celts? Celtic coins, weapons such as swords and shields, exquisite jewellery and other objects were thrown into the Thames and indeed the Walbrook. Whatever the origin of London's Celtic name, we have many other Celtic names associated with the city, not least the names of some of its ancient gates, such as Ludgate.

More important, to the argument of the river's site for votive offerings, is Billingsgate on the River Thames. The Saxons, when they arrived, recorded it as *Bilesgata*, the gate of Bíle. The Celts originally regarded Bíle as the sacred oak, Danu's consort, and he, in time, became the god who took the souls on their journey from this world to the Otherworld.

Celts often deposited their dead in the sacred river, as do the Hindus in the Ganges, and would escort the dead on their journey to the Otherworld through Bíle's gate into the "dark river" at the end of which was their rebirth. Death always came before rebirth, hence darkness before light, in both Celtic and Hindu religions. Hence the Celts counted time by the night followed by the day, and their new year was at the *Samhain* (approximating to the night of October 31 and day of November 1). So the new year started with the dark period.

Among the votive pieces in the Walbrook, there was found a pipe-clay statuette of a female Celtic goddess. Could this have been of Danu, "the divine waters", herself?

How did Walbrook receive its name from the Anglo-Saxons, and does it have anything to do with that point of the river as the place where most votive offerings have been found? The original Celtic inhabitants of London were obviously loath to leave this sacred spot and clung there even after the Anglo-Saxon conquest. They remained long enough for the Anglo-Saxons to designate the brook as *Weala-broc*, the brook of the foreigners – i.e. *Welisc* (Welsh), or foreigners, that being the name the Anglo-Saxons gave to the indigenous Britons.

Celtic mythology is essentially a heroic one but while the Irish stories belong to a more ancient "Heroic Age", the Welsh stories have received the gloss of a more medieval courtly quality. The deities in Celtic myth tend to be the ancestors of the people rather than their creators, a point that Julius Caesar observed and commented on; these deities, as well as the human heroes and heroines, are no mere physical beauties with empty heads. Their intellectual attributes have to equal their physical capabilities. They are all totally human and subject to all the natural virtues and vices. No sin is exempt from practice by the gods or humans.

In the later folklore, when the deities were being relegated into fairies or evil Otherworld folk, as Christianity grew more dictatorial in its judgment of ancient customs and beliefs, the heroes and heroines had to pit their wits more often than their brawn against the "evil magic" of such creatures. Often, when trying to escape a prophesied fate, they would simply bring that fate upon themselves.

Sometimes, impossible quests were fulfilled in the most impossible ways. The natural and the possible is often discarded for the supernatural and the impossible. The elements of fantasy, cosmic horror and the supernatural form an indispensable ingredient in the earliest folklore of the Celts. This has ever been a strong tradition, even among more modern generations of Celtic writers, who seem to have inherited the old ability to present breaks in natural laws as vivid and realistic.

However, when all the analysis is written and pondered over, when all the background is considered and digested, it is to the stories that we must turn and we should never forget that they were told for entertainment: that they were meant to be enjoyed as well as learnt from. Above all, we should not forget that a sense of mischievous fun is never far from the surface.

Before the beginning . . .

1 The Ever-Living Ones

It was the time of primal chaos: a time when the Earth was new and undefined. Arid deserts and black bubbling volcanoes, covered by swirling clouds of gases, scarred the grim visage of the newborn world. It was, as yet, the time of the great void.

Then into that oblivion, from the dull, dark heavens, there came a trickle of water. First one drop, then another and another, until finally there gushed a mighty torrent down upon the earth. The divine waters from heaven flooded downwards and soaked into the arid dirt, cooled the volcanoes which turned into grey, granite mountains, and life began to spring forth across the Earth. The dark, reddened skies grew light and blue.

From the darkened soil there grew a tree, tall and strong. Danu, the divine waters from heaven, nurtured and cherished this great tree which became the sacred oak named Bíle. Of the conjugation of Danu and Bíle, there dropped two giant acorns. The first acorn was male. From it sprang The Dagda, "The Good God". The second seed was female. From it there emerged Brigantu, or Brigid, "The Exalted One". And The Dagda and Brigid gazed upon one another in wonder, for it was their task to wrest order from the primal chaos and to people the Earth with the Children of Danu, the Mother Goddess, whose divine waters had given them life.

So there, by the divine waters of Danu, from where those waters rose and flooded through the now fertile green valleys of the Earth, eastwards towards a distant sea, The Dagda and

Brigid settled. And they called the great course of eastward rushing water after the Mother Goddess, which is Danuvius, whose children still know it as the mighty Danube. And four great bright cities they built there on its broad banks, in which the Children of Danu would live and thrive.

The four cities were Falias, Gorias, Finias and Murias.

The Dagda became their father; thus humankind call him "The Father of the Gods". And Brigid became the wise one, exalted in learning and much did she imbibe from the mighty Danu and from Bíle, the sacred oak. She was hailed as the mother of healing, of craftsmanship and of poetry; indeed, she excelled in all knowledge. She showed her children that true wisdom was only to be garnered from the feet of Danu, the Mother Goddess, and so only to be found at the water's edge.

Those who gathered such knowledge also paid deference to Bíle, the sacred oak. Because they were not allowed to speak his holy name, they called the oak *draoi* and those learned in such knowledge were said to possess oak (*dru*) knowledge (*vid*) and thus were known as Druids.

The knowledge of the Children of Danu grew and each of their four great cities prospered. In Falias they held a sacred stone called the *Lia Fáil* or Stone of Destiny, which, when a righteous ruler set foot on it, would shout with joy; in Gorias, where Urias of the Noble Nature dwelt, they held a mighty sword called the "Retaliator", fashioned before the time of the gods themselves, and which Urias presented to Lugh Lámhfada, who became the greatest warrior among the gods; in Finias, they held a magic spear, called "The Red Javelin", which, once cast, would find its enemy no matter where he hid; and in Murias they held the "Cauldron of Plenty", from which The Dagda could feed entire nations and it still would not be emptied.

For many aeons, the Children of Danu grew and prospered in their beautiful cities.

Then one day, The Dagda, Father of the Gods, and Brigid, the Exalted One, called their children to them.

"You have tarried here long enough. The Earth needs to be peopled and needs your wisdom to advise and direct them, so that they may live lives of virtue and merit. Our Mother, Danu, has directed you to move towards the place where the bright sun vanishes each evening."

"Why should we go there?" demanded Nuada, the favourite son of The Dagda.

"Because it is your destiny," replied Brigid. "And you, Nuada, shall lead your brothers and sisters, and their children, and the land that you shall come to will be called Inisfáil, the Island of Destiny. There shall you abide until your destiny is fulfilled."

"If it is our destiny," said another of The Dagda's sons, named Ogma, "then we shall accept it."

Ogma was the most handsome of the Children of Danu. From his long curly hair, the rays of the sun shone and he was called Ogma *grian-aineacg*, of the Sunny Countenance. To him fell the gift of honeyed words, of poetry and of languages, and he it was who devised how man could write in a form of calligraphy, which was named after him as Ogham.

Brigid smiled at her eager children. "I am allowed to give you one word of warning. When you reach Inisfáil, you will find another people who will claim the Island of Destiny as their own. They are the Children of Domnu, who is the sister of our mother Danu. But beware, for Domnu is not as Danu. For each sister is the inverse of the other, as winter is to summer."

"Then," Nuada said, "should we not take something to defend ourselves with, lest the Children of Domnu fight us for the possession of Inisfáil?"

The Dagda gazed at them kindly and replied, "You may take the four great treasures of the cities of Falias, Gorias, Finias and Murias."

And the Children of Danu took the treasures and they went to the mountains overlooking the headwaters of the Danuvius, the divine waters from heaven, and ascended in a great cloud which bore them westward to Inisfáil, the Island of Destiny. And among them were three beautiful young sisters, who were the wives of the sons of Ogma. Their names were Banba, Fótla and Éire and each sister nurtured an ambition that this new land of Inisfáil would one day be named after her.

Night wrapped her darkened mantle over Magh Tuireadh, which is called the Plain of Towers, which lay in the west of the land of Inisfáil. On each side of the great plain, separated by the River Unius, myriads of small campfires glowed in the gloom. Two armies had gathered for combat.

Seven years had passed since the Children of Danu had landed in their cloud on the shores of the Island of Destiny. They had fought initially with a strange race of people called the Firbolg, who challenged their right to rule in the Island of Destiny. These they had met at the Pass of Balgatan and the conflict went on for four days. And in that conflict there came forth a champion of the Firbolg, named Sreng, who challenged Nuada, the leader of the Children of Danu, to single combat. So strong and mighty was Sreng that, with one sweep of his great sword, he cut off Nuada's right hand.

But the Firbolg and their king, Eochaidh, were defeated and dispersed.

Dian Cécht, the god of all physicians, came to Nuada after the battle and fashioned him an artificial hand of silver, so strong and supple that it was little different from the real hand. Thus did Nuada receive his full name, Nuada Argetlámh, of the Silver Hand. Because he was maimed, the other children of Danu had to choose another of their number to lead them, for they had been told by Brigid that no one with a blemish must rule them.

In choosing a new leader, they made a disastrous choice. As an act of conciliation between themselves and the Children of Domnu, they chose Bres, son of Elatha, king of the Children of Domnu who were also known as the Fomorii, or those who dwelt beneath the sea. And to further consolidate the alliance, Dian Cécht married Ethne, the daughter of the foremost Fomorii warrior, named Balor of the One Eye. And the condition was that, if Bres did anything which displeased the Children of Danu, then he would abdicate and depart in peace.

Those years marked a period of strife. Bres, being a

Fomorii, refused to keep his word and began to lay heavy burdens on the Children of Danu. For a while, Bres and the Children of Domnu, the children of darkness and evil, dominated the land, and the Children of Danu, the children of light and goodness, were helpless and as slaves.

Then finally, Miach, the son of Dian Cécht, aided by his sister, the beautiful Airmid, fashioned a new hand of flesh and bone for Nuada. His hand replaced Dian Cécht's silver one and now, without blemish, Nuada reclaimed the leadership of the Children of Danu. So jealous was Dian Cécht of his son's achievement that he slew Miach. But that is another story.

Nuada chased Bres back to the land of the Fomorii, where Bres demanded that Elatha, his father, provide him with an army to punish the Children of Danu.

Thus, on the plain where ancient megaliths stood, thrusting their dark granite skywards, Magh Tuireadh, the Plain of Towers, on the evening of the Feast of Samhain (October 31), the Children of Danu faced the Children of Domnu in battle.

At dawn, the battle commenced. Combats broke out all along the line as Nuada led his warriors, both male and female, against the warriors of Bres and his Fomorii. Across the battlefield, the Mórrígán, Great Queen of Battles, with her sisters, Badh the Crow, Nemain the Venomous and Fea the Hateful, rushed hither and thither with their wailing cries which drove mortals to despair and death.

As time passed, Indech, a Fomorii warrior, approached Bres, and pointed out that whenever the Children of Danu were slain, or their weapons broken and destroyed, they would be carried from the field and, shortly after, would appear alive and well again with their weapons intact. Bres summoned his son, Ruadan, to his side and ordered him to discover the cause of the endless supply of weapons. And he summoned the son of Indech, a warrior named Octriallach, to discover how the Children of Danu, once slain, could come alive again.

Disguising himself as one of the Children of Danu, Ruadan went behind the lines of warriors and came across Goibhniu, god of smiths, who had set up a forge to one side of the Plain of Towers. With Goibhniu were Luchtainé, god of carpenters, and Credné, god of bronze workers. As each broken weapon was handed to Goibhniu, the smith-god gave it three blows of his hammer, which forged the head. Luchtainé gave the wood three blows of his axe and the shaft was fashioned. Then Credné fixed the shaft and head together with his bronze nails so swiftly that they needed no hammering.

Ruàdan went back to his father and told him what he had seen. In a rage, Bres ordered his son to kill Goibhniu.

In the meantime, Octriallach had found a mystic spring on the other side of the Plain of Towers at which stood Dian Cécht, the god of medicine, with his daughter Airmid at his side. Whenever one of the Children of Danu were slain, they were brought to the spring and Dian Cécht and his daughter plunged the body into the spring and they re-emerged alive again. In a rage, Bres ordered Octriallach to destroy the healing spring.

Ruadan returned to the forge and asked for a javelin from Goibhniu, who gave it without suspicion, thinking Ruadan was one of the Children of Danu. No sooner was the weapon in his hand than Ruadan turned and cast it at Goibhniu. It went clean through the smith-god's body. Mortally wounded as he was, Goibhniu picked up the spear and threw it back, wounding Ruadan, who crawled away back to his father and died at his feet. The Fomorii set up a great *caoine*, or keening, which was the first ever heard in the Island of Destiny.

Goibhniu also crawled away and came to the spring, where Dian Cécht and Airmid plunged him in, and he emerged healthy and healed.

That night, however, Octriallach, son of Indech, and several of his companions, came to the spring and each took a large stone from the bed of a nearby river and dropped it into the spring until they had filled it. So the healing waters were dispersed.

Bres, satisfied the Children of Danu were now mortal, and angered by the death of his son, determined that a pitched battle should be fought. The next morning, spears and lances and swords smote against buckler and shield. The whistle of darts and rattle of arrows and shouting of warriors made it seem as if a great thunder was rolling over the Plain of

Towers. The River of Unius, which cut through the plain, was stopped up, so filled was it with dead bodies. The plain was red with blood, so cruel was the battle.

Indech of the Fomorii fell by the hand of Ogma. And Indech was not the first nor last of the leaders of the Fomorii to feel the steel of the Children of Danu.

Neither did the Children of Danu go away from the battle unscathed.

To the field of slaughter came Balor of the Evil Eye, son of Buarainench, the most formidable of the Fomorii champions. He had one great eye, whose gaze was so malevolent that it destroyed whosoever looked upon it. So large and awesome was this eye that it took nine attendants, using hooks, to lift the mighty lid to open it for Balor. It happened on that fateful day of the battle that Balor came upon Nuada of the Silver Hand, the leader of the Children of Danu, and hard and fierce was the contest. Yet in the end, after shield was shattered, after spear was bent and sword was broken into pieces, it was the blood of Nuada that gushed in a never ending stream into the earth of the Island of Destiny. And not content in this slaughter, Balor turned upon one of Nuada's beautiful wives, Macha the Personification of Battles, goddess of warriors, and slew her also. Nor did Dian Cécht have the means to restore life to them.

At the death of their leader, the Children of Danu wavered and became fearful.

It was then that Lugh Lámhfada, Lugh of the Long Arm, approached the battlefield. Now Lugh was the son of Cian, which means "Enduring One", who was in turn son of Cainte, the god of speech. Now the council of the Children of Danu had forbidden him to come to the battle, for Lugh was all-wise and all-knowledgeable and it was thought that his life was too valuable to risk in battle, for his was the wisdom needed to serve humankind.

Indeed, so wise was Lugh that Nuada had let him become ruler of the Children of Danu for thirteen days, in order that they might receive his wisdom. Therefore the Children of Danu had him imprisoned, for his own safety, during the battle, with nine warriors to guard him. But on hearing

Nuada was slain, Lugh escaped his prison and his guards and, leaping into his chariot, he hurried to join his brothers and sisters on the Plain of Towers.

Bres was standing triumphantly with his Fomorii warriors when he saw a great light in the west.

"I wonder that the sun is rising in the west today," he muttered, scratching his head.

One of the Fomorii shamans approached Bres, trembling. "It is not the sun, mighty Bres. The light stems from the countenance of Lugh Lámhfada! It is his radiance."

Lugh, with his weapons sheathed, drove his chariot out from the lines of the Children of Danu; straight he drove up to the tightly packed lines of Fomorii champions. "Where is Balor?" he cried. "Let him who thinks himself a great warrior come forward and be taught the truth!"

The lines of Fomorii parted and the great figure of Balor was seen, seated on a gigantic chair. His one mighty eye was closed.

Lugh's challenge rang out again.

This time Balor heard it and said to his attendants, "Lift up my eyelid, that I may gaze upon this prattling little man."

The attendants began to lift Balor's eye with a hook. They stood well out of range: for anyone on whom that eye fell upon would perish immediately.

Lugh was ready with a sling and in it set a *tathlum*, a slingshot made of blood mixed with the sand of the swift Armorian sea. As the lid was lifted, Lugh hurled his shot into the eye. It struck it, went through the brain and out the back of Balor's head. The great Fomorii champion's eye was knocked out and fell on the ground. In its dying glint, thrice nine companies of Fomorii warriors were destroyed, for they saw its malignant gaze.

Balor fell screaming to the ground in blindness.

A great anxiety fell on the Fomorii.

Lugh now raised his sword, and the Mórrígán set up a paean of victory, "Kings arise to the battle . . . !" And so the Children of Danu took heart and, echoing the song, they began to move forward. Great was the slaughter now as they pressed back on the Children of Domnu. It is said that more

Fomorii were killed on the Plain of Towers than there were stars in the sky or grains of sand on the seashore, or snow-flakes in winter.

And Lugh came upon Bres, who was fleeing for his life from the battlefield.

"Spare my life, Lugh, great conqueror," cried the son of Elatha, sinking to his knees, for he no longer had the strength nor spirit to fight. "Spare it, and I will pay whatever ransom you require."

"What ransom?" demanded Lugh, his sword held at the throat of the Fomorii leader.

"I will guarantee that there will be no shortage of milk from the cows of this land," offered Bres.

Lugh then called the Children of Danu to him.

"What good is that if Bres cannot lengthen the lives of the cows?" they demanded.

Bres could not grant longer lives so he offered, "If my life is spared, every wheat harvest in Inisfáil will be a good one."

"We already have enough good harvests. We need no other guarantees."

Finally, Bres agreed to instruct the Children of Danu as to the best times to plough, sow and reap and for this knowledge, which they had not, they spared his life.

And when the battle was over, when the Fomorii were pursued back into their undersea fortresses, and they accepted the right of the Children of Danu to live in peace in the Island of Destiny and rule over it as gods and goddesses of goodness and light, the Mórrígán went to all the summits of the highest mountains of the island and on each summit she proclaimed the victory of the gods and goddesses of light and goodness. And she sang in triumph a paean to the Mother Goddess, Danu.

Peace mounts to the heavens
The divine waters descend to earth
And fructifies our lives
Earth lies under the heavens
We are of the Earth now
And everyone is strong . . .

And while Danu smiled on the victory of her children, her sister Domnu scowled from the depths of the earth and she chose the goddess Badh the Crow as her mouth to utter a prophecy to Danu and her children.

"All life is transitory. Even your children are not immortal, my sister. The time will come when they will be defeated. The time will come when no one will want gods and goddesses to nurture them, when they will be driven into the darkness, like my children have been this day.

"The time approaches when the summers of Inisfáil will be flowerless, when the cows shall be without milk, and the men will be weak and the women shall be shameless; the seas will be without fish, the trees without fruit and old men will give false judgments; the judges will make unjust laws and honour will count for little and warriors will betray each other and resort to thievery. There will come a time when there will be no more virtue left in this world."

Indeed, there came that time when the Children of Míl flooded into the Island of Destiny and when the Children of Danu were driven underground into the hills, which were called *sídhe*, which is pronounced *shee*, and in those mounds they dwelt, the once mighty gods and goddesses, deserted by the very people who they had sought to nourish. The descendants of Míl, who live in the Island of Destiny to this day, called the Children of Danu the *aes sídhe*, the people of the hills, and when even the religion of Míl was forgotten, when the religion of the Cross replaced that of the Circle, the people simply called the *aes sídhe* by the name of fairies.

Of the greatest of the gods, the victor of the battle on the Plain of Towers, Lugh Lámhfada, god of all knowledge, patron of all arts and crafts, his name is still known today. But as memory of the mighty warrior, the invincible god, has faded, he is known only as *Lugh-chromain*, little stooping Lugh of the *sídhe*, relegated to the role of a fairy craftsman. And, as even the language in which he was venerated has disappeared, all that is left of the supreme god of the Children of Danu is the distorted form of that name *Lugh-chromain* . . . leprechaun.

Ireland [Éire]

Ireland: Preface

The consequence of having an Irish father, and one who was a writer – indeed, who was the third generation of the family to take to the scribal art – was that, as a child, I never lacked being told legends and fairy tales. Indeed, in my early years, or so it seemed, there was almost a competition in the family as to who would tell the tale. For it was not just my father who was the storyteller; my mother was equally adept, as befitted someone from a family who had a long history of literary endeavour.

One of the first of the family whose works went into print was the brother of my mother's 11x great-grandfather. He was Thomas Randolph (1605–35), the poet and dramatist and friend of Ben Jonson. Her family also had Breton, Scottish and Welsh branches, so the Celts were well represented in my youth.

If that was not enough, I was the youngest of six, of which five of us (three girls and two boys) had survived through childhood. The eldest boy had died as a baby in a hospital during a flu epidemic. My elder sisters and brother also felt it their duty to "perform" and tell tales with me as their, often unwilling, audience.

For three years or so, when I was between five and nine years old, my father had moved us to a fairly isolated country cottage where he pounded on a large black Remington Standard typewriter, which was so heavy that I could not even begin to lift it. He produced short stories, some serials and articles for a variety of newspapers and magazines. There was no electricity in the cottage and I grew well acquainted with the warmth and light of oil lamps.

To reach the nearest village, it was a stroll across three fields and a bridge over a gushing stream, and then a walk of about three miles along a narrow country road, for the bus passed only once every hour. I walked it often, sometimes insisting on being allowed to carry the empty "accumulator" – the glass battery which ran the radio – and then trying to avoid carrying back the full one. So there was plenty of time for telling tales on such walks as well as on the dark winter's evenings.

Myths and legends were a staple fare. I remember one of my sisters adapting stories into little plays, which we would put on in a nearby disused barn for the entertainment of the other local children.

This is a long way round to saying that when I grew up, being the youngest, I had no one, in my turn, to tell the stories to and this is probably why I turned to writing them instead.

Because of my father, I grew up with stories of Irish myth and legend as part of the staple fare, so that retelling them is second nature. Our home was also full of books of such tales. I suppose Thomas Crofton Croker (1790–1854), from my father's home county of Cork, made retelling of Irish myths and legends in English popular. He produced *Researches in the South of Ireland* (1824) and *Fairy Legends & Traditions of South West Ireland* (1825), which caused the famous Brothers Grimm to translate the latter into German as *Irische Elfenmärchen*.

Lady Jane Wilde, the mother of Oscar, was an assiduous collector and her *Ancient Legends, Mystic Charms and Superstitions of Ireland* was published in 1887. Jeremiah Curtin's *Myths and Folklore of Ireland* (1890) was always a popular book on our shelves, but never replaced Lady Augusta Gregory's *Cuchulain of Muithemne* (1902) and *Gods and Fighting Men* (1904).

Perhaps the most qualified and capable folklorist was Douglas Hyde, who became the first president of the Irish Free State in 1937 under its new constitution. His collections of oral traditions have become classics, such as *Leabhar*

Sgeulaigheachta (1889), *Beside the Fire* (1890) and *Love Songs of Connacht* (1893). His *magnum opus* was, however, a *Literary History of Ireland* (1899), the first general survey of Irish literature from ancient times.

Dr Hyde laid the groundwork for many who came later and who have added important contributions to such studies. Myles Dillon's *The Cycles of the Kings*, Oxford University Press, 1946, and *Early Irish Literature*, University of Chicago, 1948. The impressive Professor Thomas O'Rahilly's *Early Irish History and Mythology*, Dublin Institute of Advanced Studies, 1946. Alwyn and Brinsley Rees's *Celtic Heritage*, Thames and London, 1961. These were some of the many titles which impressed me in sorting out the original fabric of the Irish tales.

The following stories are an amalgamation from many sources and varied versions. The first two are in the *Leabhar Gabhála*, The Book of Invasions. It contains the stories of the mythical invasions of Cesair, before the Deluge, through to the invasions of Partholón, Nemed, the Firbolg, the Tuatha Dé Danaan and finally the Milesian ancestors of the Gaels. It is regarded as the "national epic" of Ireland.

To this "Mythological Cycle" belongs the stories of *The Sons of Tuirenn* and *The Children of Lir*. *The Sons of Tuirenn* appears as *Aided Chlainne Tuirenn* and there is much spelling confusion of the name, which appears as Tuireall and Tuirill, and also uncertainty as to the identity of Tuirenn. In one text he is described as Danu's father; in another, her husband; while the goddess Brigid is also placed in this role. The narrative *Oidheadh Chlainne Lir* (The Tragic Fate of the Children of Lir) survives from a fifteenth-century text and has always been one of my favourite tales. *The Love of Fand* is based on *Serglige Con Culainn*, belonging to the Red Branch Cycle, also known as the Ulster Cycle; this is heroic myth comparable to the *Iliad* in theme and heroic tone, of which the most famous story is the saga of the *Táin Bó Cuailnge* (The Cattle Raid of Cuailnge).

Lochlann's Son belongs to the Fenian Cycle, sometimes called the Ossianic Cycle, concerning the deeds of Fionn Mac Cumhaill and his Fianna warriors, whose first bold synthesis appeared as a cohesive whole in the twelfth-century *Accamh na Senórach* (Colloquy of the Ancients). The stories are dated to the third century AD. Next to the *Táin*, the Fenian Cycle is one of the longest medieval compositions and became very popular with ordinary people during that period.

It was from the Fenian Cycle that many Arthurian stories were later embellished. Although there are nearly a dozen original Arthurian sagas in Irish, the Arthurian stories never displaced stories of Fionn Mac Cumhaill in medieval Irish popular imagination.

The Poet's Curse concerns historical personages in Mongán and the poet Dallán Forgaill. A discussion of the earliest surviving medieval texts of the story was made by Dr Eleanor Knott in *Ériu* 8, pp. 155–60. Dallán Forgaill is, by tradition, the author of *Amra Choluim Chille*, composed *c.* 600 AD, and is considered one of the oldest survivals in Irish literature.

Finally, *Cellachain of Cashel* is based on several stories I heard in West Cork in my youth and which I have cross-referenced to a couple of surviving medieval texts: *Senchas Fagnála Caisil andso sis agus Beandacht Ríg*, a fifteenth-century fragmentary story *The Finding of Cashel*, preserved in Trinity College, Dublin, and *Caithreim Cheallachain Chaisil* (The battle-career of Ceallachan of Cashel), written in the twelfth century. It was commissioned by Cormac III MacCarthy of Cashel, some time between 1127–38, and written at Cashel.

The oldest copy, dating to the twelfth century, is in the Royal Irish Academy in Dublin. These are some of the impressive texts that survive from the patronage of the Eóghanacht royal dynasty, who were kings of Munster and later Desmond, reigning from Cashel. The last regnate Eóghanacht king was Donal IX MacCarthy Mór (d. 1596).

Sadly, during this time, Sir George Carew, representing Elizabeth of England, set out not only to destroy native government in Munster but all Irish manuscripts. Many of these old manuscripts were cut up, on his orders, to make covers for English language primers. Many great works were probably destroyed, judging from that which has survived.

The *aisling* or vision tale, *The Vision of Tnugdal*, a Cashel warrior, was written in 1149 at Ratisbon (Regensburg) by an Irish monk named Marcus, carrying on the Munster literary traditions. The saga enjoyed great fame in Europe and, as well as an Irish text, some 154 manuscripts of the Latin text dating from the twelfth to the nineteenth centuries have been found in Europe, plus translations into Anglo-Norman, Belorussian, Catalan, Dutch, English, French, German, Icelandic, Italian, Portuguese, Provençal, Serbo-Croat, Spanish and Swedish.

My attempt to rescue one part of the epic of Cellachain, hopefully, puts the kingdom of Munster in its rightful place as having produced a literature equal with the Red Branch Cycle of Ulster. It is my hope that much more of that literature will be recovered.

2 *The Sons of Tuirenn*

No one knew the reason of the feud between the sons of Cainte and the sons of Tuirenn. Perhaps it had its roots in a sharp word, some affront to honour, but the result was that the three sons of Cainte and the three sons of Tuirenn had sworn to shed each other's blood, should they ever meet with one another.

So it came about that the eldest son of Cainte, Cian, whose name means "the enduring one", was crossing the great plain of Muirthemne, on his way to join the Children of Danu at Magh Tuireadh, for the news was that a great battle was being fought against the Fomorii. Cian was alone, for his two brothers, Cú and Céthen, had gone on before him.

It was as he was on the open plain, some way from any shelter, that he saw three warriors heading towards him. Standing tall in his chariot, Cian narrowed his eyes to examine them. There was no mistaking the grim visage of Brían, whose name means "exalted one", and his brothers Iuchar and Iucharba.

Now Cian realized, because he was outnumbered, that discretion was the better part of valour. But there was no cover on the plain, except for a herd of pigs feeding. Being one of the children of Danu, Cian took a Druid wand and changed his shape into that of a pig, also causing his chariot and horses to be likewise transformed.

Brían, son of Tuirenn, chieftain of Ben Eadair, paused and stared across the plain. "Brothers," he said, turning to Iuchar and Iucharba, "wasn't there a proud warrior crossing the plain, a moment ago?"

They affirmed that their brother was right.

Brían saw the herd of pigs and he realized that the warrior must have shape-changed. If this were so, then the warrior was no friend to the sons of Tuirenn. Now Brían realised that the herd of pigs belonged to Nuada himself and, if he and his brothers harmed them, Nuada would punish them. So he took his own Druid wand and touched his brothers lightly. Iuchar and Iucharba were changed into two great hounds and straightaway, baying eagerly, they made for the herd, keen noses to the ground.

Cian realized that the hounds would sniff him out and so, still in the shape of a pig, he made a break from the herd. But Brían was standing ready and cast his spear through the pig shape. Cian screamed in agony.

"I am Cian, son of Cainte, and I plead for quarter," cried the pig.

Brían, now joined by his brothers in their true shapes, stood before the bleeding pig.

"No quarter!" snapped Brían. "We have all sworn an oath that none would survive our encounters, should the sons of Cainte and the sons of Tuirenn meet."

"Then grant me a last request," cried Cian in resignation. "Let me resume my human form before you kill me."

This Brían granted.

Cian smiled triumphantly at him. "You may kill me now but remember this, sons of Tuirenn; had you killed me as a pig, your punishment would have only been the *eric* fine paid on the unlawful slaughter of a pig. Since you now kill me as a man, then you will have to pay the *eric* fine of a man. Moreover, as I am Cian the enduring, the son of Cainte, and the father of Lugh of the Long Hand, the punishment that shall be exacted will be great. Even the weapons with which you kill me shall cry out in horror at this deed."

Brían thought for a while, for it was true that Cian was one of the Children of Danu. Then he smiled sneeringly at Cian. "Then it shall not be with weapons you will be killed, but with stones of the earth."

So saying, he threw aside his weapons and picked up some stones and hurled them in hate at Cian. He was joined by his brothers and stone after stone flew until Cian was a disfigured and unrecognisable mess of a man. Then the brothers dug a grave and buried the battered body. But six times the earth refused to cover the corpse before, at the seventh time of burying, the earth accepted the body.

Yet as Brían and his brothers rode away, they heard a voice calling from beneath the earth: "The blood is on your hands, sons of Tuirenn, and there it will remain until we meet again."

The sons of Tuirenn distinguished themselves in the great Battle of the Plain of Towers, in which Bres and the Fomorii were defeated. But everyone remarked that Cian was absent from the battle, which was strange, as it was Cian's own son who had taken over the leadership of the Children of Danu when Nuada had been killed by the Fomorii, Balor of the Evil Eye. So, after a fruitless search, Lugh Lámhfada finally came to the Plain of Muirthemne and, as he was travelling across it, the stones of the earth started to speak.

"Here lies the body of your father Cian! Killed by the sons of Tuirenn. Blood on their hands, until they meet with Cian again!"

Lugh had his father's body disinterred and he called his companions together, that they might see how the deed was done. And Lugh swore vengeance. Lugh sang a lament over the body:

Cian's death, death of a great champion,
Has left me as a walking corpse
Without a soul,
Without strength, without power,
Without a feeling for life.
The Sons of Tuirenn have killed him
Now my hatred will come against them
And follow them to the ends of the world.

And Lugh buried his father's body with all pomp and ceremony and went back to the great hall of Tara, where he summoned all the people. Even the sons of Tuirenn were among them but Lugh kept his counsel. Instead, he asked those among the gods what they would do to take vengeance on those who had, with malice, slaughtered their fathers.

Each of the gods suggested ways, increasingly more horrible and more bloody, as a means of punishment. And when the last of them had spoken, the assembly roared its approval. Lugh saw that the sons of Tuirenn, not wishing to be conspicuous in the throng, were also applauding.

Then Lugh, with a scowl on his usually sunny countenance, spoke up. "The murderers of Cian have condemned themselves, for they have joined in the agreement of you all as to their punishment. But I am merciful. I will not spill blood in Tara. I claim the right to put an *eric* fine on the murderers. If they refuse to accept it, then they must meet me, one after the other, in bloody single combat at the door of Tara's Hall."

All the while he spoke he was looking at the sons of Tuirenn.

Then Brían moved forward. "It is known there was enmity between us and your father and his brothers Cú and Céthen. Your words seem addressed to us, but Cian was not killed by any weapons of the sons of Tuirenn. Nevertheless, to show that we are honourable, each one of us will accept your *eric* fine."

Lugh smiled grimly. "You will not find it difficult. I wish for three apples, the skin of a pig, a spear, two horses and a chariot, seven swine, a hound-pup, a cooking spit and three shouts to be delivered on a hill."

Not only the sons of Tuirenn stood amazed but the entire assembly could not believe their ears at the little Lugh demanded in compensation for his father's death. The sons of Tuirenn were visibly relieved and clamoured to accept the fine.

"If you think it is too heavy," Lugh added, "I will not press the fine."

"We do not consider it heavy," replied Brían. "In fact, it seems so light that I suspect some trickery. Are you intending to increase the sum?"

"I swear by our mother, Danu, the divine waters, that the

fine will not be increased. And in return for this oath, do you swear you will faithfully complete the *eric* fine?"

They did so, with mighty acclaim.

"Very well," Lugh chuckled grimly, after they had sworn. "The three apples must come from the Garden of Hesperides in the East. They are of gold in colour and have immense power and virtue. They are as big as the head of a month-old child and never grow less, no matter how much is eaten from them. They have the taste of honey and a bite will cure a sick or wounded man. A warrior can perform any feat with one for, once cast from his hand, it will return to him."

The sons of Tuirenn looked thunderstruck.

"The skin of the pig is that owned by Tuis, king of Greece. In whatever stream that pig walked, the water turned to wine, and the wounded and sick became well when they drank of it. These magical properties are enshrouded in that skin."

The sons of Tuirenn began to look grim.

"The spear is that which belongs to Pisear of Persia, and it is called 'slaughterer'. It has to be kept in a cauldron of blood to prevent it killing, for only blood cools its angry blade."

Lugh paused, but the sons of Tuirenn now stood expressionless as they realised the trap that he had set for them.

"The steeds and chariot which I require are those belonging to Dobhar of Siogair. If one of the horses are killed, it will come to life again, if its bones are brought together in the same place.

"The seven swine are those of Easal, King of the Golden Pillars, which, though killed each day for the feast, are found alive the following morning. The hound pup is Failinis, owned by the king of Ioruiadh. The wild beasts are helpless before her. The cooking spit I want is that from the island of Fianchuibhe, which is protected by mighty women warriors. And the hill on which you must give three shouts is that of Miodchaoin in Lochlainn, which is constantly guarded by Miodchaoin and his three fierce sons, Aedh, Corca and Conn. Their task is solely to prevent any person from raising their voices on the hill.

"This, sons of Tuirenn, is the *eric* fine I ask of you."

* * *

When Tuirenn heard what had befallen his sons, he was upset, but he went to them and gave them advice.

"No one can set out on this voyage without the magical ship of the god of the oceans, Manánnan Mac Lir. But Lugh owns this ship, the Wave-sweeper, which can navigate itself across the seas. But listen to me, Lugh is under a *geis*, a sacred proscription never to refuse a second request. So go to him and ask for a loan of Manánnan's fabulous horse, Aonbharr, which can gallop over land and water. He will refuse. Then ask for the Wave-sweeper, and that he cannot refuse."

And this they did and it happened as Tuirenn had said. Lugh was forced to give them the loan of Manánnan's boat. And Tuirenn and his daughter Eithne went to see them off from the harbour at Ben Eadair. Their sister Eithne sang a lament of farewell for, as much as she loved them, she knew that they had done an evil thing and therefore only evil would come of it.

The three warriors climbed into the Wave-sweeper and Brían commanded it to cross to the Garden of Hesperides. The boat leapt forward at his command and ploughed through the white-crested waves more swiftly than if the winds of spring were blowing into its sail. So fast did it travel that, within the wink of an eye, it came safely to the harbour of Hesperides on the extreme western edge of the ocean.

The three brothers climbed out. They learnt that the apple-orchards of Hesperides were so well guarded that they had no chance of entering without discovery. Then Brían drew up his Druid's wand and changed his brothers and himself into hawks. On his instructions, they rose into the air and circled high above the orchard and then they swooped down, travelling so fast that the arrows and spears of the guards could not hit them. Each in turn, they seized one of the golden apples, rose again into the air and raced back to the harbour where they had left their boat.

Now the king of Hesperides had three daughters who were sorceresses and when they heard the news, they transformed themselves into three griffins and pursued the hawks, breathing great tongues of fire after them. So fierce were the flames that the hawks were burnt and blinded and could bear the heat no longer. Then Brían used his Druid's lore and changed them into swans who were able to glide down to the sea. The griffins, confused, flew off, still looking for the hawks and the sons of Tuirenn made their way back to the Wave-sweeper.

Next, they commanded the boat to take them to Greece and entered the harbour close to the palace of Tuis.

Brían's brothers wanted him to disguise them as animals but he told them that poets from Inisfáil were well respected in Greece and they would go up to the king's palace and present themselves as such. Indeed, this was truly thought out, for the guards allowed the three "poets" into the king's palace. Tuis himself greeted them and invited them to a great feast. At the end of the feast, the king's poets rose and recited their poems. Then the sons of Tuirenn were invited to recite.

Brían stood up and intoned these verses.

I conceal not your fame, o Tuis
Great as an oak among kings,
A pigskin is a reward without meanness,
And this I claim in return for this poem.

A war may come when warriors clash
A war may be averted by a gift
And he who gives without fear,
Shall lose nothing.
A stormy army and tempestuous sea
Are weapons that no one would oppose,
But a pigskin, a reward freely given
Is that which we claim.

"It sounds an excellent poem," mused Tuis, "yet I do not understand it."

"I will interpret it," smiled Brían. "It means that as an oak excels above others trees, so do you in kingship. We claim the pigskin you have as a reward for our poem, but if it is refused it means that there will be a war between us."

Tuis stared in surprise.

"I would like your poem if you had not mentioned my

magical pigskin. You seem a foolish man, poet, to ask for it. I would even refuse the kings and warriors of your land, had they demanded it. So now I refuse you. Yet your poem is good and I will reward you with gold. And three times in gold what that pigskin will hold will be your fee."

"Generous as you are, king," Brían laughed, "let us watch while the gold is measured in the skin."

The king agreed and the sons of Tuirenn were brought to the treasure house and the skin was brought from its special place. And when the skinfuls of gold were weighed, Brían suddenly grabbed the skin, drawing his sword and cutting clean off the arm of the man who held the skin. He wrapped the skin about himself and the three brothers fought their way from the palace. In rage and fury, Tuis and his court attacked them but not one noble nor champion of Greece was able to halt them. Tuis himself fell before the slashing sword of Brían.

They fought their way back to the Wave-sweeper and straightaway they called on it to take them to Persia. It was agreed that the disguise of poets worked well for them and so they presented themselves to the court of Pisear in the same manner. Once more they were asked to recite a poem and Brían did so.

> Small esteem of any spear with Pisear
> His enemies are already broken
> Pisear has little cause for worry
> Since it is others who receive wounds.
>
> The yew is the finest tree in the forest
> The yew is king without opposition
> May the great spear shafts drive on
> Through the wounds of those they slay.

When Pisear asked Brían to spell out the meaning of the poem, Brían told him that he wanted his magic spear in payment for the poem.

When Pisear threatened to kill him and his brothers for audacity, Brían remembered that he had one of the apples of Hesperides with him. He took it from his bag and threw it at

Pisear, so hard that it knocked the king's head off, then returned safely to his hand. Then Brían and his brothers drew their swords and fought their way to the room where the blazing spear was kept in its great cauldron of blood, hissing and bubbling. They took it and went back to the Wave-sweeper.

On they went to Dobhar's kingdom of Siogair. Here they appeared before his court as three champions of Inisfáil, seeking hospitality. When asked what they wanted, they told Dobhar the king that they would serve him for payment. They spent a long time in Siogair, because they were unable to find the steeds and the chariot, which were faster than the winds of spring. Finally, Brían tricked the king into ordering that the chariot be brought to the court, harnessed and ready.

And when the sons of Tuirenn turned and demanded the prancing horses and the beautiful chariot as the price for their service, Dobhar flew into a rage and ordered his guards to kill them.

Brían sprang into the chariot, hurling the charioteer to the ground. He took the reins in his hands and unloosed the spear of Pisear so that the guards of Dobhar were slain and those who were not simply fled. And with Iuchar and Iucharba behind him, Brían drove the chariot back to the waiting Wave-sweeper.

Next, the magic boat of Manánnan Mac Lir brought them to the land of the Golden Pillars, the entrance of the Middle Sea, where Easal ruled. And when they came to the shore they saw great armies gathered, for now the fame of the deeds of the sons of Tuirenn had travelled before them, and news of their banishment from Inisfáil and the nature of their tasks had preceded them.

Easal the king came down to the harbour to meet them and he demanded to know if it was true that they had come for his swine. They told him it was. Now Easal was a peaceful man and he went and sat in council with his chieftains. Eventually, they decided that they would hand the swine to the sons of Tuirenn to avoid the slaughter of the innocent. That night, Easal invited the brothers to a feasting, where the seven pigs were handed to them. Brían sang a paean in praise of Easal's wisdom and generosity.

When Easal learnt that the sons of Tuirenn were going next to the country of Ioruaidh, the king asked that he be allowed to accompany them, for his daughter was the wife of the king of Ioruaidh. Easal promised, in return, to do his best to secure the hound-pup from the king, his son-in-law, without bloodshed.

The king of Ioruaidh would have none of Easal's advice. "You may be weak, old man, but the gods have not given strength or luck enough to any warrior to take my hound-pup by force."

Easal was saddened, for he knew what bloodshed and mayhem would follow.

A great and bloody battle began. And Brían cleaved through the warriors of Ioruaidh, throwing them back by nine times one hundred, until he reached the spot where the king of Ioruaidh stood. And he picked up the king bodily and fought his way back until he threw the craven man at Easal's feet.

"There is your daughter's husband, o king. It would have been easier to kill him than to return with him alive."

The warriors of Ioruaidh, seeing their king defeated, threw down their arms. And the king of Ioruaidh now heeded the peaceful tones of Easal and handed over the hound-pup and the sons of Tuirenn took their leave in friendship.

Now only two tasks remained to be filled.

They were to find the cooking spit of Fianchuibhe and give three shouts on the Hill of Miodchaoin.

But so excited were they at their successes that they forgot about the last two tasks. Some have it that Lugh Lámhfada had prevailed upon his Druid to send a cloud of forgetfulness to seep into the brothers' minds after they had left Ioruaidh.

Whatever the cause, the Wave-sweeper returned to Inisfáil. Lugh heard of their coming and was suddenly troubled, for he had followed the successes of the sons of Tuirenn with mixed feelings. He was happy that these gifts that they had secured were for him, but apprehensive that they might be turned against him. He was also bitter because the brothers were fulfilling the conditions of the *eric* fine which he had devised to cause their deaths.

So when the Wave-sweeper entered the mouth of the Boyne river, Lugh went to the fort of Cathair Crofinn and armed himself with the magical armour of the Ocean god, Manánnan, who was his foster-father. He also put on the cloak of invisibility of Fea the Hateful, one of the goddesses of war. For Lugh also feared their coming, thinking the three brothers might mean him harm now that they possessed such wonderful weapons.

And when they sent word to Lugh, asking him to come and take his *eric* fine, Lugh sent back asking that they hand over the spoils to the Bodb Dearg, son of The Dagda, who had now succeeded Lugh as ruler of the Children of Danu. Only when the Bodb Dearg reported that he had control of the wondrous gifts did Lugh emerge and come to examine them.

"But where is the cooking spit?" demanded Lugh, "And I did not hear the three shouts on the Hill of Miodchaoin."

The sons of Tuirenn then remembered and they were sorely grieved. So they left and spent a night with their father Tuirenn and sister Eithne, at their fortress at Ben Eadair. Now they did not have the benefit of the magical ship the Wave-sweeper, for they had foolishly surrendered it to Lugh. So they set sail in an ordinary ship, in search of Fianchuibhe. However, the task was a long one. For three months they searched, visiting many islands and asking many travellers if they knew of such a place. No one knew.

Finally, they met an old man, toothless and without eyes, for there were so many wrinkles and folds of flesh on his walnut-coloured face that they were hidden. He told them that the island of Fianchuibhe did not lie on the surface of the sea but deep down in its depths.

Brían, telling Iuchar and Iuchara to wait for him, leapt over the side of their ship and sank down into the waves. For two periods of nine days he walked the ocean bed in his search and found many houses, and great palaces. Then he entered a house with its doors open, where one hundred and fifty beautiful women were engaged in needlework and embroidery. In the middle of them lay a cooking spit.

Brían saw that the women neither moved nor spoke as he entered. So, without more ado, he walked to the spit, seized it, turned and walked out. At that point the women all burst out laughing. They rose and surrounded Brían, who saw they had a formidable assortment of weapons.

"Brave man, are you Brían, son of Tuirenn? There are one hundred and fifty of us here, every one a warrior, and each one of us able to slay you. But you are brave and courageous to make this attempt, knowing the dangers. You shall be rewarded. Take the spit, for this is one of many which we have."

And Brían thanked them and swam upwards to the ship in which his brothers were anxiously waiting. They were overjoyed.

They turned the ship northward now to the great fjords of Lochlainn, for that is what the name means, the place of lochs and fjords. They saw the great hill of Miodchaoin rising upwards and, leaving their ship, they walked to the bottom of it. But there, on the massive slopes, stood Miodchaoin, who was a mighty warrior.

Miodchaoin saw Brían and unsheathed his great sword.

"Killer of my friend and foster-brother Cian! Now you have come to shout upon this hill. You will do that deed only when I am dead."

Brían flew at Miodchaoin and the two great warriors set about one another. So fierce was their onslaught that the ringing of the swords upon their shields could be heard in every corner of the world. No quarter was asked nor given, until Miodchaoin fell dead with Brían's sword thrust through his giant heart.

Then the three sons of Miodchaoin, Aedh, Corca and Conn, having heard the noise of battle, came racing up and fell on the three sons of Tuirenn. The sky reddened and blackened, blood flowed from that mountain slope like the gushing waters of a mountain spring, and the earth trembled from the stamping of their feet, even as far to the East as Hesperides.

For three days and three nights the great combat shook the mountains of Lochlainn. Then the sons of Miodchaoin managed to find the flesh of the sons of Tuirenn with their spear points. Each one of the sons of Tuirenn, Brían, Iuchar and Iucharba, were pierced and wounded. Yet the sons of Tuirenn would not give in, for they thrust their spears into the bodies of Aedh, Corca and Conn and the three sons of Miodchaoin fell dead.

The sons of Tuirenn fell on the blood-stained grass and it seemed that a heavy veil of darkness was being drawn before their eyes. It was Brían, coughing blood, who called faintly: "Brothers, how is it with you?"

"Dead are we," they gasped. "Or as near it as makes no difference."

"We must climb the hill and give three shouts before death claims us," replied Brían. "Only then may we rest in peace."

With Brían supporting his two brothers on his mighty arms, the three went forward up the steep slopes, stumbling and moving as in a dream, until they reached the summit. Then they paused and gave three shouts; weak as they were, they were shouts nevertheless.

Brían, still supporting his brothers, then guided them to the ship and they turned her prow for Inisfáil.

In a delirium, they drifted and drifted towards the distant island. Suddenly Brían raised his head. "I see Ben Eadair and the fort of our father, Tuirenn."

His brothers raised their heads so that they might see the green hills of their home before they died. The ship gently nudged ashore and Tuirenn came down with Eithne to greet his sons.

"Father, take the spit to Lugh," instructed Brían, "and tell him that the three shouts on the Hill of Miodchaoin have been given."

And Tuirenn mounted his chariot and rode to Tara with the news. And he pleaded with Lugh to loan him the magic pigskin of Tuis which would heal the sick and wounded, or one of the apples of Hesperides, but Lugh refused him coldly. And Tuirenn returned to his dying sons and lamented:

If all the jewels of the world
Were given to Lugh to ease his anger
It would not be enough to save you
From a gloomy grave.

But Brían asked to be taken before Lugh, and when Lugh stood before him, the dying warrior begged for the magic pigskin, for humanity's sake.

"I will not give it," replied Lugh. "If you offer me the entire world and the wonders it contains, I would not give it. Your death must follow. You killed Cian, and denied him even when he pleaded for his life. You killed him cruelly and nothing less than your own deaths will compensate that deed."

So Brían returned to his dying brothers and they were laid down side by side. United, the sons of Tuirenn sighed together for the last time and their souls sped onwards by that breath into the Otherworld.

Eithne stood with her father, hand in hand, and sang a doleful lament over the bodies of her brothers. Then both she and her father Tuirenn, overcome with grief, fell beside the bodies, and departed this earth with them.

3 The Children of Lir

It happened after the Tuatha Dé Danaan, the gods and goddesses of Éireann, were defeated by the mortal sons of Míle Easpain. No one can now recall the circumstances of the conflict, except that there was a great battle fought at Tailtiu, which is now called Telltown on the north bank of the River Blackwater, in Co. Meath. A great fair was held there in ancient times and this fair was sacred to the goddess Tailtiu, who was foster-mother to the magnificent Lugh of the Long Hand. Blood stained the fields of Tailtiu for many a year thereafter, for there was a great slaughter in that place. The mortals drove the Ever-Living Ones from the face of the earth so that, ever after, they went to live in the *sídhe* – the hills – and, being lost in people's memories, they became "the people of the hills", or simply fairies.

But this was some distance in the future from the time of the sad tale of Lir's children.

It was soon after the devastation of Tailtiu that the remnants of the Tuatha Dé Danaan gathered and decided to choose a new king to rule them. The Dagda, the good god, who had ruled before, had told them that, as he had brought about their downfall, he was not fit to continue to lead them. So they choose the Bodb Dearg, who was the son of The Dagda, and he dwelt in the Sídh of Femen, which is now Slievenamon in Co. Tipperary. It fell to the Bodb Dearg to allocate the hills to the other gods and goddesses, and these were to become as their dwelling places. To Lir, the god of the ocean, fell the Sídh Fionnachaidh, that is now Deadman's Hill in Co. Armagh.

Now Lir thought he should have been chosen as ruler over all the Children of Danu, and was filled with anger and envy at the decision. He left the assembly of the gods and goddesses so angry that he would talk to no one. He showed neither respect nor homage to the Bodb Dearg.

The gods and goddesses became angry with him and were all for raising a host and marching against him. But it was the Bodb Dearg himself who prevented them.

"We have shed enough blood against the Milesians," he told them. "Let us not continue shedding blood among ourselves. Because Lir does not bow his knee to me, it does not make me any the less your king. Let me go and reason with him."

The gods and goddesses of Éireann were impressed by the compassion and wisdom of the Bodb Dearg and pleased that they had made him their ruler.

It was a while before the Bodb Dearg approached Lir, for he knew it best to let the anger die away first. Indeed, while he was waiting, it happened that Lir's wife, the mother of his magnificent son Manánnan Mac Lir, had died. Lir became lonely and bitter. More lonely was he because no other god nor goddess would visit him at his *sídh*, for they refused to speak with him after he had walked out of the assembly.

After the appropriate period of mourning, the Bodb Dearg sent greetings to Lir.

"This is the time when one stands in need of friends and kind counsel," Bodb Dearg told his fellows.

The message that the Bodb Dearg sent was to the effect that if Lir accepted him as king over the Children of Danu, he would arrange a marriage with one of his three foster-daughters – they were Niamh, Aoife and Aobh, daughters of Aillil, king of the Islands of Aran. Indeed, it was known that Niamh, Aoife and Aobh were the most beautiful women in Éireann, and the most intelligent and accomplished.

Lir was delighted, for he had grown weary of his isolation and the sadness of the loss of his dearest companion. So he set out with fifty chariots until they reached the palace of the Bodb Dearg. There he embraced his king and acknowledged him in due fashion. There was a great banquet that night, and the feasting lasted for several days. All the people of Danú were happy to see Lir back in their company.

Eventually, the three foster daughters of the Bodb Dearg were brought forward.

Lir gazed on them with awe, for each one was as beautiful as the other. Niamh, the eldest, was dark and pale; Aoife, the middle girl, was red-haired and cream-skinned; while Aobh, the youngest, was fair-haired and bright. They combined the qualities of winter, autumn and spring. And when he spoke with them, Lir was amazed at their intelligence and wit.

The choice was difficult, but Lir finally chose Aobh, for she was young and fresh and had the beauty of spring and the promise of the future.

In the fullness of time, Aobh bore Lir children. In truth, she gave birth to two sets of twins. The first set was a boy and a girl whom she called Aodh and Fionnghuala (meaning "fire" and "fair-shouldered") and the second set were two boys whom she called Fiachra and Conn (meaning "battle king" and "wisdom"). Now, in the bearing of these children, the gentle Aobh died and Lir's sadness was great. Only his children gave him joy.

However, the Bodb Dearg came to him and said: "Choose another wife from Niamh and Aoife, that they may comfort you and help you raise Aobh's children". So Lir chose Aoife of the autumn tresses and, for a while, they were happy. But Aoife grew jealous of her sister's children, for she was not blessed with children herself. More and more did she resort into confiding herself to Druids with magical powers, who taught her the secret arts. The barbs of jealousy tortured her soul and turned it to hatred for the children so that, in the end, she became obsessed with her malice.

The obsession turned into an excessive illness and for a year and a day she lay in her chamber, not coming out, not even for her husband. Her sickness overwhelmed her, so that her mind became unhinged. Then, after a year and a day, she rose from her bed and re-entered the world, professing herself cured.

Lir and his children were pleased to see her so apparently recovered.

She called the children to her and said that, as she was now so well, she was going to take them on a visit to the Bodb Dearg. Now the boys were delighted at this but Fionnghuala, with a woman's intuition, was suspicious about her step-mother. She had a dark foreboding dream that Aoife was intending them harm and that some terrible dead was lurking in her mind.

Yet everyone seemed happy. Lir was delighted to see his wife risen from her sick bed and well. Also he was pleased that she was taking the children on a trip to see the Bodb Dearg. So Fionnghuala kept her suspicions to herself, for fear that she would be scoffed at or be called an ungrateful brat.

Aoife's fine carriage came to the gates and the children went with her, with Lir bidding them a fond farewell. The carriage set off, accompanied by a bodyguard and with Aoife's personal attendants. Off they went from Sídh Fionnachaidh. They had not journeyed many a mile when Aoife contrived to stop the carriage and drew aside her trusted manservant, Conan.

"How well do you love me, Conan?" she whispered, so that no one else would hear.

The old man was puzzled.

"Didn't I come with you from your father's court at Aran to the palace of the Bodb Dearg, when you were but a child?" he demanded. "Have I not watched over you and seen you grow and never a hair of your head was allowed to come to harm?"

"Then you love me well. What would you do for me in that love?"

"There is nothing in this world, nor in the Otherworld, that I would not do," affirmed the old man.

"If I were in danger or about to suffer a great loss, would you serve me well?"

"I would so, lady. I would remove the danger and restore whatever loss you encountered."

"I am in danger of losing my husband's love," sighed Aoife.

Conan's eyes blazed. "Tell me the name of she who would steal that love, and she will not live to the sunset."

"It is no woman who has robbed me of Lir's love, Conan.

See those children in my carriage? They are the cause of his neglect to me. They have destroyed my happiness. If they were removed, all would be well."

Conan realized what she was saying. His eyes widened in horror and he took a step backwards. "But they are your sister's children, the children of your husband," he gasped. "As much as I nursed and looked after you, I have also looked after her."

Aoife's eyes were coalfires of hell as she saw his look of admonition. Hate and jealousy were so great within her that she saw it only as a personal betrayal. She turned in anger and accosted more of her personal retainers and each one of them was as horrified as old Conan had been at what she was suggesting.

Finally, they set off again, and came to the shores of Loch Dairbhreach, which is now the lake of Derravarragh in Co. Westmeath. There they encamped the night. And, that night, Aoife herself took a sword in her hand and went to the sleeping children. She was fully determined to kill them herself, but a strange emotion stayed her hand. She stood, sword raised, while her sister's blood fought with her own and she found that she could not do the deed.

But the evil in her was not to be thwarted. She went back into her own tent and came out with a magical wand which an evil wizard had given to her. The next morning, before breakfast, she suggested to the children that they go and bathe in the waters of the loch. In their joy, they cast off their clothes and ran into the waters. As they did so, Aoife touched them with her wand and sang out a cruel magical chant which turned all four into swans, with snowy white feathers.

At first, the children struggled against their new forms, bewildered and frightened. But there was no escape. Finally, they settled down and swam close to the shore where Aoife was chuckling with evil joy. But her evil spell had not worked entirely, for each of the children still possessed the power of human speech.

Fionnghuala called out:"Oh, step-mother, what have we done to you, that you should repay us with this terrible deed?"

Aoife sneered at them. "Pests! You stole the love of your father from me."

Fionnghuala lowered her swan neck in sadness. "His love for us was not the same as his love for you. Surely you know the difference between love for one's children and love for one's partner?"

Aoife stamped her foot in rage. "You will cackle with the birds on Derravarragh's shore until you die."

"Oh, Aoife, step-mother, what you have done will cry out for vengeance, as long as that vengeance takes to reach you. Foolish woman. Your punishment will be greater than our plight. One thing you may do, in virtue of the common blood we share! Tell us when this misery will end?"

Aoife smiled thinly. Her face was ugly. "It is a wiser thing not to have the answer to that question. However, as it will add to your suffering and misery, here is the answer: you will spend three hundred years on Loch Dairbhreach; three hundred more years on Sruth na Maoile, between Éireann and high-hilled Alba; and then three hundred more years off Iorras Domhnann. No power in this world, nor the Otherworld, will free you until that time is passed. Not until a Prince of Connacht marries a Princess of Mumhan. Because my spell was incomplete, you are left with the ability to make human speech and you have the gift to make sweet music which calms and soothes all who hear it. That is your only gift."

Then the evil Aoife turned and ordered her carriage to be made ready. She left with her retinue, and behind her were the four swans swimming on the lonely lake behind her. The children of Lir huddled together and raised their heads in a lament, not for themselves, but for their father.

Sad our hearts break for Lir,
red eyes searching the world for us,
hopeful in seeking shadows in forests, on mountains,
seeking forms, in skies and on land.

Seeking his lost children torn from his bosom,
Now in swan-form swimming, cold in waters of a
foamy strange shore.

Now when Aoife and her entourage arrived at the palace of the Bodb Dearg, there was great rejoicing at her recovery from her illness. A great feast had been prepared. After the Bodb Dearg had welcomed her, he peered around with curiosity.

"I thought you were bringing your sister's children with you? Where are they, your own foster-children, the children of Lir?"

Now Aoife blushed in shame, but she had a story ready. "They are not with me because Lir refused to let me bring them. He has turned against me. Likewise, he says he is no friend to you, for you usurped the love of the Dé Danaan and the title of king which should rightfully be his. He does not want his children placed in your safe-keeping, for you will surely harm them."

Now the Bodb Dearg was truly astonished when he heard these words from Aoife. "This surely cannot be? Lir knows how much I love those children, as if they were my own. How can he turn against me in this fashion?"

The Bodb Dearg was no fool and some suspicion of mischief formed in his mind. He sent a messenger immediately to Lir, telling him that Aoife had arrived alone and was saying that Lir had refused to allow the children to come with her.

Immediately he received this word, Lir mounted his fastest chariot and was away to the palace of the Bodb Dearg. In the meantime, the Bodb Dearg grew more uneasy for, when he questioned Aoife more closely, he found many discrepancies in her answers and so he summoned her servants and began to question them.

Meanwhile, Lir and his escort had decided to encamp the night on the shores of Loch Dairbhreach.

The four children of Lir, in their guise as swans, saw their father and his warriors approaching and they swam to the shallows, raising their voices in a sad song.

Lir heard the song and came racing to the shore and listened to the swans crying in human voices. Then he recognized the voice of his daughter, Fionnghuala.

"Father, dearest father, know you that I am your daughter,

Fionnghuala, and these are your sons, now changed into swans and ruined by the hatred and evil crafts of Aoife, our step-mother, sister to our own mother."

Lir raised his voice in a terrible cry of grief, at which his warriors were sure that he must have lost his reason. But, having given three shouts of grief which rocked the very mountains of the countryside, he resumed his command on sanity.

"Tell me, daughter, how I may restore you to your human form?"

"Alas, dear father, there is nothing you can do, for no one has the power to release us either in this world nor in the Otherworld. Not until nine hundred years have passed and a Prince of Connacht marries a Princess of Mumhan."

Lir, this time joined by his warriors, raised another three shouts of grief. And their grief was carried over all Éireann, so that the trees bent before it and the waves receded from the shores in terror.

"We are left only with our speech and our reason," Fionnghuala explained.

"That being so," replied Lir, "you will come and dwell with me at my palace again and still live as if you were in human shape."

"Alas, dear father, that cannot be so, for Aoife has condemned us to live on water and we are only allowed speech in order to make sweet music to those who wish to hear it."

Lir and his warriors encamped that night and the children of Lir sang and made music for them and so sweetly did they sing that they all fell into a calm sleep.

In the morning Lir went to the water's edge. "My heart is broken that I must leave you here, far from my empty hall. I now curse the first moment I saw Aoife's smiling face, that hid a cruelty which none could plumb the depths of. I shall know no rest, no sleep, from now on. I shall go into the never-ending night, for never more will I know a tranquil hour."

In tears and sadness they bade farewell and Lir rode on to the Bodb Dearg's palace.

He was greeted with respect by the Bodb Dearg and, when he met Aoife, his face was a mask to hide his feelings. Then the Bodb Dearg said: "I was hoping that you would come with your children, for I love them as if they were my own. But Aoife has told me that you refuse to let them come near me, lest harm befall them."

Then Lir turned to Aoife. "Let Aoife bear witness to the truth. She has treacherously turned them into swans on Loch Dairbhreach."

The Bodb Dearg had suspected something, especially when none of Aoife's servants would answer his questions, but he could not believe such a terrible thing. He turned to Aoife to seek her denial and saw the truth of Lir's accusation written on her guilty features.

For a moment or two, the Bodb Dearg stood before Aoife with his shoulders hunched, bowed down in sorrow and anguish. He had been foster-father to Aoife and her sister Aobh and he loved them both, just as he loved Aobh's children as if they had been his own.

Then he raised himself and his brows were creased in anger. "Aoife, once my foster-daughter, what you have done is beyond forgiveness. As bad as the suffering of the poor children of Lir is, your suffering will be worse."

Aoife, terrified, dropped to her knees, her hands held out in supplication. There was fear on her face, for she knew what vengeance the gods could take. But the Bodb Dearg's face was filled with a terrible, tormented anger and he did not heed her protestations.

"Spare my life," she cried.

"That I will, for the snuffing out of your soul is but to show you mercy. Answer this question, for you are bound to do so: of everything that is on the earth, or above it, or beneath it, of everything that flies or creeps or burrows, seen or unseen, horrible in itself or in its nature, tell me what do you most fear and abhor?"

Aoife crouched with shaking limbs. "I fear Macha, Badb and Nemain, the three forms of the Mórrígán, the goddess of war, of death and slaughter, and most of all, her blood-drinking raven form."

"Then that is what you shall be, for as long as mortals believe in the goddess of death and battles."

Then the Bodb Dearg struck her with his wand of office and she was immediately transformed into the hideous form of a croaking raven, with blood dripping on its beak. All the people in the palace of the Bodb Dearg were forced to turn away and hide their eyes from the terrible, malignant form. All save the Bodb Dearg and Lir himself, who gazed on her form without any expression at all.

The eyes of Aoife stared up from the raven head and sought mercy in their gaze, but found none. Then, with her leathery wings flapping, the blood drooling from her gaping mouth, the raven rose upwards and, croaking hoarsely, flew away into the sky, doomed to remain so until the end of time.

Then the Bodb Dearg embraced Lir and they shared their anguish and all the Tuatha Dé Danaan, all the gods and goddesses of Éireann, went down to the shores of Loch Dairbhreach and encamped there. And the Sons of Míle Easpain came from their courts, and even the misshapen Fomorii and the Nemedians, and all the people of the land of Éireann came. A great camp was made at the lakeside. There the children of Lir raised their voices and sang sweet music to them and it is said that no sweeter and sadder music was ever heard in any part of this world, nor the Otherworld.

Around the shores of the lake, the encampment became permanent and the children of Lir never wanted for company. The people remained, held by their love for the four white swans. The children of Lir talked with the people and, during the evenings, sang their incomparable songs and, no matter what trouble beset those who heard the music, they drifted into a calm sleep and awoke refreshed and at peace.

For three hundred years, the children of Lir rested on the waters of Loch Dairbhreach.

At the end of three hundred years, Fionnghuala said to her brothers: "The time has come when we must bid farewell to these waters and to all our friends, and to our father, Lir, for we must travel to the stormy waters of Sruth na Maoile which gushes in its passage between Éireann and high-hilled Alba."

So on the following morning, they spread their wings and rose, among the sadness and sorrow, and the wailing of their father.

Fionnghuala called out, as she rose: "Tears swell down our cheeks, grief in our hearts, now time dictates our departure. Sad our tears like the waters of the lake, calm deep waters we may not tread again for it is to the black storms, the endless wrath of Moyle's sea, there to linger in fear for the next three hundred years."

And all the children cried: "Our paths are drawn down the twisting road of time; destiny traps us, in spite of men and gods, and no hopes may come even in our dreams; no laughter; no wish for tomorrow, until the sorrow of our lives are ended. Though we go from here, dear father, Lir the storm-tossed, our hearts will forever remain with you."

Then they circled once more in the sky and flew away to the north-east.

Great was the sadness on the gods and men of Ireland then. Great the sadness of the goddesses and the women, too. None were so loved as the children of Lir.

The High King summoned the Brehons, the learned lawyers and, from that day forward, according to the law, no subject of the High King, nor anyone in any of the five provinces, was ever allowed to kill a swan. Thus states the law of the Fenéchus.

The children of Lir had now alighted on the Sruth na Maoile, which is the Sea of Moyle, called the North Channel which runs its turbulent way between Ireland and Scotland. It was a harsh stormy sea; cold and tumultuous. They were cold and fearful, those four poor children. The sea was not like the pleasant waters of Dairbhreach. Here the violent winds drove them up and down with sleet and snow and there was little or no food for them. No misery could be worse than the restless sea between them.

Then, one day, Fionnghuala sensed something in the air. A fierce storm was approaching. She knew it was going to be more fierce than any storm before. So she turned to her brothers.

"There is a bad tempest following and it is sure that the winds and tides will separate us. We must fix a meeting-place, so that if we are parted, we shall be sure to find one another again."

Fiachra agreed: "Sensible is that suggestion, my dear sister. Let us meet at Carricknarone, as we all know that rock."

Carricknarone was a rocky outcrop in the sea.

The storm came up abruptly. A wild, wailing wind spread across the sea, whipping at the waves, and lightning flashes split the heavens, and the sea clawed at the four poor forms which huddled together on its raging billows. Storm-tossed, wind-driven, they were hurled in the black gloom.

When dawn broke and there was an easing of the tempest, Fionnghuala found that she was alone on the waters. There was no sign of her brothers. Feeling desolate, she made her way towards Carricknarone, the rock of the seas and, cold and anguished, she reached its rocky outcrop. There was still no sign of her brothers.

"Alas, alas," she cried, "there is no shelter, no rest for us, and my heart is sundered in me. Gone are my loved ones in the bitter night; gone is everything but my grief, my cold, my hunger and my fear. These now are my constant companions."

She climbed onto the rock and peered round.

"Alas, alas, my brothers are lost in the wild tempest. Death itself would be a small mercy. Is there no pity in this world for me? Will I never see my brothers that are now dearer to me than all the human race?

"Alas, alas, no shelter for me, nor rest. Have we not suffered agony enough, nor cruelty enough, or does the depths of long anguish continue forever?"

She was so sunk into despair that she wished to die and took one last look at the grey skies before she decided to succumb to death. But in that grey darkness she saw a white speck. She peered again and there, bedraggled but flying bravely, was a tiny wind-tossed swan, making its valiant way towards the rock.

It was Conn.

With a cry of joyous recognition, she rose up towards him, urging him on. She helped poor Conn, now more dead than alive, onto the rock. Then came Fiachra, limping feebly through the shallows, and it took a mighty effort of

Fionnghuala and Conn to bring him to safety. They huddled with only the warmth of their wings to revive themselves.

Yet still Fionnghuala was sad.

"If only Aodh was here, then all would be well with us."

As if at her words, they saw Aodh coming towards them. He rode the waves proud, and he was well and radiant and his feathers dry. He came ashore and told them that he had found a welcome in a great cave on the shores of high-hilled Alba and was thus able to shelter from the fury of the storm. And he came and gave his siblings his warmth and comfort.

"Oh," cried Fionnghuala, "wonderful is it to be in life and together again. But we have three hundred years on this salt sea of Moyle and must be prepared for many such storms as this."

So it was. Alas, so it was.

For many long years, they endured on the storm-tossed sea of Moyle, first sheltering here and then there, while great winds and howling tempests tried to separate them. Though never again did it ever succeed in doing so, as it had done in that first great storm. For now they knew the cave in high-hilled Alba, they fled to it for safety at the coming of the storms.

So it came about one day that they were swimming close to the shores of Éireann, by the mouth of the River Bann and, looking towards the shore, they saw a great procession riding from the south. There were chiefs and lords and attendants and warriors who were clad in the splendour of their cloaks. They rode on white horses. Bright lights glinted on their armour, their shields and weapons.

"Who can they be?" wondered Fiachra.

"A party of warriors, perhaps?" suggested Conn.

"Warriors off to fight some great war?" hazarded Aodh.

"Let us swim closer, that we might find out the meaning of this great cavalcade," suggested Fionnghuala.

Now when the party of warriors saw the swans swimming towards the shore, they turned and went down to meet them. At their head were the two sons of the Bodb Dearg. They greeted the swans with cries of joy and happiness for, they said, they had been searching for the children of Lir for many years, travelling along the coasts of the Sea of Moyle. They assured them that they brought the love of all the Tuatha Dé Danaan to the outcasts. Most of all, they brought the love of their father Lir and of the Bodb Dearg.

The children of Lir immediately asked about the health of their father, Lir, and after him, of the Bodb Dearg.

"They are both well," said the sons of the Bodb Dearg, "and the hosts of the Dé Danaan are celebrating the feast of Gobhainn the smith-god, at your father's own *sídh*. Their happiness would be complete if you could share in those festivities. It has been so long since you left the shores of Loch Dairbhreach that they sent us in search of news of you."

The eyes of the children clouded when they heard this.

"Suffering and torment have been our lot since we have left Loch Dairbhreach. No tongue can utter what we have been through. But we will give you a song which you must remember and take back to our father and to your father and you must sing it to the hosts of the Dé Danaan."

Then the children of Lir raised their voices and sung their sad lament.

> Bleak and cold is our home,
> Ice wet are our feathers –
> No comfort to us.
> Pain and sickness is our only guide,
> The pitiless sea is our constant companion,
> Grief, grief, is our only warmth
> In the bleak heartless world which is ours.

The sons of the Bodb Dearg repeated the sad song and bade farewell to the children of Lir. The four swans returned to the icy waters of the Sea of Moyle and drifted away from the shore.

When they had vanished, the two sons of the Bodb Dearg shed a tear and turned their men, who also wept in their grief, towards their homes. They finally reached Lir's *sídh* and all the Dé Danaan gathered there to hear their news, including the Bodb Dearg. The sons of the Bodb Dearg sang the sad song of the children of Lir.

Lir was so overcome with anguish that he was unable to utter his grief and sat like a stone statue.

The Bodb Dearg put forth a hand to comfort him.

"Our power cannot help them, but they are still in life. It is good to know that one day this power will be broken and they will be free of their suffering."

For three long centuries the children of Lir suffered upon the terrible Sruth na Maoile. It seemed a time without end. But at last the time came when Fionnghuala called her brothers together.

"It is time to leave this place and fly to the west. Now we must go to Iorras Domhnann."

They took wing with trepidation, for it had been promised that their suffering off Iorras Domhnann would be even greater and yet none of them could imagine a greater suffering than what they had endured for the last three hundred years on the cold sea of the east, battered by the storm-sent winds and raging seas.

Across the kingdom of Ulaidh they flew, across the lochs and mountains, across the lands of the Cenel Conaill and the great bay which separated the Cenel mBogaine from the kingdom of Connachta, until they alighted in the seas off Iorras Domhnann, the "head of the world" which is now called Erris, Co. Mayo, for there was no point farther west that could be reached. This was where the known world ended, with the great western ocean and across it, far, far to the west was the Otherworld, the haven of lost souls, Hy Breasal. The waters were not as cold as Sruth na Maoile, but the storms were stronger, the waves harsher and the pounding on the rocky coastline was more dangerous.

Their suffering continued.

Now it happened that there was a young farmer and fisherman named Aífraic of Béal na Mhuirthead, which is now called Belmullet, and one day, while he was cultivating his land, he heard singing from the seas. Looking seaward, he saw the four swans dancing on the waves and singing their sad songs. He was entranced, for he had the soul of a poet, for the prefix to his name, *Aí*, means "poetic inspiration" and "learning". Thereafter, every day he went to the shore and sat listening to the songs of the children of Lir.

Now the day came when, having made himself known to the children, he found that they were able to converse with him. Each day he talked with them and they gradually told their story to him. He came to love each one of them and they came to love him, for he was a gentle and learned soul. Because he was a poet and storyteller he, in turn, began to tell their story to his neighbours at the evening gatherings. Although Aífraic refused to let anyone meet the four swans, for fear some harm might befall them, his tale began to spread throughout the kingdom of Connacht. We might add that, were it not for the tales of Aífraic, we might never have known the sad tale of the children of Lir.

That the children suffered still, let there be no doubt. The seas of the western ocean are not kind. So cold are they that, at times, the seas from Iorras Domhnann and around Béal na Mhuirthead froze with black ice and snow came down like a white sheet.

According to Aífraic, no other nights in the nine centuries of torment were so pitiless than the winter nights off Iorras Domhnann. Fionnghuala's three brothers confessed that they were not far away from commencing their journey to the Otherworld. Death was approaching them and, in spite of Fionnghuala's lamentations, the icy fingers of Donn, lord of death, were reaching out to transport their souls westward.

Then, in the depths of her misery, Fionnghuala felt a strange, warming feeling within her. She could not understand it. She stopped her wailing and allowed her mind to experience the strange, comforting feeling that enveloped her; it was consoling, soothing to her very soul. Words formed in her mind and the words were the great song of Amairgen the Druid. In spite of the howling wind and the crashing of the white-foamed seas on the rocks, she raised her voice and began to sing the words.

I am the Wind that blows across the Sea;
I am the Wave of the Ocean;
I am the Murmur of the Billows;

I am the Bull of the Seven Combats;
I am the Vulture on the Rock;
I am a Ray of the Sun;
I am the Fairest of Flowers;
I am a Wild Boar in Valour;
I am a Salmon in the Pool;
I am a Lake on the Plain;
I am the Skill of the Craftsman;
I am a Word of Science;
I am the Spear point that gives Battle;
I am the God who creates in the head of man the Fire of Thought.
Who is it that Enlightens the Assembly upon the mountain, if not I?
Who tells the ages of the moon, if not I?
Who shows the Place where the Sun goes to rest, if not I?
Who calls the Cattle from the House of Tethra?
On whom do the Cattle of Tethra smile?
Who is the God that fashions Enchantments –
– the enchantment of battle and the wind of change?

When Fionnghuala stopped singing the ancient chant, she found that her three brothers were also singing with her.

"I do not understand this, brothers," she said, "yet I feel that there is some power here with us which is beyond my understanding. It is great and awe-inspiring. It is the Truth and we must abide with the Truth against the World. For we will abide, no matter our fate. We will always be, no matter our shape, no matter where we are, in this world or the next. Our spark of thought, once ignited, can never be extinguished."

And in spite of the cold, the storm and the agony of their torment, their souls were renewed and hope was reborn within them.

So they remained there off Iorras Domhnann for the allotted three centuries.

The day came when Fionnghuala called her three brothers and told them:

"The appointed hour has come. We can now leave this place and fly to our father at Sídh Fionnachaidh in the warm interior of Éireann. Lir and the children of Danu, the Mother Goddess, will rejoice to see us."

With gladness in their hearts, the four swans rose from the waters of the icy sea, and, circling over Iorras Domhnann, where Aífraic had once lived – for being merely a mortal, he had long grown old and died, as had his children and his children's children – they set off eastward to the palace of the mighty Lir.

A great sadness waited for them.

There was no sign of Sídh Fionnachaidh. Desolation was there in its place. Nothing stirred there, save the wind across the hill and the rustle of the overgrown grasses. There was no sign of the children of Danu, no sign of the old gods and goddesses of Éireann. True, it was, that the descendants of the sons of Míle Easpain, the first mortals in Éireann, still lived on. But they had long ago rejected the ancient gods and goddesses, though some had vague memories of them which were greatly distorted.

But gods and goddesses exist only as long as memory and respect for them remain.

The mortals had driven the Ever-Living Ones underground into the hills and, eventually, those immortals dwelling in the hills, the *sídhe*, were relegated, in people's minds, to mere fairy folk. Even the names of the greatest of the gods were forgotten. Lugh Lamhfada, the sun god and god of all arts and crafts, who was the father of the hero Cúchulainn by a mortal woman, had gone. The mortals now remembered the great god only as a little fairy craftsman whom they called Lugh-chromain, "little stooping Lugh", which would later be mispronounced as "leprechaun".

After nine centuries of suffering, the poor children of Lir found that the mortals had finally destroyed the gods. The Tuatha Dé Danaan were all dead. Even more devastating was the fact that it was only their step-mother Aoife, in the guise of the evil demon the Mórrígán, goddess of death and battles, that people still kept alive, for they continued to take pleasure in war and bloodshed.

Horror overcame the four swans as they perched by that desolate Sídh Fionnachaidh.

They sang a sad lament.

"Whither have gone the stately palaces of our father? Weeds and nettles grow in place of the noble pillars and frescoed walls. Silence fills the desolate hill, not even the whisper of their voices remain. Where are the gods and their goddesses, where the heroes and the noble kings? Not even as mould do they lie in their graves. There is nothing left."

So they paid their sad tribute to a world that had disappeared and left them behind.

There was now no home left for them.

Fionnghuala called her brothers together.

"Little hope for us here. But the curse remains until a Prince from Connacht shall marry a Princess from Munster. So let us fly back to Connacht, to the only home we knew, which was at Iorras Domhnann. Let us go back there, in more sheltered waters, and await that day which Aoife foretold would come."

So they rose up into the air and flew back to the west and circled over Iorras Domhnann. But it wasn't to that spot they went, for Fionnghuala espied a pleasant little island and it was called Inis Gluaire, which is now Inishglory off Annagh Head. On this island was a sheltered lake, not large at all, but enough to give them shelter and food and keep them safe from the mortals who had rejected their father and the others of the Tuatha Dé Danaan.

To their surprise, they found one mortal living in a tiny cell of a hut on the island, and soon they grew to know him well. He was a kind and gentle holy man. They called him Mo Cháemmóg, which is an endearing form of Cháemmóg, which means "beloved person".

The holy hermit would listen to their singing and was in great wonder of it, for he had never heard such sweet music. Each day, he would listen to their song and knew that song was the eternal truth.

One day, the holy hermit came to them and said:

"Beloved children, you may come ashore with me, for the day has come when your enchantment shall be ended."

Having heard the story of Aoife's curse, Cháemmóg learnt that the king of Connacht, Laidgnén Mac Colmán, desired a wife. The woman he had chosen was a princess from Mumhan, Deichtine, daughter of King Fíngen of the Eóganachta of Cashel. History records their names, for Laidgnén ruled Connacht in the year AD 649 until his death in AD 655, while Fíngen of Cashel is recorded as dying in AD 629. It was Deichtine's brother, Máenach, who ruled Munster from his seat at Cashel when the marriage proposal was made. The Princess Deichtine had agreed to the marriage on one condition. This condition was that Laidgnén give her, as a wedding gift, the four singing swans dwelling in his kingdom whom she had heard so much about.

Indeed, the story of the children of Lir had long been known at the court of Connacht, from the stories that Aífraic once told. Now Laidgnén was worried when he heard this demand from Deichtine, for he knew that the children of Lir were no ordinary birds to be given as presents to appease the vain glory of any man or woman. However, the terms of the marriage contract were made plain to him by the emissary of the Princess Deichtine.

When the King of Connacht heard that Dechtine positively refused to marry unless the gift be made, he reluctantly accepted and said that if she came to his court, the birds would be waiting for her. At the same time, he sent messengers to Cháemmóg on Inis Gluaire and told him to send him the four swans.

The holy man refused and great was the anger of the King of Connacht. Not just his word to Dechtine was broken but his very pride was hurt. He turned his anger from Dechtine, who had made the impossible demand, to Cháemmóg. So he gathered his royal bodyguard, the Gamhanrhide, and set off for Inis Gluaire.

Cháemmóg met him on the shore quite calmly.

"You have insulted your king, holy one!" shouted Laidgnén. "You have refused to give up the swans so that I may present them to Dechtine of Mumhan and make her my bride."

"There is no insult, for what you ask is not in my power. I have no power to give you these poor creatures, any more than you have power to take them from me."

The king, bold in his anger, laughed harshly and signalled to one of his servants.

"No power? I will show you the power of the King of Connacht."

And he had a silver chain placed around the necks of each swan. Then, taking the ends of the chains in his hand, he began to draw them towards the boat.

Far away on the great Rock of Cashel, where the palace of the Eóganacht kings of Cashel dwelt, Dechtine had been talking with her brother, King Máenach, who was a wise man. He had heard of the story of the children of Lir and Máenach said to her: "A bad thing, is this, sister. This is no ordinary gift that you demand from the King of Connacht to appease your curiosity. In this, you mock the powers of the Otherworld."

Now Dechtine was, withal, a kindly and gracious lady, although given to the vanity that sometimes besets a person in so exalted a position. In that moment, she realised that what she had asked for was unjust. So, she agreed with her brother and sent forth a messenger to the palace of the King of Connacht, telling him that she would marry him even without the gift of the four swans. Further, she made haste to follow the messenger with all her entourage, ready for the marriage ceremony.

That was happening at the very moment when King Laidgnén was trying to drag the four children of Lir to his boat to return to the mainland.

As that happened, each of the swans began to lose their white downy coats. Slowly, before the eyes of all those gathered there, the four swans grew into human shape and stood under the light of that summer's day. But instead of returning to what they had once been – four bright, young children, the pride and love of their father, the great god Lir – they stood with the accumulation of the years of their exile. Yet there was dignity in those years, for they were, after all, the children of Lir, the children of a god of the Tuatha Dé Danaan.

When King Laidgnén saw this, his eyes filled with terror, and he fell on his knees before the aged Fionnghuala.

"Forgive me, lady. My mind was filled with vanity and avariciousness, for I wanted nothing more than Dechtine to be my wife."

Fionnghuala smiled gently at the king.

"Return to your palace, mighty king. Dechtine will be yours and even now stands at your palace gates, remorseful and penitent that she made such a demand on you. You will be happy and have a long reign."

The king and his bodyguard took to their boat, still in awe and trembling at what they had witnessed.

Not so Cháemmóg who came forward and, children of gods and goddesses or not, he embraced them with love and tenderness.

"What can I do for you, my children?" he asked, for he was not able to change his mode of addressing those he loved so well.

"We grow tired," said Fionnghuala, "and have but a few moments of life left among us. Now our torment is about to end. You must help us and bless us. While I see your sorrow at our deaths, we have long outlasted our allotted span for what was ours and our world is no more. It is right that we go, though we are also in sorrow that we should leave you, our trusted friend."

Cháemmóg was tearful. "Tell me what I must do?"

"No more than bury us all here, here in this sacred spot. Bury us in the tradition of our people, bury us standing, standing facing one another, as so often we have stood in this world."

The holy hermit dug the grave as he was instructed and, as he dug, the children of Lir sang their last song. But gone were their beautiful voices that they had had while they were swans. However, their cracked and ancient voices made the words more beautiful than any the hermit had ever heard.

"Death is near, our pain nearly ended, stretch out a hand of blessing. Soon we shall sleep, so make our bed comfortable that we may lie with the sound of the gentle waves and whispering wind in our ears. Place us together, as so often we were placed, four together, facing each other, a loving hand holding each other in eternal, unbreakable clasp. Death is near, sleep is now come as a joy to end our sorrow."

And when the last words of their song were distant whispers on the air, Cháemmóg turned and found them all locked in a last embrace. The tears fell from his eyes like bubbling waterfalls. And as he bent to them, a strange thing occurred. They were children again. Four lovely young children with golden hair and happy faces. They turned radiantly to him and gazed at him for a moment with love. Then they were gone and the bodies of the four ancient ones lay dead at his feet.

In accordance with their wishes, Cháemmóg took them and washed their bodies, which is the ritual *tonach*. Then he wrapped their poor corpses in the *racholl* or the corpse clothes. He placed them in the grave. Fionnghuala was placed at one side with Conn at her right hand and Fiachra at her left and with Aodh standing before her. Their hands were clasped in unbreakable unity. Then over the bodies he placed the traditional branches of broom.

When this was done, the sorrowing holy hermit raised a *leacht*, a sepulchre monument, and engraved their names upon the stone and sang the lamentation of sorrow which is the *Nuall-guba*.

"My eyelids drop tears and great is my anguish, it is sorrowful for me to be in life after the passing of these souls. Sad is my eye, my heart is withered, since the grave of these souls was dug."

It is said, though I cannot vouch for it, that if you still believe in the old gods and goddesses of Éireann, and your boat circles the island of Inis Gluaire on a balmy summer's evening, if you listen carefully, you may still hear the beautiful sad music of the children of Lir.

were waiting and he gave each of them one of the strange birds.

Émer was standing a little apart and Cú Chulainn had no bird to give her. He had done this deliberately as a way of punishing her for making him do a deed he was not interested in doing. But when he saw she was standing, eyes downcast and sorrowful, he began to regret his petulance.

"There is anger on your face," he said sternly, trying to throw his guilt at her.

"Why should I be angry with you, husband? I asked you to give the birds to the women and you did so. I asked as if it were I who had the power to give them the birds and so it is just that I am rebuked by you. I did it from pride in you, for you are my husband. Those women all love you and it is with them I have to share you, although no one has any share in me except yourself."

Now there was a little bitterness in her voice, for it was true that Cú Chulainn was loved by many women, although he had sought out, courted and married only Émer, because he had once said that she had the six gifts of womanhood: the gift of beauty; the gifts of sweet speech and of singing; the gift of needlework; the gift of wisdom and the gift of loving only her husband.

Émer had chosen Cú Chulainn for her husband on her own terms, and he had been made to pass strict tests to prove himself worthy of her. Her love for him was mature and deep and she knew him well. She accepted that he was pursued by women throughout his life, for he was a handsome and glamorous hero. But now and again she pointed out to Cú Chulainn that his arrogance was childish: as it was now.

The great warrior blushed with shame before her. He was sorry for his petulance. He climbed down from the chariot and kissed her hands in apology. "The next time any strange birds alight on this lake, they shall be yours, Émer," he vowed.

No sooner had he spoken when there came, out of the west, two birds of amazing colours – one had green feathers and the other had crimson. They were more beautiful than any of the strange white birds that had alighted on the lake. Their wings moved slowly and majestically as they circled the lake and their cries made sweet music that lulled the other women to sleep where they stood.

"Those are your birds, Émer," declared Cú Chulainn without vanity.

He asked Laeg for his sling but Émer reached forward and laid a hand on his arm.

"I am afraid, husband. There is something curious about those birds. Something that bodes ill for those who oppose them. Let them proceed in peace."

"I swore that they would be yours, Émer." So saying, Cú Chulainn aimed his sling and let loose. For the first time since he had taken up the profession of arms, his cast missed. He stared in astonishment.

Even Laeg was amazed. "That is a strange thing. You have never missed a cast before," observed the charioteer.

Annoyed, Cú Chulainn made another cast and yet another. Each time he missed and the strange birds circled lazily above, crying their weird song. In anger, he took up his spears and cast them. They all missed. Then the birds flew off.

A rage descended on him, almost akin to his battle-rage, and he leapt into the chariot, without waiting for Laeg and whipped up the horses, heeding neither the cries of either Émer nor Laeg. Away he went after the westward-flying birds. How long he followed them, he did not know, for he lost all sense of time. Finally, he came to a great lake and he saw the birds alight on a rocky outcrop and disappear. He searched all around the lake but there was no sign of them

It was then he realised how exhausted he was. So he lay down by his chariot, his back against an ancient pillar stone, and a weary sleep came over him. As he lay in a semi-dreaming state, he saw two women approaching him from the direction of the lake. One wore a green cloak and the other a crimson cloak. The one in the green cloak carried a rod of rowan and, laughing, she cried: "Unkind you were to cast things at us. This for that." And she beat him with the rod of rowan. When she finished, the one in the crimson cloak also beat him. Each time the rod touched him, the strength and vigour went out of his body. Then they returned back to the lake.

The next morning, Laeg and the warriors of the Craobh Ríoga came across him, stretched out by his chariot. They had been hunting for him since dawn for, when he had not returned, a great search had been made for him. They could not rouse him from his semi-sleep.

"We will take him back to Émer," Laeg suggested. "She will know what to do."

"But Émer has already departed for Cú Chulainn's fortress at Dún Dealgan, thinking that he might have gone there," replied one of the warriors.

Then Cú Chulainn began to babble and, in his fever, he told them to take him to the Speckled Hall of An Emhain and send for Eithne Inguba to nurse him.

Now his comrades were shocked for Cú Chulainn, before he had married Émer, had had a long relationship with Eithne, who loved him still. Some of his comrades suspected that Eithne might still be his mistress. They wondered what they should do. But his fever and babbling grew worse and so they decided to appease him. They took him to the Speckled Hall, where the warriors kept their most valuable treasures, and there they laid him out on a bed and put his weapons around him.

And Eithne Inguba was called for. Though she knew many helping remedies, she could do nothing for him. He lay in a strange wasting sickness, growing weaker and weaker, until they began to fear for his life.

One morning, a tall warrior of astoundingly commanding appearance came to the Speckled Hall and demanded to be taken to Cú Chulainn's sickbed.

Laeg demanded to know who he was.

"I am Aonghus, son of Aedh Abrat."

So haughty was his manner that Laeg took him for a foreign prince and they let him in. He went and knelt at the sick warrior's side and he began to intone a strange song which no one understood. Cú Chulainn heard the words, though he had no understanding of them.

You have little need to lay in sickness
When the daughter of Aedh Abrat loves you.
Tearful is she for your love.
Fand is her name.
She waits for you to come to her
And her sister, 'the beauty of women'
Will be your guide.

Then, to everyone's astonishment, he simply vanished. They asked what the song could mean. Whatever it meant, Cú Chulainn grew no better and yet grew no worse. Eithne continued with every means of healing at her disposal, but nothing changed Cú Chulainn's wasting sickness.

"There is one thing we might try," Eithne suggested.

"What is that?" demanded Laeg,

"Let us take him back to the pillar stone where this sickness began. It might change the course of this illness."

Laeg felt guilty for, in all this time, no one had been sent to Dún Dealgan to fetch Émer nor inform her of her husband's illness. But he thought that Eithne might have the right idea and Cú Chulainn, on his sickbed, was placed in his chariot, and he drove it to the spot where they had discovered him and set him against the pillar stone.

Laeg, Eithne and his friends who gathered around heard nor saw no sound nor movement.

To Cú Chulainn, however, a beautiful woman in a green cloak approached him. It was the same woman he had previously seen in his dream. The same who had chastised him.

"I am Lí Ban, the beauty of women," she greeted him in a musical voice and allayed his alarm. "Good that you are here and still in life."

"No good to me, since I am still dying," replied Cú Chulainn.

"A choice for you," smiled Lí Ban. "I am the daughter of Aedh Abrat and I have come to tell you that you may be cured, by reason of the fact that you are the beloved of my sister, Fand. She thinks of nothing but you: not even of her own husband, Manánnan Mac Lir, god of the oceans."

Cú Chulainn blinked in surprise, but he was not fearful for, it was said, that he was the mortal son of Lugh Lamhfáda, Lugh of the Long Hand and sunny countenance, who was god of all arts and crafts. Nevertheless, the love of the wife of the god of the oceans was not something to receive lightly, when such a powerful god as Manánnan might wreak a vengeance to destroy the entire human world, by causing the seas to rise and a great deluge to wipe away the lands.

"It would be a foolish man to bring down the vengeance of the ocean god," Cú Chulainn observed. "Even though my mother, Dechtíre, told me I am born of Lugh of the Long Hand."

"Manánnan has forsaken my sister Fand and now she will have no one but you as her lover. My husband says he will send Fand to you, on condition that you fight against his enemies for one day."

"And who is your husband?"

"Labraid Luathlam ar Cledeb, Labraid of the Swift Hand on the Sword, King of Magh Mell, the Pleasant Plain. He has three great enemies – Eochaidh Indh Inbher, Eochaidh Euil and Senach Síaborthe. Fight and defeat them and Fand will be yours."

"I am sick: too sick to get up let alone to fight anyone."

"You will be cured," Lí Ban assured him.

"I know nothing of Magh Mell, nor do I know of Fand, your sister. I will remain here in sickness until I know more. Take Laeg Mac Riangabur, my charioteer, and let him bring me an account, for I trust no one except Laeg in such matters."

Now it appeared to those standing round the dying Cú Chulainn, who had seen or heard nothing of this encounter, that Laeg simply wandered off and vanished. In fact, Lí Ban took the charioteer in a boat over the nearby lake and they came to an island surrounded by mist.

"You must not leave this island unless you are under the protection of a woman," said Lí Ban.

Laeg shivered. "It is not something I have ever done, but if you say it should be so, it shall be so. I wish it were Cú Chulainn here, instead of myself."

Lí Ban smiled. "True for you, and true for me."

She led him to a green mound, in which there was a doorway. They emerged through this doorway into a great house and Laeg found himself surrounded by scores of beautiful women. Lí Ban took him to a room where Fand herself was seated. He swallowed hard, did Laeg the charioteer, for Fand was more beautiful than any mortal woman. She looked on Laeg sadly, and it seemed his strength melted away before her gaze, and she let a single tear drop on his arm.

Then Lí Ban led him away from Fand's chamber and took him to the door of the house where he saw martial preparations being made.

"There will be a great battle tomorrow," said Lí Ban.

"There is a strong army here," agreed Laeg, looking around.

"But a stronger one across the plain. See in the distance there are the armies of Eochaidh Indh Inbher, Eochaidh Euil and Senach Síaborthe, gathering like ants on the distant hills. See their spears and banners, like a black tide against the blue of the sky?"

And he saw their numbers, standing silently, without a clash of weapons nor a single war cry.

Then there came the rumble, as if of thunder, and a great war chariot came rolling forward to where they stood. A tall stern-faced warrior leapt from the chariot, tossing his reins to an attendant. He strode forward. At his side hung a great two-handed sword. Lí Ban at once greeted him with a song of praise for his valour.

"No reason to praise valour before victory," he chided gloomily. "Has Cú Chulainn come yet?"

"No, my lord, but this is Laeg, his charioteer. Laeg, this is my husband, Labraid Luathlam ar Cledeb, King of Magh Mell."

Labraid greeted Laeg with enthusiasm. "Will Cú Chulainn come? See, yonder, the gathered armies of the forces of evil; the armies of the two Eochaidh's and Senach the Spectre? Unless he comes to our aid, I fear that we are fated to go down into the abyss."

"I will bear news of all I have seen back to Cú Chulainn," agreed the charioteer.

Laeg was returned to the side of Cú Chulainn and told him all he had seen. But Cú Chulainn did not rise. He seemed weak but he no longer babbled in a fever. Instead he whispered to Laeg and told him to go to his own fortress of Dún Dealgan, where Émer, his wife, had gone.

"Tell her all that has happened to me, Laeg. Tell her that my fever caused me to forget and that I have an Otherworld sickness. Ask her to come to me."

Now Eithne stood quiet when she heard him asking for his wife.

"If Eithne could not have cured Cú Chulainn with all her knowledge, how then can Émer, who does not know the herbs and spells as Eithne does?" whispered one of the warriors of the Craobh Ríoga to another.

But Laeg sped on his chariot to Dún Dealgan and soon he had brought Émer to the side of her lord. When Laeg had told her what had happened, Émer had a rage on her, the like no one had seen from her usually mild and solicitous countenance. How did Laeg and the men of Ulaidh dare keep the news of her husband's sickness from her until this time? How could they have let Cú Chulainn lie in a sleeping sickness without searching the four corners of Éireann for a cure?

"If Fergus or Conall or Conchobhar the king had been in a similar plight, would Cú Chulainn have stood by?" Émer berated them. "He would not have rested until he found a cure. As for you, Laeg, how could you have gone to the Otherworld and returned without first securing a magical cure for him? Why didn't you bring me the news earlier?"

She stepped down to Cú Chulainn's side, hands on hips, and anger in her voice. Then she saw Eithne sulking behind the warriors of Ulaidh.

"Great is the shame on you, warrior of Ulaidh," she sneered. "Great hero, who cannot rise from his bed! Shame on you, Cú Chulainn. You are no more than Coileáinín Chulainn!" That was to say that instead of being "The Hound of Culann", she told him he was no more than a "Puppy of Culann". "Rise up, brave warrior. Do you not know that weakness is a step from death itself? Take your rightful place, take your sword, your shield and spear and put on your armour. Do not shame me and yourself in front of these your comrades and countrymen. Shame is your lot if you lie there!"

She shook him by the shoulders roughly and he groaned. Then he rubbed his eyes and blinked. There was a blush of shame on him and he rose up. The strength returned to him. With a sigh, Eithne turned and left for she was no longer needed.

Émer had shamed him back into health and no other could have done so.

Émer was wise to know that her husband would only be truly released when the Otherworld folk had let him go. So when Cú Chulainn said that he was now duty bound to go to Magh Mell and fight for Labraid, she raised no objections. It was enough for her that he was recovered from the wasting sickness.

Laeg took the chariot's reins and Cú Chulainn climbed in with his weapons and they bade farewell to Émer. To the astonishment of the warriors of Ulaidh, they drove to the water's edge and vanished.

At the edge of the water of the great lake, Lí Ban was waiting for them and enveloped them in a cloud of mist and took them over to the island and through the magic portal to Magh Mell.

Labraid was there to greet them, standing tall with his sun-yellow hair tied at the back. There were the hosts of fighting men, impatient for the contest. Cú Chulainn rode out in front of the army of Labraid, Laeg guiding the chariot.

"First we should scout the enemy's forces," Laeg advised, for the advice of a charioteer is much to be respected.

"I will go and do this task," Cú Chulainn told Labraid. "Stay here with your army and when I need you, I shall raise a cry. Do not come before."

Labraid was reluctant to let Cú Chulainn ride off with Laeg and with no other warrior to support him. However, he respected the champion's request.

They moved forward and found the hills surrounding the

Pleasant Plain, filled with the black tents of the enemies as far as the eye could see. And they saw the battalions of Senach the Spectre, riding blood-red horses, moving into position. Beyond was a grey mist, through which came the moaning sounds of the demon host. Blood hung heavy on the air already.

"Today the battle will be bloody," Cú Chulainn told Laeg.

Now it happened that the Mórrígán, the triune goddess of death and battles, was allied to the demon Senach Síaborthe, Senach the Spectre. She sent her spirits, in the shape of three night-black ravens, to hover over Cú Chulainn and warn Senach and his warriors of the calibre of the warrior who came against them.

But Senach's men laughed at the birds and their warning. "There is but a single warrior of Ulaidh, a little human boy, who comes forward with his charioteer to challenge our hosts. Is that all Labraid can send against us?"

They roared with laughter and made no special defence.

Cú Chulainn spent that evening scouting and, just before dawn, he was ready for the battle. At that time, Eochaidh Euil went to bathe at a pool near his tent, to prepare himself for battle. Cú Chulainn came on him and cast his spear, transfixing him where he knelt by the water. There was a great groan from his heart, so strong that it seemed to come from a whole army and not one man. In a rage, Eochaidh Euil's bodyguard rushed forward and tried to close with Cú Chulainn. A battle-rage now rose in him.

Those who saw it and survived, of whom there were very few, said that his whole appearance altered. One of his eyes closed up so that it could hardly be seen, while the other thrust forward wide and angry; from his brows, a column of blood gushed forth, so that those it touched were scalded. His fury gave him the strength of a hundred warriors.

Within a minute, he had laid dead thirty-three of Eochaidh Euil's best champions.

Senach and Eochaidh Indh Inbher rallied their hosts and rushed forward to do battle.

"Lugh!" cried out Cú Chulainn, calling on the strength of his great immortal father.

Demon warriors fell this way and that, until Senach and Eochaidh Indh Inbher themselves were split asunder by the edge of his mighty blade.

Hearing Cú Chulainn calling on his father, the great god Lugh of the Long Hand, Labraid urged his army to roll forward on the enemy host. There was a bloody battle and soon the victory was in no doubt. Labraid was sick of the slaughter and, as the enemy were surrendering, he called for a ceasefire. But Cú Chulainn, in his battle-rage, continued in the slaughter.

Laeg left his master then and raced forward to Labraid.

"It is his battle-fury, which will not cease until he has fought himself out," he explained anxiously. "Let no man approach him, for it might be that he will turn on friend as well as foe."

"What can we do to stop him?" demanded Labraid. "For I am quite sick of senseless killing."

"Get three large vats of ice-cold water."

This they did.

Then Laeg asked for two young maidens to come forward and remove their clothes. On his instruction, they approached Cú Chulainn so that he was forced to drop his weapons before them. They led him to the first vat of ice-cold water and put him in it. It boiled over by contact with his blood-heat. Then he was put into the second vat. It became hot, but it did not boil. Then he was put into the third vat and, by this time, his blood had returned to normal and the battle-rage had left him.

Cú Chulainn emerged and was normal again.

Labraid thanked him for defeating the enemies of the Pleasant Plain.

"Now you may go to Fand, as a token of your reward."

Laeg drove Cú Chulainn to the great palace in which he had seen Fand. Cú Chulainn was taken into a room to bathe and refresh and scent himself. Then he was brought into the presence of Fand, who was waiting for him.

Cú Chulainn had never seen a woman so beautiful as Fand. Gone from his mind was Émer, gone were Eithne, Aoife and Niamh and all the other mortal women that he had ever loved. He sat by her side while Lí Ban sang songs in praise of him. Cú Chulainn, like a boy, grew boastful and juggled golden apples for Fand, and performed tricks with his sword and spear.

Fand, who was lovesick for this handsome young man, looked on him with eyes that shone with admiration. She asked him to describe his combats and battles and he was not loath to do so. She listened avidly at his feet. Finally, Fand dismissed her sister and her handmaidens and she and Cú Chulainn slept together in a lover's embrace.

Cú Chulainn stayed in the palace of Fand for a month of Otherworld time. But, as the days passed, Cú Chulainn began to remember the mortal world of Ulaidh.

"Stay with me, for no one in the mortal world misses you. No time is passing there," Fand urged him.

But Cú Chulainn began to remember more and more about the mortal world and he became increasingly restless. "I must see my home in Dún Dealgan again," he said, choosing his words carefully. "I would see the Speckled Hall of the Craobh Ríoga again."

Fand became terrified that she would lose her lover to the mortal world again.

"I must go and fight battles for my king," Cú Chulainn finally said, "for I am a hound trained for war, not a puppy to frolic at my mistress's feet."

Now having said those words, the sad accusing face of his wife Émer came into his mind's eye.

When Fand saw that he could not be persuaded to stay with her, she realised that he would have to return. She proposed that she would follow him to the mortal world and, on each quarter moon, she would meet him on the Strand of the Yew Tree's Head.

Cú Chulainn called Laeg and they bade farewell to the people of Magh Mell, the Pleasant Plain, and Lí Ban brought them back to Ulaidh, to the very spot on the lakeshore. There was great joy at their return, which seemed hours rather than the month they had spent in the Otherworld. Cú Chulainn told Émer all that had happened there, with the exception of his affair with Fand. Life returned to normal at Dún Dealgan but, on each quarter moon, Cú Chulainn would venture forth to the Strand of the Yew Tree's Head and meet with Fand.

By the shadowy light, he and Fand made love on the sandy shore, or amidst the strong oak trees, on carpets of sweet hay or on the leafy mattress of the forest floor. Fand had her magic birds sing songs so that Cú Chulainn felt himself in the comfort of her palace.

Émer was a wise woman, as we have said before. She soon learnt that her husband was meeting a strange woman and making love with her. Émer was wise but was also of flesh and blood. She found out where her husband's assignations were taking place and she gathered fifty of her handmaidens and armed each of them with a sharp dagger. Then she set out to kill Fand.

At that moment, Fand lay with Cú Chulainn in a forest glade. Being of the Otherworld, her senses were sharper than mortal ones. So she raised her head while Cú Chulainn lay sleeping.

"Laeg!" she called to Cú Chulainn's faithful charioteer, who was acting as a sentinel for his companion nearby. "Beware! There is harm coming near here."

Laeg leapt up, his bow already strung. "What is it? I see and hear nothing!"

"I hear Émer and her handmaidens coming this way. They are armed with daggers and mean me harm."

Laeg hurried off into the forest to try to distract Émer.

Cú Chulainn now roused himself from sleep, the sharpness of the exchange awaking him. He leapt up and started dressing, while Fand explained her fears.

"Do not fear, Fand, but get into my chariot. Émer shall not harm you, so long as I am here."

Just then Émer, with Laeg trying to persuade her not to continue, burst into the clearing with her handmaidens behind her.

"Put down your knife, Émer," Cú Chulainn told her quietly.

"Put it down?" sneered Émer. "This I tell you, the sun will not rise tomorrow unless I have parted you from this woman."

"I cannot fight with you," smiled Cú Chulainn sadly. "And I doubt if you will kill me, in spite of your rage."

"No? It matters not to me how I separate you."

Fand moved forward then. "You cannot love him, if you would destroy him."

"Rather would I destroy you."

"Stand aside, Émer," Cú Chulainn now told her, "for though I also love you, I have sworn to defend Fand against the daggers of our mortal world. Do you seek to destroy me? Ironic that would be, when I have survived so many combats, to be destroyed by my own wife."

Émer suddenly burst into tears. "You have shamed and dishonoured me before the women of Ulaidh and before all the five kingdoms of Éireann. What have I done to you, that you so despise me, and turned from me to a woman of the Otherworld for comfort?"

"Cannot I love Fand as well as you? She is more beautiful than any mortal, intelligent and fair and worthy of a king in any land. There is nothing under the heavens that Fand would not do for me. Cannot I love you as well? For you are both equal in your own worlds and in your own ways."

Émer dried her eyes and laughed angrily. "Are you trying to justify your capriciousness? The unknown is always more exciting than the known and this is why you think you love her. One day, red seems ordinary and white is new; the next, it is red that is exciting and white is old. Men always worship what they can't have and what they have seems worthless."

Cú Chulainn stood helpless between Émer and Fand and his face was sad. He suddenly realized that he loved both but for different reasons.

At once wisdom claimed Émer's mind.

She laid aside her knife and dismissed her handmaidens, making them take an oath never to tell what they had seen.

"I do not want him if he comes to me by claim of my position as his wife, or because of his guilt. He must come because of love."

Fand stepped forward and gazed into his eyes and then sighed deeply. She turned to Émer.

"Have no fear, Émer, daughter of Forgall. He will leave me for you. It is right, for it is you that have the greater love."

Fand blew softly on Cú Chulainn and the warrior frowned and sat down with his back to a tree and fell asleep.

"Now it is I who must go," Fand said softly, and tears were falling from her eyes.

Émer gazed at her rival sadly. "I see you truly love him, Fand. If this is so, then I will stand aside, for there is nothing the spirit can wish for that you cannot give."

And with Émer standing aside, Fand realized just how much Émer loved Cú Chulainn.

Then there was a soft sighing of the wind and a great silver chariot appeared in the forest clearing. A tall, handsome young man alighted from it. He had a noble and gentle face and he looked on them in sadness and understanding.

"Oh, my husband!" cried Fand. "It is Manánnan, god of the oceans. You were once dearer to me than the world we shared. You forsook me and I sought love elsewhere. Once we shared our lives and passed them in an unending dream."

Émer knelt before the radiant god who came and stood looking down at Cú Chulainn.

"He is a noble man, this son of Lugh," he sighed. "You chose a noble love, Fand, but he is loved already." He turned back to Fand. "We shared the same love which Émer gives to her husband. I, like him, sought a new toy to play with. I have learnt maturity. We could love again. Will you leave this land of mortals for the Otherworld and the pleasures of the Pleasant Plain?"

Fand gazed at Cú Chulainn with such distress and pain as no mortal could suffer. "I have done great harm here," she said to Émer. "I do love him, but there is no one else to whom I would release him. By standing aside for me, I know you love him well."

"Fand," demanded Manánnan, "what is it that you will do? Will you come away with me or stay here until Cú Chulainn comes to you?"

Fand simply held out her hand to Manánnan Mac Lir and the great god of the ocean reached forward and helped her into his silver chariot.

At that moment Cú Chulainn awoke.

"What is it?" he cried, as he saw Fand riding off into the sky in the great silver chariot.

"Fand is returning to her husband, as you do not love her above all others," replied Émer bitterly, for there was dismay on his features at losing Fand.

Cú Chulainn gave three great cries of grief and, ignoring Émer and Laeg, went running off along the seashore, gazing into the sea in which the silver chariot of the ocean god disappeared.

They did not see Cú Chulainn in many a month, for he took himself to the mountains, living among the wild animals, scarcely eating nor drinking nor even sleeping. He dwelt on the plains of Luchra and no one would go near him.

Then Émer went to the court of Conchobhar at An Emhain and told the king what had happened. "He still has his sickness on him," Émer said.

"I know," agreed Conchobhar, who loved Cú Chulainn as if he were his own son. "I have sent my warriors to persuade him to come back to us, several times, but he attacks and drives them off."

"Then send your best musicians. Let them sing to him and tell him of the heroic deeds that he once performed here. Let them sing to him about his companions in arms who miss him. Let them sing to him of his wife, Émer, daughter of Forgall, who once he loved and wooed and married."

And King Conchobhar sent forth his best bards and poets and, when Cú Chulainn was lulled into sleep, they brought him forth to An Emhain. Once there, Cathbad the Druid called upon Manánnan and offered prayers and the ocean god came forth and heard of the tragedy that had seared Cú Chulainn. Being a wise and mighty god, Manánnan took his Cloak of Forgetfulness and shook it between Fand and Cú Chulainn, so that each forgot the other, and thus it was ensured that they would never again meet in any time nor in any world.

Then Cú Chulainn grew well and content with the mortal world again and went back to dwell in Dún Dealgan with Émer. He had entirely forgotten about Fand.

But Émer had not . . .

She grew irritable and expressed anger on the slightest pretext. She recalled that her husband had once loved Fand to the extent that he could not choose between them and that only the intervention of the ocean god, causing him to forget, made him content with his lot. Everywhere she went, especially walking in the woods and seeing strange birds, Émer was reminded of Fand. She became more bitter with each passing day. Cú Chulainn, lacking memory, could not understand her anger to him and he grew ill, trying to recall how he could have offended her.

Émer told Lebharcham, the old nurse of Deirdre, who still dwelt at Conchobhar's palace. Lebharcham told Conchobhar and Conchobhar in turn told his Druid, Cathbad. Cathbad mixed a potion and, one evening when Conchobhar had invited both Cú Chulainn and Émer to a great feasting at An Emhain, the Druid quietly slipped three drops of his potion in each of their goblets. They drank.

Cú Chulainn and Émer were overcome with sleep and conducted to the guests' chambers and, when they awoke Cú Chulainn had no memory of his passions but there lingered in him a deep sorrow, the reason for which he could not recall. And when Émer awoke, her anger and jealousies were gone and once more she was her natural self, the sweetest and most loving of wives.

5 *Lochlann's Son*

There was once a great warrior king of Lochlann, the land of fjords and lakes which lies north-east of Éireann in cold snowy climes, which is often called the North Land, or Norway. This King's name was Colgáin Mac Teine. His country was a land of fierce warriors, who ploughed the seas in great ships and often raided and pillaged the coastal lands of Éireann. As fierce as his people were, Colgáin was the fiercest. He was a descendant of the Fomorii, the undersea dwellers, who were once the dark gods of Éireann and who had been driven north into the lands of darkness by the children of the Gael.

It chanced one day that Colgáin was feeling very dissatisfied, for he had not been on a battle voyage in many months. So he called his chief warriors about him.

"Warriors of Lochlann," he began, "do you find fault with my rule?"

They were worried when he said this, for often a challenger to the kingship of Lochlann would be met by the incumbent king with sword and buckler and soon his head would be mounted over the king's hearth.

"Not us," they all cried. "We find no fault with you, sire."

Colgáin sniffed disparagingly, for he knew there was none who would dare challenge him.

"Well, I find fault with my own rule," he declared harshly.

"What fault is that?" demanded one warrior, bolder than the rest.

"The fault is this: our ships plough the seas, raiding and

demanding tribute from all shores on which we land. All the kings of the lands within the distance of our sailing pay me tribute and call me king of all the kings of the nations."

"This is so, sire," agreed the warriors. "What is the fault in that?"

"There is one king and one people who send me no tribute."

There was an uneasy silence.

"What king would dare do that?" asked a young warrior, too young to know.

Colgáin of Lochlann turned an angry face to the young man. "Why, it is the High King of Éireann and his people. Éireann, the land which was once possessed by my ancestors. It is there that Balor of the One Eye, the first and greatest of my line, fell fighting. Éireann, which saw the graves of noble Fomorii warriors spring forth like the green grass of spring, and from which our forefathers were driven pitilessly northward."

There was a muttering of discontent among the King of Lochlann's warriors.

"I am at fault in that I have not taken our ships and brought this arrogant High King of Éireann to my obedience, and forced him and his kind to pay tribute to me and mine."

Now the warriors of Lochlann set up a clamour, banging their swords against the shields.

"We are with you!" cried one. "Let us take revenge on this upstart king."

"We shall take the gold of Éireann or we will take the heads of every male Éireannach!" shouted the young warrior, who was too boastful, not having seen a battle before.

So Colgáin, King of Lochlann, gave the orders for all the warriors of his land to gather at the shore and for all the ships that could raise sail to be there, fully provisioned. And when they had all gathered, the warriors went on board; the King of Lochlann went to his ship. Out of the fjords came the great armada, speeding over the deep dark waves, towards the green isle of Éireann. The wind filled the sails and the waves came rolling behind them, speeding the ships forward, until they sighted the green mountains of Ulaidh.

Now the Royal Branch warriors of Ulaidh told their king that the square sails of the ships of Lochlann had been sighted, approaching their shore. The king of this land was Fianchu Araide and when he heard the news, he was not dismayed.

"Send to Cormac Mac Art, who resides at Tara," he said. "After all, it is Cormac who claims the High Kingship of the five kingdoms of Éireann, so it is he and his warriors who should defend the kingdoms, not me, who am but king in Ulaidh."

It was true that, since Cormac had established himself as High King in Tara, he had wrested much of the old power of the kings of Ulaidh away from them. He and his warrior élite, the Fianna, claimed to be far stronger than any of the warriors of the kingdoms of Éireann.

So members of the Craobh Ríoga, the Royal Branch warriors of Ulaidh, went to Tara and told Cormac Mac Art that the ships of the King of Lochlann were approaching their shore.

Cormac straightaway sent to Fionn Mac Cumhaill, the commander of the Fianna, and told him that he must gather his warriors and set off to meet the men of Lochlann, as soon as they landed on the shore.

Fionn picked the greatest of his warriors and hurried to the shore, where the ships of Colgáin were beaching, spewing out their great bands of battle-hungry warriors. Without pause, Fionn and his men rushed into the conflict and a bloody battle followed. For several days it raged, without victory on either side.

Then it was that Oscar, the deer-lover, son of Oisín, the "little deer", who in turn was son of the mighty Fionn himself, found himself in single combat with Colgáin, King of Lochlann. Both men were evenly matched and strong were their weapons. Soon their spears were shattered and then their shields were split asunder so that all they had were their powerful swords. Finally, Oscar came in under the guard of the King of Lochlann and shattered his head with a hard blow.

No sooner did the head of the king roll on the floor than

the oldest son of the King of Lochlann rushed forward and fought with Oscar. To and fro they struggled, for the boy was armed with grief and anger which gave strength to his sword-arm. Finally, Oscar used his battle foresight and managed to cleave the young man so that his head was also swept from him, the body falling one way and the head the other.

The reserve battalions of the Fianna, gathering from the four corners of Éireann, had arrived. They rushed forward on the warriors of Lochlann and so wielded their weapons that none escaped back to their boats alive. There was only one son of Lochlann left alive on the battlefield. That was the youngest son of the king, whose name was Míogach Mac Colgáin. It was Fionn Mac Cumhaill himself who took charge of the boy, making him a hostage, for he was but a child who had only been brought along to witness his father's deeds of bravery. It was the custom for prisoners caught in war to become hostages and in Éireann hostages were well treated.

Fionn took the boy to live in his fortress at Almain, the Hill of Allen, whose ramparts enclosed many white-walled dwellings and a great hall towered in its midst. Here the boy grew to manhood in comfort, but with the remembrance of the defeat of his father and his brother and the men of Lochlann ever lingering.

One day, one of Fionn's great warriors, Conán Mhaol, the Bald, son of Morna, observing the brooding face of the young man, took Fionn aside. "You are doing a foolish thing, my chief," he commented.

"How so?" demanded Fionn.

"It is foolish to keep the son of the dead King of Lochlann in your company, now that he has grown to manhood. You must know how much he hates you and Oscar, your grandson. Indeed, he hates all the warriors of the Fianna. Did we not defeat and destroy his father, his brother and all the warriors of Lochlann?"

Fionn thought a moment and then nodded slowly. "You are right, Conán. What should I do?"

"It is the right of hostages of noble birth to be apportioned land to dwell upon and work as they please. Give him land

and let him remove himself there. Then he will not be a danger to you."

"That is a good counsel," declared Fionn.

Fionn told the youth that he could have such land in Fionn's domains along the Shannon as he wished. The young man chose an island in the great river and made up the total amount of the land by a small area on the mainland opposite the island. There was a reason he chose this island and the land on the shore. They were both sheltered harbours and the young man was already plotting how he could bring shiploads of warriors from Lochlann and its allies to land there and attack Fionn and his Fianna and destroy them. So great was his hatred of the men of Éireann that he had never ceased plotting his revenge, in all the years he had been Fionn's hostage.

Míogach Mac Colgáin had a fine comfortable *rath* built there and received tribute of the people dwelling there. But never did he offer hospitality there to any man of Éireann; no food nor drink would he part with to any who called at his house, unless that person was a stranger to the shores of Éireann.

Some years passed and no more was heard of Míogach, son of the King of Lochlann. Then, one day, Fionn Mac Cumhaill and the leading members of the Fianna were hunting in the southland on Cnoc Fírinne. They had paused in the hunt to take a drink and rest and, while they were doing so, Fionn espied a tall man, large of limb and strongly built, with the accoutrements of a warrior. A shield hung from his shoulder, there was a great sword at his side and he carried a spear of weight and length. He made for Fionn and saluted him.

"Greetings, warrior," replied Fionn. 'Who are you?"

Now Conán had been sitting by Fionn and he frowned. "Do you not know him?" he asked his leader in a whisper.

Fionn frowned; although there was something familiar about the young warrior, he shook his head. "I do not."

"You ought to know him," replied Conán. "It is for you to know your friends and recognise your enemies. This man is Míogach Mac Colgáin, son of the dead King of Lochlann."

Fionn rose, recognising his hostage. "You have grown into

a fine-looking warrior, Míogach. Do you mean me harm or are your intentions good?"

"My intentions, according to my lights, are good. I came to bid you accept my hospitality at my *rath*, which stands not far from here, on the shore of the Shannon."

Conán swiftly intervened. "Beware of this, my chieftain. He has never offered the meat nor drink of hospitality to any champion of Éireann."

"That is because I had no meat nor drink to offer," the young man said hastily. "Now I have the hospitality to offer, allow me to make you my first guest, Fionn."

Now Fionn liked to believe the best of people and so he was satisfied and accepted Míogach's hospitality. He told his son Oisín to take command of the Fianna when he was away and to encamp them at Sliabh na mBan. He took with him Conán, and Conán's brother Goll, and Faolán and Glas Mac Aonchearda for his companions, and they followed Míogach to his *rath*.

Now Míogach's *rath* on the banks of the Shannon was a breathtaking sight, but no more noble than its interior. Míogach led them inside and they found the walls all lined with silks of richest red. Every part was in the most spectacular colours that could be imagined. Even the surly Conán was forced to voice his praise of it. In the hallway, they put aside their armour and their weapons – for it was a prohibition of the land to enter a feasting hall with arms.

Then Míogach led them into a great wondrous dining room and pointed to their places at the long oak wood table. Míogach then excused himself, saying he had to tell the servants to make ready the meal and bring them wine, and he went out and closed the door.

For a while, the four heroes stood chatting about the splendours of the house, and then they realised that time was passing.

"Míogach has left us a considerable time without drink and food," observed Fionn.

"Míogach has not returned," pointed out Conán. "Where is he?"

"Look to the fire, Fionn," Goll suddenly cried. "The fire

that was blazing well when we entered and giving forth the sweet odour of pine and applewood, now smokes and carries the repugnant stench of rotting corpses."

"Look at the walls, Fionn," cried Faolán. "The tapestries which were of softest silk are now decaying rags and beneath them the polished red panels of yew are just rough planks of birch fastened with hazel twigs."

"Look at the doors, Fionn," cried Glas. "Where once there were seven doors in this room, there is now no door at all, save one crack to the north which lets in snow and the icy breath of the north wind, even though it was summer when we came here."

And they all realised that the polished wooden floor had gone, the table and even the chairs they had sat in had vanished and they were sprawled on the cold, damp earth.

"Rise up!" gasped Fionn. "I recognise this magic. We are in the House of Death, which is draining our souls of vigour. Let us rise up and leave this place!"

Conán tried to struggle up but could not move from his place.

"We are pinned to the earth," cried Goll.

"What can we do?" wailed Faolán, who was brave in battle, but no man was brave against the magic of evil sorcerers.

"I should have listened to Conán," cried Fionn. "The son of the King of Lochlann has long planned this revenge. We have been brought here so that we may be drained of our vitality and die."

Now in his youth, Fionn had baked the Salmon of Knowledge for Finegas the Druid, who dwelt beside the Boyne. And as Fionn had been turning the spit, his thumb had brushed the flesh of the fish and, on sucking it, he obtained wisdom. So now Fionn sucked his thumb and he knew what fate was in store for Éireann if he and the Fianna perished.

"Míogach has long been plotting his revenge, my friends. He has brought great warriors from Lochlann and all the lands allied to that north kingdom. Even Daire Donn, the King of the World, has come with all his warriors. There is Sinnsior na gCath from Greece, and twenty-six sub-kings with him; and every sub-king has twenty-six battalions of warriors and can fight twenty-six battles before they tire. Each battalion has thirty great champions in them. There are the three kings from Inis Tuile and they are equal to three evil dragons. There are Neim, Aig and Aitceas, champions who can never be taken in battle. It is Neim, Aig and Aitceas who prepared the curse of this house for Míogach. We have only one way to escape from it, only one way to sever the invisible bonds that keep us tied to the earth . . ."

"What is that?" demanded Conán.

"We have to rub our limbs with the blood of the three kings of Inis Tuile."

"More easily said than done," pointed out Faolán.

Fionn sat awhile sucking his thumb and then he said: "We are faced with death and must have courage. What is to be done, when we wait for death?"

"Why," said Conán, "nothing is left but to sing the *dord-fhiann* while we wait for death."

The *dord-fhiann* was a warrior's chant, often intoned before a battle and accompanied by the beating of the spear-shafts against the shield. But they had no spears nor shields.

"That is what we shall do," affirmed Fionn. "We will raise our voices in the *dord-fhiann* and sing as mournfully as we can when we see death approaching."

So they sang.

On the peak of Sliabh na mBan, Oisín, son of Fionn, turned to his brother Fia. "What is that humming I hear?"

Fia listened intently. "It is the *dord-fhiann*, which is sung only in time of great peril. It is Fionn's voice which is raised there: Fionn, Conán, Goll, Faolán and Glas. They are in peril."

"Go and scout the land and see what ails them," Oisín instructed.

So Fia, with Insin Mac Suibhne, rode off towards the Shannon and came to the foreshore near the house of Míogach.

"It is indeed our Fianna brethren," cried Insin.

They approached the walls of the house.

"Fionn? Are you in there?" hissed Fia through the wall, for they could find no door nor windows.

"Is that the voice of Fia that I hear?" came Fionn's response.

"Indeed, it is."

"Do not come near to us, for we are tied to the earth by some black enchantment. Beyond the ford through the river to the island is a mighty army gathering. It means no good to Éireann."

Fia turned to Insin and warned him.

"Who is that with you?" came Fionn's voice.

"It is Insin, your foster-son."

"You must leave this place and get back to your brother Oisín and tell him what has befallen us."

"It is unseemly for us to leave you here, undefended and in danger," protested Fia.

There was a silence.

"Then one of you guard us while the other goes to the camp of Míogach on the island and finds out what is being planned."

It fell to Insin's lot to go down to the ford which separated the shore of the Shannon from the island in midstream, while Fia continued on to the camp of the King of Lochlann's son on the island.

It so happened that at that very moment when Fia came to the island, Sinnsior na gCath, the King of Greece, was boasting that he would cross the ford, enter the enchanted house, take off the head of Fionn and bring it back to the gathered enemies of Éireann. He had taken a hundred of his men and began to pass over the ford. Fia missed them in the darkness of the night, for he had circled behind the camp as Sinnsior led his men from the gate.

So Sinnsior crossed the ford and, in the darkness, saw a young man waiting for him.

"Hello, boy," he growled, for Insin was young. "Will you be a guide to me and show me where Míogach's magic house is, in which Fionn and his companions are? I mean to take his head and those of his companions and bring them back to Daire Donn, King of the World."

Insin chuckled dryly. "A bad guard would I be if you did that, for I am Insin of the Fianna. Come to shore and I will greet you with a fine death."

Sinnsior gave a great battle-cry and led his warriors racing through the shallows of the ford towards the shore. And a battle-fever came on Insin and he set about him, until all one hundred warriors of Sinnsior were destroyed and only the King of Greece was left alive. Insin was now so full of wounds, having fought so furiously, that he fell dead at Sinnsior's feet. The king immediately cut off the head and took it for his own trophy.

"Now I will go back for more men," Sinnsior said to himself, seeing his warriors stretched into the water and the water red with blood. "I will fetch more men and then I will take the head of Fionn Mac Cumhaill."

So he turned and hurried back across the ford to the island.

It was at that moment that Fia, having finished his scouting, came to the river to pass back again and saw the King of Greece crossing towards him.

"Who are you?" demanded Fia.

"I am Sinnsior of Greece. I went across to get the head of Fionn Mac Cumhaill and met a great champion guarding the ford and he killed one hundred of my best men before I was able to slay him."

Sinnsior was given to boasting.

Fia pursed his lips scornfully. "I wonder that you yourself are not marked, nor that you did not fall first, leading your men."

"My strength and valour saved me," replied Sinnsior defiantly.

"If this champion fell to your sword, you must have something of his to prove it."

"I have his head." The King of Greece took it from his belt and showed it to Fia.

Fia took the head carefully and he kissed Insin's forehead. "This head was beautiful, this morning. May it remain in beauty." Then Fia turned to Sinnsior. "Do you know to whom you have given the head of this champion?"

Sinnsior shook his head negatively. "I presume that you are one of Míogach's men."

"I am not. Nor will you be, for long."

Fia drew out his sword and the two men fell on one another in wrath, hissing like venomous wild beasts, until, with a swift stroke of his sword, Fia severed Sinnsior's own head and it rolled on the ground before him.

He picked it up with Insin's head and made his way back over the ford. He reached the enchanted house and called for Fionn.

"What was the great noise and shouting at the ford?" came Fionn's voice.

"Sinnsior and one hundred warriors came against Insin while I was scouting on the island."

"Is Insin hurt?" demanded Fionn, with a heavy heart, for he knew the truth.

"He was killed, but not before he slew all Sinnsior's warriors."

"Who gave him the mortal blow?"

"Hard to tell. He died of his wounds. But one man took his head."

Fionn and his companions groaned aloud, for all knew Insin and, as the soul reposed in the head, according to the Celtic lore, Insin would not be able to seek rest in the Otherworld while his head was held by enemies. But Fia said, "Have no fear. I have Insin's head with me and have taken the head of Sinnsior, who took off Insin's head."

"Blessings on you, Fia. It was a great deed that you did. Alas, now only you stand at the ford between us and our enemies. You are our only protection until we can summon the Fianna to our aid."

So Fia went back down to the ford while Fionn and his companions raised their voices once again in the *dord-fhiann* and this time the head of Insin joined in. At the ford, Fia cut a stick of rowan and put Sinnsior's head on it, looking out to the island, as a warning to Míogach and his allies.

On the island, there was a warrior called Cairbre Cathmhíle, who had been a friend to Sinnsior. He saw Sinnsior's head and was angry.

"My friend went for Fionn's head," he exclaimed. "Now I shall complete the deed."

He went down to the shore and began to wade across, taking with him four hundred chosen warriors. They halted in midstream when they saw Fia standing there waiting for them.

"Who stands in our path?" demanded Cairbre.

"I am Fia, son of Fionn."

"Tell us, who made the great noise at this ford a while ago and who has slain Sinnsior and all his men?"

"That is for you to find out," replied Fia. "I will not tell you."

Cairbre was exceedingly angry and told his hand-picked warriors to cross and take the head of Fia. The combat was fierce and bloody and soon Fia stood surrounded by the bodies of the four hundred warriors of Cairbre. Then Cairbre, in rage, came to him and they fought until Cairbre's head joined that of Sinnsior on a pole of rowan. Then Fia knelt by the river and bathed himself, for he was full of wounds and covered in the blood of that awesome combat.

On the island, Míogach Mac Colgáin, son of the King of Lochlann, was angry that so many warriors had not even been able to pass the ford against the youngest of Fionn's warriors.

"I will go myself, with five hundred hand-picked warriors," he declared.

So Míogach took five hundred men, the best warriors of his allies, and came to the ford. He peered across at the tired and wounded warrior.

"Is it Fia who stands there?" he called.

"Indeed, it is," replied the young warrior.

"Then it is a good man who guards the ford," agreed Míogach. "In all the years I was hostage of Fionn, I never saw you bested in combat. Yet, my anger is mightier than your sword. Defend yourself or move aside."

"You grew up with the Fianna as your protectors," Fia reminded him. "Even though you were a hostage and son of our enemies, we nurtured you in your youth. You should be thankful to the Fianna and not vengeful."

Míogach laughed harshly. "Thankful? Thankful to men who slew my father and brother and the men of my country?

You must repay me for that. Revenge is a stronger principle than gratitude. I will have my vengeance."

"Did we ask your father, the King of Lochlann, to invade the sweet shores of Éireann? He came with sword and fire to destroy us and so he was answered in kind and worsted. He was destroyed by the thing he created. May you not hurt your enemy when he has struck first? Seek no vengeance for what was just, lest the vengeance rebound on you."

Míogach grew angry. "Leave the ford or stay, but I am coming across and I will not come in peace."

"It is not in peace that I will greet you, if you come with ill intent."

Míogach told his men to go forward and Fia, as wounded and exhausted as he was, met them with courage and soon he was surrounded by the bodies of three hundred. Then Míogach told the remaining two hundred to hold back and he himself, with shield and sword raised, rushed forward like a hound towards its prey.

Far away, on the peak of Sliabh na mBan, Oisín frowned.

"I still hear the moaning of the *dord-fhiann*," he said, listening. "And I hear the voice of Insin joining in. That is curious. Perhaps it is a good dinner that Fionn and his men are having with Míogach, that they are unwilling to leave. They sing songs, perhaps, to entertain their hosts."

But it was Diarmuid Ua Duibhne, the handsomest of all the Fianna, who had been fostered by Aonghus Og, the god of love, whose sharp hearing caught the sounds. "It is no song of thanksgiving, Oisín. I think Fionn and his men are in danger. I will go and find out what is happening."

"Then I will accompany you," offered Fatha Conán, another of the Fianna.

The two of them rode with great speed until they came near the ford and heard the sounds of combat and the shouting and cursing of men.

"That is the battle-cry of Fia, but he is weak and wounded," cried Diarmuid. "Let us go to his aid."

The two rode to a hill overlooking the ford. There was Fia, with all his weapons smashed and broken, his shield split asunder and nothing in his hands. Above him stood the triumphant Míogach, his sword raised to strike off his head.

"Diarmuid!" cried Fatha Conán, "quickly, save the life of Fia, son of Fionn. If I attempt to cast my spear from this spot, I do not know whether I will hit Fia or Míogach. If we wait until we get nearer them, it will be too late. Only you can cast the spear from this distance."

Diarmuid, realising the truth of his words, seized his throwing spear and drew his arm back. The cast he gave sent the spear flying through the air. It hit Míogach in the side. But Míogach was only wounded and he slashed down with his sword, taking off the head of Fia.

Diarmuid and Fatha Conán raced down to the spot but it was Diarmuid who closed with Míogach first.

"A pity it was your spear that struck me, Diarmuid," grunted Míogach. "For you were never at the battle in which my father and brother fell."

"I cast it to save Fia's life. Now I must have my vengeance on you for taking it."

The combat was fought without mercy from either man then. And, finally, it was Diarmuid who slew Míogach and took his head from him. He set it up on a rowan pole by the ford with the heads of Sinnsior and Cairbre.

Diarmuid and Fatha Conán went, taking the head of Fia with them, to the enchanted house and called out. Outside was the moaning head of Insin and they placed the head of Fia by its side.

"Who stands outside?" came the voice of Fionn.

"Diarmuid Ua Duibhne and Fatha Conán," replied Diarmuid.

"Ah, Diarmuid," sighed Fionn. "Who made that dreadful noise of combat?"

"Your son Fia stood at the ford against Cairbre and his warriors and Míogach and his warriors. He felled all who came against him except one."

"How is my son, Fia?"

"He is dead."

There was a silence.

"Who killed my son?"

"It was Míogach, son of the dead King of Lochlann. I came too late to save Fia's life."

"Did Míogach escape, after this deed?"

"He did not escape, Fionn. I took his head and placed it on a rowan pole by the ford."

"My blessing on you, Diarmuid." And Fionn told Diarmuid and Fatha Conán all that had taken place. "You are our only means of protection against the forces of Daire Donn, King of the World, until Oisín brings the Fianna to our aid."

"We will guard the ford for you."

Then Conán Maol spoke up. "The cold earth is draining me of life," he moaned. "I cannot last much longer without a bite to eat nor wine to drink."

"Plenty of food at the ford," pointed out Fatha Conán. "The warriors of Sinnsior, Cairbre and Míogach all brought provisions with them."

"Then bring that food to me, that I may last in this life until the men of the Fianna come here."

Diarmuid frowned. "Do you think of your belly at this time, while the great armies of the world march against the ford with only me and Fatha Conán to defend it?"

"Oh, Diarmuid," Conán Mhaol moaned piteously, "if I were a beautiful young woman who asked you to bring her food and drink, you would do so, no matter the risk. It is because I am a man that you scorn to do so."

Now that was true for, as Diarmuid had been raised by the god of love, Aonghus Og, it was certain that he cared more for the desires of women than for those of men. It shamed him to think so.

"Conán," he replied, "I will bring you food and drink. I vow it."

So Diarmuid and Fatha Conán returned to the ford.

"I will gather the food and take it back to the enchanted house, while you guard the ford," Diarmuid said.

"Why not I?" demanded Fatha Conán.

"Because I remember the prophecy of the Druid when you were born. It was said that you would one day dance rings around the ruler of the world. As Daire Donn, the King of the

World, is now our enemy, I have a feeling that this day has come. On yonder island stand the armies of the world against us. Do you guard the ford, while I gather food."

It was easy to find the food, for the warriors had brought provisions in wagons which now stood discarded.

But when Diarmuid came with the food to the enchanted house, Conán Mhaol rejected it.

"This is dead men's food, and I will not eat it."

Diarmuid agreed that the food had been intended for the dead warriors at the ford.

He went back to the ford. On the island, he could hear feasting of warriors.

"I will go across and take their food and drink and return with it to Conán Mhaol," he declared.

"It may cause your death and only leave myself to guard the ford, then," Fatha Conán pointed out irritably.

"Even if it causes my death, I will get the food for Conán Mhaol, that he may last in life until the Fianna arrive."

Diarmuid crossed the ford silently until he came to the island in the Shannon. There he found Borb, the son of Sinnsior, and his warriors eating their supper. Each man of them drank from a golden goblet and ate from a silver plate. Seated next to Borb Mac Sinnsior was none other than Daire Donn, the King of the World. Now Diarmuid had the gift of swiftness, as befitted one fostered by gods. So he entered into the circle of feasting, before any man could see him and he seized the great goblet of rich red wine held by Borb and passed on before Borb realized it. He went next to Daire Donn, who was feasting from a great plate of meat. He seized that, while striking the great king in the stomach, and left him winded.

"Had I not more pressing things to do," hissed Diarmuid, "I would take your heads as well, but I must return with this food to Conán Mhaol."

He came back across the ford and was puzzled when Fatha Conán made no challenge to him.

There at the ford he found Fatha Conán fast asleep among the bodies of the slain.

"If I stop to rouse Fatha Conán, Conán might perish. There

must be some curse that causes Fatha to sleep, this night. I will hasten to the enchanted house and return swiftly to rouse Fatha."

So saying, Diarmuid pressed on.

At the wall of the house, Diarmuid called to Conán. "I have brought you the food of the living, of Borb Mac Sinnsior and Daire Donn. But how may I get the food to you?"

"You must not enter the enchanted house, or you will become as we are," replied Conán. "I am lying by the north crack, where the snow is. Come there and cast the food towards me. You have not missed a javelin cast yet and so you may cast the food at me."

Diarmuid did so and he threw the dish of food into the house where Conân lay. But the plate hit Conan's nose and the food splattered all over his face.

"Forgive me. I have made you dirty."

Conán was busy scraping the food from his face and devouring it. "A hound never runs from a bone," he replied with satisfaction.

"But I can't make the same cast with the goblet of wine," Diarmuid observed.

"Indeed not. You must climb to the roof of this house. The enchantment is only on the inside, so you will not be harmed. Make a hole in the roof above where I am and pour the wine through the hole into my mouth."

Diarmuid leapt up to the roof and made the hole. However, he did not find Conán's mouth and wine spilt on one cheek and then the other. And Conán rebuked Diarmuid, telling him that if he had been a young woman, the pouring would have been more carefully done. Ashamed, Diarmuid was more careful and poured the wine into Conán Mhaol's mouth.

It was during this time that the three kings of Inis Tuile decided to raise their companies of warriors and march down to the ford.

Diarmuid raced back and tried to awake Fatha Conán from his curious sleep, but could not.

The three kings, with six hundred warriors, marched into the waters of the ford and then halted as they saw Diarmuid.

"Is that Diarmuid Ua Duibhne we see?" asked one of the kings.

"It is myself," agreed Diarmuid.

"Diarmuid, we are the kings of Inis Tuile and, as you know, there is blood which connects us."

Indeed, Diarmuid knew that he shared some ancestry in common with the three kings of Inis Tuile.

"For that and our love for you as kin and as hero, we would prefer that you did not stand against us. Will you allow us to cross the ford without opposition?"

Diarmuid smiled softly and shook his head. "I will allow you to cross without opposition on condition that you first let me cross to your island and take off the head of the King of the World."

Now Diarmuid knew that they would not allow that.

"Then we must fight our way through you, Diarmuid," cried the kings.

"You must do what you must do and I must do what I must do," replied Diarmuid, unperturbed.

The three kings of Inis Tuile started to lead their battalions of warriors against Diarmuid. He fell on them furiously and many great blows were exchanged between them. Hundreds of warriors fell beneath his sword-blade, while Fatha Conán lay oblivious in sleep.

Then Fatha Conán was at last aroused from his sleep by Diarmuid's battle-song and he sprang up, rubbing the sleep from his eyes. Around him was the terrifying combat, the splintering of shields, the cries and groaning of warriors and clang of metal on metal. He paused only a second and then seized his weapons and rushed forward to Diarmuid's side.

"A fine friend are you, who let me sleep through a battle," he said angrily.

"There is no other man on earth that I would suffer such a rebuke from!" snapped Diarmuid. "Not even the wailing of the goddess of death and battles would wake you."

Then they said no more and both turned to meet the warriors of the three kings of Inis Tuile. The fight went this way and that, and no gain was made on either side. Then slowly the numbers against them decreased. Eventually, however, the three kings themselves were left facing Diarmuid and Fatha Conán. Every blow from them was repaid by blows from the three kings. Finally, it was the three kings who measured their lengths on the ground before Diarmuid and Fatha Conán and the two heroes took the heads of the kings and raised them on rowan sticks at the ford.

When Diarmuid and Fatha Conán went back to the enchanted house and told Fionn what had happened, Fionn told them to bring the heads of the three kings of Inis Tuile to the house and toss them through the northern crack to him. They did so without delay. Fionn took the heads and rubbed the blood of the kings on himself and then on his men, except Conán Mhaol, for when they came to him there was no blood left.

So all of them were freed except Conán Mhaol.

"Is it here that you are planning to leave me?" demanded the disgruntled warrior.

"No, indeed," Fionn assured him.

They gathered round him and pulled and pulled but could not free him from the enchantment.

Then Diarmuid and Fatha Conán came and they put their hands under Conán Mhaol and, with a tremendous excess of energy, they pulled him from the ground. And the hair of his head, where he had been lying, and the skin of his buttocks and that on his shoulders were stuck to the ground as they wrenched him away. And it is from this that Conán, son of Morna, was nicknamed Mhaol or "the Bald".

It had been a terrible night and Fionn and his men were exhausted.

"The King of the World lies across the ford with his army and we are not fit to give them battle," muttered Fionn in disgust. "We must rest and recover our strength."

Diarmuid agreed. "I and Fatha Conán will go back to the ford and make sure that no one crosses until morning."

"By that time, the Fianna will surely be here," agreed Fionn.

So Fionn and his men rested while Diarmuid and Fatha Conán returned to the ford to stand guard.

Now Daire Donn and Borb Sinnsior decided it was time

that they rose up and did battle with Fionn. With them came twenty hundreds of their best warriors and they started to cross the river ford.

At this time, on the peak of Sliabh na mBan, Oisín realized that Fia, Insin, Diarmuid nor Fatha Conán had returned and now the sounds of the *dord-fhiann* were silent.

"I have waited too long for their return," he rebuked himself. "I will go and find out what is wrong myself." And he gave command of the Fianna to his son, Oscar.

At the ford, the forces of Daire Donn were beginning to cross, a great multitude of warriors, all well armed. Diarmuid and Fatha Conán stood with weapons ready and a great battle began.

It was when the first warriors' spear points were pressing towards the defenders of the ford that Oisín came to the brow of the hill and saw what was taking place. He drew his sword and raised his shield and came running down to the ford straight at Borb Mac Sinnsior. His battle-fever was so strong on him that he was able to despatch Borb with one mighty blow and take his head.

Now Fionn and his companions, having recovered their strength, came running forward to join the battle as well. Those men of Daire Donn's army who had not fallen to the swords of Diarmuid, Fatha Conán and Oisín now fell to their swords. Fionn, Goll, Faolán, Glas and even Conán Mhaol, still smarting but fit, rushed forward and despatched the battalions of the mighty king.

Daire Donn now summoned fresh hosts from the island and they began to storm forward.

Now Oisín raised his war trumpet, which Oscar heard on the slopes of Sliabh na mBan, and the great army of the Fianna, with Fionn's standard – the *Scáil Gréine* (Shadow of the Sun) – began to march forward. None could stand in its way as it swelled remorselessly on towards the enemy in closed armoured ranks.

At the ford the two great armies clashed, with spears, swords and shields locked in combat. Men fell in bloodied forms across the river.

And Fatha Conán met with Daire Donn, the King of the

World, in the very centre of the river and because the great king, though strong, was cumbersome in his movements, Fatha danced around and around him until the great king was giddy and exhausted. Then Fatha Conán gave him a mighty blow which took off his head. Thus was the Druid prophecy fulfilled. Fatha Conán raised the head of the king and showed it to the enemies of the Fianna.

The enemy warriors trembled at the sight and fled from the field of battle. The Fianna followed them, hunting them down, leaving but one man to give an account of the battle. This man was of fleet foot and scrambled through forests and across rocky hills back to his ship. Many a strong champion was left sleeping on that field; many a mother wept for her son, and wife for her husband and sweetheart for her lover. Many lost their minds after fleeing from that terror. Even the mighty Fianna did not escape unscathed. Many gave their lives, like Fia son of Fionn and Insin, Fionn's foster-son, and many others unnamed and unsung were slain or terribly wounded.

Thus was the outcome of the vengeance that Míogach Mac Colgáin, son of the King of Lochlann, had nurtured in his heart for many years. Thus it was that the words of wisdom spoken by the Druids were found to be true – that vengeance, though sweet at first, becomes a bitter cup and proves to be its own executioner. Therefore no vengeance is more estimable than one which is not taken.

6 *The Poet's Curse*

To be the subject of a curse from a poet is a terrible thing. In ancient times, the poet had high status at the king's court and could argue with the High King himself. Everyone sought the poet's praise and dreaded his satire. In the *Annals of Ulster* it is recorded that, in the year AD 1024, the chief poet of Ireland, Cuán Ua Lothcháin, was unlawfully killed in Theba. As he lay dying, he uttered the poet's curse, the *firt filed* they called it, and the bodies of his murderers were said to have rotted within the hours. To challenge a poet or displease him or her – for there were *banfíli*, women poets, equal with men in Ireland in those days – would be like playing dice with fate.

The poet's curse was not something to be chanced lightly. The *Annals of Connacht* record that, in the year AD 1414, John Stanley, the English viceroy, sent to rule in Ireland, died from a poet's curse.

When Tomás Ó Criomhthain (1856–1937) wrote his best-selling autobiography *An tOileánach* (The Islandman) he wrote that he would abandon his day's work to go to listen to the island poet, for fear of being satirised and cursed by him.

The fear of the poet's curse caused High Kings and kings to promise the poet anything that was demanded of them to avoid the curse. Let me tell you a story . . .

It happened during the years when Mongán Mac Fiachai was a king in Ulster. Mongán "of the head of abundant hair", for such was the meaning of his name, Mongán, was prince of the Dál nAraidhe who ruled from a great *ráth*, or fortress, the Ráth Mór of Magh Linne, which is now called Moylinny in Co. Antrim. Now Mongán prided himself on his court and one day he decided that, as the Chief Poet of Ireland had never graced his court with a visit, it would appear that he was lacking and this detracted from his reputation as a learned and hospitable king.

So he sent to the Chief Poet inviting him to spend a week at his court as a guest. The Chief Poet was called Dallán Forgaill, who was, of course, not of the Dál nAraidhe but of the sept of the Masraighe from Maighin, which is now Moynehall in South Cavan. Dallán Forgaill was, therefore, a stranger to the prince's land, and Mongán had no personal knowledge of him but, as he was the Chief Poet and could go wheresoever he chose and be accorded high honours among the kings of Éireann, his status was his reputation. So he came to Magh Linne and was wined and feasted and entertained at Mongán's court.

Dallán Forgaill, if the truth be not shameful, was a man of quick temper, an irascible man, proud, vain and as quick to take offence as to accept flattery. He was a repulsive-looking old man, partially blind, and most people who knew the quickness of his temper feared him.

One night, when the hearth fires were blazing high, and the feasting was over, and the warriors of Magh Linne were gathered round; when Mongán sat in his carved oak chair of office with his queen, Breothighearn – the highly noble one – at his side, her spun-gold hair reflecting the light of the flickering torches, dancing as if on fire, Dallán Forgaill was asked if he would recite some stories.

And he was nothing loath to do so.

He choose a story of the Fianna, the élite band of warriors who were bodyguards to the High King, whose leader was Fionn Mac Cumhaill. The story he chose was of the great battle in which the prince Fothad Airgtheach was killed in battle.

Most knew of the story, for there were three Fothad brothers – Fothad Airgtheach, Fothad Canainne and Fothad Cairptheach – and they found themselves as three joint rulers of the kingdoms of Éireann. But Fothad Canainne fell in love with the wife of Ailill Flann Beag, the leader of the Niadh Nask, the élite warrior corps who guarded the king of Munster. She eloped with him. But her husband caught up with Fothad Canainne and his warriors at a place called Féic, which is near Millstreet in Co. Cork, and there was a great battle. Fothad Canainne was defeated. He was captured and beheaded by the angry husband. But even after death, his head recited a poem to the woman he loved, describing his love and his death in battle.

Of the remaining Fothad brothers, a quarrel broke out between them and Fothad Airgtheach, in anger, slew his brother Fothad Cairptheach. Now as Fothad Cairptheach had been a just king among the brothers, who had ruled for a year and a day, and had also been a commander of the Fianna, it was the Fianna who now came against Fothad Airgtheach, seeking vengeance for Fothad Cairptheach's death, and fought a great battle in which he was slain.

"And this," explained Dallán Forgaill, at the end of his story, "was at Dubhthair Laighean."

Now the place he named is now called Duffrey in Co. Wexford.

At once Mongán, who prided himself on his knowledge, frowned and bent forward towards the poet. "Where, then, do you say is the burial place of Fothad Airgtheach, Dallán Forgaill?" he asked, clearly puzzled.

The Chief Poet of Ireland sniffed airily. "Why, where else but in Dubhthair Laighean? For he was buried near the spot where he fell."

"But that cannot be so, O Poet," averred Mongán, at which many drew their breath sharply, for it was not wise to contradict a poet, let alone the Chief Poet of Ireland.

Dallán Forgaill's countenance grew stony. "Not so?" he said sharply. "What do you mean, it is not so? Have not I said it is so?"

"Because it is a false enlightenment that you have given. Fothad Airgtheach, as everyone in this hall knows, fought his last battle here among the Ulaidh, indeed among the Dál nAraidhe, here in Magh Linne. When dawn rises and lights the big green hill outside this fortress, you will see that was the very spot where he fell and so that hill is a fitting place for the bones of a prince of Éireann to rest in."

Dallán Forgaill erupted in rage and fury. "You dare, little princeling, to contradict the Chief Poet of Ireland?" he cried. His brows drew together and the blood gushed in his face; his tongue was tipped with ready venom.

Mongán was taken aback by the thunderous voice of the poet.

The court was suddenly quiet.

"I may challenge you when you are wrong," Mongán replied stubbornly.

"So you deny me knowledge, kinglet? You deny me, who am versed in all the history of the dead and the living of Ireland? You dare? Very well, then I shall satirize you, and your father and your mother, and your grandfather, since it is not becoming that your word, the word of a petty king, should be taken before mine, the word of the Chief Poet of All Ireland. *Fuighleacht mallacht ort*!"

Dallán Forgaill gazed round at the pale-faced members of the court of Mongán and smiled viciously. That he had pronounced "countless curses" on Mongán was a matter which struck terror into those who had heard him.

"I will curse this court, curse the waters of this land so that no fish shall be caught in the rivers, nor in the surrounding sea, and no fruit will be borne on the trees. The plains shall remain barren of grain and cereals, and the country shall be shorn of living creatures. This I will do, Mongán of the Dál nAraidhe, because of the great insult you have shown me."

Now Breothighearn, the queen, broke in upon the ravings of the angry poet, with words like drops of honey, or the tender piping of the linnet in a hidden woodland bower.

"Stay your words, Poet of Ireland. My husband, the king, had no wish nor desire to wound you nor to vex your heart with anger. Curse us not and I will offer you a bronze cauldron filled with gold and silver and precious jewels – even if I have to strip my neck and arms of these glittering baubles. They are yours. But do not punish this kingdom by your poet's curse."

Mongán was regretting that he had contradicted the poet, even though he knew that he was right and the poet was wrong. However, the poet's curse on his people weighed heavily with him, for the people should not be blamed for his actions. So he said:

"Let me add my plea to my wife's plea – do not curse us and I will add to her gift the value of seven *cumals*, each *cumal* being the value of three milch cows, which is the honour price of a king."

Dallán Forgaill stood and folded his arms in scorn. "Are such paltry gifts worthy of my honour?" he sneered.

"Twice seven *cumals* . . ." pleaded Mongán. And when that produced no reaction he went further: "Thrice seven *cumals* . . . or if you must, take half of my kingdom to save me and my people from your blighting tongue."

Dallán Forgaill remained like a graven image, apparently unmoved by the offers of compensation. "I might consider all your kingdom as compensation," he finally conceded, "if you will say that you concede I spoke the truth of it and you lied."

Now, while Mongán was desperate to avert the poet's curse, he could not go so far as to deny the truth as he knew it. The most sacred thing a king had to undertake was to tell the truth, and the saying of the sacred oath was "the truth against the world".

There was an uncomfortable silence.

Dallán Forgaill watched the king's features and knew what was passing in his mind and he grew even more angry at this apparent affront.

"So even now you mock me, princeling!" he cried. "You deny my knowledge. Very well. I have listened to your offers of compensation and you have offered me all your kingdom, everything except one thing. I think that you must prize it above all things. Therefore, only offer me this and I will not curse you or your people."

Mongán was puzzled.

"Name it and it shall be yours."

"Your wife, Breothighearn. I shall settle for no less."

Beothighearn gave a little scream and pushed back in her chair as she gazed on the repulsive old man.

This did not even cause Dallán Forgaill to blink. He preferred people to fear him if they did not respect him.

Mongán groaned with anguish.

Breothighearn turned and clasped her husband's hand. "You have to accept, my husband, because if you do not, the whole kingdom will be cursed."

The king thought furiously. Yet he could see no other way of avoiding the curse. "Very well," he said finally.

Dallán Forgaill began to smile and move forward towards the queen.

"Yet wait!" cried Mongán. "I will agree to this but only after three days have passed. If, within those three days, I have not proved that the death place of Fothad Airgtheach was here at Magh Linne and that he is buried there, under the green hill, then you may claim my wife and I shall accept your claim."

The Chief Poet hesitated and then nodded, with a crafty smile. Being a vain man, he had implicit belief in his knowledge. He was prepared to wait three days.

"At this hour, three days from now, I shall come to claim your queen or to curse your kingdom," he said smugly and he turned from the feasting hall, while the great warriors shrank back to let him pass by.

When he had departed from the feasting hall, and those attending had left for their beds in sorrow, Breothighearn came to tears.

"Can you prove what you say, husband?" she asked between her heart-rending sobs.

Mongán was distraught. "I do not know. I tried to buy time for me to think. But do not grieve; I have a faith that help will surely come, for justice must overcome injustice."

But the days passed. The king sent throughout his land to find bards and historians who would bring testimony to the truth of the matter. But while many would say "everyone knows this" not one could offer specific proof. Proof rested with Mongán, for he was the one who had challenged Dallán Forgaill's word, and so the Chief Poet did not have to prove his contention.

On the third morning, the old poet appeared before Mongán and demanded the queen.

"Three days were agreed, until the very hour," rebuked the king. "Come back to the court when the sun is down, beyond the hour of feasting. That is the hour when the three days are up."

Disgruntled and muttering threats, the old poet shuffled off.

Breothighearn was still tearful.

"Do not be sorrowful, wife. I have faith that help will surely come," Mongán insisted.

"Three days have passed and no help has come," his wife pointed out.

Mongán smiled and tried to put a good face on matters, but he knew that she was right. No help had come to them during the three days, and now only hours separated them from the time when Dallán Forgaill would claim his prize.

He sat with his arms around Breothighearn in her chamber and, as the hours rushed by, her tears fell faster and faster.

Then, as the sun slid from the sky, Mongán suddenly raised his head, slightly to one side, as if listening.

"What is it?" demanded his queen.

"I hear the sound of footsteps, far, far away. I hear the tread of one who is coming to our aid. He comes from the House of Donn, purveyor of souls to the Otherworld."

Tech Duinn, the island where the god Donn gathered souls for their journey westward to the Otherworld, lay south-west of the kingdom of Munster.

Queen Breothighearn shivered fearfully.

Yet her husband went on: "I hear his feet splashing through the waters of the Leamhain and now, with bounds, he is crossing Loch Léin, through the lands of the Uí Fidgente, along the Suir on Moy-Fefin. His mighty stride is quickening, along the Nore, over the Barrow, the Liffey and the Boyne, across the Dee, the Tuarthesc, Carlingford Lough, the Nid and the Newry River – behold, he is scattering right and left the waves of the Larne in front of Rathmore!"

The king rose up and flung out his arms dramatically. "He is here! We will go down into the feasting hall and confront Dallán Forgaill. Have no fear, my wife. All will be well."

The feasting hall of the royal fortress of the Dál nAraidhe

was crowded. People had come from far and wide, for all had heard the news of the poet's curse. There in the middle of the hall stood Dallán Forgaill, with folded arms and a sneer on his face.

Mongán led Breothighearn into the hall, the queen looking pallid from her days of tears and sorrow, and sad was her beauty as she took her seat, her head bowed.

There was a murmur of sympathy from those gathered in the hall.

"I have come to claim what is mine by right," called the Chief Poet, moving forward. "*Mo mhallacht don lá a . . .*"

"Stay. Be not in such haste, vengeful poet," said Mongán. "There was a condition before you cursed or took my queen."

The old poet chuckled cynically. "The condition was that you prove me wrong. Where is your proof that Fothad Airgtheach was killed here and is buried in yonder green hill?"

"It is here," he said quietly.

Mongán looked to the closed doors of the fortress, which were barred from the inside, it being after dark. It was the custom to shut the gates of a royal *ráth* at dusk, to prevent lurking dangers entering. He looked at the closed doors and it was as if he were peering beyond them.

Dallán Forgaill turned and frowned, seeing only the barred doors. "Where is it?" he demanded. "Is this a trick to delay me?"

"A man is approaching from the south. He carries a headless spear-shaft in his hand. He leaps over the three ramparts which guard this fortress as easily as a bird takes flight on the wing, he comes towards the doors . . ."

Then, before the eyes of all assembled, the great wooden bolts of the doors slid back without anyone touching them. The great doors swung inwards, as if guided by unseen hands.

Standing in the door was a tall stranger. He was taller than most men of the kingdom; his figure spoke of great strength and his muscles rippled beneath his fine clothes. He wore a dark rich cloak, fastened by a beautifully crafted brooch. It flowed back from his shoulders. His face was young and very handsome and his hair was fair and curled, reaching to his shoulders. Even as Mongán had said, he carried a headless spear-shaft in one hand, with a great sword at his belt and an exquisite silver shield on his arm.

Within a few strides, he reached the centre of the hall causing, just by his presence, Dallán Forgaill to stagger away from him.

The stranger spoke in a voice so deep and ringing that it seemed all the candles in their holders shook and flickered throughout the hall. "There is trouble in this *ráth*," he observed.

Mongán rose from his seat of office and took a step forward. "Indeed, you have observed correctly, stranger."

"Tell me of it."

"Yonder is Dallán Forgaill, the Chief Poet of Ireland. He tells me that Fothad Airgtheach was slain and buried in Dubhthair Laighean. I questioned his knowledge. The traditions of my people say that he was slain here at Magh Linne and sleeps in the green hill outside."

"He affronted my station," snapped Dallán, "for which it is my right to curse him. I offered not to do so if he can prove his claim and, failing that, if he gives me his wife. The hour is now up for him to present the proof and so he must give me his wife or accept my curse."

The tall stranger looked long and thoughtfully at the poet. "Have you never heard the saying, O poet, *ná malluigh do dhuine eagnaí* – which is 'never curse a wise man'? You tell a false history. Fothad Airgtheach was not slain in Dubhthair Laighean, nor, indeed, was he killed in Leinster, nor Munster, nor Connacht nor Meath – in none of the kingdoms save in Ulster did he meet his death."

The old poet looked outraged. In spite of the way the stranger had entered the feasting hall, vanity had claimed the poet again. "Sorrow will overtake you, stranger, for now I shall include you in my curse for the contradiction which you have placed on me."

The stranger smiled softly. "I do not think your curse will trouble me, poet," he said quietly.

Mongán interrupted hastily. "Proof positive is needed."

The stranger continued to smile. "Was I not summoned for that purpose?" he asked. "I will tell you a story. I was a member of the army of Fionn Mac Cumhaill. I was of the Fianna."

Dallán Forgaill intervened with a laugh. "Fionn lived hundreds of years ago! What boastful story is this?"

"Hear me out!" the stranger calmly ordered. "Fionn and our army were campaigning in distant high-hilled Alba, when news reached us of how Fothad Airgtheach had killed his brother and set himself up as High King. Fionn was angry and he led the army back to Éireann. In the valley of the River Ollarba" (which is now the River Larne in Co. Antrim) "the Fianna and the warriors of Fothad Airgtheach engaged in battle.

"When the fight was at its fiercest and the blood was flowing on both sides, I saw Fothad Airgtheach standing at the base of a sloping hill, watching to see how the battle went. I found the shelter of a rock and, taking a stand behind it, I aimed carefully with my spear. It passed through him and its head embedded itself into the soil."

The stranger held out his spear, the one without a head. "This is the spear, for I was not able to dig out the head during the battle but only retrieved this handle. If you go to that green hill outside this fortress, you will find the granite rock from whence I cast my spear and you will find the spear-head still embedded in the soil. Nearby you will find a small cairn where Fothad Airgtheach is buried. It stands a little to the east of where the spear-head is embedded. Underneath the cairn is a stone coffin holding the remains of Fothad Airgtheach; and in it are also his bracelets of silver and his *muintorc*, his hero's golden necklace. And on the cairn, in Ogham script, it is written who lies there."

"What does the inscription say, stranger?" asked Mongán, impressed.

"It is written thus: 'Fothad Airgtheach is here, who was killed in battle by Caoilte of the Fianna'. We of the Fianna buried him, just as I have described, and it was by us that his funeral obsequies were performed."

At this, Dallán Forgaill let out a bark of cynical laughter.

"Do you claim, then, that you are Caoilte? Do you claim that you are hundreds of years old, for Caoilte was the great warrior of the Fianna and kinsman to Fionn Mac Cumhaill himself? By what marvel do you claim to have survived these centuries?"

The tall warrior turned on him in sorrow. "I have not survived. Nor can any man outlive the earthly bounds. But heroes' souls are reborn in the Otherworld, where we may sit in the hall of heroes. I have returned from the House of Donn. Why have I returned? Because we of the Fianna ever loved the truth. From the vales of the Otherworld, we sit and watch the mountains and valleys of Éireann as through a mist; we are glad in its joys and sorrowful in its grief. When doubt arises as to the past in which we were nurtured, our hearts ache.

"So sorrowful we were at the distress of the queen, Breothighearn, and the helplessness of the king, Mongán, who could not prove what he knew to be true, that the Mother Goddess relented and granted me a mortal body to return with these words of counsel and knowledge to those we left behind. At dawn, do you go and seek the cairn of Fothad Airgtheach and all shall be found as I have said. The mouth of Caoilte Mac Ronán knows nothing of falsehoods and vain boasting. The rallying call of the Fianna was – 'The Truth against the World.' Be it so!"

With that, the stranger was suddenly no longer in their midst. He had vanished like a puff of smoke.

The following morning Mongán, with his queen, a sulking Dallán Forgaill, and his entire court, left the fortress and went to the green hill, as they had been told to do. The first thing they saw was the stone rock where Caoilte had cast his spear. Then they saw the spot where Fothad Airgtheach had fallen and dug down to find an ancient spear-head. Then, a short way to the east, they found a cairn above a stone coffin and on the cairn were the words carved in Ogham, exactly as the shade of Caoilte had described them.

"Well, poet?" demanded the king, pointing to the inscription.

But Dallán Forgaill had already left the company and set off south to his own country.

Mongán and Breothighearn went back to their fortress, rejoicing with their subjects that the curse of the poet had been lifted from them.

It is recorded that this was not the first nor the last time that Dallán Forgaill had abused his office as Chief Poet. It is told that Dallán Forgaill went to Aodh Mac Duach, the king of Airghialla, and recited a poem in his praise. Then he demanded, as payment, the king's great silver shield, with gold inlay, which had, it was said, been wrought by Gobhan the smith-god.

Now the king was under a *geis*, a prohibition from the god, not to give the shield to any human. So King Aodh offered gold and silver from his own purse, but Dallán refused and threatened to curse him, as he had tried to curse Mongán, but Aodh stood firm and said he could not part with the shield as it was forbidden by the gods. So Dallán in his arrogance made his curse. But he had abused his art and the curse rebounded; the gods ensured that he lived only three days afterwards.

And of the grave of Fothad Airgtheach? Well, the hill is now called Ballyboley in the Valley of the Six Mile Water and there is still a cairn there, old and weather-worn. You cannot see now if there was Ogham carved on it or not, it is so old. The old folk thereabouts will tell you that it marks the "King of Ireland's Grave" and is a place where you must tread with reverence.

Mongán was fortunate, however, that the Fianna had heard his distress and that Caoilte was allowed back from the Otherworld to avert the poet's curse. Others have not always been so fortunate. So beware of causing the tempestuous anger of the poet to break forth. The poet's curse is a terrible thing.

7 *Cellachain of Cashel*

Caiseal Mumhan, the stone fort of Munster, which is now called Cashel in the county of Tipperary, is a great limestone rock rising from the plain some hundreds of feet, which dominates the surrounding countryside. It is a mystical place where, for twice a thousand years, the great dynasty of the Eóghanachta ruled Munster until the last regnant king, Donal IX MacCarthy Mór, passed from this earth in AD 1596 and the ancient kingdom fell to strangers, and these strangers finally drove the heirs of the Eóghanachta out of the land and into exile.

It was said that when the sons of Golamh, who was also called Míl Easpain, invaded Éireann and defeated the ancient gods and goddesses, the children of Danu, the Divine Waters, two sons of Golamh named Eber and Eremon decided to divide the land between them. To Eremon went the northern half of the island while to Eber Finn went the southern half, that is all the land from the River Boyne, south to the Wave of Cliodhna.

Now the kings of Mumhan, the land of Eber Finn, sought for a suitable capital, from which to rule the great kingdom, for many years. It had to be a high place, from where they might view their extensive kingdom and reach forth their hand to protect their people. Be it known that the very word *ríge*, meaning kingship, is the same as *ríge*, the act of reaching forth. There were many petty kings in the line of Eber and each petty king wanted the over-king of Mumhan to reside in his territory so they would have prestige.

There were two swineherds. One of them was Duirdriu,

who was swineherd to the King of Éile, while the other was Cuirirán, swineherd to the King of Múscraige. These territories were in Aurmuma, or Ormond, which simply means East Munster. The swineherds were tending their herds south along the river which rose in the kingdom of Éile, which was the Suir. They had left the course of the river and gone to where the great rock rose from the plain.

It was a great wooded country and it was said that the gods and goddesses of the Otherworld haunted the great rock and its plains. The Bodb Dearg, the son of the Dagda, who succeeded his father as the ruler of all the gods, had his palace in Munster and many women of the Otherworld married the rulers of the kingdom.

As they tended their herds by the rock, a great tiredness suddenly fell over Duirdriu and Cuirirán and they slept. It was an Otherworld sleep, for they slumbered for three days and three nights.

In their sleep they saw a vision. They saw the prince called Corc, son of Lugaidh, of the line of the Eóghanachta, and they heard voices blessing him and hailing him as the descendant of Eber the Fair, rightful ruler of all the Milesians. The voice proclaimed that the blessings Corc would have were without counting and such blessings were given to all who came to rule rightfully and in justice at Cashel.

When the two swineherds awakened, Duirdriu hastened back to his lord, who was Conall Mac Nenta Con, king of Éile. When he heard about the vision, Conall went immediately and laid claim to the land where this dream occurred, so that when the matter was reported to the prince Corc, son of Lugaidh, he would have to buy the land from Conall and Conall would obtain great prestige in having the High King of Mumhan reside on his land.

Meanwhile Cuirirán, the other swineherd, had gone straight to Lugaidh and told him about the prophecy concerning his son Corc. The old man was delighted that his seed, and his dynasty, would now be able to build a great capital and be blessed for as long as they ruled justly. So Lugaidh sent for his son Corc and told him he must go south to Cashel with Cuirirán.

Corc kindled a fire on the Rock of Cashel and solemnly laid claim to it in the name of the descendants of Eber. He sent Cuirirán to summon the under-kings of Munster and it was the king of Múscraige who came hastening first to Cashel for Cuirirán was his swineherd and so went to him before anyone else. And the king of Múscraige bowed his knee to Corc and demanded that all his line should be the first ever summoned to Cashel in time of need. This Corc said would be done.

When Conall Mac Nenta Con, king of Éile, was summoned to Cashel, he sent a messenger to Corc asking him arrogantly what profit there was in summoning him, the king of Éile, to Cashel, for it was already in his possession. He demanded to know why Corc had taken possession of Cashel without first asking his permission. Now the message came by Duirdriu. Cuirirán told Corc that Duirdriu had been with him when he had the vision and perhaps Duirdriu had reported the vision to Conall.

So when he had delivered the message, Cuirirán went up to Duirdriu as if he were an old friend and said: "You are tired from your journey. Come and drink with me, that you might be refreshed." So the swineherd of Éile drank strong ale and when the ale was upon him, he confessed to Cuirirán what he had done.

So Corc sent again to Conall of Éile to summon him to Cashel and to tell him, if he did not come, he must face Corc in a combat of truth. When Conall of Éile arrived, Corc had his carpenter, Mochta, take his axe and heat it in a fire of blackthorn. When the axe was red-hot, Corc asked that he draw it from the fire.

"Whoever speaks the truth is protected. Come here, Conall, and place your tongue on the blade of this axe. If this land was truly yours, then you will not be harmed. But if you have falsely claimed it to get tribute from me, then your tongue will be burnt."

Now Conall Mac Nenta Con, king of Éile, was a man who was brave in war but he knew that he could not stand against the gods. So truth was the victor in this contest. Conall Mac Nenta Con, king of Éile, made this prophecy: "Great my shame, true king of Mumhan. My sword will ever be in your service and, at the time of the greatest need for your seed, my seed will come to Cashel bearing poetry and sword, and both will be wrought in your cause."

That pleased Corc and he made a truce with Conall. Indeed, he made a truce with all the under-kings of Munster, except with Cass of Luimneach on the Shannon, who claimed that he was the rightful descendant of Eber Finn and should rule in Mumham. As everyone knew this to be false, they rejected Cass and his kind and had no dealings with them.

Cashel prospered and became the seat of Corc who, on the death of Lugaidh, became over-king of Mumhan and of all lesser kings and princes and chiefs. Even Duirdriu received a house at Raith na nIrlann by the lawns of Cashel, and seven *cumals*, an ivory-hilted sword, a shield, horses and many fine clothes and silver. Therefore the Uí Druidrenn became the stewards at Cashel.

Cashel was filled with even greater prosperity when the saintly Pádraig the Briton came, in the company of the holy Ailbe of Imleach, and baptised King Aonghus, son of Nad Fraích, on the Rock.

As the centuries went by, some of the petty kings became envious of the peace and prosperity of Cashel. They were stirred by the descendants of Cass, who were called the Dál gCais in northern Mumhan, which was called the kingdom of Thomond. Cass and his descendants still believed it was their right to rule in Mumhan. This dissension between the Dál gCais and the Eóghanachta pleased the other kingdoms of Eireann, because it weakened the might of Mumhan and the Eóghanachta. It also pleased the kings of Lochlann, who sent shiploads of warriors to help the Dál gCais. While pretending to be allies, Sitric of Lochlann arrived in Mumhan, and he started to carve out a kingdom for the men of Lochlann along its shores.

Mumhan was therefore rent with warfare and bloodshed and it was at that time when the King of Cashel, Lorcán Mac Coinligáin, was slain by the Dál gCais. The kingdom of Mumhan was without a king, since the death of Lorcán and the Eóghanachta had even been deprived of Cashel by

Sitric. The men of Lochlann had captured it and held it as a fortress, dominating all Mumhan.

So it was that Cennedig of the Dál gCais claimed that he should rule over Mumhan and he and his friends, the foreigners of Lochlann, laid a heavy burden on the kingdom. Cennedig sent out a summons to all the chiefs of the Eóghanachta to assemble at Glennamain. "You have been without a king of Mumhan too long. As I have more right than any other to claim the kingship, I do so. Every king and chieftain of the Eóghanachta must come to Glennamain and endorse my claim, according to the ancient law."

Now there was a princess of the Eóghanachta named Fidelma, whose husband had been the lord Buadachán, who was cousin to King Lorcán. Buadachán had fallen in combat against the warriors of Lochlann. He had left Fidelma with a son. This son was named Cellachain and the name meant "bright-headed", for he was handsome and yellow-haired. When he came to the age of choice, he was skilled in arms, in poetry and learning and, moreover, he became a man of wisdom.

When the Princess Fidelma heard Cennedig's claim, she said to her son, Cellachain: "You are of the *derbhfhine* of the Eóghanachta. You are of the generations entitled to claim the kingship. So let us go to Glennamain and challenge this upstart of the Dál gCais. You shall be king in Mumhan."

Cellachain smiled weakly. "Would not Cennedig have his men ready to counter my argument with their swords?"

"Go and find the surviving champions of Cashel, who are dispersed throughout the countryside," his mother advised him. "Bring them hither, so that they might accompany you to Glennamain."

Cellachain set out from Cashel to find those still loyal to the cause of the Eóghanachta and while he was away his mother, the princess of Cashel, also collected companies of warriors, and arms and supplies so that the Eóghanachta might become victorious over their enemies.

Then Cellachain returned and with him came Donnchadh, king of Múscraige who, by right, was the first to be summoned to Cashel's defence; then came Rígbaddán, whose name meant "royal poet", who was a descendent of Conall Mac Nenta Con, the former king of Éile; and lastly came Suilleabhán the Hawk-Eyed, who could trace his descent to the great king Oilioll Ollamh.

Now the Princess Fidelma set out to Glennamain, with her son and the champions of Cashel. However, the army they gathered remained outside the assembly place. It was Princess Fidelma who came before the assembly as they gathered to hear Cennedig's claims.

The Dál gCais lord stood before the assembly in arrogance.

"I am Cennedig son of Lorcán, descended from the seed of Nua Segamain. Did not my ancestor Toirrdelbach cut down the sacred Yew Tree at Imleach (Emly), thereby foretelling how we of the Dál gCais would one day cut down the power of the seed of Corc in Mumhan? Has this not come to pass? Now I am here wishing no more of bloodshed. I could take the crown of Mumhan with only my sword to say I was the rightful king. Yet I will not. Accept me willingly as king of Mumhan, and I will restore peace to this land."

One chieftain spoke up, and he was Brónach of the Sorrowful Countenance. "And will you ask Sitric, the king of the men of Lochlann, to depart in peace? Does not Sitric sit in splendour on the Rock of Cashel where the Eóghanachta should be, by right? And has Sitric's brother, Torna, been so assured of his right to remain here that he has married Mór, daughter of Donnchadh of Caem?"

Cennedig frowned. There was a truth in what Brónach said. For he knew that, having seized power with the aid of Sitric, he might find it difficult to dislodge Sitric and the men of Lochlann from demanding a share in the spoils of Mumhan.

"I shall indeed ask Sitric to depart in peace from this land," agreed Cennedig. "Before I do so, you must all agree that I may put my foot on the stone of destiny, so that it may roar its greeting to me as rightful king. If you agree that I may eat of the flesh of the sacred mare, so that the royal line may be continued, I shall ask Sitric to depart."

There was a muttering among the assembled chiefs and then a woman's voice rang out across the assembly place.

"If you touch the sacred stone of inauguration, it will scream out that you are a false king. If you bite into the flesh of the scared mare, you will vomit, for you are unworthy. You are a traitor king."

Fidelma, princess of the Eóghanachta, came forward to challenge Cennedig.

"Silence, woman!" roared Cennedig. "You have no right to speak here."

"Every right to speak. For I speak with the blood of the Eóghanachta!"

When Cennedig's warriors began to move forward, the chiefs rose up and surrounded her protectively.

"She has the right, Dál gCais," cried Brónach. "A right you would know, if you were an Eóghanacht."

Fidelma raised her chin and stared haughtily at Cennedig. "I repeat that you are a false king." She turned to the chieftains. "There is one here that bears rightful descent from the line of Corc and him you must choose as your king, if you would rid yourself of the jealousies of the Dál gCais and the foreigners of Lochlann."

"Name him!" cried one of the chieftains.

"Let us hear his claim!" yelled another.

The assembly of chiefs began to bang their swords on their shields. Then the Princess Fidelma called forth her son. Cellachain came, surrounded by the three champions of the Eóghanachta.

"State your claim!" roared the chiefs.

"I am Cellachain, son of Buadachán, son of Lachtnae, son of Artgal, son of Snédgus, son of Donngal, son of Fáelgus, son of Nad Fraích, son of Colgú who was king at Cashel and of the line of Corc."

"That is better qualification than Cennedig," agreed Brónach. "The line that has been recited is that of a true heir of Eóghan Mór!"

Then, with stamping feet and the banging of their swords on their shields, the chiefs called for Cellachain to be their king.

In anger, Cennedig of the Dál gCais had departed from the assembly with his men, saying that the Dál gCais would not recognise any Eóghanachta king.

Now, the stone of destiny on which Cellachain had to set his foot was at Cashel and nothing could be done until the men of Lochlann were dislodged from the Rock.

As for the flesh of the mare, a young girl brought the bowl to Prince Cellachain and held it out to him.

Cellachain took it and held it up so that all might see. Then he chanted ancient words:

I invoke the land of Mumhan,
The land of Mór Mumhan, goddess of this place.
I invoke Mumhan of the fertile shores.
I invoke Mumhan of the fruit strewn valleys.
I invoke Mumhan of the protective mountains,
Nurturing is the rivers and lake,
Fruiting and pleasing are the fields.

Land of Eber the Fair,
Bequeathed to him by the three goddesses
Banba, Fodhla and Éire of the sweet passions,
I invoke this land of Mumhan
In the name of the descendants of Corc.
In the name of the descendants of Eoghan.

And the battle cries of the Eóghanachta rang out and swords beat on shields.

Then Cellachain lowered his eyes and they met the sea-green eyes of the young girl attending him. He saw that she was beautiful and even Áine, goddess of love, nor Deirdriu, nor Étain, nor Gráinne could have such beauty to compare to hers. Then she lowered her eyes and was lost among the cheering chieftains.

Time was given over to a great festival, whereby Cellachain was given the royal diadem of Mumhan. He swore allegiance to safeguard the people of his kingdom. His great champions came before him – Donnchadh, Suilleabhán and Rígbaddán.

Then Cellachain said to his people that the time had come to chase out the Dál gCais from their great fortress at Luimneach, the bare area, which is now called Limerick. Once they had defeated the Dál gCais, they could turn on

Cashel and drive the men of Lochlann forth. As they made ready for battle, Cellachain turned to his mother, the Princess Fidelma, and asked quietly:

"That young girl who brought me the sacred flesh of the mare . . . I would know her name, mother."

Fidelma smiled knowingly. "A wise thing to know her name, o king, my son. For she is Mór, daughter of Aedh Mac Eochaidh, of the line of Bressal. It has been prophesied that his progeny will be kings at Cashel."

"Who prophesied that?" demanded her son.

"None other than Áine, the goddess of love and divine patroness of the Eóghanachta. She made this promise to the fiery Aedh, father of Mór. As Mór is his only child, whoever marries her will sire the kings at Cashel."

So Cellachain went to battle with a happy spirit. For he was in love with Mór and swore he would make her his queen.

He had his warriors march on Luimneach where the Dál gCais king, Cennedig, stood ready with his men. The Eóghanacht were in good voice. They sang a war song as they marched towards the city.

Come to Luimneach of the ships,
O Eóghanachta of the noble deeds!
Around the gentle Cellachain
To Luimneach of the riveted stones.

Defend your own beloved land,
O descendants of Oilill Olomh,
In the battle of Luimneach of the swift ships
You will set the Eóghnachta free.
You will bring peace to Cashel of the Plain.

Defend Cellachain valiantly, defend the
King of Cashel, noblest of your host.
Do not leave the battle van to him
Against the usurpers and foreigners
But wielding sword and shield
Defend our liberties.

The élite warriors bands of Cellachain advanced, surrounding their king, their standards flying, their phalanx of blue blades, golden collars and shields flashing. Against them stood the hordes of Dál gCais and with them, shield to shield, stood the men of Lochlann, led by Sitric's warlord, Amhlaibh and his sons, Morann and Magnus. They were all battle-hardened champions of the long ships of Lochlann. With their mail coats and long shields, the warriors of Lochlann took a heavy toll on the linen-tunic champions of the Eóghanachta.

Blood stained the field and the sky became grey-red as the men of Mumhan staggered under the blows of the battle-axes. The day could have been lost, but the bright-headed Cellachain rode down on the enemy with his great sword, and when he reached Amhlaibh of the Hosts, he split the champion of Lochlann's war-bonnet with one wild stroke, leaving the man bare-headed on the field.

A great shout went up among the Eóghanachta and Suilleabhán, with one hundred and fifty brave champions, cleaved a path to their Cellachain's side. Suilleabhán smote Amhlaibh dead. Then Morann and Magnus in battle fury came at him and there stood Donnchadh and Rígbaddán, shield and sword in their path.

Rígbaddán gave a shout of joy and, sword beating on his shield, he composed the following song:

Alas, for the heads without bodies,
For whom dark tears will be shed.
It was no folly to fight
Even if the heads of the race of Eóghan fall
Like leaves in autumn.

I have a head to whom women gave love.
It is the head of a brave son of the kings of Éile.
Sad should it be if this head be exhibited
On a Dál gCais pole of victory.
So a powerful slaughter there must be,
For my head I mean to keep!

Morann and Magnus fell and Cennedig fled to Cashel to seek safety with Sitric and his Lochlann men.

Meanwhile, on the gentle banks of the Suir, the lovely Mór, the tall one, daughter of Aedh of the fire, was bathing. She had offered up prayers that Cellachain of Cashel might return safely, for to him she had secretly given her heart and determined to be his joyous queen, in victory or in defeat.

She heard the soft meowing of a cat. When she peered up from her bathing, she saw a large black cat sitting on the bank.

"Who do you love, Mór?" the cat asked.

Frowning, the girl swam to the side of the bank and looked at the animal. "A strange thing is it that you, a cat, should be talking and asking such a question," she observed.

"A stranger thing if I do not, for I am Áine, your guardian in love."

Then Mór smiled warmly. "If that is so, it is a strange disguise you have put on yourself. And if so, then I may tell you it is the bright-headed one that I love."

"Then you shall be at his side, in victory or in his defeat."

Along the broad river, there came a boat and the cat leapt onto its prow. "If you truly love Cellachain of Cashel, climb in and follow me."

So Mór, full of happiness, went into the boat with the cat. A great mist came down and the boat sped away along the River Suir. And the cat began to sing:

> Peace on Sitric of the hundred curved shields.
> The Hostage of Mumhan will give him victory.
> Sitric will carry her over the sea,
> Eastwards to Lochlann of the dark ships.

In spite of herself, Mór found herself lulled into sleep at the strange words of the song and when she awakened she was in a small room in the tallest tower of the great castle on the Rock of Cashel.

A tall red-bearded giant of a warrior stood at the door.

"No fear on you, maiden," he grunted. "I am Sitric, king of the men of Lochlann, and you are now my prisoner."

Mór raised a hand to her head, for the sleep had been created by sorcery and she felt the effect of it still.

"Where is the black cat . . . ?" she began, trying to recall what had happened to her.

Sitric bellowed with laughter. He stood aside and a thin, evil-looking fellow came through the door. He was clad all in black and a great black cloak dropped from his shoulders. She blinked for, in a moment, the thin dark man had turned into a purring cat, rubbing itself at the feet of Sitric Red-beard.

"Cellachain of the yellow hair will not be your lover, lady," the cat purred. "At least, not in this world."

Then the cat grew back into the shape of a man again.

Sitric grinned at the girl.

"My brother, Torna, is a man of magic. We shall hold Cashel against the Eóghanachta. For you will be our hostage against their attack."

Then Sitric and his evil magician of a brother departed, leaving Mór to despair.

When Cellachain and his men heard word that the men of Lochlann were now preparing a last defence in the fortress of Cashel, they hastened back from Luimneach. Rígbaddán chanted as they hurried forward:

Tell the descendants of Eóghan,
Tell the heroic host,
That their high king is being carried
On victorious battlefields
Until he comes to Lochlann's standards.

Let the descendants of warlike Eóghan
Accompany him, an army without reproach,
From the Wave of Cliodhna
To Cashel's walls,
Fighting for their valiant king.

It was the Princess Fidelma who greeted her son with the terrible news that Mór, daughter of Aedh, had been taken prisoner by Sitric and was held as hostage.

"We must attack, my lord," cried stout Suilleabhán, the hawk-eyed.

"Yet if we attack, Sitric will lose his steel in the fairest maiden in the kingdom," protested Rígbaddán.

So Cellachain and his army sat down before the great grey walls of Cashel and searched their minds to find a plan as to what they could do.

Then Rígbaddán, the royal poet, went to Cellachain's tent and said: "I know the *sídh* of Drom Collchoille where the goddess Áine dwells."

Cellachain looked at the poet-warrior in curiosity.

"No one knows that," he said dismissively. "And if anyone did, what good would it avail us?"

"It is a closely guarded secret among poets," agreed Rígbaddán. "But good it might well do, for isn't it Áine who is the guardian of the Eóghanachta, and isn't it Áine who foretold that Mór would be mother to a dynasty of kings in Cashel?"

Now Áine, the love goddess, was the daughter of Mannánan Mac Lir, the ocean god. The story went that Oilill Olomh, son of Eóghan Mór, was lying asleep on a hill, the hill of Drom Collchoille, the hill of the ridge of the hazel wood, when he heard sweet music and wakened to find a maiden playing on a bronze instrument. And Oilill seduced this maiden and she begat the generations of the Eóghanachta and she was none other than the goddess of love herself. Thus Áine was patroness not only of love but of the Eóghanachta.

Cellachain saw the point and laid a hand on the shoulder of his comrade.

"Then go there, Rígbaddán. Find out if she will intercede for us."

So Rígbaddán went to the ridge of the hazel wood, which is also called Cnoc Áine, that is today called Knockainey in Co. Limerick and, it being the Midsummer Day, he sat down and concentrated his thoughts. Then he sang his best love poem, hoping to stir the interest of the goddess so that she would emerge from her dwelling under the hill.

There are arrows that murder sleep
Remembering you, my love;
Thinking of nights we spent together
Recalling our intimate secrets.

There are arrows that murder sleep,
Sharp points of love recalled,
The sweet music of a lover's tongue
Lost in the cold night air.

Suddenly, Rígbaddán realized there was someone standing at his side.

"What do you seek here, young man?" asked a low melodious voice.

Rígbaddán looked up and was shocked to see no one but an old beggar-woman looking kindly at him.

He told her that he was trying to summon Áine and why he was doing so.

"Go back to Cellachain," instructed the old woman, "and tell him on the morning of the third day from now, he may go to the gate of Cashel and knock on it with his sword-hilt three times. The door will be opened and he and his men may go inside. Mór shall not be harmed."

So Rígbaddán hurried back to Cellachain with this news.

Alone in her tower, Mór wiped the tears from her eyes and looked down on the encamped army of her lover as it gathered around the Rock. She knew that the reason why the war horns did not sound, nor swords beat on the shields, was that Sitric had said that her life would be forfeited. She was in a black despair, wondering what she could do to help Cellachain overcome the enemies of Mumhan.

She sang softly, to keep up her spirits, but the words that came forth were sad ones:

Long as a month, each day,
Long as a year, each month,
The music of the forest
Would be pleasant to me now.
Oh, why, is he separated from me by a wall?

A roaring fire
Has dissolved this head of mine.
Without him, I cannot live.

Then the door opened and an old woman hobbled in.

"If you are a maidservant in Sitric's house, I want none of you," Mór told her immediately.

The old woman chuckled. It was a curious, melodious chuckle and not really that of an old woman at all.

"I am thinking that you have no liking for Sitric?"

"Nor any man of Lochlann," avowed Mór. "I am of the Eóghanachta."

"Ah, but do you tell me right?"

"You have no reason to doubt my word. But if you do, it will not make it any the less the truth."

"True for you," the old woman agreed. "Yes, you do have the Eóghanachta sureness in you."

Mór tossed her head in annoyance. "Be about your business, old woman, and leave me to my sorrow."

"Your sorrow being that you are separated from your lover, Cellachain?"

Mór blushed but stuck out her chin defiantly. "Never my lover. Would that it be true. I saw him only once and gave him my heart. But . . ." she shrugged, "he never promised me more than a glance."

"Then you are a foolish child. Much may be read in a single glance. On such things are battles fought and won, or lost. And is it not written that you shall bear forth a line of Eóghanachta kings?"

Mór was startled as to how the old woman would know this.

"That was once foretold by the goddess Áine to my father, Aedh, when he visited Cnoc Áine."

"Indeed."

Then the old woman sang softly:

"Mór will be her name and Great will be her fortune,
She shall love the Bright-Headed son of Valour,
The daughter of Fire shall triumph and bear the
Raven-chosen king

A line of great sons who shall rule the Rock until a
woman of Red Hair,
Shall come against them
And she being of the kingdom of Britons."

"How do you know the prophecy?" demanded Mór.

The old woman shook her head sadly.

At that moment the door opened and in came Torna the Magician.

"What are you doing here, woman?" he frowned, catching sight of the old one.

"I am returning gift for gift," she replied.

"What gift has the girl given you, that you must return a gift?"

"She has given me the gift of generations of Eóghanachta," smiled the old one.

With a cry, showing that he recognised her as an enemy, Torna sprang forward, drawing his knife but the old woman dissolved into a black cat and leapt from his grasp. Torna, using his magic power, turned himself into a black cat so that there was no difference between them and jumped at the other. Then the first black cat turned into a giant black raven.

To and fro, shape-changing, the two creatures sped around the room, so that it made Mór dizzy as she attempted to keep track as to who was who.

Soon exhaustion overcame the contestants.

The magician and the old woman paused in their human forms.

"A truce," cried Torna. "And a proposition."

"What proposition is that?" demanded the old woman.

"It is unseemly for the likes of us to be fighting over this girl," Torna said. "Let us resolve the matter in a more gentle form."

"What form have you in mind, wizard of Lochlann?"

"Let us shape-change and change to a similar form and see if the girl can choose between us. If she is able to discern the difference, then, on my honour, she shall be released."

The old woman turned to Mór.

"It is for you to approve the conditions, Mór, daughter of Aedh."

With little enthusiasm, but realizing it was the only hope she had of getting out of Sitric's prison, Mór reluctantly agreed.

"Remember, your choice is for Cellachain of the bright head and does not my name also mean 'brightness'?"

Then, while Mór watched breathlessly, the old woman and Torna the wizard began to shape-change so rapidly, moving quickly around the room, that she grew dizzy again trying to keep track of who they were and where they were.

Then, when she had shut her eyes to prevent the dizziness overtaking her, she sat back on the edge of the bed and said:

"No more, no more. The changes have made me so dizzy that I cannot look upon you any more."

"We have stopped," replied a voice.

Mór looked up.

Before her sat two black cats, so identical she had no way of telling which was which.

"You may choose between us," came the old woman's voice from one cat.

"But be assured, nothing is easy," came the same old woman's voice from the other.

Mór was disappointed for she had hoped, in that moment, to have chosen the old woman. But both cats were the same.

"Come, don't take all day," said one of the cats.

Mór stared from one to another. Then she pursed her lips.

"I will choose. You are the old woman," she cried pointing to one of the cats. She did so because that cat's eyes shone more brightly than those of the other cat, and the old woman had told her that her name meant "brightness".

In a flash, the old woman was back. Mór had chosen correctly. She turned to find the evil wizard, Torna, running towards her with a knife upheld in his hand. Before she could scream, the old woman was a great raven and its claws descended into the face of the wizard. He cried loudly and went reeling backwards, dropping his knife on the floor.

Then the old woman was back and, before Mór had time to

adjust to her, a young and radiantly beautiful woman stood in her place.

"Take my hand, Mór," she said sweetly, "and trust in me, for I am Áine, protectoress of all who love truly."

There seemed to be a bright light and Mór blinked. When she opened her eyes, she was standing near a tent. Even as she looked on, the handsome, fair-haired figure of Cellachain came out. His surprise was replaced by a look of wondrous rejoicing.

He simply held out his hands to her. No words needed to be said between them.

It happened on the third morning that Cellachain went to the gates of Cashel and struck the door three times with the hilt of his sword. The door shuddered and swung open. In marched the warriors of the Eóghanachta, to reclaim their treasured castle and seat of the kingdom of Mumhan.

So the kingdom of Mumhan was wrested back from the hands of the men of Lochlann and so the Dál gCais went quietly back to Thomond. Cennedig promised to keep the peace with Cashel and this he did. Torna died of his magical confrontation, for there is no action that does not demand a counter-action. And Sitric set sail in his longships back to Lochlann's shores.

So did the fortunes of the Eóghanachta rise up once again and Cellachain and Mór gave birth to many sons. As it had been foretold, so it came to be.

Isle of Man (Ellan Vannin)

The Isle of Man: Preface

Until the eighteenth century, it is generally thought that most Manx folklore was transmitted orally. However, I would argue that, prior to the end of the sixteenth century, the evidence, fragmentary as it is, points to the fact that those islanders who were literate in their language would turn to Irish texts.

There certainly exists a poem in praise of the Manx King, Raghnal I (1187–1226), by an unknown poet, where the language is identified as Middle Irish. We also have the interesting case of Archbishop Aodh Mac Cathmhaoil (1571–1626), appointed Primate of All Ireland. Although he was born in Co. Down, it is recorded that he was sent to the Isle of Man when he was about thirteen years old "to obtain . . . the education that was denied him at home". We are told that he distinguished himself at his Manx school and remained as a teacher on the Island until he was twenty-six years old.

Now Mac Cathmhaoil's poems and prose, seen as part of the Ulster literary ethos, are still highly regarded and his works, such as *Scathán Shacramuinte na h-Aithridhe* (The Mirror of Penance), were published in Louvain in the early seventeenth century.

Most printing in Irish was carried out on the Continent during this time, as the language was being systematically repressed in Ireland. Other Irish writers, such as Tuathal Ó hUiginn (d.1450) had lived and worked on the Island. This, I believe, indicates that a standard literary Gaelic was being used.

When a distinctive Manx literature began to emerge, the similarities of theme and personality were easily observed. *Mannánan Beg, Mac Y Leirr, ny slane coontey yeh Ellan Vannin* was written down by John Kelly in 1770. This translates as "Little Mannánan, Son of Leirr, or an account of the Isle of Man". This is the earliest surviving tale of the ocean god, after whom the Island is said to have been named. Scholars analysing the text of this poem believe that it was first composed in the early sixteenth century, for it describes an event in 1504.

Even the stories of Fionn Mac Cumhaill and Ossian, the great Irish heroes, were told in the Island. *Fin as Oshin* was written down by Reverend Philip Moore in 1789. This was transcribed by Moore from the recitation of an old Manx woman and incorporated "King Orry" (the Manx king Godred Crovan – 1079–1095) into the Fenian saga.

Most of the Manx stories retold in this volume are mainly drawn from oral traditions and they have interesting echoes in tales found in both Ireland, particularly in Donegal, and in Scotland. *Island of the Ocean God* relates to the hagiography of St Maughold, who appears in the stories of St Patrick as Mac Cuill and Mac Goill.

Y Chadee, in a variant form, was first recorded by W. Ralf Hall Caine's *Annals of the Magic Isle*, Cecil Palmer, 1926. Ralf was the brother of the famous Manx novelist Thomas Hall Caine, to whom the Irishman, Bram Stoker, dedicated his novel *Dracula* (1897) for he was known as "Little Tommy" to his Manx-speaking family – i.e. "Hommy Beg". "Y Chadee" is the Manx name for the botanical plant *Anaphilis margaritacea*, which is known as "pearly everlasting", and it seems a curious transposition in the story for the name of the young woman.

The Ben-Varrey (The Mermaid) seems to be a Manx version of a tale which appears both in the Western Isles of Scotland and in Ireland and Brittany, and seems a favourite among Celtic story-tellers. This was passed on to me by Douglas Fargher. Another story he first introduced to me was *The Lossyr-ny-Keylley*, which is a goldfinch. This certainly has similarities with several stories found in Ireland.

Poagey Liaur jeh Caillagh is actually a Manx version of a Donegal tale of nearly the same title, *The Old Hag's Long Leather Bag*. But the Manx bag is not a long one. Seumas MacManus picked up the Donegal version in his *Donegal Fairy Stories* collection in 1900. The saga of *Gilaspick Qualtrough* has moments that are reflective of *Barny O'Rierdon, the Navigator*, collected in Samuel Lover's *Legends and Stories of Ireland* (1831). But Gilaspick is altogether a different character from Barny!

Most of these versions I noted down from various sources during my visits to the Island.

I first visited the Isle of Man in 1964, when the late Douglas C. Fargher, the compiler of *Fargher's English-Manx Dictionary*, 1979, introduced me to some of the tales. He also introduced me to Mona Douglas, who had been Alfred P. Graves' secretary. Graves was the father of Robert Graves and an assiduous collector of Irish folktales. Mona Douglas, in turn, was a leading exponent of the Manx language and its culture and also a collector of its folktales.

In the 1960s there was a great deal of activity on the Island in tracking down the cultural heritage, at a period when the last native speakers of the language were dying out. The last acknowledged native speaker was Ned Maddrell, who died on December 27, 1974, and is buried in his native Rushen. But, of course, a language is not snuffed out in such a fashion and many inhabitants of the island are still fluent speakers of the language.

However, many texts in Manx were published prior to that time: such as the stories of Neddy Beg Hom Ruy (Edward Faragher of Cregneash – 1831–1908), which were lodged in the Manx National Museum. Some stories were already printed in the early 1950s, due to the efforts of Arthur S. B. Davies of the Cardiff Board of Celtic Studies. These were *Skeaalyn Cheeil-Chiolllee* (1952) and *Juan Doo Shiauilteyr as Daa Skeeal Elley* (1954).

A study on Manx folklore had been published by A. W. Moore as *The Folklore of the Isle of Man*, back in 1891. However, no popular volume of Manx tales, along the lines found in other Celtic countries, was to be found. So, to some extent, Manx legends tend not to have the same "high profile" as those of other Celtic countries. Things altered somewhat when the Celtic scholar, Dr George Broderick, a Manxman himself, directed *Ny Kirree Fo Naightey* (The Sheep Under the Snow) for Foillan Films, showing what could be done in bringing Manx to people's attention.

I also spent six weeks on the Island in 1988 researching and polishing up some of the tales included here. My thanks for advice and information must go to Leslie Quirk, who was raised by his Manx-speaking grandparents at the age of three and became as near "a native speaker" as anyone can get. At the time, he was the warden of Thie ny Gaelgey, the Manx Language Centre, in the former St Jude's Schoolhouse. I also enjoyed the warm hospitality of Mrs Joyce Fargher, Douglas Fargher's widow. Douglas had been of so much help over the years. Dr George Broderick, Adrian Pilgrim, and Dr Brian Stowell were among many other Manx enthusiasts who have helped make my research tasks on the Island into a pleasant occupation.

8 Island of the Ocean God

Mac Cuill, which means "son of the hazel", was, in fact, the son of the great god of eloquence and literacy, Ogma. He had so named his son, for the hazel is a mystical tree, and Ogma used it to signify the third letter of the alphabet which he had devised. And indeed, Mac Cuill was the third son of Ogma, for his brothers were Mac Gréine, "son of the sun", and Mac Cécht, "son of the plough". The three brothers were married to three sisters; Mac Gréine was married to the goddess Éire, while Mac Cécht was married to her sister Fótla and Mac Cuill was married to the youngest sister, named Banba.

There came a time when the gods themselves fell from grace, when the sons of Míl conquered them. And it was said that Mac Gréine was slain by the great Druid Amairgen; that Mac Cécht met his end from the sword of Eremon; and that Mac Cuill was slain by the spear of Eber.

And when the gods were defeated by the sons of Míl, the wives of Mac Gréine, Mac Cécht and Mac Cuill – Éire, Fótla and Banba – went to greet the conquerors of the land of Inisfáil, the Island of Destiny.

"Welcome, warriors," cried Éire. "To you who have come from afar, this island shall henceforth belong, and from the setting to the rising sun there is no better land. And your race will be the most perfect the world has ever seen."

Amairgen the Druid asked her what she wanted in reward for this blessing.

"That you name this country after me," replied Éire. But

her sisters chimed in that the country should be named after them. So Amairgen promised that Éire would be the principal name for the country, while the poets of Míl would also hail the land by the names of Fótla and Banba. So it has been until this day.

Now the sons of Ogma were gods, and therefore "The Ever-Living Ones". They could not die completely and so their souls were passed on through the aeons. And in the rebirths of Mac Cuill, he began to lament the lost days of power, of the days he had been happy with Banba. He grew bitter and resentful with each rebirth until he was reborn as a petty thief in the kingdom of Ulaidh, which is one of the five provincial kingdoms of Éire. Each province was called *cúige* or a fifth, and the five made up the whole, and the whole, one and indivisible, was governed by the Ard-Rígh, or High King. There was no better thief in all Ulaidh than Mac Cuill, and he became the terror of the land. His deeds came to the ears of the High King himself and he sent his personal Brehon, or judge, named Dubhtach, to the provincial king of Ulaidh, saying: "Mac Cuill must be captured and punished."

Eventually, Mac Cuill the thief was caught, and he was taken before the High King's Brehon. And there was a tall, white-haired man standing by the Brehon's side. They called him by the name of an ancient god of war, which is Sucat.

"Why should we not kill you for your evil life, Mac Cuill?" demanded Dubhtach the Brehon.

Now Mac Cuill was full of guile and he smiled.

"Kill me now, Brehon. I have reached my last rebirth on this earth. I cannot descend lower than a thief. I will have been wiped from the Brandubh board of this world."

Brandubh, which means "black raven", was a wooden board game, which many compare to the eastern game of chess.

"Yet," he added with evasive craft, "kill me now and there will be no hope of redemption, no hope of reparation for my sins. Spare me and perhaps there is still some goodness in my soul, whereby I might change my life for the better."

Now Mac Cuill spoke with irony, in mocking tones, but his words held some truth. The Brehon pondered and could reach no decision. Finally, it was Sucat who said: "The decision is not for us to make, for man is often flawed in his perceptions of his fellows. What is justice for one is injustice for another. So let us leave it to the Creator to decide. You will have the judgment of the sea."

Now the judgment of the sea can be a terrifying thing. But Mac Cuill, who had lived many lifetimes, was not afraid. And Sucat had the wrists of Mac Cuill bound in a chain of iron, which he fastened by a padlock with his own hand. And he flung the key into the waves of the sea, saying: "Loose not that chain until the key be found and brought to you." The Brehon then had Mac Cuill taken to a boat, which is called a curragh. The boat was without oars and without a sail, and no food nor drink was placed in it. This boat, containing Mac Cuill, was rowed several miles from the coast of Ulaidh and cast adrift. The fate of Mac Cuill was left to whichever way the winds and tides took him. Whoever found him could make a slave of him.

Now of all the ancient gods, one of the last to live upon the Earth with their ancient powers was Manánnan Mac Lir, the tempestuous god of the oceans, who, with his angry breath, could raise large white-crested waves that could wreck entire fleets of ships. At the time of the fall of the gods, Manánnan Mac Lir had retired to his favourite island, called Inis Falga, which lay between Inisfáil and the Isle of the Mighty. Eventually, that island became called after the great Manánnan and every Manxman is called, in his own tongue, Maninagh.

Now Manánnan, seeing the plight of Mac Cuill, reborn in a weak human body, was moved to compassion. He remembered the ancient times when he and Mac Cuill and the other Children of Danu had fought the evil Fomorii on the Plain of Towers to claim the Island of Destiny. So Manánnan breathed gently on the ship and sent a current which turned its bows towards his own mist-shrouded island of Inis Falga.

But even Manánnan's breath could not break the lock of the chain which bound Mac Cuill's wrists.

After several days, the little boat, without oars or sails, and with Mac Cuill more dead than alive, bumped against a rocky shore.

Now on the island there were living two wise men named Conindri and Romuil. Both had heard the words of the Son of God, and preached the new religion of love and forgiveness. They saw the half-dead Mac Cuill and realized that his crimes must be great for him to have been cast into the sea in such a fashion. Yet they took him from the boat and laid him in their own beds and nursed him until he recovered his wit and strength.

As Mac Cuill was recovering, Conindri and Romuil spoke to him of the Creator and His Son and the new religion of love and brotherhood. And as they spoke, they did their best to unfasten the chain about Mac Cuill's wrists. But they could not do so, no matter how they tried.

Mac Cuill laughed. "In a previous life, I was a god. As I was once, so will your new God and His Son become – cast out and forgotten, when they no longer serve the needs of the people."

"You are proud, Mac Cuill. Our Lord taught: 'Blessed are the poor in spirit, for theirs is the kingdom of heaven.' "

Mac Cuill laughed again. "If poverty of spirit is a virtue, then it does man little good. When men are poor in spirit, then the proud and haughty oppress them. When I was a god, men were true and determined in spirit and resisted oppression."

"But to him that smiteth thee on the one cheek, offer also the other."

Mac Cuill sneered. "He who courts oppression shares the crime. If that is the teaching, then you are inviting further injury at the hand of the oppressor and thief."

"Him that taketh away thy cloak, forbid not to take thy coat also. Give to every man that asketh of thee . . . Blessed be the poor, for theirs is the kingdom of heaven."

Mac Cuill chuckled deeply, shaking his head. "Now this new religion is ideal for a thief such as me. It tells people to accept with good grace when I rob them. The poor in spirit will not fight me. This is a good land and here I will prosper as a thief, if all believe as you do. I will set forth to find a smithy to break my chains asunder."

Mac Cuill set out and walked along the sea-shore, leaving

the wise good men, Conindri and Romuil, in sorrow behind him.

As he walked on the foreshore, he heard a gentle singing and around a headland of rocks he came across a beautiful woman. The spot was called Langness in the parish of Kirk Malew. The girl sang sweetly.

Come to our rich and starry caves
Our home amid the ocean waves;
Our coral caves are walled around
With richest gems in ocean found.
And crystal mirrors, clear and bright.
Reflecting all in magic light.

Mac Cuill stopped and gazed upon the beautiful sad face. It reminded him of the one whom he had loved so long ago – the face of his wife in a former life – of Banba.

"Who are you, young maiden?" he demanded.

The young girl started and looked upon Mac Cuill and her eyes lit up in a smile of happiness. "I am for you, son of the hazel," she said.

"That cannot be. Nothing is for me unless I steal it. I am a thief and will take what I want."

"I am Blaanid," went on the girl and, reaching down beside the rock on which she sat, she drew forth a basket filled with coral and precious stones and other fabulous metals garnered from the ocean bed. "You may have these, for we are all thieves now."

"I will not accept that which is given when it is my place to take," cried Mac Cuill in disgust. "But if you can break the chains on my wrists, I will accept your gifts."

Suddenly, Blaanid threw her arms around Mac Cuill and so surprised was he, and so great her strength, that she dragged him to the edge of the sea and plunged in. Though he struggled, she drew him downwards to the dwellings of the merfolk that lived beneath the waves. And Blaanid took Mac Cuill to a beautiful city under the sea.

It was a place of many towers and gilded minarets and stood in all magnificence. It was deep down, beyond the region of the fishes, where there was air which was strangely clear and the atmosphere serene. The streets were paved in coral and a shining kind of pebble which glittered like the sunbeams reflecting on glass. Streets and squares were on every side. Buildings were embossed with mother-of-pearl and shells of numerous colours and there were flashing crystals to decorate their walls.

But around the circle perimeter were countless wrecks of ships. Fearful wrecks, strewn on the slimy bottom, yet the city was protected from them. And among the wrecks, Mac Cuill saw the decomposing bodies of men, women and children. There were countless eyeless skeletons, all scattered and on which the fishes gnawed. And from the dead people's skulls, which worms and fish inhabited, there arose a fearful wailing sound. The noise was so penetrating that Mac Cuill had to stop his ears.

"What manner of place is this?" he gasped.

Blaanid smiled and pointed. He could see people moving through the streets. He gasped, for he recognised his brothers and the other Children of Danu.

"This is our home now, and this could be your home. For you wish to exist by what you steal. The gods and goddesses are only left with theft in this new world. We have built our city from the ships that we entice to our mist-shrouded island and wreck upon the rocks above. Each ship comes tumbling through the seas to our city and we may take from them great heaps of pearl, wedges of gold, inestimable stones, unvalued jewels . . . thus our city prospers."

Mac Cuill swallowed hard. "And the souls of the dead sailors? Look at the bodies of the dead, of the drowned women and the children! Do you not hear their cries?"

"They are but poor in spirit," Blaanid said. "We grow accustomed to their wailing and take what we must."

Mac Cuill grew sick in his soul. He stared into the face of Blaanid and he saw in it the face of Banba. "Is this what we are reduced to?" he whispered.

Where once the Children of Danu had bestrode the earth in goodness and strength of spirit, Mac Cuill realised they had descended to thieves who preyed on the spiritual tragedy of others.

"This is but a shadow-show of the choice you can make," replied Blaanid.

"If there are choices still, then I shall choose to be released from my purgatory," cried Mac Cuill. And he held out his chained wrists.

"Alas, wealth and prosperity can be yours, but we cannot unchain your wrists," replied Blaanid. "You may remain in the realm of the Ocean God as you are, or you may be reborn in the new religion and release your soul from its eternal bitterness. Here we have only illusions of the past."

With that, he found himself back on the headland of Langness in Kirk Malew.

He found himself staring at the grey seas and thought that he heard a whispering sound.

> Come to our rich and starry caves
> Our home amid the ocean waves . . .

Slowly he retraced his footsteps to where he had left Conindri and Romuil. They were standing as he had left them, for in earthly time he had not been long gone from their sight.

They smiled joyfully at his return.

"Tell me more about your God and his Son."

And so they taught him. And he came to believe with a passion and they called him Maccaldus, for that was the form of his name in the language of the new religion. So Maccaldus, who had been the foremost thief of Ulaidh, felt repentance for his past lives and Conindri and Romuil took him to a stream and poured water over his head and confirmed him in the new religion.

That evening, Conindri was cooking a fish that he had caught and he brought it to the table to divide between the three of them. As he cut open the fish, they saw a key in its belly and Mac Cuill recognised it as the same one with which Sucat had locked the chains about his wrist. When he told Conindri and Romuil, they were astounded.

"Sucat Mac Calphurn is the foremost preacher of our faith, which is why we call him Patricius – father of citizens."

Conindri immediately unlocked the chains and they fell at Mac Cuill's feet.

The very next day, Mac Cuill went out into the island of Inis Falga and began to preach the new religion. And he went up to the Lonan stone circle, near Baldrine, where he found the Druids, set in the ancient ways, about to sacrifice a human child. A stone altar had been heated by fire and it was proposed to throw the child upon it. As the child was being flung forward, Mac Cuill threw a phial of water that had been blessed by the saints and it landed on the stone before the child and split it asunder. And the child was not harmed.

Straightaway the Druids fled, but Mac Cuill called them back and he also called before him the King of Inis Falga and told them henceforth to worship in the new religion.

One chieftain refused, and this was GilColumb, whose name meant "servant of the dove". But he was named with irony, for he was no follower of the peaceful path. And this GilColumb and his three sons desired to kill Mac Cuill, and one night they slunk stealthily to the church which Mac Cuill had built. Mac Cuill and his followers, hearing that his enemies were approaching, guided his people into the subterranean caverns beneath his church.

With loud shrieks, GilColumb and his three sons, and his followers, burst into the church.

"Where are you departed?" yelled GilColumb in anger, finding no one there.

And Mac Cuill appeared before him with his pastoral staff. GilColumb's followers stepped back in awe.

"What have you against me, GilColumb? Why have I offended you, that you should attack my sanctuary with slaughter in mind?"

"Are you Mac Cuill, the former thief?" sneered GilColumb, braver than his band of men.

"I am Maccaldus, the bishop of this land," replied Mac Cuill solemnly. "I am the servant of Christ."

GilColumb laughed and raised his sword to smite him.

Mac Cuill, however, leant forward and tapped GilColumb

over the heart with his pastoral staff. The impious chieftain uttered an horrendous shriek and then his tongue clove to his mouth. After six hours, GilColumb died in agony and all those who lived on Inis Falga realised that Mac Cuill was the one chosen to bring them to the new religion.

Therefore, one evening, Manánnan Mac Lir himself appeared before Mac Cuill on the foreshore.

"So it has come to this," the old god said. "We who were young together on the Isle of Destiny are gods no longer. Bitterness and rebirth have brought you to the human state, where now you preach a new philosophy. Our journeys through life no longer converge nor even go in parallel direction. The people no longer need the gods of their forefathers and mothers."

Mac Cuill was sad. "There is no returning. This is the destiny of the world. No footsteps back."

Manánnan shook his head. "Perhaps I could have prevented this, had I not blown you to this island, which was my last refuge."

"But that was written in the book of destiny, Manánnan son of Lir. Even before Danu, the divine waters, first moistened this earth."

"People no longer believe in me and so I am reduced to a shadow and like a shadow I will be extinguished in the light of the new learning."

"Your spirit shall abide among the grey seas and the misty mountains of this island, for so long as one person remembers you," replied Mac Cuill.

"One person?" mused the ocean god. "Where would I find that one?"

"I shall remember you," replied Mac Cuill softly.

Henceforth, Inis Falga was known as Ellan Vannin, the Island of Manánnan Mac Lir, which today is still known by the shortened version of the Isle of Man. Mac Cuill himself was known first as Maccaldus and then as Maughold and it is as St Maughold that he is still venerated in the Island of the Ocean God.

9 *Y Chadee*

There were two handsome princes, sons of the ageing King of Ellan Vannin, and their names were Eshyn and Ny-Eshyn. Eshyn was the elder of the two. He was fair and upright like his father. He was also renowned as a brave warrior who was fearless in battle and just in his judgment. All the young women of Ellan Vannin admired Eshyn and many tried to attract his attention, fluttering their eyelids and blushing as he passed by. But Eshyn was a serious young man and not given to spending time flirting with young women. He believed in true love; that one day he would meet the woman he would spend the rest of his life with and, at that moment, he would know who it was.

His younger brother, Ny-Eshyn, while just as handsome, was of a weak character. He drank too much, had affairs with many women and gambled frequently. He was also of a jealous disposition. He was jealous of his elder brother, and his jealousy made him angry and brooding. His jealousy gnawed like a knife twisting in his stomach.

One evening, Ny-Eshyn was returning across the slopes of South Barrule, on whose peak was a castle. At the castle gate stood a wizened old man who had strange eyes, one blue and one green. They could look east and west and south, but never could they look towards the north.

"*Bannaghtyn*, Ny-Eshyn," the old man greeted in the language of the island. "*Cre'n-ash ta shiu?*"

"Who are you, who asks me how I am?" returned Ny-Eshyn with discourtesy.

"That is by the by," replied the old man. "What ails you? I am merely a friend to all who are troubled and who seek joy in this life."

"I hate my brother," snapped the prince. "He has everything that makes him happy in life but I have nothing."

"Is it so?" mused the old man. "There is a proverb in this land – *Cha nee eshyn ta red beg echey ta boght agh eshyn ta geearree ny smoo*. It is not he who has little that's poor, but he who desires more."

Ny-Eshyn scowled in anger. "How dare you quote proverbs at me, little man? I tell you that my life is made miserable by my brother."

The old man sighed and shrugged. "Well, that is not anything to fret about."

"Why so?" Ny-Eshyn was much irritated, and might well have struck the old man down, had he not been intrigued by the movements of the man's strange eyes and he remembered that it was said that the *ferrishyn*, or evil spirits, had that cast of eye. So he kept his temper in check.

"Because it is a problem that can be solved." And the old man reached down, for there was a basket at his feet, and picked up the wickerwork. "Here, inside this there is a snake. All you have to do is put the basket under his bed during the day and, by evening, he will become coarse-featured and ugly and women will turn from him and men will revile him."

"Will it be so?" demanded Ny-Eshyn eagerly.

"I do not lie," said the wizened creature firmly.

So Ny-Eshyn took the basket, hearing the snake hissing within it, and went home to his father's great castle at Doolish.

That night passed and at dawn, Prince Eshyn, who was a great hunter, rose and went out to seek the red deer on the slopes of Slieau Meayll. As soon as he heard his brother depart from the castle, Ny-Eshyn took his basket and the snake and went to his brother's room and placed it under the bed.

That evening, a strange apparition appeared at the gates of the castle at Doolish: a bent figure of a man, with coarse grey skin and a protruding nose like the beak of a bird. His eyes were crossed, his hair matted and he had a permanent dribble on his chin.

The warriors on guard frowned and looked at one another, for they did not recognize him, but they saw that he rode Prince Eshyn's favourite horse.

"Who are you who rides that horse?" demanded one of the warriors. "Where is our handsome prince who owns the steed?"

The stranger stared at the warrior and called him by name.

"Do you jest?" the ugly one demanded, in a strange grating voice, which the man did not recognize. "I am Prince Eshyn."

The guard burst out laughing.

"You are mad to think you can trick us. We know our prince too well."

Then one of the warriors, more reflective than the other, said: "If this ugly horror rides Eshyn's horse, it can only mean that he must have stolen it. If he has stolen it, it means that he has worsted Eshyn in a fight. The only way he could do that would be to murder him, for Eshyn is so great a warrior he would not allow his horse to be stolen while he was alive."

And so they raised an alarm.

Eshyn began to cry out for his father, the king, as he struggled with the palace guards.

"Father! Father! They are attacking your eldest son!"

But the old king came to the battlements and looked down. "I recognise you not, stranger!" He turned back into the castle.

Still Eshyn struggled. "Mother! Mother! They are attacking your eldest son!" cried Eshyn.

The queen came and gazed on him in disgust. "Drive this evil one away and find out what has happened to my dear son, Eshyn!" she ordered.

More guards began to converge on him and so the young prince, in the hideous guise, tugged at the reins of his steed and went galloping away.

He reached a stream and stopped for water to refresh himself after the strange experience at the gates of his own castle and, as he did so, he saw his reflection in the water.

He screamed at what he saw.

Now he knew why he had not been recognized at the castle.

His heart was heavy and he sent his horse, with a slap on the rump, back in the direction of the castle. It was not fitting for someone looking like he did to ride the horse of a prince. He turned his laggardly footsteps towards the valley that lies through Beinn-y-Phott and Snaefell and, after wandering a day and a night, he came to the deep black lake which lies in Druidale, under the shadow of the black mountain, Slieau Dhoo.

Here he sat down on a great granite stone and placed his head in his hands. He did not know what had caused his shape to change, nor did he know what he should do.

He heard a sound nearby and looked up.

Along the pathway by the grim dark lake, an old woman was coming along, staggering a little under the weight of a great heavy bundle of sticks which she carried on her crooked back. Every so often, she paused to gather a handful of sticks which had fallen from the bundle, but each time she did this, more sticks fell out. But she slowly managed to build up the great bundle, which was apparently so heavy that she was bent double beneath it.

"*Moghrey mie, venainstyr*," called Eshyn for, although he had troubles, he had always been a polite and sympathetic young man. These words meant: "Good morning, madam. Do you journey far with that bundle?"

The old woman stopped and pointed up Slieau Dhoo. "My cabin is up there, near the summit of the black mountain."

It was quite a climb, but Eshyn did not even consider the difficulty. "I will carry the bundle up there for you," he said and, without another word, he took the great bundle of sticks from the old woman and slung it on his own back. They started to climb up the steep path and as they did so, Eshyn sighed deeply.

"*Vel shiu ching*? Are you ill?" asked the old woman in concern. "Is it too heavy for you, my son?"

"Not too heavy; the heaviness is in my heart," replied Eshyn sadly.

"What is it that ails your heart, my son?"

As they climbed, Eshyn told her his story: or, at least, that part of it which he knew. By the time he had finished it, they had reached the little white stone cottage, with its face towards the sun and its back to the summit of the hill.

"Put down the sticks and come into my cottage. Rest awhile while I kindle a fire to warm us."

Eshyn shook his head. "I am a young man, old woman. It is you who should rest, while I kindle the fire."

He insisted that the old woman sit down while he prepared the fire and she told him, once it was alight, to place a small kettle on the flames and put some mackerel in to cook.

As he did this, she went to the window and gazed at the sky, for it was now cloudless night and the stars were out. She considered the patterns made by the stars carefully. Then she returned inside and took the fish from the kettle and placed them on the table with bread and newly churned butter.

"Eat and grow strong, young Eshyn," she told him. "You shall be as comely as you once were and as happy. You will, however, need all your strength. So eat and rest here until morning, and then I shall tell you how you may accomplish that."

So Eshyn ate and rested, drowsing fitfully in a corner by the fire.

In the morning the old woman came to him.

"*Vel shiu er chadley dy-mie?* Have you slept well?" she asked him.

"*Cha nee feer vie*. Not very well," he replied, for he was always a truthful youth.

"Have some tea; it will refresh you. Then you must be gone. You must walk across the hills to South Barrule. At the top of the mountain is a fairy fortress. At the entrance to the fortress, you will come across a wizened old man, with one eye blue and the other eye green. They are able to look east and west and south but cannot look at the north. He will greet you with these words: '*Bannaghtyn*, Eshyn! What ails you? I am a friend to all who are in trouble and who seek joy in this life.' You can tell him what ails you. But on no account accept his advice. Whatever he tells you to do, do the exact opposite. Do you understand?"

Eshyn shook his head. "I have no understanding of it but I will do exactly what you have told me to."

So Eshyn set off towards the bald peak of South Barrule. He came to the castle and at the gate he saw the wizened old man with his one eye blue and his other one green.

"*Bannaghtyn*, Eshyn! What ails you? I am a friend to all who are in trouble and who seek joy in this life."

Eshyn told the old man what troubled him.

"A sorrowful tale, indeed. Let me go into the castle to think on this matter. In the meantime, when I am gone, if the Benrein na Shee, the Queen of the Fairies, happens to pass, go and hide yourself. Do not try to stop her nor speak to her."

The wizened old man disappeared into his castle.

As the hour was now late, the stars now shone down on the mountain top and the moon came sneaking up over a distant hill. But the night-sky was full of clouds, dark ominous storm clouds and the light of the moon was hidden behind them. The night was very dark.

Standing there in the darkness, Eshyn suddenly saw a curious sight. There was a bright white pinprick of light bobbing up and down across the mountain. It came nearer and nearer. As it grew near, Eshyn saw a group of tiny sprites, fairy people, and in their middle was a beautiful young woman, dressed in a green cloak with her golden hair held in place by a silver circlet. On her left arm was a basket, out of which the bright light shone, so that everyone in her company was illuminated.

Now Eshyn remembered what the old woman had told him and so he decided to do exactly the opposite of the instruction given to him by the old man, for he now correctly presumed that this was the Benrein na Shee, the Queen of the Fairies and her entourage.

He stepped forward into the path of the fairies.

"Greetings, Queen of the Fairies," he called.

"Why do you stop me, Eshyn?" she demanded.

It was no surprise to him that the Queen of the Fairies would know his name. So Eshyn told his sorrowful tale.

"Can you tell me what I must do?" he asked when the tale was finished.

The Queen of the Fairies went forward and examined Eshyn's appearance.

"It is the *nieu-ny-aarnieu*," she observed. "It is a serpent's venom that has wrought this evil change in you. You can be returned to what you were, but to achieve that you must come along with me."

She led him from the slopes of South Barrule towards the western sea, and it seemed to Eshyn that they had journeyed only a short distance before they were crossing the sea. Eshyn was full of wonder, for the fairy host, and he in their midst, simply continued walking over the waves, as if they were solid ground. Then they came to a sea shore which Eshyn had never seen before, so alien and curious was it.

Along this sea shore were anchored an armada of ships: ships bearing many strange devices on their sails.

The fairy queen halted the group and placed a finger on her lips.

"*Cum dty hengey*!" she instructed in the language of Eshyn's people. "Keep quiet!"

Then she pointed to a ship approaching the shore. Her voice was no more than a mere whisper. "These are the people of Yn Shelgeyr Mooar, Orion the great hunter, light of the Otherworld."

"But . . . ?"

"*Bee dty host!*" she snapped again. "Keep quiet! Listen to me carefully. In that approaching ship is Y Chadee, the Everlasting Pearl, daughter of Yn Shelgeyr Mooar, the most beautiful princess beneath the skies of this world and the Otherworld. She is the only one able to restore you to your former self."

"How can that be . . . ?" began Eshyn.

"*Hysht*!" hissed the Fairy Queen for a third time. "Keep quiet! Y Chadee, the Everlasting Pearl, shall be your wife if you are strong and do not fear. The blood of the great Ocean God, Manannan Mac-y-Leirr, whose name has been given to your island and your kingdom, flows in your veins as well as the blood of the great kings of Ellan Vannin. You must follow your destiny."

She paused and, satisfied that he no longer raised any queries, she instructed him in what he must do.

"Firstly, you must enter the cave of heroes and seize the

Slatt yn Ree, the Sword of Orion, which you will know by the name Cliwe-ny-Sollys, the Sword of Light. Take it and hold fast to it, no matter what happens, and by that means you will win what you must win."

She paused a moment and when he made no comment she continued: "Secondly, you will find a pearl of great beauty; this is the symbol of Y Chadee, the Everlasting Pearl. You must seize it and never give it up.

"Thirdly, you will find a woman of surpassing beauty, who will offer herself to you in return for the treasures you will possess. Remember this; you must never be distracted and lured from your quest by any subtle device as may distract a man. Remember the proverb of your land – *Eshyn s'moo hayrys s'moo vee echey*. He who catches most will have most."

Having said that, she pointed down a cliff path to the sea shore. "That is your path and do not let any obstacle stand in your way."

Then she bent forward and blew into her basket and the light went out and she and all her fairy host vanished.

Eshyn hesitated but a moment and then proceeded along the path, descending the cliff, as the Fairy Queen had told him to. However, he found the path blocked by a gateway which was sealed by tall iron bars. Well, if he was not to let anything obstruct his path, there was only one thing to do. He seized the bars and pulled and tugged with all his might until he twisted them right and left and made an opening large enough to squeeze through.

As soon as he found himself through the bars, he was in a great cave filled with warriors drinking and gaming with dice. Music filled the air. He noticed that the drink was taken from a central large cauldron of silver. Then, at the far end of the cave, there hung a great sword of blazing gold and silver. It shone with an ethereal light.

"That must be the Sword of Light, Orion's Sword," he muttered.

Indeed, the Cliwe-ny-Sollys or Sword of Light, was the symbol of the sum of all knowledge and put to flight every ignorance.

He sighed. It looked so high up, hanging there, that he doubted that he could reach it.

He entered the cave boldly, ignoring the warriors. But they saw him and started to shout.

"Come and drink, come and play dice with us."

Eshyn shook his head.

"That I cannot. I have come only for the Cliwe-ny-Sollys!"

At that, they all started laughing.

"It is beyond your reach, as it is beyond our reach. A brave man you must be, if you risk the wrath of the Shelgeyr Mooar by attempting to steal his sword."

Another one of the merrymakers tapped Eshyn on the arm.

"We are here to see no one takes it. But it is such an easy task to defend the sword, so we are bored and spend our time in gambling and drinking, for there is nothing else to do."

Another said: "Today we enjoy life, for who knows the cares of tomorrow? Drink to the hour that is with us now, not to the hour that may never come."

They helped themselves liberally from the brew from the cauldron and they drank and played dice and drank yet again, until they drank themselves from merriment to stupor and from stupor into a deep, snoring, drunken sleep.

Now Eshyn had waited patiently all this time, for he could not see how he could act while these warriors were capable of harming him. But now that they were all in a drunken sleep, he saw how he could act.

He pushed the tables, at which the warriors had been gambling, and the chairs to the wall on which the sword hung. He thereby built himself a means of reaching the sword. Balancing carefully, he reached upwards and carefully took the great sword by the hilt.

At that moment, a large raven swooped through the cavern and started to sound an alarm.

At once the warriors were on their feet, with weapons drawn, and gone was their drunkenness.

They saw Eshyn standing with the great Cliwe-ny-Sollys – the Sword of Light – which made him invincible. They cursed him, but none would come near him, for whoever the blade touched was despatched to the Land Beyond, whether they were mortal or immortal.

Holding the weapon in both hands, ready to defend himself, Eshyn walked slowly from the cave, keeping an eye on the angry warriors.

From the cave he passed along a narrow tunnel and then he found himself in total darkness. He blinked and, when he opened his eyes, he found a light in the passage ahead of him. He moved to it and found himself peering down at a feasting hall below. This hall had no windows; neither was there entrance nor exit. The light in this strange room was supplied by some strange source which he could not discern. From where he stood, peering down into the hall, a rope provided the only means down and, apparently, the only means up again.

There was a great table in this hall, at which many warriors sat feasting. They were all obese and indolent, in spite of their warriors' garb. Along the sides of the hall were the discarded debris and bones of many a feast. Kegs of wine, bottles and other refuse from the table were piled there. But in the middle of the table, around which the warriors were seated, was an intricate candle-holder of gold and silver and, in the spot where the candle should be, Eshyn saw a pearl of great beauty. It was the pearl itself that was emanating the light.

"That must be the pearl that I am to obtain," Eshyn said to himself. "I will seize it, but there is only one way to get down to it."

So he sheathed the Sword of Light, took the rope in both hands, and slid down into the hall. He was greeted with laughter and good humour by the warriors, who offered him the hero's seat of honour at the head of the table and said: "Eat and enjoy yourself, for we must eat today in case we cannot eat tomorrow."

Eshyn shook his head. "I have come for the pearl," he said simply.

They roared with laughter.

"That cannot be. We sit here guarding it and serve no other purpose. But we are bored and the only thing to do is to feast. No one can escape with it anyway, for they have to climb up the rope down which it is so easy to slide but impossible to climb up."

"Why is that?" demanded Eshyn.

"No harm to tell you. Once you take the pearl, this room is plunged into darkness and you will never be able to find the rope's end."

So Eshyn decided to sit down and wait. The men crammed their mouths with meat and cakes to the point of repletion. Gradually, one by one, they fell asleep in their seats, their heads on the table top, snoring away.

Then it was that Eshyn rose and reached forward and picked up the pearl, whose light immediately went out. Eshyn, however, had kept one hand on the rope and he quickly thrust the pearl into his tunic pocket and swung upwards.

At that moment, a great raven flapped through the darkness, crying out a warning.

Then the warriors were on their feet, swords out, peering into the darkness. But as it was so dark, several of them injured themselves, attacking each other. Those who realized that Eshyn had escaped up the rope were too fat to follow him and stood at the bottom, staring up into the darkness, cursing him.

Eshyn climbed back into the passageway and moved on.

He exited the passage almost immediately and came upon a great palace on the sea shore which was blazing with light. The path led into this sumptuous building and so he went in. There was a great hall hung with tapestries and lit with magnificent candelabra, with musicians playing gentle tunes. Fountains splashed lazily. Bowls of fruit stood on tables and by these there were couches on the mosaic floors. There were seven young maidens lying on the couches who greeted him with shouts of joy.

"Stay, stay with us. We have much to offer you, young prince. Make love with us."

Eshyn shook his head.

"Come, exchange that heavy sword and that dull grey pearl for our warmth and generosity," they insisted. "We can make you happier than all the women you have ever known."

Eshyn was exhausted by his adventures and sorely tempted to lay down on the nearest couch and be pampered by the beautiful maidens. But he remembered the advice he had been given and pressed on, exiting the castle by another way.

He was then on the sandy sea shore again and there was the prow of a great ship before him, beached in the shadows. On the shore before it stood the figure of a maiden.

He almost fell at her feet, so tired he was.

As he peered up he saw that she was a lady of great beauty. He had never seen her like before, and straightaway he gave his heart to her.

"You are a gallant hero," she said, staring sweetly down at him. "Indeed, you are a brave man who has overcome every hardship to obtain the Sword of Light and the Everlasting Pearl. Who are you?"

"I am Eshyn, lady; son of the king of Ellan Vannin."

"And what is your mission in the Otherworld?"

"I came to recover my lost manhood, my handsome figure, so that I could retrieve my place at the court of my father."

She threw back her white swan-like neck and laughed gently. "You are handsome, Eshyn, and you have not lost your manhood. Will you give the Sword of Light to me and the Everlasting Pearl?"

Eshyn was sorely tempted to hand them over, but he shook his head. "As sad as it makes me, I cannot. For I must retain these until the Queen of the Fairies tells me otherwise."

"You will not give them up to spend your time with me? I can show you such pleasures that you have never dreamed of."

"Who are you, lady?" he demanded.

"I am the daughter of Orion. I am Y Chadee, the Everlasting Pearl."

"Although he who holds should be ready to give, I cannot do so, even to you. I must hold these objects, for my joy in the world is more important than the shadows of this one."

The young maiden looked at him sadly. "Then rest a moment, Eshyn, and you will be returned to the world as you want."

He closed his eyes a moment and then . . . he found the sun

shining down on him and he was snuggled in the corner of the old woman's cottage, back on Slieau Dhoo.

The old woman was bending over him.

"*Vel shiu aslaynt*?" she was asking with anxiety on her brow, thinking him ill.

He sat up, shaking his head.

"*Cha vel, booise da Jee*," he replied. "No, thank God! But, old woman, where have I been?"

She smiled thinly. "Where do you think you have been, my son?"

He frowned and examined himself. The first thing he noticed was that he was wearing the great sword, the Cliwe-ny-Sollys. Then he put his hand in his pocket and found the Everlasting Pearl.

"Then it was no dream, but all was true?"

"It is true for you, my son."

At once Eshyn was sad. "Oh, then I have broken my heart. I found someone who was more lovely than any on this earth, a wonderful vision, a beautiful lady. I had the chance to exchange these baubles for her love."

"Then you would have been condemned to your ugly body and a fleeting moment in the Otherworld."

"Rather that for one more smile from her grey eyes." He frowned. "She smiled on me, as ugly as I am."

"Ugly?" The old woman handed him a mirror.

He stared at himself. There he was, as tall and handsome as ever he had been.

"How can I repay you, old woman?" he said, almost dancing with delight.

"By returning to your father's castle at Doolish and showing him these things. Then, before all the court, casting them into the dark seas beneath the castle wall. You must do this, in spite of all their pleading and offers."

"It makes me sad to bring the sword and the pearl back from the Otherworld, to bring them here when I might have exchanged them for the tender love of Y Chadee. But you have returned me to my normal state and I will do as you ask."

So Eshyn bade farewell to the old woman and set off for Doolish.

This time, the guards recognised him and greeted him with shouts of joy and bore him on their shoulders into the king's chamber. The king and queen, who had been lamenting their eldest son as dead, were beside themselves with happiness. The only angry face in the castle belonged to Ny-Eshyn, who stood sulking behind the throne, cursing the wizened old man for failing him in that his brother had returned, alive and well, and as handsome as ever.

"Where were you?" demanded the old king.

"Adventuring in the Otherworld," replied Eshyn.

"How can this be?" demanded the old king.

"Indeed, show us proof of it!" challenged Ny-Eshyn, the jealous brother. "Otherwise, I shall not believe it."

Eshyn drew the great Sword of Light, the Cliwe-ny-Sollys. "This is the Sword of Orion," he exclaimed.

He held it up so that it sparkled and shone with an ethereal light and caused the king and his courtiers to intake their breath with wonder.

Then Eshyn took out the pearl. As he held it up, it suddenly started to shine so that the king and his courtiers blinked their eyes and averted their gaze.

"This is the Everlasting Pearl."

"What great treasures you have brought back," breathed the king. "Truly, you are a son of mine."

"I have another task to fulfil," Eshyn said. "Come with me."

He led them all to the battlements. "I am here, returned to my normal shape, alive and well, and unharmed, because of a promise. That promise I mean to keep."

He went to the battlements and peered down into the angry, tempestuous seas striking the rocks below.

"Wait! Do not be hasty!" cried his father, the king. "Those things are of great earthly value."

All the courtiers, his own mother and his brother, Ny-Eshyn, cried for him to stop and offered him all manner of things if he did not part with those Otherworld treasures.

But Eshyn took the sword and the pearl and threw them over the battlements, sending them spinning into the white-crested waves below.

Perhaps it was a trick of the light, perhaps not; perhaps it was only Eshyn that saw it. It seemed that a great hand of Manánnan Mac y Leirr, the Ocean God himself, came out of the waves and caught the sword and the pearl before sinking into the Otherworld depths.

Eshyn turned back. "My promise is thus fulfilled."

"You have thrown away a great treasure," muttered his brother.

"Not so. I have gathered a treasure, for I have garnered wisdom in great store. I hold that wisdom is the greatest treasure."

The old king nodded reflectively. "He who holds, must first have discovered. He who has discovered, must first have sought. He who has sought, must first have braved all impediments. Thus did the Druids teach."

In anger, Ny-Eshyn stormed from the court.

At that moment, there was the sound of a horn outside the castle, and a gold and silver carriage was driven into the courtyard. The king and his queen and Eshyn went down to see who had arrived.

A beautiful girl stepped down.

Eshyn's heart missed a beat.

"Y Chadee!" he gasped.

Indeed, the beautiful daughter of Orion descended and stood smiling at him.

"You did not settle for treasures from the Otherworld but rather for love in this one. For the love of a man such as you, I am destined in this world and the Otherworld, for there are no barriers to true love."

There was great rejoicing in the royal house of Ellan Vannin when Eshyn announced his marriage to the Everlasting Pearl.

Yet of Ny-Eshyn, no one saw him after he left the Castle of Doolish. Some said that he had ridden off in the direction of South Barrule, cursing the *ferrishyn*, or the fairy folk, which, they reflected, was not a wise thing to do. Certainly, he was never seen again in all the length and breadth of Ellan Vannin.

10 The Ben-Varrey

Some say that the Sheading of Rushen, at the south end of Ellan Vannin, comes from the Manx word *roisen*, which means a little peninsula. The earliest mention of the name Rushen is to be found entered against the year AD 1134 in the great book known as *Chronicon Regum Manniae et Insularum* (or, in English, the Chronicles of the Kings of Man and the Islands). Rushen is partially a peninsula, bordered to the west and south by the boundless oceans. There were three parishes in the sheading : Kirk Christ, Kirk Arbory and Kirk Malew.

Now Kirk Christ is close to the sea, and all the people of Kirk Christ know the sea and its humours. They know each rock by name. Here is Creg na Neen, "rock of the girls", where two girls were caught by the tide here and drowned, being found the next morning locked together by their entangled tresses. There is Ghaw Cham, the winding creek. And there is Ghaw Jeeragh which means "the straight creek". There is Kione ny Goggyn, the headland of clefts or chasms. There is Purt ny Ding, which is from the Manx Port of Creg Ineen ny Dane which, in English, means "the rock of the Dane's daughter"; legend has it that a Danish ship was wrecked and the captain's daughter was saved after clinging to this rock.

Oh yes; every rock around this wild and turbulent coastline is named and remembered.

It can be a wild, desolate coastline, where strange things are seen but never spoken of. But the story of the Ben Varrey is told on wild dark nights before the glowing embers, after the children are safely to bed. It is a story told in hushed tones, lest the howling tempest carry the words to the deeps of the dark sea outside.

In Keeill Moirrey, there lived a fisherman named Odo Paden. He was a poor man, not making much of a living. The inclement weather did not help. One day he was casting his nets along Creg ny Scarroo, which is the rock of the cormorants, and feeling pretty desperate, for there were fishes all around him and yet not one in the bottom of his boat.

Suddenly, he found a *ben-varrey* perched on his gunwale, smiling at him enticingly. For a moment he thought he was seeing a vision and he crossed himself and shut his eyes. When he looked up again, she was still there. Now a *ben-varrey* is a sea-maiden, what some may call a mermaid.

"*Moghrey mie*, Odo Paden," she greeted. "Are you not getting enough fish?"

Odo Paden sighed.

"True enough. At this rate I shall be starving by tomorrow."

"Would you reward me if I filled your net?" asked the sea-maiden.

"I would if I had the means to do so, but I have not."

"Are you married, Odo Paden?" asked the mermaid.

"I am not, nor have I wish to be."

The mermaid pouted. "Well, if you will marry me, I will ensure that your nets are filled and that you are well provided for."

Odo Paden sniffed in disapproval. "What use are you to me as a wife? You cannot even leave the ocean."

"That I could, but only if you follow my advice. If you promise to marry me, I shall fill your nets and among the fish I will put there will be a great silver sea trout. Now you must not eat that fish but, tomorrow morning, you will take it to Port Erin and demand a golden sovereign for it. Then come back and throw the golden sovereign into the sea by Creg ny Baih."

Now Creg ny Baih was a dangerous place and means, appropriately enough, the "rock of drowning".

Odo Paden thought for a moment and found the only alternative was to remain without fish and starve.

So he promised to obey the *ben-varrey* and marry her. Before long, the nets were filled and, sure enough, there was a big silver trout there. He laid this aside when he returned home that night. The next morning he took it in a sack to Port Erin. There was a fair in Port Erin that day, and he dallied there. At the fair, he came across a great crowd gathered in a circle around a showman.

Odo Paden peered forward to see what the attraction was.

Seated on the ground was a *kayt*, which is a cat, with a fiddle and before him was a *lugh*, which is a mouse, and a *deyll*, which is a cockroach. The cat struck up a tune on his fiddle and the mouse and the cockroach began to dance. It was such a lively tune that everyone around began to clap and jig and dance and laugh and call to one another. Never was there such a happy crowd.

Then the showman picked up the cat and its fiddle, the mouse and the cockroach and put them in a sack. He held out his hat and soon it was filled with a clinking mass of coins.

The man, seeing Odo Paden watching him, gave him a friendly grin.

"You seem a sensitive sort of fellow. How would you like to buy my animals and make yourself a fortune? I've made enough money and want to retire from this life."

"I would like it fine," Odo Paden agreed, for he was still counting up how much the man must have made from the exhibition. "But I have no money."

"It's not money that I am after. Didn't I say that I have enough? But I really fancy a dish of fine sea trout. I would give the cat and the fiddle for a fish like that."

Immediately, Odo Paden showed him his sack with the sea trout.

"Now we can make a bargain. I will give you the cat and the fiddle for that sea trout."

Odo Paden frowned, remembering his promise to the *ben-varrey*.

"I rather wanted a gold sovereign for it."

"Gold sovereigns a-plenty you'll be getting, if you have the cat and the fiddle. And if you come here again tomorrow with another trout, I will exchange the mouse for it and for a third such trout, you may have the cockroach."

Now Odo Paden had never had money in his life and thought the bargain too great to miss; so he took the cat and the fiddle back to his cottage by the sea in Keeill Moirrey.

That night, the rain lashed on the windows of his cottage, rain mingled with salt sea spray and, when he went to look out on the inclement weather, Odo Paden saw the mermaid waiting on the shore outside.

"Odo Paden, you have sold the sea trout but where is the gold sovereign you promised me?" she called sternly.

"I did better than get you a sovereign," replied Odo Paden.

"What is better than I being able to get ashore?"

He held up the cat and the fiddle and set them on the window ledge and told it to play.

The mermaid looked on with a sad smile. "It is amusing, Odo Paden. How does it help me to the shore or get you with a full net?"

"Give me another silver sea trout and you shall see," replied the fisherman, firmly believing he was acting for the best.

Early the next morning, Odo Paden found another silver trout on his doorstep and hurried off to Port Erin. There was still a fair there and he saw a crowd gathered in a circle. There was the showman and on the ground before him were the mouse and the cockroach. The showman started to whistle and the mouse and the cockroach began to dance.

Soon all the crowd were whistling and dancing and laughing and never were people more happy in their lives. At the end of the dance, the man picked up the mouse and the cockroach and put them in a sack and then held out his cap and the coins flooded into it. He looked up and saw Odo Paden and grinned.

"So you are back again?" he asked.

"Back with a fine silver sea trout," agreed Odo Paden.

"In that case, I will exchange the mouse for your trout. Just think of the money you could make with the cat, the fiddle and the mouse."

Odo Paden had rather wanted the cockroach as well but he settled for the mouse.

"If you have a third silver sea trout you may have the cockroach," said the showman, repeating his promise of the previous day.

Off went Odo back to Keeill Moirrey and into his cottage.

That night, another storm lashed at his cottage windows, mingling the sea spray and rain together. Odo Paden went to the window and there, on the seashore, was the mermaid waiting patiently.

"Where is the golden sovereign which you promised, Odo Paden?" demanded the mermaid, sternly.

"I have something better," replied the fisherman.

"What is better than I being able to get ashore?"

Odo Paden took out the mouse and set it on the windowsill and then he placed the cat and the fiddle by it and told them to strike up a tune. The mouse raised itself on its hind legs and began to dance while the cat scraped away on the fiddle.

The mermaid smiled with sadness. "Fine that is, but where is my gold sovereign?" she demanded. "How am I to get to shore?"

"Give me a third silver sea trout and I'll be back tomorrow night," Odo Paden assured her.

Next morning, sure enough, there was a silver sea trout outside his cottage and into the sack it went and he went off to Port Erin. The fair was still on, and there he saw a circle of people gathered. He pushed his way through the crowd and saw the showman with the cockroach on the ground. The man whistled and the cockroach began to dance and everyone around began to dance. They laughed and smiled and never were there people so happy.

Then the showman put the cockroach in his sack and passed round his hat and, in a blink of an eye, it was filled with coins. The man spotted Odo Paden and smiled a greeting.

"Back again, Odo Paden?"

"And with another fine silver sea trout," assured the fisherman.

"Well, it is a great bargain that you have. You have

released me from the cares and worries of the fair. Yet I have made several fortunes and wish you the same."

So Odo Paden went back to Keeill Moirrey.

That night, the storm blew hard against his cottage, with the rain mixing with the salt sea spray. He went to the window and there was the mermaid waiting patiently by the sea shore.

"Where is my golden sovereign, Odo Paden? Three days are now passed and now the sovereign must be thrown into the sea at Creg y Baih."

"Now I have something which is far better than a golden sovereign," the fisherman assured her.

"Better than I being able to come ashore?" demanded the mermaid.

"Better indeed. This will keep me in riches for all my life."

He set the mouse and cockroach and the cat and the fiddle on the windowsill and told them to play.

They did so and the mermaid smiled sadly at the sight. When they had stopped and Odo Paden had put them away in the sack again, she turned her sorrowful countenance to him.

"Ah, Odo Paden, I could have come ashore and loved and taken care of you. I am a king's daughter who has to remain enchanted in the form of a mermaid until the wicked Druid, Drogh-Yantagh, the evil-doer, who did this, be paid a golden sovereign at the 'rock of drowning' or be made to laugh. As the Druid hasn't laughed in seven long years, small chance of that. Now you have thrown away my only chance of escaping from the sea and obtaining happiness."

Hearing this, Odo Paden grew sad, for he found that he was much attracted to the beautiful mermaid. He felt contrite at what he had done. He had been thinking merely of ways of raising money and not of the mermaid's welfare. When he raised his head to apologise to her, he found she had vanished in the darkness of the storm.

That night he made up his mind.

He took his belongings and set out for Creg y Baih. By that fearsome rock, he anchored his boat and shouted: "Drogh-Yantagh! If you hear me, come and show your face to me.

Don't be afraid. I am only a poor fisherman here to make you laugh!"

At once there was a tremendous sound, as if the rocks were cracking asunder and there, sitting atop Creg y Baih, was a tall, thin, dark man with flashing black eyes.

"I am not afraid of you, little man." His voice resounded like thunder. "You will have cause to regret your presumptuousness, when I feed your body to the denizens of the deep."

"No need for that," replied Odo Paden. "I am here to make you laugh."

"Laugh, is it? I have not laughed these seven years. No humour in this world do I see. Many have tried and failed and all their bodies are now particles in the deep, tasty morsels for the creatures who dwell there."

"I am prepared to try."

"Then you must obtain from me three great laughs. If you do, you shall be at liberty."

"I am at liberty now," replied Odo Paden candidly. "If I do this, I want something else from you."

"And what is that?" thundered the amazed wizard.

"I want the freedom of the mermaid who is the king's daughter. She must be free and allowed to come back and dwell on land."

Drogh-Yantagh scratched his chin thoughtfully.

"Now this is an amusing matter. It appeals to me."

He clicked his fingers and no sooner had he done so than the beautiful mermaid was sitting by his side on the "rock of drowning".

Her eyes widened with amazement when she saw Odo Paden. "What are you doing here?" she whispered. "Do you not know that you are in grave danger?"

"I have come to fulfil my word, lady," replied Odo Paden. "I mean to buy your freedom."

Drogh-Yantagh smiled; in fact, he almost laughed at the humour of it. "Of that we shall see. Commence! Try to make me laugh."

Odo Paden opened his sack and placed the cat with its fiddle, the mouse and cockroach together on the deck of his boat. Then he told them to strike up.

So surprised was Drogh-Yantagh at this exhibition that he gave a big laugh of delight.

"That is the first laugh," observed Odo Paden.

The cat continued to play while the mouse and cockroach stood on their hind legs and began to jig. Drogh-Yantagh pressed his lips together but when the jig ended and he saw the mouse bow to the cockroach, and the cockroach curtsy to the mouse, he could not hold back another bellow of laughter.

"That is the second laugh," observed Odo Paden.

Now they set up another dance and, try as they might, the Druid's face remained as graven as stone. Odo Paden was beginning to lose heart and the mermaid sighed sadly.

Then it was that the mouse came to their help, for it pirouetted on one foot and its long tail whipped round and struck the cockroach, who fell backward and upset the cat, who dropped its fiddle on the head of the mouse, who was knocked out.

Drogh-Yantagh laughed with the tears rolling down his sallow cheeks.

"That, I believe, is the third laugh," observed Odo Paden.

Immediately the Druid was angry at having laughed, but a bargain was a bargain.

The mermaid suddenly had long, beautiful legs and stepped lightly down into Odo Paden's boat. She was so beautiful that she took Odo's breath away.

When Drogh Yantagh saw her gazing on the fisherman with eyes of love, he grew even more angry.

"Bah! If you hadn't tricked me with that cat, mouse and cockroach . . ."

As he said this, the Creg y Baih suddenly split open, revealing a great fiery furnace in the middle and into it Drogh-Yantagh fell. Now the reason is plain, as all Manx fishermen know. There are certain words that it is forbidden to say when at sea. Among them is the word for cat, *kayt*, for every good Manxman will say, instead, "*screeberey*"; and among the forbidden words is the word *lugh*, for mouse, for every good Manxman will say, instead, "lonnag"; and the third word not to be spoken at sea was *deyll*, for cockroach, for every good Manxman will say, instead, "*kerog*". So when the old Druid said the three forbidden words in the middle of the sea, he was claimed by the infernal powers.

No sooner did the old Druid get swallowed by the rock than it closed up again and retained its craggy, cold appearance.

At the very same time, the cat, the mouse and the cockroach suddenly turned into an old fiddler, a young man and a girl. They thanked Odo Paden for saving them and turning them back into their real forms. It seemed that the evil Druid, Drogh-Yantagh, had turned them into the forms of the creatures because he disliked their music. While he could change their forms, he could not stop their gift to make music and dance. All three swore eternal friendship to Odo Paden and promised to dance at his wedding.

Indeed, they did. For the princess took Odo Paden, the poor fisherman, back to her father's castle. Great was the old king's joy to see his daughter return from the briny deep, where he had considered her dead, and he showered Odo Paden with great riches, made him chancellor and blessed his marriage to his daughter. And Odo Paden, the poor fisherman, eventually became one of the greatest princes of Ellan Vannin.

Yet people in Kirk Christ will tell this story only in hushed tones. When they put to sea, they will do their best to avoid the "rock of drowning", even though they know that lobsters and crabs may be found nearby and that the best fish runs lie close to the rock. They will avoid the rock, for it is thought to be a gateway to the Otherworld, where the infernal powers await and are ready to scoop up the souls of any fisherman who breaks the taboo by inadvertently using the proscribed words.

11 *Poagey Liaur jeh Caillagh*

In the parish of Kirk Lonan, above Laxey Glen, there is a wood where there is a spot called Towl Creg y Vuggane – which means "the Buggane's hole". A *buggane* is a frightful creature given to playing mischievous tricks on humankind. It is said that, if you kneel by the hole and listen carefully, you will hear a strange wailing sound coming up out of the ground.

Well, it happened long ago, before Kirk Lonan was a parish even, that Callan MacKerron died, leaving a widow and three fine young girls. Callan had been a frugal sort of man all his life and, when he passed on, he left his family well provided for. Indeed, he left them a long leather bag filled with gold coins so Iney, Callan's widow, wanted for little. She kept the bag of coins under a hearth-stone in front of the kitchen fire.

Not long after Callan's death, however, there came a *caillagh*, an old woman, knocking on the door and begging for her supper. Iney MacKerron did not like the look of the old hag, but it was unlucky to turn a beggar away, and so she invited her into the kitchen and gave her a bowl of soup. Then she remembered she had an old shawl, patched but still wearable, which the old woman might be able to use, as the weather was growing chill. So she left the old woman in the kitchen and went to fetch the shawl.

When she returned, the old woman was nowhere to be found and the dish of soup was growing cold on the table. Iney MacKerron gave a cry as her eye fell on the kitchen hearth, for the hearth-stone had been lifted and the space underneath was empty.

Lonan was searched from one end to the other but there was never a sign of the old hag who had stolen the long leather bag of gold. From this day forth, poor Iney MacKerron and her three daughters had to struggle to keep body and soul together. They were desperately poor and often needed the charity of their neighbours. Nevertheless, Iney determined to bring her daughters up and give them what education she could.

Her daughters were named Calybrid, Calyphony and Calyvorra.

One day Calybrid, the eldest, said to her mother: "Mother, I am all grown up now. Shame on me for being at home and doing nothing to help you or myself in life."

"It's true for you," sighed Iney MacKerron.

"It being so," replied Calybrid, "bake me a *soddag* and I will set off to seek my fortune."

So her mother baked the *soddag*, which was an oat cake.

"Now you can have the whole," said Iney, "without a blessing. But to have a blessing, I will have to remove a piece."

Calybrid decided to take the whole of the *soddag* without a blessing, for she felt it might be a long time before she might find food again.

So Calybrid took her *soddag* and set off to seek her fortune, telling her mother and her sisters that if she was not back within a year and a day, they were to assume that she was succeeding in making her fortune.

So off she went and the passing of time found her in the woods above Laxey Glen. There she came on a strange house and found a *caillagh* dwelling in it.

"Whither are you off to?" demanded the hag.

"To earn my way in the world," replied Calybrid.

"So you are looking for work?"

"Indeed, I am."

"I need a maid to look after me; to wash and dress me; to clean my cottage and sweep my hearth."

Calybrid was delighted by the prospect.

"There is one thing, however, that you must never do," the

hag told her. "When you clean my hearth, you must never peer up the chimney."

Now Calybrid thought that this was an odd request but agreed to it. It was no concern of hers why the old woman was eccentric about her chimney, but it did spark off some curiosity in her.

Well, the next day, Calybrid rose and washed and dressed the old woman and the hag went out. Then Calybrid cleaned the cottage and swept the hearth. Now as she was doing so, she thought it would be no harm to take one quick peek up the chimney. What did she see there but her mother's own long leather bag of gold? Calybrid reached out and took it down and then started back for home as fast as she could.

As she hurried homewards, she passed a horse in a field and the horse called to her: "Rub me down, young girl, for I haven't been rubbed these seven years!" But Calybrid was in such a hurry that she ignored the beast.

Then she passed a sheep covered in a mass of wool. "Shear me, shear me, young girl, for I haven't had my fleece trimmed these seven years!" But Calybrid was in such a hurry that she ignored the beast.

As she hurried on she came across a goat on an ancient tether. "Change my tether, change my tether, young girl, for I haven't had it changed these seven years." But Calybrid was in such a hurry to return home, she ignored the beast.

Then along the road she passed a lime-kiln. The kiln cried out: "Clean me, clean me, young girl. I haven't been cleaned these seven years!" But Calybrid was in such a hurry to return home, she scowled at the kiln and passed by.

Then she saw a cow, heavy with milk. "Milk me, milk me, young girl, for I haven't been milked these seven years." But Calybrid was in such a hurry to return home that she ignored the beast.

By this time, Calybrid was so tired hurrying, that she saw a mill and thought she would rest there for a while. The mill cried out: "Turn me, turn me, young girl. I haven't been turned these seven years!"

But Calybrid, tired, went into the mill and lay down on a sack of flour and was soon fast asleep.

Now the *caillagh* had returned home and found that the cottage was empty. The girl was gone. She ran to the chimney and peered up. When she saw the long leather bag had gone, she fell into a great rage and began to run in the direction Calybrid had taken.

When she met the horse she called: "Horse of mine, did you see a young girl with a long leather bag pass this way?"

"I did so," agreed the horse. "She passed in that direction, not long since."

On she ran until she saw the sheep. "Sheep of mine, did you see a young girl with a long leather bag pass this way?"

"I did so," agreed the sheep. "She passed in that direction, not long since."

Then the old woman met the goat: "Goat of mine, did you see a young girl with a long leather bag pass this way?"

"I did so," agreed the goat. "She passed in that direction, not long since."

The old woman came to the lime-kiln. "Lime-kiln, did you see a girl with a long leather bag pass this way?"

"I did so," agreed the kiln. "She passed in that direction, not long since."

Then she came to the cow. "Cow, did you see a girl with a long leather bag pass this way?"

"I did so," agreed the cow. "She passed in that direction, not long since."

Finally, the old woman came to the mill. "Mill, did you see a girl with a long leather bag pass this way?"

"She did not pass here, but is sleeping inside on a flour-sack," replied the mill.

The old woman lifted the latch of the mill door and took out a hazel wand and tapped the sleeping Calybrid on the shoulder. The unfortunate girl was immediately turned into stone and the old woman retrieved the long leather bag.

A year and a day passed and Iney MacKerron's second eldest daughter, Calyphony, said to her mother: "Calybrid is not home. She must be making a great fortune. Shame on me for sitting here doing nothing to help you or myself. Bake me a *soddag*, mother, and I will be off to seek my fortune."

Iney MacKerron baked the *soddag*, which is an oat cake.

"You may have the whole and go without my blessing, or I must take a piece and give you a blessing for the journey."

Calyphony said that she would take the whole *soddag* and be off, for she did not know when she might get food again. She added that if she was not back in a year and a day, it would mean that she was doing well in life and making her fortune. Then off she went.

After a while, she came to a wooded glen and found a strange cottage with an old woman waiting outside the door.

"Whither are you off to, young girl?" she wheezed.

"I am away to make my fortune."

"Are you looking for work?"

"That I am."

"I am in need of a maid. Someone to wash and dress me, clean the cottage and sweep my hearth."

"That work would suit me well."

"There is one condition. When sweeping the hearth, you must not peer up the chimney."

Now Calyphony was curious about this, but she agreed to the condition. It mattered not to her whether the old woman was crazy or not.

So the next day, Calyphony was up and washed the old woman and dressed her and the hag left the house. She cleaned the place and swept the hearth. Then she thought it would do no harm to have one peek up the chimney. What did she see there, but her mother's own long leather bag of gold? Down she took it and was away as fast as she could run back to her home.

As Calyphony hurried homewards she passed a horse in a field and the horse called to her: "Rub me down, young girl, for I haven't been rubbed these seven years!"

But Calyphony was in such a hurry that she ignored the beast. Then she passed a sheep covered in a mass of wool. "Shear me, shear me, young girl, for I haven't had my fleece trimmed these seven years!"

But Calyphony was in such a hurry that she ignored the beast. As she hurried on she came across a goat on an ancient tether. "Change my tether, change my tether, young girl, for I haven't had it changed these seven years."

But Calyphony was in such a hurry to return home, she ignored the beast.

Then along the road she passed a lime-kiln. The kiln cried out: "Clean me, clean me, young girl, I haven't been cleaned these seven years." But Calyphony was in such a hurry to return home, she scowled at the kiln and passed by.

Then she saw a cow heavy with milk. "Milk me, milk me, young girl, for I haven't been milked these seven years." But Calyphony was in such a hurry to return home that she ignored the beast.

By this time, Calyphony was so tired that she saw a mill and thought she would rest there for a while. The mill cried out: "Turn me, turn me, young girl. I haven't been turned these seven years!"

But Calyphony ignored the mill. Feeling tired, she went into the mill and lay down on a sack of flour and was soon fast asleep.

Now the old hag had returned home and found that the cottage was empty. The girl was gone. She ran to the chimney and peered up. When she saw the long leather bag had gone, she fell into a great rage and began to run in the direction Calyphony had taken.

When she met the horse she called: "Horse of mine, did you see a young girl with a long leather bag pass this way?"

"I did so," agreed the horse. "She passed in that direction, not long since."

On she ran until she saw the sheep. "Sheep of mine, did you see a young girl with a long leather bag pass this way?"

"I did so," agreed the sheep. "She passed in that direction, not long since."

Then the old woman met the goat: "Goat of mine, did you see a young girl with a long leather bag pass this way?"

"I did so," agreed the goat. "She passed in that direction, not long since."

The old woman came to the lime-kiln. "Lime-kiln, did you see a girl with a long leather bag pass this way?"

"I did so," agreed the kiln. "She passed in that direction, not long since."

Then she came to the cow. "Cow, did you see a girl with a long leather bag pass this way?"

"I did so," agreed the cow. "She passed in that direction, not long since."

Finally the old woman came to the mill.

"Mill, did you see a girl with a long leather bag pass this way?"

"She did not pass here, but is sleeping inside on a flour-sack," replied the mill.

The old woman lifted the latch of the mill door and took out a hazel wand and tapped the sleeping Calyphony on the shoulder. The unfortunate girl was immediately changed into stone and the old woman retrieved the long leather bag and went home.

A year and a day passed and Iney MacKerron's third daughter, Calyvorra, said to her mother: "Calybrid and Calyphony are not yet home. They must be making great fortunes. Shame on me for sitting here, doing nothing to help you or myself. Bake me a *soddag*, and I will set off to seek my fortune."

Iney MacKerron baked the *soddag*, the oatmeal cake, and said that her daughter could have the whole *soddag* but without her blessing or she would remove a piece of it and give her the blessing.

"I will have your blessing, mother, and you remove a piece of it," agreed Calyvorra. For she knew the old saying that a blessing will last longer than a morsel of food.

Then away she went and journeyed until she came to a wood in which was a strange house and an old woman hanging over the gate watching her.

"Whither away, young girl?"

"I am off to make my fortune," replied Calyvorra.

"Is it work you want? I am in need of a maid to wash me, dress me, clean my cottage and sweep the hearth."

"That should be good work for me," replied Calyvorra.

"There is one condition, however. When you sweep my hearth you must not peer up the chimney."

Well, this aroused Calyvorra's curiosity but it was no concern to her if the old woman was peculiar or not. So she agreed to take the job.

The next morning, she rose, washed the old woman, dressed her and the *caillagh* took herself out. Then Calyvorra cleaned the cottage and swept the hearth. Now, as she was doing so, she thought it would do no harm to take a quick peek up the chimney. And what should she see there? It was the long leather bag of gold which had belonged to her own mother. Down she took it and, without more ado, she set off as fast as she could towards her home.

As she hurried homewards, she passed a horse in a field and the horse called to her: "Rub me down, young girl, for I haven't been rubbed, these seven years!"

Calyvorra stopped immediately. "Oh, you poor horse, I'll surely rub you down." She laid down the long leather bag and gave the horse a rub.

After a while, she went on and saw a sheep covered in a mass of wool. "Shear me, shear me, young girl, for I haven't had my fleece trimmed, these seven years."

Calyvorra stopped immediately. "Oh, you poor sheep, I'll surely cut your fleece." She laid down the long leather bag and proceeded to shear the sheep.

On she went and came across a goat with an ancient tether. "Change my tether, change my tether, young girl, for I haven't had it changed, these seven years."

So Calyvorra stopped immediately. "You poor goat. Of course I'll change it for you." And she laid down her long leather bag and proceeded to change the goat's tether.

Then along the road she came to a lime-kiln. The kiln cried out: "Clean me, clean me, young girl. I haven't been cleaned these seven years."

Calyvorra stopped immediately. "You poor kiln, of course I'll clean you." And she laid down her long leather bag and cleaned the kiln.

Then she saw a cow heavy with milk. "Milk me, milk me, young girl, for I haven't been milked these seven years."

Calyvorra stopped immediately. "Oh, poor cow, of course you shall be milked." And she laid down her long leather bag and proceeded to milk the cow.

By this time, she was ever so tired. She saw a mill. The mill cried out: "Turn me, turn me, young girl, for I haven't been turned these seven years!"

"Oh, poor mill," gasped Calyvorra, fighting off her tiredness, "of course I'll turn you." She laid down her long leather bag and proceeded to turn the mill and then, eventually, she went inside, lay down on a flour-sack, and was soon fast asleep.

Now the *caillagh* returned home and found that the cottage was empty. The girl was gone. She ran to the chimney and peered up. When she saw that the long leather bag had gone, she flew into a great rage and began to run in the direction Calyvorra had taken.

When she met the horse she called: "Horse of mine, did you see a young girl with a long leather bag pass this way?"

"Have I nothing better to do than watch for young girls passing by?" replied the horse. "Seek elsewhere for your information."

On she ran until she saw the sheep. "Sheep of mine, did you see a young girl with a long leather bag pass this way?"

"Have I nothing better to do than watch for young girls passing by?" replied the sheep. "Seek elsewhere for your information."

Then the old woman met the goat: "Goat of mine, did you see a young girl with a long leather bag pass this way?"

"Have I nothing better to do than watch for young girls passing by?" demanded the goat. "Seek elsewhere for your information."

The old woman came to the lime-kiln. "Lime-kiln, did you see a girl with a long leather bag pass this way?"

"Have I nothing better to do than watch for young girls passing by?" replied the kiln. "Seek elsewhere for your information."

Then she came to the cow. "Cow, did you see a girl with a long leather bag passing this way?"

"Have I nothing better to do than watch for young girls passing by?" replied the cow. "Seek elsewhere for your information."

Finally, the old woman came to the mill.

"Mill, did you see a girl with a long leather bag pass this way?"

The mill said: "Come close, *caillagh*, so that I may hear clearly what you are asking. Come and whisper into my wheel, where I might hear the clearer."

The old woman went up to the wheel and thrust her head forward to whisper into it and just then the mill wheel twisted round and dragged her into its cogs and stone pivots so that she was ground right up and the tiny pieces were washed down the nearby hole in the ground where the water ran. And this hole was called the "Towl Creg y Vuggane" where, some say, you may hear the hag's cry even to this day.

The old witch had dropped her hazel wand and the mill called softly: "Calyvorra, Calyvorra, awake."

When Calyvorra had awakened, the mill told her to pick up the wand and touch the two stones in the corner of the mill with it. She did so and no one was more surprised than she, when the stones turned into Calybrid and Calyphony, her long-lost sisters.

The mill then told her to touch the long leather bag with the hazel wand and this she did.

"Now, no matter how much gold you take out of the bag," said the mill, "it will never be empty."

One more thing the mill told her to do, and that was to burn the hazel wand, so that no one else would grow unhappy by the use of its powers.

When that was done, Calybrid, Calyphony and Calyvorra set off home, laughing and celebrating their great good fortune.

At the gate of their home was Iney MacKerron, their mother, who had been crying in her loneliness; hearing their approach, she was waiting to greet them. Great was her joy when she saw her three daughters with Calyvorra bringing with her such great good fortune. That is the story of *Poagey Liauyr jeh Caillagh* or the Hag's Long Leather Bag.

12 *The Lossyr-ny-Keylley*

Long, long ago, there was a king of Ellan Vannin whose name was Ascon. Ascon was a fine, just and gentle king, but he was rather poor. He had three fine sons and their names were Bris, Cane and Gil. In spite of his poverty, or perhaps because of it, the king ruled wisely and well and enjoyed the love and affection of his people. In return, he, too, enjoyed life and was contented with his lot.

What he most enjoyed was the visit of a little bird which came from over the seas and alighted on his windowsill in spring, and sang until the little thing was fit to bust. It was a small golden bird and the king called it *Lossyr-ny-Keylley*, which is the Manx name for a goldfinch. It came to the castle and stayed a short while, lifting the king's spirits by its song, and then flew away to the west. The king wished that the bird would stay longer. But it never did.

The king was in his chamber one day and thinking of the future. Some day, he realized, one of his sons must inherit the kingdom, but his problem was – which one? Who was the worthiest? How could he compensate those who did not become king? There was only one thing he possessed of real value, and that was his golden crown studded with precious jewels and silver mountings. Now, as everyone knows, a crown went with being the king, so whoever inherited the kingdom would have to inherit the crown. But he had three sons and that meant that two of them would have to go without any form of inheritance. Without inheritance, how could they even marry? The Manx saying goes: *gyn skeddan, gyn bannish*! No herring, no wedding.

The king wondered whether he ought to divide the kingdom in three but, even if he did so, he could not divide the crown. It would also seem foolish if there were three kings in Ellan Vannin and only one of them ruled with a crown. That would surely be a recipe for disaster?

It was while he was considering the problem that his three sons, Bris, Cane and Gil came in.

"We were considering, father," began Bris, "our future."

"We have all reached the age when we should be married," Cane observed.

"Therefore we were wondering whether you could find us wives," added Gil.

Ascon the king grew very sad. "You have come to me with the very problem that I have been wrestling with, my sons. Because, if you are to marry, you will need some inheritance to keep your wives. Now it is hard to divide this land between you. If one inherits, then the other two will be without."

"That's all right, father," said Bris cheerfully. "Why not divide the land in three? We do not mind sharing."

"If I give you equal parts of the kingdom, the crown cannot be divided; and to be king, one must have the crown. As well as you like each other now, it could eventually lead to war between you, and that I would not have for all the world."

The boys assured the old king that they would never go to war with one another. But they did see the logic of what the king was saying. Indeed, what use was a kingdom without a crown? Indeed, the eldest son was already beginning to think – as I am the eldest, why should my younger brothers have the crown? The middle brother was thinking – as I am the brightest, why should my brothers have the crown, when I would make a better king? Only Gil, the youngest, thought that he would not mind if his brothers inherited, for he was young and fit and could surely make his own way in life.

The old king sat in thought, and then an idea struck him. He would make a test for his sons and whoever passed the test would receive the entire kingdom and the crown.

"Each year, my sons, there comes to the palace window the

Lossyr-ny-Keylley, which sings its heart out before my window. It pleases me, that little goldfinch. But then it flies off to the west. If the little bird stayed with me all year, I would be rested and happy. So, my sons, I shall set you this test. Whoever finds the home of the Lossyr-ny-Keylley, and brings it back to this land, shall inherit my kingdom and my crown."

Straightaway, his eldest son, Bris, was boastful. "I can bring the goldfinch back without hardship."

"As could I," added Cane quickly.

The young brother, Gil, smiled. "I doubt not that either of my brothers could perform this deed. Perhaps, though, I should go with them, because there might be a way of seeking my fortune in the land of the goldfinch."

The three brothers made to set out but, as they were poor, they only had one boat. After some discussion, they decided that they would leave the shores of Ellan Vannin together in that one boat.

That dawn, they set sail westward and, by nightfall of the first day, they spied an island. They came ashore to an hostel and the hostel keeper, a pleasant woman, came forward.

"Welcome, sons of King Ascon, welcome."

The three boys were puzzled.

"How do you come to know us, for we have not travelled beyond the shore of Ellan Vannin before this day?"

"I know who you are and where you are bound," the woman replied.

"Then you know more than we do, woman," Bris stated. "For we are looking for the land of the goldfinch and know not where that is."

"Tomorrow, as the sun rises, you will sail on until you strike land. Once ashore, you will come to a straight road, but do not take it. Take the small side road that leads south." The woman smiled. "From then on, your must find your own path."

So it happened the next morning they sailed on and, as the woman said, they came to land and a straight road. There they found a path south and, at the place where it began, they met an elderly man.

"*Kys t'ou*?" greeted Bris, in the language of Ellan Vannin.

"*Ta shiu cheet!*" replied the old man, in the same language. "I am Yn Oallagh. You are those seeking the land of the goldfinch?"

"What must we do?" nodded Cane.

"Do you see that chariot there?"

There was a golden chariot parked nearby with white horses pounding the road with their forefeet.

"We do," agreed Gil.

"Let Bris take the reins. Let Cane take the left side and Gil take the right. Drive on until you find a tall rock. Then dismount and take the spear on the right side and give a blow on it."

"Is that all?"

"For the time being," smiled the old man mysteriously.

So they mounted the chariot and Bris flicked the reins and away they went. Sure enough, it was not long before they came to a tall rock. Bris dismounted and examined it, while Gil came forward and took the spear on his side of the chariot. Then he gave a blow on the rock. A large piece fell from it and revealed a great opening, as if into a bottomless hole.

There, behind them, was the very same man who had directed them. How he had been able to keep up with them, they were unsure.

"Welcome, sons of the King of Ellan Vannin. This is the road by which you must go to find the land of the goldfinch."

Bris peered downwards. "How can we get down there?"

"I have a rope and may lower you down."

"Then do so," snapped Bris. "Let me down immediately, for I am the eldest and wish to bring back the goldfinch."

The old man smiled. "Is there not a saying in Ellan Vannin – *ta lane eddyr raa as jannoo*?" That meant, there is much between saying and doing.

Bris flushed in annoyance. "Do you doubt my ability?"

"You might reach the bottom, Bris. But there are dangers. You might lose your life in the descent."

Bris, in annoyance, urged the old man to let him down the rope and he went down and down in the darkness. The rope began to sway and he struck the rocks in the darkness. It frightened Bris and, before long, as he could not see the bottom, he called to be let up.

Cane was smiling cruelly at his brother's failure. "You let me down," he instructed the old man. "I'll soon find this bird, as I am the cleverest. I'll give you another saying, old man: *ta keeall ommijys ny slooid ny t'ee ec dooinney creeney dy reayll.*" That meant that wit was folly, unless a wise man had it to keep, which was a slur on his elder brother.

The old man said nothing but let him down on the rope. The same thing happened. Cane grew very frightened when the rope began to sway and he started to hit the sides of the rocky hole. He called to be let up.

Gil, the youngest, was all for turning back with his brothers, but the old man said: "Why not try your luck? There is yet another saying in your country – *ta cree doie ny share na kione croutagh.*" Now that saying young Gil could not see the meaning of, for it meant that a kind heart was better than a crafty head.

Now Bris and Cane added their voices to persuade him, thinking that if he brought up the bird, he would it give it to either one of them, as he did not want the kingdom.

So Gil was let down on the rope and, within moments, he was at the bottom and into a bright wonderful country. He set off along the road and came to a palace.

"*Bannaghtyn,*" called a voice in his own language. He looked up and saw a young woman standing at the gates of the palace. "Welcome to you, Gil, son of the King of Ellan Vannin."

"There's a wonder," remarked Gil. "How do you know my name?"

"I know you and what has brought you to this land. But there is great hardship in front of you. To find the place of the goldfinch will take you seven years, and to come back to this spot again will take a further seven years."

"Why, that's no use to my brothers, for they are waiting above for me. They will think I am dead and depart. The old man with the rope won't keep that rope dangling for me to climb back up. I should give up."

He was about to turn round and go back when the woman

held up her hand to stay him. "You can be there and back in less than a day, if you have a horse. I have a stable full of fine horses and, if you choose the right one, you may travel like the wind."

So Gil went into the stable and examined all the horses that were there.

There were magnificent horses there. But Gil, examining each of them in turn, felt that this one was too short in the leg, another was too tall, another too fretful and so on, until he came across a poor, wretched-looking mare which looked as though it stood in need of a good feed. His heart was filled with sorrow and kindness for the beast, for he felt it surely needed some exercise.

"This one will do for me," Gil said. "I shall comb and groom her and she may serve me better than those others."

So he set to and combed, cleaned and saddled the mare, then led her out of the stable.

The woman, waiting outside, was pleased when she saw his choice.

"Luck is on you, Gil, for that is the best horse in the stable. Truly, a kind heart is better than a crafty head."

Gil mounted up and set off across the countryside.

They had not gone far when suddenly the mare spoke. "Gil, son of the King of Ellan Vannin, what is it that you see around you?"

Gil, rather surprised, replied: "There is a beautiful country."

"And directly before you?"

"Before me is a great sea."

"Then, if it is your destiny, and you are the rightful heir of your father, we shall cross this sea without trouble."

So saying, the mare galloped forward across the shore and into the sea. Gil was amazed when, instead of sinking into the waves, the mare cantered easily across them as though they were nothing but dry land.

They continued on a long time until they saw, in the sea, three small islands and on each island the mare said she had to rest. Gil, being kindly, though worried about his brothers and the old man waiting for him, allowed the mare to rest as long as she liked.

Finally they came to a magnificent shore.

"What do you see now, Gil, son of the King of Ellan Vannin?" called the mare.

Gil looked along the shore. "Why, I see a splendid palace of white stone with golden currents. Who lives in this palace?"

"The King of the Land of the Goldfinch," replied the mare. "The bird that you are looking for is in that palace. But there are difficulties in finding it. Behind the castle are thirteen stables. At each of the first twelve stables, ostlers will come out and try to take me from you, saying they will tend and care for my needs. You must refuse them. Go on until you reach the thirteenth stable, and there you may dismount and lead me into it."

So it transpired as the mare said.

At each one of the first twelve stables, ostlers ran out and tried to take away the mare, but Gil told them to go away. He rode on to the thirteenth stable and there dismounted.

At that moment, a tall man with a red-gold crown came striding out. His face was wreathed in anger. "Do you dare refuse my ostlers? Are they not good enough to take care of your shabby mare?"

"Not they," replied Gil boldly. "I will rest any place, but you will not deny me the choice of stable for my mare, who has brought me through many dangers to this palace."

The King of the Land of the Goldfinch, for such he was, gave a sigh. "You are Gil, son of the King of Ellan Vannin. I know why you have come here."

"That makes my task the easier," smiled Gil.

"Not so. For you cannot take the goldfinch until you have performed twice times three deeds."

"What are they?"

"We will start with the first deed. At dawn tomorrow, I shall go off and hide. You must find me."

"Easy enough."

"If you do not find me before sunset, your head will be cut off," added the king with a smile. Then he went away, chuckling to himself.

Gil went into the stable and fed his mare and sadly

observed that his task was going to be harder than he imagined.

"You must follow my advice. Tonight, sleep in the stable, in this manger before me."

So Gil did and, in the morning, the mare nudged him when dawn came.

"Now, Gil, you must go into the palace garden. There will be many beautiful maidens there and each one will shower praise on you and give you spectacular blooms and invite you to walk with her. Do not pay any attention to them, but go straight to the end of the garden. There you will find an apple tree. On it a single rosy-red apple will be growing. Pluck it and break it in half. It is in the apple that the king will be hiding."

As the mare had said, when Gil went into the palace garden, beautiful maidens came to him and tried to give him magnificent flowers and invited him to walk with them. He kept his eyes lowered and did not even look on them. He made his way straight to the apple tree and plucked the apple.

One of the maidens came up.

"You must not take that, for that is my father's apple."

Gil smiled and took out a knife. "Then I shall take only the half of it."

So saying, he cut the apple in half and out jumped the King of the Land of the Goldfinch.

"You have beaten me today," he said sourly. "But you have not won yet. Tomorrow I shall hide again and you must find me. That is the second task."

"Easy enough," replied Gil.

"If you do not find me before sunset, I shall have your head taken off."

So Gil returned to the mare and the mare told him to sleep in the stable, in the manger, with her. And at sunrise she roused him.

"Today you must go into the kitchen of the palace. There will be many maidens there, and they will tease you, push you, or slap you with their napkins. Do not take any notice of them. Walk up to the kitchen fire and the cook will offer you a bowl of broth. Say you cannot take the broth without onions and go to the vegetable basket. You will see a three-headed onion. Cut the onion open with your knife and the king will be in there."

It happened exactly as the mare had said. He avoided the maidens, took the bowl of broth and declared that he could not drink the broth without an onion. In the vegetable basket he saw a three-headed onion and so he picked it up.

"Wait," cried one of the maidens. "That onion was one my father was keeping for his broth."

"Then I'll just take the half of it," Gil said, and took out his knife and cut it.

Out jumped the king. "You have beaten me again today," he said sourly, "but you have not won, yet. Tomorrow I shall hide and you must find me. That shall be your third task."

"Easy enough," replied Gil.

"If you have not found me by sunset, I shall cut off your head myself."

So Gil went to the stable and the mare told him to sleep with her in the manger that night. In the morning the mare awakened him.

"Harder it will be for you today, but listen to me. Take some grains of barley and go to that pond near the garden. You will find a duck swimming there. Throw the barley to the duck and she'll come towards you. While she is picking the grain, catch her and tell her to lay an egg. She will refuse, of course. Say that if she does not, you will kill her. When she lays the egg, the King will be in it."

So it happened exactly as the mare said.

He went to the pond and saw the duck. He threw the barley to the duck and, when she came ashore to peck it, he caught her and told her to lay an egg.

"I can't lay an egg when I have none," cried the duck.

"Then I shall have to kill you," said Gil, putting a hand around the duck's neck.

The duck laid an egg immediately, and Gil took it up.

"I will crack open this egg and eat it," he said.

Then the king's daughter came by and said: "You must not, for that egg is my father's."

"Then I will take only the half of it," said Gil, and cracked the egg open with his knife.

The king sprang out with a doleful countenance. "A third time you have beaten me, son of the King of Ellan Vannin. But you have not won, yet. Now it is your turn to hide and mine to seek. You will hide tomorrow and, if I find you before sunset, I will have your head."

Weary and disconsolate, Gil returned the stable and told the mare of the new development.

"You have only to best him three more times," said the mare, "if you want to win the goldfinch. So sleep here in the manger." Then, just before sunrise, she awakened him. The next minute, Gil found he had been transformed into a flea in the coat of the mare.

All that day the King of the Land of the Goldfinch looked in every place, but he failed to find Gil. At sunset, the mare turned Gil back into a man and warned Gil not to answer the king's inevitable question of where he had been hidden. Gil went into the palace and, when the king asked him where he had been hiding, Gil said: "I did not ask such a question when you were in the apple."

"True enough. Tomorrow you must hide again and, if I find you before sunset, I shall have your head."

So Gil slept in the manger again. The following morning, the mare turned him into a bee.

All day, the King of the Land of the Goldfinch searched for Gil and could not find him.

At sunset, the mare turned Gil back into his human form and told him not to answer if the king asked where he had been hiding. Gil went to the palace and the king asked where he had been hiding. Gil replied: "I did not ask you that question when you hid in the three-headed onion."

"True enough," sighed the king. "Tomorrow, you must hide again and, if I find you before sunset, I shall have your head."

Once more, Gil slept in the manger and, at sunrise, the mare turned him into one of her eye-lashes.

The king came and searched and searched and grew angry but could not find him. At sunset, the mare turned Gil back and told him not to answer the king's question as to where he was hiding. Furthermore, the mare said that the king only slept once in seven years and, as he had been so exhausted by the hide-and-seek game, he would fall asleep and his entire court with him.

Gil went into the palace and when the king asked him he replied; "I did not ask you that question when you hid in the duck's egg."

So the king bent his head forward and sighed and soon he had nodded off to sleep and his entire court with him.

Then Gil heard the voice of the mare. "Go now into the king's chamber behind the throne. There is the goldfinch in a silver cage. Seize it. I shall be waiting at the door of the castle."

So Gil went into the chamber and saw the cage and the bird. He seized it. No sooner had he done so when the bird let out a strange scream and everyone in the castle came awake. But Gil was away and at the door of the castle. There was the mare and into the saddle went Gil. The mare took off like a bird herself.

After they had galloped a while the mare called: "Look behind; what do you see?"

"The largest army I have ever seen," gasped Gil. "They have great standards and many weapons."

"What colour are the standards?"

"White."

"Then we can escape from them."

The mare galloped across the sea to the first of the islands.

"Look behind; what do you see?" she called.

"A great army, larger than the first," replied Gil. "They have great standards and many weapons."

"What colour are the standards?"

"Red."

"Then we shall escape from them."

She galloped across the sea to the second island.

"Look behind; what do you see?"

"As terrible and immense an army as I have ever seen," cried Gil. "They have great standards and more weapons than I can count."

"What colour are their standards?"

"Black."

"Then we shall escape from them."

They came to the smallest island and continued on without difficulty to the far shore.

Then they rode up to the castle from which Gil had acquired the mare. There was the young woman standing at the castle gate. She saw that he had the goldfinch in the cage and came forward, laughing with joy.

"Welcome back, son of the King of Ellan Vannin. Do you know what bird you have in your cage?"

"That I do not," confessed Gil.

"She is Princess Vorgell, daughter of Urmen, the King of the Land of the Goldfinch. The mare is the Princess Ysbal, her sister. I am the Princess Kikil, sister to them both. I have a rowan wand here and it will give back human form to my sisters. It was Urmen, our father, who changed us so, because a Druid told him that one day he would lose us to the sons of Ellan Vannin."

She struck the bird and it changed into the most beautiful woman that Gil had ever seen. Then she struck the mare and she turned into an equally beautiful woman. "Now," said the woman at the gate of the palace and she turned now into a third beautiful princess. She smiled at Gil.

"Thank you for our release, son of the king of Ellan Vannin. Now we shall go to Ellan Vannin with you. And if your father gives his approval, we will dwell with you and your brothers in your kingdom."

So they went to the foot of the opening and called up. The old man was still there with his rope, for hardly a moment had passed in the Land Beneath the Earth, which is called the Land of the Goldfinch. Gil's two brothers were there and, when they heard that Gil had been successful in his quest and had come back with beautiful princesses to grace their island, they quickly decided on a terrible plan. They turned and struck the old man dead and took his rope. Then they let it down into the hole.

So first Princess Kikil went up, and it was the eldest brother, Bris, whose eyes fell on her and who claimed her for his bride. Then the Princess Ysbal went up and it was the second brother, Cane, who claimed her.

The Princess Vorgell, who had been the goldfinch, went to the opening and peered up at the dangling rope, and she felt uneasy. She whispered to Gil that he must help her place a heavy stone on the end of the rope. The two brothers started to haul the rope up thinking that either their brother or the princess was at the other end. But now they cut the rope when it was no more than halfway up and the stone fell to the bottom and smashed. The brothers believed they had killed the princess or their younger brother or, at least, stranded them both in the Otherworld. They then set off on their chariot, with their brides, back towards Ellan Vannin.

Before they arrived at their father's court, Bris said: "Our father sent us to bring back the goldfinch and we have come back with wives. It could be that he will refuse to give us the kingdom."

Ysbal said, "I have the magic rowan wand and can change shape."

So she turned herself into the goldfinch in a moment.

Bris took charge of the magic rowan wand.

So they continued on to Ellan Vannin and came to their father's court.

The first question the old king, Ascon, asked was: "Where is my youngest son?"

Bris shrugged.

"A large rock fell on him and crushed him on the road. But, see here, we have found the bird you coveted and that is compensation enough."

He put forward the cage with Ysbal inside, in the guise of a goldfinch.

"That is not *the* goldfinch," declared King Ascon fiercely.

Now Cane had secreted the magic rowan wand from his brother and struck Kikil and turned her into a goldfinch in a cage.

"You are discerning, my father," he cried, coming forward. "It is not Bris who has the bird but myself. Here is the real goldfinch. I deserve the kingdom, for bringing it to you."

He brought forward Kikil in the cage, in the guise of a goldfinch.

Old King Ascon peered at it and shook his head.

"That is not the goldfinch. Shame on you both, for trying to deceive me in this. Leave me now to mourn for my youngest son. Neither of you shall have my crown."

Now what had happened to Gil and Vorgell after the rock had fallen?

Gil was quite upset, for now he saw how duplicitous his brothers were.

Vorgell smiled sadly at his dismay. "Wait here for me, Gil," she instructed. "I see you have a tender heart and are not used to such a betrayal."

Then she turned herself back into the goldfinch and flew up through the hole. There she turned herself into a powerful woman and let down the old man's rope to Gil. He was quickly hauled up and, when he saw the old man he bent over him and tried to help, grieving that his own brothers had been the cause of the old one's death.

Because he did so, the old man blinked and sat up.

"You have brought me back to life because your heart is good and pure, Gil, son of the King of Ellan Vannin. There is no other cure that would have made me whole again."

The old man conjured a chariot and told Gil and Vorgell to be on their way back to Ellan Vannin.

Now when they landed on the shores of Ellan Vannin, Vorgell turned herself back into the goldfinch and she flew to the window of the palace of King Ascon and set up a song for him. The mourning king heard her cry and went to the window and stared with joy mingled with sadness.

"Now if I only had my youngest son home, my joy would be complete," he sighed.

Then the goldfinch hopped into the room and changed into the beautiful Princess Vorgell.

"Look to the horizon, King Ascon. Yonder comes your youngest son, Gil, home from the Land of the Goldfinch. He has braved many dangers to save me from my enchantment."

Ascon saw his youngest son coming and gave a great shout of joy.

Bris and Cane heard it and were in dread and fear.

Great was the reunion that day at the court of the King of Ellan Vannin.

When the old king heard the true story, he fell into a rage and ordered his sons, Bris and Cane to be banished. But Ysbal and Kikil, who were now turned back into human shape, asked forgiveness. It was Gil himself who added his voice to their pleas.

"Very well, you shall be banished for seven years only," agreed King Ascon. "And you will acknowledge your brother, Gil, as the King of Ellan Vannin after me."

So Bris and Cane married Ysbal and Kikil and went off to live in a land beyond the seas for seven years. And Gil and Vorgell married. And at the end of the seven years, they all reunited and acknowledged that when old King Ascon died, Gil and Vorgell would become king and queen of Ellan Vannin . . . but that would not be for many years yet for, each afternoon, Vorgell was able to change into the goldfinch and sit and sing to the old king; and thus he was a happy and contented man; and if you are happy and contented, you live a long, long life.

13 *Gilaspick Qualtrough*

There is a saying up at Booilushag, which is the little village beyond Port Mooar, though Port Mooar is hardly "the great port" that its name implies. It is scarcely more than a cover of rocks in which ships enter at their peril, though Manx sailors are used to it. Oh, yes: the saying? The saying is, in the Manx language: *Cha bee breagerey creidit ga dy n'insh ch yn irriney*. That means, a liar is not to be believed even if he tells the truth.

Now there was a sailor of Booilushag and his name was Gilaspick Qualtrough. He was a merry sort of fellow, a lover of women, whiskey and fun. Every time he set off in his boat from Port Mooar, north round Gob ny Port Mooar or south around Gob ny Garvain, he was sure to return with wondrous tales, although, I confess, his nets were always full of fish. Off up to Ramsey he would go and the Ramsey fishermen would be amazed and even jealous at the size of his catch. Gilaspick Qualtrough knew the fishing grounds and he knew how the fish would be running; there never was a more intelligent fellow for knowing when to put out to sea, in order to return with its harvest.

But if Gilaspick Qualtrough had a fault it was this: he could never leave a story to the plain facts. He like to adorn his tales and make them even taller than they seemed at first. He was known as a teller of the tallest stories that had ever been heard from the Point of Ayre in the north to the Calf of Man in the south. Not that anyone would call him a liar, but everyone knew what a fierce exaggerator he was.

One day, when he had taken a catch to Ramsey and sold it at a good profit, he was sitting in the Elfin Arms, which stands by Elfin Glen, and talking about the dangers that he had survived in the unpredictable tides off the sharp cliffs of Traie ny Halsall. He waxed lyrical as he sipped his whiskey and began to embellish his story for the third time of its telling.

"*Loayrt ommidys*!" snapped one of his listeners, which is not a nice way of saying that Gilaspick Qualtrough was talking rubbish.

It was a man whom he had never seen before.

"Do you doubt my word?" Gilaspick demanded indignantly.

"Doubt it?" replied the man. "Instead of a fisherman lifting mackerel or catching crabs, one would think that you were Maeldún the Voyager himself. I'm never a braggart myself, but what I say is that a man who does a bit of fishing along this coast should not be boasting of his sea prowess with a man who has dared sail to Fingal and back."

Now Gilaspick had never heard of Fingal, nor did he know the nature of the place. But, if Gilaspick Qualtrough had a second fault, it was in never admitting his ignorance. So rather than admit ignorance, that he had no idea of where Fingal was, he merely said that while he respected a man who had sailed to Fingal and back, he would argue that there were just as many dangers sailing along the Manx coast from Gob ny Strona at Maughold Head down to Dreswick Point. Anyway, he was willing to go and cast his nets in the waters of Fingal any day to prove his worth.

The stranger smiled cruelly. "Is that so? Well, when you go there be sure and pick up the Blessed Bell of Ballakissak and bring the bell here and by that we will know that you have cast your nets in the waters of Fingal."

"Easy to do," cried Gilaspick boldly. He did not want to seem ignorant in front of the Ramsey men.

"When may we expect you back?" pressed the stranger, still smiling.

Now if he gave a time, it might be too long or too short because he did not know where the place was to judge time nor distance.

"It'll depend on the weather," Gilaspick replied airily. "I shan't be raising canvas in a bad wind."

The Ramsey fishermen nodded, for this was good sea sense.

"I shall return here at the next full of the moon," the stranger announced, "by which time I'll expect you to have returned. But do not forget to bring the Blessed Bell of Ballakissak. That will be the only proof I'll accept that you have been to Fingal."

"Do you doubt that I can bring this bell back?" demanded Gilaspick in annoyance.

"The proof of the pudding is in the eating of it," chuckled the stranger. "Perhaps you will take a solemn oath on the bet? If you do not return with the Bell of Ballakissak, and give up the Bell to me, relinquishing any claim you might have, I shall not only take your honour but all you possess in this land."

Now Gilaspick Qualtrough was not one to back down on a point of honour, and he immediately agreed to the wager.

Then Gilaspick Qualtrough left the Elfin Arms and trod with heavy steps to Ballure on his way south to his home. But at Ballure, he stopped off and asked if any local fishermen had heard of a place called Fingal or if they knew anything about the Blessed Bell of Ballakissak. No one had. Next he stopped off at Lewaigue under the shadow of Sleiau Lewaigue, the great hill. No one knew there. He tried at Ballacreggan and Ballasaig and Dreemskerry and Ballajora and home he came to Booilushag. But no one had heard of Fingal nor of the Blessed Bell of Ballakissak.

"Now," he said to himself, "I cannot well put to sea if I don't know where to go. If I head to sea and turn north, I might be going in the wrong direction, and if I head south, I might also be going the wrong way."

However, he knew that there was a wise old man who lived up on the hill at Baldromma Beg.

"Fingal?" the old man said, staring at Gilaspick. "That's the other side of the world, so it matters not whether you go south or north."

Now Gilaspick was a fine coastal fisherman, but he had never had to wrestle with the concept of the world being round.

"Surely I must go one way or the other, *dooinney creeney*," he said politely. It was always best to address men who had more wisdom than oneself in the most polite terms.

"No. Whichever way you go you'll find it," the old man assured him.

However, the wise old man did not know anything about the Blessed Bell of Ballakissak.

So, the next morning, Gilaspick Qualtrough provisioned up and sailed out of Port Mooar. When he came to the headland he thought he would turn south, because southern climes are more balmy than the harsh north and he did not want to enter a storm-tossed water before he had to.

Off he sailed boldly enough and then he suddenly realized that there was one question which he should have asked. How was he going to recognise the waters of Fingal when he saw them?

He gave a sigh. But it would not do to turn back now. Already the tides had put him outside of the Manx coastline. He hoisted his sail and away his boat went skimming across the waves, until a heavy sea mist suddenly came down. The curious thing was that, in spite of the mist and the thickness of it, the wind did not cease to fill out his sail and on he went, cleaving a way through the water.

With an abruptness which left him breathless, he was suddenly out of the mist and on a bright blue ocean with a yellow sandy shoreline in front of him. He peered round to examine the strange mist but, again to his surprise, he could not see sign of it at all. He shivered slightly. Then he turned back and examined the land he was approaching. It was a pleasant place and the yellow shore was lined with dark green trees and a riot of flowers of many colours.

An old woman was sitting on a rock by the shore, watching him as he brought his boat up to the beach. She had a yellow shawl around her bent shoulders.

"Good day, old woman," he cried leaping out. Then, realizing that he must be in a foreign country where Manx might not be spoken, he added: "*Vel oo loayrt Gaelg?*"

He was most relieved when she greeted him in the language of Ellan Vannin.

"*Bannaghtyn!*"

But the greeting made him think a moment. "Have I come ashore in my own land again?" he asked. "Is this Ellan Vannin?"

"No, *a mhic*," she answered. "This is not Ellan Vannin."

"Then tell me what land it is?"

She smiled cautiously. "What land do you seek?"

"I seek a place called Fingal."

"Then this is it."

Now he was fair amazed and said so. "Then tell me, where do I find the Blessed Bell of Ballakissak?"

The old woman sniffed in disapproval. "Now you ask a lot of questions, *a mhic*."

"I have promised that I would cast my nets in the waters of Fingal and bring back to my own county the Bell of Ballakissak."

"A promise is a sacred thing. If you go to the king's palace, up the path here, you will find what you seek and you may be able to accomplish what you have promised."

Then the old lady stood up and was gone. He could not swear that she had vanished because, at that moment, he had turned to make sure his boat was beached above the waterline. However, it was only a momentary glance and when he peered back, the old lady had vanished.

He went up the path that she had indicated. At the end of it, there was a great palace and apparently a feast was going on. There were noblemen a-plenty, dressed in silks and satins and gold and silver, and young ladies and great dames in bright dresses. Musicians made music and servants were carrying food here and there. Gilaspick had never seen anything so splendid in all his life. There were tables with drink and meat that would feed the entire population of Ellan Vannin, as well as cakes and sweetmeats and food for which he had no words to describe.

He turned to an old woman who was standing nearby. For a moment he thought that she was the same old woman who had been sitting on the seashore, but he noticed that she was wearing a green shawl around her bent shoulders.

"Tell me, old woman, what is happening?"

"Why, *a mhic*, it is the king's daughter who is getting married. See, there she is."

He looked across the great room and saw the most beautiful girl he had ever seen dressed in the finest wedding dress. Yet instead of appearing happy on this, her wedding day, the girl's eyes were rimmed red and it was clear that grief was on her features.

"Why is it that she grieves when everyone here is apparently celebrating and full of joy?"

"Ah, *a mhic*, it is against her will that she's marrying, for she has no love for her husband. And see him there . . . you may judge why she has no liking for him."

She pointed and he swallowed hard, for there was a hunchback dwarf with a hooked nose and green skin and his face covered in leprous spots.

"How can the king marry his daughter to that?"

"Easy enough, when a curse is placed on your kingdom and the only person who can take it off is the one who put it on. That is Prince Imshee, and perdition is his name and perdition his nature."

Now Gilaspick pitied the young princess with all his heart. You see, for all his faults, and he had a few, Gilaspick Qualtrough was a kindly and generous fellow. But he realised that he had more urgent matters to attend to than get caught up in the affairs of a strange land.

"Where might I find the Blessed Bell of Ballakissak, old woman?" he asked.

"That is none other than the Princess of Ballakissak," replied the old woman, and vanished into the crowd.

Now this left Gilaspick puzzled. What did she mean? It began to dawn on him that rather than a *bell* that rang, the strange man at Ramsey might have referred to a *belle*, being a beautiful girl.

Seeing the sobbing princess was alone in a corner of the feasting room, he went carefully over to her and bowed low. "Forgive me, lady, but are you Princess of Ballakissak?"

The young woman looked up at him with a tear-stained face. He swallowed hard when his eyes met hers, for she was, indeed, the most beautiful woman he had ever seen. There was a blush of a rose on her snow-white cheeks and honey-gold were the curls of her hair, held in place with silver combs. Her eyes were light blue.

"Good stranger," her voice was a melodious soft soprano, "surely you must know as I am the unhappiest person here. Yes, I am the Princess of Ballakissak."

"Lady, I grieve for your grief. But there is one question that I must know. Is there a *bell* of Ballakissak, that is a *clageen*, or is there a *belle* of Ballakissack, that is a *caillin*, *yn caillin s'aaley?*"

She frowned at him and, despite her red-rimmed eyes, a smile came to her lips.

"Truly, stranger, you speak in a riddle. There is no bell but I am called *yn caillin bannee.*"

Gilaspick let out a long, low sigh. "Then, lady, it is you that I have come for."

She stared at him and it seemed as if there was an expression of hope crossing her features.

He seized her up and began to dance with her through the hall, a whirling merry dance, so that they crossed the great hall towards the door without anyone crying alarm. Then out of the door they went. Gilaspick held on to her hand as they ran down the path to the sea shore.

"Where are we going?" gasped the girl, though she was eager enough to follow him.

"I am taking you with me to Ellan Vannin," cried Gilaspick.

Now there was a great outcry behind them and, casting a glance over his shoulder, Gilaspick saw the crooked little figure of Prince Imshee leaping down the path.

Quickly, he handed the princess into his boat and pushed off from the shore, leaping in and grasping his oars until he rowed the boat a little way out.

"Oh, look!" cried the princess in alarm.

As Gilaspick looked, he saw the gnome-like figure of the prince astride a bough of hazel, riding it like a great horse, and taking into the air after them.

"Ah, good sir," cried the princess, "nothing can save us now, for Prince Imshee is a *fer obbee*, a wizard of great power!"

Gilaspick Qualtrough had not been a fisherman all his life without knowing what a Manx seaman must do, when *in extremis*.

"Oh, Mannánan Beg Mac-y-Leirr!" he cried out. "God of the oceans whose island I come from! If there was ever a time when your mantle was needed to be shaken between my enemies and myself, now is the time. Shake forth your mantle, Mannanan!"

There was the sound of a great noise coming, like a whirl of wind on a storm-tossed sea, but the sea remained calm. Suddenly, they were enveloped by a thick sea mist. It was the same sea mist that had overtaken him in his outward journey. He could hardly see his hand in front of his face.

The princess looked around perplexed. "What does this mean, good sir?"

Gilaspick Qualtrough smiled nervously. "I come from the island of the Ocean God, Mannánan Beg Mac-y-Leirr, which is called Mannánan's Island. I called on the ocean god to protect me by shaking his mantle between me and the wizard, so that he might not see us. And I am no 'sir', lady. I am but a poor fisherman named Gilaspick Qualtrough of Booilushag."

The princess sighed. "Would that I was poor, dear Gilaspick. For I would rather have a life of happiness as a poor fisherman's wife than be a princess in a gold palace, who has to have a life of sadness married to such an evil thing as Prince Imshee."

Gilaspick was about to answer when he felt the wind at his back. Curiously, as before, the wind was blowing but the mist remained thick and firm. He could only suppose that it was the magic of the ocean god which made it so. Anyway, it reminded him to hoist his sail and soon they were speeding across the water.

Almost in a blink of an eye they emerged on a dark storm-tossed shore.

Gilaspick was worried. "I do not recognise this place," he muttered to himself.

It took him all his skills to manoeuvre the boat onto the wave-lashed beach.

"Look!" said the princess. "There is an old woman sitting there on that rock. She will tell us where we are."

"Greetings, old woman," cried Gilaspick, going up to the woman. He thought, for a moment, that he had seen her before, for she looked like the two old women he had seen on the island of Fingal. But then he looked closer and found that her shawl was blue.

"No greeting here for you, Gilaspick Qualtrough," replied the old woman. "No greeting for stealing Prince Imshee's wife. You had best begone and soon."

Gilaspick frowned. "I have done no such thing. For it is not stealing when someone comes willingly away."

"Is that not the Princess Ballakissak yonder in your boat?"

"It is, but . . ."

"Then know that this is Ellan Imshee, the island of the prince. You have been blown here by his will."

Now Gilaspick exclaimed in anger, for he wondered if the ocean god had played him a mean trick.

The old woman laughed sourly and spoke as if she had read his mind. "Blame not the ocean god. Prince Imshee is a great wizard. He had outwitted your Mannánan and see, here he comes."

Down came the ugly Prince Imshee, descending from the clouds. The old woman quickly scurried off.

"So, you thought that you could call on the ocean god to rescue you?" cried the evil dwarf. "Well, I merely turned the wind to bring you here and now I shall have my revenge on you both!"

The princess began to sob in terror and this irritated Prince Imshee. He pointed a long crooked finger towards the Princess Ballakissak. "This sound offends me. You will not speak, unless I tell you to."

Straightaway, the princess was struck with a magical dumbness.

Prince Imshee roared with laughter at her attempts to cry out. It seemed to please his warped sense of humour. Then he remembered Gilaspick and took a step towards the fisherman.

"Oh, Mannánan Beg, Mac-y-Leirr!" cried Gilaspick in

desperation. "Are you deaf that you have ignored my entreaty? I am a son of Ellan Vannin, your own jewel in the storm-tossed sea. Help me now!"

The crooked-backed Prince Imshee hesitated a moment but, when nothing happened immediately, he chuckled cruelly. "It seems that your ocean god has forsaken you, little fisherman."

Gilaspick was no coward, though he feared the magic of the little wizard, but he, unarmed, raised his fists and set to defend himself.

The little man stood, hands on hips, grinning scornfully. "You'll need more than two fists to fend off my spells," he sniggered.

"If the ocean god were not deaf," breathed Gilaspick, "you would not dare harm a fisherman of Ellan Vannin."

"Would I not?"

The little wizard pointed his long crooked finger at him and a bolt of lightning snaked out and sent Gilaspick flying backwards on the sand. His whole body seemed to be on fire.

"Oh, Mannánan Beg, Mac-y-Leirr!" groaned Gilaspick. "Have you no pity on the girl, if you have none for me? Help her!"

He was not sure what happened then, but there was a sudden burst of sound, like the angry tempest of the sea, and suddenly a great foamy chariot drew out of the waves. On it there stood a man which Gilaspick was sure he had seen before.

The man grinned at him. "It is a difficulty that you have found yourself in, Gilaspick Qualtrough," he remarked; his voice seemed to have a great roaring quality like the sea breaking on the rocks.

"No thanks to you!" replied Gilaspick, realizing that this must be Mannánan Beg, Mac-y-Leirr, the ocean god himself. He wondered where he had seen the ocean god before.

"Is that a way to speak to me?" rebuked the god, still standing in his chariot, his white chargers like sea foam pawing the beach.

"You did not help me when I called out to you. I thought all the sons of Ellan Vannin were under your protection?"

"True enough. But do you not know that you must call my

name three times before I can reply? Three times and then I can only help you once. So take the princess now and get to your boat and hoist your sail."

Gilaspick glanced at the enraged Prince Imshee. "What of him?" he asked nervously.

"You may leave that little wizard to me. Quick, now, for in a moment this island will sink beneath the waves when I blow on it."

Gilaspick grabbed the princess and leapt into his boat. It was already floating off-shore and he hoisted the sails. Immediately, the little vessel was speeding away across the sea and behind there was a terrible roaring and crashing as the island of the wizard was engulfed by the seas that Mannánan had brought on it.

"Well," sighed Gilaspick, "that's that. Let us hope we have a fair path home."

But she didn't reply. She opened her mouth but no sounds would come and tears were in her eyes.

"It cannot be that the wizard's spell is still working, while he rots beneath the waves?"

Princess Ballakissak nodded sadly. She reached forth a smooth white hand and laid it against his face. The tears lay on her cheeks and Gilaspick found himself tearful as well, for he could not stand the sight of this beautiful maiden in this unhappy plight. He was about to call to the ocean god again for help, but he remembered that the ocean god could only help him once, and that time had already passed.

So they sailed on in silence, with Gilaspick not knowing what to do.

Finally, he spied a temperate shore and a shingle beach and thought that he would land there, to see what help he could get. He saw an old woman seated there as he brought his boat ashore. For a moment he thought it was the same old woman who had dogged his adventures at every step of the way, but he saw that her shawl was purple.

"Greetings, old woman," he called as he helped the silent princess from the boat.

"I have been waiting for you, son of Ellan Vannin," sniffed the old woman irritably.

"Waiting for me? How so?"

"Ask no questions. Bring the girl to my house."

So Gilaspick and the Princess of Ballakissak followed her up the winding path to a white-washed old cottage on the cliff top and the sun was rising when they came to the door.

Three days they spent with the old woman and each day, at dawn, she prepared a strange potion and had the princess drink it down. Each time Gilaspick thought that there would be a cure, but each time the girl was unable to answer him when he questioned her, and the tears poured from her eyes.

It was then that Gilaspick Qualtrough realised that he had fallen deeply in love with the Princess of Ballakissak. Ah, if only she could speak.

The old woman, on the morning of the third day, as the sun was rising, came in with a herb and stripped it of its leaves and cut its stalk until a thick white juice came out of it. Then she put some water in a pot and laid the herb in and boiled the juice and gave it to the princess. A great sleep came over her and they had to carry her to her bed.

Gilaspick sat with her and, that evening, she awoke at last and looked up through the windows at the blue star-studded canopy. She yawned and stretched. Then she rubbed her eyes and said: "Where am I?"

Gilaspick was filled with joy. "I do not know, Princess. I know we are in a cottage of an old woman and that you are cured of the curse of the wizard."

Memory came to her and she jumped up with joy and gave Gilaspick a big hug and a kiss.

Gilaspick felt he would die with satisfaction and delight at her embrace.

The old woman came in and smiled knowingly. "Tomorrow you can continue on your journey to Ellan Vannin," she said.

That night, they feasted in the old woman's cottage and Gilaspick Qualtrough showered her with thanks.

"No thanks are required," said the old woman, whose name was Airmed. "I am a healer. But if you are grateful for what I have done, when you return to Ellan Vannin, you might meet an old woman selling herbs by the roadside. Do not pass her by with a curse but buy a cure from her."

Gilaspick promised to do so.

So the next morning, they set out again, both talking away as if their lives depended on it. The Princess of Ballakissak declared her love for him and he declared his love for her. Happily, they came to Gob ny Garvain and sailed into the rocky bay of Port Mooar below Booilushag.

The people of the village turned out to greet him.

"Twenty-seven days have you been gone," cried one of the fishermen of Booilushag, "and we had given you up for lost."

"So had I," cried Gilaspick, quite recovering his old spirits. And he proceeded to tell them his adventures, but no one would believe him.

"It's old Gilaspick Qualtrough telling his tall stories again," they said to one another. "However, it is a fine wife he has brought back to Booilushag. Maybe he has brought her from Onchan, or some other town in the south?"

No one quite knew where the princess could have come from, nor even that she was a princess, but as for the truth of it, well, they would not believe it.

For a few days, Gilaspick and Ballakissak were happy and then Gilaspick was reminded of his promise to go back to the Elfin Arms in Ramsey and meet the stranger. And the stranger had told him to bring the Princess of Ballakissak to him. When he explained what was troubling him to the girl, she grew unhappy.

"We must go to the Elfin Glen just as you promised, Gilaspick, otherwise you will have lost everything."

"But what if I lose you? The stranger told me that I am to hand you over to him as proof, or he would take everything I owned on this island, including my reputation."

"I will not love this stranger better than I loved the evil wizard, Prince Imshee. But your word has been given and there is an end to it."

With heavy steps they set out from Booilushag up the path to Ballajora, to Dreesmjerry and when they were passing Sleiau Lewaigue they saw an old woman by the side of the road. At first, Gilaspick thought it was Airmed, or one of the other old women he had met on his travels, but her shawl was of parti-coloured cloth and bright.

"Buy a cure, sir," she called.

Gilaspick sighed and was about to curse her. Then he shrugged. "There is no cure for the troubles that are on my shoulders," he replied.

He was about to pass by when he remembered he had given his word to Airmed, the old healer, that he would buy a cure from an old woman he met by the side of the road. So he pulled out a coin and handed it to her. "You may give me what cure you like, for nothing I know will cure a heavy heart."

The old woman gave him a bag. "That will do it. Keep it safe in your pocket until you need it."

Then he and the Princess of Ballakissak walked on slowly until they came to the Elfin Glen.

The first person he spied was the stranger, sitting on a stone outside the inn with folded arms and a smile on his face. He was so familiar that Gilaspick wondered where he had seen him before.

"So you have returned?"

"I have," agreed Gilaspick.

"Did you go to Fingal?"

"I did. But I had no time to cast my net into the waters."

"That I know. But, importantly, did you bring me the Blessed Belle of Ballakissak?"

Gilaspick, with a heavy heart, drew the princess to his side. He said no word.

"Well," said the stranger, "it seems that you are reluctant to part from her? Tell me why."

"We love one another," Gilaspick was forced to reply. "Though I promised you that I would bring her forth for you, though you force me to dishonour my pledge, I will fight you for her."

The stranger laughed good-naturedly.

"Fight me? No. I will take compensation though."

Gilaspick groaned. "I am a poor fisherman."

"Well, then, give me a bag of dried *barragyn buighey* and we will call it quits."

Now *barragyn buighey* was sea poppy and Gilaspick had as much chance of obtaining some as becoming a rich man.

His face fell.

It was the Princess of Ballakissak who said: "Good sir, we have only a cure, a bag of herbs; perhaps you will accept this."

She held out her hand to Gilaspick and he drew out the bag he had purchased from the old woman. They opened the bag and in it were the dried leaves of *barragyn buighey*.

"There, now, a bargain is a bargain," smiled the stranger. "I will take this and be on my way. I am glad I picked you for this venture, Gilaspick Qualtrough."

Gilaspick stared at him.

"*Picked me?*" he demanded. "What do you mean?"

But the stranger's visage had suddenly changed and it was clear that he was a noble prince of the Otherworld and he was mounting into a great foaming chariot, drawn by white horses the colour of foam-capped waves. Without another glance, the stranger had raced away, heading straight into the sea.

Gilaspick and the princess tripped home very happily and lived together in Booilushag for many a long year. I do hear that their descendants might still be living there to this day, although I am told that no one believes the fabulous story that Gilaspick Qualtrough told about how he brought his beautiful wife to the shores of Ellan Vannin.

Scotland (Alba)

Scotland: Preface

I have always considered that James MacPherson (1736–96) of Kingussie has been unfairly treated in popular perception. He was a graduate of Aberdeen and Edinburgh universities and, in 1760, he produced his famous *Fragments of Ancient Poetry Collected in the Highlands of Scotland*, which was followed by *Fingal* (1762) and then by *Temora* (1763). These were finally put together in a single volume as *The Poems of Ossian* in 1773.

Ossian made a tremendous impact on European literature and reawoke an interest in Celtic myth, legend and folklore. Translations were immediately made into German, French, Italian, Danish, Swedish, Polish and Russian. William Blake, Lord Byron and Lord Tennyson praised the work. The German poet, playwright and novelist, Johann Wolfgang von Goethe, admired it, as did Napoleon Bonaparte, who carried a copy of it with him on his military campaigns and took it with him into his final exile on St Helena. The English poet, Thomas Gray, was moved to comment: "Imagination dwelt many hundred years ago on the cold and barren mountains of Scotland."

However, Dr Samuel Johnson denounced it as "a literary fraud".

MacPherson had claimed the work to be translations of surviving Celtic epics. Johnson claimed that no such epics ever existed and MacPherson had made up the whole thing. Even today, you will find MacPherson denounced as a literary forger.

I feel this is unfair. When the Highland Society of Scotland set up a special committee to investigate the charges of MacPherson's critics, and it reported back in 1805, the work was declared to represent a genuine tradition, even though MacPherson had probably not merely translated from oral tradition, rather than written sources, but embellished and retold the stories. To fill out the plots and adapt the text is the lot of anyone engaged in retelling folktales. Indeed, what was wrong with that?

Furthermore, it might well be that MacPherson had access to some genuine Gaelic manuscripts which became lost or destroyed. Both during the Scottish Reformation and certainly after the suppression of the various Scottish Jacobite uprisings, many manuscripts and books in Gaelic were destroyed. Edward Lhuyd (c.1660–1709), the Celtic scholar, in a research trip to Scotland in 1699 actually catalogued a library of books in Scottish Gaelic; the catalogue survived but the library was destroyed.

From the ninth century *Book of Deer*, with its Scottish Gaelic notations, and one eleventh-century poem, we have a surprising gap until we reach the Islay Charter of 1408. The Charter not only demonstrates a sophisticated literary medium, the obvious product of a long tradition of literary endeavour, but it also proves that Scottish Gaelic was being used as a medium of legal administration. Then we have the *Book of the Dean of Lismore* leading to the first printed Scottish Gaelic book, Bishop John Carswell's *Form na h-Ordaigh* (1567).

There is no reason, therefore, why MacPherson's source material could not have existed, as Dr Johnson maintained.

Nevertheless, the literary argument has continued to this day and poor MacPherson is branded with the unjustifiable label of being a forger. If he is a forger, I, too, am a forger, because I have adapted and retold these stories just as he apparently did.

The following stories appear in many variant versions in Scotland; indeed, some of them have Irish and Manx equivalents. The story *Geal, Donn and Critheanach* is also found in Donegal, with a shorter variant of the tale collected in Seamas MacManus' *Donegal Fairy Tales* of 1900.

Perhaps the starting place for students of these tales is the work of John Francis Campbell (1822–95), a Gaelic folklorist who was known in his native Islay as "Iain Òg Ile". His *Popular Tales of the West Highlands* (1860–2) and his work on Fingal (the Scottish Gaelic equivalent of Fionn Mac Cumhaill), which was published as *Leabhar na Fèinne* (1872), are the tip of the literary mountain he left. His huge collections of stories were deposited in the National Library of Scotland and in the Dewar MSS collection in Inverary Castle. In 1940 and 1960 further collections were published from this repository, but much still remains there.

Throughout the nineteenth century, there was much done by way of collecting folktales by industrious workers in both Scottish Gaelic and in English. *Folklore of the Scottish Lochs and Springs* by James M. MacKinlay (1893) was an important study, as well as George Henderson's *Survival in Belief among the Celts*, Maclehose, Glasgow, 1911.

However, the most important worker in recording Celtic Scotland was William Forbes Skene (1809–1892), who emerged into the field editing what was then the oldest source of Scottish history as *Chronicles of the Picts and Scots* (1867). In 1868 he published *Four Ancient Books of Wales*, a two-volume study of Middle Welsh poetry. He then produced his chief work, and a most important one for Scotland – the three-volume *Celtic Scotland: A History of Ancient Alban* (1876–1880). Next to this stands another classic, which is Alexander Carmichael's *Carmina Gadelica* (Vols I and II, 1928; Vol III, 1940; Vol IV, 1941 and Vol V, 1954). There is still unpublished Carmichael material in Edinburgh University.

It is from these sources that I have drawn on the basis of the following retellings. Sometimes, one has had to cross-reference the stories with Middle Irish texts. For example *The Shadowy One*, a story of Scáthach of Skye, borrows from references to her in the ninth-century text *Aided Oenfir Aife* (Death of Aoife's Only Son), given in A.G. van Hamel's *Compert Con Culainn*, Dublin, 1933.

I would, however, like to pay a tribute to my friend as well as colleague, the late Seumas Mac a' Ghobhainn (1930–87), the historian and author, whose work on behalf of the Scottish Gaelic language, its culture and history is well known. Seumas and I went on one highly interesting trip through Scotland in 1970 and it was then that I began to make some notes on the Scottish variations of Gaelic legend and folklore. Seumas often advised me on my material. His guiding hand is sadly missed. He had an uncanny ability to make the stories leap out of the printed sources into a modern reality. *A chuid de fhlaitheannas dha!*

14 *The Shadowy One*

"A young boy is approaching the gate, Scáthach," announced Cochar Croibhe, the gatekeeper of Dún Scaith, whose great fortifications rose on the Island of Shadows in Alba, an island which today is still called the Island of Scáthach or Skye.

"A boy?" Scáthach was a tall woman, of pleasing figure and long fiery red hair. A closer look at her form showed her well-toned muscles. The easiness of her gait belied a body so well trained that, in a moment the great sword, which hung from her slender waist, would be in her hand – and that sword was not for ornament. Indeed, Scáthach was acclaimed one of the greatest warriors in all the world. No one had ever bested her in combat, which was why all the warriors who had ambition to be champions were sent to her academy, where she taught them the martial arts. Her school was famous in every land.

Cochar Croibhe, the gatekeeper, was himself a warrior of no mean abilities, for such he had to be in order to guard the gates of Dún Scaith. He shrugged.

"A boy," he confirmed, "but accoutred as a warrior."

"Does he come alone?"

"He is quite alone, Scáthach."

"A talented boy, then," mused Scáthach, "for such he would have to be, to reach this place by himself."

Cochar Croibhe conceded the fact after some thought. After all, Scáthach's military academy lay on the Island of Shadows; to reach it, one had to pass through black forests and desert plains. There was the Plain of Ill-Luck, for example, which could not be crossed without sinking into bottomless bogs, for it was one great quagmire. There was the Perilous Glen, which was filled with countless ravenous beasts.

It was with curiosity that Scáthach mounted the battlements of her fortress to view the approach of the boy. She decided that Cochar Croibhe did not lie, but the youth was more than a mere boy. He was short, muscular and handsome, and he carried his weapons as a veteran used to arms.

"He may have crossed the Plain of Ill-Luck and the Perilous Glen," sneered Cochar Croibhe, at her side, "but he still has to cross the Bridge of Leaps."

Now Scáthach's island, the Island of Shadows, was separated from the mainland by a deep gorge through which tempestuous, boiling seas flooded. And the sea was filled with ravenous creatures of the sea. The only way across was by a high bridge, which led to the gate of her fortress.

The point of this bridge was that it had been constructed by a god in a time before time. When one man stepped upon one end of this bridge, the middle would rise up and throw him off, and if he leapt into the centre, then it would do likewise, so that he might be flung into the forge to the waiting creatures of the deep. Only Scáthach knew the secret of the safe crossing, and only when her pupils had graduated from her academy and sworn a sacred oath of friendship did she reveal the secret to them.

As Scáthach watched, the youth trotted up to the end of the bridge. She smiled and turned to Cochar Croibhe. "We will wait to see if he can overcome this obstacle, to assess his worthiness."

They waited. The youth came and examined the bridge and then, to their surprise, he sat down on the far shore and built a fire, where he rested.

"He cannot cross," chuckled Cochar Croibhe. "He waits for us to go out and show him the way."

Scáthach shook her head. "Not so. I think he does but rest from his long journey here; when his strength is recovered, he will attempt the crossing."

Sure enough, when the grey mists of evening were approaching, the youth suddenly stood up. He walked back a distance and made a run at the bridge. As soon as his foot touched the end of it, it rose up and flung him backwards. He landed without dignity on his back on the ground. Cochar Croibhe laughed sourly.

"He is not finished yet," smiled Scáthach. "Look."

The youth tried once more, and again he was flung off the bridge but thankfully not into the foaming waters below. A third time he tried, and with the same result. Then the youth stood for a while in thought. They saw him walk back a distance and run for the bridge.

"My best sword as a wager that he will be thrown into the sea this time," cried Cochar Croibhe eagerly.

"Done! My best shield will answer your wager," cried Scáthach in reply.

With the fourth leap, the youth landed on the centre of the bridge. In a fraction of a second, it started to rise but the youth had made a further leap and was safely across and at the gates of Dún Scaith, demanding entrance.

"Let us go down and admit this young man, for his courage and vigour has won him a place in this academy, whatever his name and station."

Grumbling at the loss of his best sword, Cochar Croibhe went and brought the youth in and escorted him into the presence of Scáthach.

"What is your name?" she asked.

"I am named Setanta, and I am from the kingdom of Ulaidh."

Scáthach's eyes widened as she gazed on the handsome, muscular youth. "I have heard that a youth named Setanta, coming late to a feast at the fortress of Cullan, was confronted by a ferocious hound, which Cullan, thinking his guests were all in the fortress, had loosed to guard the place. This hound was so strong that Cullan had no fear of attack, save only if an entire army marched on his fortress. The story I heard was that when this youth was attacked by the hound, he killed it. And while the warriors of Ulaidh were amazed by the feat, Cullan was sorrowful that his faithful hound had died for the safety of his house. The youth Setanta then offered to guard Cullan's house until such time as a hound whelp had been trained to take its sire's place. So Setanta became Cullan's hound – Cúchullain."

"I am that Setanta, the hound of Cullan," replied the youth solemnly.

"Then you are thrice welcome, Cúchullain."

Cochar Croibhe glowered in the background, for jealousy was in his soul.

It happened that Scáthach had a beautiful daughter and her name was Uathach, which means "spectre". It was Uathach's duty to serve at the table when the students of her mother's academy were having their evening meal. One evening, therefore, when Uathach was serving meat, she came to the young man Setanta. She held out the dish of meat to him and he took it.

Their eyes met and, through their eyes, their souls found attraction.

In this moment, Setanta forgot his strength and, in taking the dish of meat from the girl's hands, his hand closed upon hers and her finger broke in his grasp.

Uathach let out a scream of anguish.

Setanta dropped to his knees before her and asked for her forgiveness. This the girl, in spite of her pain, willingly gave.

But Cochar Croibhe, the jealous doorkeeper, who had already cause to dislike the young man, came running into the feasting hall in answer to the girl's cry. Now it was known that Cochar Croibhe coveted Uathach, and his amorous suit had twice been rejected by her, in spite of the fact that he was acclaimed the bravest champion at Dún Scaith . . . with the exception of Scáthach, of course.

Straightaway he challenged Setanta to single combat, as reparation for the injury.

Uathach protested that she had already forgiven the young man, but Cochar Croibhe grew insulting and spoke of a boy hiding behind the apron of a girl.

Setanta stood quietly, for he was not one to lose his temper without just cause.

Osmiach, the physician, having heard Uathach's scream,

came into the feasting hall and set the girl's finger and applied pain-killing poultices.

All the while Cochar Croibhe, in spite of Uathach's protests, taunted young Setanta. Finally, he pointed out that everyone knew that Setanta had no father, for was it not common knowledge that his mother, Dectera, had vanished one day from the court of Conchobhar Mac Nessa and then reappeared with the boy child, which she named Setanta?

Now this was true, for Dectera had been beloved of none other than the great god Lugh Lámhfada, and the child was Lugh's gift to Ulaidh. But Setanta could not bear to hear his mother so insulted.

"Choose your weapons," he finally snapped at Cochar Croibhe, who was a master of all weapons, but was incomparable with the spear or javelin.

"Javelin and buckler!"

And with that the two went out into the courtyard of Dún Scaith.

Scáthach had the power to stop the fight but she did not. "We shall see," mused Scáthach to herself, watching from a window. "If Setanta bests Cochar Croibhe in combat, then it will mean that I am right to have accepted him, for he will become the greatest champion of Ulaidh."

And the combat commenced.

Cochar Croibhe came running forward, buckler before him, javelin held high.

Setanta merely stood there, watching his coming with a frown. He did not even raise his buckler to defend himself. Yet his muscles tightened on his javelin and moved it back into position. Then Cochar Croibhe halted in his run, halted a split second, dropped his buckler and held back his arm for the throw. At that point, Setanta loosed his own javelin. So fast and so swiftly did it cleave the air that it transfixed Cochar Croibhe before he had time to cast his own spear. Spear and buckler dropped from his grasp and he sank on his knees, staring in horrified surprise. Then he collapsed on his side.

"Dead," exclaimed Osmiach the physician dispassionately.

Setanta's gaze met that of Uathach, but she was not distressed. Admiration shone from her eyes.

Scáthach appeared, standing frowning at the young man. "You have slain my gatekeeper," she said, without emotion.

"Then as I fulfilled the duties of Cullan's hound, and guarded Cullan's fortress, let me now be your gatekeeper for as long as I stay here."

So it was, that for a year and a day, Setanta stayed at the martial arts academy of Scáthach and, each night, Uathach warmed his bed. And Scáthach herself taught Setanta all he needed to know to become the greatest warrior in all Éireann, and the fame of Cúchullain, or Cullan's hound – for as such he was better known than as Setanta – spread far and wide.

At the end of a year and a day, Scáthach drew Setanta to her and led the way down to a large underground cavern, where none but they were allowed to enter. Inside, lit by brand torches, was a great pool of bubbling sulphur, warm and liquid grey.

"Here we will make the final test," Scáthach announced. "We will wrestle and it shall be the winner of three throws who shall be the greater."

"I cannot wrestle you!" protested Setanta, for as much as he realised that she was the greatest female champion of Alba, it was against his sense of honour to wrestle a woman.

"You will wrestle as I direct, or it shall be known that you feared a challenge from me," she said simply.

So the two of them stripped off, there and then, and took their places on either side of the sulphur pool. At the first clash, Scáthach threw Setanta. The next time they touched, Setanta, no longer fearful to harm her, threw her. And then the third time they came together in the centre of the sulphur pool. They held each other so tightly in an embrace that neither could throw the other. And, after an hour, Scáthach released her hold and said: "The pupil has become the master."

Setanta then made love with her, for it is written that the apprentice must show his willingness to marry his vocation.

In return, Scáthach gave Setanta a special spear, which was called the Gae-Bolg, or belly spear. This spear was thrown by the foot. It made one small wound when it entered a man's body but then thirty terrible barbs opened so that it filled every limb and crevice with mortal wounds. Scáthach gave this to Setanta and taught him how to cast it.

And both Scáthach and Uathach knew that the time was now approaching when Setanta would leave Dún Scaith.

It happened about this time that Scáthach received a challenge to combat from her own sister Aoife, whose name means "radiantly beautiful". Now she was Scáthach's twin sister and they had both been born of the goddess of war, the Mórrígán. Each was as proficient as the other in arms, but each claimed to be the superior of the other. Sibling rivalry warped their relationship.

Aoife had sent Scáthach a message saying: "I hear that you have a new champion at Dún Scaith. Let us test his mettle. My champions and your champions will contest together."

When she read this, Scáthach was fearful for the safely of Setanta, for she knew, deep in her heart, that her sister was the greater of the two; that she was the fiercest and strongest champion in the world. But the challenge could not be rejected, and so Scáthach prepared her warriors to go out and meet her sister Aoife.

The night before they were to set forth, Scáthach called Osmiach the physician to her, and told him to prepare a potion which would send a man to sleep for four-and-twenty hours. And Osmiach prepared the sleeping draught, and it was administered in secret to Setanta.

The warriors of Scáthach set out to meet the warriors of Aoife.

What Scáthach overlooked was that the potion, which might have caused an ordinary man to sleep for four and twenty hours, only held Setanta in sleep for one hour.

As the armies gathered, great was Scáthach's astonishment when Setanta's chariot came careering up and he joined her lines, for he had followed Scáthach's army by the tracks of the chariots.

The champions met in combat and great deeds were wrought that day. Setanta and two sons of Scáthach fought with six of Aoife's mightiest warriors and slew them. Several of Scáthach's pupils were cut down, but they did not fall alone. As the day grew dark, both armies were still evenly matched.

Then Aoife challenged Scáthach directly to combat to resolve matters.

Setanta intervened and claimed the champion's right to meet Aoife in place of Scáthach and such was the ethic of the situation that Scáthach could not refuse him.

"Before I go," Setanta said, "tell me what your sister Aoife loves and values most in the world."

Scáthach frowned. "Why, she loves her two horses, her chariot and her charioteer, in that order."

So Setanta drove out into the battlefield to meet Aoife.

At first, he was amazed that Aoife was so like Scáthach, but her beauty seemed more radiant than Scáthach's and she handled her weapons with greater dexterity. It was truly said that she was the greater warrior of the two. They clashed together, Setanta and Aoife. They fought in single combat and tried every champion's feat they knew. Blow to blow, shield to shield, eye to eye.

Then skill was with Aoife. She aimed such a blow that the sword of Setanta shattered at the hilt. She raised her sword for the final strike.

Setanta cried out: "Look! Your horses and chariot have fallen from the cliff into the gorge!"

Aoife hesitated and glanced round fearfully.

At once, Setanta rushed forward, seized her around the waist and flung her to the ground. Before she could recover, there was a knife at her throat and Setanta was demanding her surrender. Angrily, she realized that she had no option but to plead for her life and Setanta granted it, on condition that she made a lasting peace with her sister Scáthach and gave Scáthach hostages for the fulfilment of the pledge.

"You are the first person who has bested me in combat," Aoife ruefully admitted, staring at the handsome youth. "Albeit, it was by a trick."

"Victory is victory, however it was achieved," replied Setanta calmly.

"There is wisdom on your tongue," agreed Aoife. "Come

and join me at my fortress, that we may get better acquainted."

To this invitation, Setanta agreed.

Scáthach and her daughter Uathach watched his departure with Aoife in sadness but in resignation of his destiny. He would become Aoife's lover and she would bear his son, Connla, whom the gods would force him to kill. In sadness, he would stride forth to become the defender of Ulaidh, his name praised in the mouths of all men; charioteers and warriors, kings and sages would recount his deeds and he would win the love of many. He would be Cúchullain. And whenever the name of Cúchullain was spoken, the name of his famous tutor would also drop from the tongue – Scáthach, the Shadowy One, ruler of Dún Scaith on the Isle of Skye.

15 Princess of the Fomorii

Long ago, in high-hilled Alba, there dwelt a band of mighty warriors called the Feans. Their chieftain was Fingal. No other warriors could stand against them, for they were the greatest champions in all the five kingdoms of Alba.

One day, returning from a quest to help the King of the Western Isles, their ship was forced to pass over the Eas-Ruaidh, the Red Cataract, but its waters were suddenly stilled. No wind blew and the surface of the sea became as clear as crystal, without the remotest ripple. The sun shone down brightly and, leaning over the railing of their ship, they could see the salmon beneath the waves, resting before their journey into the great rivers of the mainland.

As the warriors peered about, wondering why their ship had suddenly been becalmed, a further curious thing happened.

The land of the Fomorii was revealed to them. Now the Fomorii were the dwellers under the sea, and their country was suddenly seen through the crystal of the sea as if through a piece of glass – like a window. It was a fair country of deep green forests, bright flowers and silver streams. The rocks were of gold and the sands were of silver. Precious jewels were the pebbles of its shores.

In the deathly hush, the Feans looked down, enraptured but unsure of what this vision could mean.

Then one of them called softly, pointing to a boat which seemed to float up from the land beneath the waves and approach them. The boat was rowed by a woman of breath-taking beauty, who handled the oars with great dexterity, so that not even a ripple showed where she dipped them into the water. The boat approached and came alongside the warship of the Feans.

The lovely vision of womanhood stepped out and the Feans could now see that there was a deep sadness on her lovely features.

"Greetings to you, men of the Feans," she intoned sweetly.

Fingal, their chieftain, rose from his seat and came towards her, pausing to salute her, for it seemed to him that she was no ordinary woman who could row her boat from the land beneath the waves into this world.

"You are welcome, fair lady," he said. "Speak your name and tell us what country you come from and what it is that you seek among us, the Feans of high-hilled Alba."

"Thank you, Fingal the Fair," replied the young woman. "I am Muirgen, the daughter of the King of the Fomorii, the Dwellers Under the Sea. I have searched for you and the Feans for many months."

"You bear an appropriate name, Princess of the Fomorii," replied Fingal, for Muirgen meant "born of the sea". "Now tell us why it is that you have searched for us, and what it is that you require from us."

"I have come to seek your help, and I am much in need of it. I am pursued by enemies."

Fingal at once clapped his hand to his sword and his eyes darted this way and that, as if seeking the enemies she alluded to. "Fear not of enemies, Princess. You are among warriors who fear no enemy. Tell us, who is it who dares to pursue you?"

"The Tighearna Dubh is he that pursues me. The Dark Lord, who is the son of the Tighearna Bàn of the Sciatha Ruaidh. He desires to seize my father's kingdom and, not being able to do so by force, he means to make me his bride. My father, however, is now old and has no male heir and so has weakened in his resolve. He says that the Tighearna Dubh is as good as any other prince and that I must wed him. I have defied him, as I have defied the Tighearna Dubh. Great is your prowess, Fingal. I have taken an oath that none but you shall take me back to my palace under the waves and drive the Dark Lord from it."

Oscar, the grandson of Fingal, who was a great warrior and very handsome, came forward. "Princess, even if Fingal was not here, I and all the Feans would protect you from this Dark Lord. He will not dare to seize you."

As he spoke, a dark shadow suddenly fell across their ship, causing the entire seascape to be shrouded in darkness, as if it were suddenly night. The Feans peered upward, seeking an explanation, for they had not noticed any storm-clouds gathering. Indeed, the shadow was not caused by clouds, but by a mighty warrior astride a great blue-grey stallion with a white mane and tail, which pranced across the sky snorting with white foam on its nostrils and from its muzzle. On the warrior's head was a flashing silver helmet, on his left arm was a large silver shield and in his right hand was a mighty sword, whose steel surface flashed like lightning.

Faster than the mountain torrent sped his mighty horse as it came swiftly towards the ship of the Feans. Now the tranquil seas broke and the waves rose underneath the galloping hooves. The breath of the beast caused the seas to churn, as if before the gusts of an uncontrollable tempest. In fact, the waves drove the great ship of the Feans shorewards, the little boat of the Princess of the Fomorii along with it, bobbing like corks in a tub. The Feans used all their seamanship but the ship sped straight for a sandy shore and was beached. Whereupon Fingal gave the word, and his warriors leapt ashore with shield and swords at the ready to confront this mighty warrior.

Down came the great horse and its rider, halting in a spray of sand. The warrior leapt from the horse and came striding up the sandy beach to the battle lines of the Feans.

"Is this the Tighearna Dubh of whom you spoke, Princess?" demanded Fingal.

"It is none other," the Princess assured him, her voice faint. "Protect me, for his power is great."

Oscar, the youthful hero, stirred by the passionate cry of the girl, strode forward, shield and sword ready.

The Tighearna Dubh scorned to fight with him. "Move aside, *balach*," he roared, deliberately insulting Oscar by calling him "boy". His very voice made the earth quake.

However, this address made Oscar angry and he yelled back.

"Defend yourself from this 'boy', *laosboc!*" He used the most insulting term he could think of, being a "gelded he-goat".

The Tighearna Dubh laughed so that the mountains shook and landslides roared from their tops. But he ignored Oscar. He looked straight at the Princess of the Fomorii.

"I have come for you, not to fight with boys."

Enraged, Oscar seized his spear and cast it at the strange warrior. It did not touch his body but it split the ridge of the shield right in its centre.

Still the Tighearna Dubh did not respond, dismissing Oscar as a "petulant *balach*". At this, Oscar became angrier and cast his second spear at the warrior's mighty steed. It went right through the horse's heart and it fell dead. Ossian, who was the bard of the Feans, immediately composed a song about this mighty deed and some say that it still may be heard, sung in the remote places and islands of Scotland, where the language of the children of the Gael has not yet been entirely cast out by the language of the Gall.

The Tighearna Dubh was finally moved to anger by the loss of his prize horse, and he beat on his mighty shield with his sword and challenged the Feans to send fifty men of them against him and he would overcome them all. If they did not accept his challenge, then they were all weaklings who should still be supping their mother's milk.

So a great battle was fought on that strand. The Tighearna Dubh fought with tremendous strength and ferocity.

It happened that the Tighearna Dubh finally came face to face with Goll, who was Fingal's best warrior, and they closed on each other with sword and shield. Never had high-hilled Alba seen such a ferocious combat. Sharp and cunning was the swordplay. Blood stained the sands and it was a mixture of the blood of the Tighearna Dubh and the blood of Goll. It was nearly sundown when the combat ceased and then it was because the Tighearna Dubh, growing fatigued, dropped his sword-point a little and gave Goll the chance to make a lightning thrust. The Tighearna Dubh fell dead on the shore.

No mightier a warrior had ever been overcome in the history of the Feans. When the Dark Lord fell, there was a hush in the air, the whispering waters of the seas fell silent and the wind died away.

The Princess of the Fomorii turned to all the Feans with her sad smile and thanked each of them.

"I can now return to the land of the Fomorii," she said, "and return without fear, thanks to the bravery and skill of the Feans. But promise me one thing, before I go: that if ever I need the help of any of you again, you will come freely and quickly to my aid."

The Feans all promised and none more ardently than Fingal himself.

A year and a day went by. It transpired that the Feans were once more crossing the Eas-Ruaidh, the Red Cataract, when they saw a boat approaching with one person rowing it.

Oscar shaded his eyes.

"Perhaps it is the Princess of the Fomorii?" he suggested hopefully, for he still wished to prove his valour before such a beautiful maiden.

Fingal shook his head. "There is but a young man in the boat."

The boat drew swiftly alongside and the young man hailed Fingal without climbing out.

"Who are you?" demanded the leader of the Feans, peering down over the rail.

"I am a messenger from the land of the Fomorii, those who dwell under the waves."

"What is your message?"

"Muirgen, my Princess, is dying."

Now there was great sorrowing among the Feans when they heard this news and they immediately set up the *gol-ghàire*, the loud lamentation which is the tradition for the reception of bad news. But Fingal silenced them with an upraised hand.

"This is a sad message you bring," he said, addressing the young man. "Is she so ill?"

"She is and ready to die. But she sent me to bid you to remember your promise to help her in time of difficulty."

"If there is anything we can do," Fingal assured him, "then it shall be done."

"You have a healer among the Feans, whose name is Diarmuid Lighiche. Ask him to come with me, so that he may give of his healing to my Princess."

Now Diarmuid Lighiche was the handsomest of all the Feans, for his father had been none other than the love god Aongus the Ever Young. Aongus had conferred on Diarmuid Lighiche all the knowledge that he had for the curing of sickness and the healing of wounds. Only Dian Cécht himself, the great god of healing, knew more than Diarmuid Lighiche.

Diarmuid Lighiche was already moving to the young man's boat, even before Fingal had turned to him. He entered the boat and it sped off towards the sea-cave which is the entrance to the land of the Fomorii, the dwellers under the waves. On the way, they passed by an island of mosses and Diarmuid knew these to be healing herbs and so, as they passed, he reached a hand out of the boat to pick them.

He spied patches of *mòinteach*, or red sphagnum, the peat or bog moss. He plucked some of it and moved on and saw another patch where he took some more and then he saw a third clump and took another handful.

The boatman took Diarmuid straight to the palace of the Princess of the Fomorii. It was a golden castle beneath the waves, filled with courtiers who were all hushed and silent with grief. Among them was the old King of the Fomorii and his queen. And the queen seized Diarmuid by the hand and led him without a word to her daughter's bedside.

Muirgen lay on the bed, still like a corpse, with her eyes closed.

Diarmuid knelt by the bed and touched her forehead. So strong was the power of his healing that her eyes flickered open and she recognised him as one of the Feans and smiled her sad smile.

"I behold you with joy, Diarmuid Lighiche. Your touch is a

strength to me, but not strength enough to cure my illness. I am dying."

"I know your sickness," Diarmuid assured her. "I knew it the moment I touched your forehead and thereby recognized it. I have brought you three portions of red moss. I must mix them with three drops of healing water and you shall drink them. They will heal you, for they are the life-giving drops of your heart."

"Alas!" the princess exclaimed. "Dying though I am, I am under a *toirmeasg*, a sacred prohibition, that I cannot drink anything except from the Cup of Healing which belongs to the King of the Magh Ionguntas, the Plain of Wonder. Therefore, my friend, I cannot drink the healing potion."

Now Diarmuid, as knowledgeable as he was, had never heard of this Cup of Healing.

"A wise Druid has told me," continued the Princess Muirgen, "that if ever I have to drink of the three drops of the red moss of life, I can only do so from this Cup and from the Healing Water it contains. Yet it is known that no man can ever gain the Cup of Healing from the King of the Plain of Wonder. I am therefore resigned to my fate, Diarmuid. I must die."

Diarmuid Lighiche stood up; his face was filled with stern determination. "There is no man nor power in the world above or below or even in the Otherworld that will prevent me finding and taking that Cup. Tell me where I may find this Plain of Wonder, so that the sooner I may set out and the sooner I may return to you."

Princess Muirgen sighed gently. "The Plain of Wonder is not far distant, Diarmuid. If you travel westward, when you come to a great river of silver, you will find Magh Ionguntus on the other side. But, I fear, Diarmuid, you will never be able to cross the river, for that is impossible."

Diarmuid Lighiche then made some healing spells which would ensure that the Princess of the Fomorii lived until he was able to return. The King and Queen of the Fomorii were anxious at his going, but bade him a safe journey and speedy return. The courtiers were filled with hope and did their best to help him, but he had to make the journey alone.

He began to travel westward and eventually he came to a great river of silver. It was mighty and wide and Diarmuid looked up and down the shore, trying to find a ford by which he might cross. But there was no ford, no bridge nor any other means of crossing the turbulent stretch of silver water.

Diarmuid sat on a rock and put his head in his hands and tried to fathom some means of crossing. "Alas, the Princess spoke the truth. I am not able to cross over."

"Diarmuid, you are right. You are in a mighty pickle."

He looked up at the sound of a musical voice, and found a little man, clad entirely in brown, standing regarding him with a wry smile.

"That's the truth of it," assented Diarmuid, not finding it strange that the little man knew his name.

"What would you give as a reward to anyone who could help you?"

"I would give whatever one wanted, in order that I might save the life of the Princess Muirgen."

"In that case, I will help you," offered the little man in brown.

"What is it that you want in return?"

"Only your goodwill."

"That you may have and gladly," replied Diarmuid, rather amazed at the easiness of the condition.

"Then I shall carry you across the river."

Diarmuid smiled wryly. The little man was scarce a foot tall and Diarmuid was over six feet tall.

"That you cannot. You are too small."

"That I can," assured the little man. And he made Diarmuid climb on his back and Diarmuid, amazed, found it broad and roomy. Then the little man walked across the river, treading swiftly as if it were nothing but hard ground. And so they crossed the river and they passed by a curious island. Its centre appeared to be hidden by a dark mist.

"What is the name of that island?" Diarmuid asked.

"That is Inis Bàis, the Island of Death, where there is a well of healing water. But none may land on there without courting death."

They reached the opposite bank.

"This is the Plain of Wonder," the little man announced.

"It seems wrong that you have brought me here and asked for no reward," observed Diarmuid.

"I have. I asked for your goodwill," replied his companion. "You are on your way to the palace of King Iain, in order to obtain his Cup of Healing."

"That is true."

"Then may you obtain it."

The little brown man turned back to the river and was gone.

Diarmuid continued on westward and found that, although there was no sun shining on the land, it was always bright. Finally, he came to a great castle of silver with crystal spires and roofs. The doors were closed and locked.

Diarmuid halted outside and called out: "I am Diarmuid Lighiche! Open the door and let me in."

"It is forbidden!" came a voice.

"Who forbids it?" demanded Diarmuid.

"Myself it is. I am the guardian of the gate."

"Come forth, and I will fight you for the right to enter."

The gate swung open and a tall warrior came forth with drawn sword. The warrior was clad from head to foot in blood-red. Now Diarmuid was not simply a healer. As a member of the Feans, he was also a mighty champion, and he clashed with the guardian of the gate; sparks flew from their meeting weapons. It was but a short contest before the guardian lay stretched dead on the ground.

Then King Iain himself came to the gate, to discover the reason for the noise of combat.

"Who are you, and why have you slain my Red Lord?" he demanded. "He was the most skilled of my champions."

"I am Diarmuid Lighiche," replied the young man. "I slew him because he would not let me in."

"You are welcome here, son of Aongus the Ever Young," said King Iain with respect. "But there is sorrow on me that you have had to slay my guardian of the gate."

Diarmuid smiled as a ruse came to his mind. "I am a healer. I hear you possess a Cup of Healing. Why not allow me to give the warrior a drink from it? Surely he will be brought forth alive."

King Iain thought for a moment, then nodded, turned and clapped his hands. Servants appeared. "Bring forth the Cup of Healing," he ordered.

So the cup was brought forth and the king handed it to Diarmuid saying: "There is no virtue in this Cup, unless it is in the hands of a healer."

Diarmuid touched the slain warrior's lips with it and poured three drops of water into the man's mouth. The guardian of the gate sat up and blinked. Then he rose to his feet, with his wounds entirely healed.

"How may we repay you?" asked King Iain.

"I came to get this Cup to heal the dying Princess of the Fomorii. I can take it by gratitude or by force."

"Take it with my gratitude then, Diarmuid. I give you the cup freely. But little good it will now do you. You have given the guardian of the gate the three precious healing drops that were in it. It contains no more and is now useless."

Diarmuid was annoyed that he had not considered this matter.

"Nevertheless," he insisted, "I shall take the cup with me."

"I will send you a boat so that you may return across the silver river," King Iain offered.

"I stand in no need of a boat," replied Diarmuid, in anger that he had been so foolish. He felt pride crush his reason.

King Iain laughed kindly. "Then may you soon return." For he did not believe that anyone could cross the silver river without his boat.

Diarmuid bade the king and his gatekeeper farewell and returned back across the bright plain of Magh Ionguntus. He finally arrived at the edge of the river and once again started to look for a ford. Then he sat down and his thoughts were gloomy. He had obtained the Cup but spent the precious liquid. Now his pride had caused him to reject the king's offer and he could not find a ford over the river.

"Now I shall have to return in shame to King Iain, and even if I cross, this Cup is of little use to the Princess Muirgen."

"You are in a pickle again, Diarmuid," said the musical voice of the little man. He was standing looking at Diarmuid, with his head to one side.

"It is true enough," agreed Diarmuid gloomily.

"Did you get the Cup of Healing?"

"Yes, but the three drops of liquid are gone and now I cannot cross the river. I am twice defeated."

"Once defeated . . . perhaps," said the little brown man. "I can carry you back."

"Then so be it. But what do you wish of me?"

"Just your goodwill."

Then the little man hoisted Diarmuid on his broad back and began to walk across the silver river but this time, as they neared the Island of Death, surrounded by its grim, dark mist, the little man went towards it.

"Where are you taking me?" cried Diarmuid, slightly alarmed.

"Do you desire to heal the Princess of the Fomorii?"

"I do."

"Then you must fill your Cup of Healing with three drops of water. I have already told you where."

Diarmuid frowned, not understanding.

The little man was quite impatient.

"You must fill it at the Well of Healing on the Island of Death. That is why I am carrying you to the island. However, heed this warning; you must not get off my back nor set foot on the shore, or else you will never be able to leave that island. Have no fear. I shall take you to the well and kneel there while you dip your Cup into it, and thus you may carry off enough water to give the three drops to the Princess."

Now Diarmuid was delighted when he heard what the little brown man had to say. So it was that he was able to obtain a cup of healing water in this manner and the little brown man carried him to the opposite bank and place him safely in the Land of the Fomorii.

"You have a happy heart in you now, Diarmuid," observed the little brown man.

"It is true," agreed the healer.

"Then I shall add to your joy with a piece of good advice."

"Advice as well? Why have you helped me as you have?"

"I have done so because you have a warm heart and desire to do good. To heal people is better than to destroy them.

Men who do goodwill ever find friends in any land, whether it be in this world or the Otherworld."

"I thank you for your help. Now tell me your advice."

"When the Princess of the Fomorii is healed, the King of the Fomorii will offer you a choice of many rich rewards. Take no reward that he offers, but ask only for the boat to convey you homeward."

Diarmuid was a little surprised, but he nodded. "You have been a true friend to me, little man. I shall follow this advice for, truly, my healing is a gift to help others and not sold for reward."

So he bade farewell to the little brown man and returned to the great golden palace of the King of the Fomorii.

The Princess Muirgen was still alive but pale and listless. Yet she registered surprise when he came into her room bearing the Cup of Healing.

"No man has ever achieved what you have achieved," she said.

"Only for your sake have I done this."

"I feared that you would never return."

So Diarmuid mixed the healing potion, adding the three pinches of red sphagnum moss to the healing water. The princess thrice drank, sipping the three healing drops. When the last drop was swallowed, she sat up and was quite well.

There was great joy throughout the castle and a feast was prepared and entertainers came to provide music and merriment. Sorrow was put away and laughter returned to the castle of the Fomorii.

During the feast, the King of the Fomorii turned to Diarmuid and said: "You may have whatever reward it is in my gift to give you. What will you have? I will give you all the gold and silver you desire; you can marry my daughter and become heir to my kingdom."

Diarmuid shook his head sadly. "If I married your daughter, I could not return to my own land above the waves."

"True enough. But here you would spend many happy days and would be honoured by everyone."

Diarmuid shook his head again. "I have only one thing to ask of you, King of the Fomorii."

"Ask away. I promise to give you whatever you want."

"Then all I want is the boat to return me to the ship of the Feans from whence I came. My own land is dear to me, as are my kinsmen and friends, the Feans. Above all, my loyalty lies to Fingal, who is my chief."

"Then," said the King of the Fomorii, "What you desire is yours."

The entire palace came with Diarmuid to the boat and the Princess Muirgen took him aside and held his hand a moment.

"I shall never forget you, Diarmuid. You found me in suffering and gave me relief. You found me dying and gave me life. When you are back in your own land, remember me; I shall never pass an hour of life without thinking of you in joy and thankfulness."

Then Diarmuid stepped into the boat, and the boatman, who was the very same man as had come with the news of the Princess Muirgen's illness, began to row him upwards from the Land Beneath the Waves. Soon they came to the warship of the Feans. The ship was resting where they had left it, near the Eas-Ruaidh, the Red Cataract. The Feans saw him coming and came crowding round as he climbed up.

"What is the matter?" cried Oscar, coming forward. "Did you forget something?"

"You must not tarry," advised Goll, frowning. "The Princess is in danger."

When Diarmuid expressed his puzzlement at their concerns, Fingal told him that he had been gone but a few seconds. Then Diarmuid understood.

"I have been in the Land under the Waves for many Otherworld days, each day being a second of the time passed here. In the land that I visited, there is no night nor day to guide the keeping of time. Anyway, the Princess Muirgen is now alive and well and glad I am to be home among you."

Then the Feans raised sail, rejoicing, and continued in their warship until they came to the great fortress which was their home, and they feasted and celebrated the homecoming of Diarmuid the Healer.

16 *Maighdean-mhara*

There are mermaids and there are sea-maids, and the one must not be confused with the other. Mermaids can be winsome creatures, sometimes mischievous but never evil. But sea-maids, well, there's another kettle of fish. Avoid them, as your life depends on it; indeed, sometimes it will be more than your life that is at stake. The story of Murdo Sean is an example of that.

It happened long ago near Inverary, which stands on the shores of Loch Fyne, in Argyll. Inverary was once a great fishing town. Have you ever seen its town arms and its motto? "May there always be a herring in your net!" Aye, it was famed for the herring catch and its kippers, too.

Above the town, on Duniquaich Hill, stood the watch-tower of the Campbells of Loch Awe, whose castle rose black against the sky. For they say that the race of the "Crooked Mouth", which is the meaning of the Campbell name, owned the town and its people.

It happened that there was a period of poor times in the town, when the fish were not running in the waters thereabouts. Fish were more scarce than gold; indeed, not even gold could buy fish in the market of Inverary. Still, the Campbells demanded their rents and tithes from the people and there was much suffering there.

Among the fishermen out one day was Murdo Sean, or Murdo the Old, and he had no better luck than any. For weeks, his nets had come in as empty as he had cast them out. He was in despair. For the bailiff of the Campbells had sworn that, if he did not pay his rent, he and his ageing wife would be cast out of his cottage, where he and his ancestors had dwelt for many hundreds of years. His old mare and his old bitch dog would be taken away as the property of the Campbells.

Sadness was on him like a black rain cloud, when he felt his boat being rocked and, turning, he saw a sea-maid, leaning over the bow of his vessel. Yes: a sea-maid and not a mermaid.

"If I fill your nets with fish, old man," she inquired, "What will you give me?"

Murdo Sean shrugged eloquently. "There is nothing I have to give."

The sea-maid regarded him speculatively. "What about your first-born son?"

Murdo Sean laughed outright. "I have no son. At my age, I am not likely to have one."

Indeed, he was called *sean*, which means old, because he was the oldest man in Inverary.

"Tell me about your family," invited the sea-maid, still interested.

"As well as myself, there is my wife, who is well past child-bearing age, being only a few years younger than myself. Then there is my old mare and my old bitch dog. Another few years should see us all in the Otherworld, if not before, because this evening we shall be evicted by the mighty lords who dwell in the castle above the town."

"Not so," replied the sea-maid firmly. And she took from a purse around her waist twelve curious-looking grains. "Take these grain, old man. Give three to your wife, three to your mare and three to your bitch dog and plant three behind your house. In three months' time, your wife will bear three sons, your mare three foals, your bitch dog three puppies and behind your house three trees will grow."

Murdo Sean laughed. "You are joking with me, sea-maid. And why would my garden be in need of trees?"

"Not I," she replied sternly. "Indeed, the trees will be a sign. When one of your sons dies, one of the trees will wither. Away home with you now, and do as I say."

Murdo Sean laughed bitterly. "How can I do this, when my wife and I will be thrown out of our cottage tonight?"

"Cast your nets into the water. Your nets will henceforth be full of fish and you will prosper well and live a long life. But remember me. In three years' time, you will bring me your first-born son as my reward. Do you agree?"

Well, Murdo Sean had nothing to lose and so he agreed.

Now, of course, everything happened as the sea-maid had promised it would. He took home that day enough fish to pay the bailiff of the Campbells. Not only that day but thereafter.

The fisherman and his wife had three sons, the mare had three foals, the dog three puppies and three trees grew in his garden. But what is more, the fisherman's nets were always full of fish and he was prosperous and grew rich and happy. Indeed, he became very prosperous in Inverary and became independent of the Campbells entirely.

Three years passed and he knew that the time had come to repay the sea-maid. Yet he could not find it in his heart to take his first-born son to sea to give him to her.

When the time approached, he was out in his boat again when it started to rock. There at the prow was the sea-maid, leaning over the edge and regarding him with a serious expression. The old fisherman noticed that she was carrying an infant of three years of age in her arms.

"Well, Murdo Sean," she said, "the time has come. Where is your first born son?"

Murdo Sean thought hard. "Is it today that my three years are up? I had forgotten that this was the day I should bring him. Forgive me."

The sea-maid was clearly annoyed but she sighed and said: "I will be lenient with you, Murdo Sean, for I have in my arms the son of another fisherman who has fulfilled his promise to me and I cannot handle the both. I will allow you seven years more, and then you must bring him to me."

Murdo Sean continued to prosper and, seven years later, he was on his boat when it rocked and there at the prow looking at him was the sea-maid. She carried in her arms a boy of ten years of age.

"Well, Murdo Sean, where is your son?"

"Oh dear, is this the day I should have brought him to you? I had forgotten entirely."

The sea-maid looked at him in annoyance and then sighed. "I will be lenient with you, Murdo Sean, for I have in my arms the son of another fisherman who has fulfilled his promise to me and I cannot handle the both. I will allow you a further seven years. But no longer."

She dived off into the water and was gone.

Murdo Sean returned home very happy, for he was now so old that he was sure that he would be dead before the next seven years passed and that he would never again have to face the sea-maid. But, indeed, he and his wife continued well and prosperous. The seven years passed in the blink of an eye and the day soon arrived when he was due to take his first-born and give him to the sea-maid. The night before, he was troubled and restless and he sent for his first-born son, who was now seventeen; and, at seventeen, according to custom, the boy had reached the *aimsir togú* or "age of choice", when he was a man.

Murdo Sean told his son, who was called Murdo Òg, or Young Murdo, everything about the sea-maid.

"I will go and confront this sea-maid, father," he said, for he was a proud young man and no coward. "I will confront her and spare you the consequences of not handing me over to her."

But Murdo Sean pleaded with him not to go, for he knew the power of the sea-maid.

"Well, then, if I am not to face her, then I must arm myself and leave Inverary."

And he went to Gobhan, the smith, and asked the man to make him as fine a sword as possible.

Now the first sword Gobhan made was too light, and the metal blade broke, splintering into fragments, when the young man tried it out. Then the second blade broke clean in two halves. But the third stood the young man's testing. Satisfied, Murdo Òg took the night-black horse, the first-born from his father's old mare, and the black dog, the first-born of his father's old bitch dog, and he set off on the road away from Inverary.

He was not far along the road around Loch Fyne when he came across the carcass of a deer which had been freshly slain. There was no sign of anyone near to claim it. But nearby was a falcon perched on a tree and an otter on the bank of the loch and a wild dog on the land. They were hungry. The young man also felt hungry. After checking once more that no hunters were about to claim the slain deer, Murdo Òg divided the meat between the dog, the falcon and the otter. As each animal received their portion, they promised to help Murdo Òg if he ever needed it.

Murdo shared his portion with his black dog while his horse grazed in a field.

He rode on and came to the great castle of Campbell, "Crooked Mouth", the chief of his clan, and ruler of all the lands in the vicinity. The chief demanded to know what the young man sought. Murdo Òg said he wanted work, for he had refused to take anything from his father other than his clothes, sword, horse and dog. He did not want to be beholden any more than possible to the largesse of the sea-maiden.

It so happened that Campbell "Crooked Mouth" needed a cowherd for his cattle, and so Murdo Òg accepted the job. But the grass around Campbell's castle was so poor that the milk-yield of his cattle was low. Murdo Òg was very conscientious, and so he decided to search further afield for good grazing than in the fields of the chief. He moved the cattle so far that he crossed the boundaries of Campbell's territory and came to a very fertile green glen.

It was the lad's misfortune that the glen belonged to a giant of a man named Athach. The man was mean and of an irritable temper. When he saw Murdo Òg grazing the cattle in his glen, he did not even hesitate to greet him, but drew his sword and rushed on the youth with a terrible battle-cry. Now the boy was nimble with his sword and soon Athach was stretched on the green swathe with his heart pierced.

Murdo Òg saw the man's cabin not far away and, in curiosity, he went to it, finding it deserted, for none but Athach dwelt there. Inside the house there were many great riches. It seems that all mean men, like Athach, are able to gather riches and keep them. Murdo was truly amazed as he gazed on them. But, being conscientious and moral, knowing they did not belong to him, he took none of them. Indeed, he also buried Athach behind the cabin and erected a marker there, and swore that he would try to find Athach's next of kin.

He grazed Campbell's cattle in the valley and soon their milk-yield was so rich that when Campbell heard the news, he sent for Murdo Òg and told him how pleased he was with him. Murdo Òg continued to graze Campbell's cattle in the glen until the grass was exhausted and he had to move into a second glen. To his surprise, he had no sooner entered this glen but he thought he saw Athach, alive, and rushing on him with his sword and uttering a terrible battle-cry. He had to defend himself. Being nimble with his weapon, he slew the second giant of a man.

In the cabin of the second giant, he found an inscription: "this belongs to Famhair, brother of Athach". There were just as many riches in the cabin as those in Athach's cabin. Murdo Òg would take none of them and, instead, he buried Famhair behind the cabin and erected a marker, swearing he would find out who the next of kin was.

One night he returned to Campbell's castle with his cows, to find the chief's retinue in uproar. It seemed that a three-headed female monster had arisen from Loch Fyne and was demanding that the chief sacrifice his only daughter, Finnseang, who was a beautiful young maid, and the flower of Campbell's eye: for, indeed, she was his only child.

"What will happen?" demanded Murdo Òg of one of the milkmaids, who was milking the cows.

"One of the warriors, a suitor of the chief's daughter, is going to engage the monster in combat tomorrow at first light," she told him. "All will be well, for the warrior is Campbell's best champion and no man in the land has ever scratched him in combat."

So, the next day, everyone took up vantage positions along the shore of Loch Fyne and the terrible, fearsome three-headed monster appeared in its waters. The champion marched down to the shore; he looked proud and confident, with his buckler and great sword ready. But when the monster began to approach, he turned white, the sweat of fear stood on his brow and he turned, casting away his weapons, shield and sword, and fled.

The monster roared its challenge. Then it stated that the chief's daughter, Finnseang, was to be brought to the water's edge at dawn the next morning, unless any other champion could be found.

With a sorrowful heart, Campbell, the chief, knew there was no other hero in all his land better than the one who had fled before the monster. There was nothing to do but surrender to the three-headed monster that which it demanded. He bade farewell of his only child and led her down to the shore of Loch Fyne at the appointed hour. Everyone returned to the castle, including the old chief, to mourn the sacrifice, for they could not bear to witness it.

However, Murdo Òg did not return to the castle but he went to the shore of the loch and found the chieftain's daughter crying to herself as she waited for the loathsome monster to appear.

"Fear not," he told her, "I will defend you."

"But you are only the cowherd," she protested in amazement.

"A cowherd's hand is as steady as that of any warrior, and his sword is just as sharp."

She nodded, feeling remorse at having made so silly a comment. "And his heart is just as brave," she added contritely.

"But it is true, as you have said, I am a cowherd and have been hard at work. So, therefore, I am tired. I will sleep until the monster comes. Be sure that you wake me when it approaches, and you must do so by taking the gold ring which you wear on your finger and placing it on mine."

"I will do so willingly, if it wakes you to fight the monster."

He fell asleep by her side and she sat waiting and watching. Then she heard the monster rising from the watery depths, crying out that it had come to claim her. So she took off her gold ring and placed it on his finger and he awoke with a start.

The sun came up and the three-headed monster rose out of the loch.

Murdo Òg went forward with his sword ready.

The combat was long and hard but, finally, Murdo Òg managed to slice off one of the three heads. And he took the head and stuck it on a stout stick of withy, which is a branch of the osier willow. Meantime, the monster went screeching across the loch; the waters were whipped into a blood-red froth as it threshed and clawed its way without its third head.

Murdo Òg turned to the chief's daughter. "You must not tell a soul that it was I who defended you."

Finnseang took a vow not to do so. Then he returned to tend his cattle herd and she returned to the castle.

That evening he returned to the castle to find the people in an uproar.

"The monster has returned. It is two-headed now," a dairy maid told Murdo Òg. "It says that Finnseang must be sacrificed to it unless a champion comes to best it."

Murdo Òg was surprised but he was about to go to Finnseang's aid when the dairy maid said: "But fear not, for Campbell has a new champion, much braver than the other, and he has gone to defend Finnseang. For he has told Campbell that it was he who took the first head off the monster."

Murdo Òg was astonished that the warrior could make such a false claim.

"What does Finnseang say?" he asked.

"She says nothing. She does not deny it nor name anyone else."

Murdo Òg sighed. Finnseang was true to the promise that she had made him, for he had told her not to reveal that he had defended her.

So everyone went down to the loch shore to witness the combat. The second champion went out to fight with the two-headed monster. No sooner did the monster approach him than he turned white and the sweat of fear was on him. He turned, throwing aside his shield and sword and ran off and was never seen in Campbell country again.

Now the monster called to Campbell "Crooked Mouth",

the chieftain: "Place your daughter by the side of the loch before dawn and I will come for her, unless you have another brave champion to prevent me."

Sorrowfully, the next day before dawn, Campbell took leave of his daughter and left her weeping by the side of the loch. No one else remained with her, for none wanted to see the terrible sacrifice of Finnseang.

When they had all returned to the castle, Murdo Òg came to her and said: "Fear not, Finnseang, I will save you, even though I am a cowherd. But I have been tending my herd and am tired so I must sleep until the monster comes. Do you awaken me by placing one of your pearl earrings in my ear."

"Gladly," replied the girl, "if it will wake you to fight the monster."

Soon the dawn light came and the two-headed monster reared forth out of the loch.

As good as her word, Finnseang put her earring in his ear.

Murdo Òg awoke and sprang forward with his sword. Again, the fight was long, but he fought bravely and well and managed to sever a second head from the monster. This, too, he skewered on the willow branch, while the monster, screaming and threshing, returned back across the loch in a froth of blood.

"Home you go," he told Finnseang, "but give me your oath that you will not tell anyone it was I who saved you."

She promised and he went off to tend his herd while she returned to the castle.

When he returned to Campbell's castle in the evening, he found the people in uproar.

"What is it now?" he demanded.

"A one-headed monster has appeared," the dairymaid told him. "It demands that the chief's daughter be taken to it as sacrifice. But have no fear, a third champion has now come forward to slay the monster. He is much braver than the others for it was he who took off the second head of the monster this morning."

Murdo Òg was truly astonished that any warrior could make such a false claim.

"What does Finnseang say to that?"

"She neither confirms nor denies it. So Campbell, the chief, believes it to be so."

Murdo Òg sighed. Finnseang had kept her word to him and not told anyone that it was he who had saved her.

The next morning, the new champion marched down to the shore, and the people gathered round to watch the combat. The one-headed monster reared out of the lake and the champion went forward. But as the monster drew near, his face went white and the sweat of fear stood out on his brow. He suddenly turned, threw aside his shield and sword and went running off as fast as a rabbit over the hills and was not seen again.

The monster came forward.

"Since you have no champion to defend Finnseang, let her be brought to the shore of the loch before dawn tomorrow and then I will come for her."

It was truly a grief-stricken father who took his daughter to the loch shore and parted from her the next morning. No one else came, because they could not bear to see Finnseang being carried off by the monster.

But hardly had Finnseang been left when Murdo Òg appeared. "Fear not, Finnseang, for I am here and will defend you, even though I be but a herder of cows. But as I am such, I am tired and will sleep until the monster comes. Do you wake me by placing your second earring in my ear."

"If that will wake you to fight the monster, I will do so gladly," affirmed the girl.

He fell asleep. Just as dawn arrived, the one-headed monster reared out of the loch. The girl placed the second earring in his ear and Murdo Òg sprang forward, sword ready. The fight was fierce but finally Murdo Òg sliced off the third head from the monster, and this time it sank quietly into the bloody waters of the loch and never rose again.

Murdo Òg put the third head on the willow branch and placed it as a totem by the shores of the loch.

"Do not tell anyone it was I," he said.

"But the danger is gone," she protested. "Surely now I can tell my father that it was you who saved me?"

He shook his head sadly. "Your father will not accept that

a cowherd can be a champion. Nor that a cowherd can love a chieftain's daughter."

She said nothing, for she knew that there was wisdom in his statement. She watched sadly as he went off to tend his cattle. She realised that she loved him and knew that she had to act. So when she returned to the castle, where great joy awaited her, she told her father that she would marry and only marry the man who could take the monster's heads off the withy, or willow branch. Of course, with the monster dead, many came forward to try their luck, boasting their bravery. But they failed to remove the heads, for they seemed stuck tight on the willow branch. Finnseang herself knew that only the man who had put the heads on the branch could take them off.

Everyone was in despair, for it seemed no one in the castle was able to perform the deed.

Then Murdo Òg returned with his cows.

"Murdo Òg has not attempted the task yet," Finnseang told her father.

Campbell laughed uproariously, and all the warriors echoed his laughter.

"He is only a cowherd, child," rebuked Campbell.

"But he is a man," she pointed out.

Reluctantly, Campbell called Murdo Òg forward and told him to remove the heads.

Murdo Òg wondered why he was called upon to do so, for he had not heard that Finnseang had promised to marry the man who did so; he reached forward and easily removed the monster-heads from the branch.

The champions of Campbell were no more astonished at this than Campbell himself.

"What does this mean?" breathed the chieftain suspiciously.

"I cannot mention the warrior who came and saved me three times from the monster," replied Finnseang. "I am under oath not to do so. But I gave him my two earrings and my ring."

Campbell realized that Murdo Òg was wearing the earrings of his daughter and on his finger was her ring.

He went forward and clasped the young man by the shoulders.

"You are the one who saved my daughter and the man she loves. You shall marry her and be as a son to me."

Murdo Òg was well pleased and agreed.

There was a great feasting at the castle and Murdo Òg and Finnseang were wed. For three years they lived happily together.

Then a day came when the lovers were walking by the shores of the loch. Without warning, the waters boiled and the monster, with three new heads grown on it, was even more fearsome than before. It was seeking vengeance and it leapt out of the loch and seized Murdo Òg before he had time to draw his sword. The next instant, the monster had dragged the young man under the water.

Finnseang wailed and lamented and, as she did so, an old man passing by asked her what had happened. When she told him, he advised her to lay out all her best jewels on the shore of the loch and call the monster to come and look at them.

This she did. The beast surfaced suddenly and examined the fine jewels laid out on the shore.

"I'll give you any of these that you wish, if only you will give me a sight of my husband, Murdo Òg," she pleaded.

The monster's eyes glinted. It turned and dived back into the loch and soon returned with Murdo Òg, as whole and as alive as anyone.

"I will give you all my jewels if you return him to me," pleaded Finnseang.

The monster considered the request and finally agreed to the bargain.

All went well for three years until, one day, the young couple were walking by the loch shore again. This time the monster rose out and it was Finnseang who was dragged under the waters before Murdo Òg had a chance to defend her.

Murdo Òg was wailing and lamenting his lost bride when an old man walking by asked him what was wrong.

Murdo Òg told him and the old man said: "I will tell you how you can rescue your wife and destroy the monster for ever. In the centre of the loch is an island. On the island is a white-footed hind, slender and swift. If you catch the hind, a black crow will spring out of her mouth and if the black crow were caught, a trout would fall out of her beak, and in the mouth of the trout would be an egg. Now in the egg is the soul of that monster. If you crush the egg, the monster will die."

Murdo Òg was astonished, but he decided that he must try this means of rescuing his wife or do nothing at all.

There was no easy way to reach the island in the centre of the loch. Anyway, the monster was swimming the loch and any boat that passed over it would be seized. So Murdo Òg mounted his fine black horse, the first-born horse of his father's old mare, and with his black dog beside him, the first-born dog of his father's old bitch, he rode hard towards the loch shore and made a leap towards the island. Such was the power of that leap that they landed on the shore of the island.

Murdo Òg hunted the white-footed hind and finally cornered her but could not reach her. "I wish I had a great hunting dog," he thought. "Just like the dog I saw all those years ago."

No sooner had he wished it than the great dog with whom he had shared meat suddenly appeared and, between them, they captured the hind. But as they did so, it opened its mouth and a black crow sprang out and flew off.

"Ah, if only I had the help of a falcon," thought Murdo Òg, "like the falcon I saw all those years ago."

No sooner had he thought that, than the falcon he had shared meat with also appeared and chased the crow. As it caught her, a trout fell from her mouth into the loch and swam furiously away.

"Ah, if only I had the help of an otter," he thought, "like the one I saw all those years ago, then it could capture the trout."

No sooner had he thought that than the otter with whom he had shared meat appeared and was after the trout in a flash, caught it and brought it to the shore of the island where Murdo Òg waited.

The young man took the egg from the trout's mouth and put it on the ground, raising his foot ready to stamp on it.

At that moment, the great monster rose from the loch and pleaded with him not to damage the egg.

"Give me back my wife," demanded Murdo Òg.

At once, Finnseang appeared on the shore by his side.

Without hesitating, Murdo Òg brought his foot down on the egg and the monster gave one shriek and collapsed dead into the waters of the loch.

Murdo Òg and Finnseang went back to Castle Campbell to the great joy of everyone. Murdo Òg had truly become a great chieftain in the land. He and Finnseang lived happily together.

But one day, after three years had passed, when they were riding around the loch, Murdo Òg noticed a dark castle, set among the gloomy black forest, which he had never seen before.

"Who dwells there, Finnseang?" he demanded.

"Leave well alone. It is forbidden to go near it. No one has ever come back who has entered there."

Murdo Òg said nothing and they continued on their way. But if Murdo Òg had a fault, it was a great curiosity. That evening, pretending to go out hunting, he rode back towards the gloomy castle.

At the door of the castle sat a crone, a little old woman, who greeted him pleasantly enough.

"Who lives here?" he demanded.

"Why, someone you'll be happy to meet, young sir," replied the crone. "Come away inside."

Murdo Òg climbed down off his horse and went inside.

No sooner had he entered the castle than she came up behind him and struck him on the head with a club.

He fell to the ground.

At the house of Murdo Sean, the fisherman of Inverary, the old man was looking out on his garden.

"Save us!" he cried. For he saw one of his three oak trees suddenly wither and die. "That can only mean my first-born son, Murdo Òg, is dead."

"How can that be, father?" demanded Lachlan, who was his second-born son.

Murdo Sean pointed to the withered tree

"Thc sea-maid said it would be a sign. Whenever one of the trees withers, it means one of my sons has died. Sincc you and your brother are here, it can only mean Murdo Òg is dead."

"I will go in search of him and discover the truth of it," Lachlan announced, for he was as brave as his brother.

He saddled the second-born horse of his father's old mare and took the second-born dog of his father's old bitch dog and he set out. Finally he came to Campbell's castle and found it in mourning. On telling Finnseang who he was, she told him all she knew, and about the terrible dark castle in the woods. She warned him, as did her father, Campbell, but Lachlan was as warlike as his name and rode forth to the castle. Nothing would prevent him from going there. He had to see whether his brother was dead or not.

He came to the castle and saw the crone sitting by the gate.

"Who lives here, old woman?" he demanded

"Someone you'll be pleased to meet with, young sir," wheezed the old crone. "Come away in."

Lachlan entered the gate and, no sooner had he done so, than the crone slunk up behind and fetched him a hefty blow with her cudgel. He fell to the floor.

In Murdo Sean's garden, a second tree suddenly withered.

"Ah, ah," cried old Murdo Sean, "I played the sea-maid a grievous trick and now she punishes me. My second-born son, Lachlan, is dead."

"How do you know this, father?" demanded Aonghus, his third and youngest boy.

His father told him.

"Well, I must go in search of them and see for myself," he declared, for he was as brave as his brothers.

In spite of his old father's pleading, Aonghus saddled the third-born horse of his father's old mare and took the third-born dog of his father's old bitch dog and set forth. Eventually he came to the castle of Campbell, where he found great mourning and lamentation. When he told them who he was, Finnseang told him what had befallen her husband and his brother : that they had disappeared into the evil castle of gloom and had not returned.

Aonghus immediately set forth, in spite of all their pleadings for him not to chance his own life.

He reached the gates of the castle and saw the crone seated outside.

"Whose castle is this, old woman?" he demanded.

"Someone you'll be pleased to meet with, young sir. Come away in."

"I will do so, but you will proceed me," said Aonghus, who was a careful boy.

The old woman turned and began to hobble forward. Then the third-born dog sprang at her, but she had her cudgel in her hand and clubbed its head so that it fell at her feet.

Aonghus drew his sword and, with one swift cut, he took off the old crone's head. But she turned and seized it as it fell, so that it did not touch the ground. Then she stuck it back on her head.

But before she had recovered, the third-born horse reared up and struck out with flaying hooves and one hoof kicked the cudgel from her hand. It spun through the air and landed in the hand of Aonghus who, no sooner had he felt its magical properties, than he thrashed out with it, and hit her over the head. She fell onto the ground.

He began to search the castle and in the stables he found his brother's two black horses and two black dogs. Not long after, he discovered his brother Lachlan lying dead in one room and his brother Murdo Òg lying dead in another. He went to each of them and touched them with the cudgel. Whereupon they awoke, as if from a deep sleep, and were delighted to see each other once more.

They began to explore the castle and found an old man there.

"Do not harm me, sires," he cried.

"I recognise you," cried Murdo Òg. "You are the old man who told me how I could kill the three-headed monster of the loch. And you must be the same who told Finnseang how to save me from the monster."

"I am, sir. I am."

"Then what are you doing in this castle?"

"I am only the unwilling prisoner of its owner. I am her

servant and have had to serve her unwillingly for many a long century."

"The crone with the cudgel?" demanded Murdo Òg.

"None other than the sea-maid," replied the old man.

"The sea-maid?" cried the brothers, astounded.

The old man took them to where the crone lay on the floor. When they examined the corpse of the old woman, they found that she was none other than the sea-maid. This was her gloomy sea-shore castle. Further, the old man told them that the mean giants whom Murdo Òg had killed, Athach and Famhair, had been the sea-maid's foster sons, the two children that she had taken below the depths to nurture instead of Murdo Òg, when his father had pretended that he had forgotten the day on which he was to be handed over.

Finally, the three-headed loch monster was the sea-maid's special pet.

Each time she had sought to take revenge on Murdo Òg, because his father had not handed him over to her when he was a boy, Murdo Òg had been able to thwart her. Eventually she had overcome him as well as his second brother but three, being a pure number, had bested her in the end.

There was great rejoicing at Campbell's castle. No more rejoicing was there anywhere than between Murdo Òg and his wife Finnseang.

Lachlan and Aonghus were given high positions at the castle, becoming the foremost champions of the chief, Campbell "Crooked Mouth". Their father, Murdo Sean, and his wife and his animals were brought there and lived their lives in peace and prosperity.

When Campbell "Crooked Mouth" finally died, the *derbhfhine* of his family took the unusual step of acclaiming Murdo Òg as The Campbell, chieftain of the glens of Argyll, which means "the seaboard of the Gael" – *Airer-Ghàidheal.*

Beware, then, of the sea-maid, and make sure that you know the difference between a sea-maid and a mermaid, for they are dissimilar. A sea-maid may put you to the test, as she did Murdo Sean and his sons. So beware; at least they were found worthy. But not everyone may be so lucky.

17 *Conall Cròg Buidhe*

There was once a warrior who lived on Airer Ghàidheal, "the seaboard of the Gael", which some now call Argyll. His name was Conall Cròg Buidhe, which means "Conall of the Large Yellow Hand". Conall was not only a warrior of some renown, but he was known to be one of the best storytellers of the Feans, the warrior élite of the kingdom of high-hilled Alba.

Conall had three sons, who had just reached the age of choice. But they were unruly lads and needed more discipline than Conall had ever given them for Conall, it may be said, was often away at sea or engaged in wars. So his sons were sometimes lacking in sobriety and were impetuous of spirit: too fond of feasting and drinking.

It happened that, one day, Conall's three sons, after one particular feasting where the wine had circled much too freely, met with the three sons of the King of Fótla, in whose kingdom Airer Ghàidheal lay, and a joking remark led to an argument, and the argument led to a fight, and the fight led to the King of Fótla's eldest son being stretched on the ground, dead.

Conall Cròg Buidhe was summoned to the king's fortress at Dùn Cheailleann and the king was bitter in his anger. But the King of Fótla was a wise man and a just one. He finally said:

"I do not wish vengeance on you, nor on your sons, for the death of my fine, brave lad. Vengeance does not profit anyone. So I will set the terms for the compensation which you must give me for my loss."

Conall bowed his head in submission, for compensation was the basis of the law system under which all men lived. "I will pay whatever fine you place on me, my King."

"Then hear this. I will not pursue vengeance nor demand the souls of your three boys, if you will go to the land of the King of Lochlann and bring me back his famous brown horse."

The *Each Donn*, or Brown Horse, of the King of Lochlann was without peer and it had never lost a race. But the King of Lochlann was much attached to it. So, Conall reasoned, it would be no easy task, for he doubted it could be taken, except by war.

"Difficult is this request which you demand, my King," admitted Conall. "But you are fair and, rather than bring shame and dishonour on my house, I am prepared to lose my own life and the life of my three sturdy boys in the pursuit of this matter."

"That is well spoken," agreed the King. "For that, you may take your three sons with you to help you. But if you or they do not return with the horse and remain alive thereafter, my vengeance shall seek you out, no matter what corner of the world you attempt to hide in."

"That is understood," Conall said.

He returned home with his contrite sons to say farewell to his wife. She was very perturbed when she heard the demands the King of Fótla had made.

"Better to have accepted punishment than accept this quest, my lord," she told him. "It means that I will never see you again in this world."

Conall was much troubled, for he knew that the task was arduous.

The next morning, he and his sons fitted out their warship and set sail for Lochlann, the land of fjords and lochs to the north-east. The ship ploughed the grey leaping waves, whose foam-edged lips threatened to engulf them. At no time did Conall shorten his sail, so that his course was straight and true through the formidable sea towards the shore of Lochlann. His sons sat remorseful in the stern while Conall, without a word, stood in the bow, resigned to whatever fate the gods would bring.

Ashore in Lochlann, Conall asked a passer-by to direct them to the fortress of the king and point out where he might find the *tigh-òsda*, the tavern. At this tavern, Conall asked the innkeeper if he had any rooms, for he and his sons needed rest that night. They were the only guests.

Over wine that evening, Conall grew confidential with the innkeeper who, being curious – as innkeepers are about their guests – wondered what they were doing in Lochlann.

Conall told him that he and his sons had fallen out with the King of Fótla and, indeed, one of his sons had killed the king's son. Nothing would please the King of Fótla more than if he and his sons would bring back the fabulous *Each Donn*, the brown horse of the King of Lochlann.

"Perhaps you could tell me where I might find the *Each Donn* and whether I might purchase him from the King of Lochlann? You would be well paid for such a service."

The innkeeper roared with laughter. "Though I am sorry for the trouble that you find yourself in, stranger, you have come here to seek a thing impossible. The King of Lochlann will never sell his brown horse, and the only way it will be taken from him is by stealth. I will pretend that I have not heard what you said . . . provided I am compensated for my deafness."

In annoyance, Conall had to pay the man three pieces of gold in order that he did not go to the King of Lochlann and tell him.

Conall went out the next morning and he fell in with the King of Lochlann's miller. Now it turned out that the miller was a greedy man and, after Conall and he had talked a while, Conall said: "For five pieces of gold, I would put to you a proposition. Every day you and your servants take sacks of bran to the King of Lochlann's stable for the feeding of his horses."

"True enough," said the miller.

"Then put me and my sons into the sacks and carry us into the stable and leave us."

The miller rubbed his chin thoughtfully. "It is a strange request," he observed.

Conall clinked the gold coins in his hand.

The miller's eyes sparkled.

Without more ado, Conall and his three sons were placed in the sacks and the miller and his servants carried the sacks up to the King of Lochlann's stable and deposited them inside. Then they went away.

After a while Conall and his sons emerged.

"We will have to wait until nightfall," Conall told them in a whisper. "So we will make hiding places for ourselves within this stable, just in case the king's men search it at any time."

So they sought out hiding places for themselves.

Dusk came and Conall and his sons approached the stall of the *Each Donn*. Now this brown horse was an intelligent creature. As soon as they began to approach him, he kicked up his back legs and began to whinny and cry.

In the castle, the King of Lochlann heard the noise. "What ails my brown horse?" he cried, turning to his mother, who was supping with him.

"Little I can tell you of that, my son," replied the good woman. "Tell your servants to go to the stable and find out what is amiss."

So the King of Lochlann called to his servants and said: "Go down to the stable and see what is wrong with my brown horse."

The servants rushed to the stable, but when Conall and his sons heard them coming, they hid in the places they had prepared for themselves. So the servants went inside and looked around and reported back to the King of Lochlann that they had seen nothing amiss.

"Perhaps the brown horse is simply skittish," sighed the king. "Very well. Be about your business. Let us continue with our feasting, mother."

After a while, Conall and his sons came out of their hiding places and approached the *Each Donn*.

The outcry was seven times louder than before. Even the king's mother felt something was wrong. So the King of Lochlann turned to his servants.

"There is something wrong in the stable. Go and bring me word of what it is, this instant."

The servants rushed to the stable but Conall and his sons had already disappeared into their hiding places. The servants searched diligently but did not discover them. They returned again and reported that nothing was amiss.

So the king ordered the feasting to resume.

Once more Conall and his sons arose from their hiding places and approached the *Each Donn*.

Yet again did the horse make such an outcry that all the corners of the king's palace became alarmed.

"Perhaps some dark wizard is attacking us," cried the King of Lochlann's mother, who had a great fear of wizards.

The king stood up. "There is no other possibility than that someone is in the stable who has evil designs on my brown horse."

This time he ordered his servants to accompany him.

Now when Conall and his sons heard the King of Lochlann coming to the stable, they went and hid themselves once more.

The King of Lochlann entered and stood at the stable door and surveyed the place.

The *Each Donn* stood in his stall, trembling.

"Let us be wary," said the king, "for I believe that there are men within the stable. We must search them out."

Now the King of Lochlann, who was called Sigurdsson, was a clever man, otherwise he would not have been a king over such a fierce people as the men of Lochlann, whose ships were constantly raiding the seven seas. He looked at the stable floor and his keen eye picked out a stranger's footprints. He followed the footprints to the corner of the stable, the very corner where Conall himself was hiding.

The King of Lochlann stood, hands on hips, and chuckled. "I spy the shoes of a warrior of the Gael. Distinctive are they, as the colour of a man's hair. Who stands hiding there? Will you tell me, or will you die without a name?"

This angered Conall a little and he stepped forward. "My name is Conall of Airer Ghàidheal."

"Can it be Conall Cròg Buidhe who is lurking in my stable and making my *Each Donn* nervous?" asked the King of Lochlann, in good humour. "I have heard many stories of your courage and ability, but none suggest that you would come like a thief in the night to a man's stables to frighten his prize horse."

The blush of shame came to Conall's cheeks and he saw that he was surrounded by the swords of the king's bodyguard on all sides. So he stepped forward.

"It is I, Sigurdsson, who is here, indeed."

"Explain the reason to me."

Conall came out and told the King of Lochlann why and how he had come to his kingdom. "So you see, Sigurdsson, that dire necessity forced me here. Now I am under your hospitality and, hopefully, your pardon."

"You did not come first to me and ask for the *Each Donn*," reproved the King of Lochlann. "Why not?"

"I knew that I would not acquire the brown horse by asking."

"True enough," agreed the king. "We will talk more about this. But first, the cause of all this trouble must be surrendered to me. Ask your sons to step forward."

Conall told his three sons to come out from their hiding places and they were taken prisoners and escorted by the king's guard to be fed and watched over during the night.

"You will be fed this night and tomorrow at dawn you three will be hanged. I shall hang you, for you are the cause of the trouble you have placed on your father's shoulders by your insobriety and lack of thought."

Then the King of Lochlann placed his hand under Conall's arm and led him to his feasting hall, where his mother was awaiting word of what had happened. The King of Lochlann introduced Conall and then gave him food and wine.

"Now, my old enemy, Conall of the Large Yellow Hand, let us consider this matter. I shall have your three sons hanged tomorrow for attempting to steal my horse to buy their lives from the King of Fótla. I could send them back to the King of Fótla without the brown horse. Either way, your three sturdy sons will be hanged."

"Why not hang me instead?" demanded Conall. "I led them here, in an attempt to save their lives."

"What reason to hang you, Conall? You have already

absolved yourself in this matter. Necessity made you come here and I forgive you for that necessity. But faced, whichever way you turn, with your sons' deaths, can you tell me if you were ever in a more difficult situation?"

Conall was a proud man. "I was," he replied. "And in many such difficulties, and have survived them all."

Sigurdsson slapped his thigh and bellowed with laughter. "If you can tell me a more difficult situation which you overcame, I'll release the youngest of your sturdy lads."

Conall was not a stupid man, and so he asked for a drink of wine and thought rapidly. "Agreed," he said.

"Tell on, then, Conall," invited the King of Lochlann.

"When I was a young lad, and my father was then living, we had a great estate and a large herd of cattle. Among the yearling cows there was one who had just calved. My father told me to go to the meadow where she had calved and bring her and the calf home to the warm stable. It was cruel winter-time, and a shower of icy snow had fallen.

"I went to the meadow and dug out the cow and her calf and began to journey back. But snow began to fall again and so I found a herdsman's *bothan*. We went into this cabin to await the easing of the snowstorm.

"So there we were when the door opened and in came a family of cats: not one cat but ten of them, and clear, so it was, that they were one and the same family. One among the cats was very big and the red-grey colour of a fox. It had but one very big eye in its head. The others sat around the big cat and started a fearsome caterwaul.

" 'Away from this place, cats!' I cried. 'For I have no liking for your company nor the noise you make.'

"The large cat turned to me and spoke and I had understanding of its words.

" 'We shall not leave this place, for we have come to sing you a *crònan*, Conall Cròg Buidhe.'

"I was surprised that it knew my name and more surprised when they began to sing me a *crònan*."

Now a *crònan* is a croon, a dirge, often likened to the purring of the cats. Thus Conall continued to recite his story to the King of Lochlann.

"I sat amazed as those cats crooned to me. When they had finished, the one-eyed cat said: 'Now, Conall Cròg Buidhe, you must pay the fee for such a song as we cats have sung to you.'

"I was further surprised but, it is true, a bard must be paid, even the bard of the cat-people. 'I have nothing to pay your fee with,' I confessed, 'unless you take this newborn calf.'

"I had meant this as a jest but no sooner were the words out of my mouth than the cats sprang forth on the calf and the beast did not last long between their talons and sharp teeth.

"So I said to them: 'Away with you now, cats. For I have no liking for your company nor songs.' But the great one-eyed fox-coloured cat said: 'We have come here to make a *crònan* for you, Conall, and make it we will.' And the cats gathered round and sang their *crònan*. 'Now pay our fee, for bards may curse as they may praise,' said the one-eyed cat.

" 'Tiresome is this,' I replied. 'I have nothing to pay your fee, save the cow which stands here.'

" 'Suitable enough,' said the one-eyed cat. And no sooner was it said than the cats fell on the cow and it did not last them long.

" 'Away with you now, cats. I have no liking for your company nor songs, nor your devouring of honest people's cows.'

" 'Yet we have come here to sing you a third *crònan*,' replied the one-eyed cat. 'Sing it we must.'

"And they sat in a semi-circle and crooned their dirge to me.

"Then the one-eyed cat said: 'Now pay our fee, for we may sing satire as well as the *crònan*, and satires may raise blemishes on the skin and cause you to suffer the affliction of those cursed.'

" 'But I have nothing to reward you with at all, for you have had everything I can give you.'

"And the caterwauling started.

" 'Pay us, pay us the fee, pay us our reward.'

" 'I can give you nothing,' I cried.

"Then the one eyed cat said: 'If you have nothing but yourself, then we find yourself acceptable.'

"The cats began to approach me with slavering jaws and blood on their whiskers. In truth, I leapt for the window, which was framed in rowan and through it I went and down to the hazel woods beyond. I was swift and strong and my fear leant me courage. Yet I heard the *toirm*, the rushing noise of a wind, as the cats sprang after me and I knew I had not long. I reached the woods and found a rowan tree and climbed up and up into it until I was hidden from the ground.

"Below me, the wailing cats started to search through the woods. However, the rowan hid me. Soon the cats grew tired and, one to another, they called and soon gathered below the rowan.

" 'We are tired; we should return home,' cried one.

" 'We will never find him,' said another.

"Just then, the big one-eyed cat came along and stared right up at me.

" 'It is lucky for you, brothers, that I have one eye and that sees more clearly than all your eyes together. There is Conall up in that tree.'

"Now, one of the cats began to climb the rowan tree and, as I sat in it, I saw a loose branch with a sharpened end. So I grabbed this and stabbed down at the cat and transfixed it.

" '*Och-òn*!' cried the one-eyed cat. 'Alas for that! I cannot lose any more of my tribe. But we must exact our fee for the *crònan* we sang.'

"The cat sat and thought a moment. Then it said to the others: 'Gather around the tree and begin to dig out its roots, so that the tree will fall.'

"And this they did and soon the tree was swaying as they revealed its roots and began to topple it. So scared was I that I gave forth a great shout."

Conall paused in his storytelling for so long that the King of Lochlann urged him to continue.

"Well, Sigurdsson," continued Conall, "there was a druid in the wood with his twelve acolytes and he heard my cry. 'That, surely is the shout of a man in extremity and I cannot do anything but reply to it.' One of his acolytes said, however: 'Do not go, for it might be a trick of the wind. Let us wait until the shout comes again.'

"They waited and, when I gave my next cry of alarm, the druid affirmed his intention. The druid and his acolytes came towards the tree.

"It was then that the cats gnawed through another root and the tree fell with a crash and me holding onto my branch for dear life. It was then I shouted for a third time. The druid and his acolytes came to the spot and saw how the cats had severed the tree and were closing towards me. Each of them carried a hazel wand and they took their wands and ran on to the cat people. The cats, not being able to confront a druid's hazel wand, all took to their heels."

Conall paused and smiled.

"That, O King of Lochlann, is surely a more dangerous situation than facing the death of my three sturdy sons? My being torn to pieces by the cats is more dangerous for me than seeing my sons hanged tomorrow."

The King of Lochlann's mother sat by the fire and nodded her head. "I have never heard of greater danger, except once," she said thoughtfully.

Sigurdsson, the King of Lochlann, slapped his thigh and bawled with laughter. "By the beard of my god, Conall, a fine tale was that. And by it you have earned the life of your youngest son. But if you had a second tale to tell, and it was the equal of it, you could earn the soul of your middle son."

"Well, the truth is, I can tell you how I was in a more difficult situation than that."

"Tell away," invited the King of Lochlann.

"It was when I was a young lad, out hunting on my father's lands. Chance had brought me to the sea-shore where there were jagged rocks, and undersea caves and the like. All were washed by the angry foam lips of the ocean god.

"When I came to the shore, I saw a trickle of smoke arising from between two rocks. Now that is strange, I thought to myself. What could be the meaning of it? I began to climb over the rocks in my curiosity towards the smoke. It so happened that I fell. As luck would have it, no bone of mine was broken, the skin not blemished by bruising, but I had fallen down a deep cleft in the rocks. How to get out with the sea tide approaching and the hollow filling with its surging flood was my first thought.

"It was a terrible thing, to die from drowning. I knew that the sides of the cleft were too steep to climb. It was then that I heard a clattering sound. Who should it be but a giant, leading a herd of goats with a buck at their head? The giant's head popped over the rim and he stared down at me with one great eye.

" 'Hello, Conall Cròg Buidhe,' he called down. 'My knife has been rusting a long time in its sheath, waiting for the tender flesh of a human boy.'

" 'Well,' I said, 'it is not much of a meal you'll get from me, for boys do not have much meat and are sinewy in the extreme. However, if you help me out, I can help you.'

"The giant frowned.

" 'Help me? How so?'

" 'I have a gift for healing, and I see you have one eye. If you release me, I will bestow on you the sight of the other eye.'

"Now the giant thought about this a moment and then he nodded his agreement.

" 'I will release you, Conall, but only after you have given me the sight in the other eye. Tell me what I must do. If it works, then I shall pull you out.'

"Now that left me in difficulties. But I had no option but to pursue a plan. So I told him to prepare his giant cauldron and light a fire under it and boil water. And all the time my mind was working on how to achieve my freedom.

"With the water warming, I found some seaweed in the cleft. Then I told the giant that he must dip the seaweed in the cauldron and rub it in his good eye before he rubbed it on the other. Thus I convinced him that the sight of the good eye would be passed to the other eye. In fact, I knew the property of the seaweed well enough and knew that it would take the sight from the good eye and not give sight to the second eye.

"Now, when this happened, the giant was in a fearful rage. He stood, blind, but threatening over the cleft where I was trapped and he said that I would never get out or, if he caught me, I would be put in his cauldron and boiled to make my flesh tender enough for his appetite. This was no good for me, for I had hoped to escape while he was blinded. So, all through the night, I crouched in the cleft out of his reach, holding my breath at times in case he heard me.

"When it was dawn, the giant finally dropped off to sleep and I managed to climb out of the cleft. But I climbed into a pen, in which he had put his goats, and it was difficult to get out of that pen when the goats started to shift and make a noise so that the giant woke up.

" 'Are you still asleep, boy?' called the giant down the cleft, for he was still blind. Then he paused to listen: 'No, you are no longer in the cleft but you are among my goats.'

"Seeing him approaching, I killed the buck goat and began to skin it for dear life.

"The giant paused, frowning.

" 'It is one of my goats that you are killing?' he demanded.

" 'Not I,' I replied. 'It is true that I am in the pen with your goats, but I am trying to release a goat whose rope had become too tight around her neck.' So saying, I released one of the goats and let her out. The giant, feeling about, felt the goat and caught her, fondling the goat.

" 'It is true what you say, boy. I feel the goat but cannot see her. Her rope is loose.'

"I kept letting the goats loose, one at a time, and the giant, feeling each, let them go.

"Finally, I put on the skin of the buck goat and, on hands and knees, I began to crawl out of the gate away from the pen between the legs of the giant. The giant reached down and put a hand on my head and felt the horns of the buck and ran his finger down my back, feeling the skin.

" 'Well, that is my buck alive and well. Where are you, boy?'

"Outside the pen, I roared: 'Here I am, out and free in spite of you!'

"There was joy on me in my boasting.

"The giant sat down abruptly and great was the sadness on his face.

" 'You have brought me to ruin, boy. Well, I cannot help but admire you. In token of your victory, I shall give you a ring of mine and, if worn, this ring will do you naught but good. Here is the ring.'

"The giant pulled the ring from his pocket and held it up.

"I smiled sceptically, for I was a wise child.

" 'Do you throw your ring to me, for I will not come near you and be caught, giant,' I said.

" 'That is no problem,' said the giant and threw the ring across the sands.

"I went forward and picked it up. It was a fine ring of silver. I admired its craftsmanship and slipped it on my little finger of my left hand.

" 'Does the ring fit you?' inquired the giant anxiously.

" 'It fits well enough,' I assured him.

"Then the giant cried: 'Where are you, ring?'

"And the ring answered back.

" 'Here I am,' it said.

"The giant rose and came running towards the speaking ring. Now I realised what dire straits I was in, and I struggled to tear the ring from my little finger. But it would not come off. Every time the giant asked, 'Where are you, ring?', it would reply, 'I am here.' I was in such a bad extremity then, that I knew only one escape. I took out my *sgian dubh*, took the knife and cut off the little finger of my left hand on which I had placed the ring. Then I threw it far out over the cliffs into the boundless ocean.

"The giant lumbered past.

" 'Where are you, ring?' he called.

" 'I am here,' answered the ring from the depths of the ocean.

"He sprang over the cliff towards the sound of the voice and fell into the sea. It was a pleasing sight to see him drowning. I was able to return home with the herd of goats, without the buck I had slain, of course. There was great joy on my parents when I returned."

The mother of the King of Lochlann, sitting by the fire, nodded in appreciation. "I have never heard of a more dangerous situation, except once," she observed.

"It is a good tale," remarked the King of Lochlann.

"And the proof of it is here," replied Conall, holding out

his hand. "For, if you will observe, I lack a finger on which the ring was."

"I see you lack the finger so that you have spoken truly. I will reply in truth as well. By this tale, you have saved the life of your second son. Only your eldest son will be hanged tomorrow . . . However, if you have a third tale to tell me, of a harder situation than facing the death of your eldest son, and can convince me of it, I shall release him to you as well."

"It so happens, King of Lochlann, that I have. It happened when I was a young man. My father found me a wife and I was married. One day, I was out to hunt and came to a loch. In the loch was a little island and I saw game a-plenty on it. I wandered around the loch, looking for a means of getting across, and on the bank I found a boat. I took a step inside it and, before I had lifted the other leg into it, it took to the waves and sped towards the island in the middle of the loch.

"I could not believe that I had landed so swiftly on the island. I stepped ashore and found that a mist had come down, obscuring everything. I turned back to the boat and it, too, had vanished. So I went on to find shelter, but there was no shelter at all. The woods had gone and there was nothing but scrub and shrub. I suddenly saw an old cabin among this wilderness and there was a patch of clear weather round it. Before the cabin stood a cauldron, hanging over a fire.

"Seated outside was a woman with a naked baby on her knee and she held a knife in her hand. She was putting the knife to the throat of the baby and the baby was laughing in her face. Then the woman dropped the knife to the ground and began to cry. Her sobs were so heart-rending that they sent cold shivers up and down my back.

" 'What ails you, woman?' I demanded.

"She caught sight of me and started.

" 'Who are you, and how came you here?' she demanded.

"So I told her the truth of it.

" 'It was the same with myself,' she confessed. 'I came with my child.'

" 'Your child?' I asked. 'Why were you putting the knife to its throat, then?'

"She gave a low sob.

" 'Do you see that cauldron? Well, the cauldron and the fire belong to an evil wizard. The wizard has told me that I must put my baby in the cauldron and boil it for the wizard's meal by the time he returns.'

"I peered around.

" 'Where is this wizard?'

" 'Not far away, gathering herbs for the pot.'

" 'Can you not escape?'

" 'No more than you can. The boat is under the wizard's control and will not return us to the mainland.'

" 'What if you refuse?' I pressed.

" 'The wizard has sworn to put me in his cauldron instead.'

"Just then, we heard the footsteps of the wizard returning.

"The woman began to sob.

" 'Hide the baby behind those trees,' I instructed and, while she did so, I went to the cauldron and tested the water. As luck would have it, the woman had neglected to keep the fire heated and so the water was only lukewarm.

" 'I will step in the pot,' I told her, 'and do you put the cover of the pot over it when I am inside.'

"So it was I stepped into the lukewarm water and the woman placed the lid on the cauldron.

"Then the wizard came along.

" 'Ho, woman!' I heard his raucous cry. 'Have you boiled the child for me, yet?'

" 'He is still in the pot, sir,' cried the woman. 'He is not done yet.'

"I raised my voice and cried from inside the cauldron:

" '*A mhàthair, a mhàthair*, it is boiling that I am!'

"Whereupon the wizard laughed heartily.

" 'Then you shall soon be done!' I heard him heaping wood under the cauldron and it began to grow hot. I was sure that I would soon scald to death but the wizard, as luck would have it, fell asleep by the fire. As soon as he was snoring, the woman came across and raised the lid.

' "Is it alive, you are?' she demanded.

"I stood up with my face red and wet.

" 'Barely,' I gasped.

"I climbed out of the cauldron as carefully as I could and

ran to the stream to cool myself. But I scalded the palms of my hands where I gripped the rim of the cauldron.

" 'How can we kill the wizard?' I asked.

"The woman, whispering, told me that nothing could kill the wizard except his own spear, which he wore slung across his back.

"So I went to him and slowly began to draw the spear out. His snoring breath was powerful, so powerful that, on every intake, as I bent over him drawing the spear, he drew me close. It took a while to loosen the spear and finally I had it in my hand.

"But I was a warrior and could not kill a sleeping man.

"So I bent forward and gave him a prick in his face. He blinked and lifted his head. He stared at me and in that second I cast his spear. It went right through him and he fell dead on the ground. Then I took the woman and the child and went back to the boat. Because the wizard was dead, the boat no longer was possessed of magical powers and so we were able to come safely back to shore.

"The woman and her child went on their way and I returned home to my wife in Airer Ghàidheal. That was a more dangerous situation than facing the death of my eldest son tomorrow."

The King of Lochlann slapped his thigh and shook his head. "That is a fine tale. But is there proof of it? Without proof, your son will hang."

Before Conall could answer, the King of Lochlann's mother leant forward. "Show me the palms of your hands, Conall Cròg Buidhe."

Conall did so, showing the healed scalded skin whose tissue had turned to a yellow colour and which had earned him his nickname of the Yellow Hand.

"So it is you, Conall, who were there?" the king's mother said slowly.

"That I was," he affirmed.

"And that I was, too. I was the woman who was a prisoner of the wizard and that baby you saved is none other than my son, who now sits on the throne of Lochlann."

Then Conall and Sigurdsson seized each other in joy and embraced.

"Good it is, Conall Cròg Buidhe, that you have come through all these hardships. Better it is that you saved my life and that of my mother. I give you back the life of your third son. And this I add to it: you may take with you, on your return to Fótla, the *Each Donn*, my brown horse. And this I add to that: you may take a sack of gold as a token of our friendship."

So it was that the next day, Conall and his three sons embarked for the kingdom of Fótla, with the *Each Donn* and a sack of gold. And he returned first to his home and gave the sack of gold to his wife. Then he went to the King of Fótla and gave the brown horse to him. And the King of Fótla vowed he would be a friend to Conall thereafter and, moreover, Conall's three sturdy sons learnt the wisdom of prudence and sobriety and were never again given to impetuosity.

18 *The Kelpie*

The sons of all the chieftains of the Western Isles, those sons who were the tanists, which is to say the heirs-elect to their father's chiefdoms, once decided to go forth together on a great fishing expedition in the bright waters of An Cuan Barragh, which is Barra's Sound. They set out and never came back.

It was seven days afterwards that the King of the Island of Sgìtheanach sent forth messengers, to bring all the chieftains of the islands to an assembly at Port Rìgh, the harbour of the Lord of Sgìtheanach. And they came: from Arainn, Cinn Tire, Ile and Diura, from Colbhasa, Muile, Tirodh, Colla, Eige, Rum and Canaigh and from the extreme west from Barraigh, Uibhist-a-Deas and Uibhist-a-Tuath and from Na hEaradh and Leodhas – all the chieftains came in their great war-ships.

They gathered in the assembly hall, each with his sword and shield, and listened to the grim-faced lord, who stood pale and drawn. The chiefs were astonished to see that, by his side, stood Donall, the shield-bearer to the heir of the King of Sgìtheanach. He had been among the party of young chieftains' sons when they had gone fishing.

"Can it be that our sons still live?" demanded the chief of Cinn Tire.

"Shame is my portion," replied Donall, "I am the only one of the young company to escape."

They saw that his left hand was covered with a bloody bandage and realised that he had not left the others easily.

"All are perished?" demanded the Lord of Colbhasa.

"As true as I stand here," nodded Donall and there was grief in his voice.

"How could this be – who brought the curse of the *Eich-Uisge*, the feared Kelpie, upon our people?" It was the chief of Ile who spoke, voicing what they all felt a mind to ask.

The shield-bearer hesitated and looked at the King of Sgìtheanach.

"Speak on, be not afraid," grunted the king, gazing with downcast eyes as if he could not bring himself to look upon his fellow chieftains.

"It was Iain, son of my Lord of Sgìtheanach," Donall confessed. "But no blame to him," he added hurriedly. "The Kelpie appeared to us as a beautiful creature. It was as white as the froth of the waves, his mane like the restless foam around the rocks of the sea shore. He was a gentle beast and whinnied softly as he pawed with his hooves on the foreshore.

"We had seen the creature as we sailed in An Cuan Barragh and came on Eilean nam Muc. There was the beast on the foreshore and Prince Iain was the first to cry to us to go ashore and see what manner of splendid animal this white creature was. Surprise and joy was on us as we landed our ships on the shore and Iain went forward holding out his hand – you all know what pride Iain took in horses and how he loved them."

Donall paused. The great chieftains of the island were nodding to themselves.

"Speak on, Donall," cried the Lord of Diura. "Speak on, though there is pain in my heart each time you utter what must be."

"Iain stretched out his hand to the creature's muzzle and the animal nuzzled him. May the gods take pity on us."

"All our sons, our heirs . . ." The old chieftain of Colla, who had but one son, suddenly placed his old white-haired head in his hands and a sob racked his body.

"Lost, lost and soon our lands and strongholds will be no more. All lost to the Kelpie!" cried the Lord of Leodhas.

"Prince Iain would have severed his hand, had he known the outcome," cried Donall defensively.

"Would he had done so," snapped the Lord of Muile.

"But surely he knew?" The Lord of Canaigh raised the question. "Who does not know the ancient lore?"

"This is true," the Lord of Colbhasa agreed. "All of you have been taught the ancient lore, since you were able to leave your mothers' arms. You must have known!"

Donall hung his head in shame. "We knew . . . we had been taught. But we did not believe it. We thought you made up the tale to frighten us. Young men always reject the stories of their elders."

"You know, now," muttered the King of Sgìtheanach.

"And know too late to do anything," sighed the chieftain of Rum.

"We'd best hear the story out," observed the taciturn chieftain of Tirodh.

Donall called for a drink and took a sip to fortify himself. "This is the way of it," he began.

The young sons of the chieftains had seen the magnificent horse on the sands of the Island of Muc, which is the island of pigs. They had landed and petted the great white horse. The young men thought the beast must be lost, for there was no one rich enough on the island to possess such a creature. Then it was that Iain suggested that they ride on it.

He was the first to mount. But the creature stood waiting patiently and another lad mounted behind. Still the creature waited and then, one by one, all the sons of the chieftains were on his back; and all seated in comfort without crowding.

Donall, not being a chieftain's son, waited behind before he was hauled into a precarious perch at the end. Even as he was being lifted up by his companions, the great steed pounded along the sea shore and then – then it took to the sea, speeding across the waves as if they were solid ground. Away, away, towards the red-gold setting sun, flying over the choppy bright waves.

Donall did not know where they went, except that they darted through great valleys formed by waves and whirlpools of tides and still the hooves of the beast did not sink as much as half an inch into the water.

Donall confessed that it never even entered their heads to

leap off the back of the Kelpie. None could move off the broad back of the animal. It seemed that wherever their hands grasped the Kelpie, they were stuck and stuck fast.

It was then that Donall decided to act. Taking out his hunting knife with his right hand he slashed at the fingers of his left, which held tight to the young lord in front of him and the magnetism of the animal ran through each young son of each chieftain from Iain who held the mane at the front through to Donall's one hand at the back. With the fingers thus severed, Donall freed himself of the power of the beast and he sprang from the back of the creature and plunged head-down into the sea.

He peered up and saw the Kelpie, with the chieftains' sons still astride his white back, and the horse plunging down into the yawning maw of the Corrievreckan, the great whirlpool, which some said was the entrance into the Otherworld. His last sight of his companions was of youths laughing and joyous, for they did not realise their danger.

Donall swam and swam until the gentle tide washed him ashore at Dùn Bheagain and he made his way to the King of Sgìtheanach to report what had transpired.

There was another silence while the grieving chieftains reflected on his story.

"You cannot accept that there is an end to it!" cried a stentorian voice.

They looked up and saw the tall white-haired figure of Lomar, the King's Druid.

The Lord of Ile laughed, but with anger not humour. "What would you have us do?"

"Fight the Kelpie's magic with magic."

"And the Kelpie as old as the ages themselves? There is no magic that can out-magic the spell of the Kelpie!" It was the Lord of Barragh who spoke, and his wisdom was to be respected, for his land was on the western rim of the ocean. He knew the ways of the gods and goddesses, for the far west was their resting place.

"Pah!" snapped Lomar. "You would rather use the strength that you have in grieving than fight the evil that has claimed your sons and heirs."

"The Druid is right," exclaimed the King of Sgìtheanach. "But what can we do? Our ships would not dare enter the Corrievreckan, for they would be swept down into the Otherworld."

"Send a warrior to see Dall, the Blind One," replied Lomar. "He has the wisdom."

Now Dall, the Blind One, was a man of ancient wisdom who dwelt on the heights of the Hill of the Red Fox.

"He will be of no help," cried the Lord of Colla. "No one can fight the Kelpie."

"Indeed, what can he do, unless he be wise in bringing back the dead to life?" sneered the Lord of Arainn.

"That he cannot do," cried the Lord of Eige. "Once they have gathered at the House of Donn, Lord of the Dead, the souls of the departed cannot be ferried home again."

"By the Nine Wells of Manánnan, the Ocean God, I will go to see the Blind One!" cried Donall the shield-bearer, stung by their negative attitudes. "You are all old women, who would rather hide behind the walls of your fortress than take sword and shield and defy the fate that has taken away your sons. Is that all you care of them?"

The great chieftains of the islands looked at one another, full of surprise that a mere shield-bearer should berate them in such a fashion. But they made no move against him for, in truth, his words had stirred guilt within them.

"Bold young man, if you can deliver our sons, do so," sighed the King of Sgìtheanach. "But we shall not raise false hopes in our womenfolk. Not even our wives, the mothers of our young sons, must know this plan, for fear it come to the ears of the *Eich-Uisge*, the dreadful Kelpie, who has carried them off."

So it was agreed that no word was spoken of the hope that now lay within their breasts and the lusty sons of the kings of the islands were therefore mourned as dead and throughout the islands. There was a great sorrowing and a *caoineadh*, which is a keening, a great act of wailing and lamentation.

Donall took his shield and sword and set off immediately for the Hill of the Red Fox and he was not long in looking before he came across Dall, the Blind One, and told him his purpose.

"Trust is the first priority, my son."

"Trust?"

"With trust, with faith, one can go anywhere or move any obstacle."

Donall was silent.

"Do you trust me?" asked Dall.

"I . . . I have no one else to trust," admitted Donall.

Dall smiled. "Your hand is wounded. Give it to me."

Donall reached out the hand with the severed fingers.

Dall took it and held it a moment. "See that cauldron bubbling away on the heat of the fire?"

"I do," replied Donall, seeing it in the hearth of Dall's cabin.

"Put your hand into it. Have trust in me."

Donall did not hesitate but did so. There was no pain.

"Draw it out now," ordered Dall.

Great was Donall's surprise when he saw that his hand was perfectly healed and the fingers regrown.

"We will succeed!" Donall cried with enthusiasm at such a demonstration of power.

"There is only one night of the year when we might do so," agreed Dall. "In a few days' time is the feast of Samhuinn, when the sun goes down, and the Otherworld becomes visible to this world. Souls may cross from one world to another. That is our chance. We may be able to rescue those chieftains' sons and bring them home during the hour of midnight only. That feast-day and that time alone is the one time we may hope to rescue the lost chieftains' sons."

"How can this be done?"

Dall pursed his lips thoughtfully. He was not a vain man. "I do not know whether it can be accomplished. All I can pledge is that I will try, but faith is the key. If you have faith in me, then my task might be fulfilled."

"What task?"

"At midnight on the feast of Samhuinn, I shall come to the castle of the King of Sgìtheanach. I shall stretch out my hands over the waters and order the return of the souls of your lost companions from the waters of the deep. It will be my strength and knowledge against that of the Otherworld."

So Donall returned back home and, though he told the King of Sgìtheanach what old Dall had said, he did not tell the daughter of the king, who was sister to his lost friend, the prince he was shield-bearer to. This girl was named Dianaimh, for she was the "flawless" jewel of the islands, such being the meaning of the name. Now Donall and Dianaimh were close friends in the way of brother and sister and no more than that. Donall was, in fact, heartsick with love for Dianaimh's cousin, a girl named Faoinèis.

Now Dianaimh had grown up with the young princes of the islands and had every cause to lament, as had the other women, but she could not bring herself to feel sad for she, too, was in love. It had happened only a short time before these tragic events. One day, as she was sitting on the sea shore, a little distance away from her father's castle, by an inlet watching the sea birds swoop and dance in to warm sun, a handsome young man wandered by. He wore a snow-white shirt and an amazing green parti-coloured *féile-beag*, or kilt, and a *brat-falaich* or cloak. His skin was snow-white, his eyes green and his hair was the colour of the foam on the waves striking the shore.

Now Dianaimh had been singing a sad song of lost love.

Cold are the nights I cannot sleep,
Restless are the nights when there is no repose,
Thinking of you my love,
Dreaming of the nights we were together
And now you are no longer at my side.

"A sad song is that, sweet lady," said the young man. "You have brought a tear on my cheek."

Dianaimh's heart was full of sorrow for the young man who seemed so sad and handsome. He came and sat at her feet and there was, indeed, a desolation on his features.

"It is not a song of experience for me," she confided wistfully.

"But the sentiment is there. Yet reach forward and wipe the tear from my cheek and all will be well."

Now this was a bold thing to say and yet Dianaimh was not

at all upset by it. She felt an urge to do as he asked and make him happy. She reached forward and with her finger, as gently as she could, she wiped his tear. The tear stuck to her finger and as she drew her hand away, it dropped on her breast above her heart. For a moment it felt warm and comforting. She looked on the young man with eyes of love.

"Sweet stranger, tell me your name?"

"I am called the *Eich-Uisge*, the Kelpie, lord of the deeps. Do you fear me?"

"Not I," vowed Dianaimh, yet, deep within her, she knew there was a reason why she should have been scared. But the drop of a Kelpie's tear makes a mortal its slave and lover.

"You are my love, Dianaimh," the lord of the deeps said. "The beating of your heart is like the throb of my pulse."

Each morning from that day on, Dianaimh and the Kelpie had met at the sea-shore and vowed their love to one another.

They had to part at sunset. The Kelpie was always strict about this. For when the sun came near the western horizon, he had to return to the sea.

"If ever you find me resting when the sun is setting," the Kelpie admonished, "wake me and tell me to go."

It happened one late afternoon, Dianaimh and her unearthly lover lay on the sea-shore, sleeping in one another's arms. Dianaimh woke and saw the sun was near the western rim and she turned to her lover. He was so handsome and so deep in sleep that she felt it wrong to wake him. When he stirred she crooned a lullaby that sent him back to sleep. So she closed her eyes feeling there could be little harm in letting him rest a while longer.

She reached out her hand to stroke his silken hair, stroking it gently . . . gently . . . Then she became aware that the silk had a slimy touch to it. She looked with wide eyes. She lay in the arms of a strange creature, a pale horse, whose coat glistened with slime, with hoofed feet and a flowing white mane. One front hoof, where her lover's hand had fondly held her hair, was now twisted in her braid. She tried to start away but the hoof so entwined her hair that she could not move. She felt in her belt for her knife and swiftly cut away the braid, leaving it in the hoof. Then she crept away.

The magic of the Kelpie's tear had been dissolved within her breast, once she saw the *Eich-Uisge* for what he truly was. She knew that her love was impossible and that this world and the Otherworld could not be as one.

It was now that she truly realized the fate of all the young men she had grown up with and there was sadness upon her. For some days she sat wondering about them, for the story of how they were carried off by the Kelpie had spread from mouth to mouth, making the grief the harder to bear among the womenfolk of the islands.

Each day she heard the Kelpie calling her, but she was no longer its slave.

Then came the day when Dianaimh decided to challenge the Kelpie and demand to know the fate of the young men. So she answered the call of the Kelpie and went down to the sea-shore, where once they had been lovers. He stood there, in human form, as strong and handsome as ever he had been.

"I am glad you came, my love. I have been crying for you, these last few days. See, the tears lie on my cheeks. Wipe them away for me, please . . ."

Dianaimh stood with hands on hips. "I know your tricks, horse of the seas."

His sea-green eyes were bright. "I need your love, mortal maiden. I need your love and that of no other."

Dianaimh found her soul longed for the cool, strong magic of the handsome man-horse. "If you love me, *Eich-Uisge*, then you must give me a gift."

"What gift would that be, Dianaimh?"

"The gift of the safe return of the chieftains' sons."

The Kelpie let out a long, low sigh. "You will not ask me in vain, loving Dianaimh," he said softly. "Though you scorn me, I shall grant you this. Look for them on the eve when this world and the Otherworld meet."

Then suddenly a beautiful white horse stood in his place and it reared on its hind legs, as if to strike the air with its forelegs. It turned and galloped down the sandy shore and across the waves of the ocean until it was gone towards the setting sun.

"May you find love and peace, Kelpie," Dianaimh sighed softly after it.

Now, as we have said before, Donall, the shield-bearer, was in love with Faoinèis, who was Dianaimh's cousin. She was by nature a vain person, and vanity had been the very name that her father had given her. She was staying with Dianiamh at this time. She paid little heed to Donall, for she loved to flirt and dance with as many young men as pleased her. She was proud and fickle and her attitude to young men was as a hawk to its prey for, like it, she made to ensnare them, biting deep with talons that held, and then letting go so that they fell lifeless to the earth while she flew on her way.

Donall was much saddened by this behaviour and Dianaimh was saddened by her friend's sorrow. Especially as she understood what sorrow in love was. She and Donall had grown up together, as well as the fact that Donall had served her brother. She felt Donall was as much her brother as her real brother.

Now the feast of the god Samhuinn drew near. This was the great feast which marked the beginning of the New Year, the period of blackness. For it was written by the ancient ones that blackness comes before the light, that chaos precedes order, that death comes before rebirth.

One evening, shortly before the festival of Samhuinn, Dianaimh said to Faoinèis: "Donall loves you very much."

Faoinèis smiled smugly. "Many men love me," she replied and she was complacent in her vanity.

"Would it not be better to answer his plea that you may be married, so that you make a good start in this new year coming?"

"Silly, there is lots of time to consider that. Meanwhile, there are men enough that take my fancy. I am in no hurry to wed. I shall wait until a great king comes wooing me, for I am too fair to be wed to a minor king, or prince or chieftain, let alone a lowly shield-bearer such as Donall."

On the day before the great Samhuinn Féis, the festival of the new year, which started at sunset and went through until the dawn, for the people counted their days from sunset to sunset, Donall asked Faoinèis if she would marry him and she dismissed him with the same laugh that she had given to her cousin Dianaimh.

"I wait for a great king to come wooing me. I could never be content to marry a lowly shield-bearer such as you."

And the festival approached.

At sunset, the Kelpie stirred in his cold palace beneath the whirling waters of the *coire-bhreacain*, that is called today Corrievreckan, the Jura-Scarba whirlpool. He went and sat in his high-backed coral chair and looked out on his deep domain. And there Ròn Ghlas Mòr, the Great Grey Seal, came to his side. Ròn Ghlas Mòr was the Kelpie's closest friend and companion through all the aeons of time, for they were both of the wild seal-folk. He knew the Kelpie's thoughts as he knew his own and he also knew what was happening within and between the two worlds.

"Tonight is the Samhuinn Féis," he ventured.

"This I know," sighed the Kelpie.

"You are still weak for the love of Dianaimh."

"This I also know."

"There is love in her for you, in spite of all that has passed. Yet, I fear, it was a wrong choice that you made. She is not like her cousin, Faoinèis the Vain. Faoinèis drains the love of men and leaves them without strength. It would have been a better thing to have dropped your tears on her breast, for she would have no soul to challenge your love."

"It would have been the love of a lifeless statue," pointed out the Kelpie.

Then Ròn Ghlas Mòr clapped his hands and the mermaids and mermen came rushing from the depths to inquire what task was needed. They gathered round the Kelpie, seated on his coral throne, and arranged his silken moon-gold hair, and put on him his kilt and cloak of parti-coloured greens and his gold and silver jewels.

Then the Kelpie stood up. "Tonight we will release the young men of the islands, as I have promised Dianaimh. In return, I shall bring Faoinèis back here as my mortal serving-maid."

Ròn Ghlas Mòr smiled thinly. "No great exchange in that, but perhaps she will learn wisdom and you will bring warmth to that cold heart of hers."

Then the Kelpie asked the mermaids and mermen to bring him his *Falluinn na Mhuir-Bhàis*, the Cloak of Sea-Death. Also, he asked for his *Claidheamh Anam*, his soul-sword, which could cut into the hardest heart and penetrate the deepest soul without shedding one drop of blood.

Then the Kelpie sped away to the mortal world above the waves.

It was now the start of the Samhuinn Féis. Donall knew that he was soon to start his journey to the Otherworld but his heart was sick for the love of Faoinèis. Already the pipers and fiddlers were playing and the women making their ancient *puirt-a-bheul* or mouth music. Already the dancers were skirling around the hall and the fires crackled beneath the roasting joints of meat.

So Donall went to where Faoinèis was standing, next to the daughter of the King of Sgìtheanach. "I must leave soon; before I do so, give me one dance. This one dance alone is all I can give you."

Faoinèis, seeing no one more handsome in the room at that moment, turned her ready smile on Donall and pouted innocently.

"I will give you this dance, Donall, but it is bad manners, I am thinking, to quit this feasting and leave me here alone."

They had scarcely taken the floor when the door burst open and in strode a handsome young man, looking more kingly than even the High King of Scotland, who dwelt at Sgàin. He crossed the floor to where Donall and Faoinèis were dancing, forcing them to halt. Ignoring Donall, he bowed low to Faoinèis, who blushed prettily and returned his salutation.

"Dance with me, sweet maiden. Dance with me, for I have never seen a maid so beautiful in all the kingdoms over which I am lord."

Straightaway, Faoinèis went into the arms of the stranger, leaving Donall with anger on his brow.

Dianaimh came hurrying to Donall's side.

"Dearest Donall, do not be angry with her. She is but following her nature, and that nature you cannot change. And be warned . . . that foolish girl is dancing with no mortal."

They watched Faoinèis and her companion dancing. As they danced, the handsome Kelpie was smiling down at the vain girl.

"You are so beautiful that my heart stops its beating, every time I look at you."

Faoinèis smiled contentedly, for she was used to young men making such silly utterances. But, at least, this young man was a powerful king and she had promised that one day she would marry such a man; and then she would have riches and power over as many men as she liked.

"Will you wed me, maid, that I might rest content?"

Now Faoinèis' heart surged in joy at such an easy conquest, but she was not without cunning.

"How could I tell so soon what my answer would be?"

The Kelpie laughed good-naturedly. "Then I will be content to wait for an answer – but only until midnight, when I must start my journey back to my own kingdom."

"At midnight? As soon as that?"

"I will meet you on the sandy sea-shore below this castle and, at the zenith of the moon, you shall give me your answer."

Then, having completed the dance, the Kelpie bowed low, kissed her hand and withdrew.

Faoinèis was beside herself with joy at the prospect and she returned to where Donall was standing, his brow furrowed angrily, and with Dianaimh at his side.

"Still here?" she greeted him rudely. "I thought you had to leave after this dance?"

"That I do," replied Donall seriously. "But I have remained to save you from a fate no mortal can endure."

Faoinèis laughed heartily. "How dramatic you sound, Donall. Can it be that you are jealous of that handsome king?"

"Handsome king?" snapped Donall. "He is the evil spirit who has taken the souls of our companions – he is none other than the Kelpie!"

Now Faoinèis sneered at the young man. "Jealousy was written on your brow, little shield-bearer, but to come forth with such lies is beyond belief. Still, many a young man would lie, to have me smile on them. That I know."

"He tells you the truth, Faoinèis," interrupted Dianaimh. "That is indeed the Kelpie, and well I know it."

"You are like peas in a pod, both liars," sneered the girl. "You shall not spoil my happiness with such ridiculous stories. Here is the king that I one day knew I would marry." She turned and flounced off.

At the full of the moon Faoinèis went down by the seashore and there stood the proud, handsome king.

"I knew that you would come."

"I have given your plea some thought, my lord and, though there be many who desire me for a wife, I shall accept your offer."

The handsome king disconcerted her by laughing. "I knew you would accept."

Then he drew her towards him. From his pocket he took a ring of strange coral and placed it on her finger. "Now you are mine forever."

His words sounded like a bell tolling a death-knell, causing her to give an involuntary shiver. But the uncomfortable sensation lasted only a moment, for she was a very vain girl. He took her hand and suddenly she found herself on the back of a broad cold white horse, and from this horse came the sound of the Kelpie's laughter, sounding like the icy waters of a winter stream gushing over the stones.

She could not recover breath before the horse was dancing away across the dark waves of the ocean. All around her, she could hear strange sounds, as if all animal creation had joined together in a death dirge. She clung on for dear life and soon they were above the angry, boiling Corrievreckan. Straight into it plunged the Kelpie, with Faoinèis screaming on his back. Her cries were eventually lost in the sound of the briny whirling depths and drowned in the torrent of the primeval seas.

At that moment Donall had joined Dall, the Blind One, as he stood on the castle walls overlooking the seas. Around the Blind One stood the ring of silent kings and chieftains of all the islands, who had lost sons to the Kelpie. Dall raised his voice in a chanting wail. Then he stopped still and bowed his head.

"My magic is done. Come forth, you sons of chieftains, come forth from the sea! I command it."

The Kelpie had returned to his coral throne and gazed in amusement at Ròn Ghlas Mòr. "It is done and time to keep my word to Dianaimh."

"Shall I release the human souls?"

"You shall," agreed the Kelpie, for his word was sacred.

The Corrievreckan began to whirl; the waves thundered shoreward, pounding the rocky coasts; and sea birds shrieked and flew for cover. Thunder and lightning rent the dark skies. Then a wave greater than all the rest suddenly spewed itself on the shore below the great castle of the King of Sgìtheanach and there, sprawled on the shore, were the sons of the kings and chieftains of the islands, safe and sound.

Watching below, for the Otherworld has means of seeing what transpires in this world, the Kelpie laughed, a genuine deep laugh. "Dall will now go down in tradition as a great magician."

Ròn Ghlas Mòr smiled in agreement. "He had little enough knowledge to save the chieftains' sons."

"Indeed he did. Let the credit be his. We of the Otherworld do not break our word."

"And Dianaimh was . . ."

"Was mine and now is lost to me, but out of the love that once we shared, my word was made absolute."

It happened as the Kelpie foretold. Dall, the Blind One, was fêted at the courts of all the chieftains; the King of Sgìtheanach gave him a fine castle at Dùn Bheagain and enough money to keep him happy all his days. As for Donall, as he had refused to give in when lesser men might have done so, he could no longer be simply a shield-bearer to the son of the King of Sgìtheanach. So the king made him Lord of Ratharsair and showered gifts on him, as did the other chieftains.

After a while, when he was out walking with Dianaimh, Donall turned and suggested they marry. There was no passion, no lustful desire between them, but they realised that they cared for each other so much that nurturing, cherishing, comforting and sustaining was more important than anything else. So Dianaimh and Donall were married and there was great rejoicing throughout all the western islands.

Deep below the turbulent waters of the Corrievreckan, the Kelpie hid a tear when he heard the news. Then he turned to the mortal whose task was keeping his coral throne polished.

"Do not slack in your task. There is work here for a thousand years more, before you can rest."

And Faoinèis bowed her head in compliance to her lord.

19 *Geal, Donn and Critheanach*

Once, long ago, there lived a Lord of Cataibh who had three daughters. They were called Geal, which means "bright" or "fair"; Donn, which means "brown-haired" and Critheanach, which means "trembling", because people trembled at the sight of her beauty. Now the three were triplets and they looked much like one another, unless one looked more closely.

Geal had been born first. Donn had been born next and Critheanach was the youngest. Soon after their birth, their mother had died. The Lord of Cataibh never married again. He was a poor lord and did not have many riches. He could not even afford to employ any domestic servants to help him take care of his old, rambling castle. So his daughters not only grew up without a mother's love or guidance but, as they grew older, all the household chores fell to them to perform.

More and more, over the years, the Lord of Cataibh retreated into his dusty old library and took little part in how his daughters ran the affairs of the castle.

Geal and Donn were very assertive girls and, because Critheanach was the youngest, they made her do all the dirty work about their father's castle. Critheanach had to clean the kitchen, cook the meals and do all manner of disagreeable tasks. Indeed, her sisters would not let her go out until the work was done to their satisfaction and that, of course, was very seldom. They were quite tyrannical towards poor Critheanach.

Each Saturday there was a great fair at nearby Dòrnach

and, each Saturday, both Geal and Donn would dress in their finest clothes and go off to visit the fair. Now the reason why they did this was that there were often many handsome young men at the fair and the girls had reached the *aois a taghadh*, that is the age of choice, whereby they might choose a husband. Naturally, it never occurred to either Geal or Donn that their sister Critheanach was also of that age. They were more concerned in finding their own husbands.

One Saturday morning, after Geal and Donn had left for the fair, there was a knocking on the kitchen door of the castle. When Critheanach opened the door, there was an old woman standing there. And a curious old woman she was. If the truth were told, she was none other than a *sìtheach*, one of the fairy folk. She said that she was selling a *seun* or charm.

Instead of sending her away in anger, as many folk do, Critheanach smiled sadly. "Alas, I have no money to buy a charm, as much as I would like to. My two sisters need all the money in the castle to go to the fair."

Now the old woman's name was Baobh and she said: "And why are you not at the fair, young Critheanach? It is there that you should be, and not working in your father's kitchen."

"I cannot go. I have no money. Nor have I good clothes to wear at the fair. Besides, if Geal and Donn were there and saw me, they would beat me senseless for leaving the kitchen without finishing the work."

Baobh sniffed in disapproval. "Fine sisters they must be. Have no care to the work. For clothes I will give you, whatever dress you desire and a fine mare to take you to the fair, with a purse of gold to spend there."

Critheanach looked sceptical but the old woman demanded to know what dress she would like.

"A dress of brightest green, a shawl the colour of purple heather and shoes to match," cried Critheanach with a laugh.

"It is done!" cried Baobh.

Sure enough, Critheanach was dressed as she had wanted, in clothes so splendid that she looked every inch a princess. At the door stood a milk-white mare with a golden bridle and a golden saddle.

"Now you may go to the fair, but you must not speak directly to your sisters nor to any young men. And after an hour, you must ride home as fast as the mare will carry you."

So Critheanach rode to the fair and the people stared at her in astonishment. Who was this beautiful young princess who rode on such a wondrous horse and who was dressed so richly? While the young men strutted before her, to attract her attention, they were not so sure of themselves to speak to her directly and neither did she speak to them. She spotted Geal and Donn but she did not speak to them either. She rode about the fair and marvelled at it, for she had never been allowed away from home before. Then a bell tolled the hour and she knew her time was up and she turned and raced for home.

She had barely reached the door and dismounted when the horse vanished and she was dressed in her old clothes again. Hurrying inside the house, she found, to her astonishment, that all the work had been done.

Not long afterwards, Geal and Donn came in and were talking about the strange young woman at the fair.

"She was a wonderful grand lady," they said. "Never have we seen such a dress and such a horse. There wasn't a young man in all the fair who did not try to attract her attention, but she would have none of them."

They demanded that their father, the poor Lord of Cataibh, provide them with dresses of equal splendour so that the next time they went to the fair, the young men might notice them. Poor man, he had no option but to take some of his priceless books and sell them to raise the money for them.

On the next Saturday, just after Critheanach's sisters had departed for the fair in their new dresses, there was a knocking at the kitchen door.

There was the old woman, Baobh, who smiled at her. "What? Not gone to the fair today?"

Critheanach smiled sadly. "It was a great joy to be able to go last week. But I still have no clothes, no money and my sisters will still beat me if the housework is not done."

"*Bi d' thosd!*" cried the old woman, which is the equivalent to saying "tush!"

Then she said: "The work will be done, and you shall have a dress, money and a horse to take you there. But again, as before, do not speak with your sisters nor any young men, and ride home as fast as you can at the end of an hour."

Critheanach agreed quite happily.

"What dress would you like?" asked the old woman.

"I'd like the finest red satin and red shoes and a silken white cloak."

Within a blink of an eye, she was standing dressed as she desired, and outside was the milk-white mare with the golden harness.

The people at the fair were more astonished than ever to see her ride up. The young men pushed each other out of the way to get near her and smile at her. And though they doffed their caps and bowed, she said nothing to them. Nor did she speak with her sisters whom she saw at the fair. She went about the stalls and people thought that her silence denoted a haughty attitude and that she was some grand princess.

Then a bell began to toll the hour. She put her heels to the sides of her mare and had barely reached the door when the mare vanished and she was back into her old clothes again. And, going inside, she found all the work was done.

A short time later, in came Geal and Donn, full of the news from the fair. Their talk was of nothing but the mysterious and beautiful princess and her fine clothes. Geal and Donn gave their father, the Lord of Cataibh, no peace, until he promised to get them dresses that looked like the strange lady's robes. He, poor man, had to take more precious books from his library, selling them in order to raise the money for their finery.

Now on the third Saturday, just after Geal and Donn had gone off to the fair, there came a knocking on the kitchen door. Critheanach opened it and, lo and behold, it was the old woman Baobh again.

"What?" she exclaimed. "Are you still here and not gone to the fair?"

"I would willingly go if I could finish this work and if I had a dress and money to go with," replied Critheanach sadly.

"Have no care for the work. It will be done. Now, what dress would you like?"

"I'd like a dress of red silk from the waist down and white silk from the waist up, and a cloak of green silk about my shoulders, and red shoes on my feet."

Within a blink of an eye she was dressed as she had wished, and with a purse of gold to help her; outside was the milk-white mare with the golden harness.

Off she went to the fair, having been warned by Baobh to maintain the same conditions as before: not to speak to any young men, and certainly not to speak with her sisters, and be home after an hour.

Once again the people at the fair crowded around when news came that the beautiful grand lady had once more come to the fair. Everyone felt that she was a princess from a foreign country, for she never spoke. Now it happened that news of the visits of the grand lady had spread and that it had reached the ears of the Prince of Loch Abar, who was visiting Dòrnach, and he came to the fair and found himself with a crowd of young men, jostling each other to catch a glimpse of her.

Critheanach stayed at the fair awhile, but now she was not so fascinated by it, nor with the vain young men who tried to attract her attention. She did not speak to them nor to her sisters, whom she saw on the edge of the crowd, their faces clearly showing their annoyance by the lack of attention paid to them in the new dresses their father had provided. So when the bell began to toll the hour, she was rather relieved that it was time to leave the fair and resolved never to go to the fair again, for it had lost all its charm.

She had not reckoned with the tenacity of the Prince of Loch Abar, whose name was Duncan. He refused to be pushed aside by the local young men, and made his way to the front of the crowd. Having seen and fallen in love with the beautiful features of Critheanach, he decided to let nothing stand in his way in trying to make her acquaintance. Though she refused to speak to him, he ran by her horse and, when she set off at a gallop home, he grabbed for her stirrup to stay her. As he did so, he chanced to grasp her shoe and off it came in his hand. He was left behind, standing in the roadway, with her shoe in his hand.

She had barely reached her house when the mare disappeared and back she was in her own clothes.

While the work was all done, there was one difference. The old woman, Baobh, was standing in the kitchen, frowning.

"You have lost something, Critheanach."

At once the girl knew what she meant. "There is vexation on me, for I have lost one of my shoes."

"True for you," agreed the old woman. "I came to tell you that this loss is now your fortune, so do not be afraid of what will happen."

And with that, Baobh disappeared, as if she were a candle-flame being blown out.

Then Critheanach's sisters came in, angry and talking about the latest appearance of the grand lady. This time, they spoke of the young prince who had so demeaned his station as to run alongside the horse of the beautiful woman and tug off her shoe.

Indeed, at the fair, the local young men were mocking Duncan, Prince of Loch Abar.

"Do you think you can win a maiden by stealing her shoe?" they jeered.

"No, but I'll tell you this," replied Duncan. "This shoe is of such a delicate shape and size that, if I find the foot that fits it, I shall find that beautiful maiden. When I do so, that maiden I shall marry."

The young men were annoyed at this stranger's presumption, for Loch Abar lay on the western side of the land of high-hilled Alba, while Dòrnach was on the eastern coast. They felt it an affront that the Prince of Loch Abar should come and claim a maiden at Dòrnach Fair, without the local young men being given a chance to pay court to her.

"If that be so," one of them said, more boldly than the rest, "then you will have to fight us for her."

"When I find her, I shall fight you, if that is your wish," replied Duncan grimly, for he was not afraid of them. If the truth were known, he was the best swordsman from Ceann Donnchaidh in the north to Linne Salmhaigh in the south.

So the Prince of Loch Abar called his servants and, taking the shoe, they set off firstly to visit every household in

Cataibh to find anyone, high-born or low-born, who might fit the shoe. After some weeks, the prince and his retinue came to the castle of the poor lord of Cataibh. The prince had left the castle until the last, as it was known that the poor Lord of Cataibh was not so wealthy that he could send one of his daughters to Dòrnach Fair in such finery as the mysterious princess had appeared in.

When Geal and Donn heard that he was coming they, of course, insisted they should try on the shoe, even though they knew that they were not the grand lady whom he was searching for.

"It matters not, for if the shoes fits, we shall wear it. We have a right to be married to a prince."

So the Prince of Loch Abar came to the house and the shoe was tried on – first on Geal and then on Donn. But neither of them could squeeze the shoe on. Truth to tell, as it was made by a *sìtheach* or Otherworld dweller, the shoe would only accept the foot it was made for. But no mortal ever knew this.

The Prince of Loch Abar stood up with a glum face, perhaps even more disappointed than the faces of Geal and Donn.

"Well, I have tried the shoe on every woman in Cataibh and a month it has taken. I will have to travel the seven kingdoms from Baideanach to Athal and to Fiobh. I will not rest until I find the lady on whom the shoe fits."

Then the poor Lord of Cataibh spoke up. He had barely spoken until that moment, for he usually allowed his two daughters, Geal and Donn, to dominate his life, while he retired into his library.

"Prince Duncan," he said, "you have not tried the shoe on every woman in Cataibh."

"Have I not? Who has not tried the shoe?"

"My third daughter, Critheanach."

At that, Geal and Donn broke out into a peal of rude laughter. "She has no use, except for cleaning the ashes. As if the shoe could fit her. Anyway, she was never at Dòrnach Fair."

Prince Duncan sighed. "Well, let her be sent for. It must not be said I did not act fairly to every woman in Cataibh."

So Critheanach came from the kitchen in her poor clothes. Impatiently, the Prince of Loch Abar handed the shoe to one of his servants, for he only saw the poor clothes of a kitchen servant and would not demean himself by bending to her feet.

There was an astonished silence as the shoe slipped comfortably onto her foot.

Then Critheanach stood up and, lo and behold, in a blink of an eye her clothes and appearance were transformed. There stood the beautiful grand lady of the fair.

Prince Duncan fell to his knees and begged her forgiveness. "I have looked for you long and hard, lady. You are the maiden I want to make my wife."

"You have first to meet with the young men of Dòrnach," replied Critheanach quietly. She had heard the news of the challenge from her sisters. "If you return from that meeting, you will find me here."

With joy in his heart, Duncan, Prince of Loch Abar, left the house of the lord of Cataibh and rode back to Dòrnach. In the square there, he stood and beat his sword hilt on his great shield in challenge.

"What does this stranger want to challenge the men of Dòrnach for?" asked one man.

"Ah, see it is the Prince of Loch Abar," cried another.

"Did we not say he must fight us for the right to pay court to the strange grand lady who visited the fair?" cautioned a third.

"Does your challenge mean, Prince of Loch Abar, that you have found the lady?" queried a fourth.

"It does," affirmed Prince Duncan. "Now I shall fight you for her."

Nine of the young champions of Dòrnach came forward, each with their swords and bucklers. For nine nights and nine days the combat lasted. Each day a champion stepped forward and, by the end of the day, his bloody body was carried from the field. At the end, Prince Duncan stood and claimed the right to pay his court to the youngest daughter of the lord of Cataibh.

When he returned, washed and was without his warlike accoutrements, he was brought into the presence of Critheаnach. They spent a day in the garden and found they shared each other's love. So a marriage feast was proclaimed and the feasting lasted for nine nights and nine days.

However, there were two at the feast who were angered at their sister's happiness.

"She is the youngest," observed Geal. "It is not right that she should be married first."

"She was nothing but a kitchen servant," agreed Donn. "Who will tend to the chores now?"

And the envy and anger grew into hatred and the hatred became an obsession.

Now it was agreed that, before the prince took his wife home to Loch Abar, they would spent some days recovering from the wedding feast at Goillspidh, on the coast north of Dòrnach. It was here that the Lord of Cataibh had a poor hunting lodge, but it was sufficient for the needs of Duncan and his wife, Critheanach, to rest quietly away from all the festivities of the marriage celebrations.

A plan was formulated by Geal and Donn to bring no good to their sister's happiness. They offered to go with their sister to Goillspidh and act as her maids, pretending that they wanted to repay their young sister for all her kindnesses. In fact, they went to watch and wait for an opportunity to take vengeance on their sister.

We have already said that each of the three sisters was born within moments of each other and each, on first appearance, looked exactly like the others. This likeness was not remarked on, for each of the sisters tended to wear different clothing. If they were wearing the same clothes, not even their father could tell them apart.

One day, at the hunting lodge at Goillspidh, Donn was walking with her younger sister Critheanach in the garden. Her cloak caught on a thorn bush and was ripped. Now Critheanach had a warm and generous heart, unlike her sisters, and she promptly gave Donn her cloak to wear, for the wind was high and cold. Critheanach then turned to go into the hunting lodge to find out if the evening meal was ready, for Prince Duncan was returning from a day's hunting fairly soon.

Donn walked on, along the cliff tops, grinding her teeth and wondering how she could enact vengeance on Critheanach, even to the point of killing her.

As she stood on the edge of the cliff, facing the sea, and wondering what plan of slaughter could be devised, along came Geal. Geal, with equal wickedness in her heart, thought she saw her sister, Critheanach, standing on the cliff edge, misled by the cloak Donn was wearing. She ran forward and thrust with all her might. Over the edge went Donn; her scream ripped from her, down to the rocks and a watery grave.

Satisfied with her work, Geal went into the lodge and found Critheanach and Duncan in each other's arms. Her horror grew when she recognised that it was truly Critheanach and not Donn.

"Where is our sister, Donn?" asked Critheanach. "I left her a short time ago, walking along the cliff tops. I had to loan her my cloak, for she had torn her cloak on a thorn bush."

Geal swallowed hard. "A messenger came and she had to return to our father at Cataibh," she said hastily. "He is feeling poorly and she has gone to see what is amiss."

Now Critheanach was concerned, but Geal said it was not a serious matter and she expected Donn to return soon.

Now, instead of feeling guilty that she had brought about the death of Donn, Geal became more angry and her hatred of Critheanach grew deeper. But she bided her time.

The next morning, after breakfast, when Prince Duncan had gone hunting again, Geal and Critheanach were walking along the same cliff tops, looking out to sea. Critheanach was unsuspecting of her sister and bent to pick flowers on the cliff top. Geal seized her chance and gave her sister a quick shove.

Over the cliff top she went, spinning down went she to the raging sea below.

As fate would have – or perhaps at the intervention of the Baobh, who knows? – at that very moment, a great *muc-mhara*, the sea beast known as a whale, came swimming along and, looking up, he opened his great cavernous mouth. Critheanach landed on his soft great tongue and in a trice was swallowed into the cave of the whale's stomach.

Geal went back to the hunting lodge, sneaking in, so that no servant saw her, and went into Critheanach's chamber and changed into her clothes. As we have said, no one could really tell them apart now, for Critheanach was only a minute younger than Geal.

That evening, when Prince Duncan came in from the hunting, she greeted him with a kiss.

"Where is your sister, Geal?" he asked, looking round.

"Another messenger came from our father. He is worsened and needs her as well."

"That sounds bad. Should we not go to visit him ourselves?"

Geal shook her head violently. "Oh no, my prince. It gives us an opportunity to stay here alone. My sisters can take care of my father in his illness."

Now Duncan truly loved Critheanach, and he knew that it was a strange thing for her to say. He knew that she loved her father and, being of a generous spirit, would have been the first to go to see her father in his illness. There were other things which did not seem right about his wife. He could not put a finger on it. She just did not seem the same maiden that he had married.

That night when they went to bed, the feeling that all was not well made Prince Duncan pause. He was truly in doubt. So he took his sword and laid it in the bed between them.

"Why do you do that, Prince Duncan?" demanded Geal.

"If you are my true love, then this sword will grow warm between us. If not, it will remain cold."

That night the sword was cold.

Early in the morning, Dìon, Prince Duncan's shield-bearer, was walking by the shore when he came on an old woman. Now the old woman was none other but Baobh, the *sìtheach*.

"Dìon, do you truly love your mistress, the princess Critheanach?" she asked.

The young shield-bearer nodded eagerly. He was a faithful servant to his lord and had helped Prince Duncan find the beautiful maiden whose foot fitted the shoe.

"Then, when you return to the hunting lodge, call forth Duncan and tell him that Geal pushed her sister Critheanach into the sea yesterday. She fell into the maw of a great whale, the *muc-mhara*. She is there now and alive under enchantment. Today, at midday, the whale swims along the shoreline. Your prince must put out in a *sgoth*, a small skiff, with his javelin. There is a red spot under the breast fin of the whale and he must strike there. Only then can she be released from its stomach."

Now Dìon was amazed but hurried to find Prince Duncan and pass on this news.

A scowl enveloped Duncan's features. "I can believe this story, as fantastic as it is, for I had a feeling last night that the woman who claimed to be my wife was not her. Fetch me my hunting javelin and find a skiff, that we may go and do battle with the *muc-mhara*."

They waited until midday and Prince Duncan saw the dark shape of the whale swimming along. Dìon helped him launch the skiff into the waters and they rowed with all their might. The whale, observing their approach, turned to the attack, swimming quickly towards them. Prince Duncan stood in the prow of the skiff with his javelin poised. Nearer and nearer came the great whale, rising from the water to crash down on the small boat. As it rose, the small spot became visible under the breast fin.

Straight and true, Prince Duncan launched his javelin and it went home. The whale leapt with the pain of it, turning from the boat and threshing in the sea so that the water became red with blood. Then it opened its mouth to roar with pain and as it did so it threw out Critheanach straight into the skiff.

Dìon turned the small boat and raced for the shore, while Prince Duncan sought to revive his wife. She was unharmed, for the spell of Baobh of the *sìtheach* had protected her from harm.

They found Geal trying on Critheanach's clothes. She knew there would be no pity for her as she gazed from Critheanach's sorrowful but determined face to Duncan's angry countenance. They made her a prisoner and rode straight back to the house of the Lord of Cataibh.

There was already a suspicion between them that he would not be found ill but was hale and hearty, and that Donn would not be there nursing him. Geal confessed all before her father.

Sorrowing, the Lord of Cataibh blamed himself for his daughters' folly. Yet Prince Duncan pointed out that, in spite of all that Geal and Donn had done, Critheanach was also his daughter and he should be proud of her.

So judgment was passed on Geal. She was cast out to sea on an offshore tide in a small rowing boat, but without oars. She was given enough food and water for a night and a day and left to the fortunes of Manánnan the great sea god. It is said by some that she was dragged beneath the waves and became a slave to the Kelpie. Others said that she managed to reach the shore of Lochlann and married a king's son there and made him unhappy ever afterwards.

As for the Lord of Cataibh, his fortunes began to prosper and he married a fine, handsome woman, who made him very happy.

And as for Prince Duncan of Loch Abar and his wife, Critheanach, they never had a day's unhappiness in the rest of their long lives, and their children and their children's children continued to rule Loch Abar for as long as the descendants of Scota and Gàidheal Ghlas, the progenitors of the Gael, prospered there.

Wales (Cymru)

Wales: Preface

This selection of Welsh myths and legends starts with the story of Bran and Branwen, the children of Llyr. This appears in the Second Branch of the *Pedair Cainc y Mabinogi* (The Four Branches of the Mabinogi). The term *Mabinogi* originally meant a "tale of youth" and has since become simply "a tale". The stories of the Mabinogi were first made known to the English-speaking world in translation by Lady Charlotte Guest (1812–1895) as *Mabinogion* in three volumes in 1846. Her translations have been open to question for, although she learnt Welsh, she relied on the help of John Jones and Thomas Price in that field, and her task was merely to render the stories into good English. She was actually born in Uffington in Lincolnshire and became interested in Welsh matters after her marriage to Sir Josiah John Guest (1785–1852) of Dowlais, Glamorgan.

Both the *Mabinogi* and Lady Guest's work have, of course, been the subject of countless scholastic studies. The texts come from the *Llyfr Gwyn Rhydderch* (The White Book of Rhydderch, c. 1300–1325) and *Llyfr Coch Hergest* (The Red Book of Hergest, c. 1375–1425) together with the fragmentary texts in the *Peniarth Manuscript 6*, (c. 1225–35). Some scholars believe that the texts were copies from an earlier manuscript source, possibly set down about 1060, according to the scholar Sir Ifor Williams. Professor Proinsias Mac Cana and Dr Patrick Sims-Williams have argued about this dating.

A recent study, *Medieval Welsh Literature* by Andrew

Breeze (Four Courts Press, Dublin, 1997), argues that four of the eleven tales which comprise the *Mabinogi*, "Pwyll, Prince of Dyfed", "Branwen, Daughter of Llyr", "Manawydan, son of Llyr" and "Math, son of Mathonwy" were all apparently written between 1120 and 1136 by an author identified as Gwenllian (d. 1136) of Gwynedd and Dyfed. Gwenllian's father was Gruffudd ap Cynan (1055–1137), king of Gwynedd, and her husband was a prince of Dyfed. However, as intriguing as Dr Breeze's arguments are, the evidence is admittedly circumstantial. Certainly the themes and motifs of the stories are older and it is obvious that, even if Gwenllian is the author, she was merely retelling the stories.

If Gwenllian was the author of these stories, it does make a fitting image of a rather intriguing woman. When the Anglo-Normans attacked her husband's territory, while her husband Gruffydd ap Rhys was away, Gwenllian raised an army and led a counter-attack which drove the Anglo-Normans back to Cydwedi (Kidwelly) castle. Under the command of Maurice of London, the Anglo-Normans fortified themselves in the castle. Gwenllian led an attack on the castle but her men were driven off. She was killed fighting a rearguard action at the fort of Maes Gwenllian (Gwenllian's Field) in 1136/37. She had managed to drive off the initial Anglo-Norman invasion and gave her husband time to prepare his forces.

Branwen uerch Llyr (Branwen, daughter of Llyr), which she is said to have retold, is the main basis of our first tale, which is found in the Second Branch. By the time this story was written, as with the others, Christian scribes had tended to censor the fact that they were talking about the ancient gods. Bran is often referred to as *Benedigeidfan* in Welsh sources and this comes from the adjective *bendigaid* – blessed, which identifies him as a deity.

Bran of Wales seems cognate with Bran of Ireland, who journeys to the Otherworld in search of adventure. He also appears to be the source of the medieval French romance of "Bron, the Fisher King".

For the story of "Math fab Mathonwy" we also go to the *Mabinogi* and specifically to the Fourth Branch of the Mabinogi. The story not only tells of Math and the war with Pryderi but of the birth of Gwydion's son, Lleu Llaw Gyffes, and of his faithless wife, Blodeuedd. This is one of the most powerful stories in Welsh myth and, among retellings and works based on its themes, Saunders Lewis made it into one of his most memorable plays, entitled *Blodeuwedd* (1948). This appeared in an English translation by Joseph Clancy as "The Woman made of Flowers" (1985).

The next tale, "Llyn-y-Fan Fach", which is sometimes called "The Physicians of Myddfai", has survived both in ancient written form and as a folk tale handed down orally. The earliest written reference appears to be in a medieval manuscript in the British Museum, BL Add. 14912. There have been several versions of the tale and many scholastic studies.

The story of "Bedd Gellert", however, is not so widely known, surviving in oral tradition down to the end of the 18th century and then being picked up in the form of a poem by the Hon. William R. Spencer, and printed privately by him in 1800, later being reprinted in his collected poems in 1811. However, a similar story, "The Fables of Cattwg the Wise", appears in the mss of Iolo Morganwg (Edward Williams, 1747–1826). The first part of the story, concerning Rhita Gawr, bears a resemblance to a theme from the story of "Culhwch and Olwen".

"The Quest for Olwen", often called simply "Culhwch and Olwen", is one of the oldest complete story texts in the Welsh language. It is not an intrinsic part of the *Mabinogi* but found in *The White Book of Rhydderch* and *The Red Book of Hergest*. It is also the earliest recorded native Arthurian saga in Welsh, predating Geoffrey of Monmouth's *Historia Regum Britanniae* and therefore, unlike many later tales, not influenced by it.

The final story, "The Dream of Rhonabwy" (*Breudwyt Ronabwy*) is also a native Arthurian tale, the earliest copy of which is found in *The Red Book of Hergest*. The tale is set in Powys in the reign of Madog ap Maredudd (d. 1160), the last King of Powys, and it is presumed that the story was composed during his reign. This is the earliest example of the use of the dream motif, which is found in both Welsh and Irish tales.

But Rhonabwy's tale is a mystery tale, for the mystery lies in its interpretation. No satisfactory explanation has ever been given by a scholar as to the meaning of Arthur and Owain's strange board game and the symbolism of the ravens. That it has something to do with the crushing victories of the Anglo-Saxons over the Celtic Britons is clear. Politically, at the time the story was set (ie in the mid-12th century) Owain of Gwynedd had managed to unite the Welsh princes in an alliance against the attacks of Henry II. Should the story be read in that context? Did the storyteller, seeing the need for another Arthur to rise to defend the Britons, this time against the Anglo-Normans, also attempt to show, in symbolic form, the dissensions among the British Celts? The conclusions must be left to the readers.

Like the other Celts, Welsh myths and legends are full of topographical references. One cannot walk through any area of a Celtic country without coming to realize, unless one is totally impervious to atmosphere, that geographical features are intrinsic to the myths and legends. Celtic myth has much to do with place as well as with story content. As a demonstration of this, my wife and I used to spend some time on the Lleyn Peninsula, in North Wales. In the area around Trefor, where we stayed in the early 1970s, one could still find the old-style *chwedleuwr* or storyteller who maintained the oral tradition of tales. That is where I first picked up the tale of "Bedd Gellert". It was, however, on that very peninsula that the locations of the creation of Blodeuedd, the woman of flowers, is said to have happened and the spot where Lleu lived in the form of an eagle. On the north shore, Gwydyon sought a name for his son. South-west, by Bardsey Island, Branwen's starling came ashore with the sorrowful news of her fate. To the south shore, the ships of Matholwch arrived to take Branwen back to Ireland. All these events are contained in the following tales.

One simply tunes into the landscape and it is replete with tales of gods and heroes, goddesses and heroines, and of the constant struggle of good and evil.

Wales was exceptionally fortunate in having scholars and folklorists such as Sir John Rhŷs (1840–1915), appointed as the first professor of Celtic Studies at Oxford. His book *Celtic Folklore, Welsh and Manx* (two vols, 1901) and his concern with pre-Christian Celtic religion and mythology, as in his *On the Origin and Growth of Religion as Illustrated by Celtic Heathendom* (1888), were pioneering works in the field.

One could not leave this area without mention of one of the most important figures in the collection of Welsh folklore – William Jenkyn Thomas (1870–1959), who was an assiduous collector of oral tradition in Wales. A graduate of Cambridge, he lectured at University College of Bangor and published two collections of folklore: *The Welsh Fairy Book* (1907) and *More Welsh Fairy and Folk Tales* (1958).

The best general introduction to early Welsh literature is the previously mentioned *Medieval Welsh Literature* by Andrew Breeze.

20 *Bran and Branwen*

There was great rejoicing throughout the Isle of the Mighty when Bran, son of Llyr, announced that his beautiful sister Branwen, "the Fair Blossom", would be married to Matholwch, king of Éireann. It was a union that everyone rejoiced in, for it meant peace between the two kingdoms. Others rejoiced that Branwen should find a husband in the handsome warrior-king and a king so rich that he had sent no less than thirteen great ships to Aber Alaw, which is now called Aberffraw, filled with rich gifts. It was at Aber Alaw that the wedding feast was to be held.

Great pavilion tents were pitched around the sea port and for nine days and nine nights there was feasting and entertainment.

Branwen and Matholwch gazed upon one another and neither could find fault in the choice.

Bran, the king of the Isle of the Mighty, was much pleased with the match for, above all things, he desired peace for his people. But there were some in the kingdom, and within his own family, who did not. Some were ready for mischief and war. Penarddun, the daughter of Dôn, who was the mother of Bran and Branwen by Llyr, had married again to a champion called Eurosswydd. To him she bore twins. One was called Nisien and the other was Efnisien. The first grew to be a youth of gentle nature and a lover of peace, while the second was one who loved nothing better than strife and conflict.

Because this was known, Bran the king decided that Efnisien should not be invited to Branwen's wedding feast.

So enraged did Efnisien become that he came to the celebrations anyway, although he did not make his presence known. He slunk into the camp of Matholwch in disguise and proceeded to cut off the tails, ears, eyebrows and lips of all the king of Ireland's horses.

Matholwch stormed into Bran's tent the next morning and demanded an explanation for the great insult that had been paid him. Bran explained that the deed had been done without his knowledge and, as token of his good faith, Bran would replace every horse that had been mutilated. In addition, he gave Matholwch a plate of purest gold as big as his face and a staff of silver as tall as Matholwch himself. To this Bran also added a special gift. It was a magical cauldron that had been brought from Éireann.

Matholwch was mollified by these gifts. In fact, he was more than delighted with the cauldron. Matholwch knew of this magical cauldron and knew where it had once been kept, at a spot called the Lake of the Cauldron in the heart of his kingdom. Walking by that lake many years before, Matholwch had met a tall, ugly man, with a wife larger and uglier than himself. The man, who was called Llassar Llaesgyfnewis, had the cauldron strapped to his back. Every six weeks his wife, called Cymideu Cymeinfoll, gave birth to a fully armed warrior. And if any one warrior was killed, Llassar would put the corpse in the cauldron and the warrior would re-emerge, as alive as ever but lacking the power of speech.

At first they had taken service with Matholwch, but the continual growth of the warrior family, who could never be killed, and their incessant bickering caused the king of Éireann many a heartache. Finally, he could stand no more and knew that the only thing to do was to destroy Llassar and Cymideu and all their children together.

He had enticed them all into a house made of iron and had coals heaped on it, hoping that it would roast the whole family to death. But as soon as the iron walls grew white-hot, Cymideu and Llassar had burst through them but their bickering children had remained behind and were roasted to death. Cymideu and Llassar, together with their magic cauldron, had crossed to the Isle of the Mighty, where Bran had allowed them to settle and, in return for this kindness, they had given Bran the magic cauldron.

So Matholwch was well pleased at receiving the cauldron but without the fierce pair who had previously owned it and all the warriors to which they gave birth.

So the wedding feast continued and, at the end of the nine days and nights, Matholwch and his beautiful bride, Branwen, set sail for his court at Tara in Éireann. And before the year was out, Branwen bore Matholwch a son, who was called Gwern, and because he was the heir to the five kingdoms of Éireann, he was sent to be fostered among the greatest families of the land.

In the second year of their marriage, tales of the insult Matholwch had suffered at his wedding feast were made known to the people of Éireann. Stories were spread that Matholwch was weak, having accepted a token compensation from Bran. The people of Éireann, prompted by these stories, grew indignant. They demanded that Matholwch should seek vengeance. Now Matholwch was rather worried at this, for he knew that behind the stories were his foster-brothers, who were envious of his throne. They were stirring up this trouble in order to oust him as king and claim the throne for themselves.

So Matholwch decided to appease his people by publicly degrading Branwen. He had her removed to the kitchens of the palace and forced her to cook and clean and ordered the chief cook to give her a blow on the ears every day so that she would know her place. All traffic of ships between Éireann and the Isle of the Mighty was forbidden, so that no news of how Branwen was being punished should reach her brother.

For three years, Branwen bore the punishment, working from sunrise to sunset in the kitchens and being sent to sleep in a draughty attic at night. It was in the attic, in the brief period before dawn, that she found a young starling with a broken wing. She mended the wing and taught the starling how to fly. Then she wrote a letter to her brother Bran, telling him what was taking place. The starling took the message under its wing and flew up into the sky.

Away eastward from Éireann it flew, until it alighted at Caer Seiont in Arfon. Indeed, not only did it alight in Caer Seiont but it set down on the very shoulder of Bran, the king, himself.

Bran's rage grew as he read the letter from his sister and he called his son Caradawg to him and told him to send out to all the chieftains of the Isle of the Mighty to prepare a great army to invade Éireann. No less than one hundred and forty-four kings came to his aid. Leaving Caradawg to rule the Isle of the Mighty in his absence, Bran set sail with his great armada.

Messengers soon came to Matholwch, telling him that a great forest was growing on the sea and this vast wood was moving towards the shores of Éireann.

Branwen heard the news and cried in joy. "It is the masts and yards of the fleet of Britain."

The chief cook reported this outburst to Matholwch, who immediately sought the advice of his council. They decided that the army of Bran was so vast that it could not be met in battle where advantage was with it. Matholwch, however, ordered a great palace to be constructed for Bran to placate him. A great feasting would be held and all homage done to the king of the Isle of the Mighty. Branwen would be released and her son Gwern brought to the court.

However, this was an outward subterfuge. The plan was that Bran and all his sub-kings and chieftains would be invited into the new palace feasting-hall. Of course, according to ancient law, no one could enter a feasting-hall with arms, so that made the Britons defenceless. Matholwch secretly arranged that at each of the pillars behind the seats at the feasting tables were to be hung two leather bags. And in each bag would be an armed warrior of Éireann. A signal would be given and the warriors would then fall on the guests and slaughter them.

Now it chanced that Efnisien had come with Bran's army and, while Matholwch was greeting Bran and inviting him to the banquet, Efnisien entered the feasting-hall. Efnisien saw the bags and asked one of Matholwch's attendants: "What is in this bag?"

"Meal, good soul," replied the servant

So Efnisien put his hand in the bag and felt the head of the warrior inside. He squeezed the head until his fingers met together in the brain as the bone cracked. He went to the next bag and asked the same question. The attendant tried to brazen it out. But Efnisien went through the entire hall and crushed all two hundred warriors' heads while they were hiding in the bags, even the head of one warrior who was wearing an iron helmet.

When the feasting began, Matholwch made a great play of preaching peace and concord. Branwen, suitably clothed once more as a princess, was told to enter the feast and pretend to her brother Bran that her letter of despair was all a mistake. Matholwch had brought her son, the boy Gwern, to the feasting-hall and threatened to kill him if Branwen disobeyed. And when the boy was led in, Bran and his followers embraced their young nephew, in whom the kingship of Éireann rested.

But when the boy came to Efnisien, the boy's half-uncle, Efnisien seized him and flung him into the blazing fire in the hearth saying: "No son of Matholwch can be trusted, for treachery runs deep in his blood!" Branwen, with a cry of despair, would have leapt after him but Bran seized her and held her back.

Matholwch called his warriors to strike but they lay dead in their sacks.

Realising now that he had been betrayed by Matholwch, Bran ordered his men to arms while Matholwch and his nobles beat a hurried retreat from the feasting hall. Thereafter, the men of the Isle of the Mighty and the men of Éireann closed in battle and the combat continued far into that first night.

During the night the men of Éireann told Matholwch that they were losing too many warriors. And so Matholwch ordered that the magic cauldron be readied and the bodies of the dead were thrown inside. Come the next morning, the dead warriors emerged alive but without the power of speech. The fresh army of Matholwch renewed the attack on the exhausted army of Bran and there was great slaughter.

Now Efnisien, who had inherited a little of the purity of

spirit of his mother Penarddun, for he was still half-brother to Bran and Branwen, was filled with remorse for what he had done. He realised that he was responsible for everything that had come to pass since the wedding of Branwen. "It is up to me to find a way of delivering my people safely from this catastrophe," he said.

And so he hid himself that evening among the dead warriors of Éireann. He was taken up with their corpses and transferred to the hidden place of the cauldron during the night. Then he was flung inside with the others and, once inside, he rent the cauldron into four pieces so that it could not be used again. Such was the effort of his deed that his own heart burst asunder.

The men of Éireann and the men of the Isle of the Mighty continued to wage war but, finally, all the men of Éireann were slain and only five pregnant women of Éireann were left to repopulate that ravaged land. And among the warriors from the Isle of the Mighty, only seven remained. Bran himself was wounded in the foot by an arrow bearing poison and he knew that the poison was spreading through his body. So he called the remaining warriors of Britain to him.

They were Bran's brother Manawydan ap Llyr; Pryderi, son of Pwyll and Rhiannon; the great bard Taliesin; Gluneu son of Taran; Ynawg; Gruddyeu son of Muryel; and Heilyn son of Gwynn Hen.

Bran gazed at them sadly. "I am dying. Before the poison reaches my head and destroys my soul, cut off my head. Take it with you to the fortress of Llyr and bury it on the White Hill. There shall my head be placed so that it faces east, and then no foreigner will invade Britain while it is there. Once you have cut off my head, I shall remain and talk to you through my head, and be pleasant company on your sad journey back to the Isle of the Mighty. I shall remain with you until you have completed your task."

Then the seven cut off Bran's head and, together with a sorrowing Branwen, those survivors left the ravaged shores of Éireann where so many had perished. And although the head of Bran talked and was as joyful as it had been in life, the more Branwen grew mournful and depressed. And when the party reached the shores of the Isle of the Mighty and came to Aber Alaw, where she had once been so happy at her marriage feast, Branwen sat down in grief.

"Grief is on me that I was ever born. Two island kingdoms have been destroyed because of me. Though yesterday my grief was unbearable, today it is twice so."

Without another word, the beautiful Branwen groaned and her heart broke.

Softened were the voices in the brakes
Of the wondering birds
On seeing the fair body of Branwen.
Will there not be a relating again
Of that sadness that befell the Fair Blossom
At the stream of Alaw?

The seven survivors gathered round and they built her a four-sided grave on the banks of the Alaw, which spot they called Ynys Branwen.

As they journeyed eastward, the seven found that Casswallawn son of Beli had overthrown Caradawg, Bran's son, and destruction had settled upon the Isle of the Mighty. Caradawg had died of grief and only Pryderi's foster-father, Pendaran had escaped the destruction. And while Manawydan should have been king of the Isle of the Mighty, Casswallawn ruled instead, for the destiny had been laid on the seven that they first accompany the head of their beloved leader to its final resting place.

They journeyed onward, eating, drinking and feasting with the noble head of Bran.

Finally, they came to the fortress of Llyr, Llyr's dun, which is now called London, and they took the head to a hill overlooking the place, called the White Hill, where in later years the Tower of London was raised. Here they buried the head with its face to the east. And it came to pass for many centuries no conquerors truly conquered the Isle of the Mighty, and Britain remained under the rule of the descendants of the Children of Dôn.

It is said that ages afterwards, Arthur, in his Christian

pride, thought it beneath his dignity to rely on the prophecy wrought by Bran, and he had the fabulous head dug up and thrown into the sea. Within a short time, Arthur was slain at Camlann and the godless hosts of Angles and Saxons were swarming into Britain across the Northern Sea.

21 *Math fab Mathonwy*

Back in the time when the children of Dôn, the gods and goddesses, ruled the five kingdoms of Cymru, the god of increasing wealth was Math son of Mathonwy. His palace lay in Gwynedd. He was regarded as wise and powerful, but he could not exist in the human world unless his feet were held in the lap of a virgin. Only when his prowess in war or hunting were needed could he leave the virgin's embrace.

The virgin to whom Math had given the honour of being his footholder was Goewin ferch Pebin, daughter of Pebin of Dol Pebin of Arfon. She was very beautiful, chaste and entirely devoted to her lord.

Among those who dwelt at Gwynedd's great palace were the children of Math's equally powerful sister, Dôn, who had married Beli, god of death. And of these children there were two sons, Gilvaethwy and Gwydyon. They were both handsome young men.

It was not long after Goewin came to live at the palace as Math's footholder that Gwydyon noticed that his brother seemed listless and without appetite. He no longer seemed to enjoy the hunt, nor occupy his time in games of *gwyddbwyll*, the ancient board game known as "wooden wisdom". Finally, while the two brothers were out hunting, and Gilvaethwy had missed a shot at a deer that not even a child could have failed with, Gwydyon turned and demanded to know what the matter was.

"I cannot say," replied his brother.

"Nonsense!" snapped Gwydyon. "It seems obvious to me.

You've been like this since Goewin came to the palace. You have fallen in love with her."

Gilvaethwy turned around nervously and put a finger to his lips. "Don't you know that Math can hear the most intimate of whispers anywhere in Gwynedd?"

Gwydyon shook his head dismissively. "I have the power over science and light. Math may be powerful but I can distract his hearing."

"Whether you can or not matters little. What can I do? Math is powerful and I cannot best him in combat."

"You can elope with Goewin," Gwydyon suggested.

His brother looked at him as if he were stupid. "Bring down the power of Math? He is the supreme leader among our people. Is he not the brother of Dôn, the divine waters who has given us all life?"

"And are we not the children of Dôn? We have no need to be scared of Math. But we shall go about abducting Goewin for you in a more subtle manner."

Gwydyon was a sharp-minded young man.

One day, seated before Math, he remarked: "Have you heard that the people of Dyfed are talking about some curious beasts which have arrived in their kingdom?"

Math frowned. "Curious beasts? What do you mean?"

"They are unlike anything anyone has seen, smaller than cattle, fat with lots of flesh and a sweet-tasting meat."

"And what are they called?"

"*Mochyn.*" That is to say, pigs.

"Who owns these creatures?"

"Pryderi, son of Pwyll and Rhiannon, lord of Dyfed."

"I would like to own some of these creatures."

Gwydyon grimaced negatively. "Pryderi guards them with his most élite warriors. He will not part even with one. I have heard that many have offered him fortunes for them." Then Gwydyon, knowing how covetousness plays with the soul, held his head to one side and said softly: "Yet I believe that I could get them for you."

Math leaned forward eagerly. "How so?"

"I will go, disguised as one of a company of bards. We will sing Pryderi's praises and demand the pigs as our repayment."

Everyone knew that even a great king could not refuse a bard's fee, for fear that the poet might satirise the king and thereby destroy his power.

So Gwydyon, with his brother Gilvaethwy, and seven others – for nine is the powerful number – rode forth to the kingdom of Dyfed, pretending to be a company of travelling bards. Pryderi was always delighted to welcome poets and song-makers to his court and a lavish feast was prepared. Afterwards, Pryderi invited Gwydyon and his company to tell their stories and sing their songs. They did so; all through the night they held the court of Pryderi spellbound with stories and songs, and reduced them to laughter or weeping or fear, so powerful was their entertainment.

As dawn came up, Pryderi realised that the entertainment must be drawn to a close and he asked Gwydyon what his fee was. When Gwydyon asked for the pigs, Pryderi was very serious.

"I would have no hesitation in meeting your fee, bard of the north, but I have taken an oath to my people of Dyfed that I will not part with one of the pigs until they have bred twice, so that there will always be pigs in the kingdom of Dyfed. Ask what else you want and it shall be given. Of the pigs, I cannot give you one neither by gift nor by sale."

Gwydyon said that as they were all tired, he and his fellow bards would retire and sleep on the matter and let Pryderi know later that day. Now Gwydyon seized on the words of Pryderi that he would not part with the pigs by gift or sale. So being, as most gods are, a master of illusion, he created nine black stallions, saddled with silver and gold, and had them tethered in the palace courtyard.

"If you will part with your pigs neither by gift nor sale," he told Pryderi after they had rested, "exchange is a fair way of dealing with the matter, so that you do not break your oath to your people. Here are nine beautiful night-black stallions and in return I will accept the pigs."

Pryderi sought the advice of his counsellors and was told that an exchange would not break his oath.

So the pigs went to Gwydyon and the magic horses to Pryderi's stable.

Gwydyon and Gilvaethwy, with their pseudo-bardic company and the pigs, set off back to Gwynedd. Of course, as Gwydyon knew, his illusion did not last long. They had barely reached Gwynedd when the night-black stallions disappeared. An enraged Pryderi, realizing he had been tricked, mustered an army and set off after the "bards".

Math heard that Pryderi was marching on his kingdom. Gwydyon had told him only part of the story, saying that Pryderi had agreed to make a deal about the pigs but now seemed determined to break it and seize the pigs back by force. Math's great war-horn sounded, summoning all the men of Gwynedd. Because it was war, Math had to leave the side of Goewin the virgin, and lead his men out to face the men of Dyfed.

Now all the men had left the palace of Math and only the women remained behind. Knowing this, Gwydyon and Gilvaethwy left the camp of Math and slunk back to his palace at night.

"Go to, brother," grinned Gwydyon. "I shall stand here on guard while you press your suit on your lady."

So Gilvaethwy went to Goewin's chamber.

"What are you doing here?" the virgin demanded. "All the men are with my lord, Math fab Mathonwy, preparing to do battle with Pryderi of Dyfed."

"I am here because I am in love with you," replied Gilvaethwy.

Goewin was shocked. "That cannot be. I am the servant of my lord. That is my destiny."

But Gilvaethwy pressed his suit upon her. The more she refused to countenance his protestations, the more ardent he became. The more she refused his love, the more his passion grew. Finally, like a kettle boiling, he burst the constraints of manhood and leapt on her, tearing off her clothes and took away her virginity.

Next morning, before dawn, Gilvaethwy, sheepish and regretting his passion, joined his brother, who grinned lewdly and winked at him. Together they rode back to Math's army and it seemed that they had not been missed during the night. They were just in time to take their positions at the side of Math when Pryderi's war-horns sounded and the army of Dyfed moved forward. Most of the day the terrible battle raged; first Dyfed were moving forward then it was Gwynedd's turn.

Finally, Pryderi sent word to Math.

"Good women are becoming widows, mothers losing sons, wives their husbands and sweethearts their lovers. There is little good in this. Let Gwydyon the conjurer come forward and settle this dispute man to man."

So a truce was held and a single combat between Pryderi and Gwydyon was agreed on.

Now had Gwydyon been a man and not a son of the Ever-Living Ones who was steeped in magic, Pryderi might have overcome all odds, for he was a mighty warrior. But only guile and cunning won the day against him. Gwydyon set to with his magic so that Pryderi never knew where his opponent was and which was reality and which was a shadow, or from where the sword edge would fall.

Guile and magic alone killed Pryderi, lord of Dyfed, and not a warrior's skill.

Yet a great cheer went up from the men of Gwynedd and Gwydyon and his brother Gilvaethwy, who had acted as his shield-bearer in the combat, were carried shoulder-high around the army. Math himself went forward to praise his nephews. He showered them with gifts and the two triumphant young men set out to tour the lands of Cymru, to receive the honour and praise from all the kingdoms. So flushed with success were they that they forgot all about Goewin the maid.

When Math returned to his own palace he sent for Goewin, his footholder.

She came, pale and red-eyed to him.

"Lord, you may no longer rest your feet with me for I am no longer a virgin."

Math's brows gathered together. "How can this be?" he demanded sternly.

He stared into her eyes and there he saw the vision of how

Gwydyon and Gilvaethwy had concocted the plan and how Gilvaethwy had raped her. Then it was that Math knew that Gilvaethwy's passion had caused many good men, Pryderi among them, to die in a carnage of bloodshed.

Math's rage knew no bounds. He sent out orders that no one should shelter his nephews, nor give them food nor drink, until they returned to his palace. When they came in fear and trembling before him, he berated them and called them animals for the deed they had done.

"As you are animals, so you shall now have the appearance of animals."

He turned Gwydyon into a stag and Gilvaethwy into a hind.

"You will go into the forest and mate with one another and return here in a year and a day," he said. Then he ordered his servants to drive them both with blows and curses into the forests.

A year and a day later, the stag and hind returned and with them came a fawn.

Then Math changed the stag into a wild boar and the hind into a wild sow. The fawn he turned into a human boy. He called him Hyddwn, meaning "deer", and kept the boy with him.

"You will go into the forest and mate with one another and return here in a year and a day," he told Gwydyon and Gilvaethwy. He ordered his servants to drive them forth with blows and curses into the forest.

A year and a day later, they came back with a young wild boar.

Then Math changed the boar and the pig into wolves and the young boar into a human boy. He called him Baedd Gwyllt, meaning "wild boar", and kept the boy with him.

"You will go into the forest and mate with one another and return here in a year and a day," he told Gwydyon and Gilvaethwy. He ordered his servants to drive them both with blows and curses into the forest.

A year and a day later, they returned with a young wolf cub.

This time Math restored Gwydyon and Gilvaethwy to human form and the wolf cub to a human boy. He called him Bleiddwn, meaning "young wolf", and kept the boy with him.

Math glowered angrily at his nephews. "You are disgraced enough for the rape of Goewin. You have been forced as animals to go into the forests and breed children off each other – your names will be forever known for that. Now you may return to dwell in my palace, but if ever you transgress the moral code again, you shall answer to me once more and I will not be so lenient in your punishment."

Time passed and Math fab Mathonwy once more found himself without a virgin in whose lap to rest his feet.

So one day Gwydyon summoned courage to speak to his mighty uncle.

"If I may, uncle, I would make a suggestion as to where you might find a suitable virgin in whose lap to rest your feet."

Math glanced at him with interest. "Whom did you have in mind?" he asked.

"None other than my sister, the daughter of your own sister, Dôn. None other than the beautiful Arianrhod, silver goddess of the dawn."

So the beautiful Arianrhod was sent for and she came to the palace, demure and virgin-like.

Now Math was always suspicious about anything his nephews suggested, so he asked Arianrhod to come before him and asked her if it were true – was she a virgin?

"So far as my mind tells me," replied Arianrhod unsatisfactorily.

Math then put his magic rowan stick on the floor and said to her: "Step over it."

This was a test of her virginity and, as she stepped across it, two boy children with golden-yellow hair dropped from her womb.

Now Gwydyon, so quickly that no human eye could have seen him, scooped up the first child and hid it within his clothes. But he was not quick enough to catch the second yellow-haired child. The boy ran immediately to the window of the palace which overlooked the great sea and leapt for it, immediately receiving the sea's nature and being able to swim as well as any fish.

"Let his name be Dylan Eil Ton," announced Math. That name means "Sea, Son of the Wave".

And sad was his story, for he was doomed to be slain by his very own uncle, Govannon, the smith-god, brother of Arianrhod and son of Dôn. But that is another tale.

Rejected by Math, Arianrhod, the goddess of the dawn, returned to her own palace at Caer Arianrhod.

As for the child left behind, Gwydyon took on the responsibility of raising the child. The two children had shown that Arianrhod was no virgin. Moreover, no one was the father of the children but Gwydyon himself, who had slept with his own sister under the guise of a magic cloak. Gwydyon, however, proved a good father and he nursed and trained the child and soon he was a fine, strapping lad.

Now Arianrhod, filled with shame of this child of incest, swore he would never be named. Now this upset Gwydyon for it fell to a mother to name her child, otherwise ill-luck would follow.

So Gwydyon, who still had his powers of illusion, altered his appearance and that of his son, appearing in the guise of shoe-makers. They presented themselves at Caer Arianrhod and asked if they could show their shoes to the ladies of the court. Arianrhod came and did not recognise them. While the cobbler and his boy were making shoes for her, a wren alighted on a branch. The young boy threw a dart at it and hit it on the leg. The wren was a bird of augury and to capture a wren was a great portent.

"Why, bright one," laughed Arianrhod, "you have a skilful hand. What name are you known by?"

"I have no name, lady."

"Then Bright One of the Skilful Hand you shall be known as from this day on." That is, Lleu Llaw Gyffes.

Then Gwydyon and Lleu turned back into their normal form and Arianrhod saw that she had been tricked into naming her son.

"You may have deceived me this time, Gwydyon, but this boy will never carry a weapon unless I arm him. That I shall not do."

Now, unless a mother give her son his first weapon, he may never be a warrior.

The years passed by and Lleu grew to be a fine youth. He was an excellent horseman and well skilled. But he could not bear arms. One day, when Math was away with most of his retinue, Gwydyon turned himself and Lleu into the guise of youthful bards and then came to the Caer Arianrhod and asked to see her. She supplied a feast and there was much good conversation and storytelling. Well satisfied, everyone retired for the night.

At dawn next morning, Gwydyon was up early and he conjured the illusion of a great enemy fleet in the harbour just below the palace. War horns were sounded and the few men in the palace were called to arms.

Arianrhod turned to the two bards.

"I know you are bards and without arms, but we need every man and boy we can to defend our palace from this strange warlike horde outside."

"My son has no arms, lady," said Gwydyon. "But he is a fine young man and, if he had arms, he would be better use to you than he is now."

Arianrhod immediately called for a sword, shield and spear to be brought forward and gave these to young Lleu.

"Have these with my blessing," she said.

It was then that Gwydyon turned himself and Lleu back into their normal form and the enemy ships vanished.

Rage was on the face of Arianrhod when she realized that she had been tricked into giving Lleu arms.

"You have deceived me this time, Gwydyon, but now I take oath that this boy will never have a human wife, nor wife of any race that dwells in the far corners of this world."

Gwydyon was angered by this. So far he had felt it merely a game, but now his sister was taking a real vengeance on their son because he, Gwydyon, had tricked her. He swore an oath that he would secure a wife for Lleu, in spite of his sister.

Gwydyon went to Math fab Mathonwy and told him the whole story, because he realized that his uncle had grown to like the handsome young boy, who was a youth of beauty and strength and skilled in many things.

"I will help you, Gwydyon, and share my power with your magic."

Together they went into the forests and took the flowers of an oak, broom and meadowsweet. Having performed the correct incantations, they conjured a beautiful young girl. They called her Blodeuwedd, which is "flower aspect". Lleu and Blodeuwedd seemed destined for each other, in spite of Arianrhod's curse. A great wedding feast was held and there was much celebration throughout all Gwynedd. And Math, who was fond of Lleu, gave him one of his own palaces, which was Mur Castell in Cantref Dunoding, in the uplands of Ardudwy.

Time passed. And Blodeuwedd began to grow tired of Lleu Llaw Gyffes, for she was of a gentle nature and bored with the martial life of her husband.

One day, when Lleu was off on some martial expedition, a hunting party arrived at the castle.

"Who is it?" she asked her servant, seeing a handsome young man at their head.

"That is Goronwy Pebr, lord of Penllyn," the servant replied.

The party was invited in and Blodeuwedd could not take her eyes off the handsome lord, nor could he take his eyes from her. Through the feasting that night, they had eyes for no one but each other, and at the end of the feast they rose, leaving the other guests, and went straight to Blodeuwedd's bed chamber and made love all through the night. For three nights and three days they made love with one another, until Blodeuwedd realized that her husband must soon return.

Lleu Llaw Gyffes came home the very next day, stained with the blood of his enemies.

That night, when Blodeuwedd became withdrawn from his amorous advances, he asked her what ailed her.

"Nothing, lord," she said blushing, realizing that she must not show that she was in love with another.

"Come; something troubles you?"

The girl thought rapidly. "In truth, lord, I'll tell you, then. I fear that one day you might never come back from your wars. I fear that you might be killed."

Lleu put his head back and laughed good naturedly. "Well, if that is all, Blodeuwedd, rest easy. I shall let you in on a secret. As you know, my father is the god of science and light, Gwydyon; my mother was the goddess of dawn, Arianrhod the Silvery One. Therefore the blood of the Ever-Living Ones courses in my veins. I cannot be killed on horseback nor on foot. I cannot be killed indoors nor out of doors."

Blodeuwedd had a plan forming in her mind. "That is pleasing to know, husband. But I would rest happier if I knew that there was absolutely no way an enemy could kill you."

Lleu laughed heartily. "Have no fear. I can be killed only in one way and no enemy will ever know that."

"Maybe I should know of it, so as to be able to prevent it happening?" Blodeuwedd asked artfully.

"Well, first a bathing place has to be prepared for me by the bank of a river. A thatched roof has to be placed over it. A goat must be tethered alongside. Then, if I am caught with one foot on the goat's back and the other on the rim of the bath, the conditions are fulfilled. Even then, the only way to kill me is by a spear that has been a year in the crafting."

"Surely, no enemy would know that," agreed his wife, thinking hard.

"None, indeed. So your worries have no foundation. I will not be killed."

The next day, Blodeuwedd had arranged to meet her lover, Goronwy Pebr, in the forest; after they had met and made love on the leaf-strewn carpet of the forest, Blodeuwedd told him that she had a plan that would rid them of her husband. She then told Goronwy Pebr how Lleu could be killed.

"But the other conditions are impossible," complained Goronwy Pebr. "Lleu would never obligingly get in that position."

"Leave that to me," Blodeuwedd assured him.

For a year, Goronwy Pebr set to crafting the special spear.

Then the time came when Blodeuwedd's plan was to be put in motion. She told Goronwy Pebr to be at the river bank at dawn the next day.

At the palace she seemed preoccupied.

"What is it, my lady?" asked Lleu.

"Well, the truth of it is that I have been worried. Do you remember telling me a year ago how you could not be killed?"

"I do," asserted Lleu. "You are not still worrying about that, are you?"

"I am. I have forgotten how you told me that you had to stand for an enemy to kill you. If I don't know, then I couldn't protect you if the circumstances arose."

Lleu thought she was so worried and concerned that he should show her and demonstrate how it was impossible such circumstances could happen.

The next morning, a bathing place was built on the river bank, near to where Goronwy hid. A thatched roof was placed over it and a goat brought up. Then Lleu showed his wife how he had to stand with one foot on the goat's back and the other on the rim of the bath.

"See what an impossible thing it is?" laughed Lleu as he stood, balancing precariously.

"Now!" screamed Blodeuwedd.

Goronwy Pebr rushed out of his hiding place with his spear at the ready. In a flash, as if of lightning, the spear was speeding towards Lleu. It hit him between the ribs and stuck there. Now Lleu was of the Ever-Living Ones and, in the split second he saw death approaching and the penetration of the spear, he turned into a great golden eagle. Painfully, the eagle rose, crying in its anguish; he rose slowly higher and higher until he became a dark speck in the sky and flew away.

Blodeuwedd rushed into her lover's arms and they went back to the castle to celebrate. Both believed that Lleu would soon be dead.

The next morning Goronwy Pebr, lord of Penllyn, declared himself ruler of all the lands once held by Lleu Llaw Gyffes.

Now Lleu's father, Gwydyon, heard the story from some of Lleu's former servants, and he told the story to Math. But without proof that Lleu had died, they could not move in punishment against Goronwy Pebr. So Gwydyon asked Math if he could leave the palace and go in search of his son. For a year and a day, he searched the five kingdoms of Cymru.

One evening, Gwydyon was staying with a farmer when the farmer's swineherd came in and told his master that his boar was behaving oddly. Every evening, the boar went into the pigsty and disappeared. In the morning, the boar would be there in the pigsty. The swineherd thought it strange behaviour.

Gwydyon pricked up his ears and asked the farmer if he could deal with the matter, as he felt there was some magic in this. That evening, he followed the boar from the pigsty. The boar, however, raced away and it took all Gwydyon's power to keep up with it. It halted under a tree. And the name of the place was called Nantlleu, which is "Lleu's brook".

On the tree perched an eagle. Gwydyon recognised it at once. It was Lleu. Gwydyon enticed it from the tree. The boar turned out to be the fabulous Twrch Trwyth, the King of Boars, the protector of the Ever-Living Ones. It had been looking after the dying Lleu and led Gwydyon to his hiding place. Gwydyon changed the eagle back into human form.

Lleu lay near death, his cheeks blue and sunken. He was babbling about Blodeuwedd, but nothing made any sense.

Gwydyon took him in his arms, like a baby, and carried him to the palace of Caer Dathyl, where Math fab Mathonwy and Gwydyon joined their supernatural forces. There Math conjured all the Otherworld knowledge he could summon and after a long struggle – a struggle which took a year and a day – Lleu finally stood strong in health and as vigorous as ever he had been.

Now there was no other way forward but to take revenge on his faithless wife and her lover. But Goronwy Pebr had gathered large armies to protect his domains, and so Lleu led the mighty hosts of Gwynedd against them. Goronwy Pebr and his armies retreated and they became separated from Blodeuwedd and her women, who ran screaming before Lleu. They knew the mighty lord would show little mercy.

Indeed, Lleu had no mercy at all for his former wife. He and his men rode at the running lines of women. In their fear, they kept glancing behind at their pursuers and not looking ahead, and so they streamed into the River Cynfael and were drowned – all except Blodeuwedd!

She was rescued and brought trembling before Lleu.

"I will not kill you," Lleu told her. "That is too easy a punishment. For your betrayal, you will become a bird. Not just any bird, but a bird that will only emerge at night, for daylight is too bright a time for the likes of you. And all other birds will scorn you and avoid you."

So saying, Lleu turned his former wife Blodeuwedd into an owl.

Goronwy Pebr had fled with his army into his own territory of Penllyn. He sent messengers to Lleu, asking him for forgiveness and whether Lleu would accept compensation. Lleu replied that he would, but added that there was only one compensation he would accept. Goronwy Pebr must return to the spot on the river bank where he had cast his murderous spear at Lleu. There he must stand and allow Lleu to cast his spear back at Goronwy Pebr. If he refused, Penllyn would be annihilated.

Goronwy Pebr hesitated at these terms, but his people, tired of bloodshed and knowing that they would suffer much if Lleu invaded Penllyn, demanded that Goronwy Pebr face Lleu. So the lord of Penllyn went to the river bank. At first he was boastful, but when he stood before Lleu, his little courage began to leave him. He pleaded with his men to come and face Lleu with him. They all refused. Then he fell on his knees and pleaded with Lleu. They had both been victims of a faithless woman, he cried.

Lleu stood stony-faced, ready to cast his spear.

"One last request!" Goronwy Pebr cried. "You must grant me one request."

"You may be granted one last request," agreed Lleu.

"No matter what it is?" pressed Goronwy Pebr eagerly.

Lleu smiled sceptically. "Only within reason."

"It concerns only where I am to stand on this river-bank when you cast your spear."

"That is reasonable enough," agreed Lleu. "You can choose where you want to stand. Take your choice."

"There." Goronwy Pebr pointed to a large rock. "I want to stand behind that rock when you cast your spear."

Now Lleu's followers cried out that this was a blatant trick to escape his punishment. However, Lleu smiled calmly and said his word had been given.

Goronwy Pebr went and stood confidently behind the rock.

Lleu cast his spear and the cast knocked a round hole through the rock and transfixed Goronwy Pebr to the ground behind it. To this day some will take you to *Lech Goronwy Pebr* – the Stone of Goronwy Pebr – and show you the round hole caused by Lleu's great spear.

Then Lleu took back his lands and thanked his father Gwydyon and his uncle, Math fab Mathonwy. He became renowned among the Ever-Living Ones, looked to as the great patron of all arts and crafts.

As for Blodeuwedd, people say that they have heard her plaintive cry at night in the dark forests where she still dwells, never to show herself in daylight and the eternal enemy of all the other birds.

22 *Llyn-y-Fan-Fach*

In the ancient kingdom of Dyfed, in the north west of that kingdom, on the Black Mountain, there is a small, dark lake called Llyn-y-Fan-Fach, or the Lake of the Little Peak. Not more than two miles from that remote lake, near Blaensawdde, the source of the river Sawdde, three-quarters of a mile from the village of Llanddeusant, there lived the widow of a farmer.

Now this farmer, while alive, had no love for the toil of farm work and he had maintained himself as a warrior, drawn to combat and wars. As often occurs when people follow warfare, he was killed. And of his four sons, three of them were killed at his side. The fourth son had been too young to bear arms.

The widow, therefore, hearing the news of her husband's death in philosophical manner, declared: "War shall not destroy my fourth son." She taught him only the arts which a farmer should know and nothing else.

She worked hard and her son helped her and the farm prospered. Soon she had a sizeable cattle herd. It increased so well that she came to realize that her land was being over-grazed. The cattle needed more grass than she could provide. So she would send a portion of her cattle herd to graze upon the verdant slopes of the Black Mountain and a favourite place was near the small dark lake of Llyn-y-Fan-Fach.

Now this widow's son was growing to manhood and was a handsome, strapping young man who took his full share in tending the cattle. He would herd them when they went to the Black Mountain.

One day, while attending the cattle, he was sitting by the lakeside, breathing in the warmth of the evening air, when he fell to drowsing. Then in a half-waking, half-dreaming state, he heard a sweet female voice singing:

In drowsing and dreams,
Naught is as it seems.
All is an illusion
That grows from delusion.

If your true love you'd see
Then wake and see me . . .

He sat up and looked in the direction of the sound and saw, to his surprise, seated on a rock by the lakeside, was a most beautiful young girl. Her golden hair flowed gracefully in ringlets over her fair shoulders, the tresses of which were held in place by a comb. Her skin was whiter than the foam of the sea waves, whiter than snow on a winter's morning. She caught sight of him and gazed at him from sea-green eyes. There was a smile on her lips, lips as red as foxgloves, and he felt his heart leaping within him; his eyes were riveted on her beauty and he felt helpless, bewildered by the feelings which this wondrous creature stirred in him. His eyes took in all the details of the young maiden, from her resplendent jewels, to her sea-green dress, even to her dainty slippers with their gold thread laces.

All he could think of by way of conversation was to offer her the barley bread and cheese which his mother had given him for his day's meal when he left home.

The young girl laughed.

"*Cras dy fara; Nid hawdd fy nala*!" she chuckled. "Hard-baked is your bread. It is not so easy to catch me!"

Then she turned and dived under the water and disappeared. All day did the love-stricken youth sit by the lake, hoping that she would re-emerge but she did not. Disappointed, the youth returned home. Try as he would, he could not shake her image from his mind. Never, among all the fair maidens of Llanddeusant and Myddfai, had he ever seen such beauty. And beauty there was abounding among the maidens of Myddfai. Didn't the ancient poets sing of that beauty?

Mae eira gwyn
Ar ben y bryn
A'r glasgoed yn y Ferre
Mae bedw mân
Ynghoed Cwm-brân
A merced glân yn Myddfe

That means:

There is white snow
On the mountain's brow
And green wood at the Verdre
Young birch so good
In Cwm-brân wood
And lovely girls in Myddfai

For a long time the youth mooned about the farm, hardly concentrating on his work, until his mother finally demanded that he tell her what was wrong. When he explained, she advised him to go back to the lake and take with him some unbaked dough, as she reasoned that there must be some enchantment connected with the *bara cras* or hard-baked bread which caused the strange maiden to refuse it and dive into the lake.

"My bread was hard," she confessed, "but I was not expecting a goddess from the Otherworld to break her white tooth on it."

The very next morning, as the sun came up over the Fans, the peaks of the Black Mountain, the young man was at the lakeside with his mother's cattle. But his mind was not on the cattle. His eyes searched the still waters of the lake, seeking the young maiden. Yet in vain did he search for her. The breeze sent ripples over the lake, and the clouds eventually came down and hung low over the summit of the Black Mountain, adding a gloom to his tormented mind.

The hours passed and there was still no sign of her. Evening approached. The wind hushed and the clouds still hung heavy over the mountains. The youth suddenly realised that he had let his mother's cattle wander and he saw them on a precipitous rock on the far side of the lake, where they were in danger of losing their footing and falling to their death.

He sprang from his seat, impelled to race to their rescue, when, abruptly, the beautiful maiden was seated on the lake shore before him. Once again he found himself tongue-tied and went forward, only just remembering his mother's instructions, and held out his hand with the unbaked bread in it.

When she smiled at him, he suddenly found his voice and offered his heart and vows of eternal love.

The maiden suddenly chuckled. "*Llaith dy fara; ti nu fynna*!" she cried. "Unbaked is your bread. I will not have you."

Then she turned and dived back under the waters of the lake.

Distraught, the youth left the cattle to their fate and went home, scarcely looking where he was going.

His mother, by gentle questioning, learnt of his second rejection. Now she was still sure that there was some enchantment in the manner of the bread. She suggested that he go to the lake on the very next morning and this time take with him bread that was but slightly baked. If hard bread and unbaked bread caused this mysterious being to reject her son, then surely a middle way was intended?

Next morning, the youth left his mother's farm and arrived at the lakeside. He was feverish with desire. He did not even heed that the cattle, still straying among the precipitous rocky slopes of the Black Mountain, were occasionally loosening the stones and rocks, and some were falling into the lake.

He waited, his eyes searching the lake, as the freshness of the morning gave way to the sultry heat of the noon sunshine, and then the warmth of the afternoon faded into the shadows of early evening. Soon it would be dark.

Sadly, the young man rose and cast a final look across the dark waters.

Then he beheld a wondrous sight.

The cattle which had drowned, falling from their precipitous perches into the lake, suddenly appeared well and healthy on the waters of the lake and swam to shore. Every last one of those which he had lost by his inattentive attitude towards his charges, by his concentration on attempting to fulfil his desire, was saved.

Then he saw that they were herded from the lake by the beautiful maiden.

His heart leapt again and he offered her the partially baked bread. "Maiden, unless you love me, it is no better for me to live than to die."

The maiden smiled softly at him. "A pity for me to cause the death of a handsome youth such as you."

This time she took the bread and accepted his hand and sat by him awhile. When he offered her marriage, she did not say "no". But this she said: "True-baked is your bread; indeed, I'll be wed."

He pressed her to name the day and she replied: "You have been negligent in looking after your cattle, which I saved from drowning for you. So now I will make a condition for our marriage. I will only come and be your bride so long as you are not negligent to me. If you strike me three blows without cause, I shall return to the lake and leave you forever."

The youth, brimming with ardour, agreed to the conditions. Indeed, he would have consented to any condition, in order to secure the lovely maiden as his wife.

"Having agreed to that condition, there is a test which you must pass," she said.

Before he knew what was happening, she had dived back into the lake.

He sat stunned. Indeed, he was so grieved that, for a moment, he determined to cast himself into the dark waters after her and so end his life, in the element that contained the only being in the world he cared to live with.

Just as he was about to make the decision, the calm waters of the lake bubbled and out of them there appeared a large man of noble appearance and extraordinary physique. And with him came the beautiful maiden . . . except there were two of her. Two maidens exactly the same. The youth gazed on them in bewilderment.

The noble being addressed him in a low pleasant voice. "Have I been told correctly that you want to marry one of my daughters?"

"You have, sire," the youth replied. "Unless I do, it is no better for me to live than to die."

"A pity then to cause the death of a healthy, handsome youth such as yourself. I will consent to this union, provided that you can distinguish which of my two daughters you truly love. For if you love only the shell of the girl, you will not know which is which, for they are both alike. It will be only the outward appearance you like. To really love someone, you must love beneath the outward appearance."

Now this was no easy task for the youth for, as the noble spirit of the lake had said, the two were such perfect counterparts of each other. The youth knew that if he chose the wrong one, she would be lost for ever. Three times, the noble being urged him to speak up and each time he was lost for words.

He stood awhile, not being able to perceive the slightest difference between them. He was on the verge of making a guess when one of the girls slipped a foot forward. The motion was not lost on the youth and he saw that there was a slight variation in the method in which their slippers were tied. The maiden he loved, he recalled, had golden laces on her slippers. This put an end to his dilemma, for he had so impressed the details of the maiden he had fallen in love with in his mind, carefully noting every item of her dress, that he knew the peculiarity of the golden laces of her slippers.

He reached out a hand towards her.

"This is she," he said firmly.

"You have chosen correctly," said the spirit of the lake. "Be to her a kind and faithful husband, and I will cause you to thrive. You will have, as a dowry, as many sheep, cattle, goats and horses as she can count without heaving or drawing in her breath. But remember, mortal, if you prove unkind to her, or strike her three times without a cause, she shall return to me and shall bring back all her goods."

The young couple were married and as many sheep, cattle, goats and horses as the maiden could count were theirs. And the number was considerable, for the maiden chose to count by fives. She would say thus: "One, two, three, four, five," and then repeat it as many times as possible in rapid succession, until her breath was exhausted. In an instant, the fields were full of the numbers she had called.

And the young man, now having his own fortune, took a farm a mile from Myddfai, which was on a ridge which became known as Esgair Llaethdy, the ridge of the dairy, for the farm abounded in cattle and its milch cows became famous. The couple lived in great prosperity and happiness and raised three sons, who were handsome children.

A baptism was held in Myddfai one day and the couple were invited, being the most prosperous and generous people in the area. But the lake maiden was reluctant to attend, alleging the distance to the appointed place was too great a distance for her to walk. In truth, the birth of a child in this world always meant the death of a soul in the Otherworld, and this was the reason why she was reluctant to go for, instead of celebrating, as a denizen of the Otherworld she would have to mourn.

"Are you not ready yet?" cried her husband as he came bustling out of the farmhouse. "Where are the horses?"

"I shall get them, if you bring me my gloves which I left in the house."

He did so and, returning, he found that she was still standing exactly where he had left her and had not bothered to bring the horses.

"Get the horses! Hurry!" he said, in annoyance. In his vexation he gave her a tap on the shoulder to make her hurry up. "Come on, we will be late." Whereupon she turned with a frown and reminded him that he had agreed not to strike her without cause. Now he had done so and struck her for the first time. He must be more careful in the future for, if he struck her three times without cause, she would return to the lake.

A wedding was held in Myddfai and the couple were invited, being the most prosperous and generous people in the area. There was great mirth and hilarity at the wedding among the assembled guests, but the lake maiden was doleful and sad. Her husband playfully slapped her on the back and told her to cheer up for there was no cause for sadness. She turned to him and said:

"The wedded couple are entering their own troubles and your troubles, too, are likely to start, for you have struck me a second time without cause."

From then on, her husband was especially careful that he should not hit her by accident or in a playful mood. He was ever watchful, lest any trivial occurrence take place which would cause the last blow and separate them forever.

As the years passed, their three children grew apace. Indeed, they grew into handsome and clever young men. All seemed well.

A funeral was held in Myddfai and the couple were invited, being the most prosperous and generous people in the area. There was a mourning and grief at the house of the deceased.

The lake maiden, however, did not look sad. Indeed, she amazed her husband by being in the gayest of spirits. She so shocked him that he tapped her sharply on the arm saying: "Hush! It is wrong that you should laugh."

She turned to him and said: "Mourning in birth, because of the death of the soul in the Otherworld; sadness at a wedding, for it is the start of travail; joy at death, because of the birth of a soul in the Otherworld. Now the last blow has been struck, and our marriage is at an end."

She rose and left for Esgair Llaethdy, claiming her goats, sheep, cattle and horses together and in this fashion:

Mu wilfrech, Moelfrech,
Mu olfrech, Gwynfrech,
Pedair cae tonn-frech,
Yr hen wynebwen
A'r las Geingen
Gyda'r Tarw Gwyn
O lys y Brenin

A'r llo du bach,
Sydd ar y bach,
Dere dithau, yn iach adre!

Brindle cow, white speckled,
Spotted cow, bold freckled,
The four field sward mottled,
The old white-faced,
And the grey Geingen
With the white Bull.
From the court of the King;
And the little black calf
Tho' suspended on the hook,
Come thou also, quite well home!

All the cattle obeyed the summons of the lake maiden, even "the little black calf", although it had been slaughtered for the feast. And among the livestock there were four grey oxen who had been attached to a plough and who were furrowing a field driven by a ploughman. And to these she called:

Pedwar eidion glas
Sydd ar y maes,
Deuwch chwithau
Yn uach adre

The four grey oxen
That are on the field,
Come you also
Quite well home!

They left the field, still dragging their plough, and made their way to the lake maiden, leaving the ploughman with jaws agape.

Then she called the sheep, who ran to her, the rams with their curly horns and the ewes with their lambs. Then she called the goats, who came skipping from the copses and leaping from the rocks. And finally she called the horses, who came surging towards her, whinnying and swishing their tales.

All the livestock which she had brought from the Otherworld made their way to the lake maiden. She led them in procession across the Myddfai mountains. She led them by owl-light, under the watery moon, over the dark mountains, towards the lake from whence they had come. And they came to the edge of the lake and, without pausing, they entered the lake and disappeared beneath the waves, leaving no trace except the furrow marked by the plough which the oxen had drawn after them into the lake.

They say that the furrow remains to this day, as testimony to the truth of this tale. What became of the ploughman who had been tending the oxen and ploughing the field is not known. Some say he was so scared that he ran off; others claim that he was dragged into the lake, trying to save his plough.

The distraught husband of the lake maiden raced after her, but she had returned to the Otherworld under the lake. In vain, he cried for her to return, apologising for his stupidity, for his negligence and forgetfulness. But there was no reply. Then, in his despair, he threw himself into the lake. The moment he leapt into the water, it was as if a great force seized him and threw him back on shore. Twice more he tried to drown himself by leaping into the lake. Twice more he was returned to the shore and finally a great voice, in which he recognised the spirit of the lake, cried: "You are not worthy to enter here!"

What became of the distracted man, no one can say. He was never again seen in the area nor, indeed, in the length and breadth of the land of the Cymru – the land of comrades – which the Saxons were later to call the land of "foreigners" or *Wealas*.

But it is said that the three sons of the lake maiden, having grown to manhood, never lost hope of seeing their mother again. They often wandered by the lake and its vicinity and hoped that their mother might take pity on them and return to land once more.

Now the eldest son was called Rhiwallon, and it happened

that he was near the lake on the Black Mountain, at a pass which was called the Mountain Gate. A young maiden suddenly appeared before him, for the lake maiden never aged.

"Rhiwallon, it is your mother," she called.

And after the joy of seeing each other again, she told him that she had come to inform him and his brothers that they had great work to do in the world.

"What work would that be, mother?" demanded Rhiwallon.

"You will be a benefactor to the mortals, relieving them from their pain and misery and healing them from their diseases."

"But my brothers and I have no knowledge of medicine, mother. How could we do this?"

Then the lake maiden handed him a bag, which contained a great book which was filled with prescriptions for all the diseases and illnesses which could strike at mankind. She told him that if he paid strict attention, he and his brothers would become skilful physicians and their families would become great healers for the next thousand years.

"If you ever need my counsel, but only when there is no other choice, call on me, and I will return and help you. I will visit you and your brothers once more to give you further instructions."

With those words, she vanished.

The spot where she met Rhiwallon was called Llidiad y Meddygon, The Physicians' Gate, and it is still so called today.

True as her word, she appeared to her three sons at a place called Pant-Y-Meddygon – The Hollow of the Physicians. In that hollow grew the various herbs and plants which, as she showed them, had the qualities of healing. And eventually the three brothers became the most skilled healers in all Cymru and were known as "The Physicians of Myddfai". The sons of Rhiwallon and his brothers became physicians to Rhys Gryg, Lord of Llandovery and Dynefor, who gave them rank, lands and privileges at Myddfai.

Generation after generation, the fame of the Physicians of

Myddfai spread. History records that the last of the Physicians of Myddfai was David Jones, who died in 1719. He was the last to practise healing there and the last to have descended from the maiden of Llyn-y-Fan-Fach.

23 Bedd Gellert

It is not wise to spend certain nights of the year on Yr Wyddfa, which the English called Mount Snowdon, the highest mountain of Gwynedd. Especially, it is not wise to tarry in the vicinity of the tomb which is called Bedd Gellert. Why and how it came by that name is a story which I will tell you but, firstly, I should tell you how some people claim Yr Wyddfa was formed.

There were once two lords in Gwynedd: one called Nynniaw and the other was Peibiaw. Each was as vain and as arrogant as the other. They were given to placing wagers with one another as to who was the better man, or who had the best possessions. It came about that they laid a wager on who had the best fields and the best herds and flocks. Each lord said that his was by far the best.

Nynniaw it was who suggested that they meet at midnight near Snowdon; and Nynniaw it was who promised to show Peibiaw a field that he could not better.

Peibiaw arrived and demanded to know where the magnificent field was which Nynniaw had promised him.

"Look upwards then," cried Nynniaw.

Peibiaw looked up and gazed at the vast expanse of darkness speckled with a myriad of twinkling stars. "I do not understand."

"Why, easy to tell. There is the field, the wide firmament of the heavens. That is my field."

Peibiaw smiled. "Well, I can show you herds and flocks which you cannot better."

"Where?" And Peibiaw pointed upwards. "The herds and flocks are the galaxies. Do you see my milk-white cattle and sheep which are the stars? And see what a wondrous shepherdess tends them?"

"Where is she?" demanded Nynniaw.

"Why, the moon, of course, whose pale light shows them to their pastures."

"They shall not continue to graze in my field," thundered Nynniaw.

"But they shall!"

Peibiaw and Nynniaw challenged each other to a combat and each promised that one of them would be dead before either conceded the grazing rights of the heavens.

Now the kingdom of Gwynedd was ruled by a mighty warrior named Rhita Gawr. He exclaimed that the two lords were silly creatures, who would argue over such meaningless matters. As he was the mightiest king, if anyone had the rights to graze cattle anywhere in the universe it was surely he?

Tired with the squabbling of Nynniaw and Peibiaw, he called his army together and marched against the combined armies of Peibiaw and Nynniaw and vanquished them both. Even then he found them squabbling and, being a man who had studied alchemy and the magic of the Druids, he turned Nynniaw and Peibiaw into oxen of exceptional strength when pulling together, but each one apart was weak. In this manner, Rhita Gawr said that they would learn how to work together.

And this is true, for it was Culhwch's task to harness them together to plough the land in preparation for Olwen's feast; they were used to pull Afanc out of the Conwy and also to haul a large boulder so that the church of Llanddewi Brefi could be built. But these are stories which do not concern us at the moment.

Before Rhita Gawr had turned them into oxen, he had insulted them by shaving off their beards and having them stitched together to make a cap to keep his head warm.

Now this news spread to the kings of the universe where Nynniaw and Peibiaw claimed their field and flocks. They took the matter very seriously and said, "If we permit Rhita

Gawr to do this thing, which is the greatest insult against a warrior that can be made, what beard among us will be safe?"

And the twenty-seven kings of the universe joined forces and marched their armies against Rhita Gawr. Warned of their approach, Rhita Gawr raised his warriors and went forward to meet them. He defeated them and had all twenty-seven beards shaved off and stitched together to make a coat for himself.

Now it so happened that the kings of the world soon heard how their brother kings of the universe had been worsted and had their beards shaven off by Rhita Gawr. They all exclaimed: "This king of Gwynedd is too presumptuous. If we do not stop him, he will not leave a king with a beard in any country in the world nor in the Otherworld."

So a great army was gathered and set out to invade Gwynedd.

Now Rhita Gawr was sitting gazing up at the heavens and counting the value of the vast fields and grazing rights which must surely lie there. Thicker than an autumn forest came the assembled armies and they fell on Rhita. But the giant and his men were ready for them and, within a blink of an eye, all the invading kings were beaten and each king had his beard shaven off; now Rhita Gawr had enough to make himself a great cloak.

It was then that a young king named Arthur the Bear, who was dwelling in the south, came to Rhita's attention. Now Rhita Gawr had found that he had developed a passion for collecting the beards of kings and making them into clothing to keep him warm.

"I'll have no rest, until I take the beard of this youth Arthur," he said to himself.

So Rhita Gawr sent off to the kingdom of Cernyw, which was where Arthur dwelt. He brought with him his army, just in case. One fine afternoon, he arrived at Arthur's palace.

"I do not wish to harm the young king," Rhita announced, "but I will take his beard. He must also renounce all interests in the grazing rights of the heavens."

Now Arthur came to the gate of his castle and gazed up at the giant king of Gwynedd. "I have no interest in the grazing rights of the heavens," he told him "But you will never take my beard, unless by force."

Now this angered Rhita Gawr, who was clad in his cap, coat and cloak of beards as a means of putting fear into his enemies. But Arthur was not even awed by the sight. So Rhita Gawr took his sword and smote on his shield in challenge.

Arthur arranged to meet in battle with Rhita Gawr's army on the following morning.

Just before dawn, the horns summoned the warriors.

Rhita Gawr saw a strange flash of lightning spread from Arthur's encampment. "What is that?" he demanded of his charioteer.

"That's Arthur's warriors raising their spears for battle."

There came a mighty rumble like thunder. "What is that?" Rhita Gawr demanded of his charioteer.

"That's Arthur's men issuing their battle-cry."

"Ah, I will have his beard all the same!" cried Rhita Gawr, unperturbed.

The two armies met like waves colliding with one another. The battle was matched equally and, finally, Arthur, tired of the bloodshed, and following a custom among his people, issued a challenge to single combat. Rhita Gawr agreed, for no one could surpass him in combat. Rhita Gawr and Arthur strode out before their armies.

"I will still have your beard!" cried Rhita Gawr as he faced Arthur.

The young king smiled. "But my beard is that of a young man," he called. "It would be but a poor cover to the hole I see in your coat."

Rhita Gawr was not goaded by this. "True enough, but it is still a king's beard and one that I do not have."

"I know of a king's beard which you do not have and which will more than adequately cover that hole."

"Whose beard is that?" demanded Rhita Gawr, intrigued for the first time.

"Your own beard!" answered Arthur with a shout.

And with that the combat started.

It was a mighty combat and neither one of them showed any sign of weakness nor of yielding. Great valleys were carved out of the level plain on which they fought, scooped out by the pounding of their feet. The earth was so shaken, as if an earthquake was striking it, that Rhita Gawr's army lost their balance: but Arthur's men stood firm. For nine nights and nine days the contest went on.

Finally, Rhita Gawr, exhausted to the point where he could no longer lift his sword, fell to his knees before Arthur.

"You are the better man, Arthur," he conceded.

So Arthur had Cadw of Pictland come forward and shave off the beard of the giant king of Gwynedd. Then Rhita Gawr's beard was stitched to all the other beards that he had taken and the beard-mantle was draped over his shoulders. Rhita Gawr was sent back to Gwynedd and admonished never to shave anyone's beard again and never to claim the grazing rights of the heavens, which were neither Nynniaw's nor Peibiaw's but belonged to all people to gaze upon.

Rhita Gawr returned to Gwynedd with much wisdom then, and he wore his beard-mantle as a token of his service to Arthur and his promise. Sometimes, so it is said, the old folks around Snowdon would gaze up at the night sky and look at the stars and, if it was a cloudy night and the snow falling, they would remark that the sky was as thick as *barf Rhita* or Rhita's beard.

Rhita Gawr's people remained fond of their giant king, in spite of his eccentricities. When he died, they came from every corner of the kingdom to pile stones over his body, which is the local custom. Soon the pile became a great cairn above Rhita Gawr's grave. This great cairn grew and grew until they called it Gwyddfa Rhita, which is "Rhita's cairn" and this, shortened to "Yr Gwyddfa" was the first name given to Yr Wyddfa, or Mount Snowdon.

Some people will tell you that Rhita Gawr is not truly dead but merely sleeping, and now and then he turns in his sleep, causing the stones atop his body to come crashing down in great landslides.

But I have set out to tell you about Bedd Gellert. It happened this way. Many years after Rhita Gawr's death, his descendants were still kings of Gwynedd and these princes also called themselves the Lords of Eryri, which is the name of the mountainous district in which Yr Wyddfa lies. There was one prince of Gwynedd called Llewelyn who had a favourite hound named Gellert for he was a brown coloured beast, for *gell* means brown or auburn in colour. When Gellert was giving cry and chasing the fox across the mountains, the dog was as brave and magnificent as a lion, but when he was lying in front of the blazing hearth with his lord, he was as mild and gentle as a lamb.

He was so tame and gentle that Prince Llewelyn often entrusted the care of his young wife and tiny baby to the hound.

It happened one day that Prince Llewelyn set out for the hunt and blew his horn to gather his hounds. Now all the hounds answered the horn except Llewelyn's favourite – Gellert. No one knew where the hound had hidden himself and so the disgruntled prince set off on the hunt without the swiftest and most tenacious of his hounds. There was bad sport that day for the Lord of Eryri.

In a rage he returned to his castle and what was the first thing he saw? Gellert his hound, bounding joyfully to meet him. As he came nearer, Prince Llewelyn saw that the dog's muzzle was dripping with blood.

Now a terrible thought came into Llewelyn's mind, for his wife was visiting her sick mother and he had left his baby, a son no more than a year old, in his chamber, asking his servants to look in now and then. Gellert was used to playing with the child, for he was usually a docile and gentle animal within the doors of the palace.

Prince Llewelyn let out a cry as he ran to his young son's nursery. As he passed through the rooms, he saw the trail of blood thick upon the ground. Into the nursery he rushed, crying for his servants and attendants.

There was the child's cradle overturned and the covers and floor were drenched in blood.

No anguish could compare with Prince Llewelyn's despair. He and his servants searched everywhere, but nowhere was any sign of the tiny child. It was clear to him that the hound Gellert had devoured his son and heir.

There was a rage on him as he went back into the courtyard and saw Gellert sitting patiently wagging his tail, as if puzzled at his master's behaviour.

"Evil monster!" yelled the prince. "You have devoured my son, my baby and my joy!"

Without more ado, he drew his sword and struck the animal, thrusting the point into the hound's side.

Gellert gave an agonized cry, gazed for a moment into its master's eyes, and fell dead.

In that moment, as Gellert gave his dying howl, the prince heard a little child's answering cry.

Prince Llewelyn dashed back into the nursery, where the cry had come from. There, underneath the upturned cradle, where he had been asleep, was the prince's tiny son. No one had thought of looking under the upturned cot. Moreover, beside the child, who was entirely unhurt, there lay the carcass of a great, gaunt grey wolf. And the wolf was covered with blood and its throat torn out.

Now what had happened became very clear.

A wolf had entered the castle without anyone seeing it, but Gellert had sniffed out the beast and stayed to protect Prince Llewelyn's son. He had fought the great beast and slain it before it could harm the little prince.

Now Prince Llewelyn was filled with grief and remorse for what he had done. He had not only killed his favourite hound, but without just cause. The hound had saved the life of his son and trusted him, and he had betrayed that trust. Now Prince Llewelyn realised the true meaning of the old proverb: "The nut cannot be judged by the husk", for it seems that a bull with long horns, even if he does not butt, will always be accused of butting.

So sadder and wiser, Prince Llewelyn carried his faithful hound to the slopes of Yr Wyddfa and buried him. Over his grave he raised a cairn. So this is why the place is called Bedd Gellert, or the Grave of Gellert. It is said that the phantom of Gellert still hunts across the mountainside and you may hear its lonely howl on cold winter's nights. It is the howl of a trusting, loyal soul betrayed.

Some people will tell you to beware of Gellert's tomb,

especially if there is disloyalty lurking in your heart; the hound will sniff it out and take revenge. Therefore, on certain days, especially after dark, beware as you wander across the slopes, beware of a leaping phantom hound.

24 *The Quest for Olwen*

There was once a king of Cilydd who was related to the famous Arthur of Britain. This king, who also bore the name Cilydd, married a princess named Goleuddydd. As her name suggested, she was a "bright light" among her people. The marriage was a happy and a prosperous one, and soon the couple were blessed by Goleuddydd becoming pregnant. However, she visited Gwiddanes the Hag, who dwelt in a forest, and asked her fortune. The fortune was not good.

It was a troubled period for the young queen, for the foresight of Gwiddanes lay heavily upon her. Nearing the time when she would give birth, while passing through a forest, she became unhinged by the pain of childbirth and the doom disclosed by Gwiddanes. She leapt from her horse and fled into the depths of the forest, coming near a place where a swineherd was keeping his pigs. It was there that she gave birth to a handsome boy child. The name that she gave him was Culhwch, which meant one born in a "pig run".

Now all this had come to pass as Queen Goleuddydd had been warned. But in the fever of her childbirth, she saw a vision of a sorrowful goddess; and some said that it must have been Arianrhod, whose childbirth was also sorrowful. She told Goleuddydd shadows of the future, but also how they might be avoided.

Cilydd and his retainers found her and they carried her and the child back to the palace where she lay still in a fever. She knew that she would die. As her husband knelt beside her bed, she spoke sorrowfully to him: "My lord, death is approaching me. When I am gone, you will seek another wife."

The king protested, but she brushed aside his protestations of love for her alone.

"It is the nature of things, my lord. Your new wife shall be your companion and the dispenser of your gifts. Remember, however, that it is Culhwch who is your first child, your son. He must be the champion of this kingdom and its heir. So there is a promise you must make me, a sacred promise, before I die."

"Name it and it shall be as you say," vowed the king.

"Do not take this second wife until you see a two-headed briar growing from my grave."

"Easily done. I have no wish for a second wife."

"You cannot change the spinning of the world."

Now it happened that Goleuddydd had a loyal servant and she called this servant to her and told him what he should do. For the vision of the goddess Arianrhod had advised her how the future might be changed. Knowing of the evils to come, she told the servant to ensure that nothing at all grew on her grave so that King Cilydd, not seeing the two-headed briar on her grave, might never marry again and no harm would ever come to her son Culhwch. This servant promised faithfully to keep the grave clear of all growths.

So it came about that Goleuddydd, the bright light, died and the court mourned and the child Culhwch was found a nurse.

As time passed, King Cilydd overcame his grief and found that he had grown lonely and his thoughts turned to finding a new wife. But he was a moral man when it came to keeping promises. So he would go to visit Goleuddydd's grave. For seven years the grave stood bare, and not even so much as a weed grew upon it. But the servant grew old and tired. He neglected his duties and did not weed the grave. One day, when King Cilydd came to the grave, he found a briar growing there and the briar was two-headed.

"So it is now time for me to find a new wife," he said in satisfaction. He went to his palace and summoned his attendants and he asked them if they knew of any suitable prospects. None of them knew of any available princesses who were worthy of King Cilydd. Then one of his advisers, a sly fellow, said: "There is only one lady who is worthy of marriage to you, my lord. Alas, she is married already, albeit unhappily. And she has a daughter."

"Who is she?" demanded the King.

"She is the wife of King Doged."

"No hardship there," replied the King Cilydd thoughtfully. "If she is the right woman, I can see no problem. King Doged is such a weak monarch and can soon be disposed of."

So it came about that King Cilydd found an excuse to go to war with King Doged and soon slew him and claimed his wife. Now, in bringing this queen to his court, King Cilydd neglected to mention that he already had a son and heir named Culhwch. In fact, the king had sent Culhwch to be fostered, which was the practice among the kings and lords in those days, for, in fosterage, the young received their education and were taught the art of weaponry and warfare.

Now some time went by and this queen, who already had a daughter, did not bear any children to King Cilydd.

"Can it be that he cannot sire a child?" mused the queen. So she went to Gwiddanes the Hag to ask her advice.

"Lady," said the crone, "your husband already has a son and heir by his first wife. The boy's name is Culhwch."

The queen was amazed at hearing this, rewarded the old woman and hastened back to the palace.

"Husband, I was not told that you had a son. Why have you hidden this prince, Culhwch, from me?"

The king, when he saw that his new wife was not jealous, was apologetic. "I will hide him no longer but will send for him immediately."

Now Culhwch had grown into a handsome youth and, when he came to the palace to meet his stepmother, she was impressed at his beauty and his bearing. Immediately she thought that if she could marry him to her daughter it would ensure the dynastic succession and consolidate her position as the most powerful woman in the kingdom.

"You look of age to marry, Culhwch," she observed. "So is my daughter, and what better match could you make?"

Culhwch shook his head. "Lady, I am not old enough to have a wife and, if I were, I would not marry your daughter."

The queen flew into a rage immediately.

She foresaw that when King Cilydd died, she would be ousted as queen and her daughter would have no inheritance. It so happened that she had sought some other magical advice from Gwiddanes the Hag.

"As my daughter is not good enough for you," she told Culhwch, "I shall make a curse of destiny on you – you will never have a wife unless you can win the love and marry Olwen, the daughter of Ysbaddadan Pencawr, the Chief of the Giants."

Now although Culhwch had never heard of her, he was suddenly consumed with love for this unknown girl. Perhaps this had something to do with the magic of the curse that his stepmother laid upon him.

"Very well, lady," he replied, colouring at the emotion which welled in him. "You have set forth my destiny and I shall follow it."

He turned to his father, who was very unhappy at this outcome. He was sad, for he knew that a terrible burden had been placed on his son.

"Father, do you know where this Olwen and her father, Ysbaddadan Pencawr, abide?"

King Cilydd shook his head. "I do not know where they may be found. All I can give you is this advice – go to your cousin, the mighty Arthur. As your cousin, he is bound to offer you gifts. Ask of him the gift of delivering Olwen to you."

Young Culhwch embraced his father, the king, and taking his weapons, his grey-coloured warhorse and his hounds, he set off to find the court of his cousin, Arthur.

He eventually came to Arthur's court at dusk and the gates were closed, for the feasting had already begun. So Culhwch rode up to the gates and hammered on them.

It was Glewlwyd Gafaelfawr, Glewlwyd of the Mighty Grasp, who came to the door.

"Open the gate!" demanded Culhwch.

"Who are you, little boy, who speaks so arrogantly?" demanded the disgruntled Glewlwyd.

"I do not speak to gatekeepers, if such you are."

"I share the task with Huandaw, Gogigwr, Llaesgymin and Penpingion," agreed Glewlwyd.

"Then if you are the gatekeeper of Arthur, open Arthur's gate."

"I will not. The knife has gone into the meat and the drink into the horn, and there is music in Arthur's hall. None may enter now but the son of a rightful king or a craftsman or a poet. Go away, for this gate will not be opened until dawn tomorrow."

Then Culhwch leant forward, frowning. "Listen, proud gatekeeper, if you do not let me in, I shall raise three shouts as shall cause every woman in this palace to miscarry and will bring shame and dishonour on Arthur's court. Now go, tell Arthur what I have said."

So Glewlwyd of the Mighty Grasp, somewhat taken aback by the youth's persistence, scurried into the feasting hall and told Arthur of the strange youth outside the gate. "I tell you, my lord, I have never seen a youth so handsome as this one, and so forceful in manner and strong in carriage."

Arthur was annoyed but realised that Glwelwyd would not trouble him for no reason at all.

"Bring him in, then, and let us see who he is."

One of Arthur's companions, Cai, agreed. "Indeed, if he is all that is reported, it would be a shameful thing to leave so fine a youth outside our gate."

So the gate was opened and Culhwch came in. He strode straight up to his cousin and bowed. Arthur did not know who he was but greeted him civilly.

"Greetings, stranger. Share our food and drink for dusk has come and the night is chill."

"I am not here to beg your hospitality, lord king. I came to ask a favour of you," replied Culhwch.

"Ask it," said Arthur, quite intrigued at the boy's directness.

"I would have you cut my hair."

Now this was a ritual of kinship and Arthur knew then that he must be speaking to a blood relation. So he sent for a golden comb and scissors and began to trim Culhwch's hair and beard. And while he did so, they spoke of their lineage and came to the conclusion that they were first cousins.

"Excellent!" Arthur said with satisfaction. "As my blood relation, I can now ask you, what gift is it that I can bestow on you?"

"There is a curse of destiny on me, cousin," Culhwch replied. "I must win the love of Olwen, daughter of Ysbaddadan Pencawr. I must marry her and none other. I ask you to give her to me or tell me where she may be found and won."

Now Arthur confessed that he had never heard of Olwen nor even of Ysbaddadan Pencawr, the Chief of Giants. However, he invited Culhwch to stay at court with him while he sent messengers to the four corners of the kingdom to seek out the girl.

Time passed and each messenger returned saying that they had been unable to find word of Olwen. Indeed, a full year and a day went by and still there was no news of where the girl might dwell or even of who her fearsome father was. Culhwch became impatient.

"Cousin Arthur, you have given gifts to everyone who asks of you. Yet here I am, your own cousin, asking a simple gift and yet I remain empty-handed. If I leave your palace without even news of Olwen, then your honour must be called into question."

Now Cai, son of Cynyr, one of Arthur's greatest champions stood forward. Cai could hold his breath for nine nights and nine days under water and for nine nights and nine days he would go without sleep. He could change his stature at will, even growing as tall as a tall tree. He was headstrong but also quite ruthless. A wound given by his sword would never be healed by a physician.

Cai glowered at Culhwch. "It is wrong that you call my lord's honour into question. He has done all he can to seek word of Olwen. Now I suggest that we go forth ourselves to seek her. I will accompany you, on Arthur's behalf. We shall find this girl, if she exists. My oath on it."

Then Bedwyr of the One Hand, son of Pedrawg, volunteered to accompany them. He was a handsome man and, with his one hand, he could kill more warriors in battle than any three. When he thrust his spear at the enemy, it made nine more thrusts of its own.

Then came Cynddelig, the greatest guide and tracker in all the kingdoms of the Cymru. He also volunteered to help.

Then came Gwrhyr Gwalstawd Ieithoedd who, as his name stated, knew all the languages of men as well as those of the birds, beasts and fishes. He also volunteered to accompany Cai and the others.

Then came Gwalchmai fab Gwyar, whom the Saxons called Gawain and he was Arthur's nephew, who never returned without that which he had set forth to find. He, too, said he would accompany Culhwch.

Lastly, there came Menw son of Teirgwaedd, who was a Druid and a magus, who could even cast a spell that made men invisible.

So Culhwch was much impressed by these six able warriors and agreed that they should go with him in his quest. The seven of them set out from Arthur's palace at dawn the next day.

The journey was long and arduous and, initially, without any reward. No one had heard of Olwen nor of her formidable father, the Chief of Giants.

One day, however, the warriors came to a broad plain and from it there arose a large castle. They set out towards it but, after several days riding, it seemed as far away from them as it had been when they started. They were passing by a hill when they spied a shepherd on it and with the shepherd was a great hound, as big as a full-grown stallion. His breath scorched the very grass and trees before him and yet he was able to keep the flock in order. He was a fierce beast.

"Gwrhyr," said Culhwch. "As you are our interpreter, go and ask that shepherd if he has heard about Yspaddadan Pencawr?"

Gwrhyr hesitated, one cautious eye on the fierce hound. "I only volunteered to accompany Cai and the others," he muttered. "Not to put myself forward alone into danger."

Cai grinned. "Then I will come with you, in case the hound prove too fierce for you."

Menw took a step forward. "If you are worried about that hound, I will cast a spell so that it will neither see nor scent us."

So it was that they all went forward under Menw's spell and came to the shepherd without his hound scenting them or raising a cry.

"Greetings, *bugail,*" Cai said respectfully. "By the size of your flock, all goes well with you."

The shepherd snorted indignantly. "May they never be better with you than with me," he replied. The words made little sense to them and they pondered on his reply.

"Are these flocks not your own, *bugail*?" Gwalchmai asked, realizing that the shepherd might be tending them for some great lord.

"Ignorant men!" snapped the shepherd. "Do you not know in whose domains you are? These are the lands and flocks of Ysbaddadan Pencawr, whose castle lies yonder."

"Ah, of course," agreed Cai quickly. "And who are you, then?"

"I am Custennin Heusor yr Bugail, who was once a mighty warrior but am now ruled by my lord and doomed to be his shepherd." The shepherd suddenly realized that his dog had ignored the seven warriors and not attacked them. "What men are you, that my hound has not harmed you?"

Cai glanced at Culhwch and received a brief nod to indicate that he should hold no truth from the man.

"We are warriors of Arthur and we are in search of Olwen, Ysbaddadan's daughter."

Custennin looked grim. "If you wish to throw your lives away, then I shall not stop you. But better you quest for anything other than the daughter of Ysbaddadan Pencawr."

Then Culhwch spoke for the first time. "Custennin, I am Culhwch son of Cilydd, and my destiny is to marry Olwen or no woman in this world."

The shepherd started at the mention of his name. He came forward and peered carefully at him. "You are Culhwch son of Cilydd and Goleuddydd?"

"I am."

Then the shepherd threw his arms around the surprised Culhwch. "Then you are my nephew, for my wife was sister to Goleuddydd."

So Culhwch and Custennin embraced with joy.

"Where is your wife, that I might greet my aunt?" cried Culhwch.

"I will bring you to her directly, but I must warn you, my wife is the strongest woman in the world and does not know her own strength. So avoid being hugged by her until she has calmed her joy."

With that warning, Custennin ordered his hound to stay on guard over his flock and then led them to his house.

"Woman, it is your nephew Culhwch who is come to see us," cried the shepherd.

A great muscular woman came bounding out of the house. "Tender is the heart in me, for he is my sister's own flesh and blood," she thundered. Then she looked at the seven warriors who had dismounted before the house. "But which one is Culhwch?"

Her husband, realising her grasp might hurt Culhwch, pointed to Cai, who seemed the strongest. The woman rushed on him with arms outstretched. Cai, however, seized a great log and threw it at her. A second later it lay splintered where she had caught it.

Cai shook his head wryly. "Woman, had I been squeezed like that log, there would have been no further need for you to express your love for Culhwch."

The woman, realising she had misjudged her strength, looked at the splinters in dismay. "There is a lesson in this," she agreed.

Then Culhwch identified himself and all were introduced to the woman.

They went into the house and sat down to a feast. Culhwch told her why they had come and his aunt shook her great head.

"Better you find some other quest to go on, or else all your lives will be forfeit."

"I will not go unless I find Olwen," replied Culhwch firmly.

The woman's face was sad. She went to a cupboard and opened it and out stepped a handsome youth, with golden hair.

"This is Gorau, my best and only son. Once I had twenty-three fine strapping young boys. Ysbaddadan Pencawr slew them and if he finds this lad he will also slay him."

"Then I offer Gorau my protection. Let him join me and my companions and, if he should be slain, it will be because I and these six brave warriors are already dead."

Cai and the others shouted their approval and young Gorau, whose name did actually mean "best", joined their band.

"Now to our task," cried Culhwch, who was enthusiastic that his quest seemed so near an end.

"I can tell you how you may see Olwen," said the burly aunt of Culhwch.

"How?"

"See the pool and waterfall just beyond this house? It is there that Olwen comes alone, without attendants, to bathe every morning."

"Will she come tomorrow morning?"

"She will, indeed."

"Then I will wait by the pool."

So it happened that Culhwch hid himself beside the pool and, the next morning, there came to the pool a young girl. She had hair the colour of burnished gold, her flesh was whiter than the foam on the waves, foxglove-red tinged her cheeks and the juice of berries stained her lips with crimson. She wore a necklace of coral and bracelets of red gold and, wherever she walked, white trefoils grew behind her, marking her path. It was for this reason she was called Olwen, meaning "of the white track".

Culhwch lost his power of speech as he watched the girl come to the bank of the pool and, dropping her red silk dress from her, stepped into the waters, white as the snowy breast of a swan.

The young man rose and came to the bank. "Ah, maiden, it is you that I have loved all my life, although I have not seen you, not until this moment."

Olwen started in surprise but she did not cry out. She regarded him carefully as she trod water. "You have advantage of me, fair sir," she replied, for Culhwch was, as we have said, a handsome young man and she was not displeased at his greeting.

"I am Culhwch, son of King Cilydd. You are my fate. The pulse of my heart. You are my destiny, to return to my land and marry me."

"Alas, young prince, I am under a prohibition. I can never leave my father's house without his consent, for he was told that he would only live until I take a husband. Thus have the Druids foretold that when I wed, he shall die. So no man can wed me."

"Then I shall challenge him."

The girl shook her head seriously. "No; what you must do is this. Go and ask my father for my hand in marriage. He will give you several tasks to perform to prove your worthiness. If you perform them, then you will win my heart. If you do not, then I cannot go with you and you will surely die."

So Culhwch left her to her bathing and returned to tell his companions what he must do.

"You shall not go forth alone," cried Cai.

"Indeed," Bedwyr said. "We have come thus far and so we shall all go to see this Ysbaddadan Pencawr."

So, at midday, they went to the great castle. Cai and Bedwyr slew nine gatekeepers, without a man crying out, and nine great hounds, without one of them barking. And they went forward into the great hall where Ysbaddadan Pencawr, a fierce giant of a man with one great eye, reclined in slumber.

Culhwch marched forward and smote the giant on the leg with the flat of his sword to wake him.

"Who is it?" demanded Ysbaddadan, without opening his eyelid.

"I am Culhwch, son of Cilydd, and I have come to ask the hand of your daughter Olwen in marriage."

Ysbaddadan roared with laughter, causing the entire room to shake as if an earthquake had hit it.

"Where are my servants? For I would see you, you presumptuous little man."

The servants came running into the hall in answer to the giant's bellows and they had two great poles with which they raised the giant's eyelid. The one great eye glared down, red and baleful.

"So you are Culhwch?" he demanded in a roaring tone.

The young prince acknowledged his name.

"Then depart and return tomorrow at this hour. I will answer you then."

Could it be that simple? What of the tasks? Still, Culhwch turned and with his companions began to leave the hall. At this point Ysbaddadan seized a great spear next to his chair. It was tinged with poison. He cast it straight at Culhwch. But Bedwyr seized it in mid-flight and hurled it back towards the giant. It hit Ysbaddadan in the knee-cap.

The giant screamed in agony. "I shall never be able to walk again. Cursed be the smith who forged this iron and the anvil on which it was wrought!"

Culhwch controlled his anger at the sly attack. "We shall return for your answer tomorrow," he said firmly. "Let no more tricks be played on us."

They spent that night with Custennin and his wife and the next morning they went back to the giant's hall.

"I have come for your answer, Ysbaddadan," announced Culhwch.

"I cannot give it," replied the giant. "I can give no permission over the marriage of Olwen until I have consulted with her four great-grandfathers and four great-grandmothers. Come back tomorrow; I will give you an answer then."

So Culhwch and his companions turned to leave the hall.

Then Ysbaddadan seized another poisoned spear and hurled it at Culhwch. This time it was Menw who caught it in mid flight and hurled it back at the giant. It pierced his breast, coming out in the small of his back.

Ysbaddadan screamed. "I will be in pain in my chest and my back from this cast. Cursed be the smith who forged the steel and the anvil on which it was wrought!"

Then Culhwch turned in anger at the giant's duplicity. "We will return on the morrow to hear your answer. Yet I warn you again, do not vex us further."

They stayed again with Custennin and his wife and the next morning went back to Ysbaddadan's hall.

The giant's eye was closed.

"I cannot look upon you and so cannot give you my answer. Come back tomorrow and I shall do so then."

As Culhwch and his companions turned to go, the giant took up a third spear and hurled it at Culhwch, in spite of his claim not to be able to see him. This time it was Culhwch who, hearing the noise of the metal in the air, turned, caught the spear and hurled it back with such force that it pierced Ysbaddadan's eyelid and the ball of his eye.

Ysbaddadan screamed. "Oh, I shall be blinded forever. Cursed be the smith who forged the metal and the anvil which wrought it!"

"We will return tomorrow for your answer," Culhwch said angrily, "but if we do not receive it, you or we shall be dead thereafter."

So they stayed again with Custennin and his wife and the next morning went to the giant's hall.

"Cast no more spears at me, Ysbaddadan," warned Culhwch at once, "for the next time, you shall surely be slain."

Ysbaddadan called for his servants to prop up his eyelid and his one baleful eye stared angrily at Culhwch.

"You must prove to me that you are worthy of my daughter, Olwen," he thundered.

"I am willing to do so."

"Then you must promise to fulfil whatever task I set you."

"Easy to promise. Tell me what you require that I should do."

The giant smiled grimly. "The first task is to go to the great forest that lies to the east. Cut down the trees, plough the land and sow it with wheat and, out of the wheat, bake bread for the wedding guests. That task must be done in a single day."

Culhwch bowed his head. "It shall be done."

"The second task is that you find two vessels to be used at the wedding feast."

"Easy enough."

Ysbaddadan chuckled harshly. "The first vessel is the horn

of Gawlgawd and the second is the cup of Llwyr son of Llwyrion."

Culhwch bowed his head. "It shall be done."

"The third task is that you obtain a hamper for me to eat from on the wedding day."

"Easy enough."

Ysbaddadan smiled cruelly. "It is the hamper of Gwyddno Long-Shank, who ruled the Drowned Kingdom. If thrice times nine men sit around it they would not go away hungry."

Culhwch bowed his head. "It shall be done."

"The fourth task is that you get a veil for Olwen on her wedding day."

"Easy enough."

Ysbaddadan smiled thinly. "When I first met with Olwen's mother, I sowed nine hectares of flax seed in an overgrown plot. But it has vanished. The seed must be resown, grown, gathered and spun and made into Olwen's veil."

Culhwch bowed his head. "It shall be done."

"The fifth task is to bring me a razor to shave on the morning of the wedding."

"Easy enough."

"Ah," Ysbaddadan was grinding his teeth, for no task seemed to make an impression on Culhwch or cause him to be fearful or refuse it, "the razor must be the tusk of Ysgithyrwyn, the chief of boars, and the man who must shave me is Cadw of the land of the Pictii, who refuses ever to leave his kingdom. And I can only dress my beard from the blood of the Black Witch who dwells in the Valley of Grief in the uplands of Hell."

"It shall be done," agreed Culhwch.

Ysbaddadan now began to grow angry. He enumerated no less than thirteen difficult tasks, together with no less than twenty-six less difficult tasks, all to be accomplished. To each and every one of them, Culhwch agreed to perform the deed.

Ysbaddadan wanted the comb and shears that lay between the two ears of Twrch Trwyth, the king of Otherworld boars, who could not be hunted until the hound Drudwyn was obtained, and the hound could not be held until a leash owned by Cors Hundred Claws was taken. No collar would hold the leash, save that of Camhastyr Hundred Hands and only the chain of Cilydd Hundred Holds could hold both collar and leash.

No one could act as hound-keeper to Drudwyn except Mabon ap Modron, who had been stolen from his home when he was three nights old, and his whereabouts not known. Only Eidoel, his kinsman, had known where he was but Eidoel was in the secret prison of Glini, and no one in the world knew where that was. And even Mabon could not hunt Twrch Trwyth, save on Gwyn Dunmane, the steed of Gweddw, who would have to be fought for him.

Twrch Trwyth could further not be hunted until the dogs of Aned and Aethlem were obtained, for they were never unleashed on a beast they did not kill. To use the hounds, only Cyledyr the Wild Son of Hetwyn the Leper could act as huntsman. Cyledyr was nine times wilder than the wildest beast in the world. Nor could Cyledyr be obtained without the agreement of Gwyn son of Nudd, whom the gods had made guardian of the demons of the Otherworld. He could not leave his charge, in case the world was destroyed by the demons.

Further, no leash in the world would hold Aned and Aethlem, the hunting dogs, unless it was made from the beard of Dissull son of Eurei, the bearded giant. Even that would be useless, unless it was plucked from his beard while he was still alive and then with wooden tweezers. He would certainly not allow anyone to do so unless he was dead.

Neither would Twrch Trwyth be hunted until the services of Bwlch, Cyfwlch and Syfwlch be obtained, together with their three shields, three spears, three swords and their three hunting-horns that sounded so dreadful a note that no one would care if the sky tumbled on them in order to stop the sound.

However, Twrch Trwyth could not finally be slain except by the sword of Wrnach Cawr, a mighty giant, and he would never part with it. Lastly, Twrch Trwyth could not be hunted without the full backing of Arthur and all his huntsmen.

Culhwch's companions' faces were growing longer and longer at the recital of Ysbaddadan.

However, Culhwch stood his ground, calmly nodding and agreeing to every condition.

"It shall be done," he said simply.

Ysbaddadan cursed him, for he had now run out of difficult tasks.

"If you do all these things, you may marry Olwen. Fail in just one of the deeds and you shall die."

"It will not be me who meets his end, Ysbaddadan Pencawr," Culhwch said solemnly. "Count the days to your own death."

With that, Culhwch turned and left the hall, followed by his companions.

So it was that Culhwch set off to fulfil the impossible tasks placed on him by Ysbaddadan Pencawr.

He and his seven companions, for now young Gorau was journeying with them, rode for many days until they came to a great stone castle, at whose gate a giant stood.

"Whose castle is this?" demanded Cai.

The giant gatekeeper stared at them in surprise. "You are foolish men, if you do not know the castle of Wrnach Cawr. Be off with you, lest you lose your lives."

The companions exchanged glances. Getting the sword of Wrnach Cawr was an important task on the list.

"Is that a fine way to display hospitality?" Cai replied.

"No guests ever leave this castle alive," smiled the gatekeeper.

"Even so," Cai said, "Wrnach might like to bide awhile with me."

"Why so?"

"I have a craft. I am the best sharpener and polisher of swords in all the world."

Now when Wrnach was told this by his gatekeeper, he asked him to go and fetch Cai in. Cai entered the castle by himself while Culhwch and his companions waited outside.

"I have long been in need of a man who could polish my sword," cried the giant as Cai came into his presence. "Is it true that you know how to polish swords?"

Cai smiled briefly. "I have polished the greatest swords in all the world. I have even polished the sword of Arthur himself."

Then Wrnach took out his great sword and laid it before Cai. "This sword is one that I let no one have, not for money nor for favour. Can you polish it?"

"That I can," said Cai.

He took out a whetstone from his pocket and set to work. But he cleaned and sharpened one side. Then he stopped and showed the giant Wrnach.

"Is this work pleasing to you, my lord?"

Wrnach looked on it with approval.

"Indeed it is. Do the other side."

"That I will, but I noticed your scabbard stands in need of cleaning and I have a friend outside with as great a craft as mine."

"Who is this man?"

"Oh, a companion who owns a wondrous spear, whose head will spring from its shaft and draw blood even from the air before returning."

"This man I must see, especially if he will polish my scabbard."

So the gatekeeper went to summon Bedwyr. While Bedwyr was being let into the castle, Gorau, the son of Custennin, managed to secrete the key so that, while Bedwyr was being conducted into the presence of Wrnach, Gorau let Culhwch and the rest of the warriors secretly into the castle.

When Cai had finished polishing the sword and Bedwyr had finished cleaning the scabbard, Wrnach examined them in satisfaction.

Then Cai gently took the sword and the scabbard, saying: "I will check that our work is acceptable, for the sword should be able to slide smoothly into the scabbard." With the sword in his right hand and scabbard in his left, Cai raised the sword as if to sheathe it. Sheathe it he did, but into the breast of Wrnach, pressing forth with all his might. Then, as Wrnach toppled sideways, Cai cut off the giant's head.

Culhwch and his companions sacked the castle and carried off a great treasure and then they returned in triumph to Arthur's palace. There they told Arthur all about the quest and Arthur, delighted by the challenges, told Culhwch that he and all his warriors would help fulfil the list of tasks.

Now to achieve the main tasks that Ysbaddadan had set, they had to perform the deeds in a certain sequence. The next important deed was to seek Mabon, son of Modron, but to find him they first had to find his kinsman Eidoel, who was a prisoner in Glini's castle. So Arthur and his warriors surrounded the castle. Arthur summoned Glini forth by the sound of trumpet.

"What is it that you want?" demanded Glini surlily. "I have no great treasure here."

"I am come for Eidoel, whom you hold prisoner in your deepest dungeon. Surrender him to me and I shall leave you in peace. If you do not, I shall leave your castle in ruins."

So Eidoel was brought forward and asked where his kinsman Mabon was.

"This is only known by the beasts, the birds and the fishes," confessed Eidoel. "I do not know."

At this, some of Arthur's men began to chuckle. Arthur silenced them with a frown.

"Come forth, Gwrhyr Gwalstawd Ieithoedd, interpreter of all languages. Question those, even as Eidoel suggests."

So Gwrhyr came forward and set off to question the birds, beasts and fishes. For his companions he had Cai and Bedwyr. First Gwrhyr asked the Ouzel of Cilgwri, but in all her long life she had not heard of Mabon. She believed that the Stag of Rhedynfre was older and wiser than her.

So Gwrhyr questioned the Stag of Rhedynfre, but in all his long life he had not heard of Mabon. He believed that the Owl of Cwm Cawlwyd was older and wiser and might know.

Then Gwrhyr found the Owl of Cwm Cawlwyd, but in all her long life she had not heard of Mabon. She believed that the Eagle of Gwernabwy was older and wiser than her.

So Gwrhyr asked the Eagle of Gwernabwy but, in all his long life he had not heard of Mabon.

They were about to despair when the Eagle suddenly said: "But I do recall that I tried to capture a salmon once, and this was the wisest salmon in all the world. He was so strong he nearly drowned me by dragging me into his river. Eventually we made peace and I did him a favour by plucking out fifty fishing javelins from his great back. I will take you to him. If he does not know, then no one else in all the world does."

So the Eagle of Gwernabwy took them to Llyn Llyw and summoned the Salmon.

"Mabon?" the Salmon said to Gwrhyr. "I will tell you what I know. Often I swim up the river Sabrann on the tide until I come to the wall of Caer Loyw; every time I reach that spot I hear the most distressing cry that I have ever heard. I am sure this cry belongs to Mabon, who was stolen away from his mother when he was three nights old."

"Will you take us there?" asked Gwrhyr.

"That I will," agreed the Salmon of Llyn Llyw.

So Gwrhyr, Cai and Bedwyr sat on the Salmon's great broad back and he took them up river, the great river Sabrann, which is now called the Severn, to Caer Loyw, which is now called Gloucester. At the wall, they heard a great lamentation.

"Ho there!" cried Gwrhyr. "What man can make this lament?"

"It is Mabon son of Modron," wailed a voice. "I am imprisoned here, and that is cause enough for my lament. Further, none was more cruelly imprisoned than I; no, not Lludd Llaw Ereint nor Greid ap Eri had worse imprisonments than mine."

"Does your captor seek a ransom for your release?" demanded Cai.

"No. I can only be rescued by force."

With that news, Gwrhyr hastened back to tell Arthur and his warriors, but even before Arthur and his men came near to Caer Loyw, Cai and Bedwyr launched an attack at the river wall and rescued Mabon and returned him to Arthur's palace a free man.

One of the greatest problems was to find the nine hectares of flax seed, from which to grow the flax to make the white veil for Olwen. As fate would have it, Gwythyr ap Greidawl was passing a mountain slope. Gwythyr was a great warrior whose bride-to-be was Creiddylad, daughter of Lludd Llaw Ereint. She had been abducted by Gwyn ap Nudd, king of the Otherworld, and in struggling to get her back, it was decreed that once a year Gwythyr and Gwyn would fight a combat. The annual combats would last until doomsday and whoever was the victor of the combat on doomsday would have the beautiful Creiddylad.

Now Gwythyr heard a terrible lamentation as he was crossing the mountain. He saw an anthill which was on fire. Drawing his sword, he dug off the pieces that were on fire and thus prevented the fire from consuming the entire anthill.

"Blessings on you, Gwythyr; what reward can we give you?" asked the king ant.

Gwythyr thought of Culhwch's quest and, on explaining matters, he discovered that long ago it had been the ants that had carried off the flax seed. In reward for saving them, the ants agreed to return it. They did so, save one seed and finally, just before nightfall on the appointed day, a lame ant brought it to the pile.

The story went further, for when the time came for one of the annual combats, it was Gwyn who won the day and, among the hostages he took from Gwythyr, there were several people important to Culhwch's quest. Hetwyn the Leper was slain and Gwyn compelled Cyledyr the Wild, his son, to eat his father's heart, by reason of which Cyledyr went mad and fled into the wilderness to avoid the company of men.

Now Arthur was angry when he heard this and rode forth to bring about peace and, as a price of peace, he obtained Dunmane the steed of Gweddw, the leash of Cors Hundred Claws and many another of the marvels which Ysbaddadan had listed.

Another most important task was the plucking of the hair of the giant Dissull while he was alive. Ysbaddadan had said that there was no leash in the world which would hold the dogs Aned and Aethlem, save one made from the beard of Dissull. They not only had to pluck his beard while he was alive but with wooden tweezers.

It happened that Cai and Bedwyr came on Dissull cooking a wild boar over a fire. They knew that when the giant had cooked his boar and eaten it, he would fall asleep. So they waited and watched and passed the time making the tweezers.

When Dissull had fallen asleep, they dug a great pit under his feet, almost to the height of the giant. Then Cai went forward. He struck the giant such a blow as to precipitate him feet first into the pit.

While the giant slumped senseless in the pit, Bedwyr went forward and plucked the hairs from his beard. Then he and Cai killed Dissull. They made the leash and hastened back to Arthur's court. It happened that Arthur made some jest about the stealth they had used to overcome Dissull which offended both Cai and Bedwyr and they retired to Celli Wig, in the land of Cernyw, and refused to have anything more to do with the quest.

Now Ysbaddadan had decreed that he would only be shaved with the tusk of the Chief of Boars, Ysgithyrwyn. It happened that Arthur had gone in search of Cyledyr the Wild and, on the way, he managed to find Bwlch, Cyfwlch and Syfwlch and also Cadw of the Pictii, whom he persuaded to return with him. How all this happened is too lengthy to recount. Yet it was on the return that they came across the great boar, Ysgithyrwyn. It was Cadw who saw the chance and, having no horse near at the time save Arthur's own mare, Llamrei, he brought the great boar to bay. He split the boar's head in two and took into his keeping the tusk with which to shave the beard of Ysbaddadan Pencawr.

There was, however, no greater task than the hunting of the fabulous Twrch Trwyth, the Otherworld boar who made Ysgithyrwyn seem quite tame. Now this boar was said to dwell in Éireann, where it was known as Torc Triath, among the prized possessions of The Dagda and the goddess of fertility Brigid. But that does not concern our story.

When most of Ysbaddadan's requests had been fulfilled, save the great hunt, Arthur gathered his men and first sent Menw out to spy. Menw changed himself into a bird, for he had to find out where the magic boar was dwelling and whether, of course, he still had the comb and shears between his ears.

Now Menw set off and found the boar in its lair. There was the comb and shears and Menw tried his luck at snatching the marvels from his head. He managed to get a single bristle but a speck of the boar's angry spittle touched his bird feathers and, though Menw managed to get back to Arthur and report his findings, he was never without sickness from that day forth.

So all the warriors of Arthur set forth on this quest and off they went in his ship called *Prydwen*, the Fair Aspect, to Éireann. The warriors of Éireann came forward to find out why the battle array of the Britons had come to their shores and, on being told, they offered to join Arthur in his hunt for the magical boar. If the truth were known, the men of Éireann were pleased at the idea of ridding themselves of the magical boar, which was always causing trouble in their land.

At Esgeir Oerfel, they found Twrch Trwyth, surrounded by seven young pigs; each pig was as fearsome and magical as each other. As it was their territory, the warriors of Éireann went forward first with their dogs but, by evening, the magical boar had the best of them and he had laid waste one of the five great kingdoms of Éireann in revenge.

The next day, Arthur's warriors went forward and, by the end of that evening, they won nothing but death and destruction and another kingdom lay waste. On the third day, Arthur and his best warriors went against the Twrch Trwyth and, when nightfall came, there was more death and destruction and a third kingdom lay waste.

So it was that they battled with the magic boar for nine nights and nine days, yet Twrch Trwyth remained unscathed.

That evening, around their encampment, one of his warriors called on Arthur to tell them more about this fearsome creature.

"He was once a great king in this land but he thought himself too mighty and the gods transformed him into a boar."

"Then, perhaps," said the warrior, "we might be able to negotiate with him, for he would know the meaning of diplomacy, having been a king."

This was not so naive as many thought.

While they rested, Arthur decided to sent Gwrhyr the Interpreter to speak with the boar for, in truth, all they wanted were the comb and shears that lay between his ears.

However, Twrch Trwyth would not deign to answer him and it was his son, Grugyn Silver-Bristle, who told Gwrhyr to tell Arthur that he would have to take the comb and shears by force, because he had attacked first without trying to talk with him.

"Until you have killed us and Twrch Trwyth's life has run its course, the comb and shears stay where they are. Tell Arthur and his warriors to leave us in peace, or we will go to his own land and destroy it even as we have destroyed this one."

Now when Gwrhyr told Arthur, Arthur was angry and made ready to attack at dawn again. But before he could do so, he found that Twrch Trwyth and his seven young pigs had swum across the sea to the Island of the Mighty. They landed at Porth Cleis in the kingdom of Dyfed and killed all the inhabitants and cattle, except a few who managed to flee before them.

Arthur and his men set off after Twrch Trwyth and the beast led him into the mountains of Mynydd Preseli. There Arthur gathered his men on both sides of the river Nyfer, but off went the great boar and his seven pigs to Cwm Cerwyn, where he slew four of Arthur's best champions. Twice he stood and each time four great champions suffered their deaths, including Arthur's young son Gwydre. It is said that a spear-cast grazed the boar and made him draw off in anger, otherwise more would have died.

The following day, Twrch Trwyth was as fierce as ever. Huandaw and Gogigwr, Penpingion and three champions serving under Glewlwyd of the Mighty Grip went down beneath his tusks. Gwlyddyn the Craftsman, who was chief builder to Arthur, was also slain.

At Peluniawg, they almost had him, but three more champions went down and the beast burst through their ring to Gyn Ystun, where the dogs lost his scent and no one could find him.

Arthur demanded of Gwyn, son of Nudd, if he knew the beast's whereabouts, but Gwyn denied knowledge. So on moved the hunt with their dogs. An advance party came to Dyffryn Llychwr, where two of Twrch Trwyth's pigs, Grugyn

Silver-Bristle and Llwydawg Torrwr, the Hewer, burst into their camp and killed all, save one, who managed to flee back to Arthur and report.

Arthur immediately attacked these two great pigs and got the best of them. But so fierce a clamour did they set up that Twrch Trwyth roused himself from where he had been resting, and leapt forward to defend them. Life for life and death for death was the order of the day. The first of the pigs was slain at Mynydd Amanw and then others fell; Twrch Llawin, Gwys, Banw and Benwig were killed. Indeed, only Grugyn and Llwydawg were left alive with Twrch Trwyth himself.

The three magical creatures were brought to bay at Llwch Ewin, and here Twrch Trwyth slew Echil Big-hip, as well as countless other champions of lesser degree. The pigs then retreated to Llwch Tawy and here Grugyn was forced to leave them, making for Din Tywi and Garth Grugyn, where he was eventually slain, though not without destroying four more of Arthur's champions in his death-struggle.

Llwydawg went on to Ystrad Yw where he, too, was overtaken and slain, but not before he slew two great kings. One of them was Arthur's own uncle.

In rage at the loss of his children, Twrch Trwyth destroyed all the countryside and its people between Tawy and Ewyas and began to move south across the Sabrann river.

Arthur called his champions together once more.

"While I live, I shall not let this magical boar pass into the land of Cernyw. I intend to stand before him and not chase after him. Life for life and death for death. One of us shall be the victor. You may do as you will."

Not one warrior chose any other course but to stand with Arthur.

So they gathered on the banks of the great Sabrann where Twrch Trwyth stood at bay.

Then it was that Mabon, son of Modron, seized his chance. On the stallion Dunmane, with Gorau ap Custennin and the sick Menw, crying for revenge, they rode forward. Then came Arthur, and Osla Big Knife, and Manawydan ap Llyr and Cyledyr the Wild. They surrounded the great boar and, in the struggle, Mabon seized the comb from beneath the boar's ears while Cyledyr the Wild seized the shears.

Then the great boar raced forward, chased by the hounds Aned and Aethlem, along the watery course of the Sabrann and into the sea, south-west to Annwn, the Otherworld, and vanished from men's sight. Some say – and who will deny them? – that Twrch Trwyth sleeps under a giant oak in Annwn, his snout among the lush acorns that drop from it. He is only resting. One day he will return to this world to continue his fearsome contest with Arthur and humankind.

So the greatest task asked by Ysbaddadan was now completed.

But one task still remained, and that was the blood of the black witch, Dewines Du, with which Ysbaddadan wanted his beard dressed. Now she was the daughter of the White Witch who dwelt at the head of the Valley of Grief in the uplands of Hell.

So once more Arthur set off, and with him he took Cynddelig the Guide. They reached the place and found the witch's cavern which was dark and evil and the stench of putrefaction offended the warriors. Cacamwri and his brother Hygwydd went into the cavern to fight the witch, but they returned bloodied by their wounds and terrified out of their minds by her magic.

While Arthur himself wanted to go into the cavern, his men persuaded him to send in Amren and Eiddil, two more splendid warriors. They came out as worse for their wounds as the others.

Arthur could no longer be restrained. He went into the cavern and hurled his knife, flashing into the darkness, so that it cut the witch in twain. Then Cadw of the Pictii rushed forward and drew the witch's blood into a bowl which he kept.

Then Arthur asked, "Are all the tasks completed?"

Culhwch came forward and replied, "They are, my lord."

"Then I have kept my promise, Culhwch, son of Cilydd. The day when you first came to my court and I trimmed your hair, I made you a promise that if Olwen existed, you would have her. Go forth now and claim her from Ysbaddadan Pencawr."

Culhwch and his companions set off once more for the castle of Ysbaddadan Pencawr.

Ysbaddadan Pencawr sat in his hall and, when they came before him, he demanded that his servants prop up his one great baleful eye with poles.

Cadw of the Pictii came forward.

"I am here to shave you."

And he shaved and dressed his beard as Ysbaddadan had asked.

"So all the tasks are done?" inquired Ysbaddadan softly, knowing full well that this must be the case.

"As you see," Culhwch replied. "Olwen is now mine."

Ysbaddadan nodded with a surly expression.

"Yet do not think that it was any deed of yours, Culhwch. The tasks were completed because of the deeds of your kinsman, Arthur, and his champions. They obtained Olwen for you. For my part, I should have done more to ensure that you never had her for a wife."

Then the beautiful Olwen was sent for. She came willingly and with love for the handsome young prince, Culhwch.

"It is said on this day you would die," Culhwch observed, looking at Ysbaddadan.

The giant smiled sourly. "It is so, but even that task is not yours to perform."

It was Gorau son of Custennin who sprang forward and, with a single blow of his sword, struck off Ysbaddadan's head.

"True enough," he said. "It was my task to perform, to avenge my twenty-three brothers who lay dead."

He took the giant's head and raised it on a stake as a warning to all tyrants that their day would eventually come, no matter how they tried to protect their power. Then Ysbaddadan's castle became the property of Gorau. From it, Gorau ruled wisely and justly and lived to a fine old age, marrying and having many sons.

So Culhwch's quest for Olwen came to an end and he had fulfilled the destiny curse placed on him by his stepmother and was able to return to his father's palace with his bride. Here he found not only was his father dead, but also his stepmother and her daughter, and so the people rejoiced to see him alive and well and with his beautiful queen. They ruled the land wisely and justly and lived happily for the rest of their lives.

The hosts of Arthur then dispersed each to his own lands. The bards told many tales of the quests of Arthur's champions but there is none as great as the quest for Olwen.

25 *The Dream of Rhonabwy*

In the days when Madog ap Maredudd ruled over Powys, there was fighting and warfare. But Madog did his best to bring peace to his kingdom and to the neighbouring kingdoms. However, Madog's brother, Iorwerth, was jealous of his brother, for he had wanted to be king in Powys, and to cause harm to Madog's just reign he went raiding into a neighbouring kingdom.

His band of renegade warriors attacked under Madog's own standard and, by this means, Iorwerth hoped to destroy his brother's kingdom. His ravaging army threatened to overturn all the peace treaties which Madog had made. Fire and blood were seen throughout the country.

Madog summoned his loyal warriors and gave command of them to Rhonabwy. Rhonabwy was his best general and he was told to find the rebellious Iorwerth and bring him back to Powys, as a prisoner. The army set off immediately, searching for Iorwerth. It was no easy task and, indeed, Iorwerth could not be found.

Rhonabwy and his men, in their searching, came to the country of the lord Heilyn Goch, son of Cadwgawn ab Iddon. This lord's hall had burnt black in Iorwerth's raids and smoke was still rising from every blackened stone and timber. It had not only been burnt but now stood deserted; deserted, that is, except for a crone who sat in the cinders of the building, feeding a fire in a corner in order to warm herself. Night was approaching and Rhonabwy realised it was useless to continue the pursuit that day. He gave orders for his men to encamp in the grounds of the once-great hall, while he and his two fellow generals entered the ruins.

"Where is the lord Heilyn?" demanded Rhonabwy, seeing the crone. "What tragedy has overcome his hall?"

He and his men walked over to the woman's fire, but the old woman took little notice of them, sitting feeding the fire and muttering under her breath. Rhonabwy presumed that she was either deaf or stupid and, anyway, he felt that it was obvious that the lord Heilyn had been overcome by Iorwerth.

At least it was warm by the fire, in spite of the acrid smell and, seeing an ox skin spread nearby, Rhonabwy and his men took a seat on it.

"Where are the people who lived here?" asked Rhonabwy again, trying to get the woman to speak.

She was still mumbling when into the ruined hall came a man and a woman. They were a wizened old couple, toothless and almost hairless. They came with bundles of sticks which they offered to the old woman, who placed them on the fire.

Rhonabwy greeted them but they simply ignored him.

Now Rhonabwy turned to his companions to suggest that they go back to their encampment. Even a night spent on a cold camp bed was better than the putrid smells and the lack of civility of the old woman and her two new companions. But Rhonabwy found that his companions were fast asleep on the ox skin. As he looked at them, he realized just how sleepy he actually was. There was room on the ox skin and so he stretched himself out and the next minute he was fast asleep.

He felt that he had not been asleep long when a horn sounded and it was daylight. He and his two companions appeared to be alone. They ran out of the ruins and found that their army had disappeared. Furthermore, the sun was up and they realized that this hall must stand on the plain of Aryngroeg. They mounted their horses and started riding towards the waters of the great river, the Sabrann by Rhyd-y-Groes. As they rode, they heard a thunder of hooves behind them and, turning in their saddles, they beheld a strange warrior dressed all in yellow with yellow curly hair, riding a horse of yellow and holding a sword of gold. He looked extremely fierce and threatening.

"It must be a warrior from the Otherworld!" cried one of Rhonabwy's companions and put spur to his steed. The panic spread but, try as hard as they could, they could not stay ahead of the strange warrior. In fear of their lives and worse, Rhonabwy turned and ordered his companions to yield.

"We ask terms for surrender," Rhonabwy cried.

The young golden warrior halted his steed a little way from them and laughed good-naturedly. "Then you shall have quarter, in Arthur's name."

"Since you have granted us that," Rhonabwy replied, "permit me to know to whom I have surrendered."

"I am called Iddawg ap Mynio, but I am better known as Terfysgwr."

"Now that is a strange name to be called." Indeed, the name meant "mischief".

"I am so called because I make mischief," replied the other, unabashed. "I was an envoy at the battle of Camlann between Arthur and his nephew Medrawd, and I kindled all sorts of strife between them. I pretended one thing to one and another to the other. So when Arthur told me to give kind words to Medrawd, I made his message rude and harsh. When Medrawd sought to reconcile himself to Arthur, I told Arthur that Medrawd was arrogant and hot-blooded. That is why my name is Terfysgwr, the mischief-maker."

While they were speaking there came the sound of more horses. Down the road came another horseman. This time he was clad all in scarlet, and his horse was chestnut but nearing redness. Blood was on his sword and his shield. In a moment, he rode up alongside them.

"Are these little folk enemies or friends?" he demanded of Iddawg.

"You may choose. I have chosen to make them my friends."

"Good enough," agreed the other. "Friends they are."

Before another word could be said, the man spurred his chestnut-red horse on down the road.

"Who was that?" asked Rhonabwy.

"That was Rhiwawn Bebyr, a mighty warrior," replied Iddawg. "Now come with me to our encampment."

They rode on and, when they reached the great River Sabrann, they saw a mighty host encamped on its banks. The camp was a square mile in size. Pennants and banners fluttered in the breeze and there were many pavilions set up on the field. Iddawg conducted them through the encampment to a dais on which sat a tall handsome man. His hair was auburn, his skin white and he had a golden circlet around his head and a great sword in his hands.

Next to him stood a youth who was fair of skin and black of hair.

"Blessing on you, my lord Arthur," cried Iddawg, bowing before him.

The man with the golden circlet, Arthur, turned and examined Rhonabwy and his companions curiously.

"Who are these folk, Iddawg? Where did you find such little fellows?"

Iddawg laughed good-naturedly while Rhonabwy coloured hotly. He was Madog's best general and warrior and did not like to be called a "little fellow".

"I found them on the road, lord."

Arthur gazed at them and grinned as if in derision at what he saw.

"Are we amusing to you?" demanded Rhonabwy, because he was a proud man. "Do you find us a laughing matter?"

Arthur pursed his lips in a grimace. "It is no laughing matter when little men like you are the only means of keeping our people safe from the Saxon hordes, when yesterday giants guarded our shores against them."

He then dismissed them with a wave of his hand. When they had withdrawn out of earshot, Iddawg whispered to Rhonabwy: "Did you see the ring worn by Arthur?"

"The gold ring with the large stone? Yes, I saw it. What of it?"

"That is a magical stone which will force you to reveal all you have seen since first we met."

They were interrupted by the sound of cantering horses and, turning, Rhonabwy saw a troop of warriors on horseback coming into the camp. They were colourful men, with bright shields and wore nothing save red and crimson.

Iddawg, catching his look of curiosity, said: "They are the warriors of Rhiwawn Bebyr, the Shining One: he that you met on the road. None but they may pay honour to the daughters of kings in this Island of the Mighty, and their drink is honey-mead."

Then came another troop of warriors on horseback and they were clad all in white. They raced up so quickly that the leading rider drew very near Arthur, whereupon the youth, who was fair of skin and black of hair, stepped forward and smote the horse on the muzzle with the flat of his sword, causing it to rear up and halt.

"Is it an insult that you give me?" demanded the rider, a hand on his own sword.

"It is a warning that I give you. You ride near Arthur and have splashed him with mud from your horse."

"Then no insult has been made to me," said the man, thrusting his half-drawn sword back into his scabbard.

"That is March ap Meirchion," Iddawg told Rhonabwy, indicating the youth. "He is first cousin to Arthur."

Then a third troop of warriors arrived on horseback and they were clad all in black.

"Those troops are led by Edern ap Nudd," confided Iddawg.

Now a great army was around them and one of the warriors said it was marvellous to see the host of the Britons gathered in such a narrow place. His name was Caradoc.

"Remember at the battle of Badon, how each one of us swore an oath that we would meet here when we were needed?" went on Caradoc. "Now the host of the Saxons have taken over the fair land of the Britons and great is the need of our people."

"This is truly spoken," agreed Arthur. "And now we are gathered, it is time to march forth and challenge our enemies once more."

Iddawg took Rhonabwy and his companions with him and the whole host set off in the direction of Cefn Digoll.

At the entrance to a large plain, the army had halted to arrange its positions. Suddenly, a great uproar broke out in the centre of the army and there came riding through the ranks a tall man in silver armour with a white cloak and a red plume. It looked to Rhonabwy that the ranks of Arthur's army were splitting asunder to allow this single man through.

"What is it?" he demanded of Iddawg. "Are the warriors of Arthur fleeing?"

"Rhonabwy," Iddawg replied, "Arthur and his men have never yielded a foot of our sacred soil to the Saxons. If your remark had reached other ears, it would have doomed you to a traitor's death."

"For that I am sorry. Truly, I merely wanted to know what was happening."

"The horseman in silver and white is none other than Cai, son of Cynyr, the most handsome and fierce warrior in all Arthur's court. Cai is the best rider, the best warrior, the best champion. The men are making way for him and then closing in around him."

As the tumult grew, Cador of Cornwall was called for, because he was the bearer of Arthur's mighty sword. He appeared and raised it so all could see it. He held the magic sword Caladfwlch, "the hard dinter", up in its scabbard. The sword then leapt from the scabbard and whirled around like a tongue of flame and so terrifying was it that it quelled the tumult and all became quiet among Arthur's men.

Then Rhonabwy heard the named of Eiryn called. He was Arthur's servant and a big, red-headed and ugly fellow he was. He came forward and unpacked a golden chair, along with a coverlet of brocaded silk, which he spread over the chair. A table was set before it and another chair was placed there. On the table he laid out a board and gaming pieces known as Gwyddbwyll or "wooden wisdom".

"Owain, son of Urien, come forward," Arthur called.

A handsome young warrior came forward. "I am here, lord."

"Does it please you to pass an hour playing wooden wisdom with me?"

Owain smiled. "That would please me fine, lord Arthur."

So they stretched themselves on each side of the board and began to play in earnest. It was clear to Rhonabwy that Owain was an excellent player but needed to concentrate more carefully on his game to overcome Arthur. Now it happened, and no man knows why, that Cenferchyn had given Owain three hundred night-black ravens to follow him in battle. Whenever these ravens followed Owain, he became invincible in combat.

At a crucial point of the game, Owain's servant came running forward to him and saluted.

"What is this distraction?" muttered Arthur.

"He is my servant, lord."

"Then bid him speak."

The servant stood hesitating. Then he said, "Lord Owain, the king's servants are molesting your ravens."

Owain ap Urien was upset and said to Arthur, "Lord, if this be true, please call off your servants and do not harm my ravens of battle."

Arthur did not reply directly, but simply said, "It is your move in this game."

The servant was sent off and the game continued.

A little while later, the same servant came running forward to Owain.

"Lord Owain," he cried out, "is it with your permission that the king's servants are wounding and killing your ravens?"

Owain was shocked. "It is against my will that anyone should do so." He turned to Arthur. "Lord, if these are your servants that are killing my ravens, please call them off."

Arthur did not reply directly but, turning to Owain, said, "It is your move in this game."

The servant was sent away.

After a little while, the same servant came running back and called out, "Lord Owain, your favourite among the ravens has been killed, and many of the rest that have not been killed are so badly hurt that they cannot lift their wings again. It is the king's men who have done this terrible deed."

Owain ap Urien was greatly upset. "Lord Arthur, what does this mean?"

Arthur did not reply directly but, turning to Owain, said simply, "It is your move in this game."

Then Owain turned to his servant. "Go to where the battle

is hardest fought and raise my standard as high as possible. Then call the ravens and those that are able will go there."

The servant disappeared to do this bidding.

Some distance away, the battle was raging and it was seen that the bright standard of Owain ap Urien was raised on a hill. With rage and passion the ravens, seeing Owain's standard in the thick of the battle, went berserk and rose in the air, higher and higher, wounded and dying and dead as well. Down they came tearing into the battle; flesh and bone and hair were torn from those beneath their talons. Croaking with exultation, the ravens drove the enemy from the ground.

The board game between Owain and Arthur resumed in peace.

Then one of Arthur's servants came running forward and bowed to the king. "Lord king, Owain's ravens are now attacking your warriors."

Arthur looked in annoyance at Owain. "If this is so, call off your ravens."

"It is your move in this game," observed Owain, not replying directly.

The servant went off and, a short time later, returned. "Lord king, Owain's ravens are wounding and killing your men."

"If this be so, tell your ravens to stop."

Owain took no notice of the king but said, "It is your move in this game."

A third time, the servant came running back. "Lord king, now your warriors are slain and the greatest sons of the Island of the Mighty are no more."

Then Arthur said again, "Call off your ravens, Owain ap Urien."

"Lord, it is your move," replied Owain stoically.

The messenger finally said to Arthur, "The ravens have destroyed your whole war-band, lord Arthur, and left all Britain to the mercy of the Saxon army."

Arthur sprang up then and, taking the gaming pieces on the board, he crushed them in his hands until they were dust. Only then did Owain ap Urien order his battle-banner to be lowered.

At that moment, there came envoys from the commander of the Saxons, Osla Big-Knife, and he sought peace from Arthur. Surprised, Arthur summoned his counsellors – Cai, Bedwyr, Gwalchmai and Trystan and Peredur and Gwrhyr, Menw and March and they all considered what should be done. It was finally agreed that a truce be made and that there would be peace in the land.

Cai then rose up and said, "Let every man who wishes to follow Arthur be with him tonight in the kingdom of Kernow."

As they departed, Rhonabwy turned to Iddawg. "I do not understand, Iddawg. Can you tell me the meaning of the game of 'wooden wisdom' between Arthur and Owain? What was the meaning of the battle between Arthur's warriors and Owain's ravens? Why did Cenferchyn give those three hundred battle-ravens to Owain in the first place?"

Now the answer to these questions might have illuminated the darkness in Rhonabwy's mind. But, as Iddawg was about to speak, Rhonabwy's eyes flitted open and he found himself lying on the ox skin in the burnt-out shell of a hall. Alongside him were his companions. It was his men who had come to find their general who awakened them. They told them that they had actually slept for three days and three nights and nothing they could do would waken them.

Rhonabwy told them all about his dream and his companions said that they, too, had shared the dream but none could offer a satisfactory interpretation.

That there was an interpretation, it was obvious, but no one could offer it.

So Rhonabwy and his men continued in their search to find the rebellious lord Iorwerth, brother of the King of Powys. It is not recorded what happened, whether he found Iorwerth or not, nor what further adventures Rhonabwy had. All we know is that, at some time, Rhonabwy told a bard his dream and that dream was recorded: but who knows what its meaning is?

Cornwall (Kernow)

Cornwall: Preface

There is only one complete folk tale recorded in the Cornish language that has survived. This was taken down in the mid-seventeenth-century and is called "Jowan Chy-an-Horth" which is Jowan or John of Chy-an-horth. There is some scholastic discussion as to whether this was recorded by Nicholas Boson or his son John Boson. However, it was first printed in 1707 in *Archaeologia Britannica*, by the great Welsh scholar Edward Lhuyd (*c.* 1660–1709), whose work made him the most important forerunner to modern Celtic studies.

It also survived into English oral tradition and was picked by William Bottrell in his *Traditions and Hearthside Stories of West Cornwall* (1880). Robert Hunt, in *Popular Romances of the West of England* (1871), also printed a version as "The Tinner of Chyannor", but his source came from Thomas Tonkin's rather poor translation of the text, as printed by Lhuyd.

The story is in no way original to Cornwall. Versions are found in Scotland, in a story called *Na Tri Chomhairlie*, collected in John F. Campbell's four-volume study *Popular Tales of the West Highlands* (1860–62). The Breton scholar Roparz Hemon (*d.* 1978) gave a Breton version, for comparative purposes, in the Breton cultural magazine *Gwalarnn*, which he founded and edited from 1925–44. In 1938, Professor Ludwig Muelhauser had made a study of it, in *Die Kornische Geshichte von der drei guten ratschwägen*. Indeed, variants of the tale crop up in many European cultures. Nevertheless, mainly because it does survive in Cornish, Cornish people are proud of it and in 1984 it was made into a short Cornish language television film.

As Robert Morton Nance, in an undated pamphlet (*c.* 1930s, Penzance) *Folk-lore Recorded in the Cornish Language*, explained – there survives nothing else in Cornish in its entirety as regards Cornish legends. Nance described that which did survive as splinters of a great shipwreck: snatches of songs, oblique references to stories, proverbs and the like.

The story of Tewdrig, the first in this selection, as an example, is a story that now has to be pieced together from excerpts from medieval saints' lives in Latin, and from the only surviving medieval saints' play in the Cornish language, *Beuanns Meriasek* (Life of Meriadoc), the manuscript of which was written by Father Radulphus Ton, a parish priest of Crowan, near Camborne, in 1504. The manuscript is in the National Library of Wales (Aberystwyth) as Peniarth Mss 105.

The curious thing about Tewdrig (given as "Tev Dar" in the 1504 manuscript) is that, in trying to give him a suitable pagan religion, the author makes this fifth to sixth century Cornish king a follower of Islam! Obviously, by this time, a memory of the old Celtic deities had been totally lost in Cornwall. The lines, with contractions expanded in brackets, are:

Tev Dar:
Tev Dar me a veth gelwys
arluth regnijs in Kernov.
May fo Mahu[m] Enorys
ov charg yv heb feladov
oges ha pel
penag a worthya ken du
a astev[yth] peynys glu
hag in weth me[er]nans cruel.

I am Tewdrig,
reigning lord in Cornwall.
That Mahommed be honoured

is my unfailing duty,
everywhere in my land:
any who worship another god
shall endure sharp pains
and have a cruel death.

Most of the other stories given here have survived through the medium of English, some much intermixed with Cornish words, sentences and the English dialect form that displaced the Cornish language. William Bottrell, in his three-volume collection, printed variant versions of many of them.

The versions I give differ in many respects from Bottrell and also the Hunt retellings, and this is due to commentaries given me by the late Robert Dunstone and Leonard Truran, when I was living in Cornwall in the late 1960s. Between 1967 and 1968, my wife and I roamed the West Penwith peninsula, at the very end of Cornwall. Although we have been back to Cornwall for many visits, and I was honoured to be inaugurated as a bard of the Cornish Gorsedd (under the name Gwas-an-Geltyon – Servant of the Celts) as a recognition for my work on Celtic history and culture, my main work on Cornish was conducted during this period. From it, I produced *The Cornish Language and its Literature*, published by Routledge & Kegan Paul, 1974. It was gratifying that this was considered the definitive work on the history of the language and a standard text for the Cornish Language Board examinations.

There were also many in Cornwall who were happy to offer advice on my queries about Cornish folklore and I should record my appreciation of their help: to E.G. Retallack Hooper (Talek), to G. Pawley White (Gunwyn) both former Grand Bards of the Cornish Gorsedd. Particularly, with regard to the story "Nos Calan Gwaf" I would like to express my appreciation of the discussions I had with the late L.R. Moir (Car Albanek) during the time I spent in St Ives.

L.R. Moir was a fluent Cornish speaker and worked closely with Robert Morton Nance (Modron) 1873–1959, taking over, at his death, as editor of *Old Cornwall*. Moir produced many works in Cornish and was interested in folkloric themes. Among several works he published, "*An Map Dyworth an Yst*" (The Boy from the East) in 1967 won a Gorsedd prize. The story concerned the famous Glastonbury legend. As I recall, by 1968, he had made draft versions of "*Nos Calan Gwaf*," which is the Cornish for Hallowe'en, which title I have kept rather than the title of the version given by Bottrell: "An' Pee Tregeer's Trip to Market on Hallan Eve".

A variant of "The Bukkys" was first collected by Bottrell under the title "The Fairy Master". The title, used by Retallack Hooper, is the equivalent to the fairy or mischievous spirit which leads travellers astray in most Celtic fairy tales, such as *Púca* in Irish and *Pwca* in Welsh. These are the equivalents of the English *Puck*. The word is said to have come from the Norse settlements, from the word *puki*. There does not appear to be any early tradition of it.

I have left the title "Lys-an-Gwrys", which Len Truran recorded when he picked up the tale in the Lizard Peninsula. Coincidentally, the name "Lizard" comes from the word *lys* – a court or palace and *arth* – meaning high. People usually and mistakenly apply the name to the whole of the peninsula south of Helston, but it only belongs properly to the southern half, as the northern half is Meneage. The peninsula is almost an island and at its southern tip is Cornwall's (and, indeed, Britain's) most southerly town – Lizard Town. The story had a lot of Lizard topography in it. But when I first heard it, it reminded me of another tale.

Indeed, this is a similar tale, under a similar name, to one collected by Luzel on the Côtes-du-Nord, in Brittany, and told to him in 1873 by Louis Le Braz, a weaver of Prat. The name translates as "The Crystal Palace" but I have left the Cornish name in the version given here. Both stories are esoteric journeys rather than adventure stories, for they constitute a spiritual quest. Luzel believed the Breton version was pre-Christian.

26 *Tewdrig, Tyrant of Treheyl*

"Tewdrig! A strange ship has appeared in the estuary," cried Wron the Druid, bursting into the great feasting hall of Tewdrig, king of Treheyl and emperor of all Kernow, that south-western peninsula of the Isle of the Mighty that is today called Cornwall.

Tewdrig glanced up in agitated surprise. "What guards do I have, that I am not warned of the sight of a strange sail until a ship sails into the estuary?" he demanded vehemently. "I should be informed as soon as a sail appears on the distant horizon."

Wron made a dismissive gesture. "Better to learn late than learn never, my king."

"Does it come in war or does it come in peace?" demanded Tewdrig, buckling on his great sword and taking up his rounded buckler.

Tewdrig was a strong man, as tall as a spear and as straight, with long black hair and a face that was saturnine and cruel. Skill with his weapons had brought Tewdrig power and his domains spread through the land of Kernow as far east as the great River Tamar, the quietly flowing river that marked the border with the kingdom of Dumnonia.

It was not strength alone, however, by which Tewdrig had kept his kingdom secure. He believed in the gods and the old ways in a world that was rapidly changing. In the east, whole kingdoms were falling before the hordes of Saxons with their mighty gods of war. Countless tribes had fled north, west and south to escape massacre by the children of Woden.

So far, the kingdom of Kernow had been kept safe. But Tewdrig was ever vigilant. Only a battle-hardened king could keep harm from his people.

Now he hurried to the battlements of his fortress at the place of the estuary, Treheyl, and looked out across its waters. The estuary of the river, which was also called Heyl, formed a wide sac stretching two miles which, at low tide, was a stretch of mud banks on which numerous seabirds nested. The ramparts of Tewdrig's fortress rose above them.

Wron had obviously alerted the guards, for they were gathered ready, their weapons in their hands.

Tewdrig came to the battlements and halted.

Indeed, there was a ship sailing into the estuary, its sails filled before the wind. It was heading towards the quay below Treheyl.

The king's eyes narrowed. "It bears a strange emblem on the sail, Wron. Can you identify it?"

The Druid peered forward and shook his head. "I cannot identify it, my king. It is not a symbol that is familiar in this land. Though, from the cut of the vessel, I would say that it is from the western island of Ywerdhon."

Ywerdhon was the name by which the people of Kernow called the land of the goddess Éire.

Tewdrig bit in irritation at his lip, a habit he had often tried to control since childhood. "Well, if they are foreign and mean us harm, they can harm us little. There is not room enough on that little craft for many warriors and their approach is open enough."

Wron nodded. "Nevertheless, my king, it would be best to have the men stand ready."

Tewdrig turned to Dinan, chieftain of Pendinas, who was the captain of his guard, and told him to take a company of warriors to the quay to greet the strangers. Dinan was, in fact, Tewdrig's own brother and as fair as Tewdrig was dark, yet they were both born at the same hour of the same mother and father. Dinan was Tewdrig's right hand and his shield at every battle. Firm in battle and as shrewd in war was Dinan.

Some said that without Dinan, Tewdrig could not have maintained his kingdom. Though this was never said before either Tewdrig or Dinan. Further, many said that Tewdrig was as evilly tempered to those nearest to him as Dinan was amiable and obliging. Indeed, at Tewdrig's sharp commands, Dinan smiled but a gentle acknowledgment of his brother's order and went down in obedience to it.

Tewdrig turned back to examine the sail and its strange emblem again. It consisted of two curving lines which crossed each other, so that the emblem appeared as if it was meant to be the outline of a fish.

Tewdrig was seated in the great hall of his palace when Dinan escorted the visitors to him. Wron the Druid stood at his right elbow, for Wron was his chief counsellor.

There were five people who came before him: three men and two women and, while they were all clad in simple attire, they stood tall and had the look of nobility on their faces. Around the neck of each one of them there hung a silver cross on a leather thong. Tewdrig's eyes narrowed, for the cross seemed to be a badge of their fellowship.

"These, my brother, are travellers from Ywerdhon," Dinan announced.

Their leader stepped forward. He was a tall, elderly man with a regal countenance. "The Blessing of the Living God on you, Tewdrig of Treheyl," he greeted.

Tewdrig frowned before he replied. "The prosperity of each of the gods of my ancestors on you, stranger. Who are you, and what do you seek in this land?"

"I was a king in my own country, but have given up earthly pomp to follow a more glorious life. My name is Germoe."

"Welcome then, Germoe. And what is more glorious in your eyes than temporal splendour?" smiled Tewdrig indulgently, wondering if the man was mad.

"To follow the ways of the Son of God and teach His truth and peace to your people."

Wron drew his brows together. "The Son of God? The Father of the Gods had many sons, each of them gods in their own right. Of which do you speak?"

"The one and indivisible God," replied Germoe. "Him we

shall speak of anon, if you allow me and my band to stay in your kingdom."

"And who are these others?"

"I am Coan," said one of the two young men.

"I am Elwyn," announced the other.

"My name is Breage," one of the young women added.

"I am Crowan," said the last.

"We are all servants of the Living God," Germoe said. "We seek your permission to settle in peace and preach the new faith of our God."

Wron glanced at the king. "To settle in peace?" he sneered. "Yet you would preach against our faith, destroy our beliefs and our laws. Do you call this peace?"

"Once you have opened your ears to the word of our Lord in heaven, it will be peace," replied Germoe confidently. "Our God is not a God of war, strife or dissension."

"I would hear them, brother," Dinan suddenly said. "Let them go where they will in our land. For what can five people do to shake the faith of a nation?"

Wron flashed an angry glance at Dinan. "I like it not. If they must stay, let them go south, away from this place, so that they may not contaminate our good government."

Tewdrig chuckled suddenly in humour. "We will give in to our brother's urgings," he said. "For I agree – what harm can five strangers do in our midst? But Wron is my counsellor. Go southward, strangers, and preach as you wish."

They all left Treheyl and journeyed south. But Crowan was the first to break away and took an eastern road, until she came to a spot where she built a round enclosure and she prospered. They call this place Crowan, to this day.

The others continued southwards. Then Coan also turned east and found a river called the Fal. On its eastern bank, he started to preach the word of the Son of the Living God. But it is said that this land owed allegiance to Wron the Druid, who stirred up the people against Coan and, in their anger, they stoned him to death. So the place where this happened was afterwards called Merther, which stands between Tresillian and St Michael Penkevil. The word *merther*, in the Cornish tongue, means "martyr".

The others continued southwards. And first Germoe halted at the southern coast of Kernow and established a house where he taught, and the spot became named after him. The others continued to the south-east, following the coast. Then Breage stopped and, under the shadow of a fortress called Pencaire, between the hills of Tregonning and Godolphin, she built her house and began to teach, and so the place was called Breage after her. Finally, the young man named Elwyn came to the sea's edge and to a small port where he established himself and taught. The place was thereafter called Porth Elwyn, or Elwyn's port, which is now Porthleven.

Now Tewdrig watched the progress of the strangers, with their strange stories of the son of God, with anxiety on his brow. His people, who had followed the wise Druids of old, had begun to fall away from the rituals at the stone circles and the worship of the old gods. In spite of the martyrdom of Croan, the other members of Germoe's party were gaining converts throughout the southern lands of Kernow.

What Tewdrig did not realize was that his own brother had listened to the word and accepted the truth of the new faith.

It happened that a year and a day after the coming of Germoe and his followers, Wron came running to Tewdrig, who was seated in his feasting hall.

"Tewdrig! A strange ship has appeared in the estuary," cried Wron.

Tewdrig glanced up from his wine in agitated surprise. "What guards do I have, that I am not warned of the sight of a sail, until a ship sails into the estuary?" he demanded vehemently. "I should be informed as soon as a sail appears on the distant horizon."

Wron made a dismissive gesture. "Better to learn late than learn never, my king."

"Does it come in war or does it come in peace?" demanded Tewdrig, buckling on his great sword and taking up his rounded buckler.

"Perhaps it does not matter," said Wron slyly, "for the last strange ship that came here was supposed to come in peace and its honey-tongued crew have sewn dissension through the land."

They climbed to the battlements and Tewdrig's eyes narrowed. Indeed, there was a ship sailing in the broad estuary before Treheyl, a ship with its sails filled before the wind.

Tewdrig gasped and pointed. "See, Wron, look at its sail. It carries the same design as the ship of Germoe." And, indeed, he was right, for the sail carried two curving lines which crossed each other, forming the outline of a great fish.

Wron drew in a deep breath. "Then this ship is of the same nation as Germoe and his tribe. We would do well to slaughter them before they come ashore."

Even so, Tewdrig hesitated and, by the time he had made up his mind, his brother Dinan had gone down to the quay to welcome the strangers to Treheyl.

So Tewdrig hurried to the hall of his palace and slumped upon his throne while Wron stood moodily at his side.

Five strangers entered with Dinan.

"These, my brother, are travellers from Ywerdhon," he said.

Tewdrig was filled with apprehension for, though this time there were three men and two women, like the five that had come before them, they each carried a silver cross hung around their necks, and while the clothes they wore were simple, they all carried themselves with noble bearing.

"The Blessing of the Living God on you, Tewdrig of Treheyl," greeted their leader. He was a tall, handsome man.

"The prosperity of the gods of my ancestors greet you," replied Tewdrig, frowning.

"I am called Gwinear; I was a prince in my own land, but I have given up all temporal pomp to serve the true God."

"All the gods are true," snapped Wron irritably.

"There is but one God," replied the woman at Gwinear's side.

Tewdrig's eyes bulged a little as he beheld her, for never had he seen a maiden so comely as this.

Gwinear smiled, not noticing the look in the king's eyes. "This is my sister, Piala."

"My name is Ia," the second maiden said. She was as fair as

Piala was dark but as beautiful, or so Dinan thought, for he had not taken his eyes from the girl since she had set foot on the quay of Treheyl.

"I am called Erth, and I am brother to Ia," announced one of the young men.

"While I am Uny," added the third man, "brother of Ia and Erth."

"And I suppose you want to stay in my kingdom and live in peace?" queried Tewdrig, a hint of sarcasm in his voice. But the derision was taken from his voice when his eyes dwelt on the beauty of Piala.

"That is our earnest request," Gwinear responded.

"But, in doing so, you would want freedom to preach your religion?" Wron prompted.

"That is what we desire." Piala smiled sweetly in innocence at Tewdrig.

The heart of the king gave a lurch and a passion began to throb within him.

"My king, we cannot grant this," Wron leant forward and whispered into the ear of the king of Treheyl.

Tewdrig glanced up, startled. "Why so?"

Wron closed his eyes in anguish. "Have you forgotten so soon how Germoe and his followers are disrupting the kingdom in the south?"

Tewdrig bit his lip and then stared across at Piala. "Then we will allow these good people to stay with us, but provided they stay within sight of Treheyl, that we may know what they are doing."

Now this idea had occurred to Tewdrig, not because of the reason he implied to his Druid, but because he wanted to be near the beautiful Piala. Further, he rose and went down to Piala, smiling, and said: "And in good faith, and to keep you safe, I will grant you land at the gate of my fortress, and there you may preach to those of Treheyl who would hear you."

Thus did the spot where Piala set up her dwelling become known as Phillack, in her honour, yet it was under the shadow of the king's gloomy fortress at Treheyl.

Piala's brother, Gwinear, wandered a mile or so further to

the east and established himself at a spot which is still named after him. And Erth also stayed within a short distance from Treheyl and the spot where he taught also took the name of St Erth. And Uny crossed the estuary opposite to Tewdrig's fortress and the place he taught was called the enclosure of the church – Lelant.

Now Ia tarried a while with Dinan, for in those days the sons and daughters of the church could marry and did so. Love and marriage between men and women, even though they be of the church, was not then forbidden as it was in later centuries. Ia was as attracted to Dinan as he was to her. Dinan promised her that he would hand over to her a tiny island at the end of a small bay to the west, on which he had a fortress. That fortress was called Pendinas. Ia established her church on this island and there lived with Dinan.

Wron the Druid was angered by these happenings and began to wonder whether the land of Kernow was in need of a new king to govern. The preachers of the new religion were gaining converts from the old and, in teaching love and forgiveness, were allowing their enemies to rage and pillage unchecked along the eastern border of the kingdom, where ran the mighty River Tamar. Within the kingdom, there were also rumblings and dissent, and many came to call Tewdrig a tyrant and godless king.

To the south-east, Geraint, chieftain of Gerrans, was openly preaching insurrection, for he had been converted to the new religion. In spite of Wron's pleas, Tewdrig would not stir against him.

"Plenty of time to teach him a lesson," Tewdrig assured Wron. "Let him have his say. The howling of a dog at the moon will not change its course."

Tewdrig was too infatuated with Piala to notice the danger. In fact, desire still burned deep within him. Piala was polite and greeted him in friendship, not being of the world to read the depth of the craving in his eyes. Indeed, there was a fearful emotion which smouldered restlessly there. Like a dog, Tewdrig followed her about, pretending interest in her teachings in order to sit in her company for hours on end.

Wron realised that the veil of desire must be lifted from his king's eyes or else Kernow would be doomed. It would be wracked by internal dissension and then it would be attacked from without. So Wron sat and pondered the problem, and a crafty plan began to form in his mind. He would create bloodshed between Tewdrig and the Ywerdhon. If the Ywerdhon died, then well and good; if Tewdrig died, then he would be able to rouse all Kernow against all the Ywerdhon preachers there. Then Wron arose with a great smile on his thin features and, saddling his horse, he rode for the church of Gwinear.

"Greetings, Ywerdhon," he said.

"Blessings of God on you, Wron of Treheyl."

"I will come straight to the point," Wron said, as he dismounted and sat before Gwinear's fire.

"A good place to start," acknowledged Gwinear.

"My king is besotted with your sister Piala."

Gwinear at once looked troubled, for he had seen the carnal fire in the eyes of the tyrant of Treheyl. "My sister has sworn to celibacy, for she will serve no other than the Son of God."

Wron hid his contempt and simply nodded. "Very laudable," he exclaimed. "But Tewdrig has sworn to have no other woman seated by his throne."

"This is grave news. Perhaps I should speak to the king and explain our ways?"

"An excellent idea. I know that this evening, Tewdrig goes to plight his troth to Piala. Be there at the ninth hour. Tewdrig is a reasonable man and will listen to argument."

So saying, Wron mounted his horse and rode back to Treheyl. There he sought out the sulking Tewdrig.

"What ails you, my king?" Wron asked.

"I am as restive and fretful as a young man in the first vapours of love. I send Piala tokens and she dispenses them as charity to the poor. What am I to do?"

Wron's thin lips twitched, but he controlled his cunning smile. "If that is all that ails you, fret no more."

"What do you mean?" demanded Tewdrig.

"I have just come from the lady. She does return your love.

This she has told me. But she says she must act with decorum before her brother, for these Ywerdhon have strange beliefs and ways. Though under that faint cloak, they are as passionate as we. However, it is clearly fear of her brother's anger which bids her hold you at arm's length. He is the problem here."

"Speak further," Tewdrig invited, much intrigued.

"She tells me that she shares your passions. Her cloak of indifference shall be discarded if you come to her just before the ninth hour and, because of her customs, you must not heed her protest but take her like the great man and mighty king she knows you to be."

A smile of lascivious joy spread over Tewdrig's face.

Wron went off to his meal, well pleased with his day's work.

So it happened, as dusk was falling before the ninth hour, Tewdrig went to the place where Piala had set up her church, which is called Phillack. Those the beautiful maiden was instructing in the ways of the new religion had departed to their houses, and Piala was kneeling, praying before the image of a young man hanging on a cross. Two candles were lit before it.

Tewdrig entered the church, his body tingling with desire as his lustful eyes fell on the maiden.

Piala started at the noise of his entry and turned round, her eyes widening as she beheld the tyrant of Treheyl.

"Why, King Tewdrig," she said, scrambling from her knees, "what brings you here at this hour of the night?"

"That you know well," smiled Tewdrig confidently.

Piala bit her lip in agitation, for she now recognized the meaning of the many presents Tewdrig had bestowed on her during the last months.

"I must tell you the ways of those who follow the Son of God, Tewdrig!"

Tewdrig let forth an oath. "You may tell me later, for my body aches for our union."

Piala went pale as she discerned his purpose. "This must not be!" she gasped. "I am sworn to celibacy in the service of . . ."

But Tewdrig moved forward and seized her, delighting in her struggles because he believed it to be, as Wron had told him, her way of greeting his love-making.

An angry exclamation halted Tewdrig. He turned in annoyance as a figure burst into the church.

It was Gwinear, his face working in anger. "Lecherous dog! You dare the sacrilege of this place by attacking a daughter of the church?"

Tewdrig pushed Piala to one side and drew his sword. "Begone, little man! Preach not to me, for I am not of your faith."

Now it has been said that Gwinear was a king in his own land before he followed the path of the Son of God. The blood of champions still flowed in his veins and a battle-rage came upon him. He moved forward with only his wooden staff for courage. Tewdrig, whatever else he was, was a great warrior but he lacked the warrior's will to self-control. He saw Gwinear's approach and made only three strokes of his sword. The first stroke cut the staff into two useless pieces; the second stroke pierced Gwinear's heart while the third stroke decapitated his head.

Piala let forth a tremendous shriek. She rushed to her brother's side and picked up his head and kissed it fervently. The eyes of Gwinear flicked open, for the ancients rightly believed that the soul resided in the head, and his voice spoke. "I have sinned. Do not you do likewise, my sister. Unto him that smiteth thee on the one cheek, offer also the other. Remember."

With that, Gwinear's soul departed.

Piala, too, was born of the blood of champions and it burnt with a fierce fire. It is one thing to hear a philosophy with the mind, but blood is strong.

In blind vengeance, she seized the dagger which Gwinear wore in his belt, for each man must carry a means to cut his meat. She seized it and lunged forward.

It can be said for Tewdrig that he acted only out of instinct. The point of his sword met Piala's onward rush at breast level and entered it. The blood spurted from her heart and she fell to the ground.

Tewdrig stood in a daze at the swiftness of what had happened.

Then Wron entered, for the sly Druid had been watching all the time, and while he was pleased at what had befallen, he pretended horror at the scene.

"Now the remaining Ywerdhon will preach rebellion against you, Tewdrig, and join with Geraint of Gerrans. You must act to stop this rebellion, before it has time to flower and bear fruit."

Tewdrig moved in a stupor and Wron had to shout to snap him out of it.

"Take the head of Gwinear and wash it in the well, then place it on a spike and have it carried before you, so all Kernow may know your serious intent to rid the land of the Ywerdhon."

Now the reason for this was not so much to put fear in people but because of the religious symbolism of the head, wherein the Druids believed the soul dwelt. To carry the head of your enemy endowed you with the strength and valour and intellect of that enemy.

Soon, Tewdrig came to his old self and realised that Wron was right. Before the next dawn, Tewdrig and his men had ridden to the churches of Erth and Uny and the brothers were slain before they had time to raise an alarm.

"Where is Ia, the last of this breed?" Tewdrig commanded as he stood by the bloody remains of Uny.

His warriors looked uncomfortably at each other.

"Why, she is with your brother Dinan, at Pendinas," they said.

Anger was on Tewdrig's face now. "Then we will go to Pendinas and finish this job. And woe to any, brother or no, who tries to defend this Ywerdhon from my wrath!"

His army arrived at Pendinas the next day and was surprised when they found Geraint of Gerrans with an army there before them. Geraint had gathered the rebellious men of Kernow from the four corners of the kingdom. Before this great hosting stood Breage, Crowan and Elwyn as well as Ia. By Ia's side, on his warhorse, sat Tewdrig's own brother Dinan. And before all of them was Geraint, a handsome young man of princely countenance. At his side was the venerable Germoe and Germoe carried a great cross of silver to act as their standard.

Tewdrig rode forward and by his side rode Wron, who carried the pole on which the head of Gwinear was set. And Geraint came forward with Germoe riding by his side, bearing the silver cross.

"You are in rebellion against your just king," cried Tewdrig in anger.

Geraint smiled gently. "Is it not written in our ancient law – what makes a king weaker than a servant on the poorest farm? It is because the people ordain the king, the king does not ordain the people. While you sat in justice, promoting our commonweal, Tewdrig, we followed you. But a bad deed you have done and we will now have done with you."

"Then, by the gods, I challenge you to the right of single combat!" cried Tewdrig.

Both men drew their swords.

Now, as Tewdrig was about to spur forward, the head of Gwinear, set atop the great pole held by Wron, suddenly fell. It fell straight and true and struck Tewdrig on the head with such impact that his iron helm was shattered and he was knocked to the ground.

Wron dismounted and examined his king and, when he looked up, there was fear in his eyes.

"His skull has been crushed by the head of Gwinear," he whispered.

"The true God has spoken," cried Germoe. "Vengeance is mine, says the Lord. Geraint is king."

And they departed, each to his own place. The head of Gwinear was buried at the town named after him. Ia continued to preach at Pendinas with support of the prince Dinan, rejecting all worldly treasures, and eventually the spot was named after her and is known today as St Ives. Geraint became a good and just king, whose name is still spoken of today and Gerrans, named after him, still exists. He it was who encouraged many saints to come to Kernow, and soon all the land was following the faith of the Son of God.

As for Wron, he departed the field unseen and was never punished. They say he went to hide in a cold, dark granite cave, within the sound of the blustery billows of the sea, and is there waiting for his time – for he was sure that time, which was, must be and will come again.

27 *The Lord of Pengersick*

Halfway between Helston and Marazion is the village of Germoe and about half a mile south of this, near Praa Sands on the coast, stands the ruins of Pengersick Castle. Only the towers remain now and it is a dark and evil place. Many gruesome legends are told of the castle and its inhabitants. One legend has it that a murderer hid from justice there, but was himself murdered and his soul carried off screaming by devils to the Land Beyond. Pengersick Castle once stood at the head of a dark moor, a marshy bog, which few would dare to wander into in case they did not return. In the Cornish language, *pen* means "head" while *gersick*, which comes from *corsic*, means a marshy place.

The castle did not always stand in ruins. Once it was a mighty fortress dominating the countryside, and here the lords of Pengersick dwelt. The lords of Pengersick were all warriors: champions who preferred fighting in wars than tending their flocks and herds, or tilling the soil, or even digging for tin.

It is said that the last lord of Pengersick was named Gwavas, because he had a wintery countenance and lived a lonely life. One day Gwavas Pengersick, tired of the fact that there were no wars in the land, nor had been for some time, betook himself beyond the seas to find a war. He fought such a war in a far eastern land called Paganyeth, where the people worshipped a strange god called Termagaunt. The land was rich and this was the cause of the war, because some people had more gold than others and each fought to rob their neighbours of what they had. It was ruled by an old king called the Gwelhevyn.

Suffice to say that the lord of Pengersick chose the side of the Gwelhevyn simply because he was offered more gold for his services than the side of the lawless bandits who were robbing the land. The main point in this was that he fell in love with a beautiful princess of the country called Berlewen, that is "morning star". She was the daughter of the Gwelhevyn. Gwavas, lord of Pengersick, wanted to carry the princess back to the kingdom of Cornwall.

It is said that Berlewen would not have minded this, for she returned the love of the lord of Pengersick. However, Berlewen was betrothed to Prince Cadarn the Strong, a neighbouring prince. Because she was betrothed, the Gwelhevyn had his daughter, Berlewen, watched and guarded each moment of the day, for he was anxious for his daughter's honour. He did not want anything to disrupt the forthcoming marriage, as it was advantageous to his kingdom, and it was known that Cadarn the Strong was a very jealous man.

However, the lord of Pengersick was not without cunning. He found a means to visit Berlewen in the dead of night without anyone discovering him. Berlewen and her lover passed many happy hours together. Eventually, the lord Pengersick had to return home, for he had been away a long time and he was worried in case his castle and estates might have fallen to his enemies. Over the years he had been a warrior, he had made several enemies who would have liked to take their revenge on him. So he took his leave of Berlewen, promising to return as soon as he could. As he left, she took off her gold finger ring and broke it in half. One half she kept while the other she gave to him.

"If you do not return soon, I will try to find a way of following you to your castle in the distant kingdom of Cornwall," she said. "By this half-ring, you will remember your love in this far country."

Gwavas, lord of Pengersick, took the half-ring and swore by all that was sacred to him, and to Berlewen, that if he could not return, then he would wait for her and wait for seven years, during which time he would look at no other woman.

If, after seven years, she had not come to Castle Pengersick, he would know that she would never come to him.

As the lord of Pengersick was on his journey home, Berlewen gave birth to a child. A son.

When the lord of Pengersick returned home, it was not long before Berlewen was just a distant memory. Such is often the nature of soldiers. One day he went to Helston, which was then a very different place from what it is today. There was an old palace there in which dwelt a rich family. You see, Helston was then called Henliston, which means in Cornish *hen* (old), *lis* (court) *ton* (meadow) and thus was called the "old court of the meadow". Dwelling in this place was a lady called Hyviu, whose father had been a great druid, although he was now dead. Hyviu had some of her father's abilities and, moreover, she was very wealthy.

The lord of Pengersick courted her and, forgetting his oath, married her. Not long passed before Gwavas, lord of Pengersick, grew dissatisfied. He disliked the peaceful life that he and his lady Hyviu lived. Then news came of new wars in the distant land of the Gwelhevyn. He announced one day that he would return there. So he set out.

He found that Berlewen had succeeded her father and become the Gwelhevyn or ruler of her kingdom, and now the war that was being fought was against Prince Cadarn the Strong because she had refused to marry him. The lord of Pengersick enlisted in Berlewen's service, although he took good care not to tell her about Hyviu, his wife at home in Cornwall. In the joy of his arrival back in her land, Berlewen did not tell the lord of Pengersick that she had given him a son. There would be plenty of time after Cadarn the Strong had been defeated.

Now Berlewen presented the lord of Pengersick with an enchanted sword, a magic weapon, *Cledha Ruth* or the Red Sword. She said that it would bring success and invincibility to its rightful possessor. She made him general of her army and came to fight by his side.

It happened that, in spite of the *Cledha Ruth* and his warrior's eye, the army of Pengersick and Berlewen was defeated by the hordes of Cadarn the Strong. We may know that if the *Cledha Ruth* only gave invincibility to its rightful owner, then the lord of Pengersick was not so considered, because he had lied about his wife in Cornwall.

In the heat of the battle, Pengersick and Berlewen lost sight of each other. After the battle, Pengersick could not find her and, being defeated and having no cause to stay to be captured and executed by Cadarn, the lord of Pengersick took to his ship and sailed for home, without giving Berlewen a second thought. With him, he took the *Cledha Ruth*.

Berlewen, however, had escaped, took her small child, and found her way to one of her galleys on the coast. So she gave orders to the captain to find the land of Cornwall and the Castle Pengersick, knowing that if her lover had escaped the carnage, that would be where she would find him.

Meanwhile, lord Pengersick had arrived at his castle and found Hyviu, his wife, had given birth to a child in his absence. The boy, who was called Marec, was nursing at her breast. Pengersick told her off for not telling him that she was pregnant before he left for the war. She assured him that she had not been sure and feared to raise false hopes. So, once more, Pengersick settled in his castle.

Then, one cruel windswept night, there was a knock on the castle doors.

Berlewen stood there with a baby in her arms. The lord of Pengersick was alone that night, for Hyviu had gone to Helston with her child to visit her old palace.

The lord of Pengersick was amazed to see Berlewen with a child at his door.

"This is the child of our love," Berlewen announced.

Now Pengersick was guilty and his guilt made him fearful and angry.

"Stupid woman, how dare you follow me? I have been wed these many years and am already father to a boy child."

"Oh, cruel man!" cried Berlewen, aghast. "Even overlooking what has been between us, do you spurn your own son and turn me from your door, when I am alone and needy in this strange land of yours?"

Now Pengersick was fearful at her raised voice, and scared that his servants might overhear and tell his wife. So he drew her away from the castle gates and led her down towards the cliffs, in spite of the roaring and howling of the wind. He explained to her that he was taking her to a place where he would provide for her, in order to make her come away from the castle.

When they reached the cliff top, he turned and handed her a small purse with a few gold pieces in.

"You must return home," he told her.

"Faithless lover, you perjured your soul to me," cried Berlewen. "Thief who took the *Cledha Ruth* from me, on which the safety of my kingdom rested, for we would not have been defeated had you rightly possessed it."

"Go home, go back to your kingdom," cried Pengersick, anger rising in him in response to his increasing guilt.

"Alas, cruel man, I have no kingdom. Because of you, I have disgraced my people and lost them their freedom. For that, you will no longer flourish in this land. May evil meet you and bad luck follow you to the sorrowful end of your days!"

In a fury, he turned on her and threw her and the baby in her arms over the cliff top, spinning down into the restless sea below. Then he returned to his castle and told no one.

As dawn came up, the captain of the vessel which had transported Berlewen to Cornwall, which was standing offshore waiting for her return from Praa Sands, saw the body of his queen floating on the sea and on her breast was her tiny baby, fast asleep but well and happy. The captain consigned Berlewen's body to the depths and took the baby back to his own country and to his wife, where it was reared as his own son. Prince Cadarn now ruled the land and the boy would be in constant danger if the cruel prince knew that the boy was the rightful Gwelhevyn. Thus he was raised in secret.

As the days went by, Gwavas, lord of Pengersick, became moody and angry. He took to hunting wolves, which were numerous in Cornwall then. Whenever he went out to hunt, he would strap the *Cledha Ruth* to his side, for he was under the delusion that it still made him invincible. One day, he was chasing a wolf over Tregonning Hill and so hard in the chase was he that he failed to notice that night had come down and a great storm arisen. He had to pause and dismount on the hill, hoping that the great storm would pass. In the glaring white light of the lightning stroke, he saw a number of savage beasts gathering and in their midst was a large white hare, whose eyes glowed with coals of fire. The wild beasts began to howl and Pengersick's horse reared, lashed out and thundered away into the night.

The next day, when Pengersick had not returned to his castle, his steward, Gillis, had a search made. The lord of the castle was found on Tregonning Hill, more dead than alive. He no longer wore the *Cledha Ruth* buckled to his side. He was carried home and nursed by Hyviu, who used all the arts she had at her command. Slowly he recovered but, while healthy in body, he was not healthy in his mind. He was brooding and angry. He had lost the *Cledha Ruth*, the magic sword. And, in his heart, he knew that the white hare was nothing else but the vengeful spirit of Berlewen. He changed into a coward who dreaded to go beyond his castle gate and his gold was spent on bodyguards and on a druid to protect him from the evils of the Otherworld.

Yet every time he thought it safe to venture forth, with or without his bodyguards and druid, he saw the great white hare. Indeed, no one but himself could see this hare: not his druid nor his bodyguard.

The lord of Pengersick soon grew into a perverted and cruel man whose treatment of his wife Hyviu was the talk of all Cornwall. Indeed, her days were shortened by his manner and she grew sad, sick and ill and died, leaving her child Marec. Knowing that Pengersick cared nothing for the child, in her dying moments, Hyviu sent the faithful Gillis, the steward, to bring to her bedside her old nurse, who had married a local miller. The nurse had given birth late in life and her son Utar was still at her breast. Hyviu asked the nurse to take Marec also. So Hyviu died and the miller's wife shared her breast between Marec and her own son, Utar.

So the sad years passed, sorrowfully for those who dwelt in the shadow of Castle Pengersick. The lord of the castle seldom ventured forth and lived almost entirely alone. Only a few old servants, who remembered him as a strapping youthful hero, riding forth to war, remained within the gloomy halls of the castle. Among them was Gillis, the steward, who cared for his master out of duty to all the lords of Pengersick that had gone before and in the hope that Marec, the legitimate heir to Castle Pengersick, would one day come into his inheritance.

Twenty years passed. Marec had grown into a fine youth and master of all manly sports. His constant companion was Utar, his foster-brother. They became famous for their daring. Often they would steer their boat to the rocks offshore to rescue sailors in distress, when other men feared to leave the shore. Marec also had a reputation for taming wild horses, caught in the hills. He was a fine horseman and skilled in all the equestrian arts.

It was at this time that Gwavas, the lord of Pengersick, began to recover something of his lost courage and he ventured forth and began to renew his acquaintances in the land. His old friend, the lord of Godolphin, invited him to his castle and he found that Godolphin had a beautiful young daughter. Pengersick thought that if his son Marec could marry the daughter of Godolphin, it would be an auspicious match, for there was no heir at Godolphin and it would mean that the domains of Pengersick and Godolphin would become one great estate.

It so happened that the idea was not displeasing to the young daughter of Godolphin, because she had seen Marec, watching him playing hurley and win at wrestling and racing horses.

But there was one problem. Marec did not like the daughter of Godolphin. Indeed, he was rather afraid of her, for it was rumoured that she was a sorceress. The whisper throughout the countryside was that she was intimate with the witch of Fraddam, whose niece, Venna, was her favourite maidservant. Further, it was said, the two women would spend a great deal of time concocting potions and distilling herbs. Some people went so far as to say that the daughter of Godolphin had the evil eye, and they would avert their gaze and hold out forked fingers to her whenever she passed.

Since Marec himself cared nothing for her, it happened that

the lord of Pengersick was courting her more than his son. So it was Pengersick, who still retained some of his youthful ruggedness in spite of the ravages of time and fortune, who married the daughter of Godolphin. It was said by some that the daughter of Godolphin, realizing that she could not get near Marec in any other way, thought the role of stepmother to him was a better relationship than none at all. One of the conditions of her marriage, however, was that she and her children should inherit the lands of Pengersick in preference to Marec. Of all the servants in the castle, Gillis, the steward, suspected the intentions of the new wife of his master, and decided to keep a careful eye on her.

Time passed. The daughter of Godolphin soon grew bored with her morose and elderly husband, and the isolation of Castle Pengersick. Marec and his companion seldom visited the castle, preferring always to be hunting or visiting at other palaces. Neither was there any sign of her becoming pregnant. This vexed the lady Pengersick and one day she called Venna, her maidservant, and asked for some advice. Venna went to her aunt, the witch of Fraddam.

When she returned, she said this: "My aunt says that you are to seek out Marec and invite him here and be kind to him. The kinder you are, he and his comrade might visit more regularly and cheer you in your solitude."

"Marec!" snapped the daughter of Godolphin. "He is an uncouth boy who would rather chase hounds and ride wild horses than pass an hour in a lady's bower. As for his companion Utar, why, he is only a miller's son and not fit for my company."

But Venna, the witch's niece, knowing what her mistress truly felt about Marec, promised that she would prepare a potion which, if Marec took it, would soon turn him into her humble slave who would pine for her love.

So it came about that Marec was invited to a dinner, on the pretext that he should repair the relationship between his father and his father's new bride. Marec came and Venna, who waited on the table, was able to slip the potion into his drink.

Now it so happened that Venna, in her eagerness to please

her mistress, had forgotten one important thing. The potion had to be given by the person who wanted the attention of him to whom it was given. So Marec turned love-sick eyes on Venna, who was a comely enough young girl. And Marec, as was the custom with youths in that day, pressed Venna to share a drink from his wine, so that she, too, flustered as she was, was forced to wet her lips and the tip of her tongue with the potion. It was a strong potion and it was enough to make her immediately forget her duty to her mistress; she went strolling on the sea shore with Marec where they dallied in amorous embraces.

Now the lady Pengersick's love for Marec turned to hatred and her hatred into vengeance.

Next morning, over breakfast, she told the lord of Pengersick that she wanted to return to Castle Godolphin, because she was pining for fresh air. Pengersick pointed out that there was plenty of fresh air in his castle but she answered coyly that she dared not leave her room, because his son Marec was about the castle, and she went in fear of being insulted by his ungentlemanly behaviour. By subtle hints, she gave old Pengersick to understand that Marec had discovered a passion for her and was trying to make her unfaithful to his father.

Gwavas, the lord of Pengersick, raged and raved and swore that his upstart son would suffer banishment before many hours were passed.

"He does not deserve that, my lord," smiled the daughter of Godolphin. "He cannot help his ardours."

"Nevertheless, I shall have him removed from this house and put so far away that it would be years before he found his way back here."

"Let him tarry here a while longer," said his young wife. "But remember that I warned you of his intentions, so that if anything happens in future you may be prepared."

Having planted this seed of distrust between the old lord Pengersick and Marec, Godolphin's daughter went straight to Venna's room. The maidservant had returned and she grabbed the luckless girl and was about to thrust a knife into her breast, vowing to make her heart pour forth its life-blood that moment for her treachery. It so happened that Venna had already come to her senses, only having wet her lips and tongue with the potion and not drunk it. So its effects had worn off.

"Have patience, my dear mistress," cried the girl. "You may plunge your dagger into my heart, if you wish, but first let me explain what happened."

Venna then told her mistress what had befallen her and that it was all a mistake. There was another way in which the lady Pengersick might now gain Marec's love. If she could induce him into the garden in the dead of night and climb the outer stair to her chamber, Venna would then make certain arrangements. The daughter of Godolphin listened carefully and approved the plan.

The plan was to poison the lord of Pengersick that very evening at dinner for, having excited him to jealousy against Marec, they realized that he might have him abducted or sent from the country or even killed before they could act.

What they did not realize was that their plan was overheard by Gillis, the steward. Gillis had long suspected the daughter of Godolphin and it was his custom to keep a wary eye upon her and her maidservant, Venna. There were many secret passages in Pengersick Castle, and such places were known only to Gillis, who had frequented them while the lords of Pengersick had forgotten these mysterious hiding holes. Thus it was that the faithful servant overheard the diabolical plan.

That evening, as was his custom, he stood behind his master's chair to attend to his wants. The hall was dimly lit and the fading twilight was only enhanced by the sparkle from the fire on the hearth. In this twilight, while the daughter of Godolphin was suggesting that it was high time that the lamps were lit, Gillis managed to remove his lord's glass of wine, which he knew had been prepared with poison, and switch it with the lady Pengersick's glass of wine.

It happened that the poisoned draught had little effect on her, because she had long accustomed herself to imbibing poison in increasing doses, until she could withstand a quantity which would be fatal to anyone else. This custom she had started in order to guard against attempts to poison her because, as we have already said, she was feared and disliked by those who accused her of being a sorceress. So she felt only a slight discomfiture and nothing else.

When supper was over, Gillis went to search for Marec and warn him of the entire plan.

Marec, meeting the daughter of Godolphin in the corridor, showed his loathing.

"Know this, woman, I detest you and your shameful intentions. Know also that you can neither hurt me by your witchcraft nor with the blight of your evil eyes."

In anger, she hurried directly to the lord of Pengersick and told him that his son had grossly insulted her.

"Indeed, my lord, frail woman that I am, I had to defend myself with all my might to preserve my honour even to the point that I had to threaten to plunge a dagger into Marec's heart until he desisted and left my bower."

Her fabrications so incensed the lord of Pengersick that he decided to dispose of his son without another day's delay.

That evening, the wind rose across the sea and a storm blew in from the east. Marec and Utar were walking on the shore and saw a vessel in trouble on the sea.

"She will be on the rocks in a moment," observed Utar.

The two young men did not delay but went down to the shore and launched their boat, rowing towards the endangered vessel with all their might. As they drew near, they were able to warn the vessel of the approaching rocks. Thus they saved the vessel and turned back towards the shore.

Now a sudden sea mist had come down and they could scarcely make out the shore. Out of the mist they saw something floating in the water. They rowed nearer and found a sailor, exhausted, and near to drowning. They pulled him on board and Marec realized that they had only just saved him.

They rowed back to the shore and bore him to Marec's chamber, where they removed his wet clothing, rubbed him dry and placed him in sheepskins. They dropped brandy in his mouth and gradually restored him to warmth. Finally, the man fell into a deep sleep of exhaustion.

In the morning, he was awake and well and thanking his rescuers when they told him how they had taken him exhausted from the sea.

The seaman told them his name was Arluth and recalled that he had fallen from the swaying masthead of his ship into the sea. He had tried to keep himself afloat and endeavoured to raise his voice and shout for help. But no one had noticed his fall and he had despaired of ever being picked up. He said that his father was the captain of a ship from the east, which frequently traded at Cornish ports. He feared his father would be in great distress, fearing him drowned, and he wondered how he could find a sea-going ship which would catch up with his father's vessel.

Marec and Utar found him clothes, for he was a young man like themselves, and also provided him with a good breakfast.

"We will find a ship, such as you seek, at Marazion. There is a market there, Maraghas Yow, or Tuesday's Market. That is where we shall go."

So they set out over Tregonning Hill with the sailor riding one of the hunters from the Pengersick stable. As they passed over the hill, a strange thing happened. The hunter suddenly took off, as if chasing hounds. At the top of the hill, a sudden thick mist descended and the horse reared in fright and threw its rider. The sailor, unused to riding, was thrown to the ground and winded. He sat up and looked about. He found himself alone in a thick mist.

He moved towards some rocks. He was startled when a sudden flash of lightning came out of nowhere and split the rock asunder. Arluth reeled backwards. Then it seemed a voice came out of the depths of the rock.

"Fear not, Arluth, beloved son of mine," came a sweet feminine voice. "Fear not, but seize the sword of your ancestors and win back the kingdom that is rightfully yours."

There was no one near him and he looked round in astonishment. Near the rock which had been split sat a great white hare, which gazed lovingly upon him and then turned and disappeared into the crack made by the lightning. He went to the rocks, still puzzled, and where they had been severed, he found a naked sword with sparkling jewels in the hilt. It was, of course, the *Cledha Ruth*, the Red Sword.

Having recovered from his surprise, he picked up the sword. All at once the mist disappeared and he glanced up and saw Marec and Utar nearby, obviously in the process of looking for him. They held his horse with them. He told them what had happened and Marec and Utar were amazed. Now Marec, inheriting some of his mother's wisdom, for she had been the daughter of a druid, said that Arluth had discovered a magic weapon, which meant that he was destined to achieve great things.

Arluth, however, was more concerned in finding his father and the ship's company, who would think of him as dead. So they continued on to Marazion, to the great market there. In Marazion harbour, there was the very ship which had nearly been wrecked on the previous night. It was the very ship that Marec and Utar had saved and the very ship from which Arluth had been cast overboard.

However, Marec and Utar did not want thanks and so left their new friend, Arluth, to go his way while they returned home to Pengersick. Once on board, Arluth greeted the captain as his father. There was great joy on the old captain's face and those of his crew, for poor Arluth had been given up as dead. After they had all celebrated, Arluth told his father the tale of his rescue by Marec and Utar and how he had discovered the sword.

The captain's face grew sad as he examined the *Cledha Ruth*. "The time has come to tell you the truth, my boy. I am not your father. I am no kin to you that I know. However, I served your mother, Berlewen, the Gwelhevyn of our sad land. She was murdered by your father, whom she had trusted. Indeed, she had trusted him with this sword of power and he had deceived her, and thus she lost her kingdom to Cadarn the Strong."

"Who, then, is my father?" demanded Arluth in wonder.

"My son," said the old captain, "I feel that I must call you son still, though I am only a poor captain and you are, truly, a great prince . . ."

"I would have it no other way," insisted Arluth, "for you

are the only father I have known. But I must know who is responsible for the murder of my mother."

"So you shall. Your half-brother is Marec, the young lord of Pengersick. The same young man who you now tell me rescued you from the sea. The other was his foster-brother, Utar the miller's son."

When Arluth went to speak, the old man held up a hand. "No blame to him. His mother was likewise betrayed and driven to an early grave by the father you share. That same man still plots the death of Marec, his own son."

Arluth shook his head in bewilderment. "This must not be."

"It is true, but your duty now lies in returning to your land, the land of Berlewen, now that you have the magic sword which will overcome Cadarn the Strong. You must liberate your people."

"I cannot leave Marec and Utar if they are in danger. They saved my life and now I must save their lives."

"It is your duty to save your kingdom, which has been for so long rent by civil war and with no one powerful enough to overthrow the tyrant Prince Cadarn. You must take the magic sword and return," insisted the old sea captain.

Coincidence is an amazing thing. It was while the old captain and Arluth were thus engaged that none other than Gwavas, the lord of Pengersick, came on board and demanded to see the captain.

When they heard who it was, Arluth hid in a closet and the captain invited the old lord into his cabin.

Pengersick came straight to the point of his journey. He offered a large sum of money to the captain if he and his crew would kidnap Marec and Utar, who he said were a youth and his servant who were lazy and plotting to take his castle from him. He asked the captain to take them to an eastern land and sell them as slaves. For that he would be well rewarded.

The captain, in his rage, fell on old Pengersick and threw him off the ship before he realized that he could have used the coincidence to his advantage and the advantage of Arluth. However, righteous indignation won the day over subtle scheming.

Angered, the lord Pengersick went to the next ship whose captain had no scruples and, indeed, a deal was struck.

It was when they saw lord Pengersick coming from that ship with an evil smile on his face, that the old captain turned to Arluth and expressed his regret. "Had I but thought of it in time, we could have taken the evil lord Pengersick and given him a taste of the sea instead of his son."

Arluth nodded thoughtfully. "He has persuaded the other captain to take Marec and Utar as slaves and sell them in some distant land. Send one of our crew to mix with the crew of the other vessel, and see what plans are afoot."

The crewman eventually reported back that the plan was that at dawn, when Marec and Utar went fishing in their small boat, the slave-ship crew would head off by longboat and attack them, with the view of taking them prisoners.

Arluth ordered that some of the crew arm themselves and make ready in their own longboat. As soon as it was twilight, they saw a raiding party leaving the slave-vessel in their boat. Arluth urged his men to strike out after them and he unloosed the *Cledha Ruth*, which he now wore strapped in a scabbard at his side.

"May the gods be my guide, for I will use this magic sword to save my brother and foster-brother."

The boat of Arluth gave chase. They were not able to catch up with the slave-ship until after the slavers had captured Marec and Utar and had them bound. But it was only a moment later when Arluth and his men rammed the slave-vessel and came board. The victory over the slavers was easy and every evil one of them paid the price of his folly.

Marec and Utar were surprised to see their companion of the previous night, and even more surprised when Arluth told them what the old lord of Pengersick had intended for them. He told them to come away back to the old captain's ship and sail with him. The only thing he did not tell them was that he, too, was the son of the lord of Pengersick.

"Come with me and never more put foot in this evil place whilst your crafty stepmother's head is above ground," he urged.

Marec felt that he could not leave without taking with him

something of what rightfully belonged to him, for he and Utar were without any money or resources to make their way in the world.

"Don't touch anything in that accursed castle," Arluth instructed. "I'll tell you why. We go to a distant land to the east. There you have a brother, Marec. A brother who will give you gold, silver and share his last coin with you. He would shed his heart's blood for your safety. This brother of yours will soon be king in that country to which we go. Neither you nor Utar will want for anything. My word on it."

Marec and Utar were astonished at how assertive Arluth was.

"We shall seek out this brother of mine," agreed Marec, "but I wish that gods would grant that you were my brother, Arluth. I would more willingly go with you to any land." Marec was greatly fond of the young sailor.

Utar nodded agreement. "And I. I will go willingly, even now, without a brother to look after me."

"You have your foster-brother," Arluth pointed out. "And, in me, you have another foster-brother."

The three young men then swore allegiance to each other which neither men nor gods would break.

The old captain welcomed Marec and Utar on his ship and they set sail eastwards. And it fell to the old captain to tell of the adventures of lord Pengersick when he was younger and how it was that Arluth was his son. They all embraced now and swore again that they would fight for Arluth's kingdom.

On the high seas they met the slave-ship, whose captain had agreed to kidnap Marec and Utar, and Arluth led a boarding party, killing the slavers and rescuing the enslaved, who willingly agreed to form a new crew and come with Arluth to fight for the freedom of his country. Arluth took command of the new ship, with Marec as his mate and Utar with them. So now the two ships made sail for the lost kingdom of Berlewen.

In Pengersick Castle, the old lord Pengersick was told that his son and Utar had been out that morning fishing. Neither had returned but their empty boat had been washed ashore with blood in it. Gillis, the steward, who brought the news, was greatly distressed, for he knew that his master had been on board two eastern vessels the day before, and that both had sailed.

Now it was that Gillis came before the lord Pengersick and his lady and accused them of destroying Marec and Utar or worse. The daughter of Godolphin he accused of conspiring with her maidservant, Venna, to destroy not only her stepson but her husband as well. Venna was summoned and, to save herself, she turned against her mistress and confessed all. Old lord Pengersick, realising how he had been fooled, ordered both women to be thrown into the deepest dungeon at Pengersick. Then he mounted his horse and rode in haste to Marazion in search of the slave-ship which he had hired.

It is curious but he felt some link of blood kinship to his son, even though he had sought his death and ordered his kidnapping. Finding the vessel had sailed and finding no other ship to go after it, he rode back to Pengersick at nightfall in a drunken rage, fuelled by his remorse and guilt. He fully determined that at dawn, his wife, the daughter of Godolphin would hang from the tallest tower of the castle and by her side would be her maidservant Venna.

As he rode along the coast road on his hunter, there sprang from a thicket a great white hare, with flaming coals for eyes. It leapt straight into the face of his horse. The horse, terrified, turned and galloped towards the cliff top, and in seeking to escape the pursuing hare, leapt over the cliffs, down into the turbulent seas.

That was the last anyone saw in this world of Gwavas, the lord of Pengersick.

Now it happened that the daughter of Godolphin was rescued from her dungeon by her father's servants. She had developed a scaly leprous skin; some said it was the result of taking her own poison, others that it was some contagion from the dungeon, while others that it was a retribution for her evil life. None wished to look upon her and so her father had her shut in a dark chamber of Godolphin Castle, where no one would gaze on her.

As for Venna, she used magic arts and escaped back to her aunt, the witch of Fraddam.

Gillis told the people of Pengersick how his master had confessed how he had disposed of Marec, his son, and Utar. The people gave them up for lost, thinking them sold to some slave market far in the east. But Gillis refused to believe that there would be no lords left in Pengersick, and so he took care of everything. He looked after the castle and spent frugally, hoping to use the money to pay a ransom for Marec's release if he could be found alive.

Far to the east, Arluth's ships approached the shores of Paganyeth. It was noticed that, since setting sail from the coast of Cornwall, a beautiful great white bird had followed them all the way. It had often come within bowshot, but no one had dared to aim a shift at it for sailors, being superstitious folk, believed it to be the spirit of a seafarer who followed to keep them from harm. And during this voyage, Marec and Utar used to listen to all the tales of Paganyeth, which Arluth and the old captain would tell them to pass the long hours of the voyage.

On arrival in the country, they found it in great disorder, racked by wars. Few people liked the harsh rule of Cadarn the Strong. The old captain began to tell people of the birth of Arluth, and of his recovery of the *Cledha Ruth*, and soon people began to flock to his standard until he had a fair-sized army. He was proclaimed the Gwelhevyn, rightful ruler of Paganyeth.

Soon, indeed, did Arluth topple Cadarn the Strong, who died under the bright flashing blows of the *Cledha Ruth*. In truth, however, Arluth, while a good king, would have preferred the command of a good ship at sea than the cares of running his kingdom. Indeed, he regulated his rule as if he were a captain of a ship and saw to it that there were no idle hands in his kingdom, that stores were gathered and the kingdom was well provisioned.

Arluth wanted his brother, Marec, and Utar, to live with him in the palace and be his *Cusulyer* or chief advisers. But Marec had heard from the old captain that there was a part of the kingdom, high up in the mountains in a small corner, in which a people dwelt called the Pystryoryon, who were wizards of great skill and learning. He ardently desired to visit their country and learn what he could of their arts and so Arluth, with some regret, provided him with horses and warriors to go and seek them out. Utar, of course, went with him.

Marec remained a long while with the Pystryoryon, studying with them and learning many curious things. While he was there, he fell in love and married the daughter of their chieftain, a lady named Skentoleth. She was as accomplished as she was beautiful. Utar married her chief handmaiden. For some years, Marec and Utar dwelt happily in their land.

Now the old captain had returned on a voyage to Cornwall, to Marazion. He had discovered that Gwavas, the old lord of Pengersick, was dead, that the daughter of Godolphin was incarcerated in her room at Castle Godolphin and that Castle Pengersick was being looked after by the faithful Gillis, longing for the day when he might have word of Marec. Further, the old captain heard that the people of the estates of Pengersick wished for Marec's return to his rightful place and were willing to pay a ransom for that return.

When Marec heard this, his heart yearned to return to Cornwall, to his own people. He told Skentoleth all about his land to the west under the setting sun. He warmed as he told her about this land and praised its climate, its inhabitants and scenery.

"I have a strong and beautiful castle by the sea, with a green valley beyond where I will build you a bower by the murmuring shore, and where you may wander in tranquil gardens and your pleasure will be my will."

"Say no more, sweet husband," smiled Skentoleth. "As great as the delights of your land are, I would heed them not when you are by me. Your home is my home, wherever you choose to dwell. Whatever pleases you is my will. When do we depart for the west?"

So it was decided that Marec and Skentoleth and Utar and his lady would leave for Cornwall. Marec ensured that he took many books of great learning from the country of the Pystryoryon. On their way back, they stayed with Arluth, the Gwelhevyn, and his grateful brother sent seven ships to accompany him, all loaded with great bales of brocade, pearls, precious stones, gold and silver and spices from the east and so many precious things that the telling of them made people weary.

Soon this rich fleet came in sight of Cornwall and sailed for Pengersick. Marec and Utar's hearts leapt as they saw Trewavas Head and their fleet beat along the shoreline, coming into the great bay between Rinsey Head and Hoe Point. There was the great stretch of Praa Sands, with Pengersick Castle up on the hill beyond.

When the young lord of Pengersick landed with his beautiful bride and the news was spread, everyone rushed down to the shore to greet him. Bonfires were set alight on every hill to the north, east and west, and weeks were spent in feasting at Pengersick. No one could remember a time when the brooding castle had been so alive with laughter and good music. For days, contests were held in the castle grounds: contests of archery, hurling, slinging and wrestling. Minstrels and bards of all degree and description entertained.

The Lady Skentoleth was delighted in her new home and fell to with a will, learning the pleasant language of Cornwall. In the morning she would accompany Marec on the hunt, riding over the moor and hills with a hawk on her wrist or a bow in her hand. In the evening, people would flock to hear her playing the *telyn*, or harp. Such sweet music was never heard and beyond Praa Sands, in the bay, even the dolphins gathered to bask and play to its joyous strains; even fishermen, out to catch the shoals, would rest their oars and listen; even the sea birds, forgetting their hunting tasks, would seek rest and stand entranced around the castle.

The Lady Skentoleth brought joy where there had been suffering and brooding evil, for she was kind and generous and ignorant of fraud or flattering and told people truly, treating them as she found them.

Marec set to work to build the bower he promised, building two lofty towers united by a gallery on the seaside of his castle. He laid out a pleasant garden and took pleasure in improving his great castle and chasing away the ghosts that had dwelt there before.

But ghosts are strong.

Soon after Marec had returned, the daughter of Godolphin, his erstwhile scheming stepmother, had fretted herself to death in her dark chamber in Castle Godolphin. No sooner had the breath left her body than her unquiet spirit returned to Pengersick to haunt the rooms which she had formerly occupied. The howling and wailing of her ghost could be heard throughout the castle.

The young lord of Pengersick, in desperation, had that part of the castle buildings razed to the ground, but the hideous ghost continued to wander the place. So it was that Marec turned to the great books of learning and lore which he had brought with him from the wizards of the Pystryoryon. Using the forbidden knowledge of those books he captured the unquiet spirit and imprisoned it in the body of a large *nader*, a viperous snake, which he further imprisoned in a hole on the headland of Hoe Point. So beware, walking the Point, for the large adder is often seen there, even to this day, for spirits never die.

Because of that success, the young lord of Pengersick grew more and more attached to his books of magic lore. He became obsessed, indeed impassioned, by the pursuit of forbidden knowledge and time changed his character. The years passed and he was seldom seen outside his castle. He often locked himself in a tower-room for weeks on end. He could never be approached by anyone except Skentoleth or Utar and his lady, all of whom often assisted him in his experiments.

It was rumoured that he sought how to turn base metals into gold and silver and had prepared an alchemist fire which burnt all day and all night, having been lit by sparks drawn down from the sun by means of a magic crystal. It was said that, with this same crystal, he could view the events that were taking place in many distant lands.

Marec no longer paid attention to his farms and estates, which were left to Utar's management. Nor, indeed, was Marec particularly bothered, for through his magic he could now obtain riches in abundance. Then he found the ultimate forbidden knowledge. He was able to make a magic elixir, the *eva hep deweth*, which made him immortal, preserving his youthful vigour. He gave the drink to Skentoleth, and to Utar and his lady.

So Marec began to earn a reputation as the most powerful wizard in all Cornwall and he became a figure of fear. Everyone began to avoid Castle Pengersick. It was recalled that his mother had been the daughter of a druid, and this was why he had taken so obsessively to his enchantments.

It came about that a thief from Germoe, not far from Pengersick, who was reinforced by drink, one day tried to steal a sheep from the castle lands. Marec saw the thief taking the sheep, by means of his magic crystal, and with his formidable knowledge he transported the thief onto Praa Sands, where he could not move and he was forced to remain there all night with the incoming tide washing around him and coming to his bottom lip, so the man was in fear of drowning. Marec released him from the spell the next morning and gave him the very sheep the man had sought to steal, with the admonition never to covet the goods of the lord of Pengersick again.

As Marec's reputation grew, an old antagonist heard of him – Venna, who had once dallied with Marec on Praa Sands under the influence of the love potion she had administered and also tasted. When she heard about Marec, she found there was still some emotion in her heart for him. She now dwelt at St Hillary Downs. Like Marec, she had learnt the secret of immortality, but by a different means.

She enticed young women to the cave in which she dwelt and, by means of her wicked craft, she drew their life's vigour into her body. They withered and died while she grew ever younger.

Now people went to Marec and told him of this. He was basically a good man, in spite of his changing character. So he challenged Venna to meet him in a magical conflict. One night when she was brewing her hell-broth, by which she intended to poison Marec, and with the flames rising higher and higher under the cauldron, Marec caused her door and windows to be sealed by magic means so that she could not escape. Then he caused a clod of turf to fly up onto her chimney pot. The infernal vapour from her hell-fire caused her to choke to death.

Local people started to be alarmed by Marec's growing reputation. They heard he conjured spirits in unknown tongues, that he commanded unruly spirits who did his will and sometimes appeared in explosive clouds of smoke with pungent, fiery vapours. Several times, the people came to Skentoleth and asked her to intervene with her husband and subdue the fiery demons or play her *telyn*, as she had in the old days, and drive away their evil power by the beauty of her music.

Many years passed. The people grew old and died but the lord of Pengersick and his wife and Utar and his wife remained ever young. They had a great and numerous family. Their children spread throughout the world to seek their fortunes. When their children had children of their own, and their children had children of their own, the lady Skentoleth grew tired of an existence in the world in which all she had known was long dead and gone. She turned to Marec and begged him not to keep prolonging their life – for, every twenty-one years, they had to drink his elixir, the *eva hep deweth*. But the lord of Pengersick, while still young and virile to outward appearances, had grown old and ill-tempered and frightened of death. He refused.

So Skentoleth, with great regret for leaving him, pretended to take the elixir at the next appointed time but did not. Within a day, she lay under the sod and her soul went on its long-delayed journey to the Otherworld.

Marec mourned a while, but returned anew to his enchantments.

A prince of Dyfed, hearing of the magician's renown, arrived at Pengersick to seek Marec's advice on a certain matter. While this prince was at Pengersick, he fell in love and married the beautiful great-granddaughter of Marec, whose name was Lamorna. It was this prince of Dyfed who was to be the instrument of the destruction of Marec, lord of Pengersick. For the prince had brought with him a quantity of black stones which were to be found in no other place than Dyfed.

Marec had been seeking the stone for years. He, by means of his alchemy, was able to extract a liquid dark fire from the stones. But he had over-reached himself for, by some accident, in the handling of the liquid fire he placed a wrong vessel for its containment. The fire burst the vessel and instantly a great fire roared through Castle Pengersick. It consumed Marec, it consumed the faithful Utar and his lady, and all the rare books of forbidden knowledge within the castle. No one else was harmed nor hurt by it. But Castle Pengersick became the ruin which you see today.

This is why Marec was the last lord of Pengersick, why the castle has been abandoned and why no one from Germoe to Praa Sands ever ventures in the castle grounds after dark.

28 *The Bukkys*

Long ago, in the town of Carn Kenidjack, there dwelt a man called Tamblyn Trevor. He was a proud man and had a large family, and his pride was that he could support them all. Not for him was the old Cornish proverb: *Yn Haf, porth cof Gwaf* – in summer, remember winter. For he did not save a penny. He doted on all his children and gave them anything they wanted; new clothes and gifts. All were taken care of except one child.

Now that child was his eldest daughter. This daughter was called Blamey. Blamey Trevor remained at home, while her brothers and sisters went playing with the other children. She had to help her mother in the house, with the sewing and with the washing. While all her father's money went on his younger children, there was not a penny to spare for her. But Blamey did not mind and she went about her work, singing like a lark.

Blamey Trevor was a good hard-working girl, but she had one fault, and that fault was curiosity. No one had ever been able to keep a secret from her.

It turned out that, one day, a cousin took pity on Blamey and invited her to stay a few days at their house in the next village. It was then that Blamey took a sight of the beautiful dresses and jewellery for the first time. She went to a dance and saw that others had sweethearts to dance with and good clothes to go courting and fine food to eat, and when her cousin took her to Morvah Fair, she knew that she was going to be dissatisfied with returning to old Tamblyn Trevor's home and doing nothing but work.

When she returned, she began to grumble from sun-up to sun-down, and never gave her mother nor father any peace at all, always complaining about the drudgery in the house. Finally, Tamblyn and his wife agreed that they would allow Blamey to seek her fortune elsewhere and, perhaps, go into the service at the castle of a lord.

Tamblyn and his wife were not bad parents, and so her mother made her new clothes and Tamblyn found a few coins to give the girl. Then the day came for her to depart and Tamblyn warned her never to go near big cities like Penzance, for there were terrible stories of girls being kidnapped and taken on board ship and sold as slaves beyond the seas. He told her how strange sailors came to such places and passed on diseases and other evil things.

So Blamey promised she would avoid Penzance and would find a kindly lord with a big rich castle, where she could work as a maid.

Then her father warned her against certain areas of the country where, among the hills, there dwelt evil witches and small people with magic powers. He told her to avoid going there. And she promised that she would avoid such places and would find a kindly lord with a big rich castle.

Off she went.

But as she climbed the hill overlooking Carn Kenidjack, she felt her heart growing heavy at the idea of leaving home. She looked round at the village and saw the children playing and the smoke rising from the hearths and saw her own home among them. She walked on up the brow of the hill and paused once again for a final look at her home.

Then emotion overcame her and she sat on a rock on the roadside and started to cry.

In the middle of this, she heard a hollow cough.

Before her stood a kindly looking well-dressed gentleman, who peered at her with great concern.

"*Dew roy deth da dheugh-why*!" he greeted in a kindly voice, using the language of Cornwall. "Why are you weeping, young lady?"

Blamey had never been called "lady" in her life, and she felt flattered.

"*Myttyn da*!" she replied respectfully. "I have just left home, and am on the road looking for a kindly lord's castle where I might work and earn my keep."

The gentleman smiled broadly. "Well, luck may be in our way, for I am looking for a maid-servant. I had been told that there were some good servants to be had in Kenidjack, and had left my home early this morning to come and seek one."

Blamey blinked her eyes. Could it be so easy to find a job?

The gentleman sat down on the rock beside the young girl and told her that he had been left a widower with a young baby son to look after. He had an old great-aunt as well, who helped him in the house but did not live there. There he was in the house, without a maid, but there was only one cow and some poultry to look after, so the work would not be arduous.

"What do you say, Blamey Trevor?" he asked. "Why not come along home with me? You look as fresh as the dew in the morning and it will be nice to have you as a maid. At least you could come with me and if you don't like the work, or if another job comes along which you find better, then you can leave my service when you want."

Blamey thought for a moment and wondered how he knew her name, for she had not told him, but other thoughts tumbled into her mind. The gentleman was handsome and spoke kindly and was most courteous to her, and he offered her a job which was most ideal.

Being an honest girl, however, she explained that she had no experience as a domestic servant, save that which she had received in her parents' house.

"I am sure you will do well," he said, apparently not bothered by this fact.

When she told him that she had also often helped with her parents' garden, he seemed more than delighted.

"Then this is excellent. If you had time to spare, I suppose you would not object to helping me pick fruit or weed my garden?"

"There is nothing I would like better," she agreed.

"Then let us start for my home," he said.

So off they went.

On the way, he told her his name was Master Marrack Mayne.

They chatted gaily as they walked and so absorbed did she become that she did not notice the road they took, and only after a while did she realize that she had no recognition of the countryside at all. The road ran through a beautiful wood, but the flowers were strange to her.

"Why, these trees and flowers are nothing to what you will see soon," he told her. "Where I dwell, there are many such flowers and trees."

So on they continued.

"Look, sir!" cried Blamey, spotting a great palace. "Is that where the king dwells?"

Master Marrack Mayne shook his head. "No, no. No king dwells there. There are many such great houses in my land."

So on they went, until they came to a crossroads, where four roads met. They went straight on and came to a spot where a stream crossed the road. Then Master Marrack Mayne lifted her across the stream so that she might not wet her feet.

She had lost all sense of time and it seemed that she had been walking forever, yet she was not tired at all. However, she realized that the sun was setting.

"Are we near your house now?" she asked.

"We are all but come to it," the gentleman assured her.

He helped her over a river, via stepping stones, near the foot of a great towering cairn of grey rocks. Across the river, they went into a beautiful orchard of pears and apples. The trees seemed to be bent down with the weight of the fruit. Along a winding path, through the blossoming trees, they picked their way and then, without her even noticing they had left the garden, they were in an arbour. From the arbour, they stepped into a house, which was lined with beautiful plants and flowers.

In the kitchen were pots and pans of pewter which shone like silver and of fiery copper. A fire blazed in the hearth, even though it was summer time. Seated by it, on a high stool, was a sour looking and primly dressed old woman and she was knitting, her needles going clickity-clack.

"I am home, Aunt Furneth," cried Master Marrack Mayne. "I have found a new maid for us along the way."

The old woman's eyes stared at Blamey in such a way that they seemed to bore right through her. "So I see. Young and silly, no doubt. A girl who will use her tongue more than her hands."

"I will not!" cried Blamey indignantly.

"We shall see," replied the old woman.

"Where is my son?" demanded Master Marrack Mayne.

"Here I am," cried a little boy, skipping into the room. He leapt into his father's arms and kissed him. He was no more than three years old.

"I have brought a maid to look after you, Marrack Vyghan; I hope you like her."

The little boy turned and examined Blamey with a face as cunning as a fox and eyes uncommonly sharp. He examined her as carefully and as critically as the old woman. "Can't say," he said. "Too early."

"Well," said Master Marrack Mayne, "we will show her what is to be done after we have had supper."

Food was brought out and Blamey was invited to sit with them at the table while bread, cheese, apples, honey and many another nice thing was laid out before her. It was the first time that she had nothing to do in preparing a meal. When they rose, Blamey offered to start work and clean the dishes but Aunt Furneth told her to rest until the milking time.

When the time came for milking, Master Marrack Mayne told Blamey to take a pail and go to the meadow by the orchard.

"Call 'Festynneugh! Festynneugh!' and the cow will come to you."

So Blamey took the pail and went off. She looked around the empty meadow and then, feeling rather silly, she called as she had been instructed. "Festynneugh! Festynneugh!" – which meant "hurry up!" Immediately a white cow, whose coat was breathtaking, came out of the woods and walked straight to the pail. Without Blamey doing anything, it put its udder over the pail and showered down the milk so that, in a minute, it was full and almost running over.

Blamey was looking round for another pail when the cow stopped filling it and walked off.

When she returned to the house, she told Master Marrack Mayne about this wonder. He smiled and replied that a single pail would usually do but if Blamey ever wanted more, she must take extra pails with her and the cow would fill them without asking.

"Well," sighed Blamey, "that is a priceless cow you have and no want will come to this house while she is in health."

Then Aunt Furneth took her aside to tell her what she was expected to do.

"There are some things that you must learn here. Marrack Vyghan is always to be put to bed by daylight. As you share the room, you should go to bed at the same time. Never wait for my nephew's return. Do not go into any of the spare rooms. Above all, never go into Master Marrack Mayne's room. Never meddle in anything which is not related to your work. I'll tell you all that you need to know. Do not ask questions of anyone else. Always rise with the sun and take Marrack Vyghan to the stream outside. Wash him and then," she handed Blamey a small ivory box with ointment, "you must put this ointment in his eyes."

"Does he have some illness with his eyes?" the girl asked in concern.

The old woman did not reply to her question but said, "Only put a bit the size of a pin-head in each eye. No more."

Just as she had finished, Master Marrack Mayne came in and said it would not be long before it was dark and Aunt Furneth should be away to her own home.

It was then that Blamey told Master Marrack Mayne that she was not used to going to bed so early. He shrugged.

"Please yourself. Stay up as long as you have a mind to."

He obviously was not so strict as Aunt Furneth. However, he mixed her a drink which, when she took it, made her fall asleep in a blink of an eye and dream, without sorrow, about the home she had left and the brothers and sister she had been separated from.

In the morning, she was up and had completed all the work by the time Aunt Furneth arrived. The old woman looked around her with some disapproval. She was a natural fault-finder and it irritated her not to be able to find fault.

"It is a good start that you have made," the old woman finally conceded. "And you have plenty of time on your hands still."

Then Master Marrack Mayne came in and he was very pleased with what she had done.

"Come with me into the garden. Since you have done all the work about the house, I will show you how to tend the herbs that I grow. I will tell you what you must weed and what you must not touch."

Aunt Furneth showed her disapproval of the suggestion but Master Marrack Mayne took no notice.

Blamey showed she was so adept at gardening that her employer was delighted. He demonstrated his feelings by giving her a hug that night and once more giving her the warm, comforting drink that produced such a pleasant sleep.

Now Blamey was a young girl and this was her first time away from home. She had no experience with young nor old men. She found herself adoring Master Marrack Mayne, and putting herself in the way of pleasing him in every way. And now and again, when Master Marrack Mayne gave her a hug or even a kiss, when she had done something which particularly pleased him, she was almost delirious with happiness.

Aunt Furneth was not so happy. She began to find fault in everything that Blamey did but every time she went to find her, to tell her to do this and that, she found that she was always in the company of her nephew and, as he was so pleased with her, there was nothing she could do. A dislike built up between Aunt Furneth and Blamey and between Blamey and Aunt Furneth.

Even so, Blamey found her new life as a maid very pleasant and she took no account of time. Never once did she ever think of her home, of her mother and father nor her sisters and brothers. It was as if they had never existed. Her sole ambition in life was to please her master, Marrack Mayne. Each night, he would mix her the same pleasant drink which produced drowsiness and pleasant sleep, and she would awake fresh and happy in the morning.

One thing did cross her mind, however. Most mornings he dressed as if he were going hunting, with polished boots and hunting clothes. Blamey ensured the polish of his boots was so well done that they were like mirrors when he put them on. He would mount his great horse and off he would go into the woods that surrounded the house. She tried to follow his path once or twice, for she had a mind to see what the countryside was like beyond the wood and the small meadow adjacent to the house in which the milch cow was kept. But she could never come to the end of the path and always had to return, not having seen the edge of the wood.

When Master Marrack Mayne heard what she had attempted – and, of course, it was Aunt Furneth who had told him – he grew stern and said that she must never, never venture beyond his grounds again. Indeed, he laid down a rule that she should never go beyond the meadow nor beyond the orchard nor beyond his garden ever again while he was away. Furthermore, there was at the end of the meadow, where the cow grazed, a high rock. Blamey must, on no account, attempt to climb that rock for, amidst the thicket surrounding it, there was a hole which some said had no bottom.

It had never occurred to Blamey to go near the rock for, not being a boy, she had never thought to climb rocks in all her life. It now became manifest to her, however, that from the top of the rock one might see all the countryside around. It was as if Master Marrack Mayne suddenly saw the new thought that came into her mind, for he leant close to her and laid his hand on her arm.

"Truly, Blamey, take heed of my warning. That bottomless hole is the home of the Bukkys."

Now Blamey knew that the Bukkys were hobgoblins, evil spirits who delighted in stealing innocent souls to carry off to the dark depths. She shivered slightly and promised to avoid the rock.

Time passed.

One day, after Master Marrack Mayne had left, she grew tired of the same old routine and went down to the meadow. She did not call for the cow to come and give milk, which it invariably did, no matter what time of the day or night it was called. Instead she walked across the meadow to where a silvery little stream ran beside the high rock and she sat down to rest in the sun.

She was dozing there when she heard a voice calling her name softly.

Frowning, she looked up.

Near the high rock stood a short, thin little fellow. For a moment she thought it was young Marrack Vyghan and the little boy was playing tricks.

"Come over here, Blamey. I have a beautiful diamond ring to give you," called the voice.

She started up to fetch him but, as she grew near, she realized that the little figure was that of an adult with dark, diamond-shaped eyes and thin, red lips and sharp white teeth.

It was then she realized what Master Marrack Mayne had told her and, with a scream, she turned and ran as hard as she could back into the house. There she found Aunt Furneth in the kitchen. The old woman glanced at her with total disapproval.

"You have been near the high rock, I can tell. You've only just escaped being carried away by the Bukkys. I am going to tell my nephew of your disobedience to his instructions."

So Blamey waited in trepidation for Master Marrack Mayne's return and wondered how he would react when Aunt Furneth told him. However, her master was not angry.

"We will let this matter pass, as it is the first time you disobeyed me, Blamey." He spoke kindly, for he saw that she was so anxious to please him. That evening, she took her drink once again and in the morning she was happy and feeling pleasantly refreshed.

Aunt Furneth was more irritated with her than ever.

"You would do well to heed my advice, child," she told her.

Blamey, however, grew confident, for nothing she seemed to do displeased Master Marrack Mayne, in spite of the nagging of Aunt Furneth.

So confident did Blamey now become of her position that, one day when Aunt Furneth was in the kitchen and Blamey was upstairs cleaning her room, a thought suddenly occurred to her. She had not followed Furneth's rules, given to her on her first day in the house. In spite of that fact, she had never been chastised for her disobedience. There was only one rule she had strictly kept and that more out of absent-mindedness than anything else. This was the rule which forbade her to go into Master Marrack Mayne's room nor into any of the spare rooms.

Bold she was. She crept along the corridor and reached out to the handle of the master's room and slowly turned it. She peered inside and found she was in a room filled with objects which set her heart pounding in fear. Shelves lined the room and on the shelves were rows of men's heads and shoulders – no arms were attached to them. They looked almost like stone busts. By the fire-place were whole bodies of young boys and girls. They were also stone-like and whiter than corpses.

In the middle of the room was a great black wood coffin with a tiny brass plaque on it.

Though fear caught her heart, she moved forward and peered down. The plaque was obscured by dust and, nervously, she pulled out her handkerchief and rubbed it so that she could read what was inscribed there.

As she did so, a sound came out of the coffin like a soft groaning of a soul in agony. The coffin-lid moved slightly.

Blamey was so overcome with fear that she collapsed in a faint.

The sound of her falling body on the floor above caused Aunt Furneth to go racing up the stairs. She saw the door of her nephew's room open. Inside, she saw Blamey stretched on the floor by the coffin.

Aunt Furneth reached forward and grabbed the girl by the ankle and dragged her out of the room.

She said nothing to Blamey after the girl had recovered from her faint but, that evening, when Master Marrack Mayne came in, Blamey knew that he was acquainted with what had happened.

"This is the second time that you have disobeyed an instruction, Blamey," he said sternly.

The poor girl was quivering with fright. She had so wanted to please him in all things.

"It will not happen again, sir," she whispered.

"Indeed, it may not. For, if you transgress a third time, there will be no forgiveness for you. I have been kind to you and, in that kindness, you have thought that you might ignore the rules of Aunt Furneth. I have been lenient and, because I have been so easy, it seems that you have become too forward in this house."

Blamey burst out crying and it seemed that Master Marrack Mayne was struck by her contrite attitude. "We will let this matter pass, but do not let it happen again."

After this, it seemed that Marrack Mayne was distant to her and so she redoubled her efforts to please him and even to please Aunt Furneth. Finally, one evening, after she had sung a song to him and put him in good mood once again, he gave her a hug and it seemed that the past was forgiven.

Time passed and, as time passes, so the sharpness of memory fades. Blamey felt a welling curiosity about the forbidden rooms and the strange statue-like heads and shoulders and little ones inside. Then she began to think about the house and its curious inhabitants and wondered if she was missing something.

It was one morning when she was putting the ointment from the ivory box into the eyes of Marrack Vyghan that a thought crossed her mind. Marrack Vyghan had curious eyes, far older than those of a mere boy. He seemed to notice things that she did not. She wondered what the ointment could be. She decided that it was some magic balm that could improve the eyesight. She wondered whether it would improve her own eyesight.

Later that morning, when she was alone in the house, she went to the ivory box and put a tiny drop of the ointment in her eyes. At first nothing happened and then her eyes started to burn and smart. So painful was the sensation that she rushed downstairs out of the house and to the little stream in the meadow and began to bathe her eyes in an attempt to wash the ointment away.

As she finally sat back on the bank of the stream, blinking

and gazing around, she suddenly noticed something in the water before her. Her mouth dropped open in surprise. She could see an entire little world there. Trees, birds and people in such great numbers. They were so tiny.

A figure was moving there among them.

Startled, she recognized Master Marrack Mayne. He was dressed exactly as he had been when he had left the house that morning, yet he was scarcely as high as a thumbnail.

She turned aghast from the water, but realized that the tiny world was surrounding her. She could see the little folk everywhere she went: hiding in the grass, behind flowers, sitting on branches.

"This must be an enchanted place," she whispered to herself. She found that she was not fearful and her curiosity had, if anything, grown.

That evening, there was a change to the usual routine. Master Marrack Mayne arrived home with several strangers and baskets of cakes and other goods. Blamey expected him to call her to help prepare a feast for the guests. However, the master told her to take Marrack Vyghan and put him to bed and then go to bed herself.

"Be sure you take the evening drink," he called. "I have left it by your bedside."

Now a feeling of jealousy came over Blamey, for she saw Master Marrack Mayne, whom she had to admit she was in love with, take the guests, fair ladies and young men, into his chamber where the stone statues were.

For the first time, she did not take the drink which brought such restful sleep but merely poured it out of the bedroom window. She lay on the bed, fully clothed, listening to the sounds of music, laughter and the ringing of glasses, which showed that Marrack and his guests were enjoying themselves.

She waited a while and then she crept from her room and along the darkened corridor to see what was happening.

The door of Master Marrack Mayne's room was ajar and she looked in. There were the three beautiful ladies in fascinating long gowns, with diamonds glinting from their necks and ears and fingers. There were the two well-dressed gentlemen with the master and they were all dancing round the coffin in the centre of the room. As they danced around, they pounded on the coffin-lid, thumping it soundly, and from it came the sounds of music, as if there were a dozen fiddlers inside.

Astonished and unable to make any sense of what she had seen, Blamey returned to her room.

After a while, the music stopped and there came the sounds of guests departing.

She went to her bedroom window and looked down.

By the light of the moon she saw Master Marrack Mayne bidding farewell to the guests and he kissed each one of the ladies in such a manner that it brought a blush of jealousy to Blamey's cheeks. Never had she seen a woman kissed with such a passion.

She went back to her bed and cried herself to sleep, a sleep which was restless and filled with strange dreams: a sleep which she had never experienced since she had left home.

That morning, she was up with the sunrise and went through the day's chores automatically. When Master Marrack Mayne came in, he complimented her on her work and said that she was indeed a good girl and put his arm about her and give her a hug, such as he usually did.

In ordinary circumstances, Blamey would have been delighted, but now she repulsed him.

"Save your embraces for the fine ladies you danced with last night."

Master Marrack Mayne frowned. "What do you mean, girl?" he said sharply.

She told him what she had seen.

The master shook his head sadly.

"You silly, silly girl. You have rubbed your eyes with the ointment and disobeyed for the third time. You will leave this house tomorrow."

She was surprised at his reaction.

She protested that she would never find her way back to her home, so it was best that she remain.

"I will take you back to where I found you," he said sadly.

She cried and promised to obey in future. She swore that

never again would she give way to curiosity, but Master Marrack Mayne would have none of her protestations.

So, the next day, she packed and, with a broken heart, she left the house; she left the beautiful herb garden and meadow and was taken up upon a horse behind the master. Time had passed, she realized, but she didn't know how long it was, for it had seemed so fleeting. She thought perhaps it was one year since she came to the master's house. She didn't even know if there were any wages due to her.

Tears obscured her eyes so that she did not know which road they took except that, in a moment or two, so it seemed, they stood on the road above Carn Kenidjack. Master Marrack Mayne swung down from his horse and lifted Blamey to the ground, placing her on the rock where he had first met her. There he gave her a purse.

"You'll find your wages within," he told her roughly.

Then he was gone.

She stayed at the spot for a while, wondering what to do. How could she go home? Were her parents still living? How long had she been away? She had no idea.

Reluctantly, she began to walked slowly back down the hill into Carn Kenidjack.

Imagine her surprise when she found her father not looking a day older than when she had last seen him standing at the gate.

He did not cry out with joy at her appearance, but instead he seemed puzzled.

"Have you forgotten something?" he asked.

Then her mother came rushing out. "What's the matter?" she greeted.

Blamey was annoyed at the seeming indifference of their greetings.

"I have been gone these many years and you are not pleased to see me? What does this mean?" she grumbled.

"Gone these many years? Have you quit your senses, girl?" demanded her father. "It is only half an hour since you quit this house and now here you are back again?"

"*Whyst! Whyst!*" cried her mother. "The thing is obvious. When she reached the top of the hill she took fright at the big world and has returned home again."

Now Blamey didn't know what to say. She knew she must have been away for several years. She was just astonished.

"It is so," she insisted. "I have been working at the house of Master Marrack Mayne and have just been paid my wages."

Her father laughed good-naturedly.

"These wages I must see, girl. Show me what you have earned in the half-an-hour you have been gone."

Blamey took out the purse which the master had given her and emptied nine gold coins onto her father's palm.

Her parents stared at them in bewilderment.

"What are you doing, girl? Playing tricks with us?"

Even her mother grew angry and stamped her foot. "*Mowes goky!*" she rebuked. "Aren't you the silly girl? Why, there is nothing in your hand at all."

Blamey bit her tongue. "Can't you see this purse and nine pieces of gold?"

"Would I not know nine pieces of gold if I saw them?" rejoined her father. "There is nothing in your hand, I tell you."

"Then it must be the magic ointment," protested Blamey. "I can see the coins quite plainly."

"Magic ointment . . . ?" Her father opened his mouth and closed it like a fish. "Do you take us for fools, girl? You've lost half-an-hour on your journey to look for work by returning here. Now be off with you and don't return again until you have done some decent work in life. Off with you, or we'll call the parson and report your evil humour to him."

Blamey was sent away from Carn Kenidjack.

She returned up the hill and, at the top of the hill, she stood looking back and the tears were streaming from her eyes. She had been away for years and it was clear that she had been working for none other than the Bukkys themselves. Master Marrack Mayne was nothing more than a changeling and not human at all. She had been punished truly.

In the middle of her crying, there came a hollow cough.

Before her stood a tall, handsome, but kindly looking young gentleman. He was peering at her with grave concern. "Why are you weeping, young lady?" he asked.

Blamey stared at him for a moment and realized that she

could never explain the real reason, and so she said, "Why, sir, I have just left home and am on the road looking for a kindly lord's castle, where I might work and earn my keep."

The gentleman smiled broadly. "I am no lord, nor have I a castle, but the manor house in Trewinnard is mine. I am looking for a maid-servant and was on my way to Kenidjack to see if I could find one. I have a young son to be looked after, for I am a widower. The job is yours, if you want it."

Blamey was cautious. "And do you have an old aunt?"

"Not I."

"Then I shall accept."

So Blamey went to work for the young squire and she worked hard, never showed curiosity – for she had truly been cured of it – and one day the squire asked her to marry him and she did. Oh, and the Bukkys' purse of gold . . . ? Strange to relate, at the moment the squire proposed to her, it disappeared entirely from her gaze and Blamey thought it just as well that it did, for she had a better reward for her hard work than all those years in the house of the Bukkys.

29 *Jowan Chy-an-Horth*

Everyone knew Jowan who lived at Horth, near Lanlavan in Kernow. Of course, now he lives at "Chy-an-Horth", which is the big house there. But he was not always so rich nor so respectable. Indeed, there was a time when he and his wife were so poor that they were in dire straits. Jowan could not find any work at all in the vicinity of Lanlavan.

Faced with starvation, Jowan one day told his wife that he would have to leave Lanlavan and travel eastwards into the land of the Saxons, in search of work. His sister, who was married to a man who did have a job, promised to look after his wife while Jowan was gone, and see that she would not starve nor be put out on the road.

So Jowan set off, but he did not have to go as far as the River Tamar, which marked the border between Kernow and the land of the Saxons. Near to Bosvenegh, surrounded by its wild, windswept moors, he came upon an old man dressed as a farmer, seated on a log under a great oak tree.

"*Durdadha-why*, young man. Good day to you. Where are you off to?"

"I am off to Pow-Saws, the land of the Saxons, in search of work," replied Jowan. And he explained to the farmer what dire straits he found himself in.

"What work can you do?" asked the old man, regarding him carefully.

"I can turn my hand to most anything," Jowan replied, without boasting.

"*Lowena re-gas-bo*!" exclaimed the old man in satisfaction. "Then work for me. I am a farmer and, at my age, I need someone to help me on the farm."

They agreed that Jowan would work for a year and be paid three sovereigns for his work. Now three sovereigns in those days was a fair wage. So Jowan worked for a full year. At the end of the year, the old man handed him the three sovereigns. Then he said, "If you give me back those sovereigns, I will tell you something which will be infinitely more valuable."

"More valuable than three sovereigns?" demanded Jowan, who was somewhat naive and trusting. "What could that be?"

"Advice," smiled the old farmer.

Jowan thought and came to the conclusion that if advice was worth more than the three gold coins, then he'd better take it. He solemnly handed the old man back the money. "What is this advice?"

"Never leave the old road for the sake of a new one."

Jowan scratched his head and frowned. "I do not understand. How is that more valuable than three sovereigns?"

"You will see," assured the old man.

"But now I have no money to take home to my wife. I will have to find more work."

"Work another year for me and you shall have three sovereigns more," replied the old man.

So another year passed and, at the end of it, the old man handed him three sovereigns. "Give me them back and I will give you something infinitely more valuable."

Jowan was credulous. "More valuable than three sovereigns?"

"Much more."

Jowan obediently handed back the coins. "It is a piece of advice – never lodge where an old man is married to a young women."

"How is that more valuable than three sovereigns?" demanded Jowan.

"You will see," replied the old man.

"But now I have no money to take home to my wife. I must find more work."

"Work for me for another year and you shall have three more sovereigns," the old farmer invited.

So Jowan worked another three years and, at the end of it, the old man gave him three sovereigns.

"Hand me back the three sovereigns and I will tell you something which will be much more valuable."

"More valuable than three sovereigns?"

"Much more valuable."

So Jowan, still trusting, handed back the three sovereigns.

"Here it is," said the old man. "Honesty is the best policy."

"How is knowing that more valuable than three sovereigns?" demanded Jowan.

"It will be," said the old man.

Now Jowan was artless, but he was not a fool. There was a limit to his trust. "I have spent three years away from home and have no money. I must return to my wife, whether I have money or not, for she will be anxious about me."

"Do not start your journey now," advised the old man, "but start for home tomorrow. Tonight my wife is baking cakes and she shall make you a cake to take home to your wife."

Jowan gave a sigh. Yet, after three years, another day would not matter in his starting for home.

"At least bringing her a cake will be something, rather than turning up empty-handed," pointed out the old man. So Jowan agreed to stay the night and, in the morning, the old man's wife handed him a new-baked cake.

"You must take it on one condition," the old man said. "You must break it and eat it only when you are feeling most joyous. And you and your wife and no one else must eat it."

So Jowan, no richer than he had set out, turned his footsteps back to the west towards Lanlavan. He had journeyed a day when he came across three merchants from his own town who were returning with their goods from the great fair at Dyndajel.

"Good day, Jowan," they greeted warmly. "Where have you been, these last three years?"

"I have been working for an old farmer," he told them. "Have you news of my wife?"

"She is well enough and still living with your sister, but is no richer than when you left her. She will be glad to see you home, and we are glad to see you as well. Why not continue your journey with us?"

Jowan continued his journey with the merchants a while but, when they came to a fork in the road, Jowan saw one road was the old way he knew well while the other was a new road that had recently been built. The merchants said that it was a new short cut home. But as Jowan did not know it, he remembered the old man's advice and decided to stick to the old road. The merchants thought he was silly and they parted company.

Barely had they gone a hundred yards along the new road when highway robbers fell on them and they began to cry out: "Help! Thieves!"

The robbers were heavily armed and the merchants could not defend themselves.

Jowan, hearing their cries, quickly ran back to the fork and saw what was happening. He ran forward crying, "Help! Thieves!" and waving his blackthorn stick which he had cut to walk with.

The robbers, hearing his cries and seeing him running forward waving his stick, thought that reinforcements were coming and rapidly dispersed, leaving the merchants still in possession of their goods.

The merchants welcomed Jowan back with gratitude. "But for you, Jowan, we would have been lost men," cried the merchants. "We are beholden to you for rescuing us. You were right. We should have stuck to the old road. Come with us there, for there is an inn nearby and you must be our guest. Dine with us and stay the night there."

So they continued along the old road together until they came to a new inn, which was curiously sited next to an older one. The new inn seemed to be taking all the business from the old one. The old inn was dilapidated and had the air of decay and abandonment about it.

At the doorway of the new inn, a very beautiful young girl came forward to greet them. She was the wife of the host of the inn. But, attractive as she was, Jowan saw that she was lascivious and coarse. Her vulgar voluptuousness made Jowan feel uneasy as she bade the happy merchants come inside and furnished them with drink.

Inside was an old, bleary-eyed man, who was doing all the heavy work while the girl flirted with her guests.

"Who is that old man?" Jowan asked the girl. "Surely he is too old to be doing all that heavy work?"

The girl chuckled in good humour. "That old wreck? He is my husband. Don't worry about him, my handsome."

At once, Jowan recalled the old farmer's advice: *never lodge where an old man is married to a young woman*. He rose immediately and went to the door.

"Where are you going?" demanded the merchants.

"I cannot lodge here," he replied. "I will find lodgings next door in the old inn."

"No, no. Stay and dine with us, first," insisted the merchants. "We want to repay you for saving us on the road."

But he would not. The merchants, who were honest men, said that if he found lodgings in the old inn, they would pay for him.

That night, while he lay in bed in the old inn, a noise roused Jowan from his slumber. He went to his window and looked down. There were two figures in the shadowy doorway of the new inn opposite. They were engaged in conversation.

"Are you ready?" asked a female voice.

Jowan had no trouble recognizing the voice of the voluptuous young hostess of the new inn.

"As ready as I'll ever be," came a masculine voice.

"Are you agreed on the plan?"

"I will stab your husband as he lies in bed tonight and place the bloody dagger in the hands of one of those fat, stupid merchants. When they are blamed and hanged, we shall be together and owners of a fine inn."

The figures then went inside the new inn.

Now Jowan dressed and hurried to the new inn, with the thought of warning his merchant friends. He peered through the open window where he saw a light.

He was too late to save the host of the inn, for he saw the deed had already been done. Near the window, within arm's reach, stood the figure of the man, the murderer. It was then that Jowan recognized the man for he was named Lewarne, the Fox, of Chy-an-Horth, who had once refused him a job. He was the factotem, or manager, of the great estate of Lord Gwavas of Castle Gwavas. He was a vain man who wore a very distinctive purse at his belt and Jowan, who was nimble, reached in across the window-sill and managed to lift it from Lewarne's belt without him noticing it.

Soon the lecherous hostess raised a cry, claiming her husband had been murdered and that there was no one but the merchants in the house and that they must have done the deed.

Lord Gwavas, lord of the Castle of Gwavas, came riding to the new inn, for he was the administrator of justice in the area.

Lord Gwavas had the merchants marched out and told them: "You will all hang, unless one of you confesses your crime."

Each merchant cried out that they were innocent, and Lord Gwavas ordered they all be marched off to prison, to await execution.

"Wait, lord," cried Jowan. "Why not arrest the real murderer?"

Lord Gwavas stared down at him in surprise.

"Who committed the crime," he demanded, "if not these merchants?"

Jowan gave the man the purse. "The owner of that purse did the deed."

Then Jowan told Lord Gwavas all he knew.

"Why, this is the purse of my factotem, Lewarne of Chy-an-Horth. Bring him here."

Lewarne came in fear and they brought the hostess with him. Lord Gwavas saw the truth of the situation in their eyes. He ordered the merchants to be set at liberty and the hostess and Lewarne taken to prison to be hanged for the crime.

So they all journeyed on together, the merchants and Jowan, and at the foot of the hill, the hill on which Jowan's sister and her husband lived, they parted company. But not before the merchants gave Jowan a fine horse and loaded on it all manner of presents, in return for his services in saving them not once but twice. Jowan went home with wealth enough to compensate him for his three years without wages.

His wife was waiting at the gate of the cottage. After they had had their reunion and celebration, his wife said: "Jowan, you have returned in the nick of time. I have a problem. You see, Lord Gwavas passed here yesterday and, when I was going along the same path that he had been on, I came across this purse of gold. But the purse has no name on it, only a crest, so I am fairly sure that it belongs to him. Yet I have been living on your sister's charity these last three years, and the gold is such a great temptation."

Now Jowan remembered the third piece of advice which the old farmer had given him. *Honesty was the best policy.*

"No. We will take the purse to Lord Gwavas in his castle and return it to him."

So Jowan and his wife went up to the castle and demanded to see the great Lord Gwavas.

Lord Gwavas was delighted when his eyes fell on Jowan. "You went off too soon, before I could reward you for revealing the crime of my factotem."

"Well, I came with my wife, who found something of yours on the path this morning."

They gave Lord Gwavas his purse of gold. He was amazed and quite delighted. "Such honesty needs reward," he said. "Now that Lewarne is no longer my factotem, will you come and work for me in his place? I will pay you five golden sovereigns each year, and you will have the big house at Horth as your own."

Jowan was ecstatic.

"Here, then," said Lord Gwavas, when Jowan had agreed, "in token of my respect, is the purse of gold to set you up in your new home."

They thanked Lord Gwavas, but the great lord dismissed their thanks by saying that he owed them much, for he had finally found trustworthy friends to help him run his estates.

So Jowan and his wife returned to Jowan's sister's cottage and there was a great celebration. Jowan ensured that his sister and her husband did not go short, on account of the years they had looked after his wife. He paid them in gold coin from Lord Gwavas' purse. Jowan's sister and his wife prepared a big home-coming feast.

Jowan felt the most joyous that he had ever felt in his life.

It was then he remembered the cake that the old farmer had given him. He took it out and placed it on the table.

"I promised my old master that I would break and eat this when I felt most joyous. I do now and so I shall be true to my word and break it open to eat it."

His wife, his sister and brother-in-law, laughed at the humble-looking cake but Jowan broke open the cake. Then he stared in amazement, for inside the cake were nine golden sovereigns, his wages for the three years he had worked for the old farmer.

30 Nos Calan Gwaf

Pendeen, north of St Just in Penwith, in the western extremity of Cornwall, is an ancient mining village and there are many stories associated with it. Its history goes back into the time before time began, and it is regarded as the most primordial part of the country with many old sites nearby – places like Chun Quoit and Chun Castle, that date from when man first walked the land; strange underground tunnels, such as the one which is shaped like a "Y" and stretches fifty-six feet in length and is four and a half feet high, called a *fogou*, and no one knows what it is used for.

Pendeen has long been associated with the *piskies* – the mischievous supernatural creatures who haunt the remoter areas of Cornwall. Many are the people who have been *pisky*-led and have disappeared from this world or, if they have returned, been out of their mind until their dying days. Locals will tell you to avoid the nearby Wood Gumpus Common, especially at night.

Time was, down at Pendeen House, which stands out towards Pendeen Watch on the cliffs, and where the great antiquarian William Borlase was born, there was another family who were squires there. I can't vouch for their name but I have heard tell that it was Bosanko, which some say comes from the old Cornish *bosancow* – meaning the dwelling place of death! And if it were so, they dwelt at Pendeen so long ago that no one will now vouch that they were ever there.

Well, let's call the squire "Squire Bosanko", and say he had an elderly housekeeper named "Peggy" Tregear. It turned out that the old lady was a fussy kind of soul, who liked to make sure that the squire was well fed. One day, she found that she had run out of certain herbs to cook a meal with, and what could she do but get her basket and her rowan walking stick and set out across the hills to Penzance market? Now, Penzance is a fair walk from Pendeen, and you have to cross the hills from the north to the south side of the Penwith Peninsula.

Now the time and day on which she set off was noon on 31 October. Maybe some of you will recognize the significance of the date. The significance had, in fact, not occurred to the old lady. It was *Nos Calan Gwaf*, in the old Cornish calendar. That is now called Hallowe'en, when the Otherworld comes into view in this world and when spirits can come forth and wreak their vengeance on the living, and when the *pisky* folk may lead unguarded souls a merry dance.

Old Peggy Tregear, before she started her journey, went first to the house of Jan Tregher, who was the wife of the tailor over at Portheras Cove, for Peggy liked to walk in company and thought that she would see if Jan might accompany her to Penzance. Jan had the reputation of being a *peller*, which in Cornwall is a remover of charms or a white witch. Others said that she was not so "white" in her witchcraft and could curse as well as any folk. I heard tell of one man who even said that the Torpen himself, that is to say Lucifer, advised Jan Tregher and her husband when a rich wreck would come floating into Portheras Cove.

Mind you, there were plenty of wrecking places off the shore, like The Mozens or the rocks known as The Wra or Three Stone Oar. That's why, on certain days, they lit beacon fires on Pendeen Watch and along the coast at Greeb Point. Even so, there were plenty of wrecks, with or without the Devil's help. It seemed that the Treghers were always there ahead of anyone else, and rich were the pickings they had. But, of course, as is always the way, no one would challenge Jan and her husband Tom to their faces, but went around muttering darkly about the Treghers between themselves.

Now Peggy Tregear was not one to gossip unkindly. She never bothered about sorcery and the like and was always friendly to Jan. In turn, Jan would give her a good bottle of spirits as came off any of the wrecks. Come this Hallowe'en, old Peggy arrived at the Treghers' door, to find it shut: which was unusual. She heard voices raised within and so bent to the keyhole and peered in to see what she could see.

Tom Tregher was sitting on a stool with Jan rubbing his eyes with something held in a *crogen*, which is a limpet shell. Then she placed the *crogen* in the oven. Tom stood up. So Peggy gave a call to announce her presence, lifted the latch and went in. Now neither Jan nor Tom seemed pleased to see her, and Tom left with scarcely a greeting on his lips. This was unusual. He bade her a good day and left the cottage. But Jan was soon all smiles and acted as though she was pleased to see her.

"Glad I am to see you, for I have been thinking of you, Peggy. I have a choice bottle for you to take up to Squire Bosanko."

True it was that the Treghers liked to keep the squire happy with a bottle or two from the wrecks. The squire was the local justice of the peace and, if he were happy, he would not bother to chase wreckers too strenuously.

Jan went off to get the bottle of spirits and, while she was gone, old Peggy Tregear, out of curiosity, bent to the oven and looked at the *crogen* of ointment. She bent a finger in it and touched one of her eyes with it, as she had seen Jan placing it in the eyes of her husband. She could only place it in one eye before Jan was back with the bottle.

"Now take a glass for yourself," Jan invited her and, nothing loath, she did.

When Peggy Tregear told her what she had come for, Jan made an excuse and said she was busy with a meal for her husband that afternoon. She also expected some guests who were interested in buying goods from the wreck.

So Peggy Tregear, after her drink, bade her farewell and set off, basket and rowan stick, towards Penzance. It was curious that she strode out with a firm step and felt she was walking more rapidly than ever she had done before. As she trod the road, she realized how well she suddenly could see and she was tripping down the lane without the need of her stick. Faster went the ground beneath her. Even so, Penzance is a fair distance from Pendeen, and she realized that she would be returning home in the dark. Yet still it did not occur to her what the evening was.

She went to the market place to make her purchases.

Who should she see in the market but Tom Tregher? Something curious was abroad. Tom Tregher was going round the market stalls, helping himself to anything which took his fancy, picking it up and never paying a copper penny for it. Yet no one seemed to take any notice of him nor challenge him to pay. He carried a big sack into which he placed the goods which he was picking up.

Old Peggy Tregear grew quite amazed.

"Tom Tregher," she called, "what does this mean? How are you allowed to pick up such rich purchases and not pay the market-folk for them?"

Tom Tregher whirled round on her with a dark expression on his face, his eyes narrowed. "Do you see me, old dame Tregear?"

"Of course I do."

"Which eye can you see me from?" he asked.

"Both, I suppose." But when Peggy Tregear closed the eye that was not anointed, she could not see him at all.

In a trice, Tom Tregher knew what had happened.

He pointed to her anointed eye and cried: "This for poking your nose where you are not wanted. You shall no more pry with that anointed eye!" It seemed as if a needle pierced it and she fell to the ground in such agony, for she couldn't keep on her legs.

Immediately, he vanished. But she heard his voice saying: "May you be *pisky*-led this evening and not reach your bed! May the winds of retribution carry me and mine off if the *pisky* will is not fed!"

Now the market-folk gathered round to see what was amiss with the old woman. Peggy, still sitting on the ground, wailed and cried that Tom Tregher had put her eye out by his black magic and that he had been going round their stalls stealing their goods. Some accused her of drinking and others told her to get back to Pendeen and sober up.

Angered by their refusal to do anything, she decided to take herself off and went up by way of Castle Horneck and came to the high road there. When she reached there, she remembered the bottle Jan Tregher had given her for Squire Bosanko. It would be no harm to have just a wee nip from it. Just to revive her spirits. So she did. Then she started along the road and soon the darkness came down on her, for the sun was now well below the horizon and it was truly the *Nos Calan Gwaf*.

However, by this time, old Peggy Tregear had taken quite a few nips from the bottle and was not concerned at all. She just wanted to get home and report how Tom Tregher had put her eye out to Squire Bosanko, not to mention what she knew about his thieving at the market.

As she went down the lane, through the little hamlet of Tremayne and beyond, she saw, on the road ahead of her, a man on a large horse silhouetted against the rising moon. Now Squire Bosanko owned such a large horse and, in her drink-befuddled state, old Peggy Tregear immediately thought that this was the squire.

"*Dew re-sonno dhys*," she greeted. "Give 'ee a good evening, squire," she said.

The man sat still and straight in the saddle and did not reply at all, but the old woman did not seem to notice this.

"I've had a queer day, your honour," she went on and proceeded to tell him everything which had happened since she left home. However, when the man still sat there and made no reply, the old woman grew impatient.

"Now I've been long on the road today, your honour, and in spite of being footsore and leg-weary and now being blinded in the one eye by Tom Tregher, I have been hurrying back with my purchases from Penzance to cook your dinner. I think it would be a gentlemanly thing to do to take me up on the back of your horse and we can ride back to Pendeen. It would be a kindness and your dinner would be cooked the sooner."

But the man still sat there, quiet as death, without replying.

Old Peggy Tregear stamped her foot in annoyance. "Why don't you speak to me? Are you asleep? Are you and your horse taking a nap? For you are both standing so quiet there."

Still there was no reply.

Then the old woman shouted as loud as she could. "You know me, Squire Bosanko, and if you be the gentleman everyone knows you to be, then you will take me up behind you."

Yet still he did not make a murmur.

"Are you drunk, then?" demanded Peggy Tregear, raising her courage to so address her master. "Is it drunk that what you are, so still and quiet? Is it a drop too much drink that you have taken and fallen asleep there? Shame on you!"

Still there was no movement nor answer.

Hands on hips, the old woman sneered at the man. "A fine thing! Squire Bosanko drunk, and his horse as well. Well, I am as fine a lady as any Bosanko and will not be treated thus. Time was when we Tregears were first among the people of the parish and buried with the other gentry of Pendeen, when the Bosankos had never been heard of."

If she had hoped her scorn would move the horse and rider, it had no effect at all. They were still silent and immovable.

Angered beyond endurance, the old woman moved forward and gave the animal a mighty smack on the rump.

You can imagine her surprise when her hand met nothing but air, and such was the force of her weight behind the blow that she lost her balance and fell on the road. When she sat up, blinking, she saw that the horse and rider were vanished.

"A curse on Tom Tregher," she said, scrambling to her feet. "He must be bewitching me."

She gave a cautious look around in the shadowy moon-lit lane, but could make nothing out. Then she was on her feet and the soles of her shoes were slapping down the lane as fast as she could put one foot before the other. So intent was she on reaching Pendeen that, when she went over the stream at Newbridge, except there was no bridge at all at that place in those days, she did not wait to balance on the crossing stones but went splashing through the stream, so she had water up to her knees and above.

Along the road she went, drenched and sorry for herself as well as exhausted. She kept the stream to her right, for she planned to go through the hills and across the road that led by the old Standing Stone which would take her across Wood Gumpus Common.

She suddenly saw a light on her right hand and recalled that the Tregerest dwelling was there; she thought the light must be shining from the window of the dwelling. Here she could ask if she could dry her clothes and rest for a while. So off she set. She did not know how far she walked because the curious thing was that, the more she hurried towards it, the light always seemed just the same distance away. Then the light went out and left her in darkness.

She was across the hills and knew she must have been hurrying across Boswens Common and away from the main road. There she was, floundering along in boggy land. She was almost in despair. Then the moon came peeking out from behind the dark clouds and before her she saw a pig pen with a little shed for the shelter of the animals. She was so exhausted that she would have welcomed any shelter at all, to sit down and rest and be dry for a while.

Into the little shed she crawled, that she might take an hour's rest from the cold and damp of the evening. There was some straw inside and she did not take heed of the smell of the pigs. Onto the straw she went and was soon asleep.

Now the pig pen contained a dozen young suckling pigs and these came into the shed and mistook old Peggy Tregear for their dam. They crowded round, pushing her with their snouts, so that there was no way she could rest nor lay nor sit in comfort.

Tired, angry and confused, the old woman crawled out of the pig pen and then paused in surprise.

Not far away she could see a light and it seemed to come from a big barn. She heard the sound of a *fust*, a flail, being used against wheat. Now she knew that there was only one farm in that area, and that was Boslow's farm. She wondered what the farmer was doing so late in the evening, threshing corn, but she was more concerned that there was somewhere warm where she might dry and rest herself.

She made for the barn and peered in.

There was a lamp lit there, sure enough. There was the slash-staff, the beating part of the flail, going up and down, beating the wheat. But, heaven preserve her, there was no one holding it. It seemed to be doing it on its own.

She swallowed hard and blinked. Was she going mad? Being of a curious mind, she moved cautiously into the barn. So intent was she, on looking at the flail in action, that she tripped over a sack and measured her length on the ground. She felt that she had landed against something soft.

There was a cry of pain.

The next moment, she found herself looking at a little man, no higher than two feet. His face was long, the eyes great round owl's eyes, shaded by shaggy eyebrows. His mouth stretched from ear to ear and they were sharp and pointed. His teeth were long and jagged and his skin was a strange green colour.

Now Peggy Tregear was not stupid when it came to knowing the *pisky* lore.

"This is luck, indeed, for whoever espies a *pisky* threshing is sure to have a wish granted."

She sat up and was about to address the little man when she became aware that there were a number of other little people all around her. They were all engaged in threshing the wheat. She could not help but admire how professionally the wheat was cut, stacked and ready for the collection.

There was a tinge of jealousy in her.

How come farmer Boslow had this special treatment from the *pisky* folk, that they would thresh his corn for him while he stretched in front of his fire and ate his meal in comfort, without having to worry about work? Maybe she could get the *piskies* to do work for her?

So she climbed to her feet.

"A good evening to you, little folk," she said.

Suddenly all the lights went out and they vanished. But a handful of chaff dust was thrown into her eyes so that she was nearly blinded. She blinked and rubbed hard. She had forgotten the rule that, in order to speak to the fairy folk, she had to first take one by the hand and hold him, or her, fast.

Then she heard a voice hissing in her ear.

"Ill becomes she who would spy on the *pisky* at their work."

She felt suddenly afraid when she remembered that *piskies* were known to take revenge on any who stumbled across them and had no hold on them.

So she turned and went stumbling from the barn and from Boslow to the roadway, which was now lit with the moonlight. Quick she ran along the lane that led over Wood Gumpus Common. Even today it is a haunted place, with its stone circles, carns and strange earth mounds. Folk still dread to take that haunted lane. Locals will tell you that on such nights, with the full of the moon, the Torpen, which is their name for the Devil himself, rode across those grim moors with his hounds in search of restless spirits that might have strayed from the stone-walled churchyards. The hounds from hell would hunt them down and drag them off to eternal suffering. And, further, they will tell you that the Torpen was not so particular as to wait until your body was dead but would hunt out the souls of the living and drag them off as well.

Old Peggy Tregear was full of fear now as she went slapping her leather-soled way along the lane and hoping to see sight of Higher Boscaswell and the crossroads there, which would bring her down towards Pendeen Watch and the safety of Pendeen House. Ah, Pendeen House! Her mind was full of thoughts of a nice warm fire in her kitchen, of warmth and a comfortable chair and a good bottle of spirits in her hand.

But she seemed to be running for hours. Surely Higher Boscaswell was not so far from Boslow's farm?

Now she was hurrying along the lane when a curious thing began to happen. She began to hear music, fiddles scraping a merry jig and she felt she had to stop and try a few steps. The music seemed to come from behind some tall trees and there seemed to be a light there and the sound of people laughing, dancing and making music. She thought that perhaps there was an encampment of tinkers there. She would see if she could warm herself by their fire for a moment or two before continuing her journey.

She left the road and came behind the trees and what did she see? Among the trees and the rocks was a fair. But such a fair that she had never seen before. It was a *pisky* fair. Hundreds of small people were crowding around, buying, selling, drinking and dancing and eating. They were all clad in splendid little costumes and most were bedecked with silver and gold and precious jewels. They were dressed like gentry, all very smart. None of them was taller than two feet in height.

She stood quiet as she watched them, especially the dancers as they gathered round the bonfire. There were fiddlers and pipers and drummers and old Peggy never felt more inclined to get up and dance in all her life. The music seemed to have a strange hypnotic effect on her.

Then her eye fell on the stalls of the fair and she realized how beautiful were the objects being bought and sold. She determined that she must have something to take away. She saw a stall with some beautiful jewels which made her feel that she had to have them at any cost. She took a step forward towards the stall and bent down to speak with the stall holder.

As she did so, the little people began to call out in rage and point to her. As she bent to speak with them, half-a-dozen leapt onto her back. They dug their heels in and some prodded her with tiny swords, like pins. Others tripped her so that she fell flat on the ground. They began to leap all over her and she tried to bundle herself up into a ball. They pulled off her shoes, and dug their little swords into the soles of her feet and she went almost mad with their torment.

Fighting them, she rolled and rolled, and cursed them and hit out with her rowan stick. Now the rowan, as we know, has many properties, and it so happened that as she struck out, it hit the head of the king of these *piskies*. Now *piskies* are allergic to the rowan and the king screamed and went leaping away. In a moment, the others followed, the fair disappeared and all was deserted.

Old Peggy Tregear found herself sprawled on damp bracken, minus her shoes, in a bit of boggy land under the trees. She was cold and miserable and aching. The moon was now low and the stars shining. She realized to her horror that it was early in the morning and she had come down off Wood Gumpus Common by Bojewyan and could see the dark outline of Pendeen House.

She scrambled to her feet and tried to find her shoes, her hat and her basket. She found the basket, but it was empty. All her purchases at Penzance were gone. There was nothing to do but take up her stick and hobble barefooted to Pendeen House.

At the gate she paused and glanced at the sky.

It would soon be dawn and she was thinking that she should at least thank her lucky stars that she would soon be in her own bed and asleep within a minute or two.

Now, from the gate of Pendeen, you have to pass over several acres of grounds which are uncultivated. The ground goes down to the cliffs at Pendeen Watch on the north side and overlooks the rocky cove by the island rock which is called simply, in Cornish, The Enys – the island. Old Squire Bosanko, so they say, had stocked the ground with many breeds of rabbits, tame and wild, and provided a sort of sanctuary for them, where they were never hunted. Now the rabbits, eating the furze and grass, provided a nice soft path to Pendeen House and, as old Peggy Tregear now had no shoes, she thought she would tread along the soft grass instead of sticking to the rocky road which led straight up to the house.

She had crossed this route many times, both sober and drunk. This time, following the track on the grass, she found that she had wandered away from the house entirely. Each time she tried to make directly for the great shadowy outline of Pendeen House, she found herself lost among the furze and once wandering dangerously near to the cliffs at Pendeen Watch.

Finally, exhausted to the point of passing out, she sat down on the ground and vowed not to move until dawn. So she fell asleep.

At dawn the next morning, the Squire of Pendeen made enquiries from his other servants whether Peggy Tregear had arrived back or not during the night. In truth, he was worried.

He knew she was inclined to drink now and then but she had never taken herself off before and deserted the house, and especially not when there was dinner to be made. He sent his hostler out to make enquiries and the man saddled a horse to ride out into Pendeen village itself. As he rode along the path to the gate, he thought he saw a bundle of old rags on the grass and, looking closer, found it was none other than Peggy Tregear, fast asleep in the frosty dew.

Dismounting, he went over and shook her.

"Leave me alone," she muttered after a while. "It's not my time to be up. Leave me alone and be sure to shut my bed-chamber door as you go."

The hostler sent for the Squire and the two of them carried the almost unconscious old woman into the kitchen and placed her before a blazing fire.

She came round slowly and, when the Squire asked her where she had been all night, she told him in a flood of words so that he didn't understand one half and was doubtful of believing the other half. He put it down to the fact that she had drunk too much and missed her way.

Old Peggy Tregear was indignant that he should think so but Squire Bosanko, having decided on the explanation, would not be moved from it.

"Do you sleep off your drunkenness, woman," he admonished. "For tonight I have friends coming for the Golwyth Pup Sans." That being the feastingtide of All Saints.

Peggy Tregear's eyes opened wide. "Do 'ee tell me, master," she said slowly, "that last night be Hallowe'en . . . the *Nos Calan Gwaf*?"

Squire Bosanko shook his head sternly. "Don't tell me that you forgot what day it was?"

She scratched her head. "I knew before I went to Jan Tregher's place, yesterday noon," she said, trying to remember how it was she had forgotten. "No wonder I have suffered, being out alone that night."

"Nonsense," said the Squire. "Sober up and, when you have, start preparing the meal, for the feastingtide is here. And if you want anything, send the hostler into Pendeen to purchase it without tripping across the hills to Penzance."

Still shocked, the old housekeeper promised she would never go to Penzance again.

It was that evening, when she had recovered from her ordeal and the Squire's guests had been served and fed, that there came a loud knocking on the door. It was a foul night, as foul a night as ever there had been, with high seas and winds beating along the cliffs from Cape Cornwall along to Pendeen Watch and from Pendeen Watch to Gurnard's Head. There was never a night like it, and already Squire Bosanko had suggested to his guests that they should stay the night.

When the door was answered, it was a farmer from Chypraze.

"What ails you, man?" demanded the Squire, as the farmer stood shivering and drenched in his hall. "What brings you out in this weather?"

"I thought you should know, sir," replied the man. "The Tregher cottage in Portheras Cove . . . a great wind and tide has swept it clean away. Tom and Jan Tregher were in it at the time. We've searched the foreshore, but there is hardly a stone left standing on another there, and no sign of them."

Only old Peggy Tregear was not shocked by the news.

She knew that for every action there was a reaction; for every cause there was an effect. She knew that it was Tom Tregher who had set off the chain of events of the previous evening. Even the tiniest action, like the struggle of the new-born land crab to make it to the sea, makes a contribution to eternity. Hadn't Tom Tregher called down a curse that the winds of retribution should carry him and his off? Did not the old proverb go – *nyns-us gun hep lagas, na ke hep scovann*? There is no plain without an eye, nor hedge without an ear. The *pisky* folk had heard him and old Peggy Tregear knew that Tom and Jan Tregher had been punished for vainly ill-wishing her. To cause evil necessitates a consequence. And no one ever changed Peggy Tregear's mind about that.

31 *An Lys-an-Gwrys*

There was a poor family by the name of Kellow and they dwelt down by Garras in the forests near a great mansion called Chygarkye – the "house of the white dog". They worked for the lord of the manor by tending his sheep and cows. There was the husband and his wife and seven children. Six of these children were boys and one was a girl. Now the girl was called Welet, and she was the eldest of the family. The youngest boy was called Wuric, and he was a bit feeble in the head, or so his family thought.

In fact, both Welet and Wuric were picked on by their brothers, who played all sorts of mischievous tricks on them and made sure that it was they who did all the work that their parents asked them to do. Every day, at sunrise, when all the boys were supposed to be looking after the sheep and cows, it was poor Welet who found herself being sent to the fields by the forest near Chygarkye, with no more than a buckwheat cake to sustain her throughout the day. And poor Wuric was told he was too young to go out and sent to do all the cleaning of the stables and barns. And while Welet and Wuric did all the work, the five brothers lazed in bed or went off playing. Of course, they were clever and able to hide this bad state of affairs from their parents, who thought them all dutiful and well-behaved children.

One bright morning, Welet was taking the cows and sheep to the pasture on the heath when she saw a great white stallion coming out of the forests. On it was a tall young man, clad all in white, with the finest jewels and gold on him. His hair was a flaming red-golden colour, held around his head by a circlet of gold. Welet stopped and stared at him in astonishment. It seemed that the sun itself radiated from his features. He was as handsome a lord as ever she had seen.

The young man stopped his horse and gazed down at her with a smile that caused a warm glow to spread through her tired limbs.

"*Myttyn da*, young maiden." He wished her "good morning" in a low pleasant voice. "Truly, I have never seen a maid as fair as you."

Welet blushed, because she had never been spoken to in such a manner. Now it is true that some people found Welet attractive, but no more so than many a young girl on the peninsula.

"Tell me, maiden," continued the handsome young lord in earnest, "will you marry me?"

Welet was so taken aback that she nearly fell over. She was too astonished to give an answer immediately.

"I don't know," she finally stuttered, thinking that it would be a fine life to go off with the young man and leave behind the drudgery and mistreatment of her brothers: that is all except Wuric, her younger brother, whom she was very fond of.

"I'll leave you time to think. This time tomorrow, as the sun rises over the heath, you'll find me waiting here for your answer."

The sun suddenly caught her eye and she blinked and, when she opened her eyes, the young man had vanished.

All day Welet thought of nothing except the handsome young man. She went home that night, not even feeling her hunger, but skipped back with a merry little song on her lips. Her brothers were surprised and asked themselves what could have made their sister happy.

She told no one except her mother, who promptly sneered at her. "What a fool you are, to be sure, child. It is some grand gentleman playing a trick on us poor folks. Do you really think such a lord would come along and ask the likes of you to wed?"

And, to her shame, her mother told her husband and her

sons and they all laughed uproariously – all except young Wuric. He looked sad and tried to comfort his sister in her distress.

"I will agree to marry the man tomorrow if he is there," she vowed, "for, whatever happens to me in the future, I shall never be more unhappy than I am now."

Wuric pressed her hand and told her that if she had a chance for happiness, she should take it and not mind about him. One day he, too, would escape the drudgery which their brothers put on them.

The next morning, Welet was up at dawn and taking the cows and sheep to the pasture.

Sure enough, up rode the radiant young man on his white stallion. "*Myttyn da*, young maid. Have you thought the matter over? Will you be my wife?"

"That I will," replied the young girl. "That I will and right gladly."

"Then," said the young man with a beaming smile, "we shall go and make sure that your parents have no objections."

She went reluctantly with him, for she was now ashamed of her parents. They, in turn, were astonished at the arrival of the young lord so richly attired, who asked for the hand of their daughter in marriage. Her brothers stared enviously on him, except Wuric.

"We can give her no dowry," muttered her father anxiously. Could it be that the young lord thought his daughter had money?

The young lord laughed at the idea and ignored the insult. "I have no need of dowries," he replied. "If that is your only objection, then we will fix tomorrow as the day of the ceremony."

"But we don't even know your name," protested Welet's mother.

"You will know it soon enough, at the ceremony."

Then he bade them "good day" and rode off.

Well, Welet's father went to make the arrangements, but Welet's brothers still jeered – with the exception of Wuric – and laid bets that it was still all a bad joke and the handsome young man would not turn up the next day.

However, the young man did turn up: and not just himself but another handsome young man, whom he introduced as his best man. They came in a coach of solid gold drawn by seven magnificent white stallions, and everything shone in a dazzling light.

"What name shall we know you by?" asked Welet's father.

"I am called Lord Howlek, the lord of the sunny countenance."

The ceremony took place and no sooner was it over than the young man handed her up into the carriage.

"Say farewell to your family, for now you will come to dwell at my palace."

"What about my clothes?" she protested. "I have nothing ready, except that which I am wearing."

"You will find everything you want in my palace," he replied.

"Where is that palace?" demanded one of Welet's brothers, feeling it time he should take a hand.

"It is called *An Lys-an-Gwrys* . . . the Palace of the Crystal . . . and it lies eastward, underneath the rising sun."

So saying, Lord Howlek, Welet and the silent lord who was the best man climbed into the carriage, and it drove away into a sparkling light.

A year and a day passed by and no word was heard of Welet and her husband, the Lord Howlek. Welet's brothers became curious. If the truth were known, they had been hoping to have a share in their sister's newly found prosperity. They had been forced to continue to work for the great lord at Chygarkye. Now that Welet was gone, they also found that they could not put all the work on Wuric but had to do a good share of it themselves, which did not suit them at all.

But after a year and a day they decided that it was too bad of Welet not to send them any tokens of her well-being, and they announced that they would set off in search of the *An Lys-an-Gwrys*. Young Wuric wanted to go with them, but they told him to stay at home and help their parents with all the work that was to be done.

So eastwards the five brothers began to travel. Every time they stopped, they asked if anyone knew where *An Lys-an-*

Gwrys was situated. But no one knew about such a grand palace. They travelled for such a long time that they began to argue among themselves if they should give up the enterprise and turn back home.

One day, they entered a forest and were so tired and exhausted by their search that they agreed that, if they had found nothing by the time they reached the other side of its gloomy stretch, they would turn back to Garras and their home near Chygarkye. No sooner had they entered the forest than they heard the sound of a woodsman cutting trees and they came into a clearing.

"Do you know a palace called *An Lys-an-Gwrys?*" they asked of the woodsman.

The old man scratched his balding head.

"I do hear tell of such a place, for there be a road not far off called *Forth Lys-an-Gwrys*, which is the road to the palace of crystal. That ought to lead you there."

So elated were they with this news that the five brothers went off in search of the roadway immediately, with renewed vigour. They had not gone much further when a great storm broke out across the forest. Thunder and lightning crashed here and there. They could not disguise the fact from each other that they were more than a little afraid at such a fierce tempest. Soon the storm abated and they continued on their way, feeling rather sheepish.

Night came down in the forest and the sound of wild prowling beasts could be heard around them.

"We must seek shelter," suggested one of them.

Another decided to climb a tree and see if he could spot any signs of habitation. There was nothing but trees except . . . he saw the glimmering of a fire and, noting the direction in which it lay, he came down and joined his brothers.

He led his brothers in the direction and then a storm seemed to break out again above their heads. Thunder and lightning crashed around them. Then all was silent again. They calmed themselves and moved on.

In a clearing in the forest they came across an old woman, with long yellowing teeth and a skeletal look about her. She was sitting before a fire, stirring a great cauldron of simmering broth.

"Good evening, *dama-wyn*," greeted the eldest of the brothers, for it was polite to call old ladies of this age "grandmother". "We are searching for the *Forth Lys-an-Gwrys*. Do you know where it is?"

"Ah, good evening, my good sons. I know the road but my son, who travels it every day, knows it better. He often journeys to the Crystal Palace and back again."

"Is the Crystal Palace near here?" asked another of the brothers, surprised that it could be reached there and back in a day.

"It is not far. But we must wait until my son returns. Perhaps you've seen or heard him in the forest?"

"We have seen no one," they assured her.

"But you must have heard him, then?"

Suddenly they heard the thunder and lightning again. It seemed as if it was coming nearer.

"What is it?" they cried, cowering together.

"It is only my son," she assured them with a smile. "Shelter under those tree-branches until I have a word with him. He is a hungry man and he might eat you."

Rather frightened, the brothers hid themselves and the thunder and lightning grew worse until a tall man came flashing out of the sky and landed in the clearing on his two feet. He glared about him.

"*Dama, dama, yma nown dhym*." "Mother, mother, I am hungry," he cried, in the language of Cornwall.

The old woman smiled. "*Da yu genef agas gweles*," replied the old woman. "*Ny a-vyn dalleth gans yskel onyon*."

Which means: "I am glad to see you. We'll begin with onion soup."

The giant stopped and sniffed the air suspiciously.

"I do smell the smell of Cornishmen here? They'd make a tasty snack. *Nown blyth a-m-bus*. I am ravenous."

Quick as a wink, the old woman took up a cudgel and brought it down hard on the giant's foot. "If you harm my guests, I'll give you a walloping with my cudgel."

The giant trembled, as it seemed that the old woman made

no idle threat, and he took an oath not to harm the five brothers who were told to show themselves.

"Now, these are your Cornish cousins. You must take them, first thing in the morning, to *Lys-an-Gwrys*."

It was early in the morning when the giant leapt up, with a crash of thunder and flash of lightning, and woke the brothers.

"It's time to set out for the *Forth Lys-an-Gwrys*."

He told them to stand on a great sheet and then he lifted the corners, so it seemed they were in a sack, and he slung it over his shoulders and went off up into the air with thunder and lightning crashing around him. It seemed that the giant turned into a great ball of fire and sped through the skies eastward.

"Is this the road?" cried one of the brothers to his siblings.

"It is rather high up, isn't it?" said another.

It was then the eldest remembered an old saying. *Tus skentyl nu-gar fordhow ughel.* Wise men do not like high roads.

He was thinking how true this was.

Then, just as he was thinking that he ought to make a protest, they came down on a broad plain.

"This is the right road to the Crystal Palace," cried the giant, pointing to a distant speck on the horizon. "I can't take you further."

Then he was away in a blazing ball, before they could say anything else.

One of the brothers shivered slightly. "Let's go back home; I do not like this."

"We've come this far. We should see it through until the end," said the eldest.

So they began to walk on towards the spot where the giant had pointed. But it never seemed to get nearer. So, finally, they all decided to return home. It took them a long, long time but eventually they came to Garras and on to Chygarkye and came into their house. They told their parents what had transpired.

"I wouldn't have given up," declared the young Wuric. "I would have journeyed on until I found out if our sister was happy or not."

"Well, you are an imbecile," his elder brothers declared in disgust. "How could you succeed when we, who are strong and intelligent, could not?"

Wuric flushed in annoyance and stood up. "I shall set out and I won't come back until I have discovered what has happened to my sister, Welet," he declared.

"You idiot!" sneered the eldest brother. "If you think that you can succeed, then be off with you!"

"I will try. And I will find her, wherever she is." So the next day, Wuric set off alone.

He followed the same road as his brothers had followed and eventually he came to the dark forest, moving in the direction of the rising sun. He heard the terrible thunderstorm and saw the flashes of lightning as he journeyed through the forest. Finally, he met an old woman, bending over a fire.

"Good evening, *dama-wyn*," he greeted politely.

"Where are you off to, my son?" the old woman replied.

"I am trying to find the *Forth Lys-an-Gwrys*. Do you know it?"

"I know it. But my son knows it better. Perhaps you have heard or seen him in the forest?"

"I believe I have heard him."

Just then there was a most fearful noise of thunder and lightning.

"Here comes my son. Quickly, hide under those trees, or he might eat you."

"Not I!" declared Wuric.

Then into the clearing came a giant of a man.

"Good evening, mother," he said. Then he sniffed. "I smell a Cornishman, I think. *Nown blyth a-m-bus*! I am ravenous."

"Then you will have to feed elsewhere," declared Wuric. "There is not enough meat on my bones to stuff your over-sized belly with."

The giant stared at him and then began to quake with laughter. "Here, indeed, is a game one," he chuckled. "Aren't you afraid of me?"

"I was told to respect thunder and lightning when I was a child, but never to fear it," replied Wuric.

The giant slapped his knee in delight, for no man had

talked to him like this before. "Tell me what you want here, and I shall help you."

His mother told him.

"I shall take you to the *Forth Lys-an-Gwrys* in the morning," declared the giant, whose name was Taran, which means "thunder".

Sure enough, in the morning, he flew up in the sky, with Wuric on his back, and landed him on a great plain.

"I can't take you further, but keep on across this plain. Soon you will find that it becomes a broad plain of blackened earth. Keep to the road, even if you find it impassable. Do not look right nor left and, no matter what is on the road, keep to it. If you go as fearlessly as you have come, you will reach *Forth Lys-an-Gwrys*."

Wuric kept to the road that Taran the giant had indicated and stuck to it, looking neither right nor left. He came to the plain and began to trek along the blackened earth road. Then he suddenly found his way blocked by a pile of writhing snakes. He halted for a moment in fear. Then he remembered Taran's words. He began to march straight into the snakes. They wrapped themselves around his legs, writhing and biting. But he took no notice of the hideous reptiles, hissing and menacing him. He did not lose his courage and walked through them without hurt.

Next the road came to the edge of a great lake. He could not swim and there was no sign of any boat. He remembered what Taran had said and on he marched, right into the deep, dank waters. Up to his knees the cold water came; up to his armpits, then up to his chin. Finally the waters closed blackly over his head but he kept going forward and suddenly he was on the other side of the lake.

The road continued until he found himself entering a narrow defile, which was full of thorns and brambles and with no way through them. Rocky cliffs stretched upwards for hundreds of feet on either side. Then he remembered what Taran had said. Down on his hands and knees he went and began to slither on his stomach through the undergrowth until he was through it – torn, cut and bleeding and his clothes were in tatters. Yet the moment he was through the other side, his cuts and scratches were healed.

He went on and finally came on an emaciated horse standing blocking the path.

"Climb on me," the horse invited. "I'll take you onwards on your journey."

"*Dursona*!" Wuric cried. "Blessing on you, horse. I'm too exhausted to walk further."

So the horse took him off along the path. That evening, they came to a spot where there was a large stone resting on top of two other stones.

"You must dismount now," said the horse. "See those two stones? Tip the top stone over."

Wuric did so and found a tunnel entrance.

"Go into the tunnel; that is your way forward," instructed the horse.

At first Wuric thought that he would suffocate in the stench of the tunnel. It was odious in the extreme, and the tunnel was so dark that he had to grope his way forward. Then he heard a terrible sound behind him like demons baying for blood.

"I shall doubtless die here," he shivered. But he remembered what Taran had said and set his jaw firmly before hastening on. Eventually he saw a glimmer of light ahead and it gave him hope. The noises behind were getting close but he gave a spurt and then he was through into the bright sunshine, out of the tunnel, and safe and sound.

Now he found his path came to a cross-roads.

He paused, dismayed, wondering which one he should take. Then he remembered what Taran had said and he took the one which led straight ahead. Now there were many high gates across the road and each was barred or padlocked. Being unable to open them, he simply climbed over them. It was hard going, but eventually he came to the brow of a hill and the last gate. Finally he saw, in the distance, a large palace of sparkling crystal.

"Surely that is *Lys-an-Gwrys*!" he cried. "I must be near the end of my journey."

He hurried forward and, after a while, he came to the gates of the Crystal Palace with its resplendent light, which dazzled his eyes. There were a number of doors around it and he tried each one, but each one was locked. Then he found a small open hatch which led onto a chute which went downwards. It was a ventilation chute into the cellars of the palace. He did not hesitate, but climbed in and slid down into the cellars.

From there, he went up the cellar stairs into a large kitchen, and from the kitchen into a hall. The rooms of the palace were of increasing beauty and so bright with light that he had to blink his eyes. Then he came to a hall of such surpassing beauty that he was almost blinded. But there, yes – there at the end of the room was a great bed of gold with silk sheets – and there was his sister, Welet, lying asleep on the bed. She looked as if she had not aged a single hour since he had last seen her. She did not wake but lay slumbering. She was so beautiful that Wuric stood back behind the curtains, just to watch her for a while.

He had no sooner taken his stand than the door opened and the tall figure of Lord Howlek entered. He was as resplendent as ever, with his red gold hair and flashing figure. He went straight to Welet and, to Wuric's surprise, he gave her three sharp slaps across the cheek. He went to move forward and protest but then he realized that his sister had not stirred – not even blinked an eye. Then the Lord Howlek climbed onto the bed and lay down at her side.

Wuric thought it a strange way to treat his sister. Then he saw that Lord Howlek was in a deep sleep and he wondered what to do. Perhaps he should find something to eat and a room to rest in. Then he realized that although he had been weary and had a great hunger on him when he arrived at the palace, he now felt rested and replete. He could not understand it. He sat down and found that the night passed profoundly peacefully. Wuric did not even move from his hiding place.

Then, as dawn approached, Lord Howlek stood up and gave Welet three sharp smacks on the cheek and left. Still Welet did not even move.

When Lord Howlek had left, Wuric left his hiding place and went to the sleeping form of his sister. Now he feared that death had overtaken her. So still and calm she was, in spite of the resounding smacks on her cheeks. Wuric reached out a hand and felt her forehead and assured himself she was still alive. Then he bent and kissed her brow. As he did so, she gave a smile, opened her eyes and stretched languidly. Then she recognized her brother and her smile grew broader.

"Wuric! How came you here? What joy to see you!"

They embraced each other.

"Sister, I have been worried for you."

"What cause to worry, brother?"

"Where is your husband?" Wuric was anxious, lest Lord Howlek come back into the bedroom.

"Gone on a journey. You surely must have seen him, for he left my side only a moment ago."

Then Wuric realized that if his sister knew this, she must surely have been feigning stillness when Lord Howlek slapped her. "Oh, my poor sister, it grieves me to see him ill-treat you so."

"But he is my joy, brother. He does not ill-treat me at all." Welet was clearly puzzled by what he had said.

"How can you say this?" he demanded. "I witnessed him slap you last night when he came in. Three hard slaps on the cheek. When he rose this morning, the Lord Howlek did spitefully use you again by giving you three slaps on the cheek."

"You are surely mistaken, brother, for he does not give me a slap, nor three slaps. Each evening he comes and kisses me three times and each morning he bids me farewell with three kisses."

Wuric was perplexed.

Then he realized it was surely breakfast time, but he still felt replete.

"There seems neither cold nor hunger in this place, sister. I have seen no servants, nor any preparations for food. What does this mean?"

"I have no idea, brother. But it is true, for as long as I have been here, I have not experienced the desire to eat nor drink."

"Is there no one else here?"

"Oh, yes. But my lord told me that I must not speak to anyone. But I have not seen anyone since I came here."

So they spent the day together, talking about their family and what had happened in the kingdom of Cornwall since she left. That evening, Lord Howlek came to the palace and saw Wuric.

"This is my youngest brother," said Welet hastily, seeing his frown.

"Ah, I recognize you now. You have come to visit us? That is good of you."

"Not without great hardship in the journey," added Wuric.

"I can believe you. No one has ever come as far as this. But on your journey back, the road will be easier, for I shall ensure that you will be well protected over the harder paths."

So Wuric stayed with his sister, Welet, and her husband, the Lord Howlek. Each day, Lord Howlek left the palace, and he returned each night. Nor was there any cause to eat and drink, for they always felt replete. Intrigued by the manner of living at the Crystal Palace, Wuric asked his sister where her husband went each day.

"I do not know, nor have I ever asked him."

So the next morning, Welet asked her husband: "Where do you go, each day?"

Howlek frowned. "What makes you ask this question?"

"My brother is curious."

And Wuric, when asked, confirmed his curiosity. "I would like to go with you, wherever it is, for I would like to see this country before I return to the kingdom of Cornwall."

"Then you shall, but there is one condition."

"I shall respect it, whatever it is."

"You will do exactly as I say."

"No hardship in that."

"Then you must not touch anything and you must speak only with me, no matter what you see or hear."

Wuric agreed to these conditions.

So they left the Crystal Palace and started along a path that was so narrow that Wuric could only follow behind the Lord Howlek. Then they came to a vast arid plain of sand, so broad that it stretched like a great desert. There in the middle of it was a herd of big fat cattle, sitting in the sand and chewing their cud.

On they went until they came to a plain of grass, thick and tall. Here there was a herd of thin, emaciated cattle, bellowing pitifully.

"Listen, brother-in-law," whispered Wuric, "tell me, for I have never seen the like: how do cattle grow fat in a sandy desert while they grow lean in a big grassy plain. Can you explain this to me?"

Lord Howlek smiled thinly. "Know this: the fat cattle are the poor people who are content with their lot and do not covet other people's wealth. The emaciated cattle are those who are always fighting one another for wealth: fighting to increase their riches, and never satisfied because they are seeking more and more at the expense of others."

On they went until they came to a river bank where they saw two giant oak trees clashing and banging against each other so bitterly that the splinters of wood flew off them. It was so terrible that Wuric could not help himself, for he had a tender heart. He had a staff and he stretched it forward between the two trees.

"Stop this terrible fighting! You must not mistreat one another. Learn to live in peace."

No sooner had he spoken these words than the trees disappeared and in their place were two men.

"We've been condemned to fight like this for an eternity, for we were always fighting in life. Our punishment was to argue and fight until some charitable soul took pity on us. Now we can progress to the Land of the Ever Young. Blessings on you, young sir."

The two humans vanished.

Lord Howlek moved on and they came to a cave entrance. From inside came a terrible uproar. Cries, curses, screams and wailing – Wuric's blood ran cold.

"What is it?"

"That is the entrance to Purgatory. Now you must turn back, for you have disobeyed me. You should not have spoken or interfered between those two trees. Return to your sister. When I get back tonight, I will place you on the road homewards."

So Wuric returned to the Crystal Palace and his sister

asked, "Why are you back so soon, without my lord Howlek?"

"I disobeyed him."

"So you do not know everywhere he goes?"

"No. I do not." But Wuric could not suppress a shiver when he remembered the entrance to Purgatory.

That evening, the Lord Howlek returned and said to Wuric, "Because you have broken your promise, you must return to the kingdom of Cornwall and bide there awhile. One day you will return here, and then you will stay for ever. Only then will you see the extent of my journey."

"I will go," Wuric agreed. "But I must know one thing above all others."

"Ask away," Lord Howlek said.

"Why do you slap Welet instead of kissing her?"

Lord Howlek smiled. "Because I love her. Do you not know the old proverb – the spontaneity of a slap shows sincerity, whereas the ceremonial of caresses is largely convention?"

"That I do not understand."

Lord Howlek sighed. "One day, you will."

So there was a tearful parting with his sister, and Wuric followed Lord Howlek to the start of a road.

"Go without fear on this road and you will soon be home. Remember that this parting will not be for long. You will return here quite soon."

So Wuric went off along the road, a little sad and greatly puzzled. Nothing hindered him in that journey back. On he went, feeling neither fatigue nor hunger nor pain. Soon he came to Garras and on to Chygarkye, and he went to look for the house of his parents and his brothers. But he could not find them.

"This is the very spot that the house stood, otherwise I am a fool indeed," Wuric said, pausing by a field and peering around.

He saw a man walking along the road.

"Hey, fellow, I am looking for the house of Kellow and his wife and sons."

The fellow shook his head.

"Kellow? No one by that name lives here, nor any of that name since my father's father's day."

The man stared at him thoughtfully. Then he scratched his head. "But there do be a legend around the forest of Chygarkye of a Kellow and his sons who told of how their daughter married a great lord and they were but poor peasant folks. But that were many hundreds of years gone by."

Wuric felt suddenly cold. "Many *hundreds* of years ago?"

"So the legend goes."

Wuric went to the old mystical mound at The Mount above Halliggye and sat down and wept for his lost family. They found him there a few days later, the body of an ancient old man, more skin and bone than flesh. He was so great an age, that they do say his body crumbled to dust when they were taking him to be buried down at Garras.

And who is to say where his soul went?

Some hint darkly that he took the road back to *Lys-an-Gwrys* to dwell with his sister, Welet, and her Lord Howlek at the gates of Purgatory.

Brittany (Breizh)

Brittany: Preface

I have always felt a particular attachment to Brittany, or Breizh, as it is named in the Breton language. My grandmother, Sarah-Ann DuLake, was the granddaughter of a Breton political exile, Jean-Joseph DuLac, who had been employed in the office of the Procureur-Général Syndic of the États Bretagne, or the Breton Parliament. In his early years he worked under Louis-René Caradeuc de la Chalotais (1701–85) who, as Procureur-Général, had dared challenge the power of the French King Louis XV in 1764.

As the facts of Brittany's incorporation into the French state are little known in the English-speaking world, I make no apology for devoting a few paragraphs to this intriguing subject.

In the medieval period, Brittany had been an independent and prosperous trading country, but had long been the object of territorial ambition by both England and France. Finally, in 1488, the Breton armies, under Francis II of Brittany, had been defeated by the French, under Charles VIII, at Aubin St Cromer. A treaty was signed with Francis II accepting Charles VIII as his "suzerain lord". But Francis II died soon after and his daughter Anne succeeded. She tried to regain Breton independence. The Treaty of Laval emphasized Brittany's military defeat and Anne was forced to marry Charles VIII at Langeais on 6 December 1491. When Charles VIII died, Anne then had to marry Louis XII, so that the precarious "union" could be maintained. However, when Louis XII's heir François I succeeded to the throne in 1515, Anne's daughter Claude had to marry him, in order for the French to maintain that union. With that marriage, the crown head of Brittany rested in the crown of France.

This was made law in the *Traité d'Union de la Bretagne à la France* on 18 September 1532. The French promised to respect the autonomous position of Brittany within the French empire and its autonomous parliament, the États. From Henri II, in 1554, however, attempts were made to assimilate Brittany into a centralized French state.

The Bretons proved stubborn at surrendering their independence. When Louis XV made attempts to centralize financial autonomy in 1760, Procureur Général La Chalotais reminded the French in no uncertain terms as to the conditions of the Treaty of 1532. Chalotais was imprisoned for his defence of Breton independence. He was released and returned to Brittany in 1774, on the death of Louis XV, and received a triumphal reception in the Breton Parliament, which now called itself the National Assembly of Brittany.

But the end of Brittany's independence was in sight. Chalotais did not see it, as he died in 1785. Jean-Joseph DuLac did not appear to have suffered imprisonment with Chalotais.

The seeds of revolution and republicanism grew in Brittany's fertile soil and no less than 333 officers of the American revolutionary army in 1776 were Breton volunteers, men like the Marquis La Fayette, Marquis de la Rouerie, Comte Guichen and others. Enthusiastic Bretons fitted out sixteen warships and manned them for the American Revolution. The Bretons threw themselves into the revolution, thinking to rid themselves of the centralizing policies of the French kings and maintain their political independence. But the French republicans were even more centralist and succeeded where the French monarchs had not; they declared Breton autonomy "a privilege" and abolished the Breton Parliament.

The President of the Vacation Court of the États Bretagne protested to the French Constituent Assembly: "*Les Corps ont des privileges. Les nations ont des droits!*" (Parliament has privileges. Nations have rights!) Vicomte de Botherel, who had become the Procureur Général Syndic, raised the same protest in a printed manifesto. Even the Marquis La Fayette had made an impassioned plea to the French republicans to allow Brittany to retain its independence in the Breton Parliament, before giving up and accepting a place in the new French National Assembly.

His fellow Bretons did not give up so easily, led by the Marquis de la Rouerie, who had learnt his craft as a brigadier in the American Revolution, and then by Georges Cadoudal; there followed over ten years of bitter warfare in Brittany. There were no less than four armed camps: Breton republicans and Breton royalists, who wished an independent Brittany with different ideologies, and French royalists and French republicans, who wanted to incorporate Brittany in the French state but differed as to the type of French state. All four were fighting each other.

Breton autonomy was inevitably lost, for the French republicans and French royalists were in accord on one thing: that Brittany was to become part of France, and the new centralist French state emerged.

Many political Bretons fled abroad. Vicomte de Botherel went to London, where he made an annual protest at the abolition of the Breton parliament until his death in 1805. My grandmother's grandfather also arrived in England at that time, to act as Botherel's secretary and he eventually changed the name DuLac to DuLake.

Our family, therefore had Breton, as well as Irish, Welsh and Scottish branches and I was fortunate to imbibe folklore from each. I found the Breton folk tales were particularly fascinating. We had the works of Anatole Le Braz on our bookshelves, such as his *Land of Pardons* (1884). Another assiduous collector of Breton legends was Francois-Marie Luzel (1821–95) with works such as *Contes Populaires de Basse-Bretagne*, Paris, 1879. He published many editions of Breton medieval mystery plays and volumes of legends and folktales and songs in such works as *Gwerziou Breiz-Izel* (1868–74) and *Soniou Breiz-Izel* (1890).

His work provided an essential background for some of these retellings. I am also indebted to P. Sébillot's *Costumes populaires de la Haute-Bretagne, Paris*, 1886, and to the many scholarly works of the Abbé Francois Falc'hun, such as *Perspectives nouvelles sur l'histoire de la langue Bretonne* (Presses Universitaires de France, 1963).

I should emphasize that the stories chosen here are those handed down orally until the nineteenth century, when various versions were noted down, particularly by Luzel. The medieval literature of the Breton *lai* has not been used, even though some see them as an integral part of Breton legend and folklore. In fact, the Breton *lai* became popular in England during the fourteenth century. They were transmitted to England via French translations rather than directly from the Breton form.

The *lais* usually dealt with Celtic themes from the Arthurian Cycle. Marie de France (*ca* AD 1200) became famous for her Breton *lais*, versified narratives full of Celtic myths and atmosphere. Of the fifteen Breton *lais* that are extant, *Sir Launfel* is the best known. He was a warrior at Arthur's court who fell in love with a fairy. Guinevere accused Launfel of insulting her and Arthur swore to have him executed. James Russell Lowell retold the tale in his 1848 version *The Vision of Sir Launfel*.

Over the years, some notes and advice, which I have incorporated into these retellings, have come from Yann Tremel and Professor Per Denez, formerly of the University of Rennes. And there had always been the guiding hand of Philippe Le Solliec of Lorient.

The story of "The Destruction of Ker-Ys" is almost a classic and its retellings from Le Braz and Luzel and others are numerous. The version of "N'oun Doaré" given here differs in several respects from the oral tradition picked up from F.-M. Luzel in Morlaix in 1874. I am convinced that this version, for which I have to thank Professor Per Denez for referring me, shows more of the original Celtic motifs than the one Luzel copied down from the Morlaix factory worker.

The title "Prinsez-a-Sterenn" could, in fact, mean "Princess of the Pole Star," but when F.-M. Luzel collected a version in the tale in the 1860s/1870s, he rendered it into French as "Princess of the Shining Star". I have decided to keep to the Breton title, as still used in Cornouaille.

32 *The Destruction of Ker-Ys*

At the hour of the birth of Gwezenneg, Prince of Bro Érech, a holy man foretold that he would be king. But the holy man also issued a warning: that on the day Gwezenneg ate pork, drank watered wine and renounced his God, then he would surely die. And his death would come about by poison, by burning and by drowning.

Such was the nature of this prophecy that everyone at the court of Bro Érech laughed and sent the holy man away to his hermitage, with patronising smiles but also with gifts, lest he be a man of true prophecy.

The years went by and Gwezenneg grew to be a tall, handsome prince. It came about, as the holy man foretold, that he was acclaimed King of Bro Érech, a kingdom in the southernmost part of Armorica, the land by the sea, which we now call "Little Britain". Gwezenneg married a princess of Kernascleden named Gwyar, and she bore him two sons. And Gwezenneg grew in fame and sought to extend the borders of his kingdom; he fought several wars with neighbouring princes, to expand his kingdom.

All the while, however, he was aware of the prophecy made at his birth.

One day, he was hunting in the great forests of Pont Calleck, by the edge of the great lake there, when he came upon a beautiful young woman. Never had he beheld such beauty before. She sat on a log by the shore of the lake, combing her hair with a silver comb ornamented with gold. The sun was shining on her so that her two golden-yellow tresses, each one braided in four plaits, with a bead at the end of each plait, glistened like liquid fire.

She was dressed in a skirt of green silk, with a tunic of red, all embroidered with designs of animals in gold and silver. She wore a round golden brooch with filigree work decorated with silver. From her slender shoulders, there hung a cloak of purple.

Her upper arms were white as the snow of a single night and they were soft and shapely. Her cheeks had the tinge of the foxglove of the moor upon them. Her eyebrows were coloured black and her eyes were as blue as the bugloss. Her lips were vermilion. The blush of the moon was on her fair countenance, and there was a lifting pride in her noble face.

"Maiden, tell me your name," demanded Gwezenneg, alighting from his horse and going on his knees before her as a tribute to her beauty.

She smiled softly, a dimple of sport in both her cheeks, and she answered with a gentle womanly dignity in her voice. "I am called 'whirlwind', 'tempest' and 'storm'."

"Lady, I would give the kingdom of Bro Érech to know you." His children and queen, Gwyar, were all forgotten. "Lady of the rough winds, come as my mistress to my royal palace at Vannes. I will grant you anything that is in my power."

"Think well on this, O king," replied the girl. "I have warned you of the storm to come. Do you still desire me?"

"I do."

"Then I will come to your palace, on the condition that no Christian cleric shall ever set foot there, and that you must submit to my will in all things."

Without even thinking, Gwezenneg, mesmerized by the deep blue of her eyes, agreed.

So the girl, who said her name was Aveldro, the whirlwind, came to the king's palace at Vannes.

Horrified, Gwyar, Gwezenneg's queen, took her children and went straightaway to Guénolé, the bishop, and, sobbing, asked him to intervene and cure her husband's infatuation. And when Guénolé came to Gwezenneg, the king would not listen to him. The bishop then turned to Aveldro, who was sitting unconcerned by the side of her lover. He demanded whether she felt guilt.

Aveldro turned to him with a smile.

"Guilt is for the followers of your God, Gunwalloe," she said, using the ancient form of his name, so that he would know his pagan past. "Guilt is not for those who follow the old ways."

And Guénolé was enraged. "Do you not follow the Christ?" he demanded.

"I cleave not to the clerics of your church," she replied. "They chant nothing save unreason, and their tune is unmelodious in the universe."

Then Guénolé cursed King Gwezenneg and reminded him that his doom had already been foretold.

Gwezenneg grew afraid at this, but Aveldro caused a great wind to blow through the palace which swept the cursing cleric from its halls. Now Aveldro had done this feat of magic in order to put heart into Gwezenneg. But he was awed by her great power and realized that she was a *dryades*: that is to say, a female Druid. And he feared Guénolé's curse and the prophecy of his birth. So he waited until Aveldro had retired before he summoned a messenger and told him to go after Guénolé, telling the bishop that Gwezenneg would come to him as soon as he could and confess all his sins, do penance, and with his blessing would eject Aveldro from his court.

The next evening, Aveldro summoned him for the evening meal and a dish of meat was placed before the king.

"What meat is this?" he demanded of his cook, after he had chewed and swallowed a large piece. His cook looked uncomfortable.

"Why, we had no slaughtered beef nor mutton in the kitchen and so your lady," he glanced awkwardly at Aveldro, "told us to serve the pig we had slaughtered for the servants. She said that you would approve."

And Gwezenneg went white, for he knew the significance of eating pig. He reached for his wine glass to swallow the wine, in order to wash out the unclean meat from his mouth. He took one swallow before spitting out the rest of the wine in disgust.

"What weak wine is this?" he demanded of the chamberlain, who had served the wine.

His chamberlain looked awkwardly at Aveldro.

"Why, sire, we had only one flagon of good wine left in the palace and so your lady told us to add a little water to it, so that it would go that much further. She said that you would approve."

"God be damned!" swore Gwezenneg, rising up in anger from his place. Then, realizing the nature of his unthinking curse, he sat down abruptly. Gwezenneg sat white-faced and stared at Aveldro, who smiled a knowing smile.

Aveldro was a skilful Druidess, for she could read the thoughts of the King of Bro Érech just as surely as if he had spoken them aloud. She knew that he had planned to go to Guénolé and betray her. So, that same night, she evoked a vision which mesmerized him. And once more he pleaded for Aveldro to come to bed with him and make love and, in the vision, she consented.

Then Gwezenneg awoke from his lovemaking with a dry mouth and a great thirst which lay heavily on him.

"I thirst," he moaned, "but can find no water."

Aveldro smiled beside him. "I will go to the kitchen, my lover, and bring you some crystal cold water to assuage your thirst."

When she returned, she handed him a glass of water. He drained the glass and returned to sleep.

She watched his sleep and was satisfied, for she had placed poison in the glass.

At dawn, she was abruptly wakened by distant shouting. She smelt smoke and burning. It had happened that Gwyar, driven to distraction with her anger, had come upon the palace that night and set a fire under her husband's sleeping chamber.

Aveldro, taking a last look at her poisoned lover, decided to flee the palace. She had wanted to be there when Gwezenneg's body was discovered, so that no blame would attach itself to her. But with the flames licking at the walls, she decided that her journey westward to her home must be precipitate. She escaped from the burning fortress and disappeared into the dawn light.

Now Gwezenneg, drugged with the poison, was not yet dead. For he was a strong and healthy man and it took a time for the poison to work through his system. The noise of shouting awoke him and he saw great flames engulfing his chamber. In discomfort from the poison, he staggered from his bed and, standing swaying, he gazed about him, finding himself amidst the smoke and crackling fires. He sought for a means of escape. The heat was intense but he managed to flee from the bedchamber as the blazing ridge poles of the roof came crashing down.

He made his way down the stone stairs, with the stones so hot that they burnt and blistered his bare feet, and found himself in the kitchens of the palace. There he was trapped by a great sheet of flame and, in desperation, he saw the tall water vats. In an effort to escape the flames, he clambered into the first vat, which was filled with water. He plunged into its icy depth, intending to wait there until the flames had passed.

But the poison had so weakened him that he could not swim and, after a minute or two, he sank into the cold water of the vat and was drowned.

The next day, when Guénolé came to the smouldering ruins of the palace, the attendants of King Gwezenneg told him what had happened, for they had found the body of the king in the debris. Guénolé knew then that the prophecy had been fulfilled. But he knew also that the cause of it was the mysterious woman named Aveldro, the whirlwind. He vowed that Aveldro, who had denied the Living God, would have to pay reparation for this deed, if ever she was found.

The time came when Guénolé left the sad kingdom of Bro Érech and set about a journey westward to the kingdom of Kernev, which is Cornouaille, which stretched south from the Monts d'Arrée and east to the River Ellé, beyond the great realm of Domnonia. Guénolé had heard that this kingdom of Kernev was still fiercely pagan. So he set out to convert it and he built a great monastery, which is called Landévennec, and slowly the people of Kernev turned to him and accepted his teachings.

However, Kernev was ruled by an eminent king called

Gradlon. Gradlon ruled from a great city called Ker-Ys, which is "the beloved place", which was situated in what is now the Baie des Trépassés, that is the Bay of the Dead, just off the Pointe du Raz, for at the time the land of Kernev stretched over this area of the sea.

Ker-Ys was a mighty place and spoken of in awe by those merchants who had travelled to its massive walls.

Guénolé was put in a mind to see the city and to bring the word of the Living God to its king, Gradlon.

One day, seated in his cell at Landévennec, he sent for his disciple, Gwion, who had been a fisherman from Kerazan and had often sailed the western coast around Kernev.

"Tell me of this Gradlon and Ker-Ys, for tomorrow I mean to make a journey to see them."

Gwion looked slightly worried. "They hold steadfast to the old gods," he warned his master.

"So did many of us, until we heard the truth," Guénolé replied complacently.

"Gradlon is certainly a fair king," Gwion said. "A sad king, though. Once, many years ago, Gwezenneg of Bro Érech tried to extend the borders of his kingdom to the west and into the territory of Kernev. He brought an army with him and crossed the River Scorv at Hennebont, which is the old bridge.

"It happened on that day Gradlon's wife and queen, Dieub, was visiting her kinfolk at Belon. And with her was her son Youlek the Determined. Gwezenneg and his warriors came down like a plague of locusts, slaughtering all before them and leaving behind the blackened earth stained red with blood. And the blood of Gradlon's wife, Dieub, was among that which had mingled with the sorry clay. And the blood of Gradlon's son, Youlek, also drenched the earth, for Youlek had tried to protect his mother with his word. And all the generations of Dieub's family were slaughtered."

Guénolé was troubled when he heard this, for Gwezenneg had been a Christian king and unworthy to have committed such a slaughter.

"Did Gradlon seek vengeance for the deed?"

Gwion shook his head.

"No; he sent his ambassadors to Gwezenneg, asking for reparation and was refused. Each year, at the festival of Imbolc, he sent his ambassadors and they came back from Vannes empty-handed. His daughter, Dahud-Ahes, whose beauty is renowned in the west, and who, it is said, is a mighty Druidess, demanded that her father take his army and seize that which Gwezenneg refused to give. Gradlon is a wise and worthy king and refused to lower himself to the actions of Gwezenneg."

Guénolé was pleased then, for he knew that Gradlon was such a king as he could convert to the true faith. But he was worried when he heard about Dahud-Ahes.

On the next morning, he set out for the west and Ker-Ys. The further west he went, the more forbidding the country became, with bare heathland and no trees but scrubland, and little stone walls here and there, as a means of enclosing the scanty crops which grew. There came a long narrow spur of land, torn by waves on either side, overlooking the sea from a height of two hundred feet, and this was prolonged seaward into a chain of reefs. Then, to the north, there was a low green plain, protected from the sea by a long high dyke, which stretched between the Pointe du Raz and the Pointe du Van for, as we have said, this area was once land.

The great dyke had built into it two massive gates, which acted in the manner of a lock, and no one could open these gates, for they would flood the city. The gates were secured by a massive padlock, to which there was but one golden key, which Gradlon carried on a chain around his neck.

Guénolé rode up to the gates of Ker-Ys and demanded entrance and access to Gradlon. Gradlon readily admitted the man and listened to all he had to say.

"There is much that is true in what you say," Gradlon conceded, after a while. "I would learn more."

"I would not!" rang out a voice.

A most beautiful woman entered the hall and, from the way the attendants bowed low, Guénolé knew he was in the presence of Dahud-Ahes, daughter of Gradlon. As his disciple, Gwion, had said, she was a mighty Druidess.

Then Guénolé peered closer. "Are you not known as Whirlwind?" he demanded.

Dahud-Ahes smiled condescendingly. "What do you think?" she parried.

Guénolé gasped. "Yes, by the Living God. You are Aveldro, who caused the death of Gwezenneg!"

Dahud-Ahes stood without shame. "It was my right to take vengeance. Did not this Gwezenneg take the life of my mother, Dieub, and my brother Youlek? And did he not slaughter all my mother's family?"

"Yet you took his life by sorcery," breathed Guénolé, genuflecting.

"I took his life, as he took the lives of my kin," affirmed Dahud-Ahes.

Gradlon hung his head in shame. "What you have done is not justice, daughter. Vengeance is not reparation."

"Vengeance satisfies the soul," replied Dahud-Ahes. "My soul is at peace."

"We are born bound to the great wheel of life, Dahud-Ahes," warned Guénolé. "There is no action without a consequence. Just as Gwezenneg has paid for his action, so must you pay for your action." He turned to Gradlon. "King, I feel that you wish to reach out for the truth of the Living God. When the time comes, you will find me at the city of Kemper."

So he left the court of Gradlon.

That evening, Dahud-Ahes was in her bedchamber when, without warning, a young man of surpassing handsomeness entered. He was so handsome that Dahud-Ahes found herself trembling from her desire of him.

"You are no mortal man," she murmured.

"I am Maponos, the god of love," he replied with a smile. "And of all the women on the earth, I have heard that you were the most beautiful. Now I have seen the truth of it with my own eyes. And I desire you. Come away with me and dwell with me in the palace of love, which is far to the west of this place."

Dahud-Ahes lost all her rationality. Indeed, as Gwezenneg had fallen under her spell, she fell under the spell of this young man. "I will," she replied with vehemence.

Then the handsome Maponos hesitated. "I have admitted my love for you. But, before we go to my eternal palace, you must prove that you love me. The entrance to my palace is known only to myself and, if you share this secret, I need a token of your love."

"I will do anything," she replied simply.

"Then fetch the golden key of the gate in the dyke which hangs around your father's neck. Fetch it and unlock the gates."

"But the whole city will drown," protested Dahud-Ahes.

"Not so. If you believe in me, I will not let it drown. Am I not a god and cannot I stop such floods? If you desire to live with me in all eternity, then you must do this thing, to prove your worthiness."

For Dahud-Ahes, there was never any doubt of her desire and she ran straightaway to her father's bedchamber and, finding him asleep, she took the golden key and chain from around his neck. Then she hurried to the great gate where the handsome young god stood.

"Open the gate," instructed Maponos, "if you trust and desire me. Prove to me that you believe in me."

She put the key in the lock, turned it and flung open the gate. The vast green frothy sea rushed in. Dahud-Ahes turned eagerly to the young man.

"Now save the city, for I have proved my love for you," she cried.

The young man started to laugh. He laughed and, as he did so, his body was transformed into a twisted, ageing devil with the evil, sneering face of Gwezenneg. Then, with the laughter still echoing, the figure disappeared.

In terror and despair, Dahud-Ahes ran through the city of Ker-Ys, raising the alarm. The sea rushed down, its waves like hungry mouths swallowing all in their path.

"Mount up behind, my daughter!"

Gradlon rode up beside her on his fastest charger, and Dahud-Ahes was swung up behind. The king rode as hard as he could before the mighty, oncoming tide, the powerful sinews of his horse bursting with the effort. But the sea began to overtake them, to swallow them. Gradlon began to despair when he heard the voice of Guénolé.

"If you would save yourself and your people, Gradlon, throw your unworthy and shameful daughter off into the sea. She has betrayed you for her own desires."

With aching heart, Gradlon did as he was bid. He pushed his pleading daughter back into the hungry waves. The seas began to recede, although Ker-Ys remained submerged. But all the people of Ker-Ys managed to reach the safety of dry land, except for Dahud-Ahes, who was swept under the mighty waves. But because Dahud-Ahes was bound to the wheel of fate, because she was not the beginning nor the ending of its cycle, Guénolé took pity on her.

"You will live your time as one of the merfolk, living in the sunken palaces of Ker-Ys for all eternity!"

And so it is, throughout time, Dahud-Ahes, in the form of a mermaid, still lures unwary sailors, drawn on by her unsurpassable beauty, to the bottom of the sea. Thus, in the language of the Bretons, the place is called *Boé an Anaon*, or the Bay of Suffering Souls.

Gradlon, meanwhile, went on in sorrow to Kemper, which is still called Quimper to this day. And he became a convert of Guénolé. When that venerable man returned to his monastery at Landévennec, Gradlon chose Corentin as the bishop of his city, and ended his days in the odour of sanctity, guided and sustained by Corentin, who became patron of the town. And if you climb the cathedral that is in the Place St Corentin today, you will find that a statue of Gradlon on horseback stands between its two spires.

But beware of standing on the Pointe de Raz, listening to the whispering of the sea amongst the rocks: beware, lest you hear the seductive calling of Dahud-Ahes.

33 N'oun Doaré

There was once a noble chieftain of Montroulez, in Léon, one of the five ancient kingdoms of Armorica, the land by the sea. Montroulez is now known by the French form of the name – Morlaix. This noble chieftain was called Bras, for he was tall as well as important, and he ruled the adjacent territory of Coat-Squiriou. He had been to the great horse-fair in Montroulez to acquire a new plough-horse, and was accompanied by his servant.

As Bras and his servant rode back after the fair, along the dusty road towards his fortress, they heard a whimpering from the hedge. It was the cry of a distressed child. Bras was a kindly man who had not been blessed with children, although he and his wife Anvab loved and wanted children more than their rich castle and estates. So when he heard the cry of the distressed child, he halted his horse and told his servant to investigate.

The servant climbed down from the plough-horse, for that was the horse he was riding, and went to peer into the hedge. He found, to his surprise, a small boy, not more than five years old, huddled against the chill air, trying to sleep under the thorn bush.

The child had been whimpering in his sleep.

The servant prodded the boy and woke him.

The child let out a yell and cowered back, clearly frightened.

"What is it?" called Bras.

"A young knave, sir, hiding in the bushes," replied the servant.

Bras climbed down and came to investigate, himself. "What are you doing there, boy?" he demanded.

The boy cringed back. "I don't know," he replied.

"Trying to sleep, I think, sir," offered the servant.

"Who is your father, boy?" demanded Bras, wondering how such a young boy could be allowed to wander alone in the country and sleep in such a place.

"I don't know," replied the boy.

Bras raised his eyes in surprise. "And who is your mother, then?"

"I don't know," replied the boy.

Bras shook his head in wonder. "Where do you come from, then?" pressed the chieftain. "Surely you know that?"

"I don't know."

"What is your name?"

"I don't know."

"By the long hand of Lug!" snapped the chieftain, "are those the only words you know?"

"I don't know," answered the child doggedly.

Even the servant could not help but smile.

"Well, we shall call you 'I don't know', until such time as you discover your own name or earn a new one," replied Bras. And from then on the child was called *N'oun Doaré*, which means "I don't know" in the Breton language.

Bras told the child that he should come with him, and Bras and his wife would take care of him until they found who his parents were. The child did not object and so the servant took him up on the plough-horse and, with Bras leading the way, they returned to the great fortress of Coat-Squiriou.

The Lady Anvab fell in love with the young child and soon took him in hand, having him washed and given clean clothes and food. It was obvious that she saw, in the child, the baby that she could not have. And in that, Bras was also pleased to have the child around his castle. Yet he was a fair and just man. He sent his servants to the five kingdoms of Armorica and in each of them enquiries were made about the mysterious child and his parents. But no one knew him nor came forward to name him as their own.

Two years passed. N'oun Doaré drew near the age when

most sons of chieftains were sent to "fosterage" – that is when they were sent away to seek an education. Now Bras had a cousin, who was a famous Druid in Carhaix, which lay south across the hills; he decided that N'oun Doaré should go to his cousin, the Druid, for his education.

Needless to say, before the child went, Bras had to deal with some protests from his wife. But she accepted it in the end, for that was the way of things. Chieftains' sons always went away to study until they reached the "age of choice", which was seventeen years of age.

The years passed – quickly for N'oun Doaré, and slowly for Anvab and Bras. Then, one day, a handsome young man approached their fortress. He was slim, had red-gold hair and keen blue eyes. He bore himself with a noble elegance. Bras, having seen the young man approach, had gone down to the castle gates to greet the stranger and he was amazed when this youth rushed up to him and embraced him like a son.

"It is I. It is N'oun Doaré!"

Bras recovered from his surprise to call his wife, Anvab, and that evening there was a great feasting, with music and the best wine of the country to celebrate the return of the boy whom they had made their own son.

That evening Bras told N'oun Doaré how pleased he was. "Tomorrow, I shall swear before my council that I have adopted you and that you are now my heir-elect. You must win my people's hearts as you have won those of Anvab and myself."

The young man bowed his head in gratitude. According to the ancient law, Bras could name one of his family as the heir-elect, but it had to be approved by the family.

"You honour me too much. I still do not know who I am nor where I come from. I have no memory other than being awakened in that ditch by your servant all those years ago."

"It matters not," Lady Anvab told the boy. "We know all that there is to know about you. It is what you are now that counts. Not what you were."

Bras was as good as his word. The next day he made the formal announcement to his council and his chiefs and nobles were pleased, for everyone in Coat-Squiriou liked the young boy and were pleased he had turned into a well-educated young man.

"Did my cousin teach you the use of arms, as befitting a son of a chief?" asked Bras one day.

The young man nodded. "Your cousin, the Druid, taught me many things," N'oun Doaré replied. "Among them was the use of arms in order to protect the weak from any injustice caused by the arrogance of the strong."

Bras was pleased. "Then today we shall ride for Montroulez. There is a blacksmith there who makes weapons for the king of Léon himself. That is the place where we may purchase for you the best sword in the land."

So they straightaway rode off for Montroulez and it was the day of the Haute Foire, the middle of October, and there was a great market in the town. They came to the blacksmith's shop and spent a long time there, examining many fine weapons. But N'oun Doaré did not appear to be interested in any of them. None of them seemed to please him and, finally, they left the blacksmith, who was greatly irritated, without making a purchase. Bras was actually puzzled by the seemingly over-particular attitude of the youth when he examined the weapons.

They were passing through the stalls of the fair, in the main square of the town, when N'oun Doaré halted. Bras frowned, for they were among the seedier stalls of junk, away from the stalls where a chieftain like himself might expect a good purchase.

N'oun Doaré was examining a stall on which there was a lot of scrap metal, twisted and rusty items that surely no one would want. From the tangled mess of bent and rusting metal, he had extracted an ancient rusty iron sword. He weighed it in his hand as if testing the balance of the ancient metal.

The stall-holder came forward. He wore a single black robe with a cowl, shielding him from head to toe. He kept his head lowered, as if out of respect.

"Look closely at the blade, young sir. There is some writing there."

N'oun Doaré peered closely and scraped away a little of the

rust to reveal some worn lettering. He managed to decipher it. "I am invincible," it read.

He turned to Bras, who was looking on with disapproval. "This is the sword for me, Bras, my father. Will you purchase it for me?"

Bras stared at N'oun Doaré as if the boy had lost his head. "What? This is scrap. It's eaten with rust. Look at the state it is in. Besides, it's not even steel: it is rusty iron, centuries old. Who wants an iron sword that will bend and rip before a trusty steel blade? Are you joking with me? You have passed up swords fit for a king and now choose this piece of rusty scrap. It's good for nothing."

N'oun Doaré smiled patiently. He could not explain to Bras that he felt a curious compulsion to be the owner of the rusty sword. "Please, my father, buy it for me – and you will see that it is good for something."

The stall-holder, still keeping his head lowered, said softly to Bras, the chieftain: "The young man has made a wise choice, sir."

Bras sniffed in disapproval. "And I suppose that you want to rob me, now?" he said disdainfully to the stall-owner. "How much do you want for this worthless scrap?"

"The price is the handclasp of a just chieftain," and the stall-holder held out his hand to Bras.

The chieftain was so taken aback that he reached into his purse and took out a silver coin. "Here is my hand, my man, but you cannot live on that, so here is a coin to go with it."

They continued on through the market with N'oun Doaré apparently delighted with the purchase.

"I said that I would also buy you a horse," Bras reminded him. "There is the market for the horses at the far end of the square."

Indeed, there were many fine horses gathered there for sale. There were the cream of the horses from the five kingdoms, not only from Léon but from the kingdom of the Veneti (Vannes), from Poher, from Kernev (Cornouaille), from Domnonée.

Again, N'oun Doaré did not appear to find one that took his fancy. Bras showed him many fine horses, good war-horses which he knew the King of Léon would pay a fine price for, but the young man would have none of them.

So Bras and N'oun Doaré left the horse fair with Bras airing his disgust at how finicky his adopted son was turning out to be.

It was as they were taking the road back to Coat-Squiriou that they encountered a man leading a horse. He was a tall man, clad in a long black robe and cowl which covered him from head to foot. He was leading a very sorry-looking animal. The horse was thin and the bones stood out as if it were the Mare of Doom.

To Bras' surprise, the young man stopped and began to examine the steed. Then he turned. "That is the horse for me!" he exclaimed.

Bras nearly choked himself with indignation. "Are you insulting me?" he demanded. "You have turned down the finest horses in all Armorica and you now ask me to buy this horse, which seems in the last days of its life."

N'oun Doaré shook his head. "No my father. This is no insult to you, and one day I shall prove it. Please buy it for me. I will have no other than this gentle beast."

He could not explain to his father that he felt a curious compulsion to be the owner of this ancient horse.

Bras stared at his adopted son and saw the determination in the young man's eyes and sighed. Bras turned to the man who was leading the horse and then frowned. "Do you also sell scrap metal?" he demanded suspiciously.

The man kept his head lowered, but a low laugh came from his cowl. "No, sir. I sell no scrap."

Bras sniffed in disapproval. "How much do you want for this animal? Whatever it is, it will be too much."

"Too much, sir? Why, all I ask is your hand in token of the goodwill of a generous chieftain."

Bras was so surprised that he handed the man a silver coin as well. "You cannot live on a handshake," he said, "so this will provide you with a meal."

As he turned away, the man with the cowl caught hold of N'oun Doaré's sleeve and whispered: "See the knots on the mare's halter, young sir?"

N'oun Doaré nodded. "I do," he replied.

"Each time you untie one of those knots, the mare will transport you wherever you wish to go. It is a magic steed."

Now N'oun Doaré felt he could not impart that news to Bras, who was now heading along the road to his castle, muttering under his breath about the bad day at the market. N'oun Doaré returned to the castle of Bras with a smile and full of excitement.

On arriving back at the fortress of Bras, N'oun Doaré took the mare into the stable and rubbed her down and fed her. Then he took his sword into the smithy and, with the smith's permission, set to work polishing and sharpening his sword. But as hard as he tried to get the rust off by polishing hard, the more the rust clung to its iron blade. By the end of several hours, it was no cleaner than before. Yet N'oun Doaré still felt his desire to keep the weapon.

That evening, N'oun Doaré decided to try out his new horse, saddled the mare and rode off. The horse, in spite of its thinness and ancient look, was nimble and he enjoyed a swift canter along the lanes surrounding the fortress. As chance would have it, he came along the very road where he had been found as a child. Because of his enjoyment of his ride, he had forgotten the time and the hour had grown late. The moon had already risen in a cloudless sky. The pale white rays were glinting on something at the foot of an old standing stone. Had he known it, it was near the very spot where Bras and his servant had found him.

The young man dismounted and approached the stone. At the foot of the stone, the object that was causing the winking reflection was a small golden crown, which was studded with precious stones. He realized, to his surprise, that it was not just the moonlight which caused it to give out a radiance, but the very precious stones themselves shone and gave out such a light that he could see by it.

"Finders keepers," N'oun Doaré muttered, bending down to pick up the crown. He was certainly not going to leave the crown just lying there.

"Have a care, or you will regret it," came a soft feminine voice.

He wheeled round. He could see no one else in the moonlight, apart from his mare. He examined the bushes and behind the standing stone, but to no avail. With a sigh of bewilderment, he stood for a moment, wondering if he had imagined it. Having decided that he had, he bent down and picked up the golden crown. He saw that there was some writing on the golden band of the crown, but it was in a language which he could not read. He tried vainly to make a sense of the jumbled words.

"Have a care, or you will regret it," came the soft feminine voice again.

Once again, he tried to find the owner of the voice and once more he saw no one near the standing stone.

This time he hid the gold crown beneath his cloak. "The decision is now yours," came the whispering voice, for the third time. "Tomorrow you must proceed to Vannes."

Having searched thoroughly again and found no one, N'oun Doaré sat and thought a while. Now Vannes was far to the south-east from Coat-Squiriou and was a journey of many days. But he suddenly remembered what the vendor of the mare had told him.

The following morning, he told Bras and Anvab that he was going away for a few days. They questioned him about this sudden decision but he said that he would not be gone long.

He put on his best clothes, strapped on his sword and saddled his mare.

As soon as he was out of sight of the fortress, he bent forward and undid one of the knots on the halter. Nothing happened. He frowned. The mare stood waiting patiently. Then an idea occurred to him. He leant forward and whispered: "Vannes."

There was a sudden gust of wind and he blinked. He opened his eyes a moment later and found himself in the centre of a city. He did not have to be told that he was in the square of the city of Vannes.

He rode to the great palace which dominated the town, where the King of the Veneti dwelt, and peered up at its magnificent walls and the silken banners which fluttered from its turrets.

"Hey! you there!"

A harsh voice hailed him and he turned to see a couple of warriors staring at him. With them was a handsome man, some years older than he was. This man was well dressed and carried a splendid sword.

"Do you address me, sir?" asked N'oun Doaré, courteously enough.

"Yes. Why are you staring up at my palace walls? Are you planning to rob me?"

N'oun Doaré's eyes widened. "Your palace? Are you the king?"

"I am Gwion, king of the Veneti," acknowledged the handsome man.

N'oun Doaré introduced himself.

Gwion smiled and came forward with open arms, for he knew Bras and Anvab and he had heard of their adopted son. He offered the hospitality of his great castle to N'oun Doaré and feasted him. After the feast, the king offered him the use of a guest chamber for the night. But then he told him not to light any candles there during the night, for he had forbidden any lights at all to be seen in Vannes during the night, for it was rumoured that fierce Saxon pirates were roaming the coast, looking for places to raid.

Now the fact was that, in the dark, the jewels of the crown that N'oun Doaré had with him shone with such intensity that whatever the young man did, he could not disguise the light.

King Gwion's servants saw the light and raised an alarm. N'oun Doaré was seized and dragged before Gwion, who demanded to know whether he was a spy for the Saxons. He had been told not to show a light and he had been found doing so. Was he signalling the Saxon pirates?

The young man had to admit that he possessed a crown which shone with a bright light.

Now, when the king was given the crown it certainly sparkled but the light which had caused the trouble was extinguished. Gwion was suspicious. However, when he handed the crown to N'oun Doaré, it started to shine with a radiance which caused him to blink. Gwion now accused the young man of sorcery. But it was soon discovered that the crown shone in the hands of everyone except the king of Vannes.

So Gwion now called all the learned men and alchemists in his land to come and tell him the meaning of this strange phenomenon and also to decipher the words on the crown.

Meanwhile, in case there might be some trick in it, N'oun Doaré was kept in a dungeon in the palace.

No one could make head nor tail of the radiant crown nor of its writing.

N'oun Doaré was finally sent for.

Once more, he confessed he did not know. Gwion grew impatient and told his servants to take him to the stables and make him clean them out.

"You'll work at every menial job in the palace until you tell me the meaning of the crown," snapped the king.

Alone in the stables, N'oun Doaré sat on an upturned bucket in despair.

"I'll tell you the meaning of the words," a husky female voice whispered.

N'oun Doaré turned round sharply, but he was alone in the stable except for the horses, including his old mare. Puzzled the young man searched out every stall. Then, feeling like an idiot he called, "Tell me the meaning of the crown."

At once came the husky reply. "The crown belongs to Aour, the beautiful Princess of the Golden-Ram who dwells on the southern islands."

"I don't know who you are, but thanks. You may have saved my life." N'oun Doaré was a courteous young man. With this he called for the guards and demanded to see King Gwion.

However, when he explained the meaning to King Gwion, the king of Vannes told him: "This is a sign. You must go and bring me the Princess of the Golden-Ram, for if she is as beautiful as her crown, she must become my wife. If you fail in this, I shall have your life in forfeit. Do not try to hide, if you fail in this task. If you do, I shall march an army into Léon and devastate the lands of Coat-Squiriou and the lives of your adopted parents shall be forfeit instead."

Aghast, N'oun Doaré packed his clothes, took his sword and went down to the stable. Gwion had given him oats for his horse and some money to help pay for his journey. But the price of failure was a grim one. He was fearful, for he did not know where the southern islands were, nor who the Princess of the Golden-Ram was. He had merely repeated what the mysterious voice had said.

He went to saddle his old mare and the anxiety was engraved in his features.

"Do not worry," came the husky tones again. "If you do everything exactly as I tell you, then all will be well. Trust me. Didn't I warn you that if you picked up that crown at the pillar stone, you would regret it? You had free choice then. Now, from the moment you picked it up, you have to follow your destiny."

Peering round anxiously, N'oun Doaré said: "I will obey you. But who are you? I do not see you."

"Who I am is irrelevant."

Then it was that N'oun Doaré realized that it was the old mare who was speaking in a human voice, and he grew afraid.

The horse stamped a foreleg. "Do not be silly! If you want to travel through life, you will see more frightening things than an old mare being able to imitate human speech."

N'oun Doaré felt rather ashamed at his fear, and realized that the old mare had helped him so far. She had done him no harm.

The mare instructed him to mount up and they set out from the city of Vannes riding along the seashore.

They had not gone far when N'oun Doaré suddenly saw a fish on the sand, flapping about. It had obviously been stranded by a sudden ebbing tide and now lay dying above the water line. It was a sea trout.

"Quickly!" whispered the mare. "Dismount and put the fish back into the water."

N'oun Doaré was about to protest but thought better of it. He slid off the mare and picked up the fish carefully and placed it back into the water.

A moment later, the fish's head appeared and a high-pitched voice said: "You have saved my life, N'oun Doaré. I am the King of the Fish and if you ever need my help, you have only to call me by the seaside and I will come at once."

Then it dived back into the water and disappeared.

Amazed by the experience, N'oun Doaré remounted his mare and continued on.

Not long afterwards, he heard a frantic flapping of wings and saw a wooden crate which had been used as a snare, for in it was a large bird. It was a giant kestrel.

"Release that bird at once!" instructed the mare.

This time N'oun Doaré obeyed the horse immediately.

Released, the bird hopped forward and flapped its wings and then put its head to one side and spoke clearly: "You have saved me, N'oun Doaré. For that I thank you. I am the King of the Birds. If ever I or mine can return you this favour, then you have only to call into the air and I will come at once."

They reached the end of the seashore and the mare instructed him to untie another of the knots in her mane and wish that he were outside the Castle of the Golden-Ram.

There was a breath of wind and it seemed that seas, mountains, rivers and islands flashed away beneath them, but then they were in a forest clearing before a towering castle built of dark granite blocks and looking gloomy and forbidding. Outside the sinister gates there stood a great oak tree, from which there was a horrendous clamour emanating.

A man was chained to the tree, crying and struggling and causing the horrible noise.

When N'oun Doaré looked closely at the man, he grew very frightened. The man had a serpent-like body, speckled like the body of a snake. There were two horns standing out on his head and his red tongue was long and lashed from his mouth like the tongue of a serpent.

"Unchain him and set him free," instructed the mare.

N'oun Doaré shook his head. "I am afraid to go near such a terrifying thing . . . why, it is not a man at all."

The mare stamped her hoof again. "Don't be afraid! He won't harm you. Do as I say."

Reluctantly, the young man moved cautiously forward towards the shrieking apparition.

The beast-thing growled and struggled, but made no move to harm him.

N'oun Doaré unchained the serpent-man and set him free. The thing sprang away and then wheeled round to face him. But there was no hostility in the action.

"Thank you, N'oun Doaré. I am Griffescornu, King of the Demons. I'll return this favour. If ever you need help, shriek my name on the night wind and I'll come straight away."

Then he was gone in a flash of smoke and the smell of brimstone pervaded the air.

Shaken, N'oun Doaré turned back to his mare. "What now?" he demanded.

"Now, I shall go and refresh myself in that green field by those woods. You will go to the castle and demand to speak with its mistress, Aour, the Princess of the Golden-Ram. Do not take 'no' for an answer. She will welcome you and try to delay you by showing you all kinds of wondrous things. Ignore them and tell her that you have a mare at pasture in the field by the wood. Invite her to come to see it, for it knows all the dances of the five kingdoms of Armorica and it will perform them for her. Stress that only you can make the mare do this."

N'oun Doaré was about to turn away to the castle door when the old mare stayed him. "One thing you should know. The keeper to the gate of the castle will open it for you. Do not go in at his invitation. He is a Druid and will, by magic, turn you into one of the fearsome beasts they keep locked within the castle rooms."

N'oun Doaré was surprised and not a little fearful. "What must I do?"

"The old iron sword that you have – it says that it is invincible. And iron is pure and invincible over the forces of darkness. As soon as he opens the door, you must pierce him through the heart and he will vanish to the Otherworld."

N'oun Doaré went to turn away again. "A moment more," cried the old mare. "The Druid has a son, just as evil as he. You must also slay him, but do not look into his eyes or you will be finished."

"Better that I never undertook this task," muttered N'oun Doaré. "It seems that I shall not survive."

The old mare stamped her foot impatiently. "Did I not warn you about the crown? It was your free choice."

N'oun Doaré sighed in resignation. "You are right. I have brought this upon myself. I will see it through."

"Then hear me again. Never, never . . . set foot over the doorway of the castle until you are freely invited by Aour, the princess. Accept no invitation from any other person in the castle."

N'oun Doaré made his way to the gates and hammered on them with his sword hilt.

"I wish to speak to Aour, the Princess of the Golden-Ram," he said, when an elderly silver-haired servant opened the gate.

"Welcome, young sir," replied the servant. "Come in." He looked so old and frail, and held a kindly disposition, that for a moment, N'oun Doaré hesitated, thinking the advice of the old mare must be at fault. At the moment he hesitated, he heard a grim chuckle from the old servant and some instinct made him thrust out his rusty iron sword, straight into the old man's heart.

There was a shriek of terror and N'oun Doaré looked up. The old man had turned into some hideous creature, even more hideous than the King of Demons. An old, leprous man with such malignant eyes, with open sores across his features.

He stood for a moment and then – vanished. His wailing shriek remained a long time after him.

N'oun Doaré saw, to his surprise, that his rusty old sword was shining like bright silver, where he had thrust it into the old man's torso.

He waited for a moment, but there was no sound at all within the castle.

He was about to enter through the open door when the old mare's warning came to his mind. He knocked again with his sword hilt.

A young man suddenly appeared before him. He was youthful and as handsome as any he had seen.

"Forgive me, stranger. I was sure that my father had come

to open the door. I am sorry for the delay. But do not stand there: come in and tell me what it is you want."

"I want to see Aour, the Princess of the Golden-Ram," said N'oun Doaré, without stepping over the threshold. He glanced at the young man and suddenly went cold with apprehension.

Dark malignant hypnotic eyes clawed at him. He felt himself being propelled across the threshold towards the interior of the castle.

He was helpless.

Then a sudden gust of wind ruffled his hair. The young man blinked as the wind caused a speck of dust to blow into his face. N'oun Doaré dropped his gaze immediately and thrust forward with his sword, with all his might behind that thrust.

There was a scream of anguish and, as abruptly as the elderly servant had vanished, this young man also vanished.

N'oun Doaré found that he was now holding a beautiful burnished sword which would not be out of place at the hip of a great prince.

He paused again, but there was no sound from within the castle.

He banged against the lintel once more with his sword hilt.

Moments later, a beautiful young woman appeared. She had golden hair and features which caused him to swallow in nervousness. However, when he looked closely, he realized there was something hard and speculative about this girl's features: something that made him shiver slightly with apprehension.

"Who are you?" she asked, pleasantly enough.

"N'oun Doaré and I am come on a mission from Gwion, King of Vannes. If you be Aour, Princess of the Golden-Ram, then Gwion wishes to make you his wife."

"*Ouah*!" snapped the girl, which is the Breton for "fiddlesticks". Then she smiled and laid a hand on his arm. "I am Aour and invite you into my castle. I have many wonders that you will wish to see. I collect fabulous creatures."

"Such as the Griffescornu?" mused the young man, not able to hold back the jibe.

She sniffed in arrogant dismissal. "He bored me with his

shrieking. I am glad that you released him. He gave me a headache."

She smiled invitingly and tried to draw him into the castle. "Come."

N'oun Doaré shook his head. "I have a fabulous creature which you might be interested in," he said airily.

"And what might that be?"

"I have an old mare. It can do all the dances of the five kingdoms of Armorica. But it will only perform when I tell it to. If you like fabulous creatures, you will be amazed at this one."

"And where is this miraculous steed?" asked the girl suspiciously.

Noun Doaré pointed to the woods. "At pasture, in a field by those woods. Not far away at all."

The princess looked at the woods and, realizing they were so close, nodded her agreement.

The princess shut the gate of the castle behind her. N'oun Doaré saw her take a golden key out of her purse, which hung on a belt around her waist, and carefully lock the gate of the castle. Then she followed him. They found the old mare in a field by the woods, contentedly grazing.

"I have brought the Princess of the Golden-Ram to see you dance, horse," said the young man. "Perform the dances for her."

And the old mare began to perform the most varied and intricate dances for the princess, who clapped her hands with delight.

"I have collected many marvels but this is truly wondrous," she said approvingly.

Then the old mare deliberately winked at N'oun Doaré. He knew in an instant what he must do.

"There is a loose knot on the halter," he said, moving forward and untying it. Then he added: "Climb on her back now, princess, and she will happily dance with you."

The princess hesitated a moment or two.

"This will surely be a great marvel, better than any you have seen," persuaded the young man. Finally, the princess mounted the mare and, no sooner had she done so, than N'oun Doaré leapt up behind her and cried, "Vannes!"

In a trice, the horse seemed to rise into the air and mountains, forests, rivers, islands and the sea, flashed below. N'oun Doaré, as stunned as he was by the journey, saw that the princess seemed to be more in control of her faculties, for he saw her take the golden key from her purse and throw it into the sea, above which they sped, sending it down into its deep black depths. Then, as if in an instant, they were in the great square of Vannes.

"You have tricked me!" exclaimed the princess as N'oun Doaré dismounted and King Gwion and his retinue came running forward to greet them.

"I have brought you the Princess of the Golden-Ram, sir," exclaimed the young man. "Just as you ordered."

The princess looked angrily at N'oun Doaré. "You are not at the end of your trials yet, adopted son of Bras. You will weep more than once before I wed the King of Vannes." She made the threat in a sibilant voice, so low that King Gwion and his men would not hear her.

Gwion moved forward to greet her. He was overcome with her beauty and his heart was full of happiness. He feasted her that night with N'oun Doaré as a special guest of honour. The princess was charming and did not once show anything but a sweet attitude towards Gwion and the man who had abducted her.

At the end of the evening, Gwion proposed marriage to her.

"I would do so, sir," replied the princess, "but I cannot marry without first wearing the ancient ring of my race. No princess of my family has ever married without it. It is a prohibition on my family not to do so, for it means bad luck will surely follow."

"It is a reasonable request," Gwion agreed. "Where is the ring?"

"It is in my bedchamber in my castle. By the bed there is a locked cabinet, to which I have lost the key."

"Fear not. N'oun Doaré will go back and fetch it and he knows the penalty for failure."

Dismayed, N'oun Doaré went to the stables and told his mare of the latest task that he was ordered to perform.

"Why are you worried?" demanded the mare. "Don't you

remember that you saved the life of the King of Birds and that he promised to help you when an occasion arose?"

"I remember," cried N'oun Doaré.

"What are you waiting for, then? Call him."

The young man went to the stable door and called up into the sky, asking for the King of Birds to come to him.

There was a flapping of wings and the voice said from the lintel of the stable: "What is it, N'oun Doaré? How can I help?" The great kestrel stood perched on the beam.

The young man told him the problem.

"Don't worry. The ring will be brought to you."

Straightaway the kestrel called every known bird to go to the castle, but there was only one bird that was small enough to pass through the keyhole into the bedchamber of the castle, and only one small enough to squeeze itself into the cabinet and regain the ring. That was the wren. With much difficulty and the loss of most of his feathers, the wren managed to get into the cabinet and take the ring and bring it to Vannes.

At breakfast the next morning, N'oun Doaré presented it to the delighted Gwion and the angry princess.

"There you are," Gwion said, handing her the ring. "Now we can name the day."

"I only need one thing more before I can satisfy you by naming the day of our marriage. Without it, there can be no marriage."

N'oun Doaré kept his temper in check, knowing that she would ask something more difficult.

"What is it?" asked Gwion.

"I want my castle to be brought here and erected on that hill overlooking Vannes."

Even Gwion was amazed. "You want what . . . ?"

"My castle brought here intact."

"How can you expect such a thing?" demanded the King of Vannes.

"I shall have it, or you shall have no wife."

Gwion turned to N'oun Doaré. "You must find a way, or . . ." He did not have to finish the sentence.

Sadly, N'oun Doaré went to the stable.

"Well, that is no problem," the mare answered, surprising him.

"How so?"

"Did you not save Griffescornu, the king of demons, releasing him from his chains, when the princess had made him part of her collection of fabulous creatures?"

"I did."

"Very well. Summon him, and he will help you now."

So N'oun Doaré shrieked the name of the king of the demons into the howling night wind and, sure enough, in a cloud of deepest black smoke, the Griffescornu arrived, in all his awesome and hideous visage.

"How can I help you, N'oun Doaré?" hissed the apparition.

The young man told him.

"That is no problem. My demons and I will do it in an instant."

When the sun rose above Vannes the next morning, the Castle of the Golden-Ram was standing in all its grim splendour, on the very hill where the princess had indicated she had wanted it. A whole army of demons had uprooted the castle from the rock on which it had stood and whisked it through the air to stand where it now dominated the hill. The people of Vannes were in fear and trembling. But the King Gwion was delighted.

Not so the princess.

"Now, lady," Gwion said, "it only remains for you to fix the wedding day."

The Princess of the Golden-Ram thought furiously. "I need only one more thing, and then I will name the day of our wedding, lord."

Gwion was cynical. But the princess took a sacred oath that this was the last thing that she would ask.

"What is it?" sighed Gwion.

"The key to my castle. There stands the castle, but I cannot get in without the key."

"I have the best locksmiths in the five kingdoms of Armorica," protested Gwion. "They will make you a new key."

"No. No one in the world can make a key which can open

the door of my castle. It has a magic lock. I must have the key."

And so N'oun Doaré was sent for again. He was very angry, but when he heard that the princess had made this her last request and taken an oath to it, he was satisfied and went off to get his old mare. The princess had not realized that he had seen her throw the key into the sea.

He told the mare and the horse answered, "Well, you know what you must do. You saved the life of the King of the Fish."

So they went to the seashore and N'oun Doaré raised his voice and cried aloud for the King of the Fish.

"What can I do for you, N'oun Doaré?" squeaked a voice. And there was the head of the sea-trout gazing at him from the waves.

"I need the key to the Castle of the Golden-Ram which the princess has thrown into the sea."

"Never fear," replied the fish. "You shall have it."

At once, he called all the fish who rushed here and there. But none of them had seen the key to the castle. Finally, the King of the Fish called a lonely dolphin who came and presented him with the key, a golden key inset with a priceless diamond.

N'oun Doaré and his mare went straight back to the King of Vannes and presented it to him.

The princess could no longer play for time, and was forced to name the day of the wedding.

"Ask her now," whispered the mare, "to open up her castle door."

N'oun Doaré did so.

The princess seemed reluctant but even Gwion started to press her, for he also wanted to gaze on the interior of the impressive structure.

"You have had it brought all the way here, to Vannes," he said, "so it seems a shame that you will not even allow us to see inside it."

The princess was forced to go with Gwion, with N'oun Doaré and his mare, and other members of the King of Vannes' court. She opened the door with the golden key.

"Now, before you step inside," whispered the mare, "ask her to formally invite all those present to do so."

N'oun Doaré made the request.

The princess shook her head. "You may come in if you so wish – the choice is your own."

"No. It is not etiquette," insisted N'oun Doaré. "This your castle, princess, and the king and his retinue cannot come in without being formally invited."

Gwion nodded his agreement, for N'oun Doaré was only quoting the law of hospitality.

The princess sighed. "Then every one of you is formally invited to enter the castle."

And they went inside.

To their surprise, there was a nauseating smell of decay and evil in the castle, unlike the sunny countenance of the princess. It was more like a dank dark stable in its interior than a beautiful palace. Those following her stood back, all except the old mare.

The mare trotted forward to the centre of the dark room, where a stall stood, in which there was a small bundle of oats tied in a golden ribbon.

"Stop that horse!" cried the princess in terror. "I did not mean to invite it inside."

But the old mare bent forward and ate the oats in two large mouthfuls.

No one knew what exactly happened next. They knew that the castle had suddenly vanished. They were all standing on the sun-drenched green hillside overlooking Vannes. And in their midst there was a great chest of treasure, and each side of the treasure stood two beautiful women. One was the princess, whose features seemed to have softened and were more beautiful than before; while the other woman could only be her twin. The only difference was that the princess had golden hair while her twin had red-copper hair.

Everyone gaped in amazement at them.

"Where is my mare?" demanded N'oun Doaré, gazing around angrily. "If she has been hurt, there will be blood to pay for this. My mare is very dear to me."

The red-haired young woman came forward and laid a

slender hand on his arm. "I am here, N'oun Doaré," she said in the husky voice, which he recognized immediately. "I am still ready to serve you, for you are also dear to me."

Gwion of Vannes stared at his princess, so warm and attractive that she appeared a new person, and he shook his head in wonder.

"What has happened?" he asked.

"An evil Druid placed us under a spell many years ago," replied the princess. "We are sisters, you see, and our father angered this Druid. He had betrothed my sister Ruz-glaou to a young prince instead of to the Druid's son. And when the Druid then demanded my hand, my father said he would rather give me to a fabulous beast than allow me to marry him.

"The Druid slew my father and, ever vengeful, found the young prince, who was then five years old, and cast him into a far kingdom so that he would not know his name, his parents nor where he came from. My sister was turned into an old mare and transported to Kernev. And I was made to be a prisoner of our castle, my character was changed, and I was compelled to collect fabulous creatures in retaliation for my father's threat to marry me to one. The castle became an evil-smelling stable, in which the fabulous beasts were housed, and over which I had no control."

"How were you freed?" demanded N'oun Doaré.

"The Druid placed magic oats in the stall in the castle which, if my sister was ever able to get into the castle and eat them, would undo the spell. As the years passed, my sister, in the guise of a mare, was purchased by a learned Druid in Kernev. He advised her of the way in which she could remove the spell. He told her that she would be aided by the pure sword of Govan the Smith-God, cast in the days of primordial chaos."

"This one?" demanded N'oun Doaré, reaching to the bright sword at his belt.

But the sword was gone. The scabbard was empty.

"It has served its purpose," observed Ruz-glaou. "It has returned back to its owner, who gave it to you."

"So the spell has been lifted?" Gwion observed. "Then all is well. We have all played our parts."

"Will you set out to find this nameless prince that was cast away without memory?" asked N'oun Doaré sadly of the red-haired princess.

Ruz-glaou smiled. "What is your name?"

"N'oun Doaré," replied the puzzled young man. "You know that well enough."

"And what does it mean?"

"I don't know."

Ruz-glaou chuckled. "I have found my prince already," she said solemnly. "Do you want to know who you really are and where you came from?"

N'oun Doaré thought for a moment or two and then he shook his head with a smile. "I have two good parents now who have raised me. My home is in Léon. If you are content with me as I am, I am also content."

Both princesses, Aour and Ruz-glaou, were pleased with the men who declared their love for them, and they reciprocated that love. On the next day, a great double wedding was held in Vannes, and Gwion and his princess remained there while N'oun Doaré returned to his adopted parents, with his princess, where they lived in Coat-Squiriou happily for many years. In time, N'oun Doaré became the king of Léon and he was contented knowing who he was, rather than who he might have been.

34 *The Anaon*

There were two brothers who dwelt in Botsorhel. Their names, for the sake of our story, were Maudez and Primel. They were twins and very close to each other. Even as youngsters, they had never been known to argue over their toys and they shared everything, the hardships as well as the good things of life.

They shared only one bad secret, and that was when they were youths, they found an old lame beggar on the road and thought it would be amusing to steal his stick for sport. But it was no sport at all and the poor man cursed the two boys heartily, calling down the wrath of the Ankou, the spirit of the dead, on them. They finally desisted and felt ashamed of what they had done.

Thereafter, they grew up as fine young men. They even forgot the incident. That was the one bad thing that they ever did in their lives.

When they grew into manhood, everyone who knew them remarked how inseparable they were.

"Why," agreed their mother, "only death will separate those two."

"If that happens," remarked Primel to his brother, on hearing what his mother said, "let us swear an oath."

"What oath?" demanded Maudez.

"Why, whoever is the first of us to die, we must return from the Otherworld and tell the other of what has befallen us there."

"Very well," agreed Maudez.

"And we will also swear that if either one of us is made to suffer, the other will share the suffering."

So the two brothers swore this oath.

It happened sooner than expected. A malignancy struck the area and the Ankou himself, the great Death personified, walked the village of Botsorhel, choosing his victims. And it was Primel who was struck with the fever and he being scarcely twenty and five years of age. His family sent for healers but the fever gripped him and, at last, the Ankou was victorious and claimed Primel's soul to take with him to the Otherworld.

Now, during all this time, Maudez had never left Primel's bedside. He nursed and watched over his brother with such attentiveness that it broke everyone's heart to see his distress when his brother was taken by the Ankou. Nor did Maudez leave the side of the body of his brother, until the bier was taken to the burial ground; nor did he leave the graveside, until the grave digger had finished levelling the earth on top of the grave; nor did he leave the burial ground, until the bier was ritually smashed to pieces against the great oak tree that grew there. This was to prevent the evil spirits from carrying the corpse away on the bier and turning it into an Un-Dead creature which would haunt the living.

Now it so happened that the very next evening was the start of the feasting which would bring in the New Year, marking the end of one pastoral year and the beginning of the next. This festival had been altered in Christian times. It had fallen on the evening of 31 October, which was renamed the eve of All Saints' Day or All Hallows. More importantly, it was the time when spirits and ghosts could return from the Otherworld and set out to wreak vengeance on the living, on those who had wronged them in life. The fires of the village were extinguished that night and in the morning, when the sun rose in the sky, the fires would be rekindled from a ceremonial flame which would be lit by the Druids from the sun's rays.

Maudez took little part in these ceremonies and, indeed, returned sorrowfully to his house before midnight. He went to bed but could not sleep. His mind was too preoccupied with thoughts of his dead brother, Primel.

It was as he lay in bed, thinking his sad thoughts, that he heard a footstep in the yard outside. He heard the door of the house open and a foot on the stair. He knew the footsteps well. The bedroom door swung open. He could not suppress the shiver that came over him as he saw the figure silhouetted in the doorway.

"Are you asleep, Maudez?" came the familiar voice.

Maudez let out a sigh.

"No, Primel. I am not asleep. I have been lying awake here, waiting for you."

"We swore an oath, Maudez, that I would return. Get up now and come with me."

Maudez arose and started to put on his clothes. Maudez saw that Primel was still clad as last he had seen him, in his shroud.

"Are there no fine clothes in the Otherworld, Primel?" he asked with interest.

"At this time, my brother, this shroud is all I possess and wear."

"How do you find this Otherworld? Is it all that we have been told?"

"Alas," said Primel, "there is a prohibition there. I am not allowed to tell you about it. But, I am allowed to show you. That is why I have come for you. I can let you see it for yourself . . . that is, if you freely agree to come with me."

Maudez nodded eagerly. "We swore an oath. I am ready."

Primel beckoned his brother to follow him and they went from the farm of their parents to the mill-pond at Goazwed. When they reached the still dark waters, Primel turned to his brother.

"Take off all your clothes and your boots, Maudez."

"What for?" demanded Maudez, a little worried, for the night air was chill.

"You must come into the water with me."

"But I can't swim. The water of the mill-pond is deep."

"You will not have to swim. There is no need to worry."

Maudez thought a moment and then shrugged. "Very well. I am resolved to follow you, wherever you go. Lead on."

Taking Maudez's arm, Primel leapt into the dark waters

and with him went his twin brother. They sank down into the black waters until their feet touched the bottom. Maudez was astonished to find that he could breathe under the water as easily as he had in the air. But the dark waters were cold, so cold that Maudez began to shiver, and his teeth chattered almost uncontrollably.

"What now?" he demanded, when Primel made no further move.

"We wait."

After they had waited there in the black, cold waters for what seemed like hours, Maudez, feeling he could bear the chill no longer, said: "Do we have to stay here much longer?"

Primel smiled in the darkness. "Are you then in such a hurry to leave me?"

"No, not I," replied Maudez. "You know very well that I am never happier than when we are together. But, Primel, I am still alive, and I am suffering more than I can tell, for it is so bitterly, bitterly cold."

Then Primel's voice grew harsh. "Then triple your suffering, Maudez, and you will begin to feel what I am suffering."

Maudez was astonished. "Why are you suffering, Primel? We are told the Otherworld is full of light and happiness."

His twin brother did not reply for a moment or two, but then he relented. "All I can tell you is that by sharing my time here, you are shortening it. By feeling my suffering, you are reducing it."

Maudez felt great sorrow for his brother. "Then I shall stay with you for as long as it takes to relieve your suffering."

Primel shook his head. "You will be free when you hear the morning cock crow."

The time passed in that cold, stygian darkness: it passed so slowly that it seemed like days and months. Then, at last, Maudez heard the crowing of the morning cock. In a moment, he found himself at the edge of the mill-pond, dry and with his clothes on.

He heard his brother's voice echoing from below: "Goodbye, Maudez. If you have the courage and the will to help me, you will see me tonight."

"Willingly, brother," exclaimed Maudez. "I will wait for you like I did last night."

Maudez made his way slowly home, feeling cold and miserable. Nevertheless, he had sworn an oath to his brother. He ate heartily and slept and the discomfort of the night seemed to pass. But his mother noticed how pale, wan and cold he was and asked if she should bring the physician to see him. Maudez shook his head. He assured her that he was all right.

That night, around midnight, he found himself lying on his bed fully dressed.

His brother, Primel, appeared as on the previous night and conducted Maudez to the mill-pond and they went in as before. It seemed twice as cold and dank as before. The suffering of Maudez was truly great and he found that he could barely endure the endless hours of being in that black, ice-cold pond.

Yet, finally, came the crowing of the morning cock and weak, feeling ill and distraught, Maudez found himself at the edge of the pond.

Primel's voice came from the depth. "Do you have courage for one more time? Just once more, and you will have eased my pain and set my soul at liberty."

"I swore an oath and will be faithful to the end, even if it kills me."

Maudez went home. This time he was so pale, exhausted and shivering that he crawled into his bed without food in an effort to warm himself. He could not eat, even when his mother brought him hot cakes and sausage. This time, she sent for the physician, who pronounced him gravely ill.

Now his mother had looked into his room on the previous night and saw that Maudez was not there.

"He must be getting this cold from spending the night watching at his poor brother's grave," she said to the physician.

Now the physician saw how ill Maudez was and said that he would keep a watch that night and prevent Maudez from going out to the burial ground.

That night the physician, who had been sleeping in a chair

in the parlour, was awakened by strange noises. He half opened his eyes and saw Maudez coming from his bedroom and talking as if deep in conversation with someone. But there was no one about. So strange was Maudez's behaviour that the physician hung back and did not intervene, but followed at a distance. He followed Maudez to the mill pond and saw him strip off in the cold night air and leap into the pond.

He was about to give the alarm and rush forward when he suddenly noticed a second ripple on the water and now he heard a second voice. It is said by the ancients that water will reveal the sounds of the Otherworld to those with ears to hear. The physician was not just a healer but came from many generations of Druids.

Using his knowledge, the physician approached the pond and saw a rowan tree growing nearby. He used the rowan to hide behind. As it had magical protection from the spirits of the Otherworld, he was entirely safe.

From the waters, he heard the voices of the brothers, Maudez protesting that he could not last any longer and Primel urging him to hang on and be brave.

"I am weakening!" cried Maudez. "I will not last until the morning."

"You must. Be strong, my brother! A little while longer and, thanks to you, I shall be delivered from this suffering. You will have opened the path for me into the Otherworld. You will have halved my suffering."

Through the long night, the physician sat there, hearing the cries of agony from Maudez and not daring to move, though he wanted to run from that spot. Finally, the sky began to grow light and the morning cock crowed.

From the bottom of the pond came two cries.

"Primel!"

"Maudez!"

Then the physician saw a strange white smoke snake out of the waters and curl itself upwards into the bright morning sky.

When he looked back he saw Maudez, fully clothed, lying on the bank of the pond.

Maudez was ice-cold and deathly white. His breathing was

shallow. His body shivered uncontrollably. The physician threw him over his shoulder and carried him back to the farm and placed him in his bed. He tried his best to bring warmth back into his racked body. It was too late, too late. By midnight, Maudez breathed his last.

And for several nights after that, the villagers of Botsorhel swear they heard unearthly screams coming from the old mill pond by Goazwed: terrible screams of anguish and pain and suffering.

If the truth were known, Maudez had halved the suffering of his brother Primel by taking that suffering on himself. Even so, the brothers had to spend three nights in Purgatory before Primel could pass on into the light of the Otherworld. But when it came to Maudez's turn, there was no one to come and share his suffering with him and three more endless lonely nights he had to spend without comfort in that dank, dark place.

The locals of Botsorhel will tell you that the old mill-pond is a place to be avoided in the darkness of the night for in it dwell the *anaon* which, in Breton, means the spirits of the dead. One or two of the villagers remarked that the cries seemed to cease after an old, lame beggar passed by the old mill pond by Goazwed. But then, country people are always looking for symbols.

35 *Koadalan*

There was once a male child born to a forester and his wife who dwelt in the Forest of Cranou, a land of hills studded with great oaks and beeches. The forest nestles under the Mountains of Arrée, the highest hills of Brittany. The couple were not wealthy but they had enough to make them happy and were content with their life and, when their son was born, they felt their happiness complete. They felt that the child put them in complete harmony with their lives and their surroundings. That was why they decided to name him Koadalan, for *koad* means "wood", symbolising the wood in which they lived, and *alan* means "harmony".

The boy grew and the forester, whose name was Alan, and his wife, taught him all they knew about the woods and forest lore. He was an exceptionally bright boy and he learnt quickly. And as he grew, he realized that he lacked a schooling; he wanted to learn to read and write. His parents, being only foresters, could do neither. When he asked his parents if they would send him to school, they shook their heads.

"The school is a long way from here in Rumengol and it costs much money," they told him.

"But you have enough. You have a fine bull and a stallion. You could sell those, and that would pay for my schooling."

It took some convincing them but eventually, because of the boy's insistence, they finally sold their fine bull and their horse, and sent the boy to school. Three years passed by, during which time the boy learnt a great deal and his teachers were very proud of him. They swore that he had more knowledge than most boys of his age.

At the age of maturity, that is at seventeen, Koadalan returned to his parents. They, having sold their fine bull and their stallion, were now extremely poor. They had a hard time simply to wrest a livelihood from the forest. They were not unhappy, but they were practical folk.

"We can only keep ourselves with great difficulty, Koadalan," they told him. "You will have to set off to seek your fortune in life, for we cannot afford to support you as well."

The young man felt some sorrow for his parents and swore to himself that if he made a fortune, he would pay his parents back and give his parents anything they desired in life.

So he set off, going south to the kingdom of Cornouaille, which in Breton is called Kernev.

Nearing the town of Quimper, he met a sorrowful-looking youth sitting by the road.

"What troubles you?" he demanded.

The youth looked up.

"I have no money and I am looking for work," he replied.

Koadalan smiled thinly. "Well, I am in the same position. You have to make the best of it. You cannot brood about it."

"I know," sighed the youth. "But I was offered a job with a nobleman only a moment ago, and I lost it by telling a lie."

"Oh? How so?"

"He stopped me just down the road there and asked if I would like a job. So I said that I would. 'Good,' he said, 'can you read?' Now I can't, but I wanted the job, so I said that I could. Well, that I could a little," he added defensively.

"So he found out that you couldn't?" inquired Koadalan.

"No. That's the stupidity of it. The great lord said to me, if you can read then you are not the one I am looking for. I have no job for you."

"Curious," agreed Koadalan. "What does this noble look like?"

"Oh, he is dressed from head to toe in black, with a silver buckle and a brooch to fasten his cloak. He rides a night-black stallion with a black-and-silver harness."

Koadalan rose from his perch beside the doleful youth. "Well, I am sorry that you didn't get the job."

He bade farewell and went on his way into Quimper. He made his way to the market square and the first person he should see, sitting outside a tavern drinking a glass of mead, was the distinguished-looking noble clad all in black. Next to him was tethered his night-black stallion.

Now Koadalan, as we have said before, was an intelligent youth. So he went over to the noble and greeted him politely. "*Devezgh-mat!*" he said. "Forgive me, sir, for being so forward, but I am thirsty and without money, for no one will give me work. Could you spare a copper for me to buy a drink?"

The noble frowned and, turning to him, he examined Koadalan speculatively. "Would you be willing to work for me?" he asked, after a while.

"Of course, if you have work for me to do."

"That I have. But can you read?"

"I can neither read nor write," lied Koadalan, "for my parents were too poor to send me for schooling."

The noble smiled in satisfaction.

"Excellent!" he said. "You are just the person that I am looking for. What is your name?"

"Koadalan, sire. And what is your noble name?"

"I am Lord Huddour," the man replied. "And now, it is not far to my castle, so you may mount behind me. We will be there in a trice."

The dark lord mounted his black horse and reached down and swung Koadalan up behind him as if he had been a featherweight. Then he heeled his horse and it sprang forward. Koadalan blinked and, in that blinking, he found that Quimper was far behind, indeed, far behind were the mountains of Cornouaille and the Pointe du Raz, and they were away across the sea beyond the Île de Sein. Koadalan hung on for dear life to the black flapping coat of the dark lord.

Barely a moment passed before they alighted in a great avenue of yew trees on a glorious-looking island in front of a towering but splendid-looking castle. They rode up to the gates. The first thing that Koadalan noticed above the door was a scroll carved in the stone which read: "He who enters here will never leave."

Koadalan was nervous and tried not to show that he had read and understood the scroll.

"Is this your castle, sir?" he asked nervously.

"It is," replied the man who called himself Lord Huddour. "Come in."

He led the way in and Koadalan could find no excuse but to follow him through those grim portals. However, the castle was pleasant enough inside, bright and cheerfully decorated. A meal, the like of which Koadalan had never seen before, was laid out, and he dined like a king. And after supper, he was conducted to a pleasant bedroom, where he slept on a goose feather bed. Never had the son of the forester known such luxury. The one thing he did notice, however, was that there were no servants at all in the castle and yet everything appeared to be cleaned and food was served, as if by unseen hands.

Next morning, when a sumptuous breakfast had been eaten, Lord Huddour addressed him.

"Now, we shall talk about the work which you are expected to do."

Koadalan was suddenly nervous. He remembered the grim notice outside.

"You will live in this castle for a year and a day and you will lack nothing. Anything you want, you have but to say."

"But to whom should I speak?" demanded Koadalan. "I have seen no one here."

Lord Huddour took out a square of linen.

"Here is a *lien*," (which is the Breton word for a napkin). "Whenever you want to eat or drink, you only have to say, to it, '*Lien, lien* do your task, bring me this or that' and straight away what you've asked for will appear. Now I must be away on a journey. In my absence, you must perform certain daily tasks."

Koadalan began to appear happy. It seemed to him that there was a pleasant prospect to being in the castle.

Lord Huddour conducted him to the kitchen of the castle. There was a fire over which a large cauldron hung on an iron hook. It was steaming away. Lord Huddour pointed to it.

"Each day, you must place two bundles of wood on that fire under the cauldron."

"Easy enough," replied Koadalan.

"You must do this, no matter what you hear. Don't take any notice but keep the fire going all the time."

Koadalan was surprised.

"What should I hear by keeping the fire going under the cauldron?" he demanded.

Lord Huddour ignored him. "You must promise."

Koadalan shrugged. "I promise."

"There is another task. Come with me."

And Lord Huddour took Koadalan to the castle stables. "Here you see a mare."

Indeed, there was a very thin mare in the stall to which Lord Huddour pointed. In front of the mare was a spiny faggot, which had been placed in her feeding trough.

"This mare is called Berc'hed. The faggot is for her food and there is a holly stick with which you must beat her each day until you draw sweat. Take the stick now and show me that you know how to give a good beating."

Koadalan was reluctant but, observing the look in Lord Huddour's eye, he took the stick and beat the poor animal as hard as he could.

Lord Huddour rubbed his chin.

"That is good. You are not bad in the way you handle the stick. Not bad at all."

He pointed across the stable to another stall where a young foal stood.

"Now see this young foal? Well, this foal has to be given as much clover and oats as it wants."

"Very well," acknowledged Koadalan.

With that the Lord Huddour led the youth back into the castle and into the great hall, from which many doors led off.

"Do you see these two doors?" demanded Lord Huddour, pointing to them.

"I do."

"These doors must never be opened by you. If you open them, you will regret it. Do you understand?"

"I do, indeed," affirmed Koadalan.

"Good. As for the rest of the castle, you may come and go as you please and pass through any other door."

Having given Koadalan all his instructions, the Lord Huddour mounted his horse and rode away along the avenue of yew trees through which they had come.

Koadalan was left alone in the castle. For a while Koadalan wandered the splendid apartments of the castle and was amazed at its riches and wealth. He wondered who this Lord Huddour could be, for surely no one except the kings of the five kingdoms of Armorica could be so rich and powerful?

Time passed and the youth grew hungry.

Suspiciously, he picked up the linen napkin and examined it carefully.

"I wonder if it was a hoax," he said to himself. He stroked his chin and then, holding the napkin at arm's length he intoned: "*Lien*, *lien*, do your task, bring me a joint of roast beef and a bottle of good red wine!"

At once, in the blink of an eye, a great sizzling dish of roast beef and a bottle of the finest red wine were placed on the table and, moreover, the table was properly laid for the meal.

Koadalan ate and drank his fill and, feeling soporific, he fell asleep at the table.

When he woke up and noticed the lateness of the hour, he felt a little guilty.

"I'd better do the work, exactly as Lord Huddour told me."

He went to rekindle the fire under the great cauldron, causing the flames to leap higher and higher around its bubbling contents. Then he heard from the depths of the cooking pot the sound of a moaning and agonising wailing, like the crying of souls in torment. He hesitated a moment and then remembered Lord Huddour's words. So he ignored the strange sounds and went to the stables. He gave the clover and oats to the young foal and then turned reluctantly to the mare, whose name was Berc'hed. He took off his jacket, took up the holly stick and set to the task of beating the mare. He was not enthusiastic about this, for he was a kindly and considerate young man.

As the first strokes fell, the mare suddenly cried out and said: "Stop! Have mercy on me, young man!"

Koadalan took a step back in astonishment. "Do my ears deceive me?" he demanded, looking at the mare. "Did you speak?"

"Yes. I was not always in this shape, young man. I was once in human form."

Koadalan dropped the holly stick and shivered. "In what evil place am I? Can you tell me, mare?"

"You are in the Castle of Huddour, the greatest wizard in all the world. If you are not careful, you, too, will have your form changed when he tires of you. The same thing that has happened to me will also happen to you."

"Save me! Can no one escape from this terrible man?"

"It is difficult, young man. Though, if you will trust me and help me, we may both escape."

"Anything," agreed Koadalan eagerly.

"*Bennozh Doue!*" replied the mare, which is the Breton for "thank you".

"What must I do?"

"Did Huddour show you two doors, beyond which you must not pass?"

"He did."

"Then go to them. In those two rooms you will find three books bound in red leather. Two books are in the first room and the third book is in the other room. You must enter and take the three books."

Berc'hed the mare suddenly was hesitant. "I do not suppose you can read, though? Huddour does not bring any helper here who can read."

"I lied to him," admitted Koadalan. "I can read."

"Then all may be well. Read the books and, if you learn what is written there, you will become a great wizard yourself. When Huddour loses the books, he will lose all his powers."

Koadalan immediately hurried to the two doors. He opened the first and saw two red leather-bound books on a table in the centre of the room. He took these and went to the second door. Sure enough, there was a third book there, lying in the manner of the first book. He took them into the dining room of the castle and sat down and began to read them. He was amazed at what he read and, curiously, found he was able to grasp all the intricate concepts of the books.

When he had finished, he went down to the stable.

Berc'hed was waiting impatiently. The mare seemed anxious and let out a sigh when she saw Koadalan.

"You have been a long time," she admonished.

"There were three books to read," replied Koadalan defensively.

"You have read them all?"

"I have."

"Then we must leave this place. Firstly, you will find a great eagle perched on top of the highest tower of this castle. At the moment, it is sleeping with its head tucked under its wing. But if we leave, it will wake and make such a din and cry out that Huddour will hear its cry, no matter where in this world he is. So therefore, you must go to it and tie it so that it cannot raise its head from beneath its wing."

Koadalan did as she told him and found the task comparatively easy.

"Can we leave now?"

"No. Secondly, there is a great bell in the square tower of the castle, which will start to ring if we leave and its ringing will be heard by Huddour, no matter what part of the world he is in. You must go to the bell and remove its clapper."

Koadalan went and found the bell and removed its clapper, so that when the bell started to move, it made no sound at all.

"Can we leave now?" demanded Koadalan.

"No," replied the mare. "Thirdly, you must wrap straw and oakum around my hooves, so that I do not make any noise on the courtyard pavement as we leave."

Koadalan did so.

"Can we leave now?"

"That we can," replied Berc'hed, the mare. "But first, take that sponge you see in the corner, that bundle of straw, the currycomb – which is a comb of metal for dressing a horse – and, above all things, do not forget to hold tight to your three red leather-bound books."

Koadalan gathered all these things up.

"Now," said Berc'hed, "climb on my back, and we shall leave."

As soon as Koadalan was mounted, the mare left the stable and cantered through the courtyard and out of the gates and then they were away, galloping through the air. Koadalan hung on tightly with his packages.

After a while the mare called: "Look behind us; can you see if we are being followed?"

Koadalan glanced behind.

"There is a pack of hunting hounds following."

"Quick, then! Throw the bundle of straw at them."

Koadalan did so. At once the hounds leapt on it and carried it off in triumph back in the direction of the castle.

After a while, Berc'hed called: "Look behind again; are we being followed?"

Koadalan looked behind. "There's only a cloud coming towards us. But it is a black one, almost blotting out the daylight."

"Huddour is in the middle of that cloud. Quickly, throw the currycomb into it."

Koadalan did so.

Out of the black cloud he saw Lord Huddour stop and retrieve the comb and then disappear back in the direction of the castle.

After a while, Berc'hed called: "Look behind again; are we still being followed?"

Koadalan did so. "Save us, there is a great flock of ravens descending on us."

"Then throw the sponge at them!"

Koadalan did so. The ravens seized the sponge, fighting over it, and flew with it back to the castle.

There was now a river ahead of them.

"Once beyond the river, we shall be safe, for Huddour's power does not extend that far," gasped the mare, for she was now tired out. "Is anything still following us?"

Koadalan glanced around.

"Save our souls! There is a giant black dog, hard on our heels."

Berc'hed sped on as hard as she could to the river and leapt across, but as she did so the great black dog came close and managed to bite a great chunk of horse hair from her tail.

Then they were across the water and the great black dog was forced to halt on the bank behind them, spitting out horse hair. It turned into the figure of Huddour.

Berc'hed stood exhausted but safe on the far bank, while Koadalan slid from her back.

"You are lucky to escape me, treacherous youth!" thundered the wizard from the other side of the river. "Nevertheless, I am willing to forgive you, so long as you return my three books."

"I know the secret of the books, Huddour. I am not likely to return them to you."

"I will have them!" howled the wizard.

"Come and get them," sneered Koadalan.

But the magician had no powers on the far side of the river now he had lost his books and so he left, cursing and angry.

Koadalan turned to Berc'hed and made sure the old mare was recovered from her exertions and then they both continued on their way. It was not long, however, before they came to a great circle of standing stones. Berc'hed went directly into the centre of the stone circle.

"What is it?" demanded Koadalan. "Why have we stopped?"

"Because it is here that you must kill me, Koadalan," replied the mare calmly.

"God save me! Not I. I would never do such a thing. Why, you saved my life. How do you expect me to kill you?"

"You must kill me, I tell you. If you do not, everything that has been done so far will be undone. You must cut my throat and slit open my belly."

"What are you saying?" Koadalan was aghast.

"You must!"

Finally, the old mare persuaded Koadalan to do the deed and, as much as he felt repulsion, he followed her instructions. No sooner had he cut the mare's throat and slit open her belly than a most beautiful young woman emerged. She was radiant and shone with the ethereal beauty of a goddess.

"Who are you?" demanded Koadalan in astonishment.

"I have told you. I am Berc'hed, daughter of the Good God."

"You are so beautiful," gasped Koadalan.

The young woman looked at him sadly. "Yet I am not for you, Koadalan. You are destined to live in this world while I and my kind live in the Otherworld. Never fear, though, your destiny is to have a wife, and one more beautiful than I. I will tell you this much. Your wife will be the daughter of the king of Poher. However, remember this. Should you ever need help at any time, come here to this stone circle and call out three times – 'Berc'hed! Berc'hed! Berc'hed!' – and I shall return to aid you. Above all, Koadalan, remember that you must not be parted from the three red leather-bound books. Always sleep with them at night under your pillow, for this is the only way of safeguarding them from the evil ones who will try to steal them. Remember that, Koadalan."

So saying, a great white cloud descended on her and she vanished in its brilliant light.

Koadalan was very sad but he had been told his destiny, so he set off for the kingdom of Poher. On his way, he used his new-found magic knowledge to bedeck himself in fine clothes, with jewels and a good horse and weapons, so that by the time he arrived at the court of the king of Poher, he looked every inch a prince. He did not lie, but many took him for the Prince of Domnonée. So he was made welcome at King Bertele's court.

Now King Bertele of Poher was generally a good man, but he had seen the evil in the world and how young man of ambition sought to better themselves. King Bertele had a beautiful daughter, whose name was Keredwen. She was of marriageable age, but rather than expose her to all the self-assertive social climbers, seeking status and her money, he had shut her up in one of his palace towers with a maidservant to attend her wants.

Now after Koadalan had spent a few nights at King Bertele's palace, and being called *keniterv*, that is "cousin", by the king, he began to wonder why he had not seen the princess Keredwen.

"I thought you had a daughter, Bertele?" he asked one day.

"No, cousin. I have no daughter," King Bertele assured him.

It was later that day when Koadalan was walking in the palace gardens that a golden ball fell at his feet. He glanced up and saw the face of a beautiful golden-haired girl peering down at him from the window of a tower. She smiled pleasantly and it seemed that she had tossed the ball deliberately to attract his attention. But just then, King Bertele came into the garden and the girl withdrew her head immediately.

"What is this?" asked Koadalan, holding out the ball.

"Oh, it is nothing," replied Bertele, but took the ball swiftly from him.

That evening Koadalan, alone in his room in the palace consulted his three red leather-bound books. By these means, he was able to materialize before the door of the room of the Princess Keredwen. No one had heard nor seen him pass through the palace.

He tapped softly on the door.

"Who is it?" demanded the harsh voice of the maidservant. "I have taken an oath to King Bertele not to let any suitors in this room."

"The King, Bertele, calls me *keniterv*," replied Koadalan firmly.

"It is my cousin!" cried a sweet voice. "The Prince of Domnonée. Let him in."

The door was open and Koadalan was admitted to the princess's apartment.

Koadalan and Keredwen found that they had so much in common and, as Berc'hed had said, she was truly beautiful. Before they knew it, dawn had come, and Koadalan returned to his room by the same magic means.

Each day for a week, Koadalan visited the Princess Keredwen and stayed with her until daybreak.

The day came, therefore, when Princess Keredwen began to manifest signs of eccentric behaviour and the maidservant summoned King Bertele and told him that, without any doubt, the princess was pregnant.

King Bertele fell in a rage and demanded to know who the father was.

The maidservant felt she had said enough and pretended that she did not know.

King Bertele demanded to know from his daughter but she refused to tell him.

Koadalan, who was the last to learn that the princess was about to have a child, met King Bertele walking in the garden, with anxiety on his face.

"What ails you, my King?" he asked.

"Alas, I have to confess to you, *keniterv*. I do have a daughter and I have kept her from everyone's eyes, to save her from the heartache of villainous fortune-seekers. But, in spite of keeping her in an apartment in a tower, with only her maidservant for company, she is pregnant. I do not know what to do. She will not tell me who the father is."

Koadalan was a moral and responsible young man.

"I will not lie to you, my King," he said. "I discovered that you had a daughter, for it was my destiny to find her. I am the father of her child. I beg you, therefore, my King, let me marry the Princess Keredwen."

The King of Poher was amazed when he heard that and, when his surprise was overcome, he realized that he was rather pleased with the idea.

"I can do no better than give you her hand in marriage, *keniterv*," he said.

So the marriage was arranged and guests from many parts of the five kingdoms attended. It was a ceremony that was talked about for some years afterwards. For a while, Koadalan and Keredwen lived happily and she gave birth to a fine son.

"Husband," said Princess Keredwen after a while, "I could not help but notice that none of your family came to our wedding. Is it you or is it I who am out of favour with them, that they disdain us both?"

Now Koadalan had been feeling ashamed that he had not been able to produce his family or confess that he was no more than a humble forester's son. He also felt somewhat guilty that he had not returned to share his new-found wealth with his poor parents. But he dismissed that from his mind, although he was ashamed. So Koadalan decided that he would pretend to take his wife and child back to his own country but, working with his three magic books, would, in fact, take them to a magic country so that the princess could report the fact back to her father.

So Koadalan summoned a golden coach pulled by five white horses with a coachman and two footmen, all by means of a spell from one of his three red leather-bound books.

Off they went, and on their journey they went by the castle of a great wizard called Anar-Zall, the great worm. He lived in a golden castle held between this world and the Otherworld and anchored to each by four silver chains. Now Koadalan, who never suspected people's motives, was pleased when Anar-Zall stopped his coach and invited Koadalan and Keredwen to come inside and sample his hospitality before they went on their journey.

After a magnificent feast in their honour, Koadalan and Keredwen were shown to a bedroom, while a wet-nurse took their son. Now Koadalan, before getting into bed, made a great mistake. He forgot completely to place the three red leather-bound books under his pillow, for this was the only means that Berc'hed had told him would keep them safe during the night.

Keredwen had grown to accept this custom, but it irritated her and so she had placed the books under a pile of clothes and failed to remind Koadalan where they were.

So, during the night, Anar-Zall entered their bedroom as they slept and seized the three books.

With the books safely in his possession, Anar-Zall woke the luckless Koadalan and ordered his servants to throw him down a bottomless well which led from the nether lands between this world and the Otherworld. Luckily, when Koadalan finally landed, it was in the middle of a great forest in this world. No longer was he dressed in fine clothes but returned to this world in the worn costume of a poor forester's son.

Koadalan cursed himself for his stupidity. He had lost his wife and his child and he had also lost the three books of magic that had made his fortune. He wandered the forest for several days, barely sleeping and finding nothing to eat. On the third day, he found a path out of the forest and, lo and behold!, he saw a familiar plain on which was the very stone circle where he had bade farewell to Berc'hed.

He went immediately to the centre and called out: "Berc'hed! Berc'hed! Berc'hed!"

There was something like a breath of wind and a voice said softly: "Do you need my help, Koadalan?"

Koadalan swung round and there was the beautiful goddess standing behind him.

"I surely stand in need of help, if ever I did," he said. "But whether you will wish to help me is another matter. For it is my fault, my grievous fault, that has brought this fate upon me."

"I know all about it, Koadalan. If you do exactly as I tell you, you shall have your wife, your son and the three magic books back again."

Then she held out her hand. "Touch my fingertips and close your eyes."

He did so and felt a gigantic wind seize him and hurl him into the air.

"Open your eyes now," said Berc'hed's voice.

They stood before Anar-Zall's golden castle.

"Everyone inside is asleep now, for it is rest time. I will show you Anar-Zall's resting place. Go in and you'll find him sleeping with the three red books. Yet he will not awaken. Take them and return to the castle gate. By that time, I will have found the Princess Keredwen and your son."

So she showed him where Anar-Zall slept.

In the room, Koadalan tried to hide his distaste, for Anar-Zall, in repose, turned into a great blind worm, curled in circles like a snake.

Koadalan tiptoed forward and picked up the three red leather-bound books.

At the gate, the goddess Berc'hed was waiting with the Princess Keredwen and their son.

"Before we leave," the goddess said, "how do you want me to punish Anar-Zall?"

Koadalan thought. Then he shrugged. "I have my wife and son back safely, and I have the three magic books. He has done me no further harm and I wish him no ill."

Berc'hed looked on in appreciation. "That sentiment stands you in good stead, Koadalan. As repulsive as Anar-Zall, the blind worm, is to your eyes, yet you wish him no harm. Very well. Come and touch my fingertips."

The wind came again and suddenly they were in the forest near the stone circle.

Berc'hed gazed sadly upon Koadalan. "Now I must bid you farewell, Koadalan, and farewell for ever in this world, for we shall never meet here again. Next time you see me, I shall be awaiting your arrival in the Otherworld."

Then a white cloud came down and she vanished in a blaze of light.

"Who was that?" demanded Princess Keredwen.

Then it was, for the first time, that Koadalan told Keredwen the full story of his humble beginnings and how he had managed to gain wealth and power.

Keredwen sighed.

"It would not matter to me if you were still a poor forester's son, Koadalan. It is the person you should love and not their clothes."

So with renewed love in their hearts for each other, they decided to journey to see Koadalan's real parents. Koadalan felt a great joy that now he would be able to repay them for all they had done for him. But to do this, Koadalan summoned forth the magic carriage again. And in fine style they came to the forest of Cranou.

Now Koadalan's parents were overjoyed at seeing their son having made his way in the world. They were amazed that he had married a princess and had a young son. Koadalan told his parents that whatever they wanted was theirs for the asking. But they were a proud and independent couple and said that they would accept no charity from their son.

When Koadalan said he would raise a castle for them, they told him that they preferred to stay in their old thatched cottage in the forest. Likewise, they refused any gifts of money.

"You were raised in the forest, my son. You are Alan of the Woods. Yet you have forgotten your forest law."

Koadalan frowned. "What have I forgotten, father?"

"Watch the animals of the forest. They own no debt, save to the seasons. Wealth is not their ambition, but to live and enjoy the luxury of what nature provides. The vixen and the dog-fox want no gratitude; they prefer to bear, to suckle, teach and then let their offspring run: not to demand repayment."

Koadalan and Keredwen and their son stayed in the cottage and shared whatever Koadalan's parents had. But Koadalan was not satisfied with old Alan's dismissal of his wish to repay his parents.

He pored over his magic books in order to see what he could do. One evening, sitting in the clearing of the forest, by means of divination, the stars told him that three evil magicians were coming in search of him and his magic books. So Koadalan devised a plan to thwart these evil magicians and so raise money for his father and mother without them feeling that it was charity.

That same evening Koadalan's father, old Alan, was having supper when his son said to him: "Tomorrow there is a fair at Quimerc'h, and you shall go there."

His father laughed sourly. "Why should I go to the fair? I've nothing to sell there, neither horse, cow nor pig. Nor do I have money to buy anything."

"You shall have something to sell, father. You have refused offers of great wealth because you do not want to accept my charity. However, I can pay you back for the bull you had to sell to educate me. That is surely no gift which you can refuse? The return of a bull?"

Old Alan thought and admitted that if his son returned a bull in exchange for the bull he had sold to educate Koadalan, it would not be accepting his son's charity. He agreed.

"Tomorrow morning, you shall go to your outbuilding and find a superb bull there," Koadalan told him. "Take it to the fair tomorrow and ask for a thousand silver pieces for it. But do not give the rope with the steer, otherwise great harm will befall me."

Now old Alan thought his son was joking but agreed. And the next morning, the old man was astonished to find a magnificent bull in his outhouse. It was the finest that he had ever seen. There was a rope around its neck and, remembering what his son has said, he took it and went to Quimerc'h fair.

When he appeared at Quimerc'h fair, the local people crowded round to admire the bull.

"We heard that you had strangers staying with you, Alan. Fine, rich strangers. Did they give you that fine bull?"

"They did," said the old man.

"Well, it is a fine beast, indeed. What do you want for him?"

"A thousand pieces of silver."

"*Gabell!*" cried a villager, which means, in the Breton language, something like "the devil!" and is an expression of surprise. "It is a fine beast, but we cannot afford to buy it."

And, indeed, no one locally could afford to offer such a sum.

Then three strangers approached him. They were tall, dark men, clad from head to toe in black.

"A fine beast is that bull," observed the first.

"Fine indeed," commented the second.

"How much for him?" asked the third.

"A thousand pieces of silver," replied old Alan.

"It is not cheap," said the first.

"But a fine beast," commented the second.

"So we are agreed on a deal. Here is the payment," summed up the third.

Old Alan put the money in his pocket and took off the rope.

"The bull is yours," he said.

"Give us the rope then, old man," said the first.

"Otherwise, we cannot lead the beast," commented the second.

"We need the rope," summed up the third.

"I didn't sell you the rope. I sold you the animal."

"But the rope always goes with a cow or bull," said the first.

"We'll buy the rope," added the second.

"Indeed, we will," said the third.

"The rope is not for sale," said Alan stubbornly, adhering to what his son had said.

"We'll give you another thousand," said all three in unison.

"Not for ten thousand!" replied Alan, making sure the rope was firmly in his pocket.

Then the three strangers mounted the back of the bull, which straightaway began to bellow and run about as if it were crazy. It threw the three strangers to the ground. Then it abruptly turned into a great dog and bounded home towards the forest of Cranou. But the three strangers had changed into wolves and chased it. But it reached the door of the forester, Alan, and leapt over the doorstep. Immediately it became a man – indeed, it was none other than Koadalan himself. The three wolves had to halt at the door and changed back into human form.

Koadalan smiled at them. "You are a little late, my friends."

"We almost had you," said the first.

"It doesn't matter," commented the second.

"We'll get you by the scruff of your neck yet," warned the third.

"You'll have to be quicker," laughed Koadalan.

They disappeared, muttering in anger.

A little while later, Alan himself returned home.

"Well, father, did you do well at the fair?" asked Koadalan.

"I did so," agreed the father. "I sold the bull for a thousand pieces of silver but held on to the rope. Here it is. I could have sold the rope for another thousand."

"Just as well that you were not tempted," smiled Koadalan.

"I was not, for the sale of the bull has given us enough to buy cows and a bull now."

Koadalan smiled. Then he said:

"But you sold a stallion for me. It is no charity to return it."

Old Alan agreed that it was not.

"There is another fair tomorrow, at Rumengol," Koadalan said. "It is a very good fair and you should go there."

"And with what should I go? I have no livestock to take there." protested old Alan.

"In the morning, you will find a stallion in your stable. It is the best horse you will have ever seen. You must ask two thousand pieces of silver for it. But when you sell it, be sure not to give the bridle away. Keep it and return here with it."

So, the next morning, old Alan went to the stable and found a magnificent stallion there. So he took it to the great fair at Rumengol. At the sight of the stallion, many gathered around and demanded to know how much old Alan wanted. But when he said two thousand pieces of silver, they felt it too much and drifted away.

Then along came the three strangers, clad in black from head to toe.

"How much for the stallion, old man?" asked the first.

"It's a fine beast," said the second.

"Indeed, it is," agreed the third.

When old Alan asked for two thousand pieces of silver, the first one said: "It is a great deal of money."

"But it is a fine stallion," pointed out the second.

"We agree on the price," agreed the third.

Now when the agreement was made and old Alan went to take the bridle off the stallion, they did not demur.

"There is an inn across the way," pointed out the first.

"Before we conclude the deal, we can go in there and count out the money in comfort," said the second.

"And we can have a drink there," the third suggested.

So they went into the inn and called for cider, for the local cider of Rumengol is a potent brew. And before old Alan realized it, he had taken a drop too much. Indeed, he was so drunk that when the three suggested that they needed the bridle, he let them have it without demur.

The three immediately took the horse, still with the bridle, and all three mounted it. Everyone looked at them in astonishment, for the people of Rumengol work on the land and have an empathy with animals. They abhor people who maltreat them.

"What are those imbeciles doing?" demanded the village folk and the three rode off through the town, passing the sacred fountain where once King Gradlon built a chapel.

"You've less sense than your animal!" yelled one man.

"At least two of you should get down from the back of that poor beast!" cried another.

"Aren't you ashamed?" demanded a third.

And as an angry crowd began to gather, the three strangers felt it prudent to get down.

It was the chance the stallion was waiting for. It leapt into the river and changed into an eel. The three strangers, in a rage, leapt after it, changing into three big fish and set off in pursuit. The eel, realising them to be coming closer and closer, leapt from the water and assumed the shape of a dove. After it went the three fish, changing into sparrow-hawks. Across the sky they sped, with the dove getting tired as it tried to elude the hunters.

It was passing over a palace at Roc Trévezel and saw a maidservant filling a bucket at the castle well. The dove turned into a bright golden ring and fell into the bucket. It startled the maidservant, who took it from the bucket and stared at it in wonder. Cautiously, she slipped it on her finger, and then hurried inside the castle to continue her duties.

The three sparrow-hawks alighted before the castle. Now the castle at Roc Trévezel was owned by the Lord of Trévezel, a powerful noble, whose fortress dominated the whole of the five kingdoms of Armorica, for it was built on the highest point. From the castle tower, one could see north to the Léon plateau where, in clear weather, the spires at St Pol-de-Léon could be seen; to the west, one could see the waters of Rade de Brest and to the south, the line of the forest on the Menezioù Du or the Montagnes Noires. Lord Trévezel was a man to be reckoned with.

So the three strangers, who you must have realized were the three magicians who had come in search of Koadalan and his red leather bound books, decided to change themselves into three musicians, who each carried a *biniou*, which is a Breton bag-pipe. They went to the castle gate and asked if they could play to Lord Trévezel. He liked bag-pipe music and so he allowed them to play. At the end, he was delighted by their music and offered them money.

"Thank you, my lord," said the first, "but we do not seek money."

"What is it you seek then?" demanded Lord Trévezel. "Name it and you shall have it."

"A golden ring," the second musician replied.

"It was dropped by a dove and fell into the bucket of water your maidservant was drawing at the castle well," added the third.

Now Lord Trévezel was puzzled by the request and wondered how the three came to know of the ring's whereabouts, but he had given his word.

"You shall have it," he said. "Send for the maidservant."

Now the maid had gone to her room to admire the ring and she was terrified when it suddenly vanished and in its place was Koadalan. For he had been the stallion, the eel, the dove and the ring.

"Do not be afraid," Koadalan told her. "I am trying to escape from three evil magicians. I was the golden ring on your finger and your master, Lord Trévezel, has sent to ask you for it. Go to him. I shall turn myself back into the ring. You must not give him the ring, however, until he has promised to do what I am about to tell you."

The girl's fear vanished although she was still astonished by what was happening.

"Tell Lord Trévezel that he can have the ring to give to the musicians, but first he must have a great fire lit in the castle courtyard. Then he must throw the ring into the flames and tell the musicians that they must retrieve it when the fire is at its hottest."

The maidservant promised to do this.

Koadalan changed back again.

The servants came and took the girl to Lord Trévezel who asked for the ring.

"Here it is, my lord," said the maidservant, raising her hand to show it on her finger.

"Hand it to me, then, for I have promised to give it to these musicians."

"My Lord, I have been told not to do so until you agree to this demand . . ." And the girl told Lord Trévezel what he had to do.

Now Lord Trévezel, as we have said, was suspicious of the three musicians and their glib demand for the ring. He was therefore not against the girl's request. He ordered a fire to be lit and asked to be told when the fire was at its hottest. Then he took the three musicians into the courtyard and stood before the fire.

"It is at its hottest now, my lord," cried one of his servants, tending the fire.

So Lord Trévezel turned to the maid, who took the ring from her finger. She handed it to him and he threw it into the heart of the flames.

Lord Trévezel said to the musicians: "You may fetch it! Then you may keep it."

The three did not wait but turned themselves into three ghastly little fire-imps and hurled themselves into the flames.

"*Va Doue Benniget*!" exclaimed Lord Trévezel. This means, in Breton, "Good Lord!"

What those looking on did not see was that the golden ring had turned into a charred grain of wheat which was blown by the eddies of the fire away from it and, ascending on the spiralling smoke, eventually came to rest in a pile of wheat in the castle granary. The three wily magicians had seen it, though.

After it went the three imps, who turned themselves into three cock birds, which started to peck at the grain to find which was Koadalan. But the grain suddenly turned into a fox and, before the cock birds could do anything, they were set upon and killed by the fox.

So, eventually, Koadalan made his way back to the forest of Cranou.

After a while, seeing that his father and mother now had a more comfortable life, even though they refused the great riches which he could have brought them, Koadalan, Keredwen and his son returned to the castle of King Bertele.

Time passed. Old King Bertele died and Koadalan and Keredwen became king and queen in his stead. Then came news from the Forest of Cranou that old Alan and his wife had also passed on to the Otherworld. Koadalan was, however, happy with Keredwen and his son, and had possession of the three red leather-bound books, which made him the greatest magician in all the land.

However, a day came when Koadalan was away hunting,

and he learnt that Keredwen and her son had perished in a terrible plague.

Koadalan blamed himself that he had not been there to cure them. He became a changed man and grew reclusive and bitter. He buried himself more and more in his three books of magic, seeking the ultimate spell which is the achievement of immortality, placing himself on a level with the gods and goddesses of the Otherworld.

He finally grew old and achieved many things in his life. But the older he grew, the more he feared death, and the more he studied his books to wrest from them the secret of immortality.

Finally, he decided that he would perform the ultimate *sakrilach*, for that is what Breton people call it when one tries to make oneself the equal to the gods.

He called his servants together.

"You must all obey me, no matter what I tell you to do, do you understand? No matter what I ask, you must carry it out. If you do, you shall be rewarded with as much gold and silver as you could wish for."

They all thought that this seemed a good proposition.

He turned to a female servant who had just had her first-born child and had plenty of mother's milk.

"You have a great role in this, woman," Koadalan said.

"I will do as you ask," she replied.

Then he called to his manservant.

"You are to put me to death. Then you will chop up my body into sausage meat. You must ensure that all the pieces and the blood are placed in a large earthenware pot, which you must cover with a cloth. Take the pot into the garden and bury it under a heap of hot manure."

They looked at him as if he were mad, and who is to say that he was not? But he had offered them money and so it was not their concern.

He turned back to the female servant.

"The earthenware pot will remain under the manure for six months. During that period, you will come to the manure heap twice a day, both at midday and at three o'clock in the morning. You will sprinkle some of your milk over the manure, above the earthenware pot, for half an hour each time. Take care that while you are performing this deed, you do not fall asleep."

The woman also thought Koadalan was mad, but neglected to say as much. After all, he was paying her to perform this deed.

When she agreed Koadalan went on.

"After six months, you will see me come forth from the earthenware pot in one piece, full of life and in the best of health, stronger and more handsome than I have ever been in my life. I shall then live forever."

The servants made no comment.

If the master was mad, it was no business of his servants, so long as they were paid and no blame attached to them as to what he told them.

So it happened as Koadalan said.

They killed him and he felt a momentary stab of discomfort before, it seemed, he fell into a deep, dreamless sleep.

Then he awoke.

But he was not emerging from the earthenware pot. Instead, he stood on a long, low, sandy shore which stretched in both directions, with the blue sea lapping at it. Then he saw a line of people – he saw Keredwen and his son, her father Bertele, old Alan and his mother, and many other people he had known but whom he thought were dead. They were lined up along the shore staring sorrowfully at him.

Then he saw a familiar and beautiful woman walking towards him.

"Berc'hed!" he exclaimed. "What does this mean?"

She, too, regarded him with sadness. "Remember what I told you many years ago? I promised you that the next time that you saw me would be at a certain time."

Koadalan frowned as he sought memory.

"You said that the next time that you saw me would be when I entered the Otherworld, but . . ."

Then the realization hit him.

He had entered the Otherworld. If that were so, then he was surely dead!

Berc'hed nodded, as if reading his thoughts.

On earth, the woman servant had gone twice a day to the earthenware pot and sprinkled her milk on the manure heap. But there were three days to go before the six months were ended when she could not overcome the drowsiness she felt, and she fell asleep as she was sprinkling her milk.

When Koadalan's servants dug up the earthenware pot after the prescribed time, they found Koadalan's body entire. It almost seemed as if he were about to spring forth. Perhaps he might have succeeded after three days, but the wise ones will tell you that it would have been impossible. No one who dares the final sacrilege of attempting to place themselves on a level with the gods may remain unpunished.

How was Koadalan punished?

Well, when he died, the three red leather-bound books vanished. They were lost to the knowledge of humankind, so that there have been no other great wizards nor magicians after Koadalan. The wise ones will tell you that it was the gods and goddesses themselves who hid the books. But, for his impiety, Koadalan is forced to return from the Otherworld, once every year. He returns on the very night that the Otherworld becomes visible to this world, when souls can travel back to wreak their vengeance on the living. Then it is that Koadalan comes back to search for his three magic books, wailing, cursing and lamenting his sacrilege.

That night, my friends, is called the eve of Gouel an Anaon, All Souls' Day, which is known in other parts of the world as Hallowe'en. So if you have any red leather-bound books, on that dark evening, do not be surprised to see them spin in the air and then fall to the ground, nor start at the sound of a wailing cry. It is just Koadalan, searching for his lost magic books, which he is now doomed to do for ever and a day.

36 The King of Bro Arc'hant

Once there was a Breton lord named Avoez, who dwelt in a large and splendid castle on the coast. He was lord of all Breizh Izel. No one could say for sure how Avoez became lord of Breizh Izel. It was remarked that his predecessors had been kind, generous and cared for the welfare of their people and the beauty of the country.

Then Avoez had become their lord and he ruled with a harshness that made everyone dread him. He was also a man who wanted to acquire wealth, and this became an obsession to the exclusion of all else.

The once beautiful gardens of his castle at Lanaskol were ploughed up to plant crops, to grow apple trees to make sweet cider. Where once rhododendrons and camellias grew, there grew instead lawns of artichokes and green peas and crops of grain. He would have no flowers within or without his castle.

His whole estate was managed by his sister, Moravik, who was just as avaricious and acquisitive as her brother.

It was a sad day when Avoez became lord of Breizh Izel and master of Lanaskol. All the people agreed on that. Yet there was nothing that could be done.

Eventually, there was nothing which Avoez did not want for except one thing – a wife and an heir to his lands.

Now the Penmarc'h Peninsula is a low, rocky plain quite unlike the promontories of the Raz or Pen-Hir. It is an area where one is always close to the sea and constantly hearing the hammering of the waves on the impressive rocks that line the coast, rocks which are in fact called the Rocks of Penmarc'h, south from the Phare d'Eckmühl north to the beach at Pars Carn. Even four hundred years ago, the area was still one of the richest in Brittany, where fishing for the "Lenten Meat", the cod, made fortunes for fifteen thousand inhabitants. But the cod deserted the shores of Penmarc'h, and a big tidal wave swept the land and now the peninsula is poor. But all this happened long after this story took place.

In the time of Avoez, it was a rich land, ruled by Tanguy of Kertanguy. He was married and with a beautiful daughter named Litavis who was born on Gouel-Yann, midsummer's day, when the rays of the setting sun touched the great centre stone at Carnac. Litavis' beauty was a byword throughout all Penmarc'h and so Avoez came to hear of her. So one day he took himself to Kertanguy in disguise and watched and waited for Litavis to come along. Then he saw for himself that the stories of her comeliness were not exaggerated.

"I will marry this girl," he said firmly.

When he went to see Tanguy of Kertanguy and his wife to arrange the marriage, they simply laughed. For Avoez had the physique to match his parsimonious and niggardly attitude. He went away in a rage and he called his sister, Moravik.

"Tell my tax-gatherers that I want them to seek out all the debts of Tanguy of Kertanguy. I want to buy up all the unpaid debts, all the mortgages on his lands. I want to reduce the fortune of Tanguy of Kertanguy to nothing. I want this done within the year."

So it came to pass that, within a year, he owned all the lands and wealth that Tanguy had, for Tanguy, although he was not an evil man, was an impecunious man and incurred debts. One midsummer's day, when Litavis was just seventeen years old, Avoez presented himself at the house of Tanguy of Kertanguy and told him that he was ruined.

"I own you and all you once possessed."

Faced with this ruin, poor Tanguy and his wife did not know what to do.

"There is a solution," Avoez said. "I am willing to give you back half of your wealth in return for your daughter Litavis."

Now Tanguy's wife would have none of this but Tanguy, who could not bear to be poor and turned out on the roadside, agreed to the shameful bargain. It is said that Tanguy's wife then left his house and refused to return there any more.

Tanguy had his daughter brought forth and she, pale and horrified at what her father had done, could do nothing. Avoez took her back to his castle at Lanaskol and his sister Moravik prepared the feasting and the wedding. Now, because of his penny-pinching attitudes, the feasting was paid for by the people who were ordered to attend, for Avoez and his sister arranged for a fair to be held at the same time at which they sold their goods for profit, and were thus amply repaid for their feasting and wrestling matches.

Litavis remained as one in shock throughout all the ceremony. She did not smile, did not dance, and refused to take any food nor drink. She did not even pluck a flower and place it in her own hair as a symbol of the joy of betrothal.

As soon as the marriage ceremony was over, Avoez decided not to press himself upon the pure, sweet girl. He had a male pride and wanted his wife to come to the bridal bed willingly. He was prepared to wait. But he was not prepared to give her freedom to wait. He viewed everyone with jealous eyes.

Moravik, his sister, offered her advice and told her brother to lock Litavis in one of the high towers of Lanaskol, one which stood on the point overlooking the brooding Atlantic seas.

"There you may keep her, brother, and none but you will be able to visit her."

"This is an excellent idea," Avoez agreed. "We will have her well-guarded. You, my sister, will watch her by day, and at night she will be locked in. We will have Gof the Smith forge us four good locks to which only I will have the key."

"You are wise, my brother," said Moravik. "And Gof makes locks that even Merlin the Enchanter cannot undo."

What Avoez said came to pass. Litavis was locked in a high tower on the point overlooking the brooding sea. It was a small room in the tower, where she saw no one except Moravik, who watched her from dawn until dusk and then each night Avoez came to her and asked: "Are you ready to be a bride?" But each night she did not answer but stood by the window, staring out to the dark whispering seas.

Seven long years passed in this fashion. No maidservants came to help her, and she was alone. She grew ill in her despair. Her long gold braids became tangled and matted, her clothes became worn and dirty and she paced the floor in her anguish.

Now Avoez grew enraged that she would not come to the bridal bed nor conceive his child and finally his passion was dampened. Yet he saw her as a piece of his property and he was not willing to let her go.

One day, and it was the feast of Meurlarjez or Shrove Tuesday, Avoez decided to set out on a tour of inspection of his estates all over Breizh Izel. So he said to his sister, Moravik: "While I am gone, sister, you must take care that nothing happens to Litavis." He gave her the four keys with which Litavis was locked in each night. These were the keys made by Gof the Smith. "Be sure to lock her chamber each night when you leave her."

"I will do so, brother. You may trust in me."

So Avoez climbed onto his horse and started off on his journey.

In the tower, Litavis stood at the window, watching him ride away. There was no feeling in her as she watched him leaving. She did not feel the soft rays of spring sun on her skin nor the gentle singing of the birds announcing the change of season. Then one of the birds alighted on her window sill and began to sing insistently and, even in her still and silent mind, she suddenly realized that words were beginning to form.

"If you believe in life, Litavis, you must believe that all evil passes. If you believe hard enough, then what you most desire will come to be."

For the first time in seven years, she spoke.

"Who are you, bird?"

"I am the messenger of Bro Arc'hant, the Land of Silver; I am the voice of the *korrigan* who dwell under the stones of Carnac; I am the voice of the *mari-morgan*, the daughters of the sea, who frolic around the Rocks of Penmarc'h. I am the voice of those beings who have not abandoned you. Believe in us."

"This is a strange song that you sing to me, little bird," she observed.

"Believe and what you most desire shall come to be," repeated the little bird.

Then it flew off across the seas.

Litavis thought hard and long. She did want to believe. She did desire one thing above all others in the world, but she was ashamed to say it aloud. Yet even as she thought, a great hawk came flapping in her window. She was very scared indeed. It flew into her chamber and alighted in the middle of the room.

Even as she looked, the hawk turned into a tall handsome warrior, richly dressed, with bright glinting armour and weapons. His hair was fair and his eyes cool, like the grey of the sea.

Litavis gave a little cry and stumbled back.

"Flower of the Rocks of Penmarc'h, do not be afraid of me," he said gently. So gentle and sweet was his tone that she found herself losing her fear. "Litavis, you have summoned me with your heart. You called me and I have been waiting in Bro Arc'hant many long years, waiting for that call. I have loved you since I saw you playing around the Rocks of Penmarc'h."

"How can this be? Who are you?" she demanded.

"I am Eudemarec of Bro Arc'hant."

"How do you know me?"

"I have long dwelt in and around Penmarc'h. That is how I know you. Do you deny that you called for me to come to you?"

The girl knew what her secret heart desired and she had, indeed, called for a fair champion who loved her and whom she could love. She knew without further question that this was such a man.

"What if Avoez knows of this?" She was still nervous.

"Our love will be more secret than the secret words of the song of the *korrigan*," he vowed. He held out his hand to her. "Do you fear me?"

"No."

And she came to him willingly and their love was almost painful in its joy and rapture.

He stayed with her until the first glimmer of dawn, when they heard Moravik undoing the locks.

"When will you come again?" cried Litavis, as her champion turned once more into a great hawk.

"Whenever your desire calls to me, Litavis," he replied.

Litavis felt a great joy.

Just before the hawk turned to fly off, it said: "Beware of Moravik, for she is steeped in the laws of magic. Say nothing, for if I am discovered, she might encompass my death."

So each night, after dusk, Litavis' desire brought forth Eudemarec out of the Land of Silver, fluttering in the form of a hawk into her bedchamber. They lay as lovers through the starry night until dawn, when Eudemarec had to return home. Litavis grew in strength and happiness and turned once more into a radiant picture of beauty.

Then it was that Avoez, the lord of Lanaskol returned. He gazed upon his bride in name and, frowning, went in search of his sister.

"What does this mean, Moravik?" he demanded. "Why is there this change in her?"

"I do not know, brother. I swear she has been locked in her tower ever since you left."

"It cannot be," declaimed Avoez. "You must have betrayed me. She must have been outside the room."

"I have not betrayed your trust," insisted his sister.

So insistent was she, that Avoez finally believed her.

"We must discover what has happened to Litavis. I swear she must be in love and I know her love is not directed at me."

So that night, after dusk, Avoez and his sister Moravik sat up and waited and watched, and they saw a hawk fly in at Litavis' high tower window. They continued to watch and wait and saw, at dawn, that the hawk flew out again.

Brother and sister then knew what was happening for, indeed, Moravik had been a follower of the old arts of wizardry from her childhood. And a plan was hatched between them.

Avoez, curbing his anger, went to speak with Litavis the next morning, and told her that the lord of Breizh-Uhel wanted to see him and that he would be away for a while.

Moravik stood beneath the tower, calling her farewells loudly enough for her voice to climb to the high room in which Litavis was imprisoned. And Litavis herself saw Avoez riding off to the eastern hills.

Litavis was surprised, however, when Moravik came to her room with a silver tray. On the silver tray was a bottle of ruby wine and two goblets.

"I am pleased that you have recovered your health, Litavis," the cunning sister of Avoez said. "To celebrate, let us drink a glass of ruby wine and observe the pleasant spring day."

Now Litavis was a trusting and open-hearted person. There was no guile nor deceit within her, and she was not aware of the fault in others. So she accepted Moravik's ruby wine with joy and they sat sipping and observing the bright spring day together.

She did not realize that Moravik had emptied a phial of liquid into her goblet and that phial was a special potion which she had prepared with all her wizard cunning.

Soon, very soon, Litavis fell into a deep, drugged sleep.

Knowing full well that no one could rouse themselves from the effects of the potion before twelve hours had passed, Moravik left the tower room with the doors unlocked and took away the wine and goblets. Then she returned and went to hide in an old oak wardrobe, to observe what would take place.

Litavis stayed in her deep sleep a night and a day and only when it was dusk did she rouse herself, sat up and rubbed her eyes and gazed out on the restless seas beyond her window.

In her heart, she called for Eudemarec.

In a moment, the hawk entered the chamber and in a blink of an eye her lover, Eudemarec, stood beside her.

"Why did you not call for me last night?"

Litavis frowned.

"Last night?"

"You did not call for me. Does aught ail you?"

She passed a hand across her brow. "I recall drinking wine and falling into a deep sleep. But that does not matter now, my love . . . I am awake now, and you are with me."

Eudemarec and Litavis slept together until the first pale streaks of dawn and then he rose from the couch and flew away back to the Country of Silver.

Litavis, smiling, went to sleep.

Then it was that Moravik crept out of the wardrobe and crept from the tower room. She was awed by what she had seen and hurried down to the castle. Her brother Avoez had returned and was waiting to hear the news.

"She has a lover!" announced Moravik.

Avoez flew into a great anger. "Do you lie to me, sister?"

"Never, brother. She has a lover."

"Who is this lover? I will tear him to pieces . . ."

"Calm your rage. Listen to what I have to say. The lover is the hawk which turns into a noble champion when he enters her bedchamber."

Avoez was astounded. "He is a wizard, then?"

Moravik sniffed. "I am more steeped in wizardry than this one. He is a comely warrior called Eudemarec, and that is the name by which she called him."

"Eudemarec? Where does he come from?"

"It matters not. Only that when she calls for him, he comes to the chamber in the body of a hawk, and hawks can be destroyed."

"How so?"

"We deal with magic, here. I have a plan, though. Go to Gof the Smith and tell him to make four pikes that are razor-sharp."

"I shall do so."

"Have him make points that are so sharp that even the wind's breath is cut by them."

"I shall do so."

"Then have your servants wait until the girl is asleep, just after dawn tomorrow. At that time, they must fix the pikes in the window of the chamber room."

"Ah!" cried Avoez. "I see the plan. This lover will be cut to little pieces when he tries to enter."

Moravik chuckled softly. "You have the plan exactly, my brother."

The evening after the pike heads had been fixed to the window, after dusk, Litavis lay and called to her lover.

The flapping of the hawk's wings grew near and then the hawk appeared.

She let forth a scream as the bleeding bird fell into the chamber, changed into human form and staggered to the couch.

Eudemarec was mortally wounded.

With horror and grief, Litavis tried to bind his wounds, but it was little use, for he was cut to pieces.

"I give my life for your love, Litavis," he said quietly. "But despair not. You will bear a son who will grow up valiant and wise and you must call him Ywenec."

"Ywenec," repeated the girl obediently.

"He will avenge me, Litavis. Now kiss me and let me go, for my enemies must not find me here and capture me."

"I cannot bear to part with you."

"Have no fear. I shall be ever near you. You will hear my voice in the whispering night seas and feel the touch of my lips with the gentle sea spray."

"Let me die with you, Eudemarec! Let me come with you to the County of Silver."

However, Eudemarec turned into a hawk, still torn and bleeding, and flew out of the window and was gone.

Litavis was left alone and sobbing for her mortally wounded lover.

Now when the servants of Avoez had fixed the pikes in place they, being lazy and inclined to do no more than was minimal, had left their ladder against the tower wall. Litavis tugged at one of the pikes and made enough room to squeeze through and out she went onto the ladder. She came swiftly to the ground and saw the drops of blood made by the hawk forming a trail across the grass and across the fields of wheat and oats.

Onward and onward she followed the trail of the hawk's blood over hill, river and through wood, until she came to the great forest of Quénécan, whose oak and beech trees spread like a thick carpet. She wandered by the fast-flowing waters of the Daoulas, through its gorges, until she came to the shore of Lake Guerlédan, where she fell exhausted, for she had lost the trail of blood and did not know which way to go.

"Oh, Merlin! Oh wisest and greatest of all wizards, help me find my beloved," she cried in her despair.

There was a sighing across the waters and she heard a deep voice answering her. "Bathe yourself in the waters of the lake, Litavis."

Now the moon was up, round and white, in the black night sky. Thinking no more, Litavis peeled her clothes from her pale tired body, and, feeling no chill, she entered the dark waters and bathed herself.

"Gone is all impurity," sighed a voice.

And she returned to shore and put on her clothes. Then, as she turned to cry again to Merlin, she found a tall, thin elf sitting on a branch watching her.

"Who are you?" she demanded.

"I am called Bugel Noz," the elf said. "I am the shepherd of the night."

"Then, good shepherd, tell me where I must go to follow my love."

The Bugel Noz held out his hand to her and she took it, and she felt a very soporific feeling overcome her: a dream-like state.

"Hark to me, Litavis, Flower of the Rocks of Penmarc'h. Hold my hand and we will follow the drops of blood of your beloved hawk."

And she suddenly saw the blood spots again and the Bugel Noz led her onwards, following them, following them southwards and further southwards, until they came by dark forest paths to a strange, wild seashore.

She heard a singing.

At once, the Bugel Noz said to her: "Close your ears, Litavis. You must not listen to the song of the *mari-morgan*. Close your ears but look about you."

Litavis saw men and women wandering the strange shore, moving like wraiths; slowly they moved and with the look of doom on their faces.

"They will never be able to rest, for they listened to the *mari-morgan*'s song and her icy call has captured their hearts and minds."

And the elf led her onwards, along the rolling surf, breaking thunderously on the rocky seashore; and onwards again into sea grottoes, and rocky caverns, until they halted in an underwater cave.

Then the Bugel Noz put a pipe to his lips and played a wild tune.

There was a sudden flash of lightning in the cave and a voice said: "Who summons me?"

The elf replied: "I do, Yann-an-Oded. I bring Litavis and place her in your care. For she seeks her beloved."

Then the Bugel Noz was gone, playing his pipes back into his forest dwelling.

Yann-an-Oded came forward, a tiny elfin creature who danced around her shouting: "*C'hwe! C'hwe! Ra zeui a-benn!*," thus wishing her success in her task.

He took her by the hand and led her onward again, along the foam-kissed shore, passing the whispering waves which tossed bright silver fishes from one wave to another. And on those waves she saw the *morwreg*, the daughters of the sea: maidens with shining silver fish-tails who rode the breakers and played in the foam of their crests, all the while laughing and singing to each other.

"The blood drops, Litavis," called Yann-an-Oded. "Follow the blood drops of your beloved hawk."

Onwards he led her, away from the clamorous sea, over the rolling dunes, until they approached a great circle of standing stones. Menhirs, dolmens and great circles of ancient stones filled the landscape.

Yann-an-Oded halted at the edge of the circle and pointed to where the drops of blood led straight across the circle.

"I must leave you here, Litavis; follow the drops of blood. But before you go, this plough stick."

Litavis frowned. "What shall I do with that?"

"A mortal holding the stick may pass through Carnac unharmed. With this, you may pass the dancing *korrigan*. Hold it and follow the drops of blood."

With the same flash of lightning in which he had appeared, the elfin creature was gone.

Litavis began to walk through the stones. It was very bright and the moon was full and silvery.

She heard a whistling sound, high-pitched, and moving in curious rhythms.

"The *korrigan!*" she whispered, recognising the sounds of the sprites who ruled the realms of the night.

She saw them dancing in the stone circle, dancing the *jabadao*, a dance of the Breton people, laughing to themselves. Then they stopped; their diamond-shaped elfin eyes caught sight of her and stared with curiosity.

"*Diwall! Diwallit!* Beware! Watch out!" they called to one another. "Here is a human who trespasses where she should not be."

They moved towards her and she gripped the plough stick before her, gripped it tightly in her hands.

Then they began to dance swiftly around in a circle chanting.

Dilun, di meurzh, dimerc'her . . .
Lez on, lez y
Bas an arer zo gant y . . .

Monday, Tuesday, Wednesday . . .
Let her go, let her go!
She has the plough stick in her hand . . .

And their circle parted and they let her walk through their midst. She saw how beautiful the *korrigan* were, laughing and joyous and calling on her to dance with them. And she did so, still holding her stick.

"*Diyaou, digwener, di sadorn ha disul*"

"Thursday, Friday, Saturday, Sunday . . ."

"Let her go, let her go . . ."

"*Doue d'e bordono!*" they cried. "*Ra zeui a-benn!*"

And, wishing her success, they let her proceed on her way.

She finally came to a hill and she saw a door in the side of this hill, on which were splattered drops of blood. She went up to the door and tried the iron handle on it. It opened to her touch and she pushed into the blackness beyond. She could see nothing. She held out her hands to feel her way, step by step, onward down a long, dark, dank tunnel, at the end of which she saw a light. She hurried on until she came to a gate at the end of the tunnel. The gate was of pure silver and studded with many jewels.

She peered beyond the gate and saw a bright land, with meadows filled with silver flowers and bright with silvery dew.

"Merlin, oh, Merlin, wisest of all wizards, help me now," she cried as she tested the strength of the gate.

It opened abruptly and she entered.

She saw the drops of blood leading along a path through the meadow and the path led upwards towards a tall city of silver atop a hill.

She hurried on, meeting no one, until she entered the city and made her way to the harbour by a great silvery sea. Anchored there were three hundred tall masted and magnificent fighting ships. On the quay were the tell-tale drops of blood. She looked around for someone to help her, but found no one. There was no living soul in the Silver City.

She walked back into the heart of the city.

Then she saw a path leading upwards to a great palace which dominated the city. So she followed the path along an avenue which led through ancient oaks and rowan trees with many scented flowers. Now she saw that the trail of blood drops was leading her towards the palace.

At the gate stood a handsome warrior, but he was sleeping where he stood. In the hallway was a feasting table with lords and ladies asleep before their food and wine. Musicians lay in a corner, with hands on their instruments, slumbering away. Further on was a bedchamber, in which a noble lord and his lady lay fast asleep in one another's arms. The whole palace seemed asleep.

She searched each room until she came to a great royal bedchamber hung with silver chandeliers and a crystal studded ceiling. There, on a large silver bed, adorned with bright white sheets, was stretched the body of her lover, pale and reposed as in death.

"Eudemarec!" she cried, flinging herself on the bed beside him. "My life, my love . . .!"

The handsome noble stirred, fluttered his eyes and gazed sorrowfully at her.

"Litavis, the Flower of Penmarc'h, you have followed my bloody trail. You have dared to come through lands which no mortal man may see . . . you have dared much in your love for me."

"Let me share whatever fate you have."

"I fear it may not be so."

"Let me die with you. That much is a token of my love."

"It is not your destiny. You must return to Lanaskol. There is your destiny."

"Avoez will kill me if I return."

Eudemarec shook his head slowly. "He will do you no harm, my love."

He reached down and took a silver ring from his finger, a fine band almost as thin as a thread of silk. "Wear this ring. While you have it around your finger, neither Avoez nor Moravik will have any remembrance of what has passed between us."

With that he fell back.

She bent forward and kissed him. "Let me stay!"

"It cannot be," he said sadly. " Here, take the great silver sword that is by my side. Keep this in secret and keep it in safety until our son Ywenec has grown to manhood."

She took the sword from his weak hands and he smiled. "I have a moment more. I will tell you what is to be. When Ywenec reaches the age of maturity, the king of Cornouaille will summon him to make him one of his warriors. You and Avoez will accompany him to the court. On the first night of your journey, you will arrive at the oak of Guénolé. You will find a tomb under the oak . . . it will be my tomb. It is there you will give to our son this sword and tell him of his true parentage and of his father's murder at the hands of Avoez and Moravik."

"Eudemarec . . . rather would I stay here."

"No, it is not in your hands. Make haste back to the land of mortals, before the Silver City wakens, for if they do and find you here, you will surely lose your immortal soul. They will blame you for the death of their king."

Her eyes opened wide. "Are you then a king, Eudemarec?"

"I am King of the Land of Silver," confessed Eudemarec. "Now leave me, my beloved and do not grieve . . . One day, we shall meet again and we shall make love under the silver moon. Go now, for I feel the city waking. Make haste."

Litavis put the band of silver on her finger, took up the great silver sword, and bent to kiss her love one more time on the lips.

She passed swiftly through the sleeping castle. Even as she did so, it seemed that the limbs of those sleeping were moving into life. She hurried on down the avenue, through the city and across the meadows. She heard the bells tolling the death-knell of the king. Her feet seemed to hardly touch the ground when she was through the silver gate and along the dark tunnel and out into the darkness of the hillside.

Back across the stones of Carnac with the singing, dancing *korrigan*, she hastened. Then Yann-an-Oded was waiting for her and took her by the hand across the dark forests to the seashore. She heard the whispering voice of the sea. There Yann-an-Oded released her hand and she found that it was taken by the Bugel Noz.

"Hasten, Litavis," he whispered. "Soon it will be dawn and the first cock will crow."

She fairly flew through the forests, over the hills until she was under the high tower of the castle of Lanaskol.

The Bugel Noz seemed to lift her up and threw her and she found herself in her chamber. She looked around and found a hiding-place for the heavy silver sword. Then, in despair, she fell on her bed, weeping, just as the cock began to crow.

Just then the door opened and Avoez and Moravik came in and stared at her.

They appeared curious and looked from one to another.

"Why have we entered this chamber, brother?" demanded Moravik. "I knew when I opened the door, but I have forgotten now."

Avoez scratched his head. "I . . . I do not know. I know

that I meant to go hunting this morning. Perhaps I meant to ask Litavis to accompany me on the hunt."

Litavis sat up in bed and felt the tiny band of silver on her finger.

"Go hunting lord?" she asked in amazement.

"Why should we not go hunting?"

"Well . . ." she wondered how much he remembered. "I am to have a child, my lord."

Avoez stared at her in amazement and then his thin face broke into a smile.

"Moravik! Moravik! Do you hear that? I am to be a father. She is to have a child."

"Yes, brother," cried his sister. "Now you have everything you ever wanted."

From that day forward, Avoez showered Litavis with gifts and nothing was too much trouble for him. He sent her handmaidens to attend to all her wants, and no gift was too rich or fine for her to have. Yet she refused to leave her little room at the top of the tower, in spite of all his pleadings.

"My son was conceived in this small, high room, and here he will be born," she announced firmly.

Avoez enraptured, almost fawned on her. "It shall be as you say. My son . . . my son shall be called Avoez, after me."

"No, his name shall be Ywenec," replied Litavis.

"It shall be as you say . . ." Avoez agreed at once.

And so a son called Ywenec was born to Litavis in the high room, in the tower on the point overlooking the sea. And often, during those days, Litavis walked by the sea, hearing the murmuring caress of her lover's voice along the seashore and tasting his lips in the salt sea-spray as she walked.

The years passed swiftly enough.

Ywenec grew to manhood and he was handsome, the image of Eudemarec, and he was strong and brave. And soon, as Eudemarec had foretold, the king of Cornouaille asked that he come to court, so that the king could bestow on him the brotherhood of warriors. And Avoez, who was very proud, together with Litavis, accompanied the youth.

Now when the time came, Litavis took the great silver sword and hid it in the coach. They set out and on the first night they found themselves in some woods by the western shore by the oak of Guénolé.

Avoez, who did not know the area, raged and shouted at his coachmen for losing their way. For he might have changed in some things, but he had not changed in all his irritating manners.

"Well, it seems a welcoming spot to spend the night," asserted Litavis. "Look, here is a holy druid come to greet us."

A druid came out of the woods and pointed to a tavern where they might rest for the night.

"This is a holy spot, lady," he said, "for there is a tomb of a great warrior here, who was also a king in his own land."

"Where is this tomb?" sneered Avoez. "Am I not lord of Breizh Izel, that I should know the names of kings buried in my lands?"

The old druid pointed to an ancient oak tree.

"The tomb lies there, lord of Lanaskol," he said softly, emphasising the fact that, in his estimation, Avoez was no more than a petty usurper.

"And whose tomb is it?" demanded Avoez.

"He was the mighty king of the Silver City, ruling since the time when day and night were not separated."

Avoez frowned and bent forward to where the tomb slab lay beneath the oak. And it was inlaid with all sorts of precious stones and gold and silver inlays. It showed leaping animals and birds in flight and, above all, a large hawk in silver with emerald eyes and ruby claws. An ethereal light seemed to glow from the tomb.

"I have not heard of this king."

"His name was Eudemarec," said the druid.

"How came he by his death?"

"He was murdered at the tower of Lanaskol, because he loved a noble lady," the druid replied.

"Ah," nodded Avoez, "an ancient legend about my very own castle. But if he were such a great king, he would not be buried here."

"Oh yes," contradicted the druid. "He rests here, waiting for his heir."

"His heir?" sneered Avoez. "It seems he has been a long time without an heir, then?"

"But the blink of an eye."

Then it was that Litavis turned to the coach and drew out the great silver sword of Eudemarec.

"My son, Ywenec, here, by your true father's tomb, I give you his own great sword."

Ywenec stood shocked for a moment, and then he came forward and took the sword from his mother and stretched it out above the tomb. All at once, a strange light seemed to glow from the tomb and leap to the sword, travelling along the sword and down Ywenec's arm and encompassing his whole body. There was a sound of wild and joyous shouting, and the sound of silver bells ringing out somewhere far distant.

Ywenec, in that moment, knew the truth of his birth.

He turned to his mother and placed an arm around her. "Is it true?" he asked in wonder.

"It is true. There," she pointed at Avoez, "stands the man who made my life a misery, a purgatory on earth, and who murdered my own true love, your father. Now my task is complete and I may join your father."

With a smile of joy, she fell backwards across the tomb of Eudemarec. She was dead.

They thought they heard her final joyful cry. "I am here, beloved, at last!"

Ywenec whirled round to the aghast figure of Avoez and raised his sword.

"You are dead," he said simply.

One blow was enough to sever the head of the evil tyrant of Lanaskol.

It is said that when Moravik heard of what had befallen her brother, she took ship immediately, hoping to voyage eastwards away from his vengeful hands. As the ship sailed out in the bay under the tower on the point where, for so many years, the unhappy Litavis had gazed down on the murmuring billows, a great storm blew up and the ship was dashed to pieces; Moravik was dragged down to her purgatory by the eager hands of the *morwreg*, the daughters of the sea.

Ywenec had his mother buried in the tomb of Eudemarec and then he set about restoring all the lands Avoez had stolen or taken by guile from the people of Breizh Izel. There was great happiness in the land, and all wanted him to stay as their lord.

"It is not my destiny to be lord of Lanaskol," he told the people. "I have another fortune to seek."

Who may say that he did not succeed? There are some who say that the bells of the Silver City rang without ceasing for a year and a day when Ywenec found the gate into the Land of Silver and claimed his father's throne. There are some who say that he ruled in justice there . . . But, of course, no one has ever returned to tell of what befell him there.

37 *Prinsez-a-Sterenn*

There was once a young, handsome miller of Lannion who dwelt by the river Léguer, whose name was Nol an Meilher. One day, and it was in the crisp cold month of miz-Kerzu, which we now call December, and, indeed, not long before the feast of Nedelek, or Christ's birth, Nol went out to the nearby lake to see what he could get for the cooking pot. The lake was fringed with ice and there was snow on the ground.

When he came to the edge of the lake, the first thing that Nol saw was a splendid duck. She was having difficulty with the ice on the water's edge and so Nol, pleased with having a "sitting duck", drew forth an arrow, fixed it to his bow and shot it. No sooner had the arrow found his mark, and he was certain it had, than the duck disappeared in a misty cloud.

While Nol stood open-mouthed at this strange happening, he heard a gentle sigh at his side and he turned and found a tall young woman standing here. She was of fair skin, with blue eyes and golden hair and of such ethereal beauty that Nol could not help but swallow and make no greeting at all.

"*Devezh-mat!*" she greeted in his language, wishing him a "good morning". "*Bennozh Dou dit!*" Which means "thank you", in Breton.

"Who are you?" Nol demanded. "And for what are you thanking me?"

"I am one who has been kept prisoner in the enchanted form of a duck for many years."

"Who did that to you?"

"Three evil wizards from the Otherworld, demons who sought to torment me. You have broken their spell for a while and brought me back to human form. However, I am not entirely delivered from their clutches. Only you can now do so and destroy their hold over me."

Nol was much taken by the girl's beauty and so he did not hesitate to volunteer his services. "What must I do to achieve your freedom?"

"Do you see that old ruined castle up on the hill there?"

Now the place to which she pointed, so the people who dwell about Lannion will tell you, was the Castle of Tonguédec. Its gate still fronts out on a pool and it stands on a height overlooking the valley where there are, significantly enough, a large number of old abandoned mills. They say most of the castle was dismantled by the Duc de Richelieu, but much of it still stands. However, Richelieu lived over a thousand years and more after Nol stood viewing it.

Nol knew that, even then, it was regarded as an evil place where no one ever ventured. It had been ruined many generations ago, and everyone said that it was haunted, for there were weird sounds, terrifying screams and cries which emanated from it at night.

Nol shivered. "What of it?"

"To release me, you must spend three successive nights in the castle."

The miller was a little reluctant. "What is it that dwells in that old ruin? I suspect it is the devil himself."

The girl looked sympathetic. "I am afraid that there are three devils: the three wizards, the demons of the Otherworld. When you are there during the night, they will torment you in fearful fashion. You will be thrown through the house, thrown in the fire and worse things will happen to you."

"Worse things?" Nol snorted in indignation. "Are you telling me that you expect me to go there and be tortured and killed by these Otherworld wizards?"

The girl nodded. "But you must have no fear. You see, I have an ointment, an Otherworld balm, which will keep you alive and cure any injury that these wizards can do. Even if you were killed, this balm will resuscitate you; if your limbs were crushed, it will make them whole again. But only if you can endure the three nights without complaining nor speaking to the wizards, no matter what they attempt to do."

Nol was very doubtful. "What if they inflict pain so great that I cannot help but cry out?"

"You must not. Not a sound. If you can endure this, not only I shall be freed but you will come into great wealth, for under the hearthstone are three great chests of gold and three great chests of silver. You will have these as your reward and myself in marriage. But you must be man enough to face the three wizards."

Now Nol was a determined young man and, once he knew that the beautiful young girl was part of his reward, he resolved to carry out the trial.

With that, there was a puff of smoky mist and the girl disappeared. There was only a solitary duck swimming on the lake.

That night, as the sun was disappearing behind the distant forest, Nol took a bottle of cider and some firewood, thinking to keep himself warm in the old castle. He also hoped that the three wizards would not bother to visit the castle that night. He kindled his fire in an old chimney in the great hall of the castle and sat there to wait out the night.

It was midnight when he heard a strange sound, like a rushing through the skies. Something was coming down the chimney. In spite of his calm, Nol hurried to a corner of the hall and hid himself in a cupboard, peering through a crack in the wooden door.

Three strange figures burst in the hearth and out into the room. They were grotesque-looking forms, with green skins and pointed ears and red angry coals for eyes. They had tails which lashed back and forth and talons were their hands.

"What's this, brothers?" cried one of them, pointing to the fire in the hearth.

The second one sniffed, raising his head to the ceiling. "I smell human blood, brothers," he said.

The third one, his evil head on one side, began to chuckle. "I think we have a little man among us, trying to free the Princess of the Shining Star from our spell."

All three of them suddenly began to hunt through the great hall of the ruined castle, sniffing here and sniffing there. Then all three halted before the cupboard in which the miller was cowering, now very much afraid.

The three evil-faced wizards grinned.

"Hello, miller," cried one.

"Come out and join us," said the second.

"We have nice games for you to play," the third chuckled.

Nol said nothing, nor did he move. He was petrified with fear.

So one of the wizards opened the door and dragged him out by his leg.

"Ah ha, little man. So you want to rescue the Princess of the Shining Star?"

It was a surprise to Nol that the girl was a princess. But he kept quiet.

"So you want to take her away?" demanded the second wizard.

"You like pretty girls, do you?" chortled the third.

He did not reply.

"Well, brothers, let's play our game," called the first.

"It won't be to your liking, miller," the second one cried.

"But it will cure you of ever wanting to take the princess away from us," observed the third.

They seized poor Nol and began to throw him like a rag-doll from one end of the great hall to another. Nol clenched his teeth and did not utter a sound. To and fro, through the window into the courtyard, up and down, they threw him. All night long it went on and he did not utter a sound. Black and blue he was. Finally, as the cock was announcing the first light of dawn, the three wizards thought Nol must be dead, for he had uttered no sounds at all. So they left him lying there and all went scurrying up the chimney.

No sooner had they done so when the beautiful girl appeared by Nol's side and looked compassionately at him. Then she drew forth a jar and began to spread the ointment over his limbs. In a trice, he sat up and put a hand to his forehead. He was alive and fit and as healthy and strong as ever he had been.

"You ointment works well," he observed thankfully.

"But you have suffered a great deal," the girl sighed.

"That I have. I would not like to do so again."

"Yet you have to spend two more such nights, if I am to be free of those evil demons."

"I do," agreed Nol dolefully. Then he asked: "Tell me, this, are you truly a princess?"

The girl smiled and inclined her head. "I am called the Princess of the Shining Star, that is the Pole Star, which guides humankind on its way home. Alas, its light is no good to guide me back home, unless I can be free."

"Then you shall be free," Nol affirmed. "Have no fear. I will stick to my bargain with you."

And the girl vanished. Nol went home, passing the solitary duck swimming on the lake.

That night he came again, bringing firewood and a bottle of cider and hoping the wizards would not come again. But as he sat by the fire, he heard a strange rushing sound in the air and he quickly went to an old rubbish pile and hid himself under it. Down the chimney came the three wizards as evil as ever.

"I smell human blood!" cried one.

"It's the miller again!" announced the second, coming directly to the pile of rubbish and heaving Nol out by one leg.

"Why, miller," said the third, "we thought you dead, after last night's game."

"We must play a better game," said the first.

"Indeed, we must," said the second.

"It will not take long to finish you off, this time," announced the third.

And they put firewood on the fire and conjured a great cauldron which was full of oil and they brought it to a bubbling boil over the fire. Then they threw the miller into it. Nol had no time to cry out in pain, even if he had wanted to. And when the cock announced the first glimmers of dawn light, the three wizards disappeared up the chimney.

The Princess of the Shining Star appeared almost immediately and pulled the miller from the cauldron. He was cooked so thoroughly that his flesh was falling off the bone.

Yet she poured her ointment over him and he was immediately whole and healthy again.

"You have suffered much for me, Nol," she observed sorrowfully.

"I don't know if I can suffer more," he confessed.

"Yet you must, if I am to be free."

So, the third night, he took himself to the ruined castle and this time he did not even bother to hide himself but stood waiting for the three wizards before the great fireplace.

There came the rushing sound and down the chimney they came.

They pulled up in surprise when they saw him.

"Well, well, well," said the first one. "It's the miller and still living."

"Brothers," said the second, "this is the third night. If we don't finish him tonight, then we will lose everything."

"He must be protected by a wizard as powerful as we are," exclaimed the third.

"Then what should we do?" demanded the first.

Nol stood silently while they stood suggesting all manner of painful deaths. Each argued with the other about the exact manner of the death and it took a long, long time for them to agree. Finally, they built up a great fire; it was suggested that they put Nol on a great iron skewer lengthwise, so that they could turn him over the fire and baste him like a roast. However, just as they were about to do so, the cock announced the first glimmer of dawn's light and they had to rush off. They were terribly angry at having wasted all night in discussing what they should do and, in their departure, each one trying to get up the chimney before the other, they knocked down the end of the castle hall.

Nol stood shivering in relief at his escape. Then the Princess of the Shining Star appeared. However, she did not need her ointment this time.

"You have suffered much for me, Nol. Now we shall find the treasure and you will have your reward."

They went to the hearthstone and were able to push it to one side. There, just as the Princess had said, were the three great chests of gold and the three great chests of silver.

"Take it all and use it as you wish, Nol. As for me, I have to leave you . . ."

Nol began to protest, but the Princess held up her hand. "I shall leave you for a year and a day and then I will return; thereafter we shall always be together. I have to undertake a journey home first . . ." And she pointed to the glimmering Pole-Star, which had not yet quite departed from the sky. "Will you trust me to return?"

Well, Nol had little choice in the matter. However, as he had trusted her three times with his life, it would be no hardship to trust her again. So, with a touch of her hand on his, she vanished in a mist again.

The chests of gold and silver were real enough.

Nol consoled himself by removing the treasure to his house and thinking what he should do with it. His best friend was Rosko and he called him and let him into the secret. They decided that they would visit far distant lands and improve their knowledge. Nol, being a generous man, gave away his mill to his chief assistant and he and Rosko set out, denying themselves nothing. Eight months were spent in their travels and Nol finally said: "I think I must be going home. It would be bad for me if I missed the meeting with the Princess at the end of the year and a day." So Nol and Rosko set off home.

They were not far off when, passing along the road, they came on a little old woman who was selling apples by the roadside.

"Buy my apples, kind gentlemen," the old woman said, holding out large red apples that were bright and tempting.

Now Rosko, Nol's friend, was a wise young man.

"Do not buy any apples from this old woman," he advised Nol.

"Why ever not?" demanded Nol. "Look how sumptuous they are, trickling with juice."

He bought three apples.

Now, with part of his treasure, Nol had the ruined castle renovated and decked out in magnificence. The princess had informed him that the three wizards could never again come there, and so Nol had made it his splendid home, fit for a prince to live in. They reached there on the very day the princess was due to arrive.

Nol sat himself outside the castle, overlooking the lake on which he had first met the princess. Rosko sat with him. There came a gnawing in Nol's stomach that made him feel ill. Nol put it down to pangs of hunger and so he drew forth an apple and ate it. He began to feel sleepy this time, and soon he was fast asleep.

It was not long afterwards that the princess arrived, in the most beautiful star-coloured carriage drawn by twenty-seven white horses with star-bursts on their foreheads. When the princess alighted and found Nol asleep, she was distressed.

"Why does he sleep, Rosko?" she asked his friend.

"Lady, that I do not know, except that he bought three apples from an old woman on the roadside. He's just eaten one of them and this has made him fall asleep."

The princess gave a long indrawn breath.

"Alas! The old woman was the mother of the three evil Otherworld wizards that kept me captive and whom Nol overcame. This is her vengeance, for she means us evil in return for her three sons' defeat. I can't invite him into my star carriage while he is asleep. I will return at this time tomorrow. Here is a golden pear and a kerchief. When he awakens, give him these tokens and tell him that I shall return and hope to find him awake."

So saying, the princess climbed back into her star-coloured carriage drawn by twenty-seven white horses and they rose into the air and disappeared.

Now Nol eventually awoke and was distressed and angry with himself when Rosko told him what had happened while he had been asleep.

"I will not sleep tomorrow," he vowed.

He went to bed immediately, so as not to be asleep the next day.

On the following day, he went with Rosko to the spot outside the castle and sat there. Time passed and in a moment of absent-mindedness, he reached in his pocket, drew forth the second apple and ate it. He was promptly asleep again.

The princess came in a moon-coloured carriage pulled by

twenty-seven white horses, each with a star-burst on their foreheads.

When she saw Nol sleeping, she raised her hands in despair. "What? Can it be he still sleeps?"

Rosko told her what had happened.

"I shall return at this time tomorrow. But after that, I can return no more. Here is a second golden pear and a kerchief. Tell him what I have said and say that if I find him asleep tomorrow, he will never see me again, unless he crosses three powers and three seas in search of me."

She stepped back into her moon-coloured carriage and it rose in the air and disappeared.

When Nol awoke and Rosko told him what had passed, he was in despair. He told his friend to ensure that he did not sleep. So the next day, at the appointed time, Nol sat gazing out over the lake. He was aware that he was feeling hungry and absently drew out the third apple and nibbled it. At once he was asleep again. Poor Rosko. There was nothing he could do to wake his friend.

Then the princess came in a sun-coloured carriage, drawn by twenty-seven white horses, each with a star-burst on their foreheads.

She raised her hands in anguish when she saw Nol. "I can return no more. Rosko, you are a good friend to him. Tell him that I cannot return. To see me again, he must come and search for me in the Kingdom of the Shining Star. To get there, he must cross three powers and three seas. He will have to go through much heartache and pain. Here is a third golden pear and a third kerchief. Give them to him and tell him that the three pears and three kerchiefs will be useful to him in his quest."

"With all my heart, I will do as you ask," cried Rosko, for he was a true friend of Nol.

Then she stepped into her sun-coloured carriage, drawn by the twenty-seven white horses, and it rose into the air and disappeared.

When Nol awoke, he was in a rage and fury with himself.

"I'll seek her out, even should my road take me to the gates of Hell and beyond!"

"I will come with you," declared Rosko.

Nol shook his head. "This is my task and mine alone. You will stay here and look after the castle and my treasure, or such of it as remains. In my absence, you are the lord here. If I fail to return, you will continue to be lord and live here in comfort for the rest of your days."

So it was that Nol set out on his quest to find the Princess of the Shining Star.

At first he rode for many miles until he lost count of them, even losing count of the days that had passed. He had come to a great, lonely forest, which seemed to have no end. He wandered aimlessly for days and nights until he grew exhausted and, hearing the distant sound of wolves, he climbed a tree for protection. Yet from this elevation he saw a distant light and thought it must come from a house. So he climbed down and went in the direction of the light.

The place was only a poor woodsman's cottage. It was made of little more than branches and hay for the roof. Nol pushed open the door. An ancient man with a long white beard sat at the table within.

"Good evening, grandfather," greeted Nol respectfully.

The old man looked up in astonishment. "Good evening, young man. You are welcome to this place. Indeed, seeing you gives me great pleasure, for I have not laid eyes on a human being in the eighteen hundred years that I have been here. How is it with the world outside this forest?"

Nol sat himself down and told the old man the reason for his journey.

The old man offered him cider and was sympathetic.

"I'll do you a favour, young man." He turned and took two pieces of cloth which, when Nol examined them carefully, were coverings for the shoes, gaiters.

"What favour is this?" he demanded.

"They are enchanted gaiters. They were useful to me when I was your age. When you put them on and take a step, you may cover seven leagues. You should be able to reach the Kingdom of the Shining Star with these."

And Nol spent the night with the old man and told him how things fared with the world outside the forest. The next morning, he put on the gaiters and began to travel very swiftly. With seven leagues gone with each step he was soon over the forest, streams, rivers and mountains. Towards sunset on that day, he had come to another forest and to another hut similar to the first one. He was hungry and tired by the extent of his journey

He knocked at the door.

Inside was an old woman, with teeth long and yellow and she was crouching before a meagre fire in the hearth.

"Good evening, grandmother," Nol greeted respectfully. "I was hoping I might get some food here and a place to sleep for the night."

"You have ill come here. I hate strangers and have three strapping sons who will grind your bones if they find you here. That will be the best of your fortune, for they will undoubtedly eat you as well. Clear off."

"What are the names of your sons?" demanded Nol.

"They are Genver, C'hwevrer and Meurzh!"

"So you are the mother of the winds?"

"Indeed I am."

"I entreat you, by the sacred stones, grandmother, to give me hospitality and hide me from your three sons."

Nol had heard a noise outside and knew the three sons of the old woman were coming.

"That is my son Genver," the old woman said relenting. "I'll try to help you . . . I know, I'll tell him that you are my brother's son and that you've come to pay us a visit."

"Very well," agreed Nol. "Does your brother's son have a name?"

"Yes, tell them your name is Fidamdoustik."

Almost immediately, the first of the old woman's sons rushed down the chimney and peered about.

"Ha ah, mother. I smell a human. I'm hungry and cold and need a tasty morsel."

"Sit down and behave, Genver. That is your cousin who sits there."

Genver frowned. "No cousin of mine, surely?"

"It is your cousin, Fidamdoustik. Sit there while I get your supper and do not harm him, otherwise I shall have to call upon the sack."

She pointed to an old sack hanging behind the door.

So Genver sat down sulkily, and from time to time he cast covetous glances at Nol. Then he was joined by his two brothers, C'hwevrer and Meurzh, each as ugly as he. As they swept through the air, trees cracked, wolves howled and even stones flicked through the air. They puffed and blowed as they came down the chimney. The old woman told them all to behave and be kind to their cousin, Fidamdoustik. Only when threatened with the sack did they settle down in the corner.

The three sons devoured three entire cows and drank three casks of wine without blinking.

Genver finally asked: "Tell us, cousin Fidamdoustik, and tell us truly – does your journey here have no other reason than merely to visit us?"

Nol decided to be truthful in this regard.

"Well, in truth, cousin, I am on a journey to the Kingdom of the Shining Star. If you could show me the way, I would be very grateful."

"I never heard of it," replied Genver.

"I've heard of it, all right," said C'hwevrer, "but I don't know where it is."

"I know it," said Meurzh. "In fact, I blew over it only yesterday. There were great preparations in the land, for the princess is getting married tomorrow."

Nol sat bolt upright.

"Married?"

"Oh yes. They've slaughtered one hundred cows and one hundred calves, one hundred sheep, and as many chickens and ducks. A great feast it will be."

"But to whom is she getting married?" demanded Nol.

"I don't know. Why?"

"I want to get there before the ceremony. Can you tell me how I can find the Kingdom of the Shining Star, cousin Meurzh?"

"I am due to go back there for a blow tomorrow, cousin. But you won't be able to keep up."

"That I can," Nol assured him.

"Very well," Meurzh was not sure. "If you can keep up with me, I'll show you where."

So about midnight, Meurzh told him it was time to go and spun up and out of the chimney. Nol followed him with his enchanted gaiters and kept up as Meurzh whistled across the forests and finally came to a seashore.

"Wait!" cried Nol. "I can keep up with you but I cannot cross the water. Can you help me across the sea, cousin?"

Meurzh looked doubtful. "There is not one sea that stands between us and the Kingdom of the Shining Star, cousin."

"Then, I beg you, take me on your broad back and carry me over the waves."

With much grumbling, Meurzh did so. The first sea was crossed without problems. The second sea, Meurzh grumbled and said he was tired. The third sea was almost crossed when Meurzh said he was that tired he was going to drop Nol. But Nol urged him on so much that when Meurzh finally dropped him, he landed right on the sandy seashore of the Kingdom of the Shining Star.

He thanked his mighty cousin and set off towards the great city in the distance, and his enchanted gaiters helped him reach there in a moment or two.

He thought that he would go to a tavern before making his way to the castle in the centre of the city. He knew that tavern-keepers were notorious at knowing all the news of the countryside. So he found a tavern and went in and ordered food.

Sure enough, the tavern-keeper was loquacious enough.

"What is the talk of the city, tavern-keeper?" asked Nol, with an innocent look.

"Talk? Why, talk of nothing else except our princess's wedding."

"Is everyone overjoyed at it, then?" pressed Nol.

"Everyone except the princess," replied the tavern-keeper.

Nol's heart gave a quick throb. "Why so?" he whispered.

"They say the princess is getting married to someone who she doesn't like."

"Who is this person?"

"The Prince of Hent Sant Jakez." And that was the Breton term for the Milky Way.

Nol wondered how he could ever claim his princess when she was marrying such a powerful prince.

"When will this wedding take place?"

"Not long now. If you wait here, you may see it, for the wedding procession passes this very tavern."

Now an idea came into Nol's mind. On a table outside the inn, he placed the first golden pear and kerchief, that which the princess had given Rosko.

The table stood within sight of the procession. Nol went to watch what would happen from the inn window.

Sure enough, the wedding procession came along. At the head was the princess and by her side was her betrothed, the Prince of the Milky Way. The princess started when she saw the golden pear and kerchief.

"Wait, Prince," she said, stopping the procession. "I feel quite unwell. Let us put off this wedding until tomorrow."

The prince, frowning with bewilderment, finally agreed. The procession turned back to the palace and the ceremony was rearranged for the next day. Meanwhile, in her chambers, the princess sent one of her handmaidens to the inn with instructions to buy the pear and kerchief from whoever was the owner.

The handmaiden returned them to the princess, for Nol had given them to her.

The next day, the procession set out again and again passed the inn. Again Nol had set on the table outside the second pear and kerchief, while he himself looked on from behind a window. On seeing them, the princess pretended to be ill again and asked that the ceremony be postponed until the next morning. Again, the prince, though more irritable than before, agreed. The princess sent the same handmaiden to go to collect the pear and kerchief.

The same thing happened on the third day, except that this time, the princess asked her handmaiden to bring the owner back to her as well.

When Nol entered the room, she almost swooned with joy and they embraced at finding one another again.

Just then a messenger came to her chambers, saying that the Prince of the Milky Way had issued orders that, because every time the princess passed the inn she fell ill, they would have their wedding feast and afterwards the ceremony would be performed in the castle.

Trying to devise a plan, the princess went down to the feasting hall and Nol also went down and took his place with the guests. He saw the princess was as radiant as ever he had seen her, lighting the feasting hall like the sun.

As was the custom, following the feasting, there were many telling tales, each boastful and bragging.

Finally, the Prince of the Milky Way turned to the princess and said: "You have told us no tale. Soon we will be married and then it will be unseemly that you should do so. Tell us a tale before we marry."

"Well, there is a tale . . . a tale which my guests should give me advice on, for it concerns a matter about which I am much embarrassed."

This intrigued everyone.

"Tell on."

"I have a pretty little gold casket. Inside was a pretty little golden key. I liked it very much, but one day I lost the key and so had a new one made. But it happens that I've just found the old key before having even tried the new one. The old one was very good and I don't yet know if the new one would be any better. So the advice I would like is whether I should now throw away the old one and use the new or throw away the new one and stick to the old."

The guests gave their advice but the princess turned to the Prince of the Milky Way.

"It is your advice I need most in this, my lord. On your word, the decision hangs."

The Prince of the Milky Way rubbed his chin thoughtfully. "One should always regard and respect the old. Better to keep what one knows will work than experiment with something untried."

The princess stood up with a laugh. "Then I will show you these keys." And she made her way across the feasting hall and took Nol by the hand. "Here is the old key which was lost and just recovered. You, my lord, are the new key."

The Prince of the Milky Way stood up and his face was wreathed in anger.

"We have had our wedding feast!" he exclaimed.

"But no ceremony," replied the princess. "And you have advised me clearly, in front of all these guests. I must respect the old and maintain it. I'll keep my old key, therefore, and leave the new key. And by the old key I refer to this courageous and faithful young man, who delivered me from the bondage of the three evil magicians. Nol was willing to give his life for me, and then came in search of me, daring a thousand evils, leaving all that was comfortable."

Her subjects applauded and started to rejoice, for they had all known that the princess had not been happy with the prospect of her marriage.

The Prince of the Milky Way left the Kingdom of the Shining Star forthwith and returned to his twenty-seven star wives, for he did not need the companionship of the single Shining Star when he could roam the twenty-seven courts of his universe.

"We shall never again be parted," the princess assured Nol. "And for the first part of our eternity, we shall return to your land and be married there."

So in a star-coloured carriage, drawn by twenty-seven white horses, each with a starburst on their foreheads, they travelled back to the Lannion and the banks of the Léguer and the old castle, where the faithful Rosko was waiting for them. There was great joy in the land and the wedding feast far surpassed that which had been held in the Kingdom of the Shining Star.

Recommended Further Reading

To make recommendations for further reading is a hard task – hard in that there are many titles one is forced to leave out rather than in the consideration of what has to be put in. There are many books that I would be tempted to put in, such as the books of Ethne Carbery (1866–1911), which were a joy in my childhood: for example, *The Four Winds of Eirinn* (1902) and *In the Celtic Past* (1904). However, I have tried to keep to those titles which, in my opinion, will collectively serve as a good, broad introduction into the Celtic world of myth and legend.

Bottrell, William. *Traditions & Hearthside Stories of West Cornwall*, London, 1880.

Brekilien, Yann. *La mythologie celtique*, Editions Jean Picollec, Paris, 1981.

Caldecott, Moyra. *Women in Celtic Myth*, Arrow Books, London, 1988.

Campbell, John Francis. *Popular Tales of the West Highlands*, Edinburgh, 1860–62.

Campbell, John Gregerson. *Waifs and Strays of Celtic Tradition*, 3 vols, London, 1891.

Carmichael, Alexander. *Carmina Gadelica*, Oliver & Boyd, Edinburgh, Vols I and II (1900); Vols III and IV (1940–41) and Vols V and VI (1954 and 1971).

Carney, James. *Studies in Irish Literature and History*, Institute for Advanced Studies, Dublin, 1955.

Coghlan, Ronan. *A Pocket Dictionary of Irish Myths and Legends*, Appletree Press, Belfast, 1985.

Coghlan, Ronan. *The Encyclopaedia of Arthurian Legends*, Element, Shaftesbury, Dorset, 1991.

Croker, J. Crofton. *Fairy Legends and Traditions of the South of Ireland*, John Murray, London, 1834.

Cross, Tom P. and Slover, Clark H. *Ancient Irish Tales*, Harrap, London, 1937.

Curtin, Jeremiah. *Myths and Folk Tales of Ireland*, Dover, New York, 1975.

de Jubainville, H. d'Arbois. *Essai d'un de la Littérature de l'Irlande*, Paris, 1882.

de Jubainville, H. d'Arbois. *Le cycle mythologique irlandais et la mythologie celtique*, Paris, 1884. English translation – *The Irish Mythological Cycle*, Hodges & Figgis, Dublin, 1903.

Delaney, Frank. *Legends of the Celts*, Hodder & Stoughton, London, 1989.

Dillon, Myles. *The Cycles of the Kings*, Oxford University Press, 1946.

Dillon, Myles. *Early Irish Literature*, University of Chicago Press, Chicago USA, 1948.

Dillon, Myles, ed. *Irish Sagas*, Mercier Press, Cork, 1968.

Dunn, Joseph. *The Ancient Irish Epic Tale – Táin Bó Cúalnge*, David Nutt, London, 1914.

Easter, Delawarr B. *A Study of the Magic Elements in the Romans d'Aventure and the Romans Bretons*, John Hopkins University Press, Baltimore, 1906.

Ellis, Peter Berresford. *The Cornish Language and its Literature*, Routledge & Kegan Paul, London, 1974.

Ellis, Peter Berresford. *A Dictionary of Irish Mythology*, Constable, London, 1987.

Ellis, Peter Berresford. *A Dictionary of Celtic Mythology*, Constable, London, 1992.

Ellis, Peter Berresford. *The Druids*, Constable, London, 1994.

Ellis, Peter Berresford. *Celtic Women: Women in Celtic Society and Literature*, Constable, London, 1995.

Ellis, T.P. and Lloyd, John. *The Mabinogion*, Oxford University Press, 1929.

Evans, J. Gwenogfryn. *The White Book Mabinogion*, Pwllheli (1907). Reprint as *Llyfr Gwyn Rhydderch (The White Book of Rhydderch)*. Introduced by Professor R.M. Jones, University of Wales Press, Cardiff, 1973.

Flower, Robin. *Byron and Ossian*, Oxford University Press, 1928.

Flower, Robin. *The Irish Tradition*, Oxford University Press, 1947.

Ford, P.K. ed. and trs. *The Mabinogion and Other Medieval Welsh Tales*, University of California Press, Berkeley, 1977.
Gantz, Jeffrey. *Early Irish Myths and Sagas*, Penguin, London, 1981.
Gantz, Jeffrey. *The Mabinogion*, Penguin, London, 1976.
Gose, E.G. *The World of the Irish Wonder Tale*, University of Toronto Press, Toronto, 1985.
Graves, Alfred P. *The Irish Fairy Book*, T. Fisher Unwin, London
Green, Miranda. *A Dictionary of Celtic Myth and Legend*, Thames & Hudson, London, 1992.
Gregory, Lady Augusta. *Gods and Fighting Men*, John Murray, London, 1904.
Gruffydd, W.J. *Math vab Mathonwy*, University of Wales Press, Cardiff, 1928.
Gruffydd. W.J. *Rhiannon*, University of Wales Press, Cardiff, 1953.
Guest, Lady Charlotte. *The Mabinogion from Llyfr Coch a Hergest*, London (1838–1849). Everyman edition, London, 1906.
Guyonvarc'h, Christian J. *Textes mythologiques irlandais*, Ogam-Celticum, Brittany, 1981.
Gwynn, Edward John ed. and trs. *The Metrical Dindsenchas*, Hodges Figgis, Dublin, 1903–1935.
Henderson, George. *Fled Bricrend*, London, 189.
Henderson, George. *Survivals in Belief Among the Celts*, J. Maclehose, Glasgow, 1911.
Hull, Eleanor. *The Cuchulainn Saga in Irish Literature*, M.H. Gill & Son, Dublin, 1923.
Hunt, Robert. *Popular Romances of the West of England*, London, 1870.
Hyde, Douglas. *A Literary History of Ireland*, T. Fisher Unwin, 1899.
Hyde, Douglas. *Beside the Fire: Irish Folk Tales*, David Nutt, London, 1890.
Irish Text Society (Cumann na Scríbhean nGaedhilge), 57 bilingual volumes published since 1899, including the *Leabhar Gabhála*, two Irish Arthurian Romances, the *Táin Bó Cúalnge* (from the Book of Leinster) etc.
Jackson, Kenneth H. *The International Popular Tales and Early Welsh Traditions*, University of Wales Press, Cardiff, 1961.
Jacobs, Joseph. *Celtic Fairy Tales*, David Nutt, London, 1892.
Jarman, A.O.H. ed. and trs. *Y Gododdin: Britain's Oldest Heroic Poem. The Welsh Classics*, Dyfed, 1988.
Jarman, A.O.H. and Jarman, G.R. *A History of Welsh Literature*, Christopher Davies, Llandybie, 1974.

Jones, Gwyn and Jones, Thomas. *The Mabinogion*, Everyman, Dent, London, 1949.

Jones, T.G. *Welsh Folk-lore and Folk Custom*, Methuen, London, 1930.

Joyce, P.W. *Old Celtic Romances*, Longman, London, 1879.

Kanavagh, Peter. *Irish Mythology*, New York 1958–59.

Kinsella, Thomas. *The Táin*, Oxford University Press, 1970.

Lacy, Norris J. *The Arthurian Encyclopaedia*, Boydell, Suffolk, 1988.

Leahy, A.H. *The Sickbed of Cuchulainn. Heroic Romances of Ireland Series*, Vol I, Dublin, 1905.

Le Braz, Anatole. *The Celtic Legend of the Beyond*, Llanerch, 1986.

Lofflet, C.M. *The Voyage to the Otherworld in Early Irish Literature*, Institut für Anglistik and Amerikanistik, Salzburg, Germany, 1983.

Lofmark, C. *Bards and Heroes*, Llanerch Books, Llanerch, Wales, 1898.

Loomis, R.S. *Celtic Myth and Arthurian Romance*, Columbia University Press, 1926.

Loomis, R.S. *Wales and Arthurian Legend*, University of Wales Press, Cardiff, 1956.

Loomis, R.S. *Arthurian Literature in the Middle Ages*, Oxford University Press, 1959.

Loomis, R.S. *The Grail from Celtic Myth to Christian Symbol*, Columbia University Press, USA, 1963.

Loth, Joseph. *Les Mabinogion*, Paris, 1913.

Luzel, Francois-Marie. *Contes Populaires de Basse-Bretagne*, Paris, 1876,

Luzel, Francois-Marie. *Celtic Folk Tales from Armorica* (selection of tales trs. into English), Llanerch, 1985.

Mac Cana, Proinsias. *Branwen daughter of Llyr*, University of Wales Press, Cardiff, 1958.

Mac Cana, Proinsias. *Celtic Mythology*, Hamlyn, London, 1970.

Mac Cana, Proinsias. *The Mabinogion*, University of Wales Press, Cardiff, 1988.

MacCulloch, John Arnott. *Celtic Mythology*, (first published as vol. III of *The Mythology of All Races*, ed. L. H. Gray, 1918), Constable, London, 1992.

Mackenzie, D.A. *Scottish Folklore and Folk Life*, Blackie & Sons, Edinburgh, 1935.

MacKinley, James M. *Folklore of Scottish Lochs and Springs*, William Hodge & Co, Glasgow, 1893.

MacLean, Magnus. *The Literature of the Highlands*, Blackie & Sons, London, 1903.
MacManus, Seumas. *Donegal Fairy Stories*, MacClure, Phillips & Co, USA, 1900.
Maier, Bernhard (trs. Cyril Edwards). *Dictionary of Celtic Religion and Culture*, Boydell, Suffolk, 1997.
Martin, W.C. Wood. *Traces of the Elder Faiths in Ireland*, Vols I and II, Longman Green, London, 1902.
Matthews, John. *Classic Celtic Fairy Tales*, Blandford, London, 1997.
Meyer, Kuno. *The Vision of Mac Conglinne*, David Nutt, London, 1892.
Meyer, Kuno. *The Voyage of Bran Son of Febal*, 2 vols, David Nutt, London, 1895.
Meyer, Kuno. *The Triads of Ireland*, Royal Irish Academy, Dublin, 1906.
Moore, A. W. *The Folk-Lore of the Isle of Man*, David Nutt, London, 1891.
Morris, John. *The Age of Arthur*, Weidenfeld & Nicholson, London, 1973.
Munro, Robert. *Ancient Scottish Lake Dwellings*, David Douglas, Edinburgh, 1902.
Murdoch, Brian. *Cornish Literature*, D.S. Brewer, Suffolk. 1993.
Murphy, Gerard. *The Ossianic Lore and Romantic Tales of Medieval Ireland*, Three Candles Press, Dublin, 1955.
Murphy, Gerard. *Saga and Myth in Ancient Ireland*, Three Candles Press, Dublin, 1955.
Nagy, Joseph Falaky. *Conversing with Angels & Ancients: Literary Myths of Medieval Ireland*, Four Courts Press, 1997.
Neeson, Eoin. *The First Book of Irish Myths and Legends*, Mercier Press, Cork, 1965.
Neeson, Eoin. *The Second Book of Irish Myths and Legends*, Mercier Press, Cork, 1966.
Nutt, Alfred. *Celtic and Medieval Romance*, David Nutt, London, 1899.
Nutt, Alfred. *Cúchulainn: The Irish Achilles*, David Nutt, London, 1900.
Nutt, Alfred. *Ossian and Ossianic Literature*, David Nutt, London, 1900.
O'Grady, Standish James. *Early Bardic Literature in Ireland*, London, 1897.
Ó hÓgáin, Dáithí. *The Hero in Irish Folk History*, Gill & Macmillan, Dublin, 1985.

Ó hÓgáin, Dáithí. *Fionn mac Cumhail: Images of the Gaelic Hero*, Gill & Macmillan, Dublin, 1988.

Ó hÓgáin, Dáithí. *Myth, Legend and Romance: An Encyclopedia of the Irish Folk Tradition*, Ryan Publishing, London, 1991.

O'Keefe. J.G. *Buile Suibne*, David Nutt, London, 1913.

O'Rahilly, Cecile, ed. *Táin Bó Cuailgne from the Book of Leinster*, Institute for Advanced Studies, Dublin, 1967.

O'Rahilly, Thomas F. *Early Irish History and Mythology*, Institute for Advanced Studies, Dublin, 1946.

Parry, Thomas, tr. H. Idris Bell. *A History of Welsh Literature*, Clarendon Press, Oxford, 1955.

Parry-Jones, D. *Welsh Legends and Fairy Law*, Batsford, London, 1953.

Patch, H.R. *The Otherworld*, Harvard University Press, Cambridge, Mass. USA, 1950.

Pennar, M. *The Black Book of Carmarthen*, Llanerch, Wales, 1989.

Polson, Alexander. *Our Highland Folklore Heritage*, Highland Society, Inverness, 1926.

Rees, Alwyn, and Rees, Brinley. *Celtic Heritage*. Thames and Hudson, London, 1961.

Rhŷs, John. *Celtic Folk-Lore (Welsh and Manx)* 2 vols, Oxford University Press, 1901.

Rhŷs, John and Evans, J.G. *The Mabinogion*, Oxford University Press, 1887.

Roberts, Brinley F. *Y Mabinogion*, Dafydd and Rhiannon Ifans, Llandysul, 1980.

Rolleston, T.W. *Myths and Legends of the Celtic Race*, George Harrap, London, 1911.

St Clair, Sheila. *Folklore of the Ulster People*, Mercier Press, Cork, 1971.

Sebillot, P. *Costumes populaires de la Haute-Bretagne*, Paris, 1886.

Sjoestedt, Marie-Louise, trs. Myles Dillon. *Gods and Heroes of the Celts*, Methuen, London, 1949.

Smyth, Daragh. *A Guide to Irish Mythology*, Irish Academic Press, Dublin, 1988.

Spaan, D.B. *The Otherworld in Early Irish Literature*, University of Michigan Press, Ann Arbor, USA, 1969.

Squire, Charles. *Celtic Myth and Legend*, Newcastle Press, USA, 1975, Reprint of *The Mythology of the British Isles*, 1905.

Thurneysen, Rudolf. *Sagen aus dem Alten Irland*, Berlin, 1901.

Trevelyan, M. *Folklore and Folk Stories of Wales*, Eliot Stock,

London, 1909.
van Hamel, A.G. *Aspects of Celtic Mythology*, British Academy, London, 1935.
van Hamel, A.G. *Myth en Historie in Het Oude Ireland*, Amsterdam, 1942.
Wentz, W.Y. Evans. *The Fairy Faith in the Celtic Countries*, Oxford University Press, 1911.
Williams, Sir Ifor. *Pedeir Keinc y Mabinogi* (The Four Branches of the Mabinogi), University of Wales Press, Cardiff, 1930.
Wilde, Lady Jane. *Ancient Legends, Mystic Charms and Superstitions of Ireland*, Ward & Downey, London, 1888.
Wright, Charles D. *The Irish Tradition in Old English Literature*, Cambridge University Press, Cambridge, 1993.
Zaczek, Iain. *Chronicles of the Celts*, Collins & Brown, London, 1996.

Index